Reorienting the Manchus

A Study of Sinicization, 1583–1795

Reorienting the Manchus

A Study of Sinicization, 1583–1795

PEI HUANG

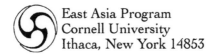

East Asia Program
Cornell University
Ithaca, New York 14853

The Cornell East Asia Series is published by the Cornell University East Asia Program (distinct from Cornell University Press). We publish books on a variety of scholarly topics relating to East Asia as a service to the academic community and the general public. Standing Orders, which provide for automatic notification and invoicing of each title in the series upon publication are accepted.

If after review by internal and external readers a manuscript is accepted for publication, it is published on the basis of camera-ready copy provided by the author who is responsible for any copyediting and manuscript formatting. Alternative arrangements should be made with approval of the Series. Address submission inquiries to CEAS Editorial Board, East Asia Program, Cornell University, Ithaca, New York 14853-7601.

Number 152 in the Cornell East Asia Series
Consulting Editor: Doug Merwin
Copyright ©2011 by Pei Huang. All rights reserved.
ISSN: 1050-2955
ISBN: 978-1-933947-22-8 hc
ISBN: 978-1-933947-52-5 pb
Library of Congress Control Number: 2010931923

24 23 22 21 20 19 18 17 16 15 14 13 12 11   9 8 7 6 5 4 3 2 1

The paper in this book meets the requirements for permanence of ISO 9706:1994.

Contents

Dedicated to the Memory of
Ssu-yu Teng (1905–1988)
University Professor Emeritus of History
Indiana University—Bloomington, IN

Qing Reign Periods

1. The Frontier State, 1616–1626

Nurhachi	Tianming, 1616–1626
Hong Taiji	Tiancong, 1627–1636
	Chongde, 1636–1643

2. The Qing Dynasty

Shunzhi	1644–1661
Kangxi	1662–1722
Yongzheng	1723–1735
Qianlong	1736–1795
Jiaqing	1796–1820
Daoguang	1821–1850
Xianfeng	1851–1861
Tongzhi	1862–1874
Guangxu	1875–1908
Xuangtong	1909–1912

List of Heavenly Stems and Earthly Branches

Chinese and Korean *Veritable Records* counted days by combining the Heavenly Stems and Earthly Branches. Data from these records are cited in the endnotes with such combined elements, known as cyclical characters.

1. Ten Heavenly Stems

Chinese	甲	乙	丙	丁	戊	己	庚	辛	壬	癸
Romanization	jia	yi	bing	ding	wu	ji	geng	xin	ren	gui
Korean Romainzation	kap	ŭl	pyŏng	chŏng	mu	ki	kyŏng	sin	im	kye

2. Twelve Earthly Branches

Chinese	子	丑	寅	卯	辰	巳	午	未	申	酉	戌	亥
Romanization.	zi	chou	yin	Mao	chen	si	wu	wei	shen	you	xu	hai
Korean Romanization.	cha	ch'uk	in	Myo	chin	sa	o	mi	sin	yu	sul	hae

3. Selected Cyclical Characters Containing the First Five Stems*

Chinese Romanization	甲子 jiazi	乙丑 yichou	丙午 bingwu	丁卯 dingmao	戊戌 wuxu
Korean Romanization	kapcha	ŭlch'uk	Pyŏngo	chŏngmyo	musul

*For a phonetical reason such Korean cyclical characters as 乙亥 and 丙子 should be romanized as ŭrhae and pyŏngja, instead of ŭlhae and pyŏngcha.

4. Selected Cyclical Characters Containing the Last Five Stems

	己未	庚寅	辛亥	壬酉	癸巳
Chinese Romanization	jiwei	gengyin	xinhai	renyou	guisi
Korean Romanization	kimi	Kyŏngin	Sinhae	imyu	kyesa

List of Illustrations and Translated Poems

A. Illustrations

B. Translated Poems

List of Maps and Tables

A. Maps

B. Tables

Explanatory Note

In this note I would like to explain the usages in the present study. Except for some well-accepted practices and a few spellings preferred by the individuals in question, I have used the *pin-yin* system of romanization for Chinese terms and names throughout the study. I render many Chinese place names according to the long-established spellings. Therefore Nanking stands for Nanching or Nanjing, Kiangsu for Jiangsu, and Sinkiang for Xinjiang. For Manchu terms and names I have consulted the *Man-Han da cidian* (Great Manchu-Chinese Cyclopedia), edited by An Shuang-cheng (Shenyang: Liaoning minzu chuban she, 1993) and the *Hakki tsūshi retsuden sakuin* (Index to the biographical sections of Baqi tongzhi). As for Korean words and names, I have followed the McCune-Reischauer system; for Japanese words and names, I have adopted the Romanji system in Kenkyusha's *New Japanese-English Dictionary* (Tokyo, 1954) respectively.[1] Chinese, Japanese, and Korean names appear in their traditional order, with the family name first and the personal name last. Dates if available are given after personal, dynastic, or event names when they appear for the first time.

Since this work attempts to be an extensive study of the subject, I have to introduce more information into the text and this requires more notes. To reduce the number of notes I place the note number mostly at the end of the paragraph. Despite its broad coverage, one can

---

1. The *Hakki tsūshi retsuden sakuin* was compiled by Kanda Nobuo, Matsumura Jun, and Okada Hidehiro (Tokyo: Toyo Bunko, 1965). For the McCune-Reischauer system, see "The Romanization of the Korean Language," *Transactions of the Korea Branch of the Royal Asiatic Society*, 29 (Seoul, 1939): 1–55 and 38 (1961): 121–28.

easily distinguish what each note refers to. Naturally the notes exclude trivial and digressive information.

While citing works in East Asian languages, I give the full names of the authors in accord with their original order. In citing Western sources by Chinese, Japanese, or Korean authors, I follow the Western practice by placing personal names first and family names last. After its first appearance, a source in whatever language will be listed by its author's last name and its shortened title if the title is long. Because the Manchus are referred to only by given names, I cite their works the same way, unless their clan names appear on the title page.

Regarding the Ming and Korean veritable records (*shilu*), I indicate first their volume (*ce*) number, then the reign title or the temple name of the ruler, the chapter (*juan*) and page numbers, and finally the date. Excluding a few cases, Qing emperors did not have voluminous veritable records. Consequently, in citations, I omit their volume numbers. In certain cases I refer to sources only by their volume and page numbers.[2] When citing *Mingshi* (History of the Ming Dynasty), I mention first the volume number and then the chapter and page numbers. As for *Baqi tongzhi chuji* (see TCCC in the Bibliography), *Baqi tongzhi* (General History of the Eight Banners), *Baqi Manzhou shizu tongpu* (see STTP in the Bibliography), and other similar sources, I give only the chapter and page numbers.

The counting of dates in traditional East Asia differed from the Western practice. Individual monarchs counted the year by their reign titles and the month in the lunar calendar, with the day by the cyclical characters. I use this dating method to cite dynastic sources. For example, in the reference of Kangxi reign 8/5/gengzi, the two numbers indicate the fifth month of the eighth year of the Kangxi reign, with the cyclical characters *gengzi* as the day identifier. A list of such cyclical characters, "Heavenly Stems and Earthly Branches," is available in this study. Because of their irregularity, I identify the reigns of Nurhaci and Hong Taiji by their temple names: Taizu and Taizong. The remaining Qing rulers are referred to by their reign titles and followed by the chapter and page numbers as well as the date. Korean kings are

---

2. *Qing shigao jiaozhu* (see *CSKC*), the *Eminent Chinese of the Ch'ing Period (1644–1912)*, ed. by Arthur W. Hummel (see *ECCP*), the *Dictionary of Ming Biography*, ed. by L. Carrington Goodrich and Chaoying Fang (see *DMB*).

mentioned by their temple names. Old Chinese and Korean books are double-leaved with the same page number. I distinguish the two sides by adding "a" and "b" to the page number. No side identification will be given if both sides of a page are covered.

I generally break long romanized names and terms that the pin-yin system tends to create. For clarity I divide them by one or two hyphens if each consists of more than eight letters. For instance, Li Chengliang, commander of the Ming army in the Liaodong region, has a long romanized personal name. I separate the two characters as Cheng-liang. The Chamberlain of the Imperial Bodyguard, a Qing official title, is known as *Ling-shiwei nei-dachen*. It would be too confusing if romanized as one word. According to the traditional way of writing, I do not break certain long names, such as Shanhaikuan, the pass strategically located between the Peking area and Manchuria. In Korean romanization some long names, for example, *Yŏnghaengnok* (Notes on China Trips), and *Simgwannok* (A Log of the Official Mission at Shenyang) remain inseparate. I treat Yongzheng as a one-word term, for it was the only reign title of Qing rulers with more than eight letters. With a few exceptions, I break names of Qing princes and imperial clansmen after the pattern as set in Arthur W. Hummel's *Eminent Chinese of the Ch'ing Period (1644–1912)*. Therefore I write Princes Yin-xiang and Yun-duan instead of Yinxiang and Yunduan. Other Manchus, such as Orong'an, Xiqing and Sungšan, are treated as one-word names. I also follow Hummel's biographical dictionary to keep such long Jurchen names as Menggebulu, Menggetimur, and Cinggiyanu intact.

Acknowledgments

I would like to take this opportunity to express my appreciation to those who have helped me at various stages of this study. My appreciation goes first to the many scholars of Qing history or Manchu studies in the United States and overseas. Their works inspired me to think more deeply and broadly about the subject. Since it would be tedious to list all of them here, I acknowledge my debt by citing their names and works in the notes to the text. For special reasons, however, a few individuals should be mentioned here: Robert H. Ferrell, Distinguished Professor Emeritus of History, Indiana University, Bloomington, Indiana, deserves my heartfelt thanks. Since 1959 he has encouraged me and showed great interest in my work. He patiently read through this manuscript and improved its style. The late University Professor Ssu-yu Teng, also of the History Department at Indiana University, was a demanding teacher and prolific scholar, under whom I completed my dissertation. He helped me acquire many photocopies of the genealogies of Manchu aristocrats from Japanese and Chinese libraries, some of which were rare. I would like to dedicate this book to the memory of him. Special thanks are due to Doug Merwin, an experienced, critical, and devoted editor. His sharp comments and careful editing improved the quality of my study.

I am grateful to Professor Philip A. Kuhn of Harvard University, who read my manuscript and made insightful suggestions. My sincere thanks are due to Jane Kate Leonard, Professor Emerita of History, University of Akron, and Chia-lin Pao Tao, Professor of Asian History, University of Arizona. Both read my manuscript and provided valuable suggestions. In particular, Leonard's comments were very crit-

xxi

ical and helpful. I am very thankful to the anonymous reader of the East Asian Program, Cornell University, for making useful comments on my work. Dr. Wei-ping Wu, an expert in the Qing Banner systems, read three chapters and provided good advice. I also want to thank Tsing Yuan of Wright State University, Beatrice S. Bartlett of Yale University, and Giovanni Stary, a well-known scholar at the University of Venice, Italy, They respectively read Chapters 3, 5, and 7 and gave valuable comments. In addition, Stary's *Manchu Studies: An International Bibliography* (Wiesbaden, Germany: Harrassowitz, 1990, 3 volumes) is essential for locating important sources. Professor Tsing Yuan also generously provided me with his pictures of the Shenyang Palace for my possible adoption.

I must express my gratitude to the following scholars for their help. The late Professor Zhonghan (Chung-han) Wang, an authority in Qing and Manchu studies at the Central University of National Minorities in Peking, kindly reproduced for me important sources such as genealogies and personnel records of the Eight Banners from the First Historical Archives. Professor Tung-kuei Kuan (Tonggui Guan), formerly Director of the Institute of History and Philology, Academia Sinica, allowed me to reproduce many rare materials from the Fu Ssu-nien library. Professor Chia-chü Liu helped me acquire many useful materials from the National Palace Museum, Taipei. Bernadette Y. N. Li, Professor and Director of the Institute of Asian Studies, St. John's University, and Dr. Chang-ch'uan Wu kindly extended their hands. Each helped me obtain a valuable Manchu genealogy from China.

I am also thankful to Drs. Tai-loi Ma, Director of the East Asian Library at Princeton University, and Martinus Johannes Heijdra, Head of Public Services of the same library. They graciously provided me with an electronic copy of the Yongzheng emperor's handwritten preface to *Zhu pi yu zhi*, a collection of memorials submitted by many officials. Moreover, during his tenure as Director of the Far Eastern Library, the University of Chicago, Dr. Ma made its collection available to Asianists, of whom I was one. Professor James Z. Lee of the University of Michigan, formerly at the California Institute of Technology, was interested in my study and sent to me two very useful books. The books given by Dr. Xiangyun Wang, a specialist in Tibetan history, are of great help because they are based on Ming and Qing archives.

My deep gratitude goes to Youngstown State University, which provided grants-in-aid, fully paid sabbaticals, and research professorships. Such generous support enabled me to lay the groundwork for my study.

I must express my appreciation to the following libraries and their staffs for their friendly assistance. Among these are Eugene Wu, Librarian of the Harvard-Yenching Library, and his successor, James Cheng. Pao-liang Chu, who did his best to find sources for me. For years I have used the resources of the Chinese, Japanese, and Korean Sections at the Library of Congress. Their staff members, especially those of the Chinese Section under Dr. Chi Wang, untiringly located materials for me. The help given by Dr. Mi Chu Wiens, a senior area specialist of the Chinese Section, saved me much time. During my 1985–86 sabbatical I did research at the libraries of Kyōto University, the Tōyō Bunko, and Tokyo University. My cordial thanks are due to their staff members.

I am equally thankful to Dr. Yuan Zhou, Director of the East Asian Library, the University of Chicago, and his staff for letting me use their books and journals. My gratitude also goes to The Family History Library at Salt Lake City for giving me access to their genealogical records relevant to my subject, and to Grace Chan, a volunteer there, for her kind assistance. I am grateful for the efficient assistance of the late Hildegard Schnuttgen, Amy Kyte, Ellen Wakeford Banks, and Jean A. Romeo, all of the Maag Library, Youngstown State University. Special thanks are also due to Mary Ann Bodnark, Maureen Wilson, and Denise Donnan, staff members of the Media and Academic Computing Center, Youngstown State University, for their help in preparing maps for my study. I also want to thank the University's Computer Services, whose Tech Desk helped fix some of my computer problems.

There are a few more individuals,who deserve my deep appreciation. Both Dr. Peter Huang of Northeastern Ohio Universities College of Medicine and Dr. Yaqin Wang of the Department of Economics, Youngstown State University, patiently solved many computer problems for me and greatly facilitated my writing. Dr. Chien Fan kindly made his pictures of the Shenyang Palace available for my possible use. My sons, Herman and Howard, located sources and made copies for me. Herman also translated two needed German sources and helped smooth out some rough spots of my writing. The assistance of my wife, Hetty, was indispensable for the completion of my study.

Finally I wish to express my thanks to four scholars for permitting me to cite from their well researched dissertations. Their names and dissertations are as follows:

Hanson Chase, "The Status of the Manchu Language in the Early Ch'ing" (Ph. D. Dissertation, University of Washington, 1979).

Samuel Martin Grupper, "The Manchu Imperial Cult of the Early Ch'ing Dynasty: Texts and Studies on the Tantric Sanctuary of Mahākāla at Mukden" (Ph. D. Dissertation, Indiana University, 1980).

Gertraude Roth Li, "The Rise of the Early Manchu State: A Portrait Drawn from Manchu Sources to 1636" (Ph. D. Dissertation, Harvard University, 1975).

Phillip H. Woodruff, "Foreign Policy and Frontier Affairs along the Northeastern Frontier of the Ming Dynasty, 1350–1618: Tripartite Relations of the Ming Chinese, Korean Koryo and Jurchen-Manchu Tribesmen" (Ph. D. Dissertation, The University of Chicago, 1995).

However, none of the above individuals are responsible for any errors in the book. If any, they are mine, and I hope they are not many.

Introduction

AN ETHNIC MINORITY IN CHINA TODAY, the Manchus enjoy a long history. The Qing dynasty (1644–1912) they founded was an apex of Chinese civilization, distinguished by its immense geographical dimensions, which contemporary China has inherited. As descendants of the Jurchens—members of the southern Tungus—they had been considered aliens by the Chinese, but this alien aspect was overstated by loyalists of the Ming dynasty (1368–1644) and by organizers of the revolution of 1911. The Manchus, one should add, have been characterized by cultural adaptability. They included both Jurchen and non-Jurchen components. Among the non-Jurchen elements were Mongols, Chinese, and Koreans. As one scholar points out, the term Manchu does not represent any "race" in a strict sense. On all accounts the Manchus were close to the Chinese, not really alien or "barbarian." With continuous accommodations to Chinese culture they became almost indistinguishable from the Chinese people.[1]

The history of the Manchus indeed is fascinating and one cannot appreciate it without considering their immediate ancestors, the Jurchens, who appeared in Manchuria, China's northeast frontier, and organized themselves into clans, tribes, and regional alliances. They founded the Jin dynasty (1115–1234), a vast kingdom covering Manchuria, part of Mongolia, and North China. In due course many Jurchens in North China accommodated themselves to Chinese ways of life. Therefore, they were classified as Northern Chinese by the Mongol conquerors. Those Jurchens who remained in their homeland— the Amur-Sungari region—divided, regrouped, migrated to southern Manchuria, and finally became the immediate ancestors of the Manchus. In the Ming period they were under China's guard-post system, a device for loose control, and comprised three groups: Jianzhou, Haixi, and Wild. Nurhaci (1559–1626) and his son Hong Taiji (1592–1643) came from the left branch of the Jianzhou tribe.[2] When unifying the Jurchens they accepted assistance from non-Jurchen elements. In 1635, for good political reasons, Hong Taiji named his group Manchus, with of course Jurchens as the core. He then founded the Qing dynasty, marking the second foreign conquest of all of China.

1. Theme and Approach

This book constitutes a study of the Manchus, attempting to show how they adopted Chinese methods of governing and ways of life and what changes occurred among them during the years 1583–1795. Studies that deal with sinicization (or sinification) of China's frontier peoples, including the Manchus, are mainly articles. As a result, my work aims at a book-length study and follows an analytical, systematic, and topical approach, with a focus on major adoptions—for example, economic, legal, and social institutions. To show the depth of Chinese influence on the Manchus, however, it occasionally covers some neglected and important aspects, such as the transformation of the *fadu*, a rustic Jurchen bag for hunters and warriors to carry food, to the *hebao*, a small and elegant Chinese pouch of an aesthetic nature. This replacement evidenced the decline of Manchu martial virtues, a major component of their cultural identity. One should point out that sinicization was never a one-way street. When receiving Chinese influence, the Manchus left their cultural marks on China. Since Manchu cultural influence should be treated as a separate subject, my study will concentrate, as the title suggests, on sinicization of the Manchus.[3] Following general practice, I select the aforesaid dates for convenience. Long before Nurhaci took up arms against the Ming in 1583, sinicization was already under way. It reached a climax during the Qianlong reign (1736–1795) and continued among the Manchus even after the end of the dynasty.

One may divide Manchu adoption of Chinese culture into two stages. The first was a Jurchen phase, with the Liaodong frontier in Manchuria as the chief setting, opening with the Jurchens's southward migration in the mid-fourteenth century from the area of Yilan in today's Heilongjiang Province and lasted until the mid-1630s. They kept in touch with China through geographical, economic, political, and social channels. It was a relationship built on mutual interests. The long and multifarious contacts helped the Jurchens improve their economy and technology, contributed to the rise of Nurhaci's frontier kingdom, laid the groundwork for the Qing dynasty, and enriched their language with many Chinese loanwords. China benefited from Jurchen products, among which were horses, furs, ginseng, and pearls. More importantly, such a relationship helped China maintain peace on its frontier. This stage came to an end when Hong Taiji forged a new ethnic identity for his subjects by changing the name Jurchen to Manchu. The following year, 1636, he proclaimed the Qing dynasty and began a second stage, the focal point of this study, with Manchus as protagonists of sinicization. Their conquest of China proper in 1644 created a new situation, which made contact easier, broader, and deeper. The Manchus now faced a prevailing Chinese society and were subject to more Chinese influence than had the Jurchens. Chinese norms, mores, and values made inroads into their cultural heritage and thus weakened their ethnic solidarity. They fell helplessly into an identity crisis, which the Qing emperors desperately tried to overcome.

The term "sinicization" first appeared in *Athenaeum*, a literary weekly published in London. When reviewing a book on Japan in 1898, a scholar mentioned that Japanese Shintoism was influenced by sinicization. Although the reviewer did not further delineate the term, it was soon adopted by scholars everywhere.[4] To make matters worse, dictionaries fail to agree on a specific definition of sinicization. *The Oxford English Dictionary* defines it as "the action or process of sinicizing" and "sinicizing" as "to invest with a Chinese character." According to *Webster's Third New International Dictionary of the English Language Unabridged*, "sinicize" means "to modify by Chinese influence." The same verb is defined as "to make Chinese in character or bring under Chinese influence" in *The Random House Dictionary of the English Language*. Even today there is little consensus among scholars about its meaning. Some define it in terms of ethnic assimilation, while some view it as adoption of institutions or cultural fusion.[5] Obviously it is difficult to define sinicization precisely. However insufficient, the definitions given by the above dictionaries are useful for my purpose, for I apply the term only as my framework to study how the Manchus were brought under Chinese influence and acquired a Chinese character. To facilitate my work, I interpret sinicization as adoption of, accommodation to, and participation in Chinese ways of life, such as attitudes, manners, ideas, beliefs, values, and various institutions.

I adopt the term sinicization because it is more suitable to my subject than two other terms, acculturation and assimilation, each with its own various theories. Acculturation is a term coined by American anthropologists when they investigated cultural change among the native Americans after the latter's contact with white colonists. In other words, the term arose from a colonial background and was characterized by conquest and Christian conversion. One may question its applicability to other societies with different backgrounds. Assimilation, a sociological term, is a process wherein a subordinate group's culture may be submerged or even destroyed by that of the dominant group. In reality, it chiefly involves individual or small groups of immigrants, who are eager to join the mainstream of the host society, but it is conditioned by many contingencies and variables.[6] Neither acculturation nor assimilation can be a paradigm for my study of the Manchus, who began as a frontier people of China and finally became its conquering minority. The Manchu experience can be more effectively treated by the theme sinicization, a term that has been well received by international academic circles since its first appearance. Further, it is a process in which China's population and history have been shaped and reshaped. For instance, it served to bring together all sorts of peoples in early China. Unification of China by the Qin dynasty in 221 BC put many ethnic groups into a single imperial framework and thus helped the molding of the Chinese. In the years 220–581 and again in 907–1234, such frontier peoples as the Xiongnu, Xianbei, Turks, Khitans, and Jurchens entered North China as immigrants or conquerors. In time they joined China's mainstream and became ethnic minorities in a larger society. What the Manchus experienced was the same process, which should be studied in terms of sinicization. One may regard this as a process of integration which is still at work in China.[7]

For example, all students in grades 1–12 must learn the official Chinese language no matter what dialects or ethnic languages they may use after school.

One cannot limit sinicization to any single aspect of Chinese culture or institutions, for it has a broad coverage and a complex nature. Therefore, whether or not a person was sinicized should not be judged by any single factor. Nor can one interpret it as an outcome of casual contact. There is no precise beginning or ending date because it is an ongoing process of contact through various channels. A sinicized Manchu was a person who had adopted certain Chinese cultural traits, but not all of them. In all likelihood, a sinicized Manchu was not aware of being sinicized because, according to specialists, ethnic identity is a subjective as well as changeable perception. What he regarded as Manchu traditions were actually the reinterpretation of a culture that had embraced Chinese elements resulting from contact.[8]

The Manchus, one may also add, were the most sinicized of all the frontier conquerors in Chinese history, and they founded the most enduring regime of the conquest dynasties. After 1644 almost all Manchus moved into China proper, a setting different from that of the Liaodong frontier. There they were numerically overwhelmed by the conquered and culturally penetrated by Chinese ways of life. With the exception of political control, they were in fact a subculture in a larger society. Nevertheless, it was not a civilizing process because the Manchus had their own cultural traditions. Nor does it mean the complete replacement of their heritages by Chinese culture. What the revolution of 1911 took away from the Manchus was their political domination, nothing else. They are an active ethnic minority group in China today, with millions of members.

The long contacts that resulted in sinicization were not planned by any individual or group. They were rather desired by both China and its frontier neighbors for reciprocal goals. Like their chiefs, Jurchen commoners played important roles in the contact. Although the commoners rarely appear in sources, their activities may be discerned from data that cover the upper levels of society. In the early days, these commoners kept in touch with Chinese and Korean frontiersmen to acquire cloth, farming tools, and many other commodities. They raided Chinese and Korean frontiers and held captives, deserters, or fugitives as slaves. With the conquest of the Ming they became the ruling class in a dominant Chinese society. But under the onslaught of Chinese culture their ethnic identity was weakened. In two or three generations, they forgot their native tongue and gave up their warrior virtues. By imperial order they, together with their officers, attended indoctrination seminars filled with Confucian ideals, which actually further diluted their cultural heritage. With the increase in their population, they were financially hard-pressed. More and more, they transformed into an interest group fighting for its survival. In such circumstances the Qing court failed to hold them together as a close-knit ethnic group; nor could it maintain their privileged status. Finally, an imperial decree in 1865 allowed them and their officers to leave the banners, choose their occupations, and register as individuals under Chinese officials.[9]

Qing rulers, one should point out, actually helped sinicization, despite their efforts to keep the Manchus as a coherent ethnic group. Unlike Nurhaci, his father, Hong Taiji took it even farther, recruiting many Chinese into his service, adopting Chinese institutions, and planning to subjugate the Ming. His successors, in particular from Kangxi to Qianlong, faced two cultural worlds: the Manchu heritage and the traditions of the conquered.[10] Through their measures, they championed Chinese culture to facilitate their rule. Perhaps the single most important measure taken by the Kangxi emperor was the founding of the palace school to teach imperial sons many subjects, among which were Chinese history and classics. Yongzheng patronized Chan Buddhism; his son, Qianlong, sponsored Chinese scholars, artists, literary men, and publication projects. But they were not captives of Chinese culture, for they were conscious of the political importance of their ethnic identity. They repeatedly exhorted the Manchus to return to their cultural heritage as a close-knit ethnic group. Since they had internalized Confucian precepts through education at an early age, they integrated them with those of the Manchus.[11] Their exhortations were in fact couched in Confucian terms. They unconsciously accelerated what they desperately tried to stop.

Some Asianists, loosely known as the "New Qing" scholars, have recently dismissed the term sinicization as biased, misleading, and conceptually flawed. Many of their criticisms seem to have resulted from their misinterpretation of the term, possibly because of its vague connotation. For example, they consider "circularity" a "conceptual flaw" inherent in sinicization. Yet it also exists within culture change, mainly as a process of constant cultural mutation. They also relate sinicization to Han Chinese chauvinism and "twentieth-century China's nationalism." These links can be debated because the term was a European creation when China was under intense pressure from foreign imperialism. It involved no Chinese chauvinism or nationalism.[12] As a major regional power with more people and richer natural resources, China was attractive to its frontier neighbors. Through migration, invasion, or occupation, newcomers, like immigrants in the United States, adopted the culture of their hosts and joined the mainstream. This was a voluntary action in their own best interests and had nothing to do with the China-centered concept. The mischaracterizing of sinicization for Chinese chauvinism or nationalism may also have arisen from its Chinese rendering, *Hanhua* (transformation into Han Chinese). The translation does not seem appropriate for the so-called Han Chinese, not a monolithic or changeless group as one may believe, but one having numerous dialects and diverse customs. Such differences have both geographical and ethnic implications. Although the Han make up the majority of the Chinese population, more than fifty other ethnic groups exist in China today.[13] Whatever the origin of this conception, the term sinicization in no way minimizes the significant contribution of the Manchus to Chinese history. As a matter of fact, the Chinese context speaks the more forcefully for the importance of the Manchu legacy.

Another criticism concerns the relationship between sinicization and the Manchu identity. Contrary to the views of the "New Qing" scholars, the two may go side by side, for their relationship is not dichotomous. The Qing rulers adopted Chinese culture, hoping to win Chinese support. At the same time they tried to maintain their Manchu identity as a coherent ruling group. These two goals were driven by the same impetus and were not in conflict. For realistic purposes, their Manchu subjects adopted Chinese culture and joined the mainstream of the conquered, but they retained membership in the Manchu ethnic group. Specialists in ethnic studies agree that the traditional culture of an ethnic group undergoes changes in the course of contact with other groups. Consequently some of its elements trail off into oblivion, some others are recentered, and new ones are adopted.[14] This is applicable to the concept of sinicization, essentially a gradual process, which does not work to replace any group's ethnic identity *in toto*.

"New Qing" scholars also dismiss sinicization on the grounds that in the eighteenth and nineteenth centuries the Manchus remained in high offices and that for security reasons, many Qing official documents were still written in Manchu.[15] Their contentions do not seem relevant. Sinicization did not have to exclude the Manchus from high offices, for they were, first and foremost, the ruling class. Most Manchu high officials were loyal both to Qing emperors and to Confucian values. Language alone is not enough to prove one's ethnic identity or deny the role of sinicization. From 1644 more and more Manchus, elite and commoners alike, had become interested in Chinese and forgotten their mother tongue. Two of Qianlong's nephews, for example, could not speak Manchu. During the Qianlong reign, one may reasonably infer, the imperial clans divided into two linguistic subgroups, Chinese and Manchu.[16]

Written Manchu was in the same situation. After the 1860s Manchu commanders were no longer required to submit military reports in Manchu unless they did not know Chinese. The late Qing monarchs required Manchu documents largely as an ethnic symbol of the ruling class. Indeed, most of the Manchu archives have not been used by researchers. While they may contain some important messages, as the "New Qing" historians speculate, there is also a possibility that these documents do not carry any information about sinicization. The case can be made that many materials, such as the bulky Manchu confidential memorials submitted by Manchu commanders and high provincial administrators during the Kangxi and Yongzheng reigns, are accessible today. They did not contain any data against the notion of sinicization or in favor of the arguments of the "New Qing" scholars. It is safe to say that once the contents of the Manchu archives are known to the scholarly community, the general picture of the Qing dynasty will remain the same, even though certain specific aspects may change.[17]

The last issue is the Chinese animosity toward the Manchus, which the "New Qing" scholars stress in an attempt to invalidate the concept of sinicization.[18] Once intense and widespread, this hatred faded with time. By the nineteenth century the Chinese-Manchu ethnic boundaries were blurred. Both the Chinese and the Manchus rallied around the Qing rulers against foreign imperialism. Like previous revolts in Chinese history, the mid-nineteenth century rebellions, especially the Taipings, who denounced the Qing dynasty in ethnic terms, essentially meant to overthrow the government, which happened to be under the Manchus. One should remember that all these mid-century revolts were suppressed by such Chinese armed forces as the Hunan and Anhui armies. The Hunan Army further recovered Sinkiang (Xinjiang) from Moslem rebels. The Guangxu emperor (r. 1875–1908) closely worked with Chinese scholar-officials to implement constitutional reforms. After the defeat of the reforms, these Chinese officials organized the Emperor Protection Society, active at home and abroad. To counteract its influence the revolutionaries under Sun Yat-sen (1866–1925) reminded their countrymen of Manchu cruelty during the conquest of the Ming dynasty and the Qing inability to defend China from foreign encroachment. Violent actions against the Manchus around the time of the fall of the Qing were sporadic and soon died down. While mentioning it as an alien regime responsible for China's many problems, Chinese scholars greatly admired the Qing as an empire-builder, a promoter of Chinese culture, and so on.[19]

To the "New Qing" scholars there were close links between the Manchu ethnicity and the Inner Asian regions. With such links, they believe, the Qing emperors were able to draw on various ideologies and practices from the Mongols, Tibetans, and Moslems to create the Qing empire and rule it in different capacities.[20] But historical evidence has not confirmed this theory. China played an indispensable role in the Qing empire. It was the empire's geographical, political, and financial foundation. The Qing monarchs governed it from their throne in Peking. When they died they were buried in the metropolitan area, not anywhere else. Clearly China was the center of their lives and careers. Moreover, my study does not deal with Mongolia, Sinkiang, or Tibet, focusing only on the Manchu accommodation to Chinese ways of life.

Sources indicate that the "Inner Asian" commonality, especially the Mongols, did not play an important role in the Qing conquest of China. The conquest resulted chiefly from the actions of the Manchus and their Chinese collaborators, whose artillery units greatly contributed to the defeat of Ming forces during the reign of Hong Taiji. By 1593 three Mongol tribal chiefs joined forces with six Jurchen tribes in an attempt to overwhelm Nurhaci. In later years many Mongols, such as some Chahar tribes, fought on the Ming side. There is ample evidence that Manchus succeeded in controlling Mongolia, Sinkiang, and Tibet by diplomacy and war, not by their Inner Asian connection or by their Mongol allies. With the fall of the Yuan dynasty (1279–1368) the Mongols were divided and dispersed. Those in Manchuria were mainly the Qorčins, at first opposing Nurhaci and Hong Taiji. By means of war and marital ties the latter won the support of some Qorčin tribes. The rise of the Chahar Mongols under the Lindan Khutuktu Khan (1592–1634?), an ambitious and oppressive ruler, pushed such Mongol tribes as the Tümed, the Qaračin, and the Naiman to seek Manchu protection. After several expeditions, the Manchus destroyed the Lindan Khan's power and controlled Inner Mongolia.[21]

The Eleuths (Oirats) provided a more complicated case of Manchu-Mongol relations. Under their aggressive rulers they invaded the Khalkha Mongols in Outer Mongolia, occupied Tibet, and posed a serious threat to the northern and western frontiers of the Qing. To safeguard their empire the Qing monarchs from Kangxi to Qianlong waged a long war against the Eleuths. A considerable number of Chinese soldiers from the Green Standard units joined each Qing task force, whose provisions were collected and transported from China proper.[22] The defeat of the Eleuths enabled the Qing to control Outer Mongolia, Sinkiang, and Tibet. Suffice it to say that the founding and defending of the Qing empire depended to a large extent on military strength, to which China's contribution was indispensable.

It should also be noted that early Qing rulers did not trust the Mongols. Nurhaci twice lashed out at some Mongol allies for their looting and killing in his frontier state. Hong Taiji entertained even more suspicions of the Mongols, forbidding people to give or sell weapons to them. He lodged many lengthy complaints against Oba, a Qorčin tribal leader, for deceptions, assistance to enemies, and failure to take joint action against the Chahar Mongols. The Kangxi emperor regarded the Mongols as greedy, mean, and wretched.[23] The imperial mistrust was justified by the revolts of the Sunid, Cecen, and Chahar Mongols in 1646 and 1675, when the Qing was engaged in a life-and-death struggle against the Rebellion of the Three Feudatories (1673–1681). During the Qing campaigns against the Zungar (Dzungar) tribe of the Eleuths in the mid-1750s, the Khalkha Mongols revolted.[24]

Nor did any Inner Asians except the Manchus play a major part in the Qing imperial administration. At the top of the Qing imperial bureaucracy were the Grand Secretariat and the Grand Council. In particular, the Grand Council exercised considerable influence over Mongolia, Sinkiang, and Tibet. But throughout the dynasty there were only ten Mongol Grand Secretaries, and nine Mongol Grand Councilors. The nineteen names made up a tiny portion when compared with the number of their Manchu and Chinese colleagues. Moreover, because five people served in both offices, the actual number of top Mongol officials was fourteen. The Mongols did not even play a major administrative role in the Court of Dependent Peoples (*Lifan yuan*), an office originally created to deal with Mongol affairs. During the period of 152 years (1644–1795), however, there were as few as eleven Mongols made presidents of the court. Altogether, their tenures lasted for seventy-seven years only.[25] There were no Tibetan or Uigher officials in the highest imperial bureaucracy. On all accounts the Inner Asian commonality did not contribute as much to the Qing empire as the Manchus or the Chinese did.

The above analysis shows that the Manchu ethnicity or Inner Asian approach to the study of Qing history would unlikely change anything significantly about the Qing dynasty or about the status of the Manchus as an ethnic minority in China today. Contrary to the views of the "New Qing" scholars, the sinicization approach did not diminish the Manchu role in Chinese history. As defined by the standard dictionaries, the concept of sinicization does not contain any notion of Chinese cultural or moral superiority. All additives seem to have been introduced into the term by some scholars because of misinterpretation. Therefore, what should be questioned is not the term itself, but the way to use it. If judiciously applied, it is a useful instrument for explaining Chinese history, specifically, China's relations with frontier peoples.

2. Contents and Sources

This study is organized into eight chapters, with an introduction and a conclusion. Since the Introduction is being presented here, no summary of it is further needed. The first chapter seeks to explain the long and complex Manchu ethnic strands, with Jurchens as the core and the non-Jurchen components—Mongols, Chinese, and Koreans—as the outer layers. The Jurchens laid the groundwork for the sinicization of the Manchus. The second deals with creation of a frontier power by Nurhaci. His two brilliant sons, Hong Taiji and Dorgon, (1612–1650) founded the Qing empire and accelerated Manchu accommodation to Chinese ways of life. On the whole, these two chapters establish the framework of Manchu adoption of Chinese culture.

In Chapter III, I discuss the ecological system of Manchuria and the effect of agriculture, frontier markets, and tributary trade on the Jurchen economy. Economic activities improved their life, broadened their contact with Ming China, and facilitated their adoption of Chinese culture.

Chapter IV treats the status of Liaodong as a frontier society, centering on frontiersmen and transfrontiersmen. Their activities helped introduce Chinese culture to the Jurchens. Administrative and legal institutions are covered in Chapter V. Early Qing rulers from Hong Taiji on adopted the Ming ruling machinery and legal code. These Chinese institutions improved the Qing governing institutions, which were also marked by certain Manchu innovations. Transformation of the Manchu social institutions, including marriage, funerals, and naming practices, is the focal point of Chapter VI. Such changes greatly weakened the Manchu martial virtues.

Chapter VII traces changes in such aspects of Manchu culture as language and literature. The importance of the Manchu language diminished with time. Although it retained official status to the end of the dynasty, it was "lifeless." As a result of education Manchu writers, mainly poets and essayists, wrote in Chinese characters and according to Chinese literary rules. The last chapter deals with the influence of Chinese aesthetic taste, religious belief, norms, and mores on the Manchu ethnic heritage. Construction of the Yuanming Yuan repre-

sented a climax of Chinese aesthetic impact. For political considerations, early Manchu rulers patronized Chinese Buddhism, popular
cults, and Confucian teachings. The hortatory writings of Kangxi and
Yongzheng were inculcated on Chinese and Manchus at lecture sessions nationwide.

The Conclusion seeks to summarize this study and also offers further insights on sinicization. One such idea is that Chinese culture
and Manchu heritage do not exclude each other. However sinicized,
Qing political institutions maintained some Manchu features. Even
today the Manchus are able to preserve some ethnic heritage in their
daily life. Another idea concerns that the Manchus left indelible marks
on Chinese ways of life. Geopolitically, for example, modern China
inherited from the Qing empire such important frontier regions as
Mongolia, Sinkiang, and Tibet. Chinese culture and history had to be
reinterpreted with the addition of the Manchu component. The last
idea is about the Manchu reaction to sinicization.

My sources divide into categories: basic and monographic. In the
first are archival materials, official compilations, collected memorials,
local histories, genealogical records, and accounts by contemporaries.
On the whole, they provide information on the ethnic composition,
economic life, social structure, political development of the Jurchens,
and the changes resulting from Chinese cultural influence, all important to the rise and sinicization of the Manchus. The old- and new-
script Manchu archives, respectively known as *Jiu Manzhou dang* and
Manwen laodang, are of a political nature, showing frontier relations
between the Jurchens and Ming China. So are the two bulky batches
of Ming-Qing archival materials published by the Academia Sinica in
Taipei. The collected confidential Manchu memorials of the Kangxi
and Yongzheng reigns contain a variety of important data, such as
the heirdom struggle, Kangxi's printing of the Chinese classics, the
military campaigns in the Northwest, the language problem, and the
imperial sensitivity to ethnicity. Equally important are the collected
Chinese confidential memorials, entitled *Gong-zhong tang* and arranged by reigns from Kangxi to Qianlong. All published by the National Palace Museum in Taipei. Both collected Manchu and Chinese
confidential memorials testify to the weakening of Manchu cultural
identity and the imperial efforts to revive it.. Comprising genealogi-

cal, hereditary, service, and miscellaneous files, the *Eight Banners Archives* (*Baqi dang*) provide useful biographical data on Manchu elites. Of the archival sources the *Collected Liaodong Archival Compilation of the Ming Period* (*MLTT*) proved the best because it sheds light on many aspects of the region, among which were frontier markets and Jurchen raids and immigrants. These activities facilitated the sinicization of the Jurchens, Also very useful is *Zhongguo Ming-chao dang'an zonghui*, a multivolume collection of Ming archival materials, published in 2001.[26]

The Ming and Qing governments sponsored many types of official works. Among them were the *Shilu* (veritable records), a chronological account of important state affairs. The veritable records of the Ming dynasty (*Ming shilu*) contain data on appointments of Jurchen chiefs, tributary missions, immigrants, Chinese deserters and fugitives, all contributing to the sinicization of the Jurchens, ancestors of the Manchus. The *History of the Ming Dynasty* offers background information for my work. The Qing *Shilu* for the early reigns, including its Manchu version for the Nurhaci era, occasionally reveals changes in Manchu values. Their deficiencies in economic and social information are complemented by the Korean veritable records of the Yi dynasty (1392–1910), which have two versions: one published in Seoul in 1955–1958, the other in Tokyo in 1953–1967. Of the Yi records, those on the reigns from T'aejo to Injo (1392–1649) are the most useful for my study.[27]

Two works on the Eight Banners, a Qing official project printed in 1739 and 1799 in both Manchu and Chinese, are very useful. They contain, among other things, biographies of more than four thousand officers and officials. Accounts of filial and righteous individuals and model women disclose much adoption of Chinese culture. Under Yongzheng's auspices three companion works on banner affairs appeared, with imperial edicts and memorials from banners. On the whole the three compilations show signs of sinicization. In 1783 the Qing court published a small compilation on the origins of the Manchus. Chapters 16–20 reveal much Chinese influence on Manchu social, cultural, and economic life.[28]

Other sources are collected memorials by Ming and Qing officials. *Chou-Liao shihua* (Great plans for Liaodong) consists of memorials by Ming officials, some of whom worked in or toured the region in 1618–1620. The Qing government prohibited printing or circulation, since the memorials recorded unfavorable information about the Manchus. In the years 1632–1635 Chinese staffers of the Literary Office (*Wen-guan*) made suggestions to Hong Taiji about adoption of Ming institutions. Ninety-seven of their memorials are available. Individual officials had their own collections of memorials. The collected memorials by Xiong Tingbi (d. 1625), who twice defended Liaodong against Nurhaci, are worth studying. In his memorials He Erjian, once an inspector of the region, related that many Chinese fled to Jurchen lands and created the Village of One Thousand Families (*qianjia zhuang*).[29]

Local histories provide data on the physical and human environment of the Liaodong frontier not found in other sources. The *Liaodong Gazetteer* is the most useful local history, with two editions: *Liaodong zhi* and its enlarged version, *Quan Liao zhi*, each revised. They supply information on census figures, local customs, frontier interpreters, Jurchen culture, and more. Completed around 1620, the *Illustrated Gazetteer of Kaiyuan*, a fortified city and frontier market, details the Four Hūlun Tribes, intertribal affairs, and the tribes' relations with China.[30]

Manchu genealogies provide data on Manchu kinship structure, marriage relations, burial customs, and interest in civilian posts, with hints of Chinese influence. They also disclose a change in Manchu names. Since the Kangxi period, Manchus had adopted Chinese naming conventions. Most Manchu genealogies, official and private, appeared after the early 1740s. The Qing imperial family records (*yudie*) are in both Manchu and Chinese, with many branch records. *Genealogy of the Manchu Clans in the Eight Banners*, an official compilation printed in 1745, with Manchu and Chinese versions, has more than seven thousand short biographies of bannermen, containing invaluable information.[31]

Private genealogies seem to have been begun by Chinese bannermen and became common in the nineteenth century. Scholars have recently discovered many Manchu genealogies in Liaoning. Politically the Manchus needed records to substantiate their claim to inheritance of titles or offices. Influenced by Chinese tradition, they compiled genealogies to maintain family values.[32] Well organized and repeatedly revised, the family records of Eidu (1562–1621), a great warrior from the Niohuru clan, are full of information and became a model for some genealogical works, such as the *Genealogy of the Gūwalgiya Clan of Hada in the Manchu Plain Red Banner*.[33]

When the situation in Liaodong deteriorated after the sixteenth century, the Jurchens attracted the attention of Chinese and Korean scholars, many of whom were officials. The best Chinese account was *A Brief Survey of the Eastern Barbarians* by Mao Ruizheng (fl. 1597–1636). It contains data on the settlement, life, and customs of Jurchen tribesmen, frontier markets, and the rise of Nurhaci. A high official in the late 1630s, Fang Kongzhao (1591–1655) wrote *A Brief Account of China's Frontiers*, with a chapter on Chinese deserters and runaways and Jurchen influence on Chinese inhabitants. Qu Jiusi (1546–1617) wrote biographies about such people as rebels, bandit leaders, minority groups, and frontier tribesmen, devoting the eleventh chapter to the rise and fall of Jurchen chiefs, their relations with China, and their commercial activities.[34]

Some Korean sources are firsthand accounts. One of these was *An Illustrated Account of the Journey to Fe Ala*, written by Sin Ch'ung-il (1554–1622) after a visit with Nurhaci in 1596. Yi Min-hwan (1573–1649), a scholar-official on the staff of the Korean army dispatched to help fight Nurhaci at the Battle of Sarhū in 1619, was taken prisoner by the Jurchens. Based on observations and inquiries made during his captivity, his book covers nearly all aspects of Jurchen life and identifies Chinese and Koreans who joined the Jurchens.[35] After capitulation, the Yi dynasty sent three princes as hostages and liaison officials to Shenyang, then the Manchu capital. They dispatched reports to the Yi court from 1637 to 1644. Out of these reports came three documentary compilations containing information on Manchu customs, Korean captives, and descendants of Jurchens who married Koreans. *Shenyang zhuangqi* includes the above dispatches, mostly to the Royal Secretariat, while *Shenyang riji* covers daily activities of the Korean office. The last compilation, *Shenguan lu*, was an abridged version of the first two.[36]

The vast body of sources available to me consists of monographic studies by both Asian and Western specialists. Because of space limitations, the works to be analyzed below must be highly selective. Most studies do not focus on sinicization of the Manchus, but I was able to draw from them bits and pieces of data, especially fresh ideas, to enrich my work.

Works that deal with sinicization of China's frontier peoples, including the Manchus, are in the main articles. Wang Tongling's study briefly covers the subject. The article by Mao Wen discusses the influence of the Chinese language on Manchu. By the 1950s Yao Congwu, an expert on China's frontiers, published a series of studies on the Khitans of the Liao state and the Jurchens of the Jin dynasty. He argues that the expansion and continuation of Chinese history resulted from adoption of Chinese culture by successive groups of frontier people. In the 1960s more progress was made in the study of Manchu sinicization. The articles by Guan Donggui, another specialist, define the meaning of sinicization, analyze the importance of agriculture to Jurchen adoption of Chinese culture, and cover sinicization of Manchuria, the native land of the Manchus. Bernd-Michael Linke's study concerns Chinese influence on bureaucratization of the Manchu state during the time of conquest. The article by Ping-ti Ho is a systematic study of sinicization throughout Chinese history, with special reference to the Qing dynasty. Most recently, Guo Chengkang wrote an article viewing sinicization in terms of cultural fusion.[37]

Almost all Chinese works, such as *Qingdai shi* (History of the Qing period) and *Qingchao tongshi* (General history of the Qing dynasty), complain about the Qing's inability to defend China against foreign imperialism during the second half of the nineteenth century, but they affirm the Manchu contribution to China. There are fine studies on the history of the Jurchen and Manchu peoples as well as their relations with China and Korea by such scholars as Kawachi Yoshihiro, Wada Sei, Mitamura Taisuka, Sun Jinji, and Li Yanguang. Frederic Wakeman's *The Great Enterprise* sheds light on the frontier society of the Liaodong region, the rise of the Manchus, the founding of the Qing dynasty, the conquest of China, the creation of a governing machinery, and the Chinese influence on them.[38]

Many works center on Qing rulers from Nurhaci to Qianlong, covering their efforts to retain the Manchu ethnic identity, as well as their role in adopting Chinese culture. Some scholars considered Hong Taiji a cultural and institutional reformer since he took over from his father a Jurchen-Mongol-oriented frontier state and turned it into a centralized, bureaucratic empire after the Chinese style. Under the guidance of Fan Wencheng (1597–1666) and Hong Cheng-chou (1595–1665), as recent studies point out, Confucian values were adopted during the Shunzhi reign. During the Kangxi and Yongzheng reigns (1662–1722, 1723–1735) sinicization made further progress. To historians, Kangxi was a great monarch, for he maintained China's unification, defeated the Eleuth Mongols, adopted more Chinese institutions, and printed books on the Chinese classics. Scholars agree that Yongzheng was an efficient, hardworking, and benevolent autocratic ruler. He wrote long commentaries on the Sacred Edict, sixteen commands issued by Kangxi and based on Neo-Confucian tenets, and inculcated them in all his subjects. The Qianlong emperor, a prolific poet, loved Chinese art, collected rare books, and strove, as his ancestors did, to keep Manchu ethnicity intact.[39] But the Manchu tradition he tried to enforce had already embraced Chinese cultural components.

Of Chinese studies on Manchu political, legal, and social institutions, *History of the Manchu State, Law, and Government Institutions before 1644* by Zhang Jinfan and Guo Chenkang is the best. It treats the subject mainly from a Manchu perspective. Also important is Liu Xiaomeng's *Tribe and State of the Manchus*, which deals with clan, village, and tribal institutions and their transformation into a frontier state. Among Japanese scholars, Kanda Nobuo studied the Manchu Literary Office while Oshibauchi Hajime discussed criminal laws under Nurhaci and Hong Taiji. The article by Fang Chaoying explores ultimogeniture, an important Manchu social institution, which trailed off in the early eighteenth century. The work by Yang Yingjie covers almost all aspects of Manchu society.[40]

Manchu is a subgroup of the Tungusic language family, which, as Zhao Zhencai concludes after studying ethnological, archaeological, and documentary sources, shares common linguistic elements with Chinese. Some scholars believe that Chinese loanwords contributed to popularization of the Chinese language among the Manchus. Naturally, Manchu translations of the Chinese classics helped spread Chinese culture. According to J. R. P. King's study, the dot and circle that distinguish the new Manchu script from the old was adopted from the Korean writing system.[41]

Some scholars have recently become interested in Manchu literature. According to Zhang Jiasheng, by the second half of the seventeenth century, Manchu poets had emerged, first from aristocratic families with official status, and then from private individuals. Despite their diverse backgrounds, Manchu poets had something in common. They learned poetry from Chinese teachers, wrote in Chinese, and observed the rules of Chinese poems. Singde (1655–1685), the most important lyric poet of the Qing dynasty, is representative of the aristocratic poets. The other category of poets, such as Funing and Canghai, appeared late and pursued literary achievement, not an official career.[42]

The influence of Chinese architecture on Manchu palaces, temples, and imperial tombs has been confirmed by Asian and Western scholars. Murada Jirō provided a detailed and illustrated study of the Shenyang palaces. Tie Yuqin, a specialist on Qing history of Manchu descent, believes that Chinese architecture affected the structural evolution of Manchu palaces at Liaoyang and Shenyang. An article on palaces and mausoleums in Shenyang by Paula Swart and Barry Till reached the same conclusion.[43]

Some scholars study religion and philosophy. The Manchus practiced Shamanism and Chinese Buddhism. Based on fieldwork and covering the history, rituals, and training of shamans, *A Study of Manchu Shamanism* is the most informative study. Shunzhi and Yongzheng were patrons of Chan Buddhism. To control the Mongols and Tibetans, however, the Qing court sponsored Lamaism.[44] Qing patronage of Confucianism began with Hong Taiji and reached a peak during the Kangxi reign. Many recent studies, including those by Lü Shipeng, Liu Zhiyang, and especially Ping-ti Ho, agree that this patronage was important to sinicization.[45]

Notes

1. Owen Lattimore argues that the Tungus people were noted for "cultural adaptability." See his *Manchuria: Cradle of Conflict* (New York: MacMillan Company, rev. ed., 1935), 18–19. As members of the southern Tungus, one may assume, the Manchus shared the same characteristic. For the quoted word, see Li Chi, "Manchuria in History," *Chinese Social and Political Science Review*, 16. 2 (1932): 227.
2. For the evolution of Manchuria as a geographical and political identity, see

Mark C. Elliott, "The Limits of Tartary: Manchuria in Imperial and National Geographies," *Journal of Asian Studies*, 59. 3 (2000): 603–46. In Chinese the guard-post system is *weisuo*. From the Jianzhou Jurchens stemmed the left and right branches. The Haixi group is alternatively known as the Four Hūlun tribes. The Wild Jurchens are referred to as the *Yeren*.

3.   For a discussion of the *fadu* and its transformation, see the last few pages of Chapter VI. For Manchu influence on China, in particular in the Peking area, see Aixin Gioro Ying-sheng, *Lao Beijing yu Manzu* (Peking: Xueyuan chuban she, 2005), 19–30 ff. The book provides many examples and anecdotes and also covers Chinese influence on the Manchus. Although it is intended for the general public, the book is informative and useful. I am grateful to Dr. Wei-ping Wu for reminding me of the above book and lending it to me

4.   For its first appearance, see *Athenaeum* (26 November 1898): 747 (3rd column). Among scholars who adopted the term were Paul Pelliot, René Grousset, Herbert Franke, Jaques Gernet, John K. Fairbank, Mary C. Wright, to name only a few. For Pelliot, see Karl A. Wittfogel and Chia-sheng Feng, *History of Chinese Society: Liao, 907–1125* (Philadelphia: American Philosophical Society, 1949), 4. René Grousset used the words "Sinicized" and "Iranized" to describe invaders and conqerors in Chinese and Persian histories. See his *The Empire of the Steppes: A History of Central Asia,* trans. Naomi Walford (New Brunswick, NJ: Rutgers University Press, 1970), xxlx. The term appears in *The Cambridge History of China*, Volume 6: *Alien Regimes and Border States, 907–1368*, eds. Herbert Franke and Denis Twitchett (Cambridge and New York: Cambridge University Press, 1994), 240, 244–45. For Gernet, see *A History of Chinese Civilization*, trans. J. R. Foster (Cambridge and New York: Cambridge University Press, 1990, reprint), 186, and Chapter 16. For Fairbank, see Edwin O. Reischauer and John K. Fairbank, *East Asia: The Great Tradition* (Boston: Houghton Mifflin, 1960), 152–53ff. For Mary C. Wright, see her *The Last Stand of Chinese Conservatism: The T'ung-chih Restoration, 1862–1874* (Stanford: Stanford University Press, 1957), 50–56.

5.   For its original meaning, see *The Oxford English Dictionary* (Oxford: Clarendon Press, 2nd ed., 1989, 20 volumes), 15: 529; *Webster's Third New International Dictionary of the English Language* Unabridged (Springfield, MA: Merriam Company, 1971), 2125; *The Random House Dictionary of the English Language Unabridged* (New York: Random House, 2nd ed., 1987), 1785.

     Among those who stress ethnic assimilation are Jing-shen Tao and John W. Dardess. See Tao, *The Jurchen in Twelfth-Century China: A Study of Sinicization* (Seattle and London: University of Washington Press, 1976), xiii; Dardess, *Conquerors and Confucians* (New York and London: Columbia University Press, 1973), 3. Included in the group of works on institutional adoption are Robert B. Oxnam, *Ruling from Horseback: Manchu Politics in the Oboi Regency, 1661–1669* (Chicago and London: University of Chicago Press, 1975), 2; David B. Honey, "Stripping off Felt and Fur: An Essay on Nomadic Sinification," *Papers on Inner Asia* (Bloomington, IN: Research Institute for Asian Studies, Indiana University), 21 (1992): 1–39; and Peter K. Bol, "Seeking Common Ground: Han Literati under Jurchen Rule," *Harvard Journal of Asiatic Studies,* 47. 2 (1987): 483–84. Bol is critical of the term sinicization.

6.   For assimilation, see *Encyclopedia Americana* (Danbury, CT: Grolier, 2003, International ed., 30 volumes), 2: 530; for the contingencies and variables about assimilation, see *International Encyclopedia of the Social and Behavioral Sciences* (Amsterdam; New York: Elsevier, 2001, 26 volumes), 2: 848.

7.   For relations between China and these frontier peoples, see Honey, "Stripping off Felt and Fur," 18–26; Thomas J. Barfield, *The Perilous Frontier: Nomadic Empires and China* (Cambridge, MA: Basil Blackwell, 1989), chs. 2–5. For their occupation and migration, see *CKMT,* 10–15. For sinicization as a process in the making of Chinese history, see Ping-ti Ho, "In Defense of Sinicization: A Rebuttal of Evelyn Rawski's 'Reenvisioning the Qing'," *Journal of Asian Studies,* 57. 1 (1998): 125, 130–35, 143, 151–52, and his "The Significance of the Qing Period in Chinese History," *Journal of Asian Studies,* 26. 2 (1967): 189–95.

     For the Xiongnus, see Ying-shih Yu, "The Hsiung-nu." In Denis Sinor, ed., *The Cambridge History of Early Inner Asia* (Cambridge and New York: Cambridge University Press, 1990), 118–50. For the Xianbei nomads, see *CKMT,* 182–203; Gernet, *A History of Chinese Civilization,* 190–95. For Jurchen migrations to North China and their sinicization, see Tao, *The Jurchen in Twelfth-Century China,* 47–51, and ch. 4; Yao Congwu, *Dongbei shi luncong* (Taipei: Zheng-zhong shuju, 1959, 2 volumes), 2: 31–64, 118–74.

8.   For these specialists, see Jack David Eller, *From Culture to Ethnicity to Conflict: An Anthropological Perspective on International Ethnic Conflict* (Ann Arbor: University of Michigan Press, 1999), 9; William C. McCready, ed., *Culture, Ethnicity, and Identity: Current Issues in Research* (New York: Academic Press, 1983), xxi; David Y. H. Wu, "Culture Change and Ethnic Identity among Minorities in China." In Chien Chiao and Nicholas Tapp, eds., *Ethnicity and Ethnic Groups in China* (Hong Kong: New Asia College, The Chinese University of Hong Kong, 1989), 11.

9.   For relations between ethnic groups and interest groups, see Ivan Light, "Ethnic Succession." In Charles F. Keyes, ed., *Ethnic Change* (Seattle and London: University of Washington, 1981), 55–56. For the imperial decree of 1865, see *CSL,* Tongzhi reign, 144: 2b–3b, 4/6/jiawu.

10. For Manchu adoption of Chinese political and legal institutions, see Chapter V below. For Hong Taiji's policy toward the Chinese, see Gertraude Roth, "The Manchu-Chinese Relationship, 1618–1636." In Jonathan D. Spence and John E. Wills, Jr., eds., *From Ming to Ch'ing: Conquest, Region, and Continuity in Seventeenth-Century China* (New Haven and London: Yale University Press, 1979), 6–7, 22–24. When discussing the two cultural worlds that the Qianlong

era faced, Philip A. Kuhn uses the term "two rhetorical arenas." This can be applied to the earlier reigns of the Qing. See Kuhn, *Soulstealers: The Chinese Sorcery Scare of 1768* (Cambridge, MA, and London: Harvard University Press, 1990), 60.

11.   For exhortations of the three emperors, see Chapters VI–VIII. For steps taken by Qing rulers from Kangxi to Qianglong, see Chapter VIII.

12.   Pamela Kyle Crossley is vehemently against the term because it is "archaic," "conceptually flawed, intellectually inert and impossible to apply to real history." See Crossley, "Thinking about Ethnicity in Early Modern China," *Late Imperial China*, 11. 1 (1990): 1–5, 22. For her view of circularity, see ibid., 2. Similar criticisms also appear in Crossley, *The Manchus* (Cambridge, MA: Blackwell, 1997), 5 and 13. Mark C. Elliott considers the term "misleading." See his *The Manchu Way: The Eight Banners and Ethnic Identity in Late Imperial China* (Stanford: Stanford University Press, 2001), 28.

Evelyn S. Rawski regards the term as "a twentieth-century Han nationalist interpretation of China's past." See her "Presidential Address: Reenvisioning the Qing: The Significance of the Qing Period in Chinese History," *Journal of Asian Studies*, 55. 4 (1996): 831–32, and 842, and her *The Last Emperors: A Social History of Qing Imperial Institutions* (Berkeley: University of California Press,1998), 2–8, especially 2–3.

13.   For the origin and evolution of the term Han, see *CKMT*, 149, 155–56; Jia Jing-yan, "'Han-ren' kao." In Fei Xiaotong et al., *Zhonghua minzu duoyuan yiti geju* (Peking: Zhong-yang minzu xueyuan chuban she, 1989), 137–52. For the diverse composition of the Han Chinese and their culture, see Li Xun and Xue Hong, eds., *Qingdai quanshi*, volume 1 (Shenyang: Liaoning renmin chuban she, 1991), 331–32. For the meaning of the term under the Yuan dynasty, see Yao Cong-wu, *Yao Congwu xian-sheng quanji* (Taipei: Zheng-zhong shuju, 1982, in 10 volumes), 7: 1–3.

14.   For these specialists, see note 8 above.

15.   For Manchu domination of the imperial bureaucracy, see Rawski, "Presidential Address," 829–42, especially 832–33; for Manchu as a security language, see Pamela Kyle Crossley and Evelyn S. Rawski, "A Profile of the Manchu Language in Ch'ing History," *Harvard Journal of Asiatic Studies*, 53. 1 (1993): 63–102.

16.   For Qianlong's nephews, see *CSL*, Qianlong reign, 992: 12a–13b, 40/10/xinsi.

17.   There are two articles on the Manchu archives. On the Grand Council's archives is Beatrice S. Bartlett, "Books of Revelations: The Importance of the Manchu Language Archival Record Books for Research on Ch'ing History," *Late Imperial China*, 6. 2 (1985), 25–36. Mark C. Elliott covers many Qing archives. See his 'The Manchu-language Archives of the Qing Dynasty and the Origins of the Palace Memorial System," *Late Imperial China*, 22. 1 (2001), 1–35.

For military reports in Chinese, see *CSL*, Tongzhi reign, 305: 4a, 10/2/xin-wei. For Manchu memorials, see *Kangxi chao Manwen zhupi zouzhe quanyi*, trans. and ed. Zhongguo diyi lishi dang'an guan (Peking: Zhongguo shehui kexue chubanshe, 1996); *Yongzheng chao Manwen zhupi zouzhe quanyi*, trans. and ed. Zhongguo diyi lishi dang'an guan (Hefei, Anhui: Huang-shan chuban she, 1998, 2 volumes).

18. For instance, see Pamela Kyle Crossley, *A Translucent Mirror: History and Identity in Qing Imperial Ideology* (Berkeley, Los Angeless, London: University of California Press, 1999), 342, 352–53, and the same author's *Orphan Warriors: Three Manchu Generations and the End of the Qing World* (Princeton: Princeton University Press, 1990), 197.

19. For unity of Chinese and Manchus during the second half of the nineteenth century, see Wright, *The Last Stand of Chinese Conservatism*, 50–56. For positive opinions of Qing contributions to China, see *MTTS, 452–500*; Xiao Yishan, *Qingdai tongshi* (Taipei: Taiwan shangwu yinshu guan, 1962), I: 773–855; Zhu Chengru, *Qingchao tongshi* (Peking: Zijin cheng chuban she, 2002–2003, 14 volumes), volume 6: Kangxi chao, ed., Wang Sizhi, chs. 9, 11–13.

20. For the Inner Asian links and the important role played by the Mongols, see Rawski, "Presidential Address," 829–42, especially 831–34. For a refutation of Rawski's view, see Ho, "In Defense of Sinicization," 123–155. For denunciation of sinicization, see Crossley, "Thinking about Ethnicity in Early Modern China," 2–5; for drawing on ideologies and practices from other Inner Asian members, see Mark C. Elliott, *The Manchu Way*, 4–5, 355.

21. For example, the artillery units under Tong Yangxing and Kong Youde helped defeat Ming defenders in many cities, including Jinzhou. See *CSKC*, 10: 8064 and 8124–25. For the three Mongol tribes, see *Qing taizu wu huangdi Nuerhaqi shilu* (Peiping: Palace Museum, 1932), 1: 10b–11a. For Mongols on the Ming side, see *CSKC*, 1. 29, 33. For Qorčins' hostility toward Nurhaci, see Yan Chong-nian, *Nuer-haci zhuan* (Peking: Beijing chuban she, 1983), pp. 49–52. For the marital diplomacy, see Manchu-Mongol nuptial links, Chapter I, Section 3. For Hong Taiji's expeditions against the Lindan Khan, see Yuan Senpo, "Lun Huang Taiji tongyi Chahaer di douzheng," *Qingshi yanjiu*, 6 (1988): 38–61.

22. For Chinese soldiers in the Qing forces, see *Qinzheng pingding shuomo fanglue*, Wenda (Unda in Manchu) et al., comps. (Peking: Zangxue chuban she, 1994, reprint of 1708 edition, 2 volumes), 1: 6: 37b–38a, Kangxi 29/6; 1: 11: 1a, Kangxi, 30/7; 2. 39: 5a, Kangxi 36/3. For provisions from China proper, see *Qinzheng pingding shuomo fanglue*, 1: 25: 28b–29a, Kangxi 35/5.

23. For Nurhaci's complaint, see Guang Lu and Li Xuezhi, *Qing Taizu chao lao Manwen yuandang* (Taipei: Institute of History and Philology, Academia Sinica, 1970–71, 2 volumes), 2: 231–36. For Hong Taiji's order, see *CSL*, reign of Taizong, 1: 19a, Tianming 11/12/gengzi. For Hong Taiji's complaint, see *CSL*, reign of Taizong, 1: 19b, Tianming 11/12/gengxu; 4: 23a–26a, Tiancong 2/12/ dinghai. For a translation of the document, see Nicola Di Cosmo and Dalizha-

bu Bao, *Manchu-Mongol Relations on the Eve of the Conquest: A Documentary History* (Leiden and Boston: Brill, 2003), 55–61, document #12. For Kangxi's contempt for the Mongols, see *Kangxi chao Manwen zhupi zouzhe quanyi*, 745, edict attached to document #1793, Kangxi 50/2/16; 962, document #2465, Kangxi 53/7/16; 1435, document #3461, Kangxi 58/8/22.

24.   In 1646 the Sunid nomads in Inner Mongolia joined the Cecen tribe in Outer Mongolia in revolt. See *CSKC*, 15: 11896, 11940. For the revolt of the Chahar Mongols under Burni in 1675, see *CSKC*, 10: 8386; *ECCP*, 1: 304–305. For the Khalkha revolt, see C. R. Bawden, "The Mongol Rebellion of 1756–1757," *Journal of Asian History*, 2. 3 (1968): 1–31.

25.   For the Mongol Grand Secretaries and Grand Councilors, see Qian Shifu, *Qingdai zhiguan nianbiao* (Peking: Zhonghua Book Company, 1980), 2–132 and 136–56, respectively.

26.   The *Jiu Manzhou dang* (see *CMCT*) has been partially translated, with two versions. One is entitled *Qing Taizu chao lao Manwen yuandang* by Guang Lu and Li Xuezhi. The other version is *Jiu Manzhou dang yizhu*, sponsored and published by the National Palace Museum in Taipei. The *Manwen laodang* has three renditions, two Chinese and one Japanese. In 1929 Jinliang translated some documents from it under the title *Manzhou laodang bilu* (Peiping: 2 volumes.).For comments on his translation, see Jin Yufu, "Manwen laodang kao," *Shenyang bowu yuan choubei weiyuan hui huikan*, 1 (1947): 8. For the second Chinese rendition, see *MWLT*. For the Japanese translation, see *MBRT*.

The earlier collection of Ming-Qing materials is known in Chinese as *Ming-Qing shiliao*, published in different formats and dates. The Chinese title for the later collection is *Ming-Qing dang'an,* ed., Chang Weiren (Taipei: Institute of History and Philology, Academia Sinica, 1986–92, 261 volumes). For the confidential Manchu memorials of the Kangxi and Yongzheng eras, see note 17 above. For the collected Chinese confidential memorials, see *Gong-zhong dang: Kangxi chao zouzhe* (Taipei: National Palace Museum, 1976, 7 volumes); *Gong-zhong dang: Yongzheng chao zouzhe* (Taipei: National Palace Museum, 1977–80, 27 volumes); *Gong-zhong dang: Qianlong chao zouzhe* (Taipei: National Palace Museum, 1982–86, 75 volumes). For the collected Liaodong archival source, see *MLTT*. The eight banners archives are available in the First Historical Archives in Peking. *Zhongguo Mingchao dang'an zonghui* was edited by Zhongguo diyi lishidang'an guan and Liaoning sheng dang'an guan (Guilin, Guangxi: Guangxi sifan daxue chuban she, 2001, 101 volumes).

27.   The best edition of *Ming shilu* was published by the Academia Sinica in 1962–1968 and collated by Huang Zhangjian (see *MSL*). In addition to the text, it has twenty-one volumes of appendices and twenty-eight volumes of critical notes. For a discussion of the work, see Wolfgang Franke, comp., *An Introduction to the Sources of Ming History* (Kula Lumpur: University of Malaya Press, 1968), 3–23, 30–33. *Mingshi* (History of the Ming Dynasty) was compiled by Zhang

Tingyu et al. and completed in 1739. Its best edition is punctuated and attached with commentaries (Peking: Zhonghua Book Company, 1974, in 28 volumes).

There are two versions of *Qing shilu*. One, *Da Qing lichao shilu,* appeared in the traditional format in 1936, with reprints (see *CSL*). The other, *Qing shilu,* in sixty volumes, is a better version, printed in 1986 by the Zhonghua Book Company in Peking. The Manchu version of *Qing shilu* for the Nurhaci reign is known as *Daicing gurun i manju yargiyan kooli* (Taipei: Hualian chuban she, 1964, reprint) in one volume.

Entitled *Chosŏn wangjo sillok* (see *CWS*), the Seoul edition is better than the other version, for it is indexed, with dates and chapter (*juan*) number on the margin of each page. The Tokyo edition—*Yijo sillok*—was published by the Gakushuin, Tōyō Bunka Kenkyūjo in 56 volumes.

28.   One of the two multivolume works is known as *Baqi tongzhi chuji,* with two reprints. The earlier reprint came out in Taipei in 1968 (see *TCCC*); the later one, a nicer reprint, appeared in 1985 (see *TCCC, 1985*). Their Manchu version, *Jakūn gūsai tung jy sucungga weilehe bithe* (prefaced in 1739), is available. The other multivolume work, *Baqi tongzhi,* included data for the years 1727–1799 (see volumes 38–40 and 41–44, respectively). One of the three works on banner affairs is *Dergi hese jakūn gūsa de wesimbuhengge* (Late Yongzheng period, 10 volumes), with a Chinese version known as *Shangyu baqi* (1723–35, palace ed., 10 volumes). Another is entitled *Shangyu qiwu yifu* (Yongzheng period, 8 volumes). Its Manchu version is referred to as *Dergi hesei wesimbuhe gūsai baita be dahūme gisurefi wesimbuhengge* (10 volumes). The last is *Hesei yabubuha hacilama wesimbuhe gūsai baita* (10 volumes). It also has a Chinese version, *Yuxing qiwu zouyi* comps. Yun-lu et al. (palace ed., 5 volumes). The Chinese title for the work on the origins of the Manchus is Agui and Yu Ming-zhong, *Qinting Manzhou yuanliu kao* (Taipei: Wen-hai chuban she, 1966, CCST, No. 14, volume 131).

29.   The collected memorials by Ming officials, originally compiled and printed by Cheng Kaihu in the seventeenth century, is a reprint (Peiping: National Peiping Library Rare Books Series 1, 1936, prefaced in 1620, 44 volumes). The ninety-seven memorials were compiled by Luo Zhenyu as *Tiancong chao chengong zouyi,* available in his *Shiliao congkan chubian* (N. p.: Dongfang xuehui, 1924, volumes 2–3). Recently, it was included in Pan Zhe, Sun Fangming, and Li Hongbin, comps., *Qing juguan qian shiliao xuanji* (Peking: Chinese People's University Press, 1989), 2: 1–116.

The Chinese title for Xiong's collected memorials is *An-Liao sugao,* in twelve volumes, available in microfilm in the Library of Congress. For the *Qian-jia zhuang,* see He Erjian, *An-Liao yudang sugao,* ed. by He Ziquan and Guo Liangyu ([Zheng-zhou]: Zhong-zhou shuhua she, 1982), 36–37.

30.   The *Liaodong zhi* was first compiled in 1443 by Bi Gong, an assistant military commissioner of the region. The *Quan Liao zhi* was compiled by Li Fu in 1565,

with six chapters and in six volumes. Both are included in the Liaohai congshu, Series 2, 1934, volumes 1–4, 5–10, respectively. Compiled by Feng Yuan, the illustrated gazetteer is known as the *Kaiyuan tushuo* (HLTS ed., 1941, volumes 26–27).

31. For example, the *Nayin Fucha shi zengxiu zhipu* compiled by Dexing (N. p., 1889–1890, handwritten) indicates that almost all the male members of the 12th generation shared the character "*chang*" as the first part of their names. See the section marked by "12th Generation." This had long been a Chinese naming tradition. The Kangxi emperor was the first Manchu throne to adopt the Chinese way of naming. Other Manchus follow suit.

    The imperial genealogy is known as *Aixin juelo zongpu*, comp. Aixin juelo xiupu chu (Shenyang: 1938, 8 volumes). Its first volume is entitled *Xingyuan jiqing*. Among such branch records in the Tōyō Bunko is the genealogy of the Dorgon line, see *Taizu Gao huangdi wei xia hoshi Ruizhong qinwang zhi zisun* (handwritten, 3 volumes). For more branch records, see Taga Akigorō, *Sofu no kenkyū* (Tokyo: The Tōyō Bunko, 1960), 185–86.

    The Chinese title of this genealogy is *Baqi Manzhou shizu tongpu* (see *STTP*). Its new printing has a biographical index (Shenyang: Liao-Shen shushe, 1989). Its Manchu version is entitled *Jakūn gūsai manjusai mukūn hala be uheri ejehe bithe* (26 volumes).

32. For instance, *Zhangshi jiapu*, comp. by Zhang Chaolin and Chang Chaozhen and prefaced in 1679. *Liushi jiapu* was compiled by Liu Anguo in 1684 (N. p.: various page numbers). For the new discoveries in Liaoning, see Li Lin, ed., *Manzu jiapu xuanbian* (Shenyang: Liaoning minzu chuban she, 1988); Li Lin, Hou Jinbang, et al., *Benqi xian Manzu jiapu yanjiu* (Shenyang: Liaoning minzu chuban she, 1988).

    Mark Elliott offers a long discussion about reasons for the Manchus' compilation of genealogies. See his *The Manchu Way*, 326–29. But he seems to have overstated the imperial attempt to retain the Manchu identity.

33. There are at least four editions of the Eidu family records. (1) *Baqi Manzhou Niuhulu shi tongpu*, comp. by Noqin (prefaced in 1747, handwritten, in 12 volumes, with the first six in Chinese and the rest in Manchu); (2) *Xiang huangqi Niuhulu shi Hongyi gong jiapu*, comp. by Aligun (1765, in 10 volumes) as a revised edition of the above compilation; (3) *Kaiguo zuoyun gongchen Hongyi kong jiapu*, comp. by Fulang (handwritten, 1786, in 16 volumes); (4) *Xiang huangqi Manzhou Niuhulu shi Hongyi gong jiapu* (handwritten, 1798, in 15 volumes), with no compiler's name.

    The Chinese title for the Hada Gūwalgiya genealogy is *Zheng hongqi Manzhou Hada Guaerjia shi jiapu*, comp. by Enling (prefaced in 1849, in 8 volumes). In the explanatory note (*fanli*), the compiler acknowledged that he took a leaf from the Eidu family records.

34. Mao wrote with the pen name "Diao-shang Yugong." Its Chinese title is *Dong-yi kaolüe* (HLTS, 1991, volumes 94–95). Some other scholars may have drawn on Mao's book. Peng Sunyi (1615–73) seems one such scholar. His book is entitled *Shan-zhong wenjian lu* (Yujian zhai congshu, 1910? volumes 4–5, in various editions). See *ECCP*, 1: 615. Fang's book is known as the *Quanbian lüeji* (Peiping: National Peiping Library, 1930, in 6 volumes).

   The Chinese title for the book by Qu is *Wanli wugong lu* (Taipei: Yiwen yinshu guan, 1980, reprint, 5 volumes). For a penetrating discussion of Qu and the book, see the foreword of the book, 1: 1–13.

35. Sin's account is known in Korean as *Kŏnju kijŏng togi*, originally a long report to the ruler of the Yi dynasty included in *CWS*, vol. 22, reign of Sonjo, 71: 640–44, 29/1/chongyu. It is available in various formats. One appears in *Chin-tan Hakpo*, 10 (1939): 160–75, with annotations and comments by Yi In-yŏng. The Korean title for Yi's book is *Chaam sŏnsaeng munjip* (N.p., postscript in 1886, 3 volumes). For its coverage, see 6: 1–7 under the subtitle "Kŏnju mun'gyonnok." When checked against other sources, this account is accurate.

36. One royal prince, known as Hyojong (r. 1650–59), later succeeded the Korean throne. The two others were Yi Wang and Yi Jun. The *Shenyang zhuangqi* is known in Korean as *Simyang changgye*, with the second compilation as *Simyang ilgi* (*Shenyang riji* in Chinese). The Korean title for *Shenguan lu* is *Simgwannok*. All the three are reprints and included in the Qingshi ziliao, Series 3, Kaiguo shiliao (3), respectively as volumes 7, 8, and 9 (Taipei: Tailian Guofeng chuban she, 1970). The Royal Secretariat was called *Sŭngjŏngwŏn* in Korean.

   For data on Manchu customs about death and hunting, see *Shenyang riji*, 429 and 494–500; for Korean captives and children of Jurchen-Korean wedlock, see *Shenyang zhuangqi*, 23–25, 87–89, respectively.

37. The article by Wang is entitled "Shina ni okeru Gairai Minzoku no Kanka ni tsuite, " *Shigaku zasshi*, 47. 11 (1936): 1277–98. For its English abstract, see *Harvard Journal of Asiatic Studies*, 2 (1937): 38. For Mao's study of the Manchu language, see his "Manwen Hanhua kaolüe," *Guoxue lunheng*, 9 (1937): 52–76. For a survey on Manchu sinicization, see Li Yuping, "Qing ruguan qian di Hanhua—Taizu Taizong shiqi" (*Shixue huikan* (Shida), 23 (1979): 53–65.

   For Yao's first article, see "Guoshi kuoda mianyan di yige kanfa." In his *Dongbei shi luncong*, 1:1–27. For the second and third articles, see "Jinchao Shang-jing shiqi di Nüzhen wenhua yu qian-Yan hou di zhuan bian." In ibid., 2: 31–64, and "Jin Shizong duiyu Zhong-yuan Han-hua yu Nüzhen jiusudi taidu." In ibid., 2: 118–74. The fourth article, a special lecture, is entitled "Nüzhen Hanhua di fenxi," *Dalu zazhi*, 6. 3 (1953): 91–103.

   For Guan's works, see "Manzu ruguan qian di wenhua fazhan dui tamen houlai Hanhua di ying-xiang," *Bulletin of the Institute of History and Philology, Academia Sinica*, 40. 1 (1968): 255–79. His second article is entitled "Guanyu

Manzu Hanhua wenti di yijian di taolun," *Dalu zazhi*, 40. 3 (1970): 94–97. For his third article, see "Manzu di ruguan yu Hanhua," *Bulletin of the Institute of History and Philology, Academia Sinica*, 43. 3 (1971): 445–88. For the study by Linke, see *Zur Entwicklung des mandjurischen Khanats zum Beamtenstaat: Sinisierung und Bürokratisierung der Mandjuren während der Eroberungszeit* [The Evolution of the Manchu Khanate into a Bureaucratic State: Sinicization and Bureaucratization of the Manchus during the Period of Conquest] (Wiesbaden: Franz Steiner, 1982), chs. 1, 3–5. For Ho's articles, see "In Defense of Sinicization," 123–55, and his "The Significance of the Qing Period in Chinese history," 189–95. For Guo's study, see his "Yetan Manzu Hanhua," *Qingshi yanjiu*, 2 (2000): 24–35.

38.   There are many general studies on important Qing accomplishments. Two examples are given here. A reprint of Meng Sen's *Qingdai shi* came out in 1960 (Taipei: Zheng-zhong shuju), part 2, chs. 2–3 and pp. 340–70; Zhu Chengru, ed., *Qingchao tongshi*, volume 6: Kangxi era, chs. 9, 11–13. For studies on the Jurchen and Manchu peoples, see Kawachi Yoshihiro, *Mindai joshinshi no kenkyū* (Kyoto: Dōhōsha, 1992); Wada Sei, *Tōashi kenkyū: Manshū hen* (Tokyo: Tōyō bunko 1955); Mitamura Taisuke, *Shinchō zenshi no kenkyū* (Kyoto: Tōyōshi kenkyūkai, 1965); Sun Jinji et. al., *Nüzhen shi* (Chang-chun: Jilin Wenshi chuban she, 1987), see *NCS*; Li Yanguang and Guan Jie, *Manzu tongshi* (Shenyang: Lioaning minzu chuban she, 1991), see *MTTS*. Wakeman's book was published by the University of California Press (Berkeley, 1985, 2 volumes).

39.   Yan, *Nuer-hachi zhuan*; Sun Wenliang and Li Zhiting, *Qing taizong quanzhuan* (Chang-chun: Jilin renmin chuban she, 1983); Jin Chengji, "Lun Shunzhi," *Wen-shi-zhe*, 5 (1984): 42–48. Bai Xinliang, ed., *Kangxi huangdi quanzhuan* (Peking: Xueyuan chuban she, 1994). For Yongzheng, see Pei Huang, *Autocracy at Work: A Study of the Yung-cheng Period, 1723–1735* (Bloomington, IN: Indiana University Press, 1974); Yongzheng's commentaries on the *Sacred Edict* is known as *Shengyu guangxun*, with a Manchu version, *Enduringge tacihiyan be neileme badarambuha bithe* (1724). Sun Wenliang et. al., *Qianlong di* (Chang-chun: Jilin Wenshi chuban she, 1993).

40.   For the book on Manchu state, law, and government institutions before 1644, see Zhang Jinfan and Guo Cheng-kang, *Qing ruguan qian guojia falü zhidu shi* (Shenyang: Liaoning renmin chuban she, 1988). Liu's book is entitled *Manzu di buluo yu guojia* (Chang-chun: Jilin Wenshi chuban she, 1995). Kanda's study is "Shinsho no bunkan ni tsuite," *Tōyōshi kenkyū* 19. 3 (1960). Oshibauchi's works include "Shin Taiso jidai keisei kō." In *Haneda hakushi shōju kinen Tōyōshi ronsō* (Kyoto: Kyoto University Tōyōshi kenkyūkai, 1950) and "Shin Taisō jidai keisei kō," *Jimbun kenkyū*, 2 (1951).

Fang's article is "Qingchu Manzhou jiating lidi fenjiazi he wei fenjiazi," *Guoli Beijing daxue wushi zhounian jinian lunwen ji* (Peiping: Peking University Press, 1948), College of Arts, No. 3. For the work by Yang, see *Qingdai Manzu fengshu shi* (Shenyang: Liaoning renmin chuban she, 1991).

41. Zhao wrote a long article entitled "Tonggusi—Manyu yu wenhua," *Manyu yanjiu*, 1 (1986): 58–69; 2 (1986): 64–73; 1 (1987): 74–80. For foreign influence, see Teng Shaozhen, "Ming-Qing liangdai Manyu Manwen shiyong qingkuan kao," *Minzu yuwen*, 2 (1986): 13; Ji Yonghai, "Lun Manyu zhongdi Hanyu jieci," *Manyu yanjiu*,1 (1985): 22. For the article by King, see his "The Korean Elements in the Manchu Script Reform of 1632," *Central Asiatic Journal*, 3–4 (1987): 252–86, especially 260–67. In addition to Ji Yonghai, some other scholars also study Chinese loanwords. For instance, see Tong Yonggong and Guan Jialu, "Lun Manwen zhong di Hanyu jieci," *Manxue yanjiu*, 1 (1992): 270–79.

Stephen Durrant argues that Manchu translations of Chinese texts were not motivated by sinicization. See his "Sino-Manchu Translations at the Mukden Court," *Journal of the American Oriental Society*, 99. 4 (1979): 653–61.

42. Among Western scholars interested in Manchu literature are Giovanni Stary. See his "Fundamental Principles of Manchu Poetry." In *Proceedings of International Conference on China Border Area Studies*, ed. Lin En-shean (Taipei: National Chengchi University, 1985): 187–221, and Denis Sinor, "Some Remarks on Manchu Poetry." In the same author, ed., *Studies in South East and Central Asia, Presented as a Memorial Volume to the Late Professor Raghu Vira by Members of the Permanent International Altaistic Conference* (New Dehli: International Academy of Indian Culture, 1968), 105–14. Zhang Jiasheng discusses both categories of Manchu poets. See his "Qingchu Manzu ciren ji chengjiu," *MANT*, 3 (1991): 46–55 and 21, and his "Qingdai qian, zhong qi Manzu buyi shiren shulüe," *SHKH*, 1 (1990): 140–45. This article covers twelve private poets. Zhao Xiuting provides a critical study of Singde's works, centering on his lyric poems. See his "Nalan Xingde zhuzuo kao," *MANT*, 2 (1991): 53–62; 3 (1991): 56–69 and 37; 4 (1991): 47–54.

43. For Murada, see his "Hōten kyūden kenchikushi kō, "*Manshū gakuhō*" (1933): 1–5 2. The articles by Tie is "Lun Qing ruguan qian ducheng chengguo yu gongdian di yanbian." In *Ming-Qing shi guoji xueshu taolun hui lunwen ji* (Tianjin: Tianjin remin chuban she, 1982), 637–58; for *The Palaces at Mukden*, see Jiang Xiang-shun and Tong Yue, *Sheng-jing huang-kong* (Peking: Zijin cheng chuban she, 1987), chs. 1–3. For the article by Swart and Till, see "Nurhachi and Abahai: Their Palace and Mausolea, the Manchu Adoption and Adaptation of Chinese Architecture," *Arts of Asia*, 18. 3 (May-June 1988): 148–57.

44. For a fine work on shamanism, see *A Study of Manchu Shamanism* by Fu Yükuang and Meng Huiying under the Chinese title, *Manzu saman jiao yanjiu* (Peking: Beijing daxue chuban she, 1991).

For Shunzhi's interest in Chan Buddhism, see *ECCP*, 1: 257. For Yongzheng's patronage, see Qing Shitzong, *Yuxuan yulu* (Palace edition, 1733, 14 volumes). For the study by Wang Jun-zhong, see his "'Manzhou' yu 'Wenshu' di yuanyuan ji Xizang zheng-jiao sixiang zhong di ling-xiu yu Fupusa," *Bulletin of the Institute of Modern History, Academia Sinica*, 28 (1997): 89–130. For the writing of Samuel Martin Grupper, "The Manchu Imperial Cult of the Early Ch'ing Dynasty: Texts and Studies on the Tantric Sanctuary of Mahakala at Mukden" (Ph. D. Dissertation, Indiana University, 1980), ch. 4.

45.   For Lü's view, see his "Qingdai di chongru yu Hanhua." In *Zhong-yang yan-jiu yuan Guoji Han xue huiyi lunwen ji* (Taipei: Academia Sinica, 1981, 7 volumes in 10), 3A: 533–42. The article by Liu Zhiyang is entitled "Qing zhengfu jianli hou Han wenhua dui Manzu wenhua di ying-xiang," *Heilong jiang minzu congkan*, 4 (1992): 83–87. Ho's views are best represented by two articles: "The Significance of the Ch'ing Period in Chinese History," 191–92; "In Defense of Sinicization," 141–44.

Chapter I

The Ancestry and Ethnic Composition
of the Manchus

THE MANCHUS ORIGINATED IN CHINA'S NORTHEAST, a vast region known to the West as Manchuria. They emerged in the 1630s as a political entity, characterized by a long and intricate ancestry, as well as diverse ethnic components. Early Manchuria was isolated in certain areas and displayed cultural disparity and political disunity, but it was accessible to the nomads of the steppes and deserts from its west and northwest. The Chinese came from the south. In the seventeenth century Nurhaci and his successor, Hong Taiji, unified the region. They laid the basis for the Qing dynasty, which at its greatest extent included China proper, Manchuria, Mongolia, Sinkiang, and Tibet, an immense area second only to the Yuan empire in Chinese history.

1. Manchuria: Its Geography and Early Inhabitants

Manchuria borders the Korean peninsula and the Gulf of Liaodong on the south. Before the nineteenth century its northern border reached far beyond the Amur River, the current boundary between Manchuria and Siberia. The middle course of the Amur lies next to the Lesser Khingan range. The Long White Mountains (Changbai shan), sacred to the Manchus and some of their predecessors, together with the Ussuri River, skirt the eastern border, which once touched the seas of Japan and Okhotsk. Standing majestically in the west are the Greater Khingan Mountains, the divide between the region and Mongolia.[1]

The land inside the boundaries is a rolling plain, drained by the Liao and Sungari river systems. The Liao River, the artery of the southern

31

part of the plain, runs eastward from Jehol, a strategic wedge between North China, Manchuria, and Mongolia. The Liao valley was settled by Chinese farmers because its land and climate are much the same as those of North China. The Sungari and its tributaries, such as the Nonni (Nunjiang) and the Mudan (formerly Hurha or Hurka), form a system linking southern and northern Manchuria. The Sungari-Nonni valley makes up the northern part of the plain, which becomes "more and more like that of the steppes of Mongolia."[2] With the exception of its southern areas, Manchuria was marked by internal isolation and disparity. In the east and north the forest-clad mountains hindered accessibility. All this was compounded by a continental climate, which brings the long winters and cold winds from Siberia. Frozen and snow-covered, the northern Manchurian plain has a short growing season, unfit for regular farming. Inhabitants had to respond in different ways. When temperatures decreased from south to north, aridity increased from east to west. Different regions give rise to different ecologies.[3] Ecological differences contributed to internal isolation. Many kinds of animals flourished in the mountains and forests, attracting hunters and trappers. The waterways are intricate, good for fishermen and pearl collectors. Dogsleds followed the lower Amur; reindeer herders were active in its middle and upper sections; horses provided transportation in the northwest. Chinese farmers inhabited the alluvial valleys of the Liao River. Each region thus tended to develop economic specialization and its own society. Early Manchuria consisted of numerous dispersed centers, which made political unification difficult.[4]

Manchuria was subject to diverse cultural influences. Because the elevation of its western borders dropped toward the Mongolian steppes, nomads from Mongolia and Central Asia overran it. Among them were the Xiongnu in early times, Turkic peoples around the sixth century, and much later the Mongols. Invaders stayed, for Manchuria was the eastern end of their long thrust. There was interplay between the steppe-pastoral tradition and forest-hunting. The northern part of the plain was the locale of the nomads.[5]

In prehistoric times southern Manchuria and China maintained cultural relations. Using recent archaeological evidence, a scholar has confirmed that Chinese Neolithic culture spread from North China, possibly via Jehol and the Liaodong peninsula. Since the Warring

States period (403–221 BC) the region has been associated with China.[6] But the Chinese cultural and political influence could not penetrate northern Manchuria. After the collapse of the Tang dynasty (618–907) a succession of frotier warriors—Khitans, Jurchens, Mongols—occupied Manchuria and weakened China's influence there. With the rise of the Ming dynasty, China reestablished its control over southern Manchuria and made great efforts to extend its influence to the north.

Korea looked northward to Manchuria, separated from it by the Yalu and Tumen rivers. When the region lost its political balance, invaders and migrants such as Khitans and Jurchens moved down from the north to Korea or its adjacent areas. Southern Manchuria served as a bridge, over which China's politics and culture were transmitted to Korea. From its early history Korea had been under Chinese influence. Chosŏn (3rd cent.–108 BC), for example, was a sinicized state and Korea's earliest documented kingdom, partly located in southern Manchuria. The subsequent Korean kingdoms, including Koguryŏ (2nd cent.–668), even adopted more Chinese culture. Although Korea developed its own tradition, Chinese political, social, and cultural institutions remained influential. Therefore Korea also helped the Jurchens keep in touch with the Chinese cultural tradition.[7]

Early Manchuria thus was characterized by regional differences, cultural diversity, and political disunity. There were influxes of newcomers from China, Mongolia, Siberia, and as far as Central Asia. Owen Lattimore correctly related that "Historically Manchuria is part of the great migration ground of eastern and central Asia." Different ethnic groups brought diverse cultures. One scholar has observed that the Sungari valley was the meeting place of four prehistoric cultures: the Yellow River valley, the Mongolian desert and steppe, the Pacific coast, and the taiga area around Lake Baikal.[8]

There were three groups of people in northern Manchuria, with the Amur valley as the center. Inhabitants of the western section included the proto-Mongols, known in Chinese sources as the Donghu (Eastern Nomads). Those in the central portion were the Paleo-Asiatics, likely native settlers and a branch of the Dongyi (Eastern Barbarians). In Chinese records the Dongyi people spread from the eastern coast of China to Manchuria. According to a Russian scholar, they transmitted

Map 1. Physical Characteristics of the Northeast.

1. Kaiyuan	2. Fushun	3. Shenyang
4. Liaoyang	5. Guang-ning	
6. Yilan	7. Peking	

Chinese bronze culture from Manchuria north to the Trans-Baikal region. The southern Tungus, also a main branch of the Dongyi, inhabited the eastern part of the region.[9]

Among early inhabitants in Manchuria were, in chronological order, the Sushen, Yilou, Wuji, and Mohe. They were all related to the Dongyi people and closely connected with the southern Tungus linguist family. Active in the Amur-Sungari-Ussuri region, they engaged in hunting, fishing, and farming, and shared such traditions as swine-

tending and dugout dwelling. But they were not unified or homogeneous, as Chinese dynastic histories and some recent studies have
argued. Nor were they the same groups with new names. Each group
was a conglomeration of people, without well-defined boundaries between them. They were influenced by Chinese bronze culture, as V. Ye
Larichev maintains, and underwent changes in their social and political structures. The most powerful tribe, one may suppose, acted as the
leader. When power shifted, political dominance changed, and so did
names. Because a recent study has covered this subject, the following
pages will summarize its content.[10]

The Sushen were contemporary with the Shang and Zhou periods
(1766–256 BC). With decline or migration of the Sushen around the
first century AD, the Yilou people appeared on the scene. They were
coeval with the Former and Later Han times (202 BC–AD 220). Recent
archaeological finds along the Wanyan River in Suibin, Heilongjiang
Province, seem to be of their cultural remains.[11]

The Wuji people were active in the fifth and sixth centuries. They
mixed with other inhabitants and divided into regional groups. Overshadowed by the Mohe people in the sixth century, they migrated to
the forested regions in eastern Manchuria. The emergence of the Mohe
people marked the end of the early Manchu ancestral line. They were
an aggregate of seven tribes. The strongest and most primitive of them
was the Heishui, from whom arose the Jurchens, the recent Manchu
ancestors.[12]

All the inhabitants of Manchuria formed the early ancestors of
the Manchus. This relationship can be explained from various per-
spectives. The swine was economically and religiously important not
only to the early peoples but also to the Manchus. The Manchu word
"yeru," whose sound is close to "Yilou," connotes "cave," "pit," and, by
extension, "dugout," the traditional dwelling in early Manchuria. As
stated, after the rise of the Mohe people, the Wuji became the forest
residents. In the Manchu language the term comes close to pronunciation of "weji," which means forest. More importantly, the Manchu
males braided their hair into queues, a style first adopted by the Sushen people.[13]

But the bird or origin myth provides the most convincing connection between the Manchus and the early peoples. As early as the Neolithic era, birds, especially the eagle, had been an object of worship in

the shaman cult because the Tungusic people believed that the shaman was descended from the eagle. The royal house of the Shang dynasty (1766–1122 BC) is said to have originated from a divine black bird. The State of Yan, at first a satellite of the Zhou dynasty (1122–256 BC) and then a powerful kingdom, consisted of Shang culture and controlled the Liao valley. The character "yan" means a swallow or black bird. The same legend perhaps influenced the people of Sushen, a term suggesting a falcon or wild goose. Among artifacts of the Sushen recently excavated in Heilongjiang Province is an eagle head.[14]

The Manchus had a similar bird myth about the origin of their imperial house. While bathing in a lake with two other heavenly maidens, Fekulen swallowed a red berry that a divine magpie put on her clothes. She became pregnant and gave birth to Bukūri Yongšon, the founder of the Manchu imperial house. This bird legend developed into two versions, both intending to show the uniqueness of Manchu genesis. Shorter and simpler, the unofficial version appeared earlier and circulated among the Jurchens in the Amur valley. The longer and refined account was adopted by Hong Taiji as the official version. Later the magpie became the subject of other stories. One such story tells that a magpie saved the life of Fanca, a descendant of Bukūri Yongšon, by misleading his enemy. As a result the magpie was revered by the Manchus as a divine bird not allowed to be harmed.[15]

The link between early inhabitants and the Manchus has appeared in recent archaeological findings. Most excavations were made in their homeland, the Amur-Sungari-Ussuri valley. From Xituan Hill near Jilin City, archaeologists discovered the bones of swine on the lid of stone coffins, as well as human skeletons that had the features of the Tungus people. The shallow dugout dwellings, birch-bark quivers, and other items found in 1963–1964 in Dongkang, Heilongjiang Province, are believed to represent Yilou culture. Similar dugouts together with stone tools, discovered in 1973 at Tongren, also in Heilongjiang, match products of the Wuji and Mohe groups in the fifth to seventh centuries.[16]

2. The Role of the Jurchens

The Manchus had been known as the Jurchens before the change to the present name in 1635. As mentioned, the Jurchens came from the Heishui people, one of the seven Mohe tribes and inhabitants of the middle and lower Amur valley. The Heishui were first under the influence of the Tang dynasty and became the subjects of the Khitans, founders of the Liao dynasty (947–1125). It was under the Khitans that they received the name "Jurchen," also written as Jürčed, Nüzhen, Nüzhi, and so on. The term possibly means the "gerfalcon of the east" (*haidong qing*).[17]

The Jurchens underwent stages of evolution, the seventh to the tenth centuries being their formative period. During the early Liao era they inhabited the area east of the Amur-Sungari confluence and migrated toward the west and south, spreading as far as the valleys of the Tumen and Yalu. Migration provided an opportunity for acquiring components and created problems of identification. Chinese, Khitans, and Koreans classified them in geographical or cultural terms. Among such classifications were Eastern Sea Jurchens, Civilized Jurchens, and Northern and Southern Jurchens.[18]

The tenth and eleventh centuries saw the rise of the Wanyan (Wanggiya in Manchu) tribe, possibly related to the Thirty Jurchen Tribes of the Long White Mountains in the Tumen-Yalu valley. In the tenth century it moved north to the region around the Amur-Sungari confluence and gradually dominated other Jurchens. In the effort to conquer the Khitans, the Jurchens recruited allies from such non-Jurchen settlers in Manchuria as the Chinese, the Bohai people, the Wure tribes, and the Tieli. Under their leader, Aguda (1068–1125), the Jurchens founded the Jin dynasty and, more importantly, created in 1119 their own written language. The kingdom ruled a vast area that covered Manchuria, North China, and part of Mongolia. In the 1120s they removed tens of thousands of Chinese to their heartland, the Harbin region in Heilongjiang Province. The Chinese captives and their descendants, one may assume, became Jurchens. By the end of the Jin dynasty many Jurchens in North China were sinicized. Typical was a member of the Nüxilie (Niohuru in Manchu) clan. Descended from an aristocratic family, he studied the Confucian classics, took a Chinese wife, changed his name to Gao Sirong, and became a prominent member in his community. Recently, news reporters discovered many people of Jurchen origin among Chinese residents in central Honan Province. They identified themselves as descendants of Aguda's fourth son, a noted commander. They have lived there for centuries and were indistinguishable from other Chinese.[19]

The Jurchens of the Jin dynasty passed much of their heritage to the Manchus. The banner institution, founded by Nurhaci, was surprisingly similar to the Jin system of *mengan* (chiliarchy) and *mouke* (century), basically a military institution, with political and social functions. Men and officers in the institution were hereditary. Nurhaci took the dynastic designation "Jin" as the name of his frontier kingdom. *Aisin*, a component of the Manchu imperial family name meaning "gold," which the term "Jin" denotes. Attacking the metropolitan area of Peking in 1629, Hong Taiji sent a prince to offer a sacrifice to the tombs of two Jin rulers. The Manchu and Jurchen languages had similar elements. Most importantly, ninety-four Manchu surnames trace back to Jurchen origins. The Manchus were linked to the Jurchens by similar greeting gestures, religious traditions, funeral practices, sports, and hairstyle.[20]

The emergence of the Mongols ended the dominance of the Jurchens. Many Jurchens perished during the transition. Some helped the Mongols to found the Yuan dynasty and were admitted to the ruling class. Those who had adopted the Chinese way of life and remained in China were classified by the Mongols as Northern Chinese. A small group returned to the Harbin region, united with their kinsmen there, and became powerless subjects of the Yuan. It was from this group that the Manchus stemmed and they finally founded a great empire.[21]

During the Yuan dynasty the Jurchens underwent regrouping. In southern Manchuria they grouped themselves with their Chinese and Korean neighbors, from whom they learned advanced farming and, therefore, transformed their ways from hunting and fishing.[22] But the Manchus were descended from the northern Jurchens, who were economically and culturally behind their cousins in the south. Among their neighbors were the Wuzhe and Shuidada (Water or Fishing Tartars) tribesmen. The Wuzhe were active in the area east of the Amur-Sungari confluence. Spreading over a wide area, the Water Tartars were a people of controversial identity. Some sources regard them as non-Jurchens; some scholars take the opposite stance. In all likelihood they commingled with neighbors during the latter part of the Yuan period.[23]

The Yuan dynasty controlled northern Manchuria through the myriarchy (*Wanhu fu*), a Mongol regional garrison unit, and the Office of the Eastern Expedition Marshal (*Zheng-dong yuan-shuai fu*), the highest military command in the region. Under the myriarchy was the chiliarchy, divided into the century. Five myriads related to the Jurchens. Of the five, Odoli, Hurha, Taowen—in particular the first two—were ancestors of the Manchus. These myriads spread over the lower Sungari, with Yilan, a district in Heilongjiang, as their center. The tribesmen kept their institutions and received assistance during natural disasters. In return they had to provide the Mongols with soldiers and such tributes as furs and gerfalcons. Because the Yuan court made excessive demands, Jurchen and other tribesmen revolted in the 1340s. The revolt resulted in the destruction of Tuo-wo-lian and Boku-jiang, two of the five myriads.[24] Shortly afterward the Ming dynasty drove the Mongols out of China, the last stage of the evolution of the Jurchens.

During the Ming dynasty the Jurchens experienced frequent regrouping. Since its beginning the Ming had relied on the guard-post system, an institution of Yuan origin, to keep the Jurchens in line. One type was the Liaodong Military Commission (Liaodong dusi), created in 1375, but not completed until after 1387. Staffed by Chinese bureaucrats, it had jurisdiction over Chinese, Koreans, and Jurchens in southern Manchuria. The other, the Nurkal Military Commission (Nuergan dusi), was organized in 1409 and led by tribal leaders. It exercised indirect control over the Jurchens in Northern Manchuria and far-flung tribes around the lower Amur and beyond. Among the far-flung tribesmen were the Wuzhe, the Gilyaks (also as Jilimi in Chinese records and Nivkhis in Russian sources), and the Guwei, who resided mainly in Sakhalin.[25] After the mid-fourteenth century, the Jurchens in northern Manchuria began a long process of southward migration because they were threatened and sometimes even displaced by Mongol looters from the west and tough Wuzhe tribesmen from the east. But economics was probably another reason for their migration.[26] Southern Manchuria had a warmer climate, more food, and greater technological know-how, with Liaodong, the valley east of the Liao River, as its center. It was the economic base of such frontier powers as the Bohai Kingdom (731–926) and the Liao and Jin dynasties.

The importance of southern Manchuria to the northern tribes was enhanced by the transportation network the Yuan and Ming dynas-

ties constructed. The system facilitated not only troop movements but
commerce. Chinese and Korean traders were active, and postal stations developed into markets. In 1374 an official of the Koryŏ dynasty
(935–1392) sent slaves to trade with the Mongols through this network.
The same system brought salt and iron tools to the Jurchens in northern Manchuria, but the insecure situation during the transition from
Yuan to Ming disrupted the flow of such commodities.[27]

Historically, tribes emerged, migrated, accommodated, and amal-
gamated on China's frontiers, including Manchuria. The Odoli, Hurha,
and Taowen Jurchens followed the same pattern. Their southward migrations were a complicated population movement, marked by regrouping and integration, with profound effects on China and Korea.
Unfortunately, one only can provide here a sketch, since there is dearth
of sources. Likely the three myriarchies began individual journeys
from the area of Yilan. They followed the Mudan River and stayed in
many places on their way south. At the end of the Mudan River they
seem to have taken different routes.[28]

Under the leadership of Aqača (d. 1409) the main body of the Hurha
Jurchens reached the northern bank of the Tumen. In 1403 the Ming
government organized them into the Jianzhou Guard. Led by Boersun,
a detachment of Hurha tribesmen settled between Kyonghung and
Hoeryong, two Korean cities near the Tumen. To accommodate them
the Ming created the Maolian Guard in 1406. The Taowen Jurchens
seem to have settled around the Tumen, but in about 1412 merged with
the Jianzhou Guard.[29]

On their southern journey the Odoli Jurchens under their chieftain, Fanca, may have sojourned in Dunhua, a city in Jilin Province. At
last they settled in the area of Hoeryong and were incorporated into
the Jianzhou Guard. Menggetimur (also Mengke Temur; Mengtem,
d. 1433), grandson of Fanca, was important to the Odoli tribe because
he maneuvered between China and Korea and attracted the attention of both. In 1412 the Ming created the Left Jianzhou Guard and
made Menggetimur regional commissioner. As a relative of the consort of the Yongle emperor (r. 1403–24), Menggetimur was repeatedly
promoted. More importantly, he was founder of the Manchu imperial house, known in Qing sources as the Primeval Emperor and First

Ancestor (*Zhaozu Yuan-huangdi*). Nurhaci, a sixth-generation descendant, unified the Jurchens and founded the second kingdom.[30]

To solve a power struggle within the Left Jianzhou Guard, Ming authorities in 1442 produced from it the Right Jianzhou Guard, with Menggetimur's brother, Tong Fanca, as its chief.[31] Although this resulted from the Ming policy of divide and rule, the Odoli Jurchens benefited because they controlled two guards. Altogether, the Hurha and Odoli Jurchens had three branches. With the Maolian tribesmen they laid the groundwork for revival of Jurchen power.

There was another Jurchen group composed of tribes of the Haixi region, a loose term, whose connotation changed with time. Originally involving the middle and lower Sungari, its coverage extended by the mid-Ming to the lower Amur valley. But later Ming sources referred to the tribesmen around the Fulahun (today, Hulan) River as the Haixi Jurchens. From the name Fulahun came the term Hūlun (Hulawen). During the fourteenth to sixteenth centuries, like many other Jurchen tribes, they migrated south. By the mid-sixteenth century they settled in the area between northern Liaoning and southeastern Jilin provinces. There they mingled with the natives, built forts, and became regional powers known as the Four Hūlun Tribes: Hada, Ula, Yehe, and Hoifa.[32]

The Four Hūlun tribes distinguished themselves from other Jurchens. They adopted the same clan name, "Nara," and were related to one another. Their leaders had been made officials of the Ming guard-post system. Singgen Dargan, progenitor of the Yehe tribe, served as the principal official of the Talumu guard; Suhete (d. ca. 1533), a chieftain of Hada, was a high official of the Left Tashan guard. All the four tribes kept close relations with the Qorčin Mongols.[33] The Four Hūlun tribes became protectors of Liaodong from raids by the Mongols and less developed Jurchens, for they were strategically located on trading and transportation lines between southern and northern Manchuria. The Ming government depended on them for peace in the region. They formed a powerful bloc against Nurhaci for twenty years. The conduct of Yehe and Ula best illustrates the case. Their chieftains—Gintaisi (d. 1619) and Bujantai (d. ca. 1619)—kept complex marriages with Nurhaci, but were his archrivals.[34] Because of China's decline and the intratribal conflict of the Hūluns, Nurhaci was able to conquer the four tribes one after another. When tribesmen joined his rank and file, their leaders became his high officials. Their support was essential to the unification of Manchuria begun by Nurhaci and completed by his heir, Hong Taiji.[35]

Ming sources classify the Jurchens in three categories: the Jianzhou branches and the Maolian, the Four Hūlun Tribes, and the Yeren. The Jianzhou and the Hūlun tribesmen were regarded as "civilized" Jurchens (shu Nüzhen) because they were more developed and kept closer relations with China. The term "Yeren," literally meaning "savage," "wild," or "less civilized," is frequently misused in Ming sources. In correct usage the term means the far-flung Jurchen tribes whose leaders did not regularly receive official titles from China or send tribute to the imperial court.[36]

The "Wild Jurchens" divide into two groups: Amur River and Eastern Sea (Donghai), each composed of subgroups. But the division is not always clear-cut because geographically the lower Amur valley could be considered part of the Eastern Sea region. Tribes spread from one region to another, and they might be classified in either group. It was difficult to subjugate them. Not until the eighteenth century were the Qing rulers able to pacify them. Among the Amur River group were tribes from the course of the upper Amur to as far as Sakhalin. The forested upper Amur valley was penetrated by steppe pastoral settlers from Mongolia. In its war against the Mongols the early Ming made the region an outpost. The Sahalcas, Oronchons (Evenks in Russian sources), O-wen-kes (known to the Russians as Yakuts or Evenks), Dahurs, and Solons were active in the area. Some of these groups were related to the Mongols, but in time they were intermingled with neighboring Jurchens. They were hunters, later organized into the Manchu banners.[37]

Inhabitants of the mid-Amur valley included the Hurha and Sahalien tribes. Although at first only natives of the Yilan area, the Hurhas expanded to cover tribes from the Mudan valley to the middle and lower Amur regions and also to the Ussuri. The Sahaliens were a subgroup of the Hurha people, and both spoke the Tungusic language. Subjugated by Nurhaci and Hong Taiji, the two tribes, as well as those in the upper Amur region, were organized into the banner system and became known as the New Manchus.[38]

The Lower Amur valley was the home of the Heje (Nanays, Gold, or Goldi), the Gilyaks, and to the north the Oronchons, all Tungusic people. Both the Heje and Gilyaks were fishermen and relied on dogsleds for transportation. Like their kin in the upper Amur valley, the Oronchons were hunters and reindeer users. Nurhaci and his successors recruited many warriors from these Lower Amur tribesmen.[39]

The Eastern Sea Jurchens inhabited the region between the Ussuri River and the Sea of Japan. Besides the Weji and some Heje tribesmen, there were the Warka and Kurka (Kuyala) tribes, both of which seem to have been related to the Hurhas. Nurhaci repeatedly campaigned in

Map 2. The Jurchens before the Rise of Nurhaci.

1. Yilan	2. Kaiyuan	3. Fushun
4. Shenyang	5. Liaoyang	6. Guang-ning
7. Jinzhou	8. Ningyuan	9. Peking

the region during the years 1598–1625 because he wanted soldiers from among the tribesmen and also sought to prevent their alliance with the Four Hūlun Tribes. He was able to control the entire region by the time of his death in 1626.[40]

3. Components

The Manchus comprised Jurchen and non-Jurchen ethnic strands. This heterogeneity was an important catalyst for sinicization. Of the Jurchen components the Jianzhou and Maolian tribesmen were the nucleus, with the Four Hūlun Jurchens making up the next layer. The Wild Jurchens constituted the outer layer. Among the non-Jurchen elements the Mongols were a major component. The Mongol influence resulted from geographical and historical factors.[41]

On the fringe of the upper Amur, the Mongols were vassals of the Jurchens during the Jin dynasty. Nine years after unification of Mongolia in 1206, Jenghiz Khan (1162–1227) made Manchuria part of the Mongol empire. From then on Mongols had settled everywhere in Manchuria. After collapse of the empire, the Ming defeated the remnant Mongol forces in Manchuria and organized them into the Three Uriyangqad (Wu-liang-ha) Guards: Taining, Duoyan, and Fuyu. Under the pressure of the Eleuth Mongols in the early fifteenth century they moved southward from northwestern Heilongjiang to the Liao valley. There they were able to keep in touch with Jurchen neighbors, especially the Hūlun Jurchens. According to Lattimore, on the eve of Manchu conquest of China Mongols occupied one-fourth to one-third of Manchuria. No wonder Mongols influenced many aspects of Jurchen life, such as rituals, terminology, and tribal organization. More importantly, Nurhaci adapted Mongol symbols for the Manchu script in 1599.[42]

Some Jurchen clans were actually of Mongol ancestry. The Gorolos descended from a Qorčin Mongol who migrated to Zhanhe, a place near Xinbin in Liaoning Province. There he organized Jurchen people into a village. He and his offspring were accepted as Jurchen. Six generations after him the clan was led by two brothers, Cangšu (Cangšiu in Old Manchu, fl. 1580s–1620s) and Yangšu (also Yangšiu, fl. 1580s–

1620s). With their support, Nurhaci was able to defeat Nikan Wailan (d. 1586), a Jurchen chieftain and his rival, in 1586. Yangšu and his son married the female members of Nurhaci's house.[43]

Jurchen-Mongol relations were so close that in some cases it was difficult to tell their ethnic origins. Possibly beginning with the Yuan dynasty, as many as twenty-two clans spread across borders. Juchen clans such as the Magiya, Hešeri, Joogiya, and Wanggiya had branches in the tradtional Mongol territory. Mongol clans, including Borji, and Kerde, founded small settlements in Jurchen lands and were classified in the rare Manchu clan surnames. As a result, compilers of the *Genealogy of Manchu Clans in the Eight Banners* listed them under both Jurchen and Mongol sections. This cross-border relationship enabled the Jurchens to absorb more Mongol components. In the early stage the Four Hūlun Tribes had the closest relations with the Mongols. The four tribes shared the same clan name, Nara, a powerful clan with thirty-eight branches. As indicated in Table 1, some clansmen lived among Mongols and were regarded as Mongols. Meanwhile, each of the four tribes had Mongol subjects. Among Hada's residents were two Mongol clans, the Urate and the Jokis. Most members of the Bayote clan lived with fellow Mongols, while a small branch settled in Hoifa. The Oltute clan left other Mongols behind and claimed Ula for its home locality. The Sartu clan resided in Yehe. Under its patriarch, Bede, the clan fought bravely for Nurhaci and Hong Taiji, and many clansmen held high offices.[44]

Out of the Hūlun Tribes the Yehe, Ula, and Hada derived from the Mongols. Singgen Dargan, founder of the Yehe clan, was a member of the Tumed Mongols. Marriages followed between Yehe tribesmen and the Mongols, generation after generation. The mother of Jaisai, ruler of the Khutuktu Mongols, was the daughter of Gintaisi, a chieftain of the Yehe tribe. The powerful ruler of the Chahar Mongols, Lindan Khutuktu Khan, married the granddaughter of Gintaisi.[45] Bujantai, the last Ula ruler related to Nurhaci by marriage, was of Mongol ancestry, according to Hong Taiji's testimony. The ruling houses of Ula continued marriages with the Mongols. Hada seems also of Mongol origin, because it shared a common ancestry with the Ula. The ethnic relations between the Hūlun Jurchens and the

Table 1. Clans with Cross-Border Settlements*
Based on the *Genealogy of Manchu Clans*
***in the Eight Banners* (STTP)**

Name	Manchu	Mongol
Magiya	7: 1a–16a	69: 6a
Hešeri	Chs. 9–10	71: 12b
Nara	Chs. 22–24	69: 9a
Wanggiya	28: 1a–23a	68: 22a
Ujala	30: 1a–19a	71: 5b
Joogiya	31: 1a–13a	69: 7a
Ligiya	33: 1a–11b	69: 5b–6a
Hūwangiya	33: 3a–15a	70: 9b
Bayara	38: 1a–13b	69: 2b–3a
Janggiya	40: 1a–11b	69: 6b
Ojo	46: 1a–7b	68: 18a
Monggolji	51: 12	67: 4
Ulhan	53: 2a	70: 5a
Kerde	56: 7b–8a	69: 11a
Jugiya	57: 12a	70: 3b
Ugiya	57: 4b	71: 5a
Liogiya	57: 3a–4a	68: 10a
Šuru	58: 13b	67: 11a
Baiyiya	59: 8a	69: 9a
Borji	63: 1a	69: 4b
Toogiya	63: 3b	70: 14b
Hūgiya	63: 8a	70: 4a

*In the Mongol section the Chinese characters for the Magiya, Joogiya, Janggiya, Jugiya, Ugiya, and Šuru clans are slightly different, but they are the same in *Jakūn gūsai manjusai mukūn hala be uheri ejehe bithe,* the Manchu version of the *Genealogy of Manchu Clans in the Eight Banners.*

Mongols can be further substantiated by the Ilari clan, originating from the Naras. Its clansmen spread all over the Four Hūlun Tribes, especially in Ula and Yehe. The Ilaris in Yehe preserved the Mongol practice of performing shamanistic services. After being conquered by Nurhaci, the Hūlun Jurchens constituted part of the Manchus. Naturally, the Mongol component passed to the Manchus.[46]

The Mongol component was augmented during the reigns of Nurhaci and Hong Taiji. Of the Mongols the Qorčin tribesmen were the most important. As the easternmost branch of the Mongols, the Qorčin tribesmen settled in a region stretching from the Hailar River to the Liao valley and made up the major portion of Mongol residents in Manchuria. They were in the neigborhood of the Yehe and Ula tribes to the east and southeast. The geographical location made their involvement in intertribal relations of the Jurchens inevitable. In 1593 they joined with two other Mongol tribes and five Jurchen tribes in an attempt to defeat Nurhaci.[47] In their efforts to win, the Qorčin Mongols, Nurhaci and Hong Taiji, undertook a veritable marriage diplomacy. Nurhaci took two Mongol concubines and married a daughter, a niece, and a grandniece to Mongol nobles. His sons and nephews married Mongol noblewomen. These relations reached their height during the reign of Hong Taiji. Of his empresses and concubines, seven were of Mongol origin. One Mongol empress was the mother of the Shunzhi emperor (r. 1644–1661). Hong Taiji gave one sister, seven daughters, and one foster daughter to Mongol noblemen. Altogether there were sixty-eight marriages, which involved forty-one Mongol brides and twenty-seven Manchu princesses during the reigns of Nurhaci and Hong Taiji. But two other scholars argue that these marriages numbered over a hundred.[48]

By the Qianlong period Manchu-Mongol nuptial bonds had extended to almost all Mongol tribes. In the years 1691–1820, one scholar maintains, the Qing court married 229 imperial clanswomen to Mongol aristocrats.[49] To be sure, Manchu imperial clansmen took approximately the same number of Mongol brides. These relations produced generations of children of both Manchu and Mongol elements. Doubtlessly such ties also existed between other social strata and strengthened the Mongol constituency of the Manchus.

But the Chinese component was more important than the Mongol to the making of the Manchus. During the Liao dynasty, for political safety, the Khitan ruler selected from the developed Jurchens the most powerful families and clans and moved them from the Amur region to the Liaodong area. In their settlements, these Jurchens intermixed with natives, among whom were Chinese. Many of these people were absorbed by the Jurchens, who moved into the same region during the late Yuan and early Ming dynasties. After conquering the Northern Song dynasty (960–1127), the Jurchens took a large number of Chinese dyers, carpenters, blacksmiths, silversmiths, and some others as slaves to the Harbin region in Heilongjiang Province.[50] These Chinese slaves and their descendants, one may believe, became new components of the Jurchens.

During Ming times the Jurchens acquired more Chinese components through many channels. Because of economic and social development, they took a vast number of Chinese as slaves for productive and domestic work. Many such slaves took great risks to escape to Korea. During his reign (1419–1450) Sejong indicated that Korea returned more than a thousand Chinese to China. His successor, Munjong (r. 1451–1452), pointed out in 1452 that his government had sent back to China 834 people and recently 169.[51] But these fortunate captives were only a fraction of those taken. More Chinese captives must have remained among the Jurchens. Korean records provided cases of marriages between captives and Jurchens. In due time all of these Chinese and their offspring became part of the Manchu constituency.[52]

During the war of conquest Nurhaci took many Chinese captives, slaughtered the soldiers, and awarded civilian captives to his officers and men. When he captured Fushun city in 1618 he took tens of thousands of Chinese residents as slaves. They worked for their masters, registered under their masters' name, and were among the fifty surnames of the "Fushun Chinese" (in Manchu *Fusi nikan*). The number of Chinese captives greatly increased under Hong Taiji. After invading North China in early 1639, he brought back about half a million, a figure that represented a small percent of civilians captured during his reign. Although ethnically not Manchus, legally they were. Many of them belonged to the 156 Chinese surnames in the Manchu Eight Banners.[53]

For various reasons Chinese frontiersmen in Liaodong joined the Jurchens. Since its beginning, the Ming had sent people to Liaodong as hereditary soldiers and military farmers. It also banished there criminals and other offenders from all over the country. Sources suggest that exiles made up a sizable portion of the population.[54] Hardships of frontier life and administrative problems allowed the rise of protesters, deserters, rebels, fugitives, and displaced farmers. They were eager to collaborate with the Jurchens. Protests began even in the Yongle period, the high point of Ming strength. During the Xuande reign (1426–1435), Chinese soldiers twice deserted. The first group, 500 deserters, fled to the Hūlun Jurchens; the other group, an uncertain number, went to the Jianzhou region. On a mission to the Hūlun tribes in 1443, a Ming official encountered many Chinese working for the Jurchens, some of whom must have been commoners. Many deserters were repatriated, but some remained with their Jurchen hosts.[55]

There were more Chinese collaborators when the late Ming administration lapsed into oppressiveness and inefficiency. Ming garrisons revolted in such strategic posts as Liaoyang and Guang-ning in the years 1509–1539. In 1608 a large crowd of soldiers and people took part in a riot against the tax collector, a corrupt and ruthless eunuch. It is possible that rebel soldiers, military farmers, and others crossed the frontier and collaborated with the Jurchens. They seem to have made up a large number of residents in the "Chinese Quarters" (*Manzi cheng*), specially built by Nurhaci.[56]

Among Chinese collaborators were transfrontiersmen, who cut their original cultural and social roots and lived among the Jurchens. The Qing official genealogical compilation contains ample evidence. For generations, many Chinese established enclaves among Jurchen settlements. There were Chinese even in the Ussuri region. They adopted Jurchen names and lifestyle. One may reasonably infer that they and their descendants intermarried with the Jurchens. They were among the earliest warriors of the Eight Banners and were treated as Manchus.[57]

Sinicized Jurchens provided another kind of Manchu component. During the Ming era Jurchen leaders petitioned the imperial court,

individually or in groups, for immigration. Early in his reign the
Yongle emperor founded in Kaiyuan two special communities, Kuai-
huo zhou and Zizai zhou, to settle his new Jurchen subjects. The Kuai-
huo community was renamed Anlezhou, while the other moved to
Liaoyang. After that the Ming government had settled thousands of
Jurchen tribesmen in these two places, especially Zizai zhou. In an entry from 1452 the *Ming Veritable Records* mentioned more than four
hundred households of immigrants settled in various places. Immigrants were given houses, clothing, tools, and money when assigned
to settlements. There they intermarried and became sinicized. The rising number of immigrating tribesmen alarmed Ming officials. When
Nurhaci conquered the region, sinicized Jurchens rejoined their com-
patriots.[58] They, together with the Chinese component, contributed to
the quick sinicization of the Manchus.

Koreans were also a non-Jurchen component. Manchuria had
been a link between China, Korea, and the Jurchens. Before 668 the
northern region of Korea, between P'yongyang and the rivers, was frequently occupied by such tribesmen as the Wuji people and the Bai-
shan branch, one of the seven Mohe divisions. During the Liao dynasty
some Jurchen groups—notably the Thirty Tribes of the Long White
Mountains and the Wanyen clan—kept intimate contact with Korea.
Until recent centuries, one scholar points out, Koreans were the sole
inhabitants of central and southern Jilin Province and the first people
the Jurchens had to deal with after arriving in the area on their south-
bound journeys toward the end of the Yuan.[59] These Koreans and their
descendants became Korean components of the Jurchens.

But the Korean population was concentrated in southern Manchuria. When they invaded Korea in 1254, the Mongols took more than
206,800 Korean captives, most of whom seem to have been settled in
Liaodong. In the 1260s, thousands of Koreans, led by Hong Bok-won
(fl. 1240s–1260s), a high official, surrendered to the Yuan dynasty. The
Mongols let them stay in the area between Liaoyang and Shenyang.
Many Koreans fled to Liaodong, especially the region later known as
the Dongning Guard because of excessive labor obligation. As a result,
the Koryŏ court repeatedly asked the Mongols to repatriate the Koreans. In the mid-fifteenth century a Ming source indicated that Chinese constituted 70 percent of the population in Liaodong, the rest

being Korean and Jurchen residents. On the basis of this estimate, an official of the Yi dynasty reported to the throne in 1464 that in Liaodong during the Yongle period Korean military deserters alone reached 40,000 people.[60] Korean settlers intermingled with Chinese as well as Jurchens.

During its early years the Yi dynasty and the Jurchens kept contact through many channels. Koreans and their Jurchen neighbors engaged in frontier trade. To protect its northern frontier the Yi dynasty competed with China to pacify the Jurchens through diplomacy, naturalization, and trade. It encouraged immigration, bestowed titles and luxury items on the chiefs, and supplied tribesmen with their daily needs. The Maolian and Jianzhou Guards frequented the Hoeryong area in northern Korea and established settlements. A large number of Jurchens were thus inside the Korean frontier. They farmed or traded, married Koreans, and were treated by the Yi government as citizens. Without question, they and their descendants constituted the Korean component when they rejoined the Jurchens after the subjugation of Korea by Hong Taiji in 1627–1637. Mafuta (fl. 1620s–1640s), a member of the Tatara clan, was a case in point. He and his clansmen moved to Korea from Warka, a region between southeastern Jilin and the Tumen River. Around 1637, he led 133 men to offer their services to Hong Taiji, and were organized into a company.[61] Of course, they were not only warriors, but transmitters of Korean culture.

The institution of bodyguards was the most sophisticated measure taken by Korea to keep contact with the Jurchens. It was begun by Yi Song-gye (r. 1392–1398), founder of the Yi dynasty, and continued by his successors. The Yi rulers invited Jurchen chiefs, or approved their requests, to serve as royal bodyguards. Both Menggetimur and Aqaču were Yi Song-gye's bodyguards. These chiefs were showered with royal favors and allowed to take Korean wives.[62] One may infer that this institution provided the opportunity to acquire the Korean component.

Korean captives played a role in the non-Jurchen constituency of the Manchus. Despite the Yi dynasty efforts at pacification, the Jurchens often raided Korea for booty and captives. In considering geographical and historical factors one may believe that the number of Korean captives was sizable. The Jurchens forced captives to do domestic and farming work, sold them, or set prices for returning them.

During the last decade of the fifteenth century each Korean captive
was worth twenty oxen or twenty horses. By the early sixteenth century the price dropped to fifteen, but the Yi court agreed only to pay
five bales of cotton cloth. Many captives joined the Jurchens and married Jurchen women. There were forty-three Korean surnames in the
Manchu Eight Banners.[63]

Students of early Qing history unavoidably confront the origin
and meaning of the name Manchu. Since its adoption by Hong Taiji
in 1635, scholars have attempted many interpretations, which fall into
three categories: linguistic, connotative, and miscellaneous. Each consists of subgroups, and altogether there are more than twenty. Because
all the interpretations have been recently reviewed, in the following
paragraphs I will offer a few observations.[64]

In all likelihood, the term originated in the old Manchu archives. It
was not an invention by Hong Taiji, as some scholars suggest. After its
first reference in 1613, the term appeared more often, especially from
1628 onward.[65] This frequent reference shows its importance and pop-
ularity. Such a term would help win acceptance from all ethnic groups.
It was only logical for Hong Taiji to choose it as the new ethnic label
of his subjects.

Adoption of the term Manchu by Hong Taiji was a result of internal and external developments. The Jurchens called themselves
"Jušen" collectively or individually. As a consequence of sociopolitical
transformation, the name Jušen was downgraded and confused with
slaves (aha in Manchu). It was no longer appropriate for his subjects
of multiethnic components. At the same time, external factors encouraged a new name. As stated, in the twelfth century the Jurchens
founded the Jin dynasty, which overthrew the Northern Song and
made its last two rulers captives. The name Jin was also the designation of the frontier state he inherited. On the eve of conquering China,
he must have become aware that the words Jurchen and Jin would remind the Chinese of their past humiliation and strengthen their resistance. Naturally he would prefer a term that already appeared in
documents and transcended ethnic, geographical, and historical barriers. Such a name would suit his internal and external needs and, more
importantly, would be an ethnic marker of his diverse subjects.[66]

One should point out that the scarcity of reputable primary sources created these issues regarding the term Manchu and encouraged speculation. Of the three categories of interpretations, the second seems more reasonable because of its connotative nature. But it is as speculative as the others, for it is insufficiently documented.[67] Without good evidence it would be futile to attempt new interpretations. The problem will continue to perplex scholars and new theories will arise.

Many Qing sources classify the Manchus in two categories: Old and New. Since official records do not provide definitions, interpretations of these classifications are ambiguous. The Old Manchus were mostly members of the Jianzhou and Hūlun tribes from today's Liaoning and Jilin provinces. They joined Nurhaci and Hong Taiji before 1636.[68] Among these were the most powerful clans, such as Gūwalgiya, Niohuru, Šumuru, Donggo, Nara, and so on. As the core of the ethnic composition of the Manchus, they were the nucleus of the banner forces. For their contributions to the conquest of China, they and their descendants occupied high offices and held hereditary titles.

The New Manchus were chiefly the Wild Jurchens, such as the Hurhas, Kurkas, Warkas, Hejes, and Dahurs from the Amur, Nonni, and middle Sungari valleys. They mostly belonged to small and obscure clans—the Isu, the Niju—to name only two. The *Genealogy of the Manchu Clans in the Eight Banners* (chs. 59–65) classifies such clans in the category of "rare clan surnames" (*xixing*), of which there were 351. They joined the banner forces during and after the latter part of Hong Taiji's reign. By 1673 the Kangxi emperor had organized these tribesmen into forty New Manchu companies (*niru* in Manchu; *zuoling* in Chinese).[69]

There was a three-stage training program for the New Manchus. They were transferred from their homeland to Ningguta, present-day Ningan in Heilongjiang Province, or another such place. After staying there a few years they and their families were moved southward to Mukden (Shenyang), the center of Qing administration in Manchuria. There they sojourned for two years, learning more about Manchu culture and military discipline. They then were organized into the banner units and moved to Peking. After completion of the training programs they became the New Manchus.[70] Although they did not play a significant part in the founding of the Qing dynasty, they served as special units or garrison forces to protect China's frontiers.

Despite their long ancestral line, the Manchus emerged in 1635 as a new people composed of four ethnic groups: Jurchens, Mongols, Chinese, and Koreans. Their integration had strategic and cultural significance for the rise and development of the Qing empire. Strategically, Nurhaci and Hong Taiji needed the support of non-Jurchen peoples. With Mongol collaborators they were able to safeguard their flanks when they confronted the Ming army in Manchuria. Nevertheless, they did not place confidence in the Mongols because of their lack of discipline and dependability.[71] Chinese collaborators were essential to the organization of artillery units, which contributed to the destruction of Ming fortresses in the Liaodong region. They also helped Hong Taiji achieve political centralization and operate the Chinese pattern of administrative machinery after 1644. Korean supporters added strength to the Eight Banners and provided advice when Hong Taiji was confronting the Yi dynasty.

The cultural effect of integration was even more important. Mongol culture, especially its writing system and martial arts, influenced the Manchus. Although Chinese and Korean components adopted some Jurchen traditions, they exercised greater cultural influence on the Manchus. The Chinese component was essential to the economic and social transformation of the Manchus. At the suggestion of his Chinese advisors, Hong Taiji adopted the Ming political system and paid attention to Confucianism. However different, the Korean and Chinese traditions shared common elements, such as the writing system, Confucian values, and political and social institutions. Therefore the Korean element was helpful for the sinicization of the Manchus.

Notes

1. R. R. C. de Crespigny, *China: The Land and Its People* (New York: St. Martin's, 1971), 89, 96–97. For the evolution of the term Manchuria, see Elliott, "The Limits of Tartary," 604–607.
2. For the environments of the Liao and Sungari-Nonni valleys, see Owen Lattimore, *Inner Asian Frontiers of China* (New York: American Geographical Society, 1951, 2nd ed.), 107.
3. For aridity, isolation, and climate, see George Barcock Cressey, *China's Geo-

graphic Foundations: A Survey of the Land and Its People (New York and London: McGraw-Hill, 1934), 232–33, 236–37, and 226.

4. For the transition of economic and social life in various regions, see Lattimore, *Inner Asian*, 110–15.

5. For the gentle change of elevation, see de Crespigny, *China*, 96–97. For contact between steppe-pastoral and forest-hunting cultures, see Lattimore, *Inner Asian*, 107, 113–14.

6. For China's prehistoric cultural influence over southern Manchuria, see Chang Kwang-chih, "Dongbei di shiqian wenhua" in the Institute of History and Philology, Academia Sinica, and Chinese Ancient History Editorial Committee, *Zhongguo shanggu shi daiding gao*, Vol. 1: *Shiqian bufen* (Taipei: Academia Sinica, 1972), 413. For a succinct article, see Li, "Manchuria," 226–53. See also *TMSL*, 1–13ff.

7. For the relations between early Korea and Manchuria, see Li, "Manchuria," 238–44; *TMSL*, 19–24, 41–46, and 65–67. For the sinicization of early Korea, see Reischauer and Fairbank, *East Asia*, 399–414.

8. For the quote, see Lattimore, *Studies in Frontier History: Collected Papers, 1928–1958* (London and New York: Oxford University Press, 1962), 307. For the four prehistoric cultures, see Kwang-chih Chang, "Neolithic Cultures of the Sungari Valley, Manchuria," *Southwestern Journal of Anthropology* 17.1 (1961): 56–74, especially 56. A Russian archaeologist is of similar opinion. See V. Ye. Larichev, "Neolithic Remains in the Upper Amur Basin at Ang-ang-hsi in Tungpei." In Henry N. Michael, ed., *The Archaeology and Geomorphology of Northern Asia: Selected Works* (Toronto: University of Toronto Press, 1964), 181–231.

9. For the three ethnic groups in northern Manchuria, see *HLCM*, 53, 110–11; *TMSL*, 7–13; also my "New Light on the Origins of the Manchus," *Harvard Journal of Asiatic Studies*, 50. 1 (1990): 241–43. For the Dongyi, see *CKMT*, 102–109. For the early Chinese settlers, see *TMSL*, 2–6. For the northward transmission of the bronze culture, see V.Ye. Larichev, "Ancient Cultures of Northern China," in Michael, *The Archaeology and Geomorphology of Northern Asia*, 240–45.

10. Chinese bronze culture helped tribes reduce local cultural differences and brought about social and political changes. See Larichev, "Ancient Cultures of Northern China," 245. Yang Baolong insists that the Yilou people were just a new name of the Sushen. See his *Sushen Yilou hekao* (Peking: Zhongguo shehui koxue chuban she, 1989), ch. 1. Some other scholars are opposed to Yang's interpretation. See *NCS*, 2–5. For comments on the issue, see Huang, "New Light," 241, 248–49.

11. For the Sushen people, see *NCS*, 10–19, 25–26; *HLCM*, 95–110; Huang, "New Light," 246–50. The name Sushen is also written as Jishen or Xishen. For the Yilou, see *HLCM*, 177–85; *NCS*, 20–29.

12. For the Wuji, see *NCS*, 30–31. For their culture and relations with China, see *HLCM*, 204–11. For the Mohe people, see *CKMT*, 408–19.

13. For the four groups of inhabitants and the relations between them, see Huang, "New Light," 246–53. For the cultural links between the Manchus and the four groups of people, see ibid. For the importance of the swine to the early inhabitants, see *TMSL*, 16, 56, 70, and 84. For the role of the swine in the life of the Manchus, see *Manzu shehui lishi diaocha*, comp., "Minzu wenti wuzhong congshu," Liaoning sheng bianji weiyuan hui (Shenyang: Liaoning renmin chuban she, 1985), 30–31, 52, 166, and 199. For the linguistic linkage, see Huang, "New Light," 249–51.

14. For a pioneer study on the bird myth among the Dongyi people, see Fu Sinian, *Fu Mengzhen xian-sheng ji* (Taipei: National Taiwan University, 1952, 6 volumes), II: 32–41. For the myth in the Shang and Zhou periods, see Kwang-chih Chang, "A Classification of Shang and Zhou Myths (Abridgement)," *Bulletin of the Institute of Ethnology, Academia Sinica*, 14 (1962): 89–92. For the bird myth among the early inhabitants and relations between the eagle and the shaman cult, see Fu and Meng, *Manzu saman jiao yanjiu*, 18, 20, and 208–23.

15. For the official version, see *Daicing gurun i manju yargiyan kooli* (Manchu veritable records of the great Qing, Taizu reign) (Taipei: Hualian chuban she, 1964, reprint), 2–3. For the unofficial version, see *CMCT*, IX: 4242. For a comparative study, see Stephen W. Durrant, "Repetition in the Manchu Origin Myth as a Feature of Oral Narrative," *Central Asiatic Journal*, 22.1–2 (1978): 32–43. The article by Wang Zhonghan regards the Long White Mountains region as the place of the origin myth. See his "The Question of the Place Where the Manchu Ancestors Originated," *Central Asiatic Journal*, 35: 3–4 (1991): 279–301. See also Matsumura Jun, "The Founding Legend of the Qing Dynasty Reconsidered," *Memoirs of the Research Department of the Tōyō Bunko*, 55 (1997): 41–60.

    For the story about Fanca, see Huang, "New Light," 245. For the Manchu protection of the magpie, see *Manzu da cidian*, eds. Sun Wenliang, Liu Wanquan, and Li Zhiting, (Shenyang: Liaoning University Press, 1990), "Divine Magpie," 568.

16. For the Xituan Hill excavations, see Jia Lanpo and Yan Yin, "Xituan shan rengu di yanjiu baogao," *Kaogu xuebao*, 2 (1963): 101–109. For the findings from Dongkang, see Heilong jiang sheng Bowu guan, "Dongkang yuanshi shehui yizhi fajue baogao," *Kaogu*, 3 (1975): 158–68. For the artifacts from the Tongren site, see Zhang Taixiang," Cong zuixin kaogu xue chengqiu kan lishi shangdi Sushen Yilou ren," *Dongbei shida xuebao: Zhexue shehui koxue ban*, 5 (1982): 28–29; Wang Chengli, "Mohe di fazhan he Bohai wangguo di jianli," *CLST*, 3 (1979): 69–73.

17. For their origins, see Franke, "The Forest Peoples of Manchuria," 413; *NCS*, 74–89. But one study is against this theory. See *NCS*, 50–51. The name "Jurchen" may have appeared even in the seventh century. See *CKMT*, 466. For the meaning of the term, see *CKMT*, 466–67.

18. For their early history, see *TMSL*, 108–10; Sun Jinji, "Nüzhen yuanliu kao,"

Shixue jikan, 4 (1984): 52–54; Xu Mengxin, *Sanchao beimeng huibian* (Taipei: Wenhai chuban she, 1962, 4 volumes), 1. 3: 1a–2b. For their names and classifications in Chinese, Korean, and Khitan sources, see *NCS*, 52–3, 54–60.

19.   For the Thirty Jurchen Tribes, see Ogawa Hiroto, "Sanjūbu Joshin ni tsuite," *Tōyō gakuhō*, 24. 4 (1937): 561–601. For the unification of the Jurchens and the founding of the Jin dynasty, see Tao, *The Jurchen in Twelfth-Century China*, 16–20; Hok-lam Chan, *Legitimation in Imperial China* (Seattle: University of Washington Press, 1984), 55–58. For the creation of their written language, see *Jinshi*, comp. Tuotuo et al. (SPPY ed., 4 volumes), 1. 2: 8b.

For various groups of people, see *NCS*, 90–105. For their diverse ethnic composition, see Sun, "Nüzhen yuanliu kao," 54–55; *NCS*, 8. For Chinese captives taken to Manchuria, see Sun Zhanwen, *Heilong jiang sheng shi tansuo* (Harbin: Heilong jiang renmin chuban she, 1983), 74–75; Xu, *Sanchao beimeng*, 2. 99: 3b, 6b–8a, 10a. For sinicization of the Jurchens in North China, see Tao, *The Jurchen in Twelfth-Century China*, chs. 4 and 8. For Gao's case, see Hu Zhiyu, *Zishan daquan ji* (Peking: Zhongguo shudian, 1990, Sanyi tang congshu ed., ed. Zhang Fengdai, volumes 51–60), 56. 18:15, "Yinshi Gao jun muzhi ming." For the descendants of the Jin imperial family, see Niu Zhonghan and Wang Jiandang, "Yue Fei Jin Wuzhu houren shouci jushou bajiu gonghua tuanjie yu hexie," *Sina News* (Internet) (27 February 2007). Global News.

20.   For the *Meng'an* and *Mouke* institution, see *CKMT*, 473–77. For the sacrifice to the two Jin rulers, see *CSL*, reign of Taizong, 5: 46b, Tiancong 3/12/xinyu. For the linguistic similarity and surname connection, see *Manzhou yuanliu kao*, 18: 13b–16a and 7: 5b–8b. For anthropological aspects, see Song Dejin, "Jindai Nüzhen zushu shulun," *Lishi yanjiu*, 3 (1982): 145–59.

21.   For the Jurchens during the dynastic transition, see *CKMT*, 495–97. For their sinicization, see Tao, *The Jurchen in Twelfth-Century China*, chs. 4 and 8; Morris Rossabi, *The Jurchens in the Yüan and Ming* (Ithaca, NY: Cornell University Press, 1982), 3–4; Luo Xianyou, "Jin-Yuan shiqi Nüzhen ren di neiqian ji yanbian," *MTYC*, 2 (984): 24–30.

22.   For Yuan rule over southern Manchuria, see Yang Baolong, "Qiantan Yuandai di Nüzhen ren," *MTYC*, 3 (1984): 19; *TMSL*, 125–27.

23.   For sources that regard them as non-Jurchens, see *NCS* (151–52) and *MTTS* (14). But Yang Baolong regards the Water Tartars as members of the Jurchens. See his "Qiantan Yuandai," 17 and 19. This view is supported by Yang Mousheng, "Guanyu Shuidada di fenbu yu zushu wenti," *Dongbei difang yanjiu*, 2 (1989): 41–47.

24.   For the five myriarchies, see *Yuanshi*, comp. Song Lian (Taipei: SPPY ed., 1965, 10 volumes), 4. 59: 4a; Ch'i-ch'ing Hsiao, *The Military Establishment of the Yüan Dynasty* (Cambridge: Council of East Asian Studies, Harvard University, 1978). 186 notes 179–80 and 182. Odoli is also known as Wodolian; Hurha also as Huligai. For the Office of the Eastern Expedition Marshal, sometimes also written

as *Dong-zheng yuan-shuai fu.* See *Liaodong zhi*, 9: 10b; Yang Yang, Yuan Lükun, and Fu Langyun, *Mingdai Nuergan dusi jiqi weisuo yanjiu* (Zheng-zhou: Zhong-zhou shuhua she, 1982), 17.

The following three works share similar views about the locations of the five myriads. See *NCS*, 145–46; Yang, "Guanyu Shuidada," 42–43; and Wang Zhong-han, *Qingshi xinkao* (Shenyang: Liaoning daxue chuban she, 1990), 2–3. One source argues that the two myriads—Tuo-wo-lian and Boku-jiang—were not populated by the Jurchens. See *NCS*, 146.

For the excessive demands and the revolts, see Wada, *Tōashi kenkyū*, 261–63. For the discontinuation of the two myriads, see *MTTS*, 17.

25.   For the guard-post system, see Romeyn Taylor, "Yüan Origins of the Wei-so System" in Charles O. Hucker, ed., *Chinese Government in Ming Times: Seven Studies* (New York: Columbia University Press, 1969), 23–40. For early Ming administration of Manchuria, see Wada, *Tōashi kenkyū*, 260–447. The Liaodong and Nurkal Military commissions first appeared in 1371 and 1404, respectively, and were later stabilized in 1375 and 1409. See Yang, Yuan, and Fu, *Mingdai Nuergan*, chs. 2–7. Also see Yang Yang, *Mingdai Liaodong dusi* (Zheng-zhou: Zhong-zhou guji chuban she, 1988), 8–57. For actual completion of the Liaodong dusi, see Feng Jichang, "Mingdai Liaodong dusi jiqi weisuo jianzhi kaobian," *Lishi dili*, 14 (1998): 176–85. Phillip H. Woodruff offers a long discussion on many aspects of the Nurkal Commission. See his "Foreign Policy and Frontier Affairs along the Northeastern Frontier of the Ming Dynasty, 1350–1618: Tripar-tite Relations of the Ming Chinese, Korean Koryo, and Jurchen-Manchu Tribes-men" (Ph. D. dissertation, The University of Chicago, 1995), 88–106.

For these far-flung tribes, see Sei Wada, "The Natives of the Lower Reaches of the Amur River as Represented in Chinese Records," *Memoirs of the Research Department of the Tōyō Bunko*, 10 (1938): 41–102; Hsiao, *The Military Establish-ment of the Yüan Dynasty*, 186 notes 179–80 and 182.

26.   The following work emphasizes the security concern as a chief reason for their migration. See Li Jiancai, *Mingdai dongbei* (Shenyang: Liaoning renmin chuban she, 1986), 91–92. For the economic motivation, see Xu Zhongshu, "Mingchu Jianzhou Nüzhen judi qianxi kao," *Bulletin of the Institute of History and Philol-ogy, Academia Sinica*, 6. 2 (1936): 169–70.

27.   For the Mongol postal stations in Manchuria and their economic importance, see *TMSL*, 131–34. For the Ming transportation network, see Li, *Mingdai dong-bei*, 106–35. For the Koryŏ official's trade, see Chŏng In-ji, *Koryŏsa* (Seoul: Yŏnsei taehakkyo, 1955, 3 volumes), 1. 44: 867.

28.   There is no agreement among scholars about the beginnings and routes of the migrations. A few studies insist that the Hurha and Odoli tribes began to mi-grate at the same time. For example, *NCS*, 183–84. *CKMT* (pp. 684–85) seems to share this view.

29.   Aqača and Boersun appear in sources also as Yuxuchu and Boyisuo. For works

on the Hurha and Odoli Jurchens, see Sonoda Kazuki, *Mindai Kenshū Jochoku shi kenkyū* (Tokyo: Kokuritsu shoin, 1948), chs, 2, 4, and 5; Kawachi Yoshihiro, "Kenshō Jochoku no ido mondai," *Tōyōshi kenkyū*, 19.2 (1960): 86–155; Jiang Xiusong, "Shilun Jianzhou Nüzhen di jiju he zuhe," in Bai Shouyi, ed., *Qingshi guoji xueshu taolun hui lunwen ji* (Shenyang: Liaoning remin chuban she, 1990), 60–73. For the Maolian Guard, see *NCS*, 193–202; for the Taowen Jurchens, see *NCS*, 188. For a summary of the controversies about their sojourns and final settlements. See Li, *Mingdai Dongbei,* 71–92.

30.   In his *Qing Zhaozu zhuan* (Shenyang: Liaoning renmin chuban she, 1991), 12–14, Dong Wanlun argues that the Odoli Jurchens were led by Fanca, grandfather of Menggetimur. For their sojourn at Dunhua, see Ying Yunping, "Manzu jiujing fayuan yu hedi," *MTYC*, 2 (1986):34. For the beginning and change, see Xu Jianzhu, "Lun Jianzhou zuowei di jianli yu bianqian," *SHKH*, 1 (1983): 92–100. For Menggetimur's family line and biography, see *MTTS*, 76–88; Dong, *Qing Zhaozu*, 39–52; *DMB*, 2: 1065–67. For Yongle's policy, see Henry Serruys, *Sino-Jürčed Relations during the Yung-lo Period (1403-1424)* (Wiesbaden: Otto Harrassowitz, 1955), ch. 5.

31.   For the rise, division, and migration of the Left Jianzhou Guard, see Kawachi, *Mindai Joshin shi no kenkyū*, chs. 2 and 6. For the creation of the Right Jianzhou Guard and Tong Fanca, see Dong, *Qing Zhaozu*, 183–85; 222–28, and 232–33. In most sources, Tong Fanca is simply referred to as Fanca.

32.   For the Hulawen Jurchens, see Kawachi, *Mindai Joshin shi*, ch. 8. For the meaning of the term Haixi, see Wang, *Qingshi xinkao*, 2 and 8. For the origin of the term Hulawen and the formation of the four Hūlun tribes, see Cong Peiyuan, "Hūlun sibu xing-cheng gaishu," *MTYC*, 2 (1984): 8–17; *NCS*, 210–29. For their rise and geographical locations, see Imanishi Shunjū, "Jušen kokuiki kō," *Tōhōgaku kiyō*, 2 (1967): 89–120.

33.   For information about Singgen Dargan and Suhete, see Cong Peiyuan, "Hūlun sibu shixi kaosuo," *KHCH*, 2 (1984): 200–12. For a detailed genealogy of the Yehe ruling house, see *Yehe Nalan shi baqi zupu*, comp. Etenge (N. p.: handwritten, unpaged, 1823). For further information, see note 44.

34.   For their importance, see Li, *Mingdai Dongbei,* 147–160. For biographies of Gintaisi and Bujantai, see *CSKC*, 10: 7890–95; 7895–99.

35.   For example, Hada under its chieftain, Wan (also Wang Tai, d. 1582), loyally maintained frontier peace for China. For his career, see *MTTS*, 122–25; *ECCP*, 2: 799–800.

36.   Tanaka Katsumi, "Minmatsu no yajin Jochoku ni tsuite," *Tōyō gakuhō*, 42. 2 (1959): 1–24; *TMSL*, ch. 5; *Dongyi kaolüe*, 94: 4a; *NCS*, 229–34.

37.   In some sources the "Wild Jurchens" are recorded as the "Eastern Sea Jurchens." This is confusing and geographically it cannot cover the upper Amur valley. For the two groups, Amur River and Eastern Sea, see Yan, *Nuer-hachi zhuan*, 73–96. For the influence of steppe pastoralism, see Lattimore, *Inner Asian*, 113–14.

The Oronchons and O-wen-kes, both referred to as Evenks in Russian sources, were of the same origin. See Wang Xiaoming and Wang Yongxi, "O-lun-chun yu O-wen-ke zu tongyuan kao," *Heilong jiang minzu congkan*, 1 (1987), 44–50. For their being regarded as the Solons, see *TMSL*, 172. For more information about the O-wen-kes, Oronchons, Dahurs, and Sahalcas, also see Fang Yan, ed., *Heilong jiang shaoshu minzu jianshi* (Peking: Central College of Nationalities Press, 1993), 49–53, 78–82, 180–84.

38. For the history of the Hurhas, see Jiang Xiusong, "Qingchu di Huerha bu," *KHCH*, 1 (1981): 137–42. For efforts made by Nurhaci and Hong Taiji, see Yan, *Nuer-hachi zhuan*, 83–90; Anami Korehiro, "Shin no Taisō no Kokuryōkō seitō ni tsuite," *Bōei Daigakkō kiyō*, 6 (1962): 1–9.

39. For these groups, see Wada, "The Natives of the Lower Reaches," 41–102; *TMSL*, 175–80.

40. Some scholars identify the Warkas and Kurkas as the Hurhas. See Jiang, "Qingchu di Huerha bu," 137–42. Jiang also regards the term "Weji" as the name for all the Eastern Sea Jurchens (ibid., 138). See also Wang Bin, "Heizhe zu yu Donghai Nüzhen," *Zhong-yang minzu xueyuan xuebao*, 2 (1988): 38–42. For Nurhaci's campaigns, see Yan, *Nuer-hachi zhuan*, 73–83.

41. Cf. de Crespigny, *China*, 96–97.

42. For a brief history of the Three Uriyangquad Guards, see Li, *Mingdai Dongbei*, 54–58, 136–39. For Lattimore's conclusion, see his *Studies in Frontier History*, 325. For Mongol influence, see Liu Xiaomeng, *Manzudi shehui yu shenghuo* (Peking: Beijing tushu guan chuban she, 1998), 379–85; Peter C. Perdue, *China Marches West: The Qing Conquest of Central Eurasia* (Cambridge, MA and London: The Belknap Press of Harvard University Press, 2005), 125–27. For Nurhaci's adaptation of the Mongol script, see *ECCP*, 1: 213, 225–26.

43. Among these sources are *STTP* (32: 1a and 2b) and *Guololo shi shizong tongpu* (N. p.: n. d., handwritten, unpaged [26 sheets]), 3rd page. Caku was the founder of the Jurchen branch. See *Guololo shi jiazhuan bing lao baqi tongpu* (N. p. 1877, handwritten, unpaged [33 sheets]), first two pages. For their marriage with Nurhaci's family, see *CSKC*, 10: 7970 and 7972. But this contradicts the account of *Nuer-haqi shilu*, 2: 3b.

44. For the Nara clan's origins, see Liu, *Manzu di buluo*, 13 (in Ch. 1). For its clansmen among the Mongols, see *STTP*, 69: 9a. Some Urates remained in the region of the Qorčin Mongols (see *STTP*, 69: 12b). For the Jokis clan, see *STTP*, 70: 11b. For the Bayotes, see *STTP*, 68: 2a–4b, especially 4b. For the Oltute and Sardu clans, see *STTP*, 68: 21a and 67: 1a–3a. The Ilari clan should be another case.See Liu Housheng, *Qingdai gongting saman jisi [yanjiu]* (Chang-chun [?]: Jilin wen-shi chuban she, 1992), 31–32.

45. For the Mongol origin of the Yehe tribe, see *Yehe Nalan shi baqi zupu*, first page; *STTP*, 22: 1a; Teng Shaozhen "Shilun Mingdai Nüzhen yu Menggu di guanxi," *MTYC*, 4 (1983): 42. For the Yehe-Mongol matrimonial relations, see Feng, *Kai-*

yuan tushuo, 2: 3b. For the Gintaisi family's marriage relations with Jaisai and the Lindan Khan, see Yuan, "Lun Huang Taiji tongyi, 40.

But some scholars argue that Yehe and the three other Hūlun tribes were of Jurchen origins. See Li Qi and Jin Jihao, "Yehe bu shi chutan," *MTYC*, 3 (1983):11–12; Zhao Dong-sheng, "Guanyu Yehe buzu shouling di zushu wenti," *MANT*, 4 (1995): 55–60.

46. For Bujantai's Mongol ancestry, see *CSL*, reign of Taizong, 15: 20b–21a, Tiancong 7/9/guimao. The Hada and Ula tribes were from the same origin. See Cong, "Hūlun sibu shixi," 200–205. The Lindan Khan and his ancestors also kept matrimonial relations with the ruling family of Hada. See Yuan, "Lun Huang Taiji tongyi," 40. For the case of the Ilari clan, see the last reference of note 44 above.

47. For the allied campaign of 1593, see *Nuer-haqi shilu*,1:10a–11b.

48. For these figures, see Huang Pei, "Qingchu di Manzhou guizu: hunyin yu kaiguo (1583–1661)." In Tao Xisheng xian-sheng jiuzhi rongqing zhushou lunwen ji bianji weiyuan hui, ed., *Tao Xisheng xian-sheng jiuzhi rongqing zhushou lunwen ji* (Taipei: Shihuo chuban she, 1988, 2 volumes), 2: 610–13; Hua Li, "Qingdai di Man-Meng lianyin," *MTYC*, 2 (1983): 45–54, 79. Liu Lu contends that the marriages numbered 115. See his "Qing Taizu Taizong shi Man-Meng hunyin kao," *Gugong bowu yuan yuankan*, 3 (1995): 88–91. The study by Zhuang Jifa gives 103 marriages, including forty-three Manchu princesses and sixty Mongol brides. See his *Qingshi lunji* (Taipei: Wen-shi-zhe chuban she, 1997, 2 volumes), 2: 277–302.

49. The figure is based on Du Jiaji, "Qingdai huangzu yu Meng-Han guizu lianyin di zhidu he zuoyong," *Nankai xuebao: Zhexue shehui kexue ban*, 4 (1990): 23. For the importance of these marriage relations, see Kang Yuming, "Man-Meng guizu lianmeng yu Qing diguo," *Nankai xuebao: Zhexue shehui kexue ban*, 2 (1986): 59–66.

50. For the relocation of the Jurchens during the Liao dynasty, see *NCS*, 51–60. For Chinese captives taken to the Harbin region, see Sun, *Heilong jiang sheng shi tansuo*, 74–75.

51. See *CWS*, vol. 4, reign of Sejong, 78: 87, 19/7/kapo; vol. 6, Reign of Munjong, 13: 487, 2/4/ kyemi.For a statistical table, see Kawachi, *Mindai Joshin shi*, 111.

52. I found a case about a Chinese runaway who was born in captivity and later married a Jurchen wife. See *CWS*, vol. 7, Reign of Sejo, 36: 698, 11/8/sinsa. One may assume that there were other similar cases. For a detailed discussion of the Chinese component of the Manchus, see Zhu Chengru, *Guankui ji: Ming-Qing shi sanlung* (Peking: Cijing cheng chuban she, 2002), 1–16.

53. For the captives from Fushun, see Guang and Li, *Qing Taizu*, 1: 85; for the *Fusi nikan* surnames, see *STTP*, ch. 80. For the 1639 figures, see *Shinkan ichiroku*, ed. by Murayama Shio and Nagane Hyosai (1860 ed., 8 volumes), reign of Taizong, 7: 12b–13a, 4/3/bingyin. *Qingdai dang'an shiliao congbian*, 14 (1990), 27ff, contains many other cases. The genealogical compilation contains 247 Chinese

names. But after eliminating the duplicates, there are 156 names only. For the Chinese surnames, see *STTP*, chs. 74–78, and its Manchu version, *Jakūn gūsai manjusai mukūn hala be uheri ejehe bithe*, comps. Ortai and Zhi (Palace ed., 1745, 26 volumes), chs. 74–78.

54. For causes and number of exiles, see *Mingshi*, 8. 93: 2301–02; Yang, *Liaodong dusi*, 63–81.

55. For the case in the Yongle period, see Yang, *Liaodong dusi*, 89. The first Xuande desertion happened in 1432 when 500 soldiers fled from their shipyard in Jilin Province to the Hūlun region. See *MSL*, vol. 20, Xuande reign, 90: 2a, 7/5/bing-yin; 95: 10b, 7/9/jiashen. The second occurred in Kaiyuan around 1433. See *MSL*, vol. 21, Xuande reign, 99: 6b, 8/2/wushen; *CWS*, vol. 3, Reign of Sejong, 61: 503, 15/(intercalary) 8/muo. Kawachi Yoshihiro believes the deserters in this case were Chinese soldiers. See his *Mindai Joshin shi*, 113. For the Ming mission to the Hūlun region, see *MSL*, vol. 27, Zhengtong reign, 103: 8b–9a, 8/4/gengxu.

56. For the army revolts, see Yang, *Liaodong dusi*, 222–30. For the tax collector, see Zhao Lianwen, "Kuang-shui jian Gao Huai luan-Liao shiping," *Dongbei difang shi yanjiu*, 3 (1991): 65–71. For these Chinese, see *DMB*, 1: 826; *MSL*, vol. 27, Zhengtong reign, 103: 8b–9a, 8/4/gengxu; *Wanli bielu* (handwritten, unpaged, housed in the Fu Sinian Library, Academia Sinica, Taipei, 9 volumes), entry of Wanli 40/5/renyin. For the Chinese Quarters, see *MSL*, vol. 119, Wanli reign, 524: 4, 42/9/renxu.

57. For Chinese in the Ussuri region, see Walter W. Kolarz, *The Peoples of the Soviet Far East* (Hamden, CT: Archon Books, 1969), 43. For details about Chinese transfrontiersmen, see Section 3 in Chapter IV. Gong Zhenglu seems a case in point. A tea trader from Chekiang Province, he was seized by the Jurchens and later served as Nurhaci's secretary. Possibly he married a Jurchen woman. For his story, see *CWS*, vol. 22, Reign of Sonjo, 70: 608, 28/12/kyemyo; Wada Sei, "Shin no Taiso no komon Kyō Seiriku," *Tōyō gakuhō*, 35. 1 (1952): 40–49; see also Wada's "Kyō Seiriku den hosei," *Tōyō gakuhō*, 40. 1 (1957): 110–11.

58. For the Jurchens in the Chinese service, see Serruys, *Sino-Jürčed Relations*, ch. 15. For the two communities, see Qi Wenying, "Lun Mingchao neiqian Nüzhen anzhi zhengce—yi Anle, Zizai zhou weili," *Zhongyang minzu daxue xuebao* (Zhexue shehui kexue ban), 29. 2 (2002): 51–56. Ejima Hisao, "Anraku jizai nishū ni tsuite," *Shien*, 48 (1951): 55–82.For the large number of immigrants, see Yan Congjian, *Shuyu zhouzi lu* (Taipei: Taiwan Huawen shuju, 1969, reprint, Zhonghua wenshi congshu Series 3, volumes 36–37), 24: 1b–2a. For the four hundred households, see *MSL*, vol. 33, Jingtai reign, 220: 11b, 3/9/gengxu. Alarmed by the increasing number of immigrants, some Ming officials petitioned the throne to disperse such immigrants into China proper. See *MSL*, vol. 18, Xuande reign, 35: 4a, 3/1/jihai; vol. 32, Jingtai reign, 27: 7a, 2/2/dingchou.

59. For various tribes in northern Korea, see *CWS*, vol. 1, Reign of T'aejo, 8: 87–88,

4/12/kyemyo. For the Jurchens in northern Korea, see ibid.; Tao, *The Jurchens in Twelfth-Century China*, 16–17. For the Thirty Tribes, see Ogawa, "Sanjūbu joshin," 561–601. For the Koreans in central and southern Jilin, see Lattimore, *Manchuria*, 20.

60. For the number of Korean captives in 1254, see Chŏng, *Koryŏsa*, 1. 24: 488. For Koryŏ dynasty's requests for repatriation of Koreans, see ibid., 1. 25: 509, 31: 640–41. For a brief history of the Hong family, see ibid., 3. 130: 818–19; *Qinding Sheng-jing tongzhi*, comp. Lü Yaozeng and Song Yun (Taipei: Wenhai chuban she, 1965, Zhongguo bianjiang congshu Series 1, 3 volumes), 31: 23.For the surrendered Koreans, see *Yuanshi*, 4. 59: 3. For the Ming source, see *Liaodong zhi*, 1. 1: 21a. For the Korean account, see *CWS*, vol. 7, reign of Sejo, 34: 642, 10/ 8/ino.

61. For offices, titles, marriages, see *CWS*, vol. 1, reign of T'aejong, 7: 297, 4/5/kimi; vol. 4, reign of Sejong, 89: 282, 22/4/pyŏng; vol. 7. Reign of Sejo, 19: 379, 6/3/ kimyo; 21: 415, 6/8/imsul. For providing daily needs and treating the Jurchens as citizens, see vol. 4, reign of Sejong, 90: 313, 2/8/muja, 82: 152, 20/7/kich'uk. For Mafuta, see *STTP*, 11: 20b. For the Yi dynasty's efforts to control Jurchens by diplomacy, naturalization, and trade, see Kenneth R. Robinson, "From Raiders to Traders: Border Security and Border Control in Early Chosŏn, 1392–1450," *Korean Studies*, 13 (1992): 97–101. Kyung Moon Hwang discusses the Jurchens inside the northern frontiers of the Yi dynasty and their intermingling with the Koreans. See his "From the Dirt to Heaven: Northern Koreans in the Chosŏn and Early Modern Eras," *Harvard Journal of Asiatic Studies*, 62. 1 (2002): 141–43, 147–50.

62. For Jurchen bodyguards, see Kawachi Yoshihiro, "Ri-chō shoki no Joshin jin jiei," *Chōsen gakuhō*, 14 (1959): 381–422.

63. For Korean captives and their prices, see *CWS*, vol. 9, Reign of Sŏngjong, 54: 213, 6/4/ulyu; vol. 11, Reign of Sŏngjong, 250: 695, 22/2/kapcha. For the issues about the captives and prisoners of war, see Morioka Yasu, "Chōsen horyo no Shinkoku no kaku ni tsuite," *Tōyō gakuhō*, 66. 1–4 (1985): 455–80; Zhang Cunwu, "Qing-Han guanxi, 1631–1636," *Hanguo xuebao*, 1 (1981): 91–93. For the forty-three Korean surnames, see *STTP*, chs. 72–73.

64. For its being officially adopted in 1635, see *CSL*, reign of Taizong, 25: 29a, Tiancong 9/10/ gengyin. For a detailed review of all the twenty interpretations, see Huang, "New Light," 272–82. For linguistic interpretations, see S. M. Shirokogoroff, *Social Organization of the Manchus: A Study of the Manchu Clan Organization* (Shanghai: n.p., 1924), 161–67; Meng Sen, *Ming-Qing shi lunzhu jikan, xubian* (Peking: Zhonghua Book Company, 1986), 1–3; Xiao, *Qingdai tongshi*, 1: 52–53; Wang, "'Manzhouyu' 'Wenshu' di yuanyuan," 89–132. Erich Hauer, trans., *Huang-Ts'ing k'ai-kuo fang-lüeh* (Berlin and Leipzig: Walter de Gruyter & Co., 1926), 592; Tang Bangzhi, *Qing huangshi sipu* (Taipei: Wenhai chuban she, 1966, reprint, CCST, Series 8, volume 71), 1.1b; Sun Wenliang, "Lun Manzu di jueqi," *MTYC*, 1 (1986):14–15; Ch'en Chieh-hsien, *Manzhou congkao* (Taipei: College of

the Arts, National Taiwan University, 1963), 18–24.For the phonetic relation between the two names "Sushen" and "Manchu," see *CSL*, Qianlong reign, 1039: 4b,
42/8/renzi.

Among connotative views are Kim Kyŏng-mum, *Yonghaengnok sonjip*
(Seoul: Sung Kyun Kwan University, 1960–62, 2 volumes), 2: 351; Zheng Tianting, *Qingshi tanwei* (Peking: Peking University Press, 1999), 389–90; Wula Xichun, "Cong yuyan lunzheng Nüzhen, Manzhou zhi zucheng," *Manzu wenhua*,
14 (December 1, 1990): 60–61; Giovanni Stary, "Manzhou jiuming xinshi,
"*Zhong-yang minzu xueyuan xuebao*," 6 (1988): 17–18.

For the miscellaneous category, see *Zhongguo tongshi jianbian*, ed. by
Zhongguo lishi yanjiu hui under Fan Wenlan (Shanghai: Huadong renmin chu-
ban she, 1952), 620. For the views of two Japanese scholars, see Mitamura
Taisuke, "Manju koku seiritsu katei no ichi kōsatsu," *Tōyōshi kenkyū*, 2.2 (1936):
17–35; Kanda Nobuo, "The National Name 'Manju'," *Proceedings of the Fourth
East Asian Altaistic Conference* (Taipei: December 26–31, 1971): 152–55.

65.   For its first appearance, see *CMCT*, 1: 81; Guang and Li, *Qing Taizu*, 1: 33. For its
use after 1628, see Gertraude Roth Li, "The Rise of the Early Manchu State: A
Portrait Drawn from Manchu Sources to 1636" (Ph. D. dissertation, Harvard
University, 1975), 10. For the name of the state founded by Bukūri Yongson, see
CMCT, 9: 4242; *CSL* (Manchu edition), reign of Taizu, p. 6. For frequent appear-
ance after 1628, see Stary, "Manzhou jiuming," 18.

66.   For the meanings of the word "Jušen," see Xue Hong and Liu Housheng, "'Jiu
Manzhou dang' suoji Daqing jianhao qiandi guohao," *SHKH*, 2 (1990): 83–86.
According to Zhou Yuan-lian, the status of Jušen finally sank to that of the *aha*.
See his "Cong "'Zhushen' shenfen di bianhua kan ruguan qian Manzu di shehui
xingzhi," *SHKH*, 1 (1979): 115–26. Another study provides a balanced view about
the status of *aha*. See Wang Mouhe, "Zaoqi Manzu shehui di aha shenfen wenti,"
Nankai xuebao, 5 (1982): 53–61.

For the change in the meaning of the term "Jušen," see Li Xuezhi, "Shi Manwen zhi 'zhu-shen' yu"aha," *Bian-zheng yanjiu suo nianbao*, 12 (1981): 1–34;
Hideo Ishibashi, "On Iregen, Jušen and Aha in the Early Ch'ing," *Acta Asiatica*,
53 (1988), 24–38.After adopting the term Manzhou, Hong-taiji redefined the
word "Jušen." See *Shinkan ichiroku*, reign of Taizong, 5:15a, Tiancong 9/10/
xinchou.

67.   Even new studies are still speculative. See Ma Yueshan, "Manzhou zuming yanjiu zongshu," *MANT*, 3 (1988): 18–20; Teng Shaozhen, "'Manzhou' ming-cheng
kaoshu," *MTYC*, 4 (1996): 70–77.

68.   For a general discussion of the two classifications, see Huang, "New Light,"
265–66; Wang, *Qingshi xinkao*, 48–50; *Jilin tongzhi*, comp. Chang-shun *et al.*
(Taipei: Wenhai chuban she, 1965, Zhongguo bianjiang congshu, Series 1, 10
volumes), 51: 3a–4a, 5a. Old Manchus are also known as *chen*, *jiu*, or *fe* Manchus,
while the New Manchus as *xin* or *ice* Manchus.

69. For the New Manchus, see Robert H. G. Lee, *The Manchurian Frontier in Qing History* (Cambridge, MA: Harvard University Press, 1970), 33–34; Liu Xiaomeng, "Guanyu Qingdai 'Xin Manzhou' di jige wendi," *MANT*, 3 (1987): 26–32; Wang, *Qingshi xinkao*, 49–50. For the forty new companies, see *TCCC*, 3: 6. Actually the clan names in chapters 50–59 of *Jakūn gūsai Manjusai mukūn hala be uheri ejehe bithe* may be considered rare surnames because their members seldom held high offices. Moreover, many such clans are squeezed into the same chapter. For the two clan names, see *Jakūn gūsai Manjusai mukūn hala be uheri ejehe bithe*, chs. 64 and 65. I studied the geographical origins of all the Manchu clans included in the genealogical compilation.

70. For their training, see Wang, *Qingshi xinkao*, 50; Liu, "Guanyu Qingdai 'Xin Manzhou,'" 30–31.

71. For Nurhaci's opinion of the Mongols, see *MWLT*, 1: 124–26 and 181. For Hong Taiji's complaints, see *CSL*, reign of Taizong, 4: 23a–26a, Tiancong 2/12/dinghai; 5: 1b–2a, Tiancong 3/1/ renxu; *MWLT*, 2: 912–14.

Chapter II

The Founding of the Qing Dynasty

THE QING DYNASTY EMERGED AS A RESULT of the Manchu conquest of China, which was of great importance to both China and the Manchus. But the transition from the Ming to the Qing was a lengthy and painful process for both the Manchus and the Chinese. To China it meant the second time the country had come under an alien minority from the frontier. The new empire now encompassed Manchuria, Mongolia, Sinkiang, Tibet, and Taiwan. More importantly, the conquest left an indelible mark on Chinese culture. To the Manchus it signified the most glorious chapter of their history. They became the makers of Chinese history. Long before the end of their dynasty, however, they came to participate in the Chinese way of life.

1. The Rise of Nurhaci

The Manchu conquest of China was mainly attributable to Nurhaci and his sons, Hong Taiji and Dorgon, each representing a stage of development. Nurhaci was the groundbreaker of this great enterprise. A sixth generation scion of Menggetimur and the eldest son of his family, he was born and grew up in Fe Ala, in what is now Xinbin in Liaoning Province. His grandfather, Giocangga (d. 1582), and father, Taksi (d. 1582), were minor chiefs of the Left Jianzhou Guard. There are no reliable data about Nurhaci's early life. One can only provide a sketch based on bits and pieces gleaned from various sources.[1]

Like other young Jurchen males, Nurhaci must have practiced archery and horseback riding to prepare himself for adulthood. He does not seem to have had a happy boyhood, for he lost his mother when he was ten. With a stepmother, he had to work collecting forest products and digging ginseng roots. He had to overcome many challenges and cultivate perseverance, thus becoming a tough young man.[2]

As the son of a Jurchen chief, Nurhaci was allowed to frequent the frontier market at Fu-shun, founded in 1439 for Jianzhou tribesmen. He must have learned some Chinese, and he is said to have been interested in the *Romance of the Three Kingdoms* (*Sanguo zhi yanyi*) and *The Water Margin* (*Shuihu zhuan*), popular vernacular Chinese novels on loyalty and heroic deeds. Late Ming sources maintain that he served as a bodyguard of Li Cheng-liang (1526–1618), commander-in-chief of the Ming army in Manchuria, or was even fostered by the latter.[3] Although this needs further documentation, it is possible that Li turned to this capable young man for political purposes.

Nurhaci finally unified the Jurchens and founded the frontier state from which the Qing dynasty emerged. In Ming times, no other Jurchen leader had succeeded in doing this. Wang Tai (also Wan, 1510s?–1582), a powerful Hada chieftain descended from the ruling family of the Ula tribe, was able to exercise influence over all the Hūlun and Jianzhou Jurchens during the late 1560s and early 1570s. Capable and loyal, he won China's support. He took the title of Khan, and was the unifier of the Jurchens, so to speak, setting a model for Nurhaci. But Fortune was no longer on his side when he was old and challenged by rivals. His death coincided with the rapid deterioration of Liaodong's situation. Fraught with factions, financial problems, and discontent, China was unable to maintain frontier peace. The Jurchens, meanwhile, underwent new social and political developments. The kinship system, once the basis of social and political structures, gave way to the territorial units, which were largely of a political nature. There were too many tribes, branches, and tribal alliances in constant struggle for land and power, but there was no effective leader for them to rely on. Nor could they look upon China as protector or arbitrator. They had to seek their own solutions to problems that confronted them.[4]

Opportunity came to Nurhaci in 1582 when the Ming army attacked Gure, a citadel near his birthplace. It was the stronghold of Adai (d. 1582), the son of Wang Gao (1529–1575), an ambitious chieftain of the Right Jianzhou Guard. Nurhaci's grandfather and father sided with the Ming, but the Chinese army killed them, perhaps by mistake. This incident gave Nurhaci an excuse for taking up arms the following year. Since he was not strong enough to challenge China at that time, he focused on Nikan Wailan, a petty Jurchen chieftain who, having helped the Ming army destroy Adai, became influential. His emergence created suspicion and fear among other Jurchen leaders. Early on, Nurhaci had only a small army.

One may divide Nurhaci's rise into two stages, with the year 1616 dividing them.[5] The first stage began when he defeated Nikan Wailan in 1583 and ended with the founding of a frontier kingdom, Later Jin (Hou Jin), in 1616. It was basically a "tribal phase," as one scholar puts it. From his base around Fe Ala Nurhaci concentrated on defeating rivals and unifying the Jurchens. The decade of 1583–1593 was crucial because with only a few followers he confronted rivals that included members of his own clan. But he overcame these obstacles with courage and strategic brilliance. As a fighter, he was able to attract warriors. Among the earliest lieutenants he recruited, Eidu, Anfiyanggu (1559–1622), Fiongdon (1564–1620), Hohori (1561–1624), and Hūrhan (1576–1623) were the best known. Fiongdon and Hohori brought in hundreds of kin and villagers, who made good soldiers. The five men, later made the Five Councilors (*wu dachen*), formed a loyal cohort that helped create a favorable situation for Nurhaci.[6] By 1593 he had unified the Jurchen groups of the old Jianzhou tribes. The Four Hūlun tribes—Hada, Hoifa, Ula, and Yehe—became his next target. Despite matrimonial ties with Nurhaci, these tribes were apprehensive of his rise to power. They organized a nine-tribe alliance, including the Neyen, Guwalca, Sibe, and Qorčin tribes, to invade his territory. This was the most critical battle he had fought during the first stage. With superior strategy his army routed these allied forces. The victory paved the way for his conquest of the Hūlun tribes and the creation of a frontier kingdom.[7]

Nurhaci's effort to unify the Jurchens identified with the struggle for imperial patents, was related to the guard-post system, which was operated by the Ming not only as a means of controlling the frontier tribes but also as an instrument of political participation by local chiefs. After receiving an appointment to office by the Ming, each Jurchen chief was given a patent, which carried political and economic privileges as well as Chinese values. As a certificate of appointment it

strengthened the status of the holder as ruler of tribesmen and was required for promotion and inheritance in the guard-post hierarchy. It
also functioned as a passport to enter China for trade or to send tributary missions. In the final analysis it served as an instrument of sinicization. Because of its importance, beginning with the early sixteenth
century the patent caused many problems, such as counterfeiting, intertribal rivalry, and even frontier raids, each affecting the Jurchens
and their relations with the Ming.[8]

The scramble for the patent among Jurchen chiefs facilitated the
rise of Nurhaci. With the weakening of the Ming, the struggle inten-
sifed from the 1570s on. The victor seized from the vanquished not
only patents but the latter's people and land. At the height of its power,
the Hada tribe controlled all 999 patents of the Hūlun tribes. Nurhaci
was the last man standing after the long war for the imperial patents.
He claimed ownership of all 500 patents from the Jianzhou tribes after he unified them. With the subjugation of the Hada tribe in 1599 he
acquired 363 patents.[9] The shift of patent ownership made Nurhaci the
most powerful Jurchen leader.

To build his military strength, around 1601 Nurhaci founded the
Eight Banners system, an institution characterizedby Inner Asian elements because it resembled the *Meng'an* and *Mouke* institutions of
the Jurchens under the Jin dynasty. There were also similarities between it and the Mongol military system. Above all, it can be traced
back to a traditional Jurchen social institution with a far earlier history. For hunting, the Jurchens organized able-bodied male members
of the same clan into ten-man teams known in Manchu as *niru*, meaning "a large arrow," which carried military, political, and social significance. One of the ten was the team commander, referred to as *niru
ejen* in Manchu (after 1644 as *zuoling* in Chinese). Each team functioned as warriors and broke up after hunting. It is clear that the teams
were units in kinship and tasks. The banner system was essentially
a modification of this institution and served as a fearsome war machine. According to Franz Michael, the banner system shared common characteristics with the Ming guard-post system, for both were
of a bureaucratic nature and took charge of civil and military affairs,
to mention just two similarities. But not until the Yongzheng period
did the banner system begin to become bureaucratized.[10]

When he began his career in 1583, Nurhaci tried every means to expand his army. As a rule, he took two measures to deal with a tribe, whether it submitted on its own or was conquered. One measure was to remove the entire tribe from its home base, however far away, to the area under his control. Without a home base, the power of its chief was undermined. All members of the tribe were now organized into the banner system. While tribesmen became common warriors, chiefs were made officers according to their merits. With a large membership a big clan could muster more *niru* or companies. He combined two or even three small clans to make up one *niru*. All served Nurhaci at his pleasure, not allowed to act as freely as before. The other measure was to raze the tribe's shamanistic center and even kill its shaman, who enjoyed spiritual and political leadership. Obviously, Nurhaci's goal was to prevent the divided loyalty of his new followers, for without their own shamanistic center they had to throw themselves at the feet of their new lord, Nurhaci.[11]

Many Jurchen tribes disappeared with the progress of Nurhaci's unification effort. Although existing within the framework of the banner, the clan system differed from its earlier incarnation. This can be seen from the dissimilarity between old and new nobilities. The old nobility—clan and tribal heads—owed their status to their ancestors. Each was a ruler in his own right, competing with others and making unification difficult. The new nobility, banner officers, obtained their status from Nurhaci and were dedicated to fighting for the realization of their master's dream. Through the banner system Nurhaci was able to achieve unification of the Jurchens.

As the basic unit of the banner system, the first *niru*, or company, was possibly created in 1583. After a reform in 1601 each company had 300 men, but this numerical strength was not strictly enforced, especially during the Kangxi and Yongzheng reigns. Nurhaci had sixteen and two half companies before 1588, and more than forty by 1601. With each new conquest Nurhaci acquired more companies. He organized the banners (*gūsa*) when the number of the companies increased. At first he had only one banner, and toward the end of the 1580s a second. The third appeared when he conquered the Hada tribe; the fourth after conquest of the tribe of Ula. Around 1615 Nurhaci added four more, and these were referred to as the Manchu Eight Banners, the centerpiece of the banner system and the model of the Mongol and Chinese branches.[12]

The system of banners was an all-inclusive institution in organization and function. All the Jurchens under Nurhaci, whatever age or sex, were made lifetime members. Fundamentally a military instrument, the banners permeated every aspect of its members' lives. Among these functions were the training and evaluation of warriors, political control, economic matters, and such social matters as the registration of marriages, births, and deaths. The banners preserved certain clan elements, which had been weakened by a bureaucratic ingredient, especially since the Yongzheng reign. In the beginning, five companies made up a *jalan* (later *canling* in Chinese). In reality a *jalan* consisted of many more companies. A banner comprised five *jalan*, each equivalent to a regiment.[13] During the last years of his life Nurhaci began to organize the Mongol banner system, but not until 1635 was it completed by Hong Taiji. By 1642, Hong Taiji possessed the Chinese Eight Banners. The banner system had twenty-four banners. Indispensable to the rise and consolidation of Manchu power, the banners lasted to the end of the dynasty, with social consequences for the residents of Liaodong.[14]

Nurhaci was a skillful manager of marriage alliances. He married off women from his clan not only to friends and followers but to rivals. Out of the Five Councilors, Eidu, Hohori, and Fiongdon married his sister, daughter, and granddaughter, respectively. He even gave more than one female member of his clan to the same person. To win over the Ula tribe, which was strategically located on the way to the Amur region, Nurhaci gave its chieftain, Bujantai, two nieces and a daughter.[15] At the same time, Nurhaci, his brother, and his sons took wives from chieftains of other Jurchen tribes. He also tried to win over Mongol tribes as allies through matrimonial relations. There were twenty-three such marriages under his sponsorship. Marriage played an important role in the founding of Nurhaci's frontier state.[16]

In addition to the above achievements, Nurhaci had another major accomplishment during the first stage. In 1599, while devoting himself to the unification of the Jurchens, he made efforts to devise a writing system based on the Mongol script. The significance of the Manchu script can be explored from several aspects. With the new instrument,

Nurhaci was able to record his oral commands and important events as political and historical documents, such as *Jiu Manzhou dang* (old-script Manchu archives). While the Eight Banners he organized served as a framework to hold together his subjects of diverse origins, the Manchu script, as a common means of expression, provided a further bond among them. It also broadened, as Peter Perdue ably argues, the Jurchen cultural horizons and helped maintain their distinct identity.[17]

During the second stage, from 1617 to his death in 1626, Nurhaci made efforts to drive the Ming out of Manchuria. He conquered the four Hūlun tribes one after the other. Because their population was larger than that of the Jianzhou tribes, their conquest provided him with more manpower. Divided, the Mongols were incapable of stopping him. China remained formidable, for it controlled more resources and exercised considerable influence in Manchuria. The existing economic and political issues between China and the Jurchens provided Nurhaci with a rationale to take action.

Trade was a major issue between Nurhaci and China. Ginseng was a chief product of the region under his control; pearls and sable furs were largely commodities of the Wild Jurchens. To protect his income Nurhaci punished and even executed trespassing Chinese ginseng diggers. After his rise, he tried to monopolize the ginseng trade as well as the pearl and sable markets. Ming officials in Liaodong attempted to manipulate trade in these products. Sometimes they closed the ginseng market to force Nurhaci into submission because ginseng was usually immersed in water for preservation and thus easily went bad. A great quantity rotted as a result of the suspension of the market in 1607–1609. Nurhaci introduced dry preservation to make ginseng storable for a long time.[18] In addition, he led eight tributary missions to Peking, which provided opportunities for trade and generous rewards from the court.[19]

Another conflict concerned disputable farmland close to the Chinese frontier. The land in question was in two areas. Like a wedge strategically driven into the settlements of the Jianzhou Jurchens, the southeastern part included six forts constructed by the Ming in 1573.[20] As a result of Nurhaci's challenge, Ming frontier authorities finally pulled back from the forts in 1606. The other area was the borderland of the Hada tribe. Without China's permission Nurhaci sent people to farm it. When China protested in 1615, he replied with threats.[21] What he fought for was not only political independence but economic autonomy. His economic needs were echoed the more clearly in the Seven Great Grievances (*qi dahen*) announced on the eve of his attack on Fushun in 1618. In them he accused the Ming of slaughtering his father and grandfather, sending Chinese soldiers across the fixed frontier line, and failing to prohibit the Chinese from transgressing his territory. Among other grievances were China's expelling of his subjects from their farms near the frontier, taking sides with Yehe, and forcing him to give up Hada, which he had conquered.[22] He needed food, salt, and cloth to support his followers, whose number increased with time.

To obtain provisions he established relations with Chinese merchants—notably Tong Yang-xing (Tung Yang-sing in Manchu, d. 1632), a resident of Liaodong, and Li Jixue, a native of the same region. They later became his high officials. When he conquered a city, he seized Chinese food and valuables. When economic crises occurred in the 1620s and 1630s, he and Hong Taiji sent troops to raid Liaodong and China proper. Clearly, political and military success hinged on economic strength, while economic problems called for aggressive solutions. In short, Nurhaci waged a two-front war, and he succeeded.[23]

The Ming court was alarmed by the growth of Nurhaci's strength, especially when he took the title of "kingdom" for the frontier region in 1616. Chinese officials in Peking, divided on many important matters, took a hard line toward Nurhaci. His sack of Fushun in 1618 marked his first direct attack on China and therefore prompted punitive action by the Chinese at Sarhū, a place in the district of today's Fushun.[24]

Fought in mid-April 1619, the Battle of Sarhū was a life-and-death struggle for Nurhaci's newly founded kingdom,. The Ming made Yang Hao (d. 1629) commander-in-chief, with his headquarters at Liaoyang. Chinese forces, together with their Korean and Yehe allies, totaled about 90,000. They divided into four routes, all aimed toward Hetu Ala, the political nerve center of the Jurchen state. Nurhaci mobilized around 60,000 men, but he won because he emphasized intelligence, centralized operations, and geographical advantage. The battle was a milestone in Jurchen relations with the Ming.[25]

The next goal of Nurhaci was to acquire the region west of the Liao River. In 1626 he led about 130,000 men to attack Ningyuan, present-day Xing-cheng in Liaoning Province. It was the stronghold of the Ming forces under Yuan Chong-huan (1584–1630), a young and brave commander. With determination and cannon the defenders beat off the attackers. Because it was his first defeat Nurhaci was frustrated, and he took ill and died the same year. But he had laid the foundation for the Qing dynasty, and his work was completed by his brilliant sons, Hong Taiji and Dorgon.[26]

2. Hong Taiji's Leadership

Hong Taiji represented the second phase of the frontier state, the stage of reorientation. His contribution was fourfold: improvement of economic and social conditions, expansion of the kingdom, centralization of power, and creation of administrative machinery. He was the eighth son of Nurhaci and a resourceful man, a good archer, and a warrior who participated in many campaigns. At age twenty-four he became a senior prince (*beile*) and master of a banner. He was the planner of the surprise attack on Fushun in 1618 and field commander in the Battle of Sarhū the following year. He played a role in capture of Shenyang and Liaoyang, as well as in the conquest of the Yehe tribe, the last member of the Hūlun-Jurchen bloc.[27]

In addition to ability, an unexpected event helped Hong Taiji become the second ruler of the Manchu state. Of the four senior princes, he and Daišan (1583–1648) were the most influential. In 1620 Daišan was disgraced owing to inappropriate conduct. As a consequence, Hong Taiji moved to the fore and ascended the throne in 1626.

The most challenging problems for Hong Taiji were the economic and social conditions, which were working to destroy the newly forged frontier state. With too much emphasis on military affairs, Nurhaci unconsciously created serious economic and social problems. As mentioned earlier, it was his policy to resettle the Jurchen tribes, clans, or villagers from their home regions to Liaodong after their submission. These new adherents brought new demands for food and clothing, which to alleviate, Nurhaci took measures, among which were farming, purchasing, appropriating, rationing, and frontier raids. Problems persisted, however, and were aggravated by natural disasters during the last six years of his reign.[28]

Associated with the economic trouble was social unrest. During the conquest of the Liao valley the Manchus were destructive. They were eager to take part in war because it provided opportunities for booty. Soldiers took away valuables, destroyed property, and massacred Chinese, including noncombatants. Those who survived were made slaves. A Korean eyewitness testified that even a private owned slaves. Without any legal protection, the slaves were at the mercy of their masters.[29]

After 1621, Nurhaci issued orders to improve the conditions of the Chinese, possibly because he realized their importance to his state. As conquerors, the Manchus did not mean to change their behavior. At the same time, Nurhaci continuously imposed harsh demands. The Chinese had to perform such services as construction and transportation. Relocation was perhaps the harshest of the demands. For economic and political purposes, Nurhaci relocated many Chinese from west of the Liao River to the east and from city to countryside. During relocation they suffered hunger and death. In the new settlements, they were organized with strangers into co-occupant households, a measure creating abuse, inconvenience, and disputes.[30]

Fear and despair motivated the Chinese of the Liao valley to take action. Flight seemed the most popular choice. Some tried to take refuge in Korea or on islands in the Yellow Sea. The majority rushed back to China proper and caused concern in the Ming court. Some even tried to poison, revolt against their Manchu masters, and recover the cities.[31] After reentering these cities the Manchus massacred more Chinese. Social unrest further disrupted the economy. These problems brought the frontier state to the verge of disintegration.

To solve such problems, Hong Taiji had to redirect his state. His first priority was to pacify the Chinese. He prohibited the Manchus from being high-handed, discontinued the requirement of co-occupant households, and carried out a segregation policy, which allowed Chinese to register as independent households. Chinese collaborators were organized into banners under commanders appointed from among them. While his father enslaved or slaughtered Chinese scholars, he freed many of them, from whom he recruited advisors or officials. With their assistance, Hong Taiji sponsored translations of the Chinese classics, encouraged the veneration of Confucius, and ad-

Shanhaikuan

■ Battle Sites

• Important Cities

Map 3. Major Battle Sites.

1. Sarhū	2. Ningyüan	3. Jinzhou
4. Fushun	5. Shenyang	6. Liaoyang
7. Guang-ning	8. Kaiyuan	9. Peking

opted more Ming institutions. As a whole, the pacification of the Chinese subjects contributed to stability, facilitated recovery, and helped political centralization.[32]

Hong Taiji gave attention to farming, commerce, and trade with Korea, China, and the Mongols. He reduced the corvée so as to let his subjects devote time to farming. He urged them to reclaim deserted land and marshland.[33] Since 1624, Nurhaci had collected a 10 percent

sales tax on commodities, but Hong Taiji cut it to 3 percent. The Liaodong region restored its bustling commercial activities. Shenyang became the commercial center of the region. Trade was an important
reason for his invasions of Korea in 1627 and 1636. Manchu merchants
traded with Chinese merchants at markets in Inner Mongolia. Trade
relations also existed between the Manchus and the Mongols.[34]

Under Hong Taiji the Manchu state expanded and prepared for the
conquest of China. For all his efforts Nurhaci did not control the middle and upper Amur regions. Through diplomatic and military means,
Hong Taiji was able to control the tribes in these areas. He and his successors recruited warriors from among them. In 1632, he defeated the
ruler of the Chahar Mongols, the Lindan Khutuktu Khan, who supported China against the Jurchens. Three years later he pacified the
remaining followers of the khan and became overlord of Inner Mongolia.[35] He thus safeguarded his rear, obtained easy access to North
China, and made Qing control of Outer Monglia possible. In 1636 he
proclaimed himself emperor of the Qing dynasty.

Korea was another target of Hong Taiji because, like the Mongols,
it posed a threat to the rear of his state. Even after the conquest of the
Liaodong valley by Nurhaci, Korea remained loyal to China. It provided asylum for Chinese refugees and helped Mao Wenlong (1576–
1629), a Ming commander who engaged in guerrilla warfare against
the Jurchen state. At the same time, Hong Taiji needed grain and other
supplies from Korea.[36] He launched two campaigns against that country. The first, to separate Korea from China and rout Mao Wenlong's
guerrillas, occurred in 1627. But Korea refused to cut off its relations
with China. Nor did the campaign wipe out Mao. Later new issues
arose regarding trade, fugitives, etc. He reached the limit of his patience when Korean envoys refused to follow the prescribed ritual at
his imperial inauguration in 1636. By the end of the year an army under his command invaded Korea and brought it to terms.[37]

Like his father, Hong Taiji tried to conquer the valley west of the
Liao River, which connected Liaodong with Shanhaikuan—the outpost guarding Peking. Shortly after his first Korean campaign he attacked Jinzhou and Ningyuan. He was beaten off, for the two cities
were defended by the best Ming troops under qualified commanders and with "foreign guns" introduced by the Jesuits. Since a frontal

attack failed, he repeatedly raided North China, with the purpose of looting and demoralizing, while planning for a second assault.[38]

The second battle at Jinzhou and its surrounding area was critical, and both sides were prepared. After subjugating Korea and Inner Mongolia, the conquest of China was the only goal that Hong Taiji had not achieved. In 1639 he set out to attack Jinzhou again. With the exception of the initial stage, he adopted a tactic of encircling and isolating Chinese defenders. In its many communications, the Ming Board of War (*Bingbu*) confirmed this tactic. In 1642 Hong Taiji annihilated the Chinese troops and captured their field commander, Hong Chengchou.[39] The Battle of Sarhū in 1619 enabled the Jurchens to wrest the Liaodong valley from China. The Battle of Jinzhou brought the Manchus to the doorstep of Peking.

The home front was also important to Hong Taiji. He made efforts to reorient the state toward centralization because he shared rule with his powerful brothers Daišan, Amin (d. 1640), and Manggūltai (1587–1633). He and the three brothers were known as the Four Senior Princes during the reign of Nurhaci. Each was a fighter, had influence in the banner, and participated in decisions. Of the Manchu Eight Banners, Hong Taiji likely controlled the Plain and Bordered Yellow Banners, many of whose members were from such powerful clans as the Gūlwalgiya, the Niohuru, the Hešeri, and the Tunggiya, which were ready to fight for him. Daišan commanded the Plain Red, while Manggūltai commanded the Plain Blue and Amin the Bordered Blue.

In the first five years of Hong Taiji's reign, the state was under a tetrarchate. Although it helped achieve the transition, it created a struggle among its members. Naturally Hong Taiji was looking for a pretext to terminate the tetrarchy so as to place himself above the other princes.[40] The opportunity came when in 1630 Amin abandoned four cities without fighting the Ming army. Amin was charged with cowardice and imprisoned. Next disgraced was Manggūltai for displaying anger before Hong Taiji in 1631, and later Daišan was humiliated.[41] By 1632 Hong Taiji had become an unchallengeable monarch.

Hong Taiji was the founder of the early Qing administrative machinery. The institutions Nurhaci organized were simple, even primitive, and characterized by Mongol influence. The banner system he introduced mainly consisted of Manchu units, tinted with tribal traditions. The offices, such as the Five Councilors and the Ten Jargūci (*Du-tang*), were supposed to care for judicial and administrative affairs, but their responsibilities were not defined. In contrast Hong Taiji rounded off the state machinery left by his father and shifted from a Mongol predisposition to Chinese institutions. He added Mongol and Chinese units to the banner system. In each banner he placed a commander, two associate commanders, and two administrators.[42] With these appointments he strengthened the bureaucratic element of the banner system.

Four other institutions Hong Taiji founded carried out administrative functions. The first was the Literary Office, which took shape during the reign of Nurhaci and was institutionalized in 1632. Staffed by Manchu and Chinese scholars, it dealt with secretarial, translation, compiling, and advisory matters. More importantly, it helped Hong Taiji achieve consolidation of power. In 1636 it branched out into the Three Inner Courts (*Nei sanyuan*), from which finally emerged the Grand Secretariat *(Neigo)*. Created in 1631, the *Liubu* (Six Boards) took charge of the offices of personnel, revenues, rites, military affairs, punishment, and public works. The Court of Dependent Peoples and the Censorate (*Ducha yuan*) were founded in 1636. For efficiency and smooth operation, in 1638 Hong Taiji reorganized the Six Boards, the Court of Dependent Peoples, and the Censorate. He issued rules and by-laws to guide the operation of these new offices. Despite their Chinese origin, as a noted specialist points out, many Qing offices revealed Manchu characteristics. Hong Taiji died in 1643 but by then had made a gigantic step toward the Manchu takeover of China, a transition from the primitive Jurchen state to the Qing empire.[43] The Literary Office, the Six Boards, and the Censorate will be discussed further in Chapter V.

3. Takeover

Dorgon was the last of the three individuals of great importance to the Manchu conquest. He was the 14th son of Nurhaci and a full brother of Ajige (1605–1651) and Dodo (1614–1649). All three were born fighters, forming a powerful bloc among the princes. Dorgon participated in many campaigns and showed leadership abilities at an early age. In 1628 he was under Hong Taiji in the expedition against the Chahar

Mongols. Because of his performance he was given the title "*Mergen daicing,*" meaning wise or outstanding warrior. During the 1630s he commanded the army that invaded Inner Mongolia and China. A general and a statesman, he was indispensable to the founding and consolidation of the Qing.[44]

The importance of Dorgon was apparent in four ways: his aversion to a war of succession, the march toward Peking, the adoption of the Chinese form of government, and the safeguarding of the conquest. The death of Hong Taiji brought a crisis because he did not designate a successor. Among the candidates were Dorgon, Hooge (1609–1648)— the eldest son of Hong Taiji—and Dodo, each a respectable warrior with his own followers. Dauntless and resourceful, Dorgon was the most renowned and very likely to be the new emperor. But Hong Taiji's men in the Plain and Bordered Yellow Banners appeared at the deliberation with drawn swords. They demanded that the new ruler come from among sons of their deceased master. Tensions ran high and a war of succession loomed large. At this moment, Dorgon disqualified himself and nominated the six-year old Fulin (1638–1861), ninth son of Hong Taiji. Dorgon and Prince Jirgalang (1599–1655) were made regents of the child emperor.[45] Dorgon's statesmanship appealed to all parties, and so an internecine war was averted.

Domestic events in China helped the Manchus pass through Shanhaikuan, the eastern terminus of the Great Wall and the impregnable fortress blocking their way to Peking. The situation in China was chaotic, with rebels, freebooters, and displaced people everywhere. In early 1644 Chinese rebels under Li Zicheng (1605?–1645) founded their own dynasty called "Dashun." When they took Peking the Chong-zhen emperor (r. 1628–1644) committed suicide. This effectively brought an end to the Ming dynasty.[46] Although he did not know the latest developments in Peking, Dorgon was prepared to take action. Shanhaikuan now faced attack from Li Zicheng, on the one hand, and the Manchus, on the other. Its garrison commander, Wu Sangui (1612–1678), decided to collaborate with the Manchus. In response to a request for help, according to a Korean eyewitness, the Manchus raced to battle against the rebels.[47]

The Battle of Shanhaikuan in the early spring of 1644 was the third major Manchu encounter with the Chinese army. When the battle between Wu's garrisons and Li's rebels reached a critical stage Dorgon unleashed his Manchu horsemen to help Wu. The allied forces routed the rebels, but the situation completely changed. Now the Manchus dominated the scene. They controlled not only Shanhaikuan but also Wu Sangui and his garrisons. It was a development that Wu Sangui perhaps did not expect.[48]

The engagement at Shanhaikuan further demonstrated Dorgon's wise leadership because he was the planner and commander. Li Zicheng left the battlefield for Peking, the city soon taken by the Manchus. Ignoring the opposition of powerful Manchu nobles who preferred Shenyang, Dorgon made Peking the capital of the Qing. From there the new Manchu rulers proclaimed themselves to be the recipients of the Mandate of Heaven.

The defeat of Li Zicheng at Shanhaikuan virtually marked the end of the Dashun regime. Chased by Dorgon, Li stayed on the run, lost one place after another, and died in mid-1645. While pursuing Li and his followers, the Manchus encountered—and defeated—another group of rebels led by Zhang Xian-zhong (1605–1647).[49] The more places the Manchus took from the rebels meant the greater the conquest of China.

With the Battle of Shanhaikuan the configuration of power changed. Prior to 1644 there were the Ming, the Manchu frontier kingdom, and the Chinese rebels. Dorgon once considered the rebels his potential allies against the Ming and had contacted them. This common ground disappeared with the fall of the Ming. The Manchus and the Chinese rebels became rivals. After winning the Battle of Shanhaikuan Dorgon was quick to make this new configuration an asset to attract Chinese collaborators. The Manchus did not, he announced, conquer the Ming dynasty because the rebels had overthrown it. Therefore, he continued, the Manchu army defeated the rebels to avenge and save the Chinese people. This argument was repeated by later Qing rulers to justify the Manchu takeover.[50]

During his regency (1644–1650) Dorgon adopted more Chinese political elements. Capable Chinese, regardless of their political background, were made officials. In a fifteen-month period, from 1643 to 1645, for example, there were more than a hundred recommendations and appointments. Dorgan prohibited princes from interfering with state affairs and curtailed tribal and clan forces in the government. In short, he created a condition enabling Chinese officials to conduct administrative affairs in a way similar to that of the Ming bureaucracy. In provinces and localities he took over the Ming administrative machinery *in toto* and staffed it mostly with Chinese officials. To recruit qualified bureaucrats, he held Chinese civil service examinations. In the years 1646–1649 there were three metropolitan examinations, which were usually given once every three years. More than a thousand students passed these examinations and were placed in appropriate offices.[51] Thus, the Qing political structure by-and-large imitated that of the Ming and operated in almost the same way. This helped narrow the cleavage between the Chinese and their Manchu masters.

Dorgon devoted his regency to clipping the wings of princes and their banners. This deserves our attention because it was conducive to the centralization of power, a feature of the political process during the early Qing dynasty. As stated, he warded off a political crisis by selecting Fulin to succeed Hong Taiji. But this did not exactly quench the thirst for power among the princes, including Dorgon. Suspicion and hatred smoldered and in time burst into flame. The first two targets of Dorgon were Hooge and Jirgalang. Hooge had participated in many expeditions to Inner Mongolia and China. His exploits won commendations from his imperial father, Hong Taiji, and other warriors. It was under his command that Manchu forces were able to crush Zhan Xianzhong and his followers in 1647.[52] Power and fame brought Hooge into confrontation with Dorgon. A shrewd politician, Dorgon mobilized all resources and applied all measures, even intrigue.

As early as the spring of 1644, Dorgon stripped Hooge of his princely rank on the ground that he made disrespectful remarks about the imperial regent. Soon, however, Dorgon restored his princely rank and commissioned him to suppress bandits and rebels. At the same time, Dorgon, using punishments and rewards, tried to disperse Hooge's supporters. After returning from the front in 1648, Hooge was put in prison on the charge of wrongdoing and died there.[53]

Next to fall under Dorgon's axe was Jirgalang, whose strength lay in the Bordered Blue Banner, once controlled by Amin, his brother. The steps Dorgon took to deal with Jirgalang differed from measures he applied to Hooge. At first he maneuvered to demote Jirgalang from co-regent to assistant, and achieved this goal in 1644. Three years later

Jirgalang was demoted again and fined for encroachment on the imperial privilege. He was further humiliated by being forced to share the assistant regency with Dodo. At last he was excluded from the assistant regency and charged with six criminal counts, most of which concerned factionalism. After Dorgon's death he reemerged and, with the cooperation of some other princes, destroyed the Dorgon faction. But he could not recover all the power he had lost and thus transferred complete power to the Shunzhi emperor.[54]

The years 1644–1650 were crucial to the Qing dynasty, as it was challenged by various groups of rebels, including, as stated earlier, Zhang Xian-zhong and the remnant followers of Li Zicheng in North China and the southwest. In the meantime, moreover, six descendants of the Ming ruling house had assumed imperial titles in South China. The Prince of Fu (d. 1646) was the first of the group to sit on the throne in Nanking in 1644, with the reign title of Hong-guang. Zhu Youlang (1623–1662), generally known as the Prince of Gui or the Yongli emperor, took the title in 1646. His regime was the last of the six to be crushed by the Qing.[55]

Ofttimes, Chinese collaborators staged revolts to denounce their Manchu masters. The revolts of Jin Sheng-huan (d. 1649) and Jiang Xiang (d. 1649) were typical, both having been army officers of the Ming. Jin commanded the army in Nanchang, capital of Kiangsi Province. His revolt of 1648 threatened Qing control over Central China, a hotbed of anti-Manchu forces. Jiang Xiang was commander of Datong, a fortress that was near the Great Wall and overlooked Inner Mongolia. When he rose in revolt in early 1649, the entire region joined him. The importance of his revolt can be seen from the fact that Dorgon twice offered favorable conditions for his surrender and twice took personal command of Qing forces to attack the Datong area.[56]

Mongol tribes took advantage of the troubled times to reject Manchu suzerainty. Led by Tenghis and a few others, the Sunid Mongols joined the Cecen tribe of the Khalkha Mongols to challenge the Qing in 1646. The Sunids were nomads in Inner Mongolia, while the Khalkhas were active largely in Outer Mongolia. It had been a policy of Manchu leaders to separate the Mongols in these regions. Naturally, the alliance of Sunid and Cecen Mongols was against the interest of the Qing. Each of the above events posed a threat to the newly founded dynasty.

With the guidance of Dorgon, however, the Manchu regime was able to survive.[57] There were several reasons for Dorgon's masterful action during crises. The first related to his personal character, his leadership. A noted warrior, he experienced many hard times and was firm in his decisions. As imperial regent, he demonstrated the same character in managing state affairs. This enabled him to deal with numerous challenges.

He kept his mind open to suggestions of advisors, notably Hong Cheng-chou and Fan Wen-cheng. Before the Battle of Shanhaikuan Hong had presented a memorial on how to defeat Li Zicheng and conquer China. He suggested that the Manchus should combine the forces of their cavalry and infantry to attack Li Zicheng. During the Shunzhi period Hong held high office, both civil and military. Fan Wencheng, a native of Fushun, must have been familiar with both Chinese and Jurchen cultures. Since 1618 he had associated with the Jurchens and served as an advisor trusted by Manchu rulers. He worked out plans to win over the Chinese and helped Dorgon create the machinery of state. Fan repeatedly received titles of nobility during the reigns of Hong Taiji and Shunzhi.[58]

A third reason for Dorgon's success in handling crises was his ability to select the right people, including rivals. The forces under his command always included Manchu and Chinese units, and in some cases Mongol soldiers. In 1644 his elder brother—Prince Ajige—and Wu Sangui were sent to clear the region near Peking of Li Zicheng's rebels. His younger brother Dodo led an army to destroy the regime under the Prince of Fu in 1645. Dodo was again made commander of the army to defeat rebellious Mongols the following year. Prince Hooge, an irreconcilable rival of Dorgon, commanded the Qing forces to surprise Zhang Xian-zhong and killed him. Jirgalang, once co-regent and Dorgon's competitor was commissioned for operations against anti-Manchu forces. In 1645 Hong Cheng-chou pacified the Nanking area and raised funds for Manchu armies in the south.

Weaknesses of the anti-Qing forces contributed to the success of Dorgon. Imperial claimants to the defunct Ming house competed and sometimes fought among themselves. Most were shortsighted and many corrupt. Rebel bands of Li Zicheng and Zhang Xian-zhong continued to fight the Qing dynasty after the death of their masters, but

most became occasional marauders. Despite their anti-Manchu sentiments, Jin Sheng-huan, Jiang Xiang, and others once collaborated with
the Manchus and victimized people under their jurisdiction. They
could not rally the support of the Chinese they had brutally treated.
The Sunid and Cecen Mongols were defeated because many other
nomadic peoples of the area were allies of the Qing. A skillful politician, Dorgon transformed the weaknesses of the anti-Manchu forces
into strengths of the Qing dynasty and thus helped it weather many
storms.[59]

As the discussion above indicates, there were three phases to the
founding of the Qing dynasty. Nurhaci was the central figure of the
first phase. His rise coincided with the decay of the Ming dynasty, and
he overcame mounting difficulties to unify most of the Jurchen tribes.
From the ruins of the clan he organized tribesmen into the banner system, which also included Mongol and Chinese members. Under his
leadership his followers had a common direction, although there were
geographical and even ethnic differences among them. Using military
and diplomatic means he carved a frontier kingdom out of Ming territories in Manchuria, thus laying the groundwork for the Qing dynasty.

Hong Taiji, who represented the second phase, was an empire
builder and institutional molder. He subjugated Korea and Inner
Mongolia and wiped out the last Ming forces in Manchuria. He broke
up the power of the senior princes and changed the status of the Chinese, whose cooperation was important to him. He enlisted officials
from among Chinese scholars, who then became his loyal supporters. His military and administrative structures became the foundation
of the Qing administrative machinery. With patience and persistence
he transformed a small and primitive frontier state into a centralized
kingdom.

By establishing Manchu ethnic identity, Nurhaci and Hong Taiji
left another important legacy for the Qing dynasty. The Manchu script,
which Nurhaci devised in 1599, enabled the Jurchens to emerge from
the shadow of Mongol cultural influence, a step essential to the emergence of their own cultural identity. For example, they used the script
to record early Qing documents, including the foundation myth of the
imperial clan, which was the conceptual basis of Manchu ethnic identity. It also served as an instrument for translating a large number of

Chinese books, thus expediting the Manchus' adoption of Confucian ideals and values. Under Hong Taiji, the writing system was perfected with more Manchu features. After that it became the official Qing script and a major building block of the Manchu ethnic identity. The other building blocks, archery and horsemanship, were inherent in the Eight Banner system because every banner warrior was trained to be a skilled archer and fine horseman. The term "Manchu," which Hong Taiji gave his people in 1635, meant not merely a new designation, but the rise of a new ethnic identity in Chinese history.[60]

Dorgon played a dominant role in the third phase because he shaped Qing policy and Manchu destiny. Under his regency the Manchus moved to Peking, suppressed bandits, defeated anti-Qing forces, and established Manchu rule over all China. He clipped the wings of many princes and their associates. Weakening them contributed to the political centralization of the early Qing. He appointed Chinese scholars to high office and borrowed Ming political institutions, which naturally hastened the sinicization of the Manchus. His leadership resulted in a central, bureaucratic empire that lasted more than two and a half centuries.

One may liken the founding of the Qing to the journey from Manchuria to Peking. With these three guides it took the Manchus sixty-one years (1583–1644). Nurhaci began the journey with a small group of people and carefully navigated many rugged roads. Under the guidance of Hong Taiji, a man with clearer ideas about the destination, the journey continued and attracted Mongols and Chinese adherents. Fortune favored Dorgon, a farsighted guide. With the new situation in Peking helping to smooth the way, he reached the destination and completed the dynastic transition from the Ming to the Qing.

Notes

1. For the lineage from Menggetimur to Nurhaci, see the *Daicing gurun i manju yargiyan kooli* (*Manchu Veritable Record*) for the reign of Taizu, 10–21. But a recent study argues that this lineage was falsified; see Xue Hong, "Nuer-hachi di xing-shih he jiashi," *Qingshi yanjiu tongxin*, 4 (1989): 1–5. For a succinct survey of Nurhaci, see Frederic Wakeman, Jr., *The Fall of Imperial China* (New York: The Free Press, 1975), 75–78.

2. For his early life, see Teng Shaozhen, *Nuer-hachi ping-zhuan* (Shenyang: Liao-

ning renmin chuban she, 1985), 32–34. For his stepmother, see *CSL*, Manchu version, reign of Taizu, 20. For his English biography, see *ECCP*, 1: 594–99.

3. For the beginning of the market at Fushun, see Chen Qi, "Mingdai Liaodong mashi jiqi lishi ying-xiang," *Dongbei shida xuebao (Zhexue shehui kexue ban)*, 1 (1987): 49. For Nurhaci's ability to speak and read Chinese, see Huang Dao-zhou, *Bowu dianhui* (N.p.: prefaced 1635, 6 volumes), 6. 20: 14b–15a; *Dongyi kaolüe*, 94: 11b; Yan, *Nuer-haci zhuan*,19; Jin Qicong, "Shilun Qingdai di Man-Meng-Han guanxi." In *Qingshi guoji xueshu*. 274. For Nurhaci's relationship with Li and interest in the two Chinese novels, see Peng, *Shan-zhong wenjian lu*, 1.1: 1a; Agui et al., *Huang-Qing kaiguo fanglüe* (Taipei: Wenhai chuban she, CCST, Series 14, 2 volumes), 1.1: 10b.

4. For the rise and decline of Wang Tai and the situation among the Jurchens, see *ECCP*, 2: 799–800; *Wugong lu*, 4. 11: 996a–1000b; Wang Dongfang, "Ming Liao-dong Nüzhen Han—Wang Tai," *Dongbei difang shi yanjiu*, 4 (1986): 45–51.

5. For Wang Gao, see *Wugong lu*, 4. 11: 1036a–43b. For his dates, see *Manzu da zidian*, 61. For Nikan Wailan, see *ECCP*, 1:591–92; Wakeman, *The Great Enter-prise*, I: 49–53. Thomas J. Barfield succinctly divides early Manchu history un-der Nurhaci into two periods, with the year 1619 as the dividing point. See his *The Perilous frontier*, 252.

6. For the term "tribal phase," see Barfield, *The Perilous Frontier*, 252. For these five people, see *ECCP*, 1: 222, 13, 247, 291, and 375–76. See *also CSKC*, 10: 7924–28, 7935–37, 7929–31, 7933–34, 7938–39. For their relationship with Nurhaci, see Liu, *Manzu di buluo*, 123–27. In the same book (p. 126), Liu insists that Anfi-yanggu should be written as Fiyanggu. For a study on Hohori, see Sun Wen-liang and Li Zhiting, "Qing kaiguo xunchen Heheli," *KHCH*, 2 (1984): 227–34. For a work on Fiongdon, see Guan Jialu, "Qingchao kaiguo xunchen Fei-ying-dong jianlun," *Gugong bowu yuan yuankan*, 1 (1985): 65–69.

7. Nurhaci had matrimonial relations with Hada, Yehe, and Ula. For his defeat of the allied forces and conquest of the Hūlun tribes, see Yan, *Nuer-hachi zhuan*, 43–72.

8. For Ming trade and tribute in Manchuria, see T. C. Lin, "Manchuria Trade and Tribute in the Ming Dynasty," *Nankai Social and Economic Quarterly*, 9.3 (1936): 855–92. For the importance of the patent and the struggle for it, see Cong Peiyuan, "Mingdai Nüzhen di chishu zhizheng," *Wenshi*, 26 (1986): 191–213; Jiang Xiusong, "Mingdai Nüzhen di chigong zhi," *MTYC*, 4 (1984): 17–29. For falsification of the patents, see Fang, *Quanbian lüeji*, 10:14a.

9. For the number of patents controlled by the Hada tribe at the climax of its power, see Cong, "Chishu zhizheng," 201–203. For the number of patents Nurhaci possessed, see ibid., 205–208. For the patents from Hada, see *MSL*, vol. 119, Wanli reign, 519: 6b, 42/4/dingyou. But according to *Dongyi kaolüe* (94: 29b), Nurhaci seized 367 patents from the Hada tribe. For the distribution of the 363 patents among Nurhaci and his followers, see *CMCT*, 5: 2199–2279; *MBRT*, vol. 3, Taizu, 79–81: 1173–1220.

10. For the origin and significance of the *niru*, see Liu, *Manzu di buluo*, 151–73; El-liott, *The Manchu Way*, 56–63. A recent article points out that Nurhaci orga-nized his *niru* as early as 1583. See Fu Kedong and Chen Jiahua, "Qingdai qianqi di zuoling," *KHCH*, 5 (1982): 164–73. For the *meng'an* and *mouke* system, see *CKMT*, 473–77. Peter C. Perdue seems to have overstated its Mongol element. See his *China Marches West*, 123–24. Franz Michael maintains that the banner system was adapted from the Ming guard-post institution. See his *The Origin of Manchu Rule in China: Frontier and Bureaucracy as Interacting Forces in the Chinese Empire* (Baltimore: Johns Hopkins University Press, 1942), 65–67. For the bureaucratization of the banner system, see Huang, *Autocracy at Work*, ch. 7.

11. For destruction of the shamanistic center, see Fu and Meng, *Manzu saman jiao yanjiu*, 53.

12. For example, Cangšu and Yangšu, two leaders of the Gorolo clan, began to col-laborate with Nurhaci in 1583. Their men were organized into the *niru*. See *Guo-lolo shi shizong tongpu*, 3rd page. But in his *Manzu di buluo* (pp. 151–55), Liu argues that the first *niru* was created in 1601.

   There are some fine studies on various aspects of the *niru*. For instance, see Ch'en Wen-shih, "The Creation of the Manchu Niru," *Chinese Studies in His-tory*, 14. 4 (1981): 11–46; Abe Takeo published three long articles entitled "Hakki Manshū niru no kenkyū." The first two appeared in *Tōa jimbun gakuhō*, 1. 4 (February 1942): 35–111, and 2. 2 (July 1942): 26–90; the third one in *Tōhō gakuhō*, Kyoto, 20 (1951): 1–134. For a most recent study, see Elliott, *The Manchu Way*, 56–63.

   For the creation of the Manchu Eight Banners, see Nakayama Hachiro, "Hakki engen shishaku," *Jimbun kenkyū*, 10 (1959): 74–95; Tanaka Hiromi, "Shin Taiso jidai no hakki seido," *Bōei Daigakko kiyō*, 53 (1976): 29–45; Mita-mura Taisuke, "Shoki Manshū hakki no seiritsu katei ni tsuite—Mindai Kenshū Jochoku no gunsei." In *Shimizu hakushi tsuitō kinen Mindaishi ronsō*, ed., Shi-mizu hakushi tsuitō kinen Mindaishi ronsō hensan iinkai (Tokyo: Daian, 1962), 315–55; Liu, *Manzu di buluo*, 173–82; Elliott, *The Manchu Way*, 74–78. A recent study argues that the Manchu banners began in 1588. See Li Xinda, "Guanyu Manzhou qizhi he Hanjun qizhi di shi jian shijian wenti," *Qingshi luncong*, 4 (1982): 216–23.

13. For the organization, completion, and transformation of the Manchu banners, see Chen Jiahua, "Baqi zhidu yanjiu shulüe," *SHKH*, 5 (1984): 109–16; 6 (1984): 113–20; Meng, *Qingdai shi*, 20–100; Li, "The Rise of the Early Manchu State," 24–29. For a work in English, see Elliot, *The Manchu W ay*, ch. 1.

14. For the founding of the Mongol Eight Banners, see Anami Korehiro, "Tensō ku-nen no Mōko hakki seiritsu ni tsuite," *Rikishi kyōiku*,13. 4 (1965): 50–55; Zhang and Guo, *Qing ruguan qian*, 263–84.

   For the Chinese Banners, see Liu Chia-chü, "The Creation of the Chinese Banners in the Early Qing," *Chinese Studies in History*, 14. 4 (1981): 47–75;

Xie Jingfang, "Baqi Hanjun di jianli jiqi lishi zuoyong," *SHKH*, 3 (1987): 69–74; Elliott, *The Manchu Way*, 74–78. One scholar maintains that the Chinese banners began in 1631. See Li, "Guanyu Manzhou qizhi," 220–23. For the banner system's social conseqences, see James Z. Lee and Cameron D. Campbell, *Fate and Fortune in Rural China: Social Organization and Population Behavior in Liaoning 1774–1873* (New York: Cambridge University Press, 1997), chs. 8–9.

15. For Bujantai and his matrimonial relations, see *ECCP*, 1: 17–18; *CSKC*, 10: 7895–99.

16. For the importance of matrimonial relations to the unification of the Jurchens, see Wang Dongfang,"Lianyin zhengce zai Nüzhen tongyi zhong di zuoyong," *SHKH*, 5 (1987): 58–63; see also Huang "Qingchu di Manzhou guizu: Hunyin yu kaiguo," 2: 601–19. For the number of marriages with Mongols, see Liu, "Qing Taizu Taizong shi," 90.

17. For the importance of the Manchu script, see Perdue, *China Marches West*, 125–27.

18. For his effort to monopolize pearls and sable furs, see *Chou-Liao shihua*, vol. 3, "Memorial of Zhang Tao," 2: 5; for trespassing Chinese ginseng diggers, see ibid., vol. 14, "Memorial of Chen Wangting," 16: 10b; Tong Zheng, "Cong Nuer-hachi di jingji yaoqiu kan Ming yu Hou-Jin jian di guanxi," *SHKH*, 6 (1987): 61. For the ginseng trade between the Jurchens and the Ming, see Van Jay Symons, *Qing Ginseng Management: Qing Monopolies in Microcosm* (Tempe, AZ: Center for Asian Studies, Arizona State University, 1981), 71–75.

   For the Ming effort to force Nurhaci into submission by controlling the ginseng trade, see *MSL*, vol. 120, Wanli reign, 531: 8a, 43/4/bingshen. For his loss of ginseng, see Zhou Yuanlian, *Qingchao xingqi shi* (Chang-chun: Jilin wenshi chuban she, 1986), 67 and 71. For his introducing the dry preservation method, see *Nuer-haqi shilu*, 2: 2b.

19. Yan Chong-nian, "Nuer-hachi rujing jingong kao," *Qingshi yanjiu tongxin*, 2 (1983): 2–5. There are various interpretations, one of which maintains that he led only seven missions. See Liu Dan, "Lun Nuer-hachi yu Mingchao di guanxi," *Liaoning daxue xuebao: Zhexue shehui kexue ban*, 5 (1978): 60. For details about the eight missions, see Table 2 in Chapter III.

20. For details of the problem, see Dong Qichang, comp., *Shenmiao liuzhong zoushu huiyao* (N. p.: Ming period, handwritten, microfilm, Library of Congress), ch. 11, Memorials of Song Yihan and Zhao Jie, 17a–23a and 23b–31a.

21. For China's concession of 1606, see *Mingshi*, 20. 238: 6191. For Nurhaci's response to the Ming protest, see *Nuer-haqi shilu*, 2: 7b.

22. For these grievances, see Guang and Li, *Qing Taizu*, 1: 79–81; *MBRT*, vol. 1, Taizu, 6: 86–88; *ECCP*, 1: 597.

23. For Tong Yangxing, see *STTP*, 20: 3b; Hou Shou-chang, "Qianlun Tong Yang-xing," *Lishi dang'an*, 2 (1986): 105–10. For Li Jixue, who was born in Qinghe, see

TCCC, 184: 2a; *CSKC*, 10: 8168; *MWLT*, 2: 923. Both men and their descendants were trusted officials of the Qing. Another example was Xiao Yongzao. Born to a merchant family which did trade in the Liaodong region, he served as a grand secretary. See *TCCC*, 198: 12a–19b; *ECCP*, 1: 305. For the economic crises, see Li, "The Rise of the Early Manchu State," 31–35, 101–109, 114–17, 155–75.

24. For his attack on Fushun and other places in 1618, see Guang and Li, *Qing Taizu*, 1: 82–85; Yan, *Nuer-hachi zhuan*, 176–81; *MBRT*, vol. 1, Taizu, 6: 90–93.

25. There are many works on the numerical strength of the contesting armies. Zhang Deyu, for example, mentioned that each side had about 100,000 men. See his "Saerhu zhiyu Hou Jin canzhan bingli zaitan," *MANT*, 3 (1989): 12–14. Ray Huang believed that the Ming, with allied forces, totaled about 100,000 soldiers, while Nurhaci had about 50,000–60,000 men. See his "The Liao- tung Campaign of 1619," *Oriens Extremus*, 28. 1 (1981): 30 and 33. Another study is Ren Chang-zheng, "Qing Taizu, Qing Taizong shidai Ming-Qing hezhan kao (1)," *Dalu zazhi*, 14. 4 (1957): 118–20. A Qing official source exaggerated that the strength of the Ming army reached 200,000 men. See *Taidzu hūwangdi Ming gurun i cooha be Sarhū alin de ambarame efulehe baita be tacibume araha bithe* (A record of the defeat of the Ming army by Emperor Taizu at the Battle of Sarhū), 1b–2a.

26. For Yuan's biography, see *ECCP*, I: 954–55; *Mingshi*, 22. 259: 6707–19. For Yuan's rise and fall, see Wakeman, *The Great Enterprise*, I: 78–86 and 126–31.

27. For his ability, princeship, and role in various battles, see Sun and Li, *Qing Taizong quan-zhuan*, ch. 2. The three other senior princes were Daišan, Amin, and Manggūltai. There are different views about the specific banner under his control. According to *ECCP* (1: 1), he probably controlled the Plain and Bordered Yellow Banners. Two other scholars maintain that he was the master of the Plain White Banner. See Li Hongbin and Guo Cheng-kang, "Qing ruguan qian baqi zhuqi beile di yanbian," *KHCH*, 5 (1982): 154–63.

28. Ch'en Wen-shih, *Ming-Qing zhengzhi shehui shilun* (Taipei: Taiwan xuesheng shuju, 1991, 2 volumes), I: 340–61; Yan, *Nuer-hachi zhuan*, ch. 10. For natural disasters, see Li, "The Rise of the Early Manchu State," 78, 101–17. For frontier campaign for grain, see *MBRT*, vol. 1, Taizu, 15: 236–37. In 1627 and 1637 the Manchu state was plagued by famine. As a result, food prices were intolerably high. See Li, "The Rise of the Early Manchu State," 156, 160.

29. For the massacre of the Chinese, including noncombatants, see Teng, *Nuer-hachi*, 303–304; for the slaughtering of the Chinese soldiers in the battlefield, see Guang and Li, *Qing Taizu*, 1: 116: 2: 108, 111. For slaves among the Manchus, see Yi, *Chaam Sŏnsaeng munjip*, 6: 3a. For conditions of the slaves, see Li, "The Rise of the Early Manchu State," 55–56.

30. For the orders to improve the conditions of the Chinese, see *MBRT*, vol. 2, Taizu, 44: 642–43; 46: 673, 677; and 51: 753. For his demands on the Chinese, see Yan, *Nuer-hachi zhuan*, 250–54.

31. For their act of poisoning, see *MBRT*, vol. 1, Taizu, 22: 334–36; for their rebellion, attacking, and flight, see ibid., vol. 3, Taizu, 66: 991–92; *CMCT*, 4: 1935–38.

32. The people he tried to pacify were mainly the Chinese. See *CSL*, reign of Taizong, 1: 9b–11a, Tianming 11/9/jiaxu, bingzi, and dingchou; Sun and Li, *Qing Taizong*, 154–64; Perdue, *China Marches West*, 119. For the Chinese banners, see the last paragraph in note 14 above. For the Chinese scholars emancipated and recruited by Hong Taiji and their importance to him, see Yuan Lükun et al., *Qingdai qianshi* (Shenyang: Shenyang chuban she, 2004, 2 volumes), 2: 561–74.

33. *CSL*, reign of Taizong, 1: 10a, Tianming 11/9/bingzi; Wei Jianxun, "Huang Taiji shiqi Hou Jin zheng-quan di xingzhi," *SHKH*, 5 (1980): 99.

34. For his encouragement of commerce and trade, see Chen Kejin and Teng Shaozhen, "Lüelun Huang-Taiji di lishi zuoyong," *SHKH*, 2 (1982):115–16. For Manchu trade with Korea, see Zhang Cunwu, *Qing-Han zongfan mouyi (1637–1894)* (Taipei: Institute of Modern History, Academia Sinica, 1978), 4 and 7–8.

35. For his pacifying the middle and upper Amur regions, see Anami, "Shin no Taisō no Koku- ryūkō seitō no tsuite," 1–29. For his subjugation of the Chahar Mongols, see Yuan, "Lun Huang Taiji tongyi," 38–61.

36. Sun and Li, *Qing Taizong*, 189–92; Li Hongbin, "Shilun 'Dingmao zhi yu,'" *KHCH*, 4 (1987): 192–98. For a brief biography of Mao, see *ECCP*, 1: 567–68. For his guerrilla warfare, see Mao Chengdou, comp., *Dong-jiang shujie tangbao jiechao* (Combined with two other titles) (N. p.: Zhejiang guji chuban she, 1986), 1–136. This book is a primary source, but its information is rather exaggerated. For the need for grain and other supplies, see *CSL*, reign of Taizong, 3: 41a–42a, Tiancong 1/12/renyin.

37. For the relations between the Manchus and Korea in 1631–1644, see Zhang, "Qing-Han guanxi: 1631–1636," 75–98, and his "Qing-Han guanxi (1636–1644)," *Gugong wenxian*, 4. 2 (1973): 13–35; for the two Korea campaigns, see Liu Chiachü, *Qingchao chuqi di Zhong-Han guanxi* (Taipei: Wen-shi-zhe chuban she, 1986), 1–48, 99–147.

38. For the first battle at Jinzhou, see *MBRT*, vol. 4, Taizong, 5: 59–73; Jiang Ning, "Lun Ningjin dajie," *Qingshi yanjiu tongxin*, 1 (1989): 7–14. For Manchu raids on China, see Sun and Li, *Qing Taizong*, 227–32.

39. For a detailed study of this long warfare, see Liu Jianxin, "Lun Ming-Qing zhiji di Songjin zhizhan," *Qingshi yanjiu ji*, 4 (1986): 1–47. Also see Chen-main Wang, *The Life and Career of Hung Ch'eng-ch'ou (1593–1665): Public Service in a Time of Dynastic Change* (Ann Arbor, MI: Association for Asian Studies, Monograph and Occasional Paper Series, Number 59, 1999), ch. 4. The Ming Board of War left many communications on the Battle of Jinzhou. See *Zhongguo Ming-chao dang'an zonghui*, vol. 35, documents #2600, 2614, 2650ff. For a Qing official record of the battle, see *Taidzung hūwangdi Ming gurun i cooha be*

Sung šan de ambarame efuleme afaha baita be ejeme araha bithe (An account of the defeat of the Ming army by Emperor Taizong at the Battle of Songsan), 1a–15a.

40. For brief biographies of Amin, Daišan, and Manggūltai, see *ECCP*, 1: 8–9, 214, and 562–63. For the tetrarchate, see *CSL*, reign of Taizong, 2: 1b–2a, Tiancong 1/1/jisi. The above interpretation about the distribution of the banners among the Four Senior Princes is based on Meng, *Qingdai shi*, 40–55, but some other publications disagree. For example, Li and Guo, "Qing ruguan qian baqi," 154–63, and Meng Xiangang, "Baqi qizhu kaoshi," *MANT*, 2 (1986): 35–37. The last two studies also argued that Daišan controlled the Plain and Bordered Red Banners. They drew on the Korean source (*CWS*, vol. 33, Reign of Kwang-hae'gun, 169: 403, 13/9/musin).

41. For a study of his measures for political centralization, see Ch'en, *Ming-Qing zhengzhi*, II: 423–525; for the conflict between Hong Taiji and his co-rulers, see Li Zongtong, "Qingdai zhong- yang zheng-quan xingtai di yanbian," *Bulletin of the Institute of History and Philology, Academia Sinica*, 7. 1 (1967): 84–125. For the termination of the four-man rule, see *CSL*, reign of Taizong, 10: 36b–37b, Tiancong 5/12/bingshen; 11: 1b–2b, 6/1/jihai; Yuan, *Qingdai qianshi*, 2: 521–35.

42. The Five Councilors and Ten Jargūci were appointed in 1615. See *CSL*, reign of Taizu, 4: 21, yimao (1615)/11/guiyou. For their function, see Piero Corradini, "Civil Administration at the Beginning of the Manchu Dynasty," *Oriens Extremus*, 9.2 (1962): 133–38. For the influence of Mongol institutions on Nurhaci and Hong Taiji's switch from it, see Liu, *Manzu di buluo*, 144–50 and 223–24; 313–26, respectively. For the Mongol and Chinese Banners, see note 14 above. For the new appointments in each banner, see *CSL*, reign of Taizong, 1: 11a–12a, Tianming 11/9/dingchou.

43. For the rise of the Literary Office, see *CSL*, reign of Taizong, 5: 11b–12a, Tiancong 3/4/bingxu. But a recent study argues that the office was actually institutionalized around 1632, instead of 1629. See Yuan, *Qingdai qianshi*, 2: 566–69. For the Six Boards, see CSL, reign of Taozong, 9: 11b–12b, Tiancong 5/7/gengchen. The Censorate and the Office of Mongol Affairs were very likely founded in 1636. See respectively CSL reign of Taizong, 29: 6a–7a, Chongde 1/5/dingsi, and 30: 9a, 1/6/bingxu. The Office of Mongol Affairs was renamed the Court of Dependent Peoples in 1638. See CSL, reign of Taizong, 42: 2a, Chongde 3/6/gengshen. For their being reorganized, see CSL. Reign of Taizong, 42: 21a–24a, Chongde 3/7/bingxu. See also Chang and Kuo, *Qing ruguan qian*, 50–71, 79–99. Ning Chia's work focuses on the Inner Asian rituals of the *Lifan yuan*. See her "The Lifanyuan and the Inner Asian Rituals in the Early Qing (1644–1795)," *Late Imperial China*, 14. 1 (1993): 60–92.

   For a different view about the creation of the Six Boards, see Guang Lu and Li Xuezhi, "Qing Taizu chao 'Lao Manwen yuandang' yu 'Manwen laodang' zhi bijiao yanjiu," *Zhongguo Dongya xueshu yanjiu jihua weiyuan hui nianbao*, 4 (1965): 148–65. For the Manchu ethnic features of many Qing offices, see Wang Zhonghan, *Qingshi xukao* (Taipei: Huashi chuban she, 1993), 321–48.

44. For English biographies of Dorgon, Ajige, and Dodo, see *ECCP*, 1: 215–19; 4–5; 215. For a detailed study of Dorgon, see Erich Hauer, "Prinz Dorgon [Prince Dorgon]," *Ostasiatische zeitschrift*, 13 (1926): 9–56. For Dorgon's military performance, see *Qingshi liezhuan* (Peking: Zhonghua Book Company, 1987, 20 volumes), 1. 2: 22–26. For Dorgon's new title, see *CSL*, reign of Taizong, 4: 8b, Tiancong 2/3/wuchen. For his military exploits, see Zhou Yuanlian and Zhao Shiyu, *Huangfu shezheng wang Doergun quan-zhuan* (Chang-chun: Jilin wenshi chuban she, 1986), 80–90. For the Manchu occupation of Peking under Dorgon, see Wakeman, *The Fall of Imperial China*, 79–82.

45. For the succession struggle, see *CSL*, Shunzhi reign, 22: 11a–13b, 2/12/guimao; 37: 8b–14b, 5/3/jihai; 38: 3a–4a, 5/4/guiyou. For an English biography of Fulin, see *ECCP*, 1: 255–59. For biographies of Hooge and Jirgalang, see *ECCP*, 1: 280–81 and 397–98; *Qingshi liezhuan*, 1. 2: 52–56; 59–72.

46. For English biographies of Li Zicheng and the Chong-zhen emperor, see *ECCP*, 1: 491–93, 191–92. For the rise of Li Zicheng, see Li Wenzhi, *Wan-Ming minbian* (Hong Kong: Yuandong tushu gongsi, 1966), ch. 5; James Bunyan Parsons, *The Peasant Rebellion of the Late Ming Dynasty* (Tucson: University of Arizona Press, 1970), 90–142. For conditions and events toward the end of the Ming, see Albert Chan, *The Glory and Fall of the Ming Dynasty* (Norman, OK: University of Oklahoma Press, 1982), ch. 12.

47. For Wu's biography, see *ECCP*, 2: 877–80; *Qingshi liezhuan*, 20. 80: 6632–46. In recent years many scholars have debated about his collaboration with the Manchus. Most agree that Wu surrendered to the Qing. For instance, Li Shilong, "Wu Sangui xiang Qing shi lishi shishi," *Beifang luncong*, 2 (1987): 74–78, 83. One scholar insists that Wu was fundamentally against the Qing dynasty. See Zuo Shue, "Zailun Wu Sangui 'xiang Qing' wenti," *Beifang luncong*, 3 (1987): 69–75. For an objective analysis of Wu, see Angela N. S. Hsi, "Wu San-kuei in 1644: An Reappraisal," *Journal of Asian Studies*, 34. 2 (1975): 443–53. For the Korean eyewitness, see Yi Jun, *Songgye Simyang illok* (N. p., handwritten, unpaged) [p. 38].

48. For the battle, see Li Hongbin, "Doergun yu Shanhai-guan dazhan," *Qingshi yanjiu ji*, 5 (1986): 66–86.

49. For the downfall of Li Zicheng, see Li, *Wan-Ming minbian*, 152–59; Parsons, *The Peasant Rebellion of the Late Ming Dynasty*, 161–67; for the rise and fall of Zhang Xian-zhong, see Li, *Wan-Ming minbian*, ch. 4 and pp. 159–61; Parsons, *The Peasant Rebellion of the Late Ming Dynasty*, 142–85.

50. Dorgon proposed to some rebel leaders that they cooperate with the Manchus to conquer China. For his letter, see *Ming-Qing Dang'an*, vol. 1, Doc. 1: B1. For his use of this asset, see *CSL*, Shunzhi reign, 9: 3b–4b, 1/10/yimao; Jiang Liangqi,

Donghua lu (Peking: Zhonghua Book Company, 1980), Shunzhi reign, 4: 65–66, 1/7/? Later Qing rulers—the Yongzheng emperor, for instance—repeated the same argument. See, Huang, *Autocracy at Work*, 219.

51. For the Qing government under Dorgon's regency, see Adam Lui, *Two Rulers in One Reign: Dorgon and Shun-chih 1644–1650* (Canberra: Faculty of Asian Studies, Australian National University, 1989), ch. 2. For the three examinations, see *CSL*, Shunzhi reign, 25: 6, 3/3/jiazi; 31: 6b, 4/3/wuwu; 43: 15b, 6/4/jiachen. Altogether, they passed 1,097 students, but according to *Ming-Qing Jinshi timing beilu suoyin*, comp. Zhu Bao jiong and Xie Peilin (Shanghai: Shanghai guji chuban she, 1980, 3 volumes), 3: 2626–31, 2632–35, there were only 1066 students who passed the examination.. For cases of recommendations and appointments, see *Qingdai dang'an shiliao congbian*, 13 (1990): 1–110.

52. Hooge was commissioned to suppress Zhang Xian-zhong in 1646. See *CSL*, Shunzhi reign, 23: 9a, 3/1/jisi.

53. For his use of disrespectful remarks and its consequence, see *CSL*, Shunzhi reign, 4: 1b–4b, 1/4/wuwu. He was given back the same rank toward the end of 1644. See ibid.,10: 3b, 1/10/dingmao. For the punishments of his supporters, see ibid., 20: 12b–16b, 2/8/dingwei; 37: 11a–13b, 5/3/jihai. For his imprisonment, see ibid., 37: 14b–15b, 5/3/xinchou.

54. For Jirgalang's demotion and lower status, see *CSL*, Shunzhi reign, 3: 4b, 1/1/jihai; 10: 3b, 1/10/dingmao. For his demotion and fine, see *CSL*, Shunzhi reign, 30: 12, 4/1/gengwu. Dodo was made Assistant Regent Prince on August 2, 1647, and four days later an imperial decree indicated that Jirgalang was no longer an assistant regent. See *CSL*, Shunzhi reign, 33: 1b–2a, 4/7/xinchou; 3a, 4/7/yisi. For the six counts and his punishment, see *CSL*, Shunzhi reign, 37: 2a–10b, 13a, 5/3/jihai. For punishments of his supporters, see *CSL*, Shunzhi reign, 37: 10b–11a, 13b, 5/3/jihai. For Jirgalang's reemergence and its aftermath, see Lui, *Two Rulers in One Reign*, chs. 3–4

55. For the bands of Li Zicheng and Zhang Xian-zhong after 1644, see Li Guangtao, *Mingji liukou shimo* (Taipei: Institute of History and Philology, Academia Sinica, 1965), 101–26. For the Southern Ming regimes, see Lynn A. Struve, *The Southern Ming, 1644–1662* (New Haven and London: Yale University Press, 1984), chs. 1, 3, and 5–7; Xie Guozhen, *Nan-Ming shilüe* (Shanghai: Shanghai renmin chuban she, 1988 printing), chs. 3, 6–9.

56. For biographies of Jin and Jiang, see *ECCP*, 1: 166–67 and 138. For the revolts of Jin and Jiang, see Zhou and Zhao, *Huangfu shezheng wang*, 240–49. For his personal command of the campaigns, see *Shunzhi shilu* (N. p.: handwritten, housed in the Fu Sinian Library, Academia Sinica, n.d., 119 leaves), 27b, Shunzhi 5/12/bingwu; 30a, 32b–33a, 6/2/guimao and xinwei.

57. For the Sunid Mongols and their revolt, see *CSKC*, 15: 11896, 11926, 11940; Zhou and Zhao, *Huangfu shezheng wang Duoergun quan zhuan*, 336–39.

58. For Hong's advice, see Wang, *The Life and Career of Hung Ch'eng-ch'ou*, 132. For his high office, see ibid., chs. 6–7. For Fan's biography, see *ECCP*, 1: 231–32; *CSKC*, 10: 8086–90. For Fan's importance to the Qing, see Walter Fuchs, "Fan Wen-ch'eng, 1597–1666, und sein Diplom," *Shigaku kenkyū*, 10.3 (1939): 14–31; Jin Chengji, "Fan Wencheng jianlun," *Lishi yanjiu*, 5 (1982): 155–66. Sources usually point out that Fan willingly joined Nurhaci when the latter conquered Fushun in 1618. But a recent study forcefully argues that Fan was taken as a captive. See Zhang Yuxing, "Fan Wencheng gui Qing kaobian," *Qingshi luncong*, 6 (1985): 135–46.

59. For an analytical article on the Dorgon regency, see Li Ge, "Doergun yu Qing-chao tongzhi di jianli," *Qingshi luncong*, 3 (1982): 117–29. For a good book, see Lui, *Two Rulers in One Reign*, chs. 1–2.

60. For creation and defects of the old-script Manchu, see Guan Kexiao and Wang Peihuan, "Man yuwen di xing-shuai ji lishi yiyi." In *Qingzhu Wang Zhonghan xian-sheng bashi shouchen xueshu lunwen ji*, 208–11; *ECCP*, 1: 225–26. Under Hong Taiji's direction, Dahai, a scholar of possible transfrontier Chinese family, added dots and circles to the old-script Manchu. For more information about the new-script Manchu, see the first section and note 3 in Chapter VII in this volume. For the foundation myth of the Qing imperial house, see the first section and note 15 in Chapter I above. For the importance of the Manchu writing system, see Perdue, *China Marches West*, 125–27.

Chapter III

Economic Forces

SINICIZATION OF THE MANCHUS BEGAN long before their conquest of China in 1644. From early Ming times the Jurchens, their most recent ancestors, had set the process in motion. Economic forces provided channels of contact and therefore played a major role in sinicization. This chapter focuses on agriculture, frontier markets, and tributary relations, each of which helped the Jurchens improve their daily life. Combined, they brought about significant political and social changes among the Jurchens. Sinicization became an undercurrent that engulfed the Jurchens as well as the Manchus. After 1644 this undercurrent rose to the surface and became a tide that nothing could reverse. Of course, economic forces were consequences of the region's geography.

1. The Influence of Geography

Manchuria has almost everything—rivers, seas, hills, plains, steppes, swamps, forests, even snow-capped mountains. Ecological differences emanate from geography, which in turn creates economic specialization.

With the exception of a narrow passage to the sea in the south, the region is surrounded by mountains. Many are densely forested. The northern border shares the climatic features of Siberia and once stretched to the frozen land north of the Amur River. Western and northwestern Manchuria linked up with the steppes and deserts of Mongolia and formed "the traditional route," as R. R. C. de Crespigny points out, for successive nomadic invaders. Its eastern border is wooded and mountainous.[1] Because of geography, Manchuria played a historic role in Asia. It marked the eastern end of the nomadic expansion from Central Asia. It was China's military outpost, political frontier, and cultural beachhead.

Manchuria once contained a variety of river systems extending far beyond the Amur and the Ussuri, its northern and eastern boundaries today. Extending all the way from Siberia to the Sea of Okhotsk, the Amur was the region's largest river system.[2] Its northern valley was the home of reindeer herders, dogsled tribesmen, and horse breeders. Upper and middle regions south of the river connected with the Sungari-Nonni river system, their lower southern valley being mainly populated by the Heje and Gilyak tribes, referred to as Wild Jurchens during the Ming dynasty. The Ussuri, a tributary of the Amur, formed another river system, along which lived other Wild Jurchens such as the Weji, Warka, and Kurka tribes. A fertile lowland suitable for farming surrounded Lake Khanka (Xingkai-hu in Chinese), a reservoir of the Ussuri.

But the Sungari-Nonni and Liao river systems are the most important, for they shaped the Manchurian (Song-Liao) Plain, the agricultural center of the region. Its northern part, drained by the Sungari and Nonni, is noted for black soil, grassland, and a short growing season. Inhabitants included the Qorčin Mongols, O-wen-kes, Oronchons, Sibes, Dahurs, and later, the four Hūlun Jurchen tribes.[3] The plain's southern portion lies in the valley of the Liao, historically the domain of Chinese culture and China's administrative center in Manchuria. Later it was home of the Jianzhou Jurchens, from whose descendants the Qing imperial house emerged.

Manchuria's geography conditioned the economic activities of its inhabitants. The Manchuria Plain provided fertile land for the inhabitants and facilitated the rise of political power in the area. The Bohai kingdom, a Tungusic and highly sinicized state in southern and eastern Manchuria, largely based on the Plain's agriculture, influenced later states in the area. The Jurchens founded the Jin on the same economic base. To support officials and garrison troops in Manchuria, the Ming government established military farms in the southern part of the plain.[4] Agriculture played a role in the lives of the Jianzhou and Hūlun Jurchens and assisted their sinicization.

Rivers in Manchuria abounded in fish—sturgeon, trout, salmon, and many more. In his book, Alexander Hosie names more than twenty species. Some rivers produced pearls, but fishing was the chief occupation of the Jurchens along the rivers. The Heje people in the lower Sungari and Ussuri Rivers were referred to as the "Fish-skin Tartars" (*Yupi dazi*).[5] Place names demonstrate the importance of fishing. The Suzi River near Xinbin district was known to the Manchus as *Suksuhu*, also the name of a Jurchen tribe, both meaning "osprey." The Manchus referred to the Mudan River as the Hurha, which suggests a large fishing net.[6]

In mountainous and wooded areas the Jurchens engaged in hunting and gathering, and hunters were held in high esteem. In many cases clan heads and tribal chieftains were hunters, as well as fighters, attracting loyal followers. Nurhaci was such a hunter and fighter who won the support of young warriors even before his rise to power. They hunted deer, leopards, tigers, bears, lynxes, badgers, and sables among other game. In addition to meat, the animals provided skins. Sable skins were in demand in both Chinese and Korean markets.[7]

Because of the association with hunting, some people, tribes, places, and titles took the names of animals or their attributes. The name Nurhaci suggested the wild boar's skin in the Manchu language. Dorgon, the prince regent discussed earlier, was the Manchu word for the badger. Sahalca, the name of a tribe in the upper Amur, connotated a black sable skin in Manchu. Loosa (d. 1641) was a brilliant fighter and hero (*baturu* in Manchu) born to the Gūwalgiya clan. Hong Taiji conferred upon him the title *songkoro baturu*, meaning a hero like the gerfalcon, a large hunting eagle.[8]

In wooded mountain areas the Jurchens collected fungi, nuts, pine kernels (*songzi*), and honey from wild bees. The most valuable product was ginseng, a member of the *araliaceous* family, which grew wild in the forests. The Long White Mountains have long been the ginseng-producing area. Natural ginseng has always been treasured because it is difficult to find and also because its root offers pharmaceutical benefits.[9] The Jurchens made it available in frontier markets, from which it was transported to dealers and pharmacies throughout China. Because of the profits ginseng generated, both China's frontier administrators and Jurchen chieftains tried to control the trade. The success of Nurhaci was in no small measure a result of the Jurchen monopoly of the ginseng trade.

The economy of Manchuria necessitated exchanges between communities. Before the fifteenth century many Jurchen tribesmen were hunters, fishermen, gatherers, and producers of furs, pearls, and ginseng. Their products found their way to the frontier markets or to China proper through traders or tribute missions. From frontier markets or tributary missions Jurchen traders purchased much of what they needed, such as salt and textiles. Among other goods they sought out were iron farming tools and draft oxen, both important to agriculture. Along with these the Jurchens brought back Chinese culture as well.[10]

2. The Agricultural Effect

Agriculture was a notable agent in bringing the Jurchens into contact with Chinese culture. The Jurchen people in the Manchurian Plain had engaged in agriculture, as well as hunting, fishing, and gathering as early as the twelfth century. A recent study points out that in some areas the Jurchens depended mainly on farming. They raised pigs, used iron farming tools, and grew grain, including wheat and millet, and this way of life persisted through most of the Yuan dynasty. Jurchen tribesmen near China and Korea made more progress in agriculture.[11] The transition from the Yuan to the Ming delivered a blow to agriculture. Marauding Mongols launched incursions into the Manchurian Plain from north and west. In the eastern end the more advanced Jurchens were pressed by less developed Wuzhe tribesmen.

Because of the insecurity created by this situation, many Jurchen tribes migrated in search of protected land. Migrations of the Odoli, Hurha, and Taowen tribes, beginning in the mid-fourteenth century, were typical. Their journeys ended when they reached the southern Manchurian Plain, the best farmland of the area. There, agriculture began to play a remarkable role in their lives. In 1423, Menggetimur, later chief officer of the Left Jianzhou Guard, revealed that as early as the 1390s he and his tribesmen, with the help of Koreans, had started farming in the Tumen River valley.[12]

Korean sources show many instances of the development of Jurchen agriculture. In 1437 the Korean government sent an agent to gather intelligence on the Jianzhou tribe. He reported that he saw Jurchen farmers and draft oxen everywhere on both sides of the lower Yalu. Considering punitive campaigns against the Jurchen in 1433 and 1461, some Korean officials twice proposed bringing them to terms by disrupting their agriculture.[13] In all likelihood, by the fifteenth century the Jurchens of the southern Manchuria Plain were predominantly farmers.

With the rise of a farming economy the Jurchens achieved new cultural status. They preferred a sedentary life and engaged in spinning and weaving as well as farming. Grain seems to have become their staple. In describing the Jurchens of the southern Manchurian Plain, private Ming sources indicate that their way of life resembled that of the Chinese, differing utterly from the nomadic tradition. Such was evident to a Chinese high official after an inspection of the frontier. Because of the Jurchens' cultural status, the Yi dynasty allowed them to live among the Koreans inside the northern frontier. They were permitted to marry Koreans and treated as new subjects.[14]

In spite of the economic progress, the Jurchens needed to further improve their agricultural skills. They achieved this largely through Chinese captives. From the fifteenth to the sixteenth centuries, they took many captives from Liaodong and provided asylum for fugitives or deserters because these Chinese were mostly experienced farmers. Korean dynastic records include countless entries about Chinese captives and their escape to Korea. One shows that during the decade from1423 to 1433 the Yi government repatriated more than 1,000 people to China. Ming official documents provide similar data. Dated 1567, one entry indicates that as many as 1,050 Chinese returned to the Liaodong area from captivity. It is safe to say that far more Chinese remained and farmed for their Jurchen masters. These captives became transmitters of the Chinese way of farming. For example, Jurchen farmers would plant seedlings in big bundles, which were widely separated. The shortcomings of this technique were obvious. Crowded conditions hindered growth of young plants, and even a few stunted seedlings would affect the entire bundle. Besides, it took more space when bundles were widely dispersed. Finally, since their farming method netted less grain, the Jurchen farmers adopted—through captives, fugitives, and others—the Chinese way, planting seedlings individually, with very narrow spaces in between.[15]

In addition to farming skills, the Jurchens sought to import agricultural tools from frontier markets. The *Collected Liaodong Archival Compilation of the Ming Period* (Mindai Liaodong dang'an huibian) offers details about such imports. An entry from 1583 lists a purchase by Jurchens of 335 spades in a single day; another entry from early 1584 shows 1,134. There were many purchases of plow oxen. One case involved a trading company of 709 Hūlun Jurchens, who bought 103 oxen and calves. Another describes a group of 950 Yehe traders who purchased, among other things, 95 oxen. In some cases the Jurchens obtained such things as gifts from the Ming government. Giocangga, Nurhaci's grandfather, visited the frontier market three times. Twice he and his companions received oxen from Ming officials.[16] To make effective use of these tools and animals, the Jurchens had to adopt Chinese skills and technology. .

The rise of Nurhaci marked a new stage in the agricultural development of the Jurchens. For his military and political needs, he had to establish an agricultural foundation. The first task was to unify and discipline the Jurchens who were plagued by intratribal feuds, attacks from other tribesmen, and punitive campaigns from China and Korea.[17] During the years 1583–1626 he unified most of the tribes, prohibited clansmen from fighting, and made them warriors to clear the way for his state-building. Because the numbers of his subjects inreased, he needed more food to feed them.

Nurhaci tried to increase the area of cultivated land. The Jurchens farmed not only the plains but the hills, as reported in 1596 by Sin Ch'ung-il, a Korean official, after a visit with Nurhaci.[18] The more area Nurhaci conquered, the more farmland was available to him. It was only natural that he would need more manpower for farming. He relocated many tribes, including the far-flung Jurchens, to the eastern Liao valley. He even sent people to farm the controversial borders. The significance of such steps did not escape the eyes of Ming officials, who petitioned the throne for counteraction.[19]

Chinese farmers in the Liaodong region contributed in no small measure to Nurhaci's agricultural success. They reclaimed wastelands, cleared marshes, and opened wooded areas. As a result they greatly expanded the cultivated area to roughly 173,400 acres (12,386 *qing*) in 1388. This figure was doubled by the early fifteenth century. All the land was later taken over by Nurhaci for his military farms and hamlets. His first goal was to organize military farms for the Eight Banners. Each farm consisted of ten males, mainly Chinese farmers, and four plow oxen. From among the Banner officials Nurhaci selected people to supervise and record the production and consumption of grain. By 1625 he had founded many hamlets, each composed of about 600 *mou* of farmland (6.6 *mou* equal an acre), run by thirteen males, also chiefly Chinese farmers, with seven oxen. Naturally, Chinese farmers applied Chinese farming methods to the farms or hamlets and shared them with their Jurchen counterparts. In other words, they spread the Chinese way of life among the Jurchens. Although Nurhaci enforced his farm policy using harsh measures and often sparked Chinese resistance and rebellion, he achieved his goal.[20]

Nurhaci's success in improving agriculture changed the mode of Jurchen production. With Chinese slaves as the chief source of labor, more able-bodied Jurchen men were released from farming for fighting. A Korean eyewitness reported in 1624 that Chinese did the farming while the Jurchens devoted themselves to military matters. One may believe that many noncombatant Jurchens also engaged in farming. Grain was no longer the only crop, as new ones were introduced. In 1616 Nurhaci ordered his people to grow cotton and engage in sericulture.[21] Cotton and sericulture were usually the undertakings of farmers in China's advanced agricultural regions. Their introduction into the Jurchen area marked significant progress of their agriculture.

The importance of agricultural life to the sinicization of the Jurchens deserves further investigation. Hunters and fishermen lived with many uncertainties. Their lives and values differed from those of farmers, attached to the soil as they were. Regardless of ethnic origins, farmers shared similar norms, mores, and values. The Jurchens were thus allowed to live among the Korean farmers by the Yi dynasty. The closer the Jurchen settlements to the Liaodong frontier, the more developed their agriculture. As stated, Chinese slaves provided labor and brought the Chinese way of farming. The Jurchens purchased farm tools and plow animals from frontier markets. The more the progress in Jurchen agriculture, the more the transmission of Chinese culture. There is no better testimony to this fact than the statement by Nurhaci in 1619 about differences between Mongols and Jurchens. He pointed out that the Mongols raised stock, ate meat, and wore hides, whereas the Jurchens relied on farming and consumed grain.[22] This eloquently testifies to his preference for farming.

From the experience of the Jurchens, one may partially explain the difficulties the Mongols experienced in adapting to Chinese culture. Mongolia is a plateau enclosed by mountains, with scant rainfall and bitterly cold winters. Situated in its center is the Gobi, one of the world's largest deserts, which forms a wide depression. Vegetation in Mongolia is very limited. The grassy steppes provide the grazing land for animals, not farms for people. Mongolia is mainly a country of herdsmen and nomads, whose lives and values were at variance with those of farmers. Nor did Mongols have many products for exchange with the Chinese. The Great Wall exacerbated the differences between Mongols and Chinese and hindered their contacts.[23] Thus cultural relations were greatly curtailed, which of course affected sinicization.

3. Frontier Markets

Frontier markets consisted of two kinds of trade, official and private. They were of great economic and cultural importance to both the Jurchens and the Chinese because trade satisfied their needs. For instance, the Chinese valued such Jurchen products as horses, furs, pearls, and ginseng. The farming tools the Jurchens bought were indispensable for the improvement of their agriculture. More importantly, frontier trade involved a great number of people and provided opportunities for contact. Jurchen and Chinese traders met at both official and private frontier markets, exchanging commodities as well as ideas and values that made their products possible. They interacted not only as individuals but as members of their respective ethnic groups. It was through this interaction that the Jurchens were able to adopt, among other things, Chinese words. When combined with the Jurchen words the Chinese borrowed, these loanwords developed into a lingua franca, used first along the Liaodong frontier and then in Peking.[24]

Ming frontier markets in Manchuria evolved over a long period. The first two markets were founded in Guang-ning (present-day Beizhen) and Kaiyuan in 1406 at the request of Mongols in the Fuyu Guard, one of the Three Uriyangqad units. Both places were Chinese

Map 4. Sites of Ming Frontier Markets.

1. Kaiyuan	2. Guang-ning	3. Fushun	4. Qinghe
5. Aiyang	6. Kuandian	7. Yizhou	8. Shenyang
9. Liaoyang	10. Jinzhou	11. Ningyüan	12. Peking

military and administrative centers. But Kaiyuan was more important, for it was the hub of the Ming transportation network in Manchuria. Composed of four main lines and two extensions, the network reached almost all regions, including northern Korea and the Lower Amur valley. It facilitated the travel of Jurchen traders and tributary missions. In 1407, the Ming admitted Hūlun Jurchen tribes to the Kaiyuan market. The Ming added a few more places to the list of frontier markets and granted the Jianzhou Jurchens the same trading privileges. Of these Ming markets, Yizhou, created in 1595 and located southwest of Guang-ning, was the last trading center for the frontier tribes. While the number of these markets had never been great, they prospered and lasted until the early seventeenth century, or more than two hundred years.[25]

The Ming court founded frontier markets to pacify tribes and safeguard China's frontiers. Contiguous with its less developed neighbors, especially tribesmen on the northern frontier, China had confronted frontier problems since the dawn of its history. In most cases China adopted the loose-rein policies (*jimi*) that the Ming followed. As a component of this policy, frontier markets operated according to Chinese rules.[26] From the markets, the Ming government acquired cavalry horses essential to the defense of the northern frontier. In Chinese sources these trading centers were often referred to as "horse markets."

Ming frontier markets were important to the daily life of the Jurchens. There they sold their products and purchased grain, cloth, salt, and other commodities. They made profits from the trade and received gifts from the Ming government. As long as tribesmen were peaceful and cooperative, the Ming kept the markets open. If they behaved differently, the markets would be closed. From 1465 to 1487 China excluded the Hūlun Jurchen tribes from the markets because of the latter's raids on the frontier. In 1574 the Ming prohibited Wang Gao and his Right Jianzhou tribe from trading in the Fushun market. Under financial stress, according to Ming sources, his lieutenants even took menial jobs with Chinese families. Only after they pledged to change their conduct were they re-admitted to the markets.[27] Toward the beginning of the seventeenth century the Ming could no longer control the frontier markets in Manchuria. Rules became ineffective, and the official markets were overshadowed by private ones.

The purchase of tools evoked strong reactions from China and Korea. The Chinese were concerned that the Jurchens might convert iron tools to weapons. Some Korean officials even attributed the economic decline of the country's northern frontier to the sale of oxen and spades to the Jurchens.[28] Despite prohibitions by the Chinese and Korean governments, oxen and iron spades continued ending up in Jurchen hands.

Jurchen traders played an important part in sinicization, and the frontier trade was chiefly a group undertaking. The *Collected Liao-dong Archival Compilation of the Ming Period* remains the best source for researching the frontier markets. Although it is incomplete, it helps us understand the trading activities of the Jurchens, for example, the size of their trading parties varied from twenty to 1,180 people and seemed to increase with time; there were fifty-nine trading tours, which involved 18,363 Hūlun and Jianzhou tribesmen visiting the markets at Guang-shun, Zhenbei, and Fushun. One may argue that many more Jurchen traders would have been included if the compilation were complete. The first two frontier markets, located near Kai-yuan, were reserved for the four Hūlun tribes, with Fushun for Jianzhou tribesmen. On average, each tour brought 311 Jurchen traders. Of course, the larger the party the more contacts.[29] Table 2 indicates the number of the Hūlun and Jianzhou traders visiting the three markets.

When Jurchen traders arrived at frontier markets, they had to contact Chinese officials first. The Ming government regulated the markets, such as designating business days, setting horse prices, classifying standards for horses into five grades, and setting tax rates. Jurchen merchants were required to show trading permits and present horses and other commodities to market officials for evaluation and taxation. The Ming government paid for horses in dry goods. To show China's good will it wined and dined traders and distributed gifts to their leaders.[30]

Table 2. Statistics of Jurchen Traders in the Frontier Markets*

Date	Guang-shun	Zhenbei	Fushun	Total
1550	1,710	2,776	—	4,486
1578, 1583–84	4,050	7,822	2,005	13,877

Grand total: 18,363

Source: *MLTT*, 2: 715–847.

*This table only includes the Jurchens engaged in trading, not those entertained by the frontier government. In one case (see *MLTT*, 2: 721–22) a party of 480 Jurchen traders visited two markets (Guang-shun and Zhenbei) at the same time. Only the first market is counted. Trading data of the Fushun market were included in 1578 (see *MLTT*, 2: 808–10). The size of a party on page 810 (first line) is inferred as fifty by context.

There were other factors at work. Frontier markets needed the services of language specialists (*tongshi*), mainly selected from the Dongning Guard near Liaoyang, whose residents—Chinese, Koreans, and Jurchens—intermingled. While Chinese was the official language of communication, the Koreans and Jurchens there conversed in their native tongues. Language specialists worked in imperial and frontier governments. Those in the central bureaucracy were members of the Translators Institute (*Siyi guan*), an office of the Court of Imperial Sacrifices (*Taichang si*). In the frontier government they served as translators, interpreters, messengers, and negotiators.[31] What they brought to frontier markets were not only Chinese regulations but also Chinese norms and mores.

The frequency of trading tours was another factor. A Ming document of April 1584 showed four entries on trading tours under Menggebulu (d. 1599), a leader of the Hada tribe. The largest tour consisted of 1,100 Jurchens, the smallest 400. Cinggiyanu (d. 1584), chieftain of the Yehe tribe, headed groups of 995 and 1,180 doing business in the northern market at Kaiyuan. Both the Hada and Yehe Jurchens purchased many farming tools. The more frequent the Jurchens visited the markets, the more they were exposed to Chinese culture. They seem to have been the first to adopt the Chinese language. This may explain why some Hada tribesmen, such as Kūrcan (d. 1633), Šose (fl. 1630s–1640s) and Hife (1589?–1652), became versed in Chinese. They served Nurhaci and Hong Taiji as high officials, advisors, and diplomats. They and a few others advised Hong Taiji to adopt Chinese political institutions. Kūrcan even advised Hong Taiji to adopt the Chinese style of dress. Hife translated three dynastic histories from Chinese into Manchu.[32]

Equally important to contacts between Jurchen traders and China was the frequency of the markets' operation. Ming frontier markets functioned rather like fairs because they did not operate on a daily basis. In their early stage they operated semimonthly or monthly. Frontier markets near Kaiyuan opened once a month, lasting five days, while the Guang-ning market opened twice a month, also five days each. The frequency of later markets increased. By 1549 the Kaiyuan markets operated once every three or four days, and during the early

Wanli era (1573–1620), once every one or two days.[33] Increased frequency enhanced contacts between the Jurchens and the Chinese.

Private trade played an important part in Ming frontier markets. It developed to fill the gap left by official trade, which was restricted by many regulations, As early as 1434 the Ming court allowed frontier markets to carry on limited private transactions between Chinese and Jurchen merchants. In time, such transactions grew in size and value and were conducted alongside official markets and also outside the frontiers walls.[34] Finally the Ming government recognized this fact and in 1576 founded three markets in Qinghe, Kuandian, and Aiyang. They were located in southeast Liaoning and were operated mainly for the Jianzhou tribes. From the second half of the sixteenth century onward private trade overshadowed official trade.[35] Officials in these markets kept public order, handled disputes, and collected taxes. The Jurchens offered furs, ginseng, pearls, honey, and many other products in exchange for woks, jars, pots, textiles, and cattle. The bustling trade attracted Chinese merchants from various parts of China[36]

There was another kind of trade: business deals between the Ming court and the Jurchens. In 1462 the Tianshun emperor (r. 1457–1465) sent court officials to Kaiyuan. There they waited on the Jurchens to escort them across the frontier, planning to trade in the latter's settlements. It is likely that the Ming ruler wanted to buy such luxury items as pearls and sables for himself and his harem. The plans failed because Jurchen escorts were fully armed and came into conflict with Chinese officials.[37] Although it is the only case I have found, this in no way excludes the possibility of others.

Frontier trade, official or private, created a vibrant Jurchen merchant class. Owing to the high profits generated by trade, it was virtually monopolized by the Jurchen upper class. Jurchen leaders who frequented the frontier markets may be considered prominent members of this new class. Among them, other than Cinggiyanu and Menggebulu, were Yangginu and Bujai, two Hūlun leaders, and Giocangga—Nurhaci's grandfather—and Jucangge, both of the Jianzhou tribes.[38] Although not included in the Ming archival compilation, Wang Tai, Wang Gao, and Nurhaci must have been members of this elite group. As a leader of the Hada Jurchens and loyal ally of the Ming,

Wang Tai and his people carried on trade at the Guang-shun market. Wang Gao, chieftain of the Right Jianzhou tribe, participated but displayed unruly conduct while trading there. Nurhaci himself frequently visited the Fushun market.[39] One may believe that there were many other Jurchen merchants whose names are not mentioned in the sources.

Jurchen traders bought the most profitable commodities from other Jurchens, including the producers of the goods, and sold them at frontier markets. Wang Tai once sent more than twenty people to buy pine kernels from the Sungari region. Laili-hong, an associate of Wang Gao, made a profit from buying and selling sables, ginseng, and pine planks.[40] Nurhaci was engaged in similar activities and even tried to monopolize the pearl and sable trade of the Jurchens. In one case he dispatched thirty people to purchase sables and pearls in the Amur valley and made these items available in the Fushun market. He also operated a business from his home to deal with Mongol traders.[41]

Korean sources mention another kind of Jurchen merchant, obscure but active. These Jurchens traveled nineteen days from settlements near Korea's frontiers to the lower Sungari in the north to buy sables directly from hunters.[42] In Jurchen regions there were hotels for travelers. After escaping captivity in the lower Sungari region, a Korean revealed that his Jurchen master was a major sable and horse dealer, trading from his house. Jurchen merchants stayed a few days in the hostel run by the master and carried away their commodities on two or three horses.[43]

Clearly, frontier trade contributed to sinicization. Commodities such as the farm tools and cloth the Jurchens purchased were connected with Chinese ways of life. For the convenience of business, as mentioned earlier, Jurchen merchants wanted to learn Chinese words, ideas, and values. Consequently, some Jurchens understood the Chinese language. Besides the above cases of the Hada, Wang Gao was another example. According to a contemporary source, he knew Chinese and was a master of Chinese divination. It is safe to say that he learned these from the Fushun Market, which he frequently visited. Yangginu and Cinggiyanu, the two chieftains of the Yehe tribe, stalked the Zhenbei Market with their tribesmen. On one occasion, they planned to raid China's frontier. Before raiding they dispatched a small task force, some of whose members spoke Chinese, to trick the frontier guards.[44] Language is more than a tool of communication; it is a way of establishing links to other aspects of culture.

Chinese traders at the frontier markets played a part in cultural transmission. The Ming archival compilation cites forty-two names, of which fifteen were associated with the Zhenbei Market, eleven with the Guang-shun Market, and fourteen with the Fushun Market. Because this study focuses on the Jurchens, the fifty-five Chinese merchants who actively dealt with the Uriyangquad Mongols in the Xin'an Market are not discussed here.[45]

Most of the above-mentioned Chinese traders carried on business at one market, with the exception of four people who were active at both the Guang-shun and Zhenbei markets. But because the frontier trade was lucrative, it had a nationwide effect. When he took Fushun in 1618, Nurhaci captured sixteen merchants who were from various provinces, including some in South China.[46] Whichever markets they were active in and whatever their geographical origins, they were merchants as well as cultural transmitters, from whom Jurchen traders learned something about Chinese culture.

Chinese merchants even joined the Jurchens and served as high officials in the early Qing government and the Eight Banners. They brought Chinese culture right to the heart of the Manchus. Li Jixue (also Li Qingshan; Lii Gi-hiyo in Manchu, fl. 1600s–1620s) was such an individual. Because of the dearth of sources one can only sketch his background. Li seems to have become familiar with the Jurchens through the Qinghe Market in the Liaodong region. Yang Hao, the commander of Ming forces in a campaign against the Jurchens, sent Li on a diplomatic mission to the headquarters of Nurhaci before the Battle of Sarhū in 1619. The mission failed, and two years later Li threw himself at Nurhaci's feet when the latter captured Liaoyang, the base of Li's commercial operations. Because of his loyalty and dutifulness, he won the confidence of Nurhaci, and many of his descendants served the Qing as high officials.[47]

The line of Li Jixue lasted throughout the Qing dynasty. His son Li Guohan (d. 1658), was perhaps the most renowned member of the family. A great warrior, he was made a *mergen hiya* (superior bodyguard) by Hong Taiji. Several times he commanded an army in defeating Chinese forces loyal to the Ming. For his contribution he was awarded the hereditary title of marquis. His sons Hairtu (d. 1687) and Sangge (d. 1686) were both commanders fighting for the consolidation of Qing power.[48] Altogether twelve members of the Li family inherited the title of nobility left by Li Guohan.

But the Tong (Tung in Manchu) clan is the best case in point. Possibly of Chinese descent, the clan had long been natives of the Liaodong region. Because its clansmen frequently intermixed with non-Chinese frontiersmen and adopted their culture, their ethnic origin became controversial. During the early Ming one clansman, Darhaci (fl. 1370s–1410s), also known as Dong Dali in Chinese, engaged in frontier trade, first in Kaiyuan and then in Fushun. Perhaps he had both Jurchen and Chinese ethnic traits. He was later made an official by the Ming to deal with the Jurchens. After centuries of living on the Chinese side of the frontier, his offspring further branched out and joined the mainstream of Chinese culture. Many of them sided with Nurhaci when the latter rose against the Ming. According to a new study, Nurhaci took a Tong clanswoman, Tong Chunxiu (Hahana Jacing in Manchu), as a consort, and she became the mother of his first two sons. Tong Yangze (d. 1643), another descendant, was imprisoned by the Ming for collaborating with Nurhaci. He escaped from prison, fought for the Manchu cause, and was awarded a hereditary title.[49]

A descendant of Tong Dali in the eighth generation, Tong Yangxing founded a prosperous merchant house. Its members and many clansmen of other branches helped Nurhaci and thereby rose to high office. Tong Yangxing cast guns and organized the first artillery unit for Nurhaci. He was rewarded by being given a princess as his wife. Several female members of his clan became consorts of Manchu rulers, and one of his grandnieces gave birth to the Kangxi emperor, the first Manchu ruler to print many Chinese books, adopt Chinese naming practices, and found a school to systematically teach imperial princes Chinese subjects. Of the direct descendants of Tong Yangxing and his cousin, Tong Yang-zhen (d. 1621), about 159 people served as Qing officials in the years 1644–1722. Some were ministers, grand secretaries, and high-ranking councilors allowed to participate in the decision-making process. Beyond all question, therefore, Chinese ways of life penetrated the Qing imperial family through the Tong connection.[50]

Trade with Korea lent additional force to sinicization of the Jurchens because that country shared many cultural traits with China.
Because of geographical propinquity Korea had long traded with people in Manchuria. In 1374 a Korean official sent slaves to trade with
the Mongols, possibly also with the Jurchens. As soon as the Jurchens
reached Korea's borders at the end of their southward migration in the
second half of the fourteenth century, they began to exchange commodities with the Koreans.[51] Such trade, at first private, expanded.

In their transactions, the Jurchens traded furs for Korean grain,
oxen, cloth, and tools. Of the furs, the Koreans most desired sable because their rulers, officials, and the wealthy demanded it. By the second half of the fifteenth century, the wearing of sable had become a
symbol of status and wealth. Without such adornments, official Yi
dynasty sources recount, Korean women did not want to attend even
small parties.[52] The sable trade was so booming that many people became involved. Jurchen merchants made journeys from the Korean
border to northern Manchuria to buy sable skins from producers and
sell them to competing Korean customers, some of whom traveled
from as far away as Seoul to the northern frontier.[53] The trade continued long after the founding of the Qing dynasty.

In conclusion, the frontier trade with China and Korea contributed
to the economic, political, and cultural transformation of the Jurchens.
They changed from a mixed economy of hunting, gathering, fishing,
and farming to a dominantly agricultural one. This change made the
rise of Nurhaci possible. In the course of his conquest, Nurhaci emphasized both agriculture and trade. It was also through trade that
Chinese norms, mores, and values spread.

4. Tributary Relations

Tributary relations put a premium on Jurchen adoption of Chinese
culture prior to the founding of the Qing dynasty. Such relations
resulted from the tribute system, a time-honored institution of a
Sinocentric, ritualistic, and political nature. Since its beginning in
the Former Han dynasty (206 BC–AD 8) the system had functioned
in tandem with other means, such as diplomacy and war, to maintain
China's frontier stability and the Chinese world order. By the Ming,

the system had reached maturity and sophistication, with a multi-tude of rules and relationships determined by historical, political, cultural, and geographical factors. As a consequence, Korea, Inner Asian peoples, Southeast Asian states, and maritime countries had to follow different rules to initiate or renew relations with the Ming court. For its complexity, the tribute system should be treated by monographs—indeed there are many studies on the subject. The following pages will cover its effect on the Manchu adoption of Chinese culture.[54]

The Ming guard-post system in Manchuria and other border regions was designed to keep frontier peace and involve local chiefs in political affairs under China's guidance. Among such affairs were tributary relations, which were conducted within the framework of the guard-post system. As stated, guards and posts were administered by two military commissions, Liaodong and Nurkal. Staffed mainly by Chinese officials, the Liaodong Military Commission consisted of twenty-five guards and two special units. Its jurisdication was present-day Liaoning Province, and its residents were made up of Chinese, Korean, and Jurchen settlers. The Yongle emperor extended the system to all Manchuria and in 1409 created the Nurkal Military Commission, which in its final form comprised 384 guards and some special units and governed non-Chinese residents, chiefly the Jurchens.[55]

Through the guard-post system the Ming court invested many Jurchen tribal leaders with titles relevant to their original status. Associated with the titles were privileges such as trade, inheritance, and protection. Since recipients were allowed to keep their tribal affiliation, the titles strengthened their control. Each recipient was given an imperial patent, ceremonial attire, and an official seal. The imperial patent verified the holder's status and vested him with privileges and obligations. Ceremonial attire suggested the dignity and hierarchy of the imperial bureaucracy, while the seal symbolized the authority of office. In return, title holders were expected to maintain frontier order, follow China's rules, and send tributes to the imperial court.[56] The guard-post system contributed to the sinicization of the Jurchens because it required them to follow Chinese ritual and political practices.

Of the regulations attendant to the guard-post system, tribute sending was perhaps the most effective cultural transmitter. Among the rules of the tribute system were frequency, routing, place of entry, and size of the tributary mission. There were regulations regarding ceremonial aspects, native products the mission was allowed to carry, and length of stay in Peking. Many of these rules were revised over time, but their principles and goals remained the same.

After 1435 the Jianzhou and Hūlun tribes were asked to send tribute once a year. Tributary articles included horses, sables, lynx skins, and the gerfalcon. The Wild Jurchens did not have to send tribute frequently, for they were far from China proper.[57] Tribute missions set out during the last three months of the lunar calendar, entering China at a designated place. For example, the Ming designated Fushun as the place of entry for the tribute missions of all Jianzhou tribes. Each mission was of considerable size. In the case of the Jianzhou Jurchens, the entourage ranged from 200 to 600 people. After checking patents, frontier officials arranged trips to the capital via appropriate routes. It was a long and tedious journey; a round trip took two months. The tribute bearers were sent by the official postal system and provided with interpreters, meals, and protection. Besides the postal stations, arrangements were frequently made for them to pass the night in private homes. The long journey and the private accommodations furnished members of the missions with opportunities for contact with Chinese and for learning their ways of life.[58]

In Peking the tribute bearers received intensive indoctrination in Chinese values, especially those of political norms. They stayed in the International Hostel (*Huitong guan*), an institution under the Board of War. There they were provided with, among other things, interpreters and physicians. To show China's grace and superiority, the Ming government bestowed upon the missions two kinds of rewards, one for their tribute articles and one for bearers commensurate with their status in the guard-post system. They were given extra rewards if they made a contribution to frontier peace. In presenting tributes and receiving rewards the bearers had to go through elaborate ceremonies, which helped expose them to Chinese norms, mores, and values. The case of Nurhaci is worth mentioning. During the years 1590–1615 he headed tribute missions to Peking eight times, while his younger brother Šurhaci (1564–1611) led four missions of his own. When in Peking, they must have heard or witnessed various Ming imperial ceremonial usages and rules. As early as 1596, a Korean source indicated, Nurhaci wore the robe with five colored dragons, as did Chinese emperors. In 1612 he imitated another Chinese imperial practice

Table 3. Tributary Missions Led by Nurhaci, 1590–1615*

Time	Date Wanli Reign		Source: *Ming shilu (MSL)* or Tan Qian, *Guoque* (vol.	huan	page)
First	1590	18/4/gengzi	*MSL* 106	222	7b
**Second	592	20/8/dingyou	107	251	5b
Third	1597	25/5/jiachen	110	310	4a
Fourth	1598	26/10/guiyou	110	327	6a
Fifth	1601	29/12/yichou	112	366	2b
Sixth	1609	36/12/yimao	116	453	1a
Seventh	1611	39/10/wuyin	118	488	3b
Eighth	1615	43/3/dingwei	*Guoque* 5	82	5080

*For more about the missions, see note 58 above.
**Although the record is not quite clear, it is likely that Nurhaci led the mission in person.

by sitting under a yellow umbrella, and accompanied by a band of musicians. Shortly afterward, his banner forces marked their flags with colored dragons. This established a precedent for his successors, who adopted even more Chinese imperial formalities.[59] These examples evidenced the influence of Chinese political culture on the Jurchen tribute senders.

The influence of Chinese culture on Jurchen tribute missions became stronger for two reasons: their size and the length of their stay in Peking. As mentioned, the Ming court showered tribute bearers with gifts. The larger the tribute mission, the more the gifts. Members made even more profit from trading associated with the mission. Since tribute sending was a profitable undertaking, the Jurchens competed to increase the size and frequency of the missions. In the months from February 1426 to January 1427 there were about 4,000 Jurchen tribute bearers who experienced Chinese culture and carried it back to their settlements.[60]

The prolonged stays of tribute missions in Peking helped augment the influence of Chinese culture on their members. In 1580 the court limited their stay in the capital to a month and ten days, but there were too many tribute senders to be put under effective control. The missions were also involved in commercial activities and the transactions created conditions or excuses for prolonging their stays. It was under these circumstances that some missions stayed in Peking for more than ten months.[61]

The importance of the tribute missions to Jurchen adoption of Chinese culture can be further examined from their commercial activities. Mainly conducted in Peking by the tribute bearers, such commercial transactions differed from the trading at the frontier markets, also from the seacoast trade by maritime states. One may divide the history of the Jurchen tribute missions into stages: 1403–1435, 1435–1541, 1541–1618. The first stage and the early part of the second marked the peak because of Ming encouragement. As early as 1393 the Hongwu emperor (r. 1368–1398), founder of the Ming dynasty, invited Jurchen chiefs to send tribute and allowed them to sell their nontributary goods to the imperial government in Peking. His successor, the Yongle emperor, pursued the same policy more vigorously. All these made Jurchen chiefs aware of the economic benefits of sending tribute missions to Peking. With the increase of the missions in size and frequency, the volume of their trading amplified.[62]

The trade of the Jurchen tribute missions in Peking grew steadity and even expanded beyond. At first they carried on business from the International Hostel, where the missions stayed. Gradually they began to sell commodities to the people in the capital and in the second half of the fifteenth century they extended the trade to the streets outside the hostel. In 1477 the Ming court legalized this street trade, for it was too booming to be stopped. This expansion was also the results of two major developments. The first was the trade carried on by the Jurchen tribute bearers on their homebound trips, and likely on their way to Peking. What they purchased included oxen, tools, and materials for bows and arrows. In consideration of frontier peace and the needs of the Jurchens, the Ming set rules in 1459–1476, permitting them to buy oxen and making metal tools contraband. These traveling commercial activities expanded not only their economic benefits but their contact with the Chinese residents along their way.[63]

The last development was conversion of the nonmonetary rewards to silver. The two kinds of rewards—those for tribute articles and those for the bearers—were chiefly silks. Because silver offered convenience of transaction, the Jurchens preferred it to silks. Initially the conversion appeared in individual cases but soon it became a trend. During the 1527–1534 period the Ming government took steps to make all rewards for tribute articles convertible and by 1564 permitted conversion to silver of those for tribute bearers. With silver the Jurchen tribute senders could purchase a large quantity of goods, including contraband, in Peking and on their homeward journey. Shen Defu (1578–1642), a noted Ming scholar, provides a vivid description of the tribute missions' trade. On every homebound journey, he records, the Jurchen tribute missions brought carriages of freight piled up to more than thirty Chinese feet high. Sometimes they packed chinaware in several dozen carriages. Jurchen tribute missions in the late sixteenth and early seventeenth centuries probably were trading caravans. Without doubt, expanded purchasing power not only increased their contact with the Chinese but also widened their access to Chinese culture.[64] As stated, the years 1455–1541 marked the second stage in the history of Jurchen tribute missions. After the mid-fifteenth century the Ming found it burdensome to host and reward the large number of tribute missions. When the imperial court tried to reduce the size and frequency of the missions and their trade, the Jurchens took countermeasures, such as petitions and frontier raids. The Ming finally restricted the number of tribute bearers to 1,500 each year: 1,000 for the Hūlun Jurchens and 500 for the Jianzhou tribes. But the Ming government was unable to enforce this restriction. The Sino-Jurchen tribute system was brought to an end with the capture of Fushun by Nurhaci in 1618. Gone with the system were the tribute missions and their trading activities[65]

   To sum up, economic forces were of great importance to the sinicization of the Jurchens, ancestors of the Manchus. The Jurchens struggled to improve their agriculture by purchasing farm tools and seizing a large number of Chinese and Koreans as laborers. From these captives the Jurchens learned advanced farming technology and certain Chinese cultural traits. With progress in agriculture, they developed a way of life similar to that of Chinese farmers. Through frontier markets, official and private, they sold their products and purchased their daily needs. They met not only with Ming frontier officials but Chinese merchants from many parts of China. Thus the frontier markets served as centers of cultural exchange. Some active merchants such as the Li and Tong houses even spread Chinese culture to the Manchu ruling circles. Tribute bearers were also tributary traders. Their missions, which invovled long trips and possibly a lengthy stay in Peking, enabled them to contact more Chinese officials and common people. The more they kept in touch with the Chinese, the more they learned from their hosts.

Notes

1. For the quote, see de Crespigny, *China*, 97. For the general geographical features, see T. R. Tregear, *A Geography of China* (Chicago: Aldine Publishing Co., 1965), 273–76.

2. For the Amur River, see Ivar Lissner, *Man, God and Magic* (New York: G. P. Putnam's Sons, 1961), 126–27.

3. Owen Lattimore uses the term "Manchurian Mongolia" to indicate the large Mongol population in the region. See his *Studies in Frontier History*, 325. These Mongols were mainly the Qorčin tribesmen. For the O-wen-kes, Oronchons, Sibes, and Dahaurs, see Fang, *Heilong jiang shaoshu minzu*, 51–52, 79–82, 141–42, 180, 183–84.

4. For the Bohai kingdom, see *TMSL*, 85–92. For the Jin dynasty, see Tao, *The Jurchen in Twelfth-Century China*, 7–8. For the Ming military farms, see Li, *Mingdai Dongbei*, 39–48.

5. For the list of fish, see Alexander Hosie, *Manchuria: Its People, Resources, and Recent History* (Boston and Tokyo: Millet Company, 1910), 113–14. For the Heje settlements, see Fang, *Heilong jiang shaoshu minzu*, 114–18. But the most detailed work on the Heje people is Ling Chun-sheng, *Songhua jiang xiayou di Heizhe zu* (Nanking: Academia Sinica, 1934, 2 volumes), vol. 1.

6. For the Suksuhu River, see Zhao Zhenji, "Qingshi guoyu jie," *Xueyi zazhi*, 15. 4 (1936): 375. For the other three terms, see Huang Xihui, "Manyu diming fanyi di yuyuan, yinbian wenti," *Manyu yanjiu*, 2 (1991): 98 and 108. These words can also be found in Haneda Toru, *Manwa jiten* (Taipei: Xuehai chuban she, 1974, reprint of 1937 ed.), 387, 199, and 473. For the word *Hurha*, see Jerry Norman, *A Concise Manchu-English Lexicon* (Seattle and London: University of Washington Press, 1978), 140.

7. In Korea both officials and common people, especially women, regarded sable skin garments as a status symbol. See *CWS*, vol. 9, Reign of Sŏngjong, 57: 242, 6/7/sinyu.

8. For the meaning of Nurhaci, see Wang Huo, "Manzu renming di minshu te zheng he yuyan tezheng," *MANT*, 4 (1993): 72. For the Manchu terms dorgon

and sahalca, see Zhao, "Qingshi guoyu jie," 375 and 377. For the word *songkoro*, see Haneda, *Manwa jiten*, 402 and 472.

9. Van Jay Symons provides a good description about its usefulness. See his *Qing Ginseng Management*, 1–8.

10. For the Jurchen products, see Liu Shizhe, "Mingdai Nüzhen jizhong wuchan shuchu shuyi," *MTYC*, 6 (1984): 39–46. For the commodities the Jurchens bought from China, see the same author's "Mingdai Nüzhen wuchan shuru jizhong," *Heilong jiang wenwu congkan*, 4 (1984): 30–35, 29; Yuan Tsing, "Qingjun ruguan qian Nüzhen zu di jingji qianli," *Qingshi yanjiu*, 1 (1996): 90–92 and 110.

11. For Jurchen agriculture during the Jin dynasty, see *NCS*, 105–106. For their agriculture under the Mongols, see *NCS*, 148–49. Rossabi suggests that in the Yuan dynasty the Jurchens began to transform to an agricultural economy. See his *The Jurchens in the Yüan and Ming*, 6 and 9.

12. Dong Wanlun forcefully argues that by the fifteenth century the Jianzhou Jurchens had relied mainly on agriculture for a living. See his *Qing Zhaozu zhuan*, 322–31. For Menggetimur, see *CWS*, vol. 2, Reign of Sejong, 20: 546, 5/6/kyeyu.

13. For the intelligence report, see *CWS*, vol. 4, Reign of Sejong, 77: 80, 19/6/kisa. For the two proposals, see *CWS*, vol. 3, Reign of Sejong, 59: 445–46, 15/2/kihae; vol. 7, Reign of Sejo, 24: 465, 7/5/ulch'uk.

14. For their sedentary life, farming, and so on, see Zheng Xiao, *Huang-Ming siyi kao* (Peiping: Wendiango, 1933, *Guoxue wenku* No. 1), 1: 38. In a report on his life among the Jurchens, a Korean captive frequently mentioned the importance of rice to their daily life. See *CWS*, vol. 12, Reign of Sŏngjong, 255: 70–71, 22/7/chonghae.

    For a description of the Jurchen life, see Ye Xianggao, *Siyi kao* (Peiping: Wendian go, 1934, *Guoxue wenku* No. 13), 34; *Wugong lu*, 4. 11: 996a. For the Ming official's verification, see *MSL*, vol. 81, Jiajing reign, 234: 1b, 19/2/dingmao; *CWS*, vol. 1, Reign of T'aejo, 8: 87–88, 4/12/kyemyo.

15. For cases of fugitives and deserters, see *MSL*, vol. 20, Xuande reign, 95: 10b, 7/9/jiashen; vol. 27, Zheng-tong reign, 103: 8b–9a, 8/4/gengxu. For the Korean account of Chinese captives, see *CWS*, vol. 4, Reign of Sejong, 78: 87, 19/7/kapo; vol. 7, Reign of Sejo, 21: 415, 6/8/imsul. For their farming labor, see *MSL*, vol. 27, Zheng-tong reign, 103: 9a, 8/4/gengxu. For the occupational background of the captives, see Mo Tongyin, *Manzu shi luncong* (Peking: Sanlian shudian, 1979, reprint of 1958), 47–48. For the Ming entry, see *MSL*, vol. 92, Longqing reign, 7: 14b, 1/4/xinhai. For the Chinese planting method the Jurchens finally acquired, see Jiang and Tong, *Sheng-jing huang-gong*, 84.

16. The source (*MLTT*) is composed of four parts. Section 7 of the first part covers frontier markets. For purchase of iron spades, see *MLTT*, 2: 816 and 818ff. For plow oxen, see ibid., 2: 717–18ff. Korean documents supply data on the purchases of spades and oxen. See *CWS*, vol. 1, Reign of T'aejong, 11: 349, 6/2/kimyo. For the cases of Giocangga, see *MLTT*, 2: 809, 812, and 814. Two short

studies on the subject are helpful. See Yang Yulian, "Mingdai houqi di Liaodong mashi yu Nüzhen zu di xingqi," *MTYC*, 5 (1980): 31–32, and Liu, "Mingdai Nüzhen wuchan shuru jizhong," 31–33.

17. For the case of intratribal feuds, see the disputes between Fanca and Tungsan
(also as Cungsan), both closely related to Menggetimur, as mentioned in *DMB*,
2: 1066. In 1433, another Jurchen tribe attacked the Left Jianzhou tribe, killing
its leader, Menggetimur, and his eldest son. See *Siyi kao*, 35. In 1450 Esen led his
Eleuth Mongols, who overran the Hūlun Jurchen tribes. See *DMB*, 1: 419. China
and Korea cooperated in 1467 to attack the Jianzhou tribes for their raids on
the borders. See *DMB*, 1: 839–40.

18. For Sin's account, see the text in Inaba Iwakichi, ed., *Kōkyō nidōkashi kyūrōjō*
(Chang-chun: Kenkoku daigaku kenkyūin, 1939), 83.

19. For his assignments of some wild Jurchens to do farming, see *CWS*, vol. 25,
Reign of Sŏnjo (revised version), 41: 700, 40/2/kapo. Nurhaci sent his men to
farm the land taken from the Hada tribe. See the memorial of Xue Sancai in
MSL, vol. 119, Wanli reign, 507: 2b, 41/4/jiawu. For his cultivating the controversial borders, see the memorial of Xue Guoyong, in *MSL*, vol. 119, Wanli
reign, 519: 6b–7a, 42/4/dingyou.

20. For the increase in cultivated area to roughly 173,400 acres (12,386 *qing*) in 1388
and in the early fifteenth century. See *Da-Ming huidian*, 1. 18: 8a. But according
to another study, the acreage decreased during the mid-sixteenth century. See
Jiang Shoupeng, "Mingdai Liaodong jingji," *KHCH*, 3 (1990): 103. The word
qing is roughly equivalent to 15 acres. For military farms, see Guang and Li,
Qing Taizu, I: 24 and 51. In 1621, Nurhaci began to distribute deserted land
among Jurchen and Chinese males. See Wang, *Qingshi xukao*, 198–217. Wang
forcefully argues that the land was distributed mainly among the bannermen.
For the hamlets, see *MBRT*, vol. 3, Taizu reign, 66: 990–91.

For harsh measures Nurhaci took to enforce his orders, including the farm
policy, and the resulting disturbances, see Zhou Yuanlian, *Qingchao kaiguo shi
yanjiu* (Shenyang: Liaoning renmin chuban she, 1981), 142–69. For a comprehensive study of the agricultural progress under Nurhaci, see Ch'en, *Ming-
Qing Zhengzhi*, 1: 335–61.

21. For the report of the Korean eyewitness, see *CWS*, 33, Reign of Injo, 7: 662,
2/12/pyongsu. For his 1616 order, see Guang and Li, *Qing Taizu*, 1: 63.

22. Guang and Li, *Qing Taizu*, 2: 186.

23. For discussion of Mongolia's geography, see de Crespigny, *China*, 104–109.
The same author considers the Gobi "one of the world's largest deserts." See
ibid., 106.

24. There were many Chinese loanwords in the Manchu language, written and
spoken, largely a result of activities at the frontier markets. Chinese traders also
borrowed Jurchen words. When combined, these loanwords developed into a
hybrid speech, known as the Shenyang dialect. See Guan Jixin and Meng Xianren, "Manzu yu Shenyang yu, Beijing yu," *MANT*, 1 (1987): 73–81.

!

25.   For the beginnings of the frontier markets, see *MSL*, vol. 10, Yongle reign, 40:
       2a, 3/3/guimao; 52: 3b, 4/3/jiawu. For later developments, see Li, *Mingdai Dong-
       bei*, 174–77; Lin Tingqing, "Lun Mingdai Liaodong mashi cong guanshi dao
       minshi di zhuanbian," *MTYC*, 4 (1983): 50–57. For the market at Yizhou,
       known as Yixian today, see *MSL*, vol. 113, Wanli reign, 375: 2a, 30/8/jiawu. For
       bustling trade in late Ming frontier markets, see Ejima Hisao, "Mimmatsu
       Ryōtō no goshijō," *Shien*, 90 (1963): 67–94. For the transportation network, see
       Li, *Mingdai Dongbei*, 106–35.

26.   For China's loose-rein policy, see Lien-sheng Yang, "Historical Notes on the
       Chinese World Order." In John King Fairbank, ed., *The Chinese World Order:
       Traditional China's Foreign Relations* (Cambridge: Harvard University Press,
       1968), 28–33. For early history of China's frontier trade with nomadic tribes,
       see Ying-shih Yu, *Trade and Expansion in Han China: A Study in the Structure
       of Sino-Barbarian Economic Relations* (Berkeley and Los Angeles: University of
       California Press, 1967), chs. 2 and 5.

27.   For the Uriyangquad Mongol case, see *Mingshi*, 28. 328: 8507. For the Jurchen
       case, see Li Yunxia, "Shilun Mingdai Guang-ning di mashi," *MANT*, 4 (1984):
       16. For the case of Wang Gao's lieutenants, see *Wugong lu*, 4. 11: 1039; Fan Jing-
       wen, *Zhaodai wugong bian* (Bingbu, ed., 1638–642, 10 chs.), 8: 27b. For impor-
       tance of the frontier markets, see Chen, "Mingdai Liaodong mashi," 47–52.

28.   For Chinese action, see *MSL*, vol. 46, Zhenghua reign, 159: 7a, 12/4/guihai; vol.
       59, Hongzhi reign, 195: 6a–8a, 16/1/jiawu. For Korean reactions, see *CWS*, vol.
       7, Reign of Sejo, 31: 585, 9/8/kapo; vol. 20, Reign of Myongjong, 29: 657, 18/8/
       kyech'uk; vol. 21, Reign of Myongjong, 33: 124, 21/10/sinsa.

29.   For these statistics, see *MLTT*, Document #186, 2: 716–27; Document #192, 2:
       808–14; Document #193, 2: 815–16; Document #194, 2: 816–31. Some *MLTT*
       documents also appear in *Manzu lishi dang'an ziliao xuanji*, comp. Zhongguo
       kexue yuan minzu yanjiu suo Liaoning shaoshu minzu shehui lishi diaocha zu
       (N.p.: 1963), 1–38.

30.   For example, in 1405 the Ming government set the horse price. See *MSL*, vol.
       10, Yongle reign, 40: 4a, 3/3/jiayin. For taxation and treatment, see *MLTT*, 2:
       718–19ff.

31.   For the geographical origin and qualifications of the language specialists, see
       Liaodong zhi, 2. 5: 28a; 3. 6: 21. For the Translators Institute and its function, see
       Mingshi, 6. 74: 1797–98. These language specialists were active in the frontier
       administration in Manchuria. See *Wugong lu*, 4. 11: 1008a and 1009a. For Kore-
       ans and Jurchens in the Dongning Guard, see Kawachi Yoshihiro, "Mindai
       Ryōyō no Tōneii ni tsuite," *Tōyōshi kenkyū*, 44. 4 (1986): 117–18, 124.

32.   For the Hada and Yehe traders, see *MLTT*, Document #194, 2: 816, 818, 828–29,
       831. Kūrcan and Šose were brothers from the Hešeri clan. See *CSKC*, 10: 8004,
       8353. The three people were all on the staff of the Literary Office, whose mem-
       bers, especially those of Chinese origin, were in favor of Chinese political insti-

tutions. For Kūrcan's suggestion, see *CSL*, reign of Taizong, 32: 9a, Chongde 1/11/ guichou; 34: 26b–27a, Chongde 2/4/dingyou. Hife was a grand secretary and translated the histories of the Liao, Jin, and Yuan dynasties from Chinese into Manchu. See *Qingshi liezhuan*, 1. 4: 189–91.

33. For the changes of the operation schedules, see Yang, "Mingdai houqi," 28.

34. For the rise of such private markets, see Lin, "Lun Mindai Liaodong mashi," 51–56, Cong, "Chishu zhizheng," 196.

35. For the limited private trade in the frontier markets, see *MSL*, vol. 21, Xuande reign, 113: 6b, 9/10/dingsi. For the founding of the three markets, see Lin, "Lun Mingdai Liaodong mashi," 54; *NCS*, 247; Zhao Duo, *Qing kaiguo jingji fazhan shi* (Shenyang: Liaoning renmin chuban she, 1992), 67–74. But another source only mentions two markets, Kuandian and Yongdian. See *Wugong lu*, 4. 11: 1028–29.

36. For Ming officials in the private markets, see *NCS*, 248 for Chinese products purchased by the Jurchen traders, see Lin, "Lun Mingdai Liaodong mashi," 53–54.

37. *MSL*, vol. 38, Tianshun reign, 341: 6a, 6/6/renchen.

38. For Yangginu, see *MLTT*, Document #193, 2: 816, and Document #194, 2: 820. For Bujai, see ibid., Document #194, 2: 819 and 827. The same source keeps three entries on Giocangga. The first is on his trade, while the remaining entries are about the gifts and treatment he and his fellow traders received. See *MLTT*, Document #192, 2: 809, 812, and 814. For Jucangge, see ibid., Document #192, 2: 808 and 810.

39. For a biography of Wang Tai, see *ECCP*, 2: 799–800; *Wugong lu*, 4. 11: 996a–1000b. For Wang Gao, see *Wugong lu*, 4. 11: 1036a–43b; *MTTS*, 114–18. For Nurhaci's frequent visits with Fushun, see Yan, *Nuer-hachi zhuan*, 18–19.

40. For the commercial activities of Wang Tai and Laili-hong, see *Wugong lu*, 4. 11: 1015a, and 4.11: 1048b–49a.

41. For his effort to monopolize the pearl and sable fur trade of the far-flung Jurchens, see *Chou-Liao shihua*, vol. 3, Memorial of Zhang Tao, 2: 5a–6b. For his purchase of these items from the Amur valley, see Guang and Li, *Qing Taizu*, 1: 64; *MBRT*, vol. 1, Taizu, 5: 68, 71, and 75. For his business from home, see *MSL*, vol. 124, Tianqi reign, 6: 20, 1/2/yichou.

42. For the peddling case, see *CWS*, vol 7, Reign of Sejo, 34: 659, 10/11/kyongsin; for the long journey to the lower Sungari valley, see ibid., vol. 9, Reign of Sŏngjong, 66: 331, 7/4/kimyo.

43. For the testimonies of the Korean, see *CWS*, vol 12, Reign of Sŏngjong, 255: 70, 22/7/ chonghae; Kawachi, *Mindai Joshinshi*, 645–46.

44. For the case of Wang Gao, see *Wugong lu*, 4. 11: 1038b, 1043b; for the two Yehe leaders, see ibid., 4. 11: 1017b.

45. For their names, see *MLTT*, vol. 2, Section 7 (horse markets), 715–847. Seven names are not complete, but they are counted here.

46. These four merchants were Ji Yingju, He Zhu, Yang Jingshi, and Xu Yue. See
    MLTT, 2: 717, 721–22, 715, 790, and 819. Li Jiugao was active in three markets
    (ibid., 827 and 830–31). The unaffiliated merchant was Delu by his first name.
    See ibid., 790.

    For the sixteen merchants, see Guang and Li, "*Qing Taizu*, 1: 85; *MBRT*, vol.
    1, Taizu, 6: 93. Of the seven places listed, "Hexi" could mean both Shensi and
    Kansu provinces or just one of them. The term "Hedong" suggests eastern
    Shansi. Yizhou was in Hopei Province today.

47. For Li Jixue, see *TCCC*, 184: 2a; *CSKC*, 10: 8168. For his involvement in the dip-
    lomatic mission, see Guang and Li, *Qing Taizu*, 1: 109; 2: 88.

48. For Li Guohan and his two sons, see *TCCC*, 184: 2a–13a. For a table of the Li
    clansmen who inherited the nobility titles, see *CSKC*, 6: 4914.

49. The Tongs repeatedly crossed the ethnic line, but they were regarded to be of
    Chinese origin. See Zhang Deyu, *Manzu fayuandi lishi yanjiu* (Shenyang: Liao-
    ning minzu chuban she, 2001), 342–56. For Darhaci, Tong Dali, and Hahana
    Jacing, see ibid., 349–53. For Tong Yangze, see *TCCC*, 231: 12b–13a.

50. For Tong Yangxing, see *TCCC*, 182: 10b–12a; *ECCP*, 2: 797–98; Wang Gesheng,
    "Qingchao kaiguo gongchen Tong Yangxing," *Beifang luncong*, 6 (1985): 34–
    37; Yang Xuechen and Zhou Yuanlian, *Qingtai baqi wanggong guizu xing-shuai
    shi* (Shenyang: Liaoning renmin chuban she, 1986), 78–82. For the measures
    taken by Kangxi, see Chapters VI and VII.

    For the figures of the Tong clansmen in Qing officialdom, see Fu Bo et al.,
    "Mingmen wangzu Tongjia shi, aiguo qinmin yu zhonghua." In Fu Bo et al,
    Manzu Tongjia shi yanjiu (Shenyang: Liaoning minzu chuban she, 2003), 22;
    another study gives a slightly different figure. See Zhang, *Manzu fayuandi lishi
    yanjiu*, 351.

51. For the case of 1374, see Chŏng, *Koryŏsa*, 1. 44: 867. For the early frontier trade,
    see ibid., 3. 135: 718; Zhao, *Qing kaiguo jingji fazhan shi*, 30, 77–79.

52. For the importance of the sable skin wears in Korea, see *CWS*, vol. 9, Reign of
    Sŏngjong, 57: 242, 6/7/sinyu; vol. 15, Reign of Chungjong, 29: 231, 12/9/ulmi. For
    the Jurchen-Korean trade, see Kawachi, *Mindai Joshinshi*, ch. 18. For a terse
    treatment of the sable trade, see Kawachi Yoshihiro, "Mingdai dongpei Ya di
    diaopi mouyi." In *Qingzhu Wang Zhonghan xian-sheng bashi shouchen xueshu
    lunwen ji*, ed. Qingzhu Wang Zhonghan xian-sheng bashi shouchen xueshu
    lunwen ji weiyuan hui (Shengyang: Liaoning daxue chuban she, 1993),
    497–99.

53. For the traveling Jurchen traders, see *CWS*, vol. 7, Reign of Sejo, 34: 659, 10/11/
    kyongsin; vol. 9, Reign of Sŏngjong, 66: 331, 7/4/kimyo. For the Korean mer-
    chants, see ibid., vol. 9, Reign of Sŏngjong, 57: 242, 6/7/sinyu; vol. 13, Reign of
    Yonsan'gun, 19: 308, 4/4/kyemi.

    For the continuation of the Korea trade, see Zhang, *Qing-Han Zongfan mouyi*, pp. 4–10, and chs. 2–3; Terauchi Itarō, "Kyōngwon kaishi no Konshun," *Tōhōgaku*, 70 (July 1985): 76–90.

54. For the early development of the tribute system, see Yu, *Trade and Expansion in Han China*, chs. 3 and 5. For its conceptual foundation, see Yang, "Historical Notes on the Chinese World Order," 20–33. For its actual working during the Qing dynasty, see John King Fairbank and Ssu-yu Teng, *Ch'ing Administration: Three Studies* (Cambridge: Harvard University Press, 1960), 107–78. There are several fine studies on China's tributary relations with maritime states, especially South and Southeast Asian countries. One of the best such works is by Jane Kate Leonard, *Wei Yuan and China's Rediscovery of the Maritime World* (Cambridge: Council on East Asian Studies, Harvard University Press, 1984), ch. 6.

55. For these two Military Commissions, see Yang, Liaodong dusi, chs. 1–2; Yang, Yuan, and Fu, *Mingdai Nuergan*, chs. 3 and 8.

56. For all these aspects, see Yang, Yuan, and Fu, *Mingdai Nuergan*, ch. 8.

57. For these details, see *Da-Ming huidian*, comps. Li Dongyang et al. and revised by Shen Shixing et al., (Taipei: Dongnan shubao she, 1964, 5 volumes), 3. 107: 7b–8b. But a Japanese scholar argues that before 1435 they sent tribute missions more than once a year. See Ejima Hisao, "Min Seitōki ni okeru Jochoku chōkō no seigen, " *Tōyō shigaku*, 6 (1952): 27–44.

58. Before 1464 Jurchen tribute bearers entered China at Kaiyuan. After that date the Hūlun missions entered at the same place; the Jianzhou people entered China by way of Fushun. See Cong, "Chishu zhizheng," 195. In the beginning, the Jurchens sent their tributes to Nanking, which was the capital of the Ming. But after 1417 Peking became the destination of the tribute missions. See Ejima Hisao, "Minsho Jochoku chōkōni kansuru nisan no mondai," *Shien*, 58 (1953): 71–93. For the size of the Jianzhou missions and the accommodation in private homes, see *MSL*, vol. 29, Zheng-tong reign, 158: 8b, 12/9/yimao; vol. 40, Chenghua reign, 17: 2a, 1/5/yimao.

59. For their life in the hostel, see *Da-Ming huidian*, 3. 109: 1a–3b; for various ceremonies, see ibid., 3. 111: 16a–17a. For their rewards, see *NCS*, 175–76. This office is sometimes rendered as College of Interpreters or Bureau of Translators. For a fine treatment of the office, see Chiu Ling Yeong (Zhao Lingyang), "Ji Mingdai Huitong guan," *Dalu zazhi*, 41. 5 (September 15, 1970): 151–64.

For the eight tribute missions, see Teng, *Nuer-hachi*, 387–95 ("Chronological Table"); Yan, *Nuer-hachi zhuan*, 313–19 ("Chronological Table"). In his book Yan does not clearly indicate the seventh mission, but in an article, he lists eight missions. See his "Nuer-hachi rujing," 2–5. Another specialist argues that there were only seven missions, for Nurhaci was not on the eighth mission in person. See Liu, "Lun Nuer-hachi," 60. On the whole, the first seven missions are recorded in *MSL*, with the eighth one in Tan Qian, *Guoque* (Peking:

Guji chuban she, 1958, 6 volumes), 5. 82: 5080. Šurhaci led four missions in 1595–1608. See Yan, *Nuer-hachi zhuan*, 314–17 ("Chronological Table").

For these instances, see *CWS*, vol. 22, reign of Sonjo, 71: 641–42, 29/1/chŏngyu and *MWLT*, 1: 12. Later some of Nurhaci's army units carried flags with colored dragons. See *CWS*, vol. 33, reign of Kwanghaegun, 169: 9a, 13/9/musin. Finally all the Manchu Banners had flags with colored dragons.

60.   For their size in the early stage, see *Da-Ming huidian*, 3. 107: 8a. For the increase in size, see *MSL*, vol. 112, Wanli reign, 373: 10b, 30/6/wushen; vol. 119, 530: 1a, 43/3/dingwei; for the estimate, see Ejima Hisao, "Mindai Jochoku chōkō bōeki no gaikan," *Shien*, 77 (1958): 11; also *NCS*, 241–44. For their frequency before 1435 and later Ming efforts for restrictions, see Ejima, "Min Seitoki," 27–44.

61.   For Ming restrictions, see *Da-Ming huidian*, 3. 108: 31a; Cong, "Chishu zhizheng," 198. For their prolonged stay, see *MSL*, vol. 118, Wanli reign, 495: 4b, 40/5/renyin.

62.   For the decree of 1393, see *Da-Ming huidian*, 3. 113: 7a. Ejima Hisao divides its history into four stages: (1) 1403–1435, (2) 1435–1464, (3) 1464–1541, and (4) 1541–1616. For clarity and simplicity, I combine his second and third divisions as my "middle stages." See his "Mindai Jochoku chōkō," 1–25. My division is similar to that of Jiang, "Mingdai Nüzhen di chigong zhi," 17–26. But Jiang does not see the close relations between tribute and tributary trade.

63.   For the missions' trading in Peking and its expansion, see *Da-Ming huidian*, 3. 108: 29. For their purchases on their homebound trips, see *MSL*, vol. 37, Tianshun reign, 300: 6b, 3/2/gengwu; vol. 46, Chenghua reign, 159: 7a, 12/11/guihai.

64.   The individual conversion case appeared in 1522. See *MSL*, vol. 71, Jiajing reign, 12: 3a, 1/3/jiayin. For changes in 1527–1534, see *Da-Ming huidian*, 3. 111: 16a–17a; 3. 113: 6a. For the imperial order of 1564, see *Da-Ming huidian*, 3. 111: 16b. For Shen's account, see Shen Defu, *Wanli yehuo pian* (Peking: Zhonghua Book Company, 1959, 3 volumes), 3. 30: 780.

65.   For their frequency before 1435 and later Ming efforts for restrictions, see Ejima, "Min Seitoki," 27–44.

Chapter IV

Frontiersmen and Transfrontiersmen

As China's northeastern frontier, Manchuria was a meeting place for cultures and peoples, even in prehistoric times. It was the "ocean gateway" of Mongolia and the end of the eastern drives of the nomads from as far away as Central Asia. It stood as a bridge, over which Chinese culture and politics reached Korea.[1] Within its boundaries, the mountains, rivers, wooded areas, and administrative barriers created internal frontiers. Tribes, clans, and clusters of communities were dispersed. Their economic activities differed with their ecological conditions, developing into specializations and bringing trade among communities and with more advanced states, such as China and Korea. Out of these international and domestic frontiers emerged a frontier society, from which arose frontiersmen and transfrontiersmen, who helped further the sinicization of the Manchus.

1. Frontier Society of Liaodong

The word "frontier" is hard to define because it may be associated with geographical, political, economic, military, and scientific fields, individually or in combination. Historians have not achieved a definition. Herbert Franke and Denis Twitchett interpret it as "a broad transitional zone in which identities, loyalties, and authority were constantly changing and striking new balances." In his *Studies in Frontier History* and *Inner Asian Frontiers of China*, Owen Lattimore defines the frontier as the edge of a zone, or the geographical area between communities, shaped by material and cultural conditions and changeable. The *Encyclopaedia of the Social Sciences* contains a long entry entitled "Frontier," dealing with the subject in terms of American history. Some scholars identify it as a sphere of transition or a zone of interaction between distinctive cultures or ways of life. It is also interpreted as "a linear border dividing two states."[2]

It seems advisable to specify how the word is used in this book. Here the term "frontier" is considered to be a transitional border between different cultural, economic, or political institutions. There were frontiers between Chinese and Jurchens, between Jurchens and Koreans, Jurchens and Mongols, Chinese and Mongols. Lands that separate communities of similar instituions, such as those between Jurchen tribes, are here regarded as clan or tribal boundaries. Of course, the distinction between frontier and boundary is not always clear, for there are also various interpretations of the term "boundary."[3]

China's presence in southern Manchuria must begin with the coming of Chinese Neolithic culture, represented by the Yangshao and Longshan cultures. These relations brought political contact. Because of its geographical proximity and long connection with China Liaodong became the center of Chinese culture. Since the Warring States period (403–221 BC), the region had been integrated with the kingdom of Yan, one of the seven contending states. Despite vicissitudes of China's control, it remained a hub of Chinese culture.[4] With the rise of the Ming dynasty, China strengthened its position there, and from it Chinese culture radiated to other parts of Manchuria.

The Ming government devoted the last three decades of the fourteenth century to clearing the Yuan army from Manchuria and stabilizing control there. During the early years of the fifteenth century the Yongle emperor aggressively pushed the Chinese frontier north to the Amur River, all the way from the Mongolian border eastward to Sakhalin. For the first time, the government established dominance over all of Manchuria. It was put under special administrative structures and peopled by diversive groups.

The administrative structure in Manchuria was known as the guard-post system, fundamentally a military institution installed throughout the Ming empire. Under its commander (*zhihui shi*) a guard unit functioned at the district level, with 5,600 men. Below the guard were chiliarchy units—each composed of 1,120 soldiers—and century units of 112 each. At the top of the system was the Military Commission *(dusi)*, headed by the regional commander *(du zhihui shi)*, who supervised guards under him and took charge of military affairs at the provincial level.[5]

There were two varieties of the guard-post system in Manchuria: the Liaodong Military Commission and the Nurkal Military Commission. Geographically, the Liaodong Military Commission covered southern Manchuria, roughly the province of Liaoning today. It took charge of civilian and military affairs, with such cities as Guangning and Liaoyang as administrative centers. Among places under its jurisdiction were Anle zhou and Zizai zhou, two districts inhabited chiefly by Jurchens. In time, a regular administrative structure, such as the offices of governor *(xunfu)* and governor-general *(zongdu)*, was introduced.[6] It functioned together with the guard-post system. The administration was bureaucratic and centralized, and although the region was much like a regular province, it remained a frontier.

The Nurkal Commission covered northern Manchuria, southern Siberia, and the area from the Ussuri valley southeastward to the Tumen. It was less developed but much larger than the Liaodong region. By the late sixteenth century it administered 384 guards and dozens of subunits, primarily comprised of Jurchens. Among the guards were the three Jianzhou and the Maolian tribes. These four tribes later made up the nucleus of the Manchus.[7] China's control over the region was indirect because of its immense size and underdevelopment. Mainly officered by tribal chiefs and their descendants, the Nurkal Military Commission was like the headman institution *(tusi zhidu)* in China's southwestern frontiers. Under it the Jurchens remained hunters, fishermen, and gatherers even after their counterparts in southern Manchuria had made agriculture essential to their life. The Liaodong region had long attracted Chinese migrants from North China, especially the Shantung peninsula, which was separated from Liaodong only by a narrow gulf. Its climate was comparable with that of the North China Plain and, more importantly, its soil was good for agriculture. It was a land for Chinese migrants in peacetime and refugees during domestic turbulence. During the Former Han period (202 BC–AD 8) it had a population of more than 270,000. As a result of chain migration caused by China's disunity in the early fourth century, as many as 200,000 households moved to the Liaodong region from present-day Hopei Province.[8] It is reasonable to assume that the numbers of Chinese residents increased with time and eventually dominated the region.

The Chinese population in the Liaodong region was affected by political disturbances and natural disasters, but it would stabilize after the troubles were over. Although the war at the end of the Yuan dynasty decimated the region's population, this situation changed with the early Ming rulers, who defeated the remnants of the Yuan armed forces, dispatched garrisons to keep peace, encouraged agriculture, and sent migrants. By the early fifteenth century, its inhabitants, civilian and military, numbered more than 306,000, and according to the 1565 edition of the *Liaodong Gazetteer*, had increased to 381,532 by around that time.[9] Although not necessarily accurate, these two figures give a sense of Liaodong's growth, which resulted from births, migrations, exiles, sojourning traders, and the admission of Jurchen settlers. At its peak the population may have reached more than two million people.[10]

Liaodong's frontier population was characterized by a rather complicated mix. Military families were the dominant component because the Liaodong Military Commission was the chief admininstrative machinery in the area. Soldiers were members of military households tied to military farms and obligated to provide warriors. While soldiers rotated to guard frontiers and to work on the military farms, their families helped. According to a local history, compiled in 1443, soldiers and people of other occupations numbered about 125,000, while family members and relatives totaled 281,887; those who were registered as civilian households numbered 7,102. Out of the 381,532 mentioned in the Liaodong gazetteer of 1565, only 10,323 were from civilian households. For all their faults, these figures show the importance of the military households in Liaodong's population structure.[11]

Part of Liaodong's population consisted of convicts, among which were officials, military personnel, common people, and individuals of ethnic minorities.[12] Since its beginning the Ming government had banished lawbreakers to the frontier or other remote areas. Many ended up in the Liaodong region as soldiers or military farmers. Ming dynastic records preserve data about such exiles. One entry, dated 1428, records 1,635 people exiled to Liaodong and other northern frontiers. Although many died before reaching their destination, a great number did, one may assume, survive the hardship and resettle in the region.[13]

Merchants made up a small percentage of Liaodong's population. Since soldiers and their families formed the centerpiece of society, the region's economy was military. Regular commerce gave way to trade in the frontier markets, designed to pacify the tribesmen. Because of the potential profits, the frontier markets attracted merchants from all around China. With permits from Ming frontier authorities, they carried on trade with Jurchen tribesmen and perhaps also served as the latter's guides. There were merchants from among local residents. He Qin (1437–1511), a noted thinker and official, was born to a local merchant family.[14] Toward the end of the fifteenth century, private and contraband trade began to prosper in Liaodong. It enticed more merchants from outside, for it was much less restricted by Ming authorities. In the beginning the outside merchants were only sojourners, but they eventually became residents.

Liaodong's population was also marked by non-Chinese components, of which, the Jurchens were the most important. They mostly resided along the Amur valley. For economic or security reasons tribesmen took southern journeys, with Liaodong as their destination. This southern drive had been the major theme of their migration.[15] With the founding of the Jin dynasty by the Wanyan (Wanggiya in Manchu) clan, the Jurchens became masters of Manchuria. But, as mentioned, in the chaotic years of the late Yuan period the Odoli, Hurha, and Taowen Jurchens repeated the historic pattern, moving down to Liaodong. It was from there they finally founded their own state.

In the Liaodong region the Jurchens formed two major blocs. The three Jianzhou tribes and the Maolian branch constituted a bloc, settling in the area between Shenyang (Mukden) and the Tumen River. Ofttimes they moved around their settlements for various considerations. They kept contact with Chinese and Korean authorities but formed communities in the valleys and hills away from the frontiers. In 1423 the Left Jianzhou leaders notified the Korean authorities of their migration, which involved about 7,500 people. But this was not necessarily its total population because it seems possible that people remained in the old settlements. A Korean source disclosed in 1451 that the three Jianzhou tribes had more than 2,300 households. Assuming each household had six members, there would be 14,000 people. The figure should have been much larger because each Jurchen household possessed a few slaves. The population greatly increased in the sixteenth century. Wang Gao, a powerful chieftain, deployed 3,000 horsemen to threaten China in 1572; Wang Wutang, another Jurchen leader, mustered 7,000 fighters in 1580.[16] Although not a reliable yardstick to measure a tribe's population, the size of these armies is suggestive.

The other Jurchen bloc consisted of the Hūlun or Haixi tribes. Like the Jianzhou and Maolian Jurchens, they migrated to the south and regrouped. Their new settlements were located in the area between Kaiyuan and the sharp bend of the Sungari River. Geographically speaking they were mostly outside of Liaodong, but under the Chinese frontier government in the area. They formed four regional powers: Hada, Ula, Yehe, and Hoifa, known as the Four Hūlun Tribes. Because they linked southern and northern Manchuria, they attracted tribesmen from other clans and played an important role in Liaodong's frontier affairs.

It is difficult to provide demographic figures for the Four Hūlun Tribes since there are no data available. An examination of events suggests that population also grew in the sixteenth century. Wang Tai, an influential chieftain of the Hada tribe, would bring 10,000 warriors under his banner when his strength reached its zenith in the 1550s–1570s. By 1572, Yangginu and Cinggiyanu, the two leaders of the Yehe tribe, were commanders of 20,000 horsemen. Confronted by Nurhaci in 1613, Bujantai, the Ula chieftain, put 30,000 soldiers in the battlefield. Of course, these warriors—mostly able-bodied young men—were far fewer than old people, youngsters, and women. In the sixteenth and early seventeenth centuries the population of the four tribes might have been between 80,000 and 100,000.[17]

Among non-Chinese settlers in Liaodong were Koreans. Since their early history the Koreans had been active in southern Manchuria, once a land of contention between China and Korea. The Yalu and Tumen rivers had never been effective borders. Dissatisfied with burdensome taxes and corvée, Koreans frequently crossed the Yalu and made Liaodong their homes. Korean fugitives also took shelter there. In a memorial of 1464, a Korean official reported 30,000 Koreans in the Dongning Guard in Liaodong during the last three decades of the fourteenth century. Some 40,000 Korean army deserters fled to the same region during the first twenty years of the next century. The Koreans, the memorialist continued, lived in the Liaoyang area and spread east and south, constituting 30 percent of Liaodong's population, perhaps an exaggeration.[18]

The aforesaid peoples—Chinese, Jurchens, and Koreans—were the principal elements of Liaotong's frontier society. There were two distinctive ways of life, Chinese and Jurchen, separated by walls, forts, beacon-mounds, and natural barriers, all forming the frontier. On the Chinese side there were cities, offices, towns, shops, villages, and schools. Among major cities were Kaiyuan, Guangning, Shenyang, Fushun, and Liaoyang. A network of water and overland transportation lines and postal stations connected the region. Constructed for government purposes, such facilities encouraged trade and travel by common people. Within the frontier, the Chinese way of life took precedence because the Chinese inhabitants made up about 70 percent of the population. It was a Confucian-oriented society like any community in China proper.[19]

Inside the Chinese frontier there were also Korean and Jurchen residents, centering in the Dongning Guard. Although they had their own heritage, the Koreans for the most part partook in the Chinese way of life. They are the ancestors of the sizable Korean ethnic group in Manchuria today. Under the Ming government the Jurchens established settlements largely in the Kaiyuan and Liaoyang areas, with Anle zhou and Zizai zhou as centers. They intermingled with Chinese and Korean neighbors.[20]

On the Jurchen side of the frontier was a different world, less developed and sparsely populated. There were small, dispersed communities, with mud and thatched houses, in the hills, valleys, and forests. These communities were virtually isolated from one another because there were only trails for travel and transportation. Generally, a community had fewer than fifty farming households, composed of family members and slaves.[21] The small size of the community was due to several factors, among them geography because small hills and wooded areas were not amenable to large communities.

By the fifteenth century, farming had become the economy of the Jianzhou and Hūlun Jurchens, who further benefited from trade in frontier markets.[22] Economic development contributed to population growth and facilitated the rise of clan and tribal chiefs able to build fortresses as headquarters and control more land. By the next century they engaged in wars and acquired subjects from other groups. Combined, economic and political forces weakened the traditional clan structure. Common ancestry was no longer a bond among members of the same clan, whose conduct was determined by self-interest. For natural, economic, or political reasons, a big clan split into many branches. The Irgen Gioro, Gūwalgiya, Fuca, and Hešeri clans had 109, 101, 65, and 56 branches. Under their leaders, these offshoots acted independently, moved from one place to another, and founded pockets of settlers. Some were even able to control small clans in the area. Out of the 645 Manchu clans, there were 351 small clans, which bore rare surnames and mostly did not have a branch. A small area was inhabited by several clans or their branches.[23]

The *Genealogy of the Manchu Clans in the Eight Banners*, known in Chinese as *Baqi Manzhou shizu tongpu*, is an invaluable source. It records 1,170 Manchu, Mongol, Chinese, and Korean surnames, their origins and home villages, and brief biographies of their eminent members. The 645 Manchu clans spread over Manchuria and altogether had about 600 communities, which possibly combined into 548 places. Almost all such places were small, and in many cases were settled by people of different lineages. The area of the Four Hūlun Tribes was a center of habitation, where tribesmen from 232 clans founded 351 settlements, many of which were in Liaodong. Thirty-four Jurchen groups, with thirty-one surnames, settled in Fe Ala and Hetu Ala, both in the region now known as Xinbin. It was the first area that Nurhaci conquered and established as his base. In Fushun and its vicinity, including Sarhū and Jaifiyan, there were nineteen groups, with sixteen surnames. There were twenty-five Jurchen groups, with the same number of clan names, in the Shenyang area.[24] So many clans and settlements crowding in a limited area left no room for large communities. The following table summarizes the above discussion.

Table 4. Select Centers of Jurchen Settlements* Based on STTP

Location	Settlements	Surnames	Sample References
Fe Ala (27) and Hetu Ala (7)	34	31	4: 15a; 31: 8b; 18: 5a; 35: 11b
Fushun (4), Sarhū (4), Jaifiyan (11)	19	16	27: 9a; 11: 23b; 4: 14b
Shenyang	25	25	15: 18b; 6: 26b
Four Hūlun Area: Hada (61), Hoifa (56), Girin Ula (61), Ula (81), Yehe (98)	351**	232	9: 14a–20b; 52: 14a; 20: 20b; 35: 9b; 18: 3a, 6b

*See note 24 above. STTP stands for *Baqi Manzhou shizu tongpu*.
**There were 357 groups, of which six were Mongols. Two Mongol groups were among the Hada and Yehe Jurchens each, and one Mongol group among the Hoifa and Girin Ula each. The Mongols are excluded here.

The Jurchens observed ancestral customs and followed clan and tribal rules. They were horsemen, archers, warriors, shamanist believers, and wearers of queue braids. In 1587 Nurhaci created a primitive code outlawing burglary, fraud, and violence.[25] In time their traditions were undercut by Chinese political and cultural influences. Leaders received titles and offices from China through the guard-post and tributary systems. Unconsciously they were introducing Chinese influences. They brought to their communities even more influence from the frontier markets they were allowed to visit. Since they needed manpower to perform domestic and especially productive functions, the Jurchens acquired a large number of Chinese and Korean slaves by means of purchase and frontier raids. The slaves lived with their masters, some even establishing marital ties with the latter. Because of their cultural background and numerical strength, these slaves were able to introduce some Chinese words and their ways of doing things to the Jurchens.[26]

The Liaodong frontier hence was shaped by environment and history. It mainly consisted of two societies, Chinese and Jurchen. Despite differences and clashes such as cross-frontier raids and punitive campaigns, the two societies were interdependent.[27] For frontier peace, China exercised indirect control over Jurchens through the guard-post and tributary institutions. Frontier markets were places where the residents on both sides exchanged products and interacted. The Jurchen settlements gave refuge to Chinese deserters, fugitives, and overtaxed individuals. Optimum conditions on the Chinese side of the frontier attracted Jurchen immigrants. Frontiers, as William McNeill argues, are dynamic places for different cultures and for transforming them.[28] It was under these circumstances that the two societies influenced each other. As members of the Liaodong frontier society Chinese and Korean frontiersmen greatly furthered the sinicization of the Jurchens.

2. Frontiersmen

The word "frontiersmen" is defined here, in a broad sense, as people active on or near a frontier. All settlers in Liaodong could be considered frontiersmen, for the Ming dynasty treated the region as a frontier. Because of differing historical backgrounds, one should not associate them with frontiersmen in American history. There were Chinese, Korean, and Jurchen frontiersmen.

For all their differences, these Chinese, Korean, and Jurchen frontiersmen shared characteristics. They were energetic, restless, adaptable. What concerned them most was a better life. They enjoyed freedom, but remained under restrictions imposed by government or tribal authorities. To improve their lives they took part in frontier warfare. They put self-interest ahead of political loyalty.[29] Their lives were influenced by the frontier, but their activities molded society and transformed cultures.

For political and military purposes, Liaodong's Chinese frontiersmen were chiefly the creation of the Ming dynasty. There were old inhabitants and some Mongols who survived the dynastic transition from Yuan to Ming. Unfortunately, it is almost impossible to unravel their demographics. But, as mentioned, garrison soldiers, military farmers, and their families made up the majority of frontiersmen. The first Ming army arrived in Liaodong as early as 1371. It defeated the remnant Yuan forces, installed military farms, defended the region, and consolidated control. As Ming military households were hereditary units, when a soldier deserted, died, was disabled, or captured by tribesmen, his family was to provide a replacement.[30]

A large portion of Chinese frontiersmen consisted of exiles and their offspring. Because the Ming penal code was harsh and not concise, many people from regions throughout China were exiled to the frontiers. In 1392, for instance, Liaodong received 157 exiles from as many as 100 districts, belonging to twelve provinces. The Fan clan, which had been settled in the district of Leping, Kiangsi Province, for centuries, was an example. During his service as a vice magistrate in Hupei Province in the Hongwu period (1368–1398), Fan Yue, a clansman, and his family were banished to Shenyang. His descendants claimed Shenyang as their home locality. Fan Wencheng, a high official and influential advisor to Hong Taiji and the Shunzhi emperor, was six generations removed from Fan Yue.[31]

There were two categories of banishment. One was punishment imposed on the lawbreaker; the other extended to descendants. The Ming government began to send exiles to Liaodong during the early years of the dynasty. Later Ming rulers added banishment regulations to the penal code. There were twenty-two during the Hongwu reign, and 213 in 1550. Among them were robbing and instigating litigation. Regulations and related imperial decrees were so many that they filled two chapters in the Ming statutes. More people were caught up and exiled.[32]

Although their number was small, Chinese merchants were important frontiersmen. They exercised economic and political influence on the founding of the Qing dynasty. Merchants from Shansi Province were a case in point. They gathered in Fushun and traded with Nurhaci. One of them was of the Fan family, which became a powerful merchant house. Its members kept strong ties with the Qing imperial house and remained influential during the Qianlong period.[33] The Xiao family of Shantung Province was another example. It engaged in trade, using Liaoyang as its headquarters. The Xiaos seem to have brought in textiles, grain, and other profitable items from Shantung in exchange for such luxury goods as ginseng and furs. They likely

shipped commodities by sea, cheaper and faster than overland transportation through Shanhaikuan. When Nurhaci captured Liaoyang in
1621, the Xiaos became his adherents and were later organized into
the Chinese Banners. Xiao Cheng-en may have as a company leader
(*zuoling*). With imperial blessing. his son, Xiao Yongzao (1644?–1729),
became a grand secretary, the highest office in the Qing bureaucratic
hierarchy.[34]

Most Chinese frontiersmen, one should add, were the product of
compulsory migrations enforced by the Ming for many reasons. Beyond question, exiles were forced migrants. So were soldiers recruited
from various regions and dispatched to Liaodong. From diverse backgrounds, these migrants—convicts, soldiers, and others—reached
Liaodong and became frontiersmen. They brought together local traditions and shaped a new society, that of the frontiersman. Even contemporaries were heedful of this fact. While discussing customs of
inhabitants, compilers of the *Liaodong Gazetteer* observed: "The people are largely migrants."[35]

Genealogical records provide numerous cases of compulsory migrations. Liu Jie, a company commander from Kiangsi Province, was
sent to Liaodong in the beginning years of the Ming. He was founder
of the Liaodong branch of the Liu clan, with Shenyang as its base.
The Zu clan, with a long and notable pedigree, settled for centuries
in northern Anhui Province. Some clansmen joined the rebels under
Zhu Yuan-zhang (1328–1398), founder of the Ming dynasty. A successful army officer, Zu Shirong went to Liaodong in 1424 and became
guard commander of Ningyuan. He and his relatives founded a military house, whose members served in the Ming army to defend the
Liaodong frontier near to the end of the dynasty. Zu Dashou (d. 1656)
was a resourceful army officer, able to defeat the Manchus, including
Nurhaci, several times. He won respect from Hong Taiji, also a brilliant warrior. He and other members of the Zu clan were made high-
ranking officers in the Chinese Banner forces by Hong Taiji a few years
before the collapse of the Ming.[36]

The case of the Cao clan may interest both historians and students of Chinese literature. During the last years of the Yuan dynasty

clansmen armed themselves to protect their settlements in Yang-
zhou, northern Kiangsu Province, and became a detachment under
Zhu Yuan-zhang. Before long, Cao Jun was made a guard commander
for his good work and sent to Liaodong. He settled in Shenyang and
founded a branch of the clan. Descendants spread throughout Liaodong and repeatedly served as ranking officers of the Ming garrison
troops. Like many other clans Cao clansmen switched allegiance to
the Jurchens toward the end of the Ming and became imperial bondservants of the Qing. Cao Zhan (also known as Cao Xueqin, d. 1763),
a member of the fourteenth generation from the fourth branch and a
man of learning, was the author of the *Honglou meng* (*Dream of the
Red Chamber*), a famous novel in the vernacular style.[37]

For various reasons a great number of Chinese frontiersmen became Jurchen slaves. Indeed, a significant portion of the Jurchen
population was composed of slaves. In terms of their origins, there
were two kinds of slaves before the conquest of Fushun by Nurhaci
in 1618. One kind consisted of captives taken by the Jurchens during
frontier raids. The Yi dynastic records provide countless cases of such
slaves and their escape to Korea. When identified as Chinese, escap-
ees were sent back to the Ming authorities. The other kind of slaves
included fugitives, outcasts, displaced farmers, hard-pressed individuals, runaway soldiers, and military mutineers. They fled into the Jurchen settlements and were enslaved. Although they may have been
fewer in number than the captives, their cases cannot be overlooked.
While on a special mission to the Hūlun tribes in 1443, a Ming official met with many Chinese slaves, among them fugitives. When
they lost their land or were overburdened with government demands,
numerous Ming farmers crossed the frontier and ended up in slavery. Chinese soldiers ran away to the Jurchens in 1422 and 1432 and
were made slaves. During the late sixteenth and early seventeenth
centuries there were mutinies, and the mutineers fled to the Jurchen
world. While some possibly joined the Jurchen army, some were
made slaves.[38]

From 1618 onward Jurchen slaves mainly came from among the
conquered Liaodong residents. When he took Fushen, for example,

Nurhaci enslaved about 300,000 inhabitants and divided them among his followers. After conquering the Liaodong region, he founded military farms and hamlets, operated by the Chinese, who also provided the labor force for construction of Nurhaci's first two palaces. Hong Taiji, during his reign, repeatedly raided North China and brought back hundreds of thousands of Chinese captives. Although they were not frontiersmen, their presence expanded the enslaved population in the Liaodong region. There were also Chinese civilian and military defectors. Some were made slaves, while some joined Nurhaci's banner forces. A Ming official complained that army defectors taught the Jurchens the Chinese way of war. They and their families worked for Nurhaci and made up almost half the residents around his headquarters, as a Korean witness reported in 1619.[39]

In various capacities, Chinese frontiersmen and their offspring took part in sinicizing the Jurchens. Since the part played by farmers and traders has been discussed in Chapter III, there is no need for further discussion here. The following pages will concentrate on the enslaved frontiersmen because their role is important and worth exploring.

Enslaved Chinese frontiersmen played a unique part in spreading Chinese culture among the Jurchens. Some were freed by Hong Taiji for political and/or military reasons, and some were still in servitude. They are treated here as the same group, for they shared a similar experience. Whatever work they did for their masters or however long they stayed with them, they interacted with the Jurchens on the inside. They had another advantage. Since they were individuals of diverse social backgrounds, from the lower to upper classes, they were able to influence the Jurchens at both levels. The majority of slaves belonged to lower social groups. As stated, their labor was essential to the development of Jurchen agriculture. From them, the Jurchens learned Chinese farming methods and perhaps certain aspects of Chinese culture. They also contributed to the rise of the Chinese Eight Banners. In 1633 there were 1,580 Manchu households, each having ten or more able-bodied Chinese in servitude. Hong Taiji took one slave from each household and organized them into the first Chinese Banner units. More Chinese, including prisoners-of-war and Ming military defectors, were later added to the Chinese Banners, which were completed in 1642.[40]

Members of these Banners maintained working and marital relations with their Manchu counterparts.

There were countless cases of marriage between the Manchu and the Chinese in the banner system. Eidu was one of the five famous councilors of Nurhaci and the patriarch of the Niohuru clan. Four of his sons, in particular Celge (1589–1647) and Ilden (1596–1663), kept marital ties with Chinese bannermen. In three generations Celge's descendants gave away seven female members to young aristocratic Chinese bannermen. In four generations, five clanswomen of the Ilden branch married Chinese bannermen. With the progression of time, cases of mixed marriages increased in number. This trend may be detected from the Neyen branch of the Fuca clan. Its genealogy recorded clansmen's careers and marriages from the fourth to the tenth generations (1630s–1830s). Altogether male members married forty-two women from the Chinese Banners. The fourth and fifth generations had one case each. But the number increased to six, eleven, ten, and twelve, for the sixth to ninth generations, respectively. There was only one case in the tenth generation because toward its end the record offered little information about its members. The Sakda clan of the Hoifa branch provided similar evidence, for it too kept cross matrimonial bonds with the Chinese Banners. From the 1750s to the 1850s its members took ten Chinese wives and married off ten women to young Chinese bannermen. In a few cases, clansmen had Chinese concubines from outside the banners.[41]

Intermarriage created generations of people of mixed origins, readier than their forebears to adopt Chinese customs and values. It is true that the Chinese Banners were influenced politically and, to a certain extent, culturally by the Manchus. It is equally true that in a Manchu family, when submerged in its heritage, a Chinese wife was in no way to help sinicize the Manchus. But in a prevailing Chinese society, it should be noted, the Chinese Bannermen were able to retain their major traditional values, while the Manchus, in their own best interest, were steadily moving toward the mainstream. The addition of so many women, either from the Chinese Banners or from the ordinary Chinese families, to the Manchu community doubtlessly created a new social context that encouraged the maintenance of contact with Chinese and their ways of life.

The above-mentioned Sakda clan is a case in point. Chang-ling (1745–1817), a member of the eighth generation, took a Chinese bannerwoman as his second wife after the death of his first one, also a Chinese bannerwoman. The two wives mothered four sons, three of whom, including Zhong-xiang, the oldest, married women from the Chinese Banners. Zhong-xiang's son, grandson, and great-grandson were all born of Chinese mothers. The Fuca clan of the Neyen branch followed the same pattern. Fuliang, a clansman of the seventh generation, married a woman from a Chinese Banner. All of his three sons took brides of Chinese descent; one of them even married a third Chinese woman after the first two died. Fuliang had eight grandsons, six of whom took Chinese wives. Beyond question the ever-increasing number of children by Chinese mothers accelerated the process of sinicization. In the Sakda clan, for instance, from Zhong-xiang onward, all members, male and female, were given Chinese names. Generally each given name was composed of two characters, with one as the generation indicator. Moreover, every male descendant had a poetic courtesy name, a time-honored practice followed by educated Chinese.[42]

Among the enslaved Chinese frontiersmen were scholars, from whom Hong Taiji selected advisors and officials. Take Fan Wencheng, for example. An obscure scholar from the Fushun branch of the Fan clan. he was made a slave of the Bordered Red Banner when Nurhaci conquered his city. Eleven years later, he was freed with other scholars, such as Ning Wanwo (d. 1665), by Hong Taiji and entered government service. Because of his ability and loyalty, he became Hong Taiji's chief advisor. In all likelihood, it was through his advice that Hong Taiji built a Confucian temple in Shenyang in 1636 and sent him to offer sacrifices to the sage. This marked the beginning of the official Qing commitment to Confucianism. Fan was also an important strategist of Dorgon. Following Fan's counsel, Dorgon adapted the Qing government to the Chinese political system. Fan remained an influential official during the Shunzhi reign. By all accounts, he played a significant role in the sinicization of the Manchus.[43]

Another contributor to sinicization of the Manchus was Ning Wanwo, who became a slave when his hometown, Liaoyang, was captured by Nurhaci. After emancipation he served as a member of the

Literary Office. He advised Hong Taiji to adopt Chinese political and examination systems, and his advice was put into effect. During the next reign he was a grand secretary, was in charge of the metropolitan examinations three times, and translated Chinese books into Manchu. Among such books was the *Romance of the Three Kingdoms* (San-guo zhi yanyi), a popular Chinese historical fiction filled with tricks, maneuvers, heroic deeds, and Confucian ideals. The importance of its translation can be seen from the fact that its completion in 1650 was one of the reasons the throne awarded him a minor hereditary title. *Romance of the Three Kingdoms* soon became a sourcebook from which Manchu officials and officers drew inspiration for argument and action. Therefore "it is considered one of the most important works to the sinicization of the Manchus."[44]

Some educated Chinese slaves became tutors of imperial sons or grandsons. The case of Gong Zhenglu is worth mentioning. A tea trader active in Liaodong, he was captured by Jurchens and later served as Nurhaci's secretary. According to a Korean account dated 1595 he also taught classes to Nurhaci's children, possibly including the Chinese language and history. Hong Taiji was likely one of these students. In an expedition to North China the seventh son of Nurhaci, Abatai (1589–1646), brought back thousands of captives, most of whom were enslaved. He chose scholars from among them to teach his sons. Consequently, prominent poets, dramatists, and artists after the Chinese style emerged from the Abatai house. Of these talented clansmen, Yun-duan (also Yue-duan, 1671–1704) was the most famous.[45]

Through various means, Korean frontiersmen also contributed to sinicization of the Jurchen people. Because of treacherous geographic conditions Korea's northern territories were almost indefensible. The Tumen and Yalu Rivers that separated the country from northern tribesmen could not keep Korean frontiersmen in or Jurchen neighbors out. Jurchens, especially those of the three Jianzhou tribes, frequently crossed the frontier and established settlements. They and their descendants intermingled with the natives and became an important component of local population. From there they kept in touch with their kin across the frontier and passed onto them the Korean way of life, which was already sinicized. It was also easy for the Jurchens to raid Korean frontier communities for goods and slaves. There were many Korean slaves working for Jurchen captors. Moreover, hard-pressed, poor Korean frontiersmen left the country and labored for the Jurchens. The profitable sable fur trade attracted not only Korean fron-tiersmen but merchants from the southern part of the country. Korean traders sold oxen and iron farming tools to Jurchen partners for sable skins.[46]

For the security of its northern territory, the Yi dynasty made ef-forts to control the Jurchens near its frontier. The policy was worked out by the dynasty's founder, Yi Song-gye (r. 1392–1398). Born, grow-ing up, and serving in the northern region, he had acquired adequate experience to safeguard its frontier and deal with the Jurchens. Among the measures he undertook were immigration, trade, and ceremonial appointment of Jurchen chiefs. The Yi government invited immigrants and provided them with necessities and made frontier markets avail-able to Jurchen tribesmen. In the period 1432–1443, for instance, the Hūlun tribesmen dispatched 127 trade missions. From the beginning of the fifteenth century onward the Yi rulers frequently made Jurchen leaders royal bodyguards and showered them with clothing, servants, and luxury items. They performed ceremonial functions. As special appointees, they could resign at any time and their sons might receive the same offices. King Sejong (r. 1419–1450) made more than ninety such appointments. Another measure taken by the Yi dynasty was to encourage Jurchen chiefs to visit its royal court. There were more than 730 such visitors in the early reign (1455–1468) of King Sejo. Korea's aggressive Jurchen policy alarmed the Ming emperor, who issued de-crees to reprimand the Yi ruler twice within two months in 1459.[47]

Korea and China shared the same written language, Confucian values, and had similar political institutions. What Koreans transmit-ted to the Jurchen tribesmen eased the way for the latter to adopt Chi-nese culture. Jurchen settlements inside Korea and Korean captives, fugitives, and poverty-stricken frontiersmen among the Jurchens had the same experience. They created conditions for transmitting Korean culture to Jurchen society. Royal appointments by the Korean govern-ment and visits to the Yi Court by the tribal leaders provided a chan-nel for Jurchens to be receptive to Korea's culture. Of course, trade also created opportunities for Korean culture to permeate every stratum of the lives of the Jurchen people.

3. Transfrontiersmen

The Liaodong frontier created a group of individuals, whom one may define as transfrontiersmen. They crossed the border between one ethnic group and another, cutting their social roots and adopting local ways of life. The term, originating in African studies, relates to European maritime expansion, and may be applied to situations beyond Africa. The frontiersmen could become transfrontiersmen, but were not always identical. The distinction is that frontiersmen, under indigenous influence, did not lose touch with their social and cultural roots.[48]

Chinese and Korean sources show many cases of transfrontiersmen, undoubtedly of Chinese descent. These sources provide different kinds of cases. Chinese data contain information on transfrontiersmen mainly as a group, with stress on family or clan. Korean sources record individual transfrontiersmen, most of whom had been in long captivity by the Jurchens. Taken together, these complementary cases provide a clearer picture of an important aspect of the sinicization of the Manchus.

The best Chinese source for the transfrontiersmen is *Genealogy of the Manchu Clans in the Eight Banners*, a monumental compilation indispensable for the study of the Manchu aristocracy. Included are 247 Chinese surnames from 156 clans. The bearers of these surnames shared common characteristics. They were largely from the area between Shenyang and Liaoyang, which was where most of the transfrontiersmen came from. With few exceptions, the genealogical record does not specify when they began to collaborate with Nurhaci. Two scholars suggest that they went over to Nurhaci in 1603–1619.[49] Some members from these Chinese clans held high offices in the Eight Banners and the government; most served merely as warriors or attendants and minor officials in the Office of the Imperial Household. The Qing government treated them as Manchus, but the genealogical compilation groups them under the Chinese section (chapters 74–80). Many of their descendants took Manchu names.

There were more than a dozen Chinese families or clans dispersed among the Jurchens. Perhaps for free land these families moved from the Chinese side of the frontier to the wild valleys and forests on the other side. In time they were surrounded by Jurchen settlers as a result of the latter's subsequent southern migrations. Eighty Jurchen clans and two Chinese families, Ya and Luo, resided in Ula, an area around today's Jilin City in Jilin Province. Seventy-one Jurchen clans, together with eleven Chinese households, spread over the valley of the Long White Mountains. Zhanhe, a small region near Xinbin, was crowded with ten Jurchen communities and two Chinese families, You and Zhao. Ningguta was the homeplace of the Ni, Liu, and Yu sibs, which mingled with twenty-four Jurchen groups.[50]

Amid the Jurchen tribesmen these Chinese families became enclaves. A case can be made that from the beginning for three or more generations, members of these families did not take Chinese-style names. The Wang branch in the valley of the Long White Mountains was started by Sungta, a Manchu name. For four generations from Sungta's son onward, all six members of the family took Manchu names. Another case was Gahana, also a Manchu name, the founder of the Yu clan in Ningguta. All family members, from sons to great-grandsons, adopted Manchu-style names.[51] Since they had adopted the Jurchen way of life, some were no longer farmers, as were most Chinese. Now they served as chief herdsmen, horse groom supervisors, and bow-making inspectors.[52] These assignments were pertinent to the Jurchen traditions; their low official positions may suggest that they had kept in touch with their counterparts—Jurchen commoners. Although they were immersed in the Jurchen way of life, it is safe to infer that their ancestors, as pioneers, introduced Chinese culture to their Jurchen neighbors.

Table 5. Chinese Enclaves among Jurchen Settlements*

Location	Jurchen Settlements	Chinese Enclaves	Source: *STTP*
Zhanhe	10 settlements: Šumuru, Tatara, Gorolo, etc.	You and Zhao	6: 22a, 27a; 11: 22b; 32: 1a–6a; 79: 6a, 6b.
Ligiya-holo	2 settlements: Joogiya and Ligiya	Liogiya	31: 13a; 33: 5a–7b; 57: 3a, 3b.
Long White Mountains	71 settlements: Irgen Gioro, Wanggiya, Joogiya, etc.	Liu, Li, Zhao, Dai, Zhu, Ren, Ji, Qin, Wang, Yang	15: 7a, 9b; 28: 20a, 21b; 31: 10b; 74: 7a; 75: 7a, 10a; 76:14b; 77: 16a, 17b; 19a, 21a; 78: 2b–3a; 79: 1b, 3b
Ningguta	24 settlements: Magiya, Ujala, Ningguta, etc.	Yu , Ni, Liu	7: 12b; 30: 18a; 41: 1a–5b; 77: 11b; 78: 3a; 79: 2b
Shang-yang bao	1 settlement, Gūwalgiya	Lü	4: 13b–14a; 78: 10b
Sintun	1 settlement, Gūwalgiya	Liogiya	4: 18b; 57: 3b
Ula	80 settlements: Fuca, Nara, Usu, etc	Ya, Luo	79: 4b, 5b
Wang-to-lo-shu	2 settlements: Bayara and Wanggiya	Li	38: 13b; 75: 7b

*This table contains the aforesaid Chinese enclaves and other cases. The references mentioned in the table can be compared with notes 50–53 in this chapter.

Even in the Manchu section of the aforesaid genealogical compilation one can identify transfrontiersmen of Chinese origin. The Lio-giya sib, listed as a Manchu clan name, consisted of nine branches, two of which were unmistakably Chinese. The branch under Lio Sang-c'ai (Liu Shangcai in Chinese) was in a small valley with two Manchu communities. Its members joined Nurhaci in the early years of his rise to power. Lio Jy-heng (Liu Zhiheng), patriarch of the other Chinese family, resided in another small place, also the home of a Gūwal-giya branch. Both Lio families were obscure because the genealogical record provides only sketchy information.[53] This does not obviate their status as transfrontiersman, however.

Korean records contain the names of many individual and obscure Chinese transfrontiersmen, mainly second- or third-generation captives. Created under coercive circumstances, they adopted the Jurchen way of life; some were even assimilated. But the first-generation captives, one may say, had brought Chinese customs to their captors. For freedom, they crossed the Korean frontier to escape their Jurchen masters. One case involved twenty-one people who fled to Korea. They did not understand Chinese; nor did they remember home villages or the names of their fathers. This perplexed Korean frontier officials, who had to decide whether these people were Chinese.[54] Beyond dispute they were transfrontiersmen.

Whatever assignment they received and however obscure, these transfrontiersmen worked for the cause of the Manchus. The case of Loohan is a perfect example. He was the patriarch of the Liu clan in the valley of the Long White Mountains and joined Nurhaci in early stage of the latter's career. For five generations he and his offspring took Manchu names. A warrior and bodyguard, he was so loyal that to defend Nurhaci he fought off an attacker barehanded and was seriously injured. To show his gratitude, Nurhaci granted him the status of a member of the collateral line of the imperial house, while the Shunzhi emperor gave him a posthumous title.[55]

Individual transfrontiersmen deserve study because they provide intriguing cases helpful for analyzing their contribution to the sinicization of the Jurchens and their successors, the Manchus. First is Dahai (Taehae in Korean), a famous linguist serving as Nurhaci's secretary who translated Chinese books into Manchu. Under Hong Taiji he improved the Manchu script, worked in the Literary Office, and carried out missions. Although the genealogical compilation registers him as a Giolca clansman of Manchu origin, there is reason to call this into question. Contemporary Korean sources, especially the book by Yi Min-hwan, identify Dahai as a native of Liaodong, namely, a person of Chinese origin. A scholar-official, Yi was sent with the Korean army to help the Ming against Nurhaci at the Battle of Sarhū in 1619. With the defeat of the Korean army, he was imprisoned for nineteen months by the Jurchens. A keen observer, he made friends with his jailers, from whom he acquired much information. He regarded Dahai as Chinese. Recent studies also consider Dahai the descendant of a transfrontiersman.[56] The location of the Giolca settlement leads to the same conclusion. The Giolcas had long resided in the Xinbin area, a frontier region near Fushun, a prosperous frontier market and important Ming garrison post.

Dahai's bilingual capacity furnishes another clue to the transfrontiersman's background of the Giolca family. According to his biographies, Dahai had mastered both Manchu and Chinese at nine *sui* (age eight). It is highly unlikely that he could have achieved this without a Chinese background. He rendered Chinese works on the penal code, military science, history, and more, into Manchu, all very difficult to translate. On several occasions he was instrumental in bringing Chinese defenders to terms, for he could speak the language. Combined with information from the Korean data, this ability proved that he was descended from a transfrontiersman of Chinese origin.[57]

Dahai was a transfrontiersman of great importance. He mastered the language of the Chinese people and showed appreciation of their traditions, such as their fashion of dress. While many other transfrontiersmen kept in touch with Jurchen commoners, he transmitted Chinese culture to their leaders. He had begun his career as a translator during the reign of Nurhaci. He translated Chinese books at the order of Nurhaci and Hong Taiji for administrative and military purposes. In his study of Mongol rule in China, Herbert Franke considers translation an important step to acculturation.[58]

Another individual was Liu Xingzuo (d. 1630), a warrior once trusted by Nurhaci and on China's most wanted list. To the Manchus he was known as Lio Aita, while the Koreans referred to him as Yu Hae

(Liu Hai in Chinese). Suffice it to say that these names manifest the controversial nature of the person. Since his early history was wrapped in myth, it is difficult to identify his ethnic origin. Fortunately, one can tap information from a few valuable and less-utilized sources.

It is likely that Liu was from a frontiersman's family in Kaiyuan. He was the second son and had five brothers. At an early age he drifted from the Chinese side of the frontier and lived with the Jurchens. It seems that at first he was an attendant to Nurhaci and then served him as a ranking officer and an advisor on Chinese and Korean affairs. All his brothers also worked for Nurhaci, perhaps after his rise to power. Liu and Dahai are frequently mentioned in Korean records as Nurhaci's interpreters and assistants. His devotion to the Manchu cause was recognized by Hong Taiji with the bestowal of imperial credentials. Obviously, Liu was a transfrontiersman. He finally decided to return to the Chinese world because, as he indicated in a communication to Korean officials, he disapproved of the destructiveness of the Jurchens. But the reason for his decision, as Hong Taiji revealed in 1635, was the abusive conduct of Daišan, the powerful senior prince and Liu's master.[59]

There are reasons to believe that Kūrcan (d. 1633), a member of the Niohuru clan, was from a transfrontier family. His ancestors originated in the valley of the Long White Mountains, but later migrated to Yengge. Since the new settlement was near both Kaiyuan and Fushun, there is no doubt that they were exposed to Chinese culture. Some clansmen were active in—and received protection from—the Hada, a Hūlun tribe in close touch with China. It is possible that in these circumstances the Niohuru branch was transformed into a transfrontier group. Under their leader, Lailuhūn, these Niohurus joined Nurhaci when the latter took up arms against the Ming in the 1580s. Kūrcan, grandson of Lailuhūn and fond of learning, attracted the attention of Nurhaci, who subsequently raised him. He later became a linguist and served Nurhaci as a secretary and advisor. With the rise of Hong Taiji as the new ruler, Kūrcan worked in the Literary Office with Dahai and a few others. He could speak Chinese and loved Chinese culture. Several times he and Dahai advised Hong Taiji to replace the Manchu style of dress with that of Chinese. It is only natural that Hong Taiji considered this advice inappropriate. Moreover, Kūrcan was a close friend of Lio Aita, identified above. He was perhaps the only person to show confidence in Lio Aita even after the latter had become an enemy desperately wanted dead or alive by Hong Taiji. Kūrcan was finally executed because of his special relationship with Lio Aita.[60]

The Tong and Shi clans, perhaps the best examples of transfrontiersmen, are worth looking into. Both were characterized by controversial ethnic origins and ambiguous political loyalty. Likely the problem resulted from the fact that they had mixed Sino-Jurchen origins, frequently crossed frontiers, and changed their names. The Tong clan appeared in Liaodong around the fifth century and from the beginning intermixed with non-Chinese frontiersmen, such as the Jurchens. By the early Ming dynasty the clan spilled over both sides of the frontier and intermingled with Mongol and Korean components. Its Jurchen members largely bore the surname Tunggiya and dispersed to twenty-nine locations. One may divide them into two branches, the Jianzhou and the Nurkal. The Jianzhou branch covered the line from Menggetimur to Nurhaci. It was not until after the founding of the frontier kingdom, Later Jin, that Nurhaci adopted a new surname, Aisin Gioro. The other Tunggiyas belonged to the Nurkal branch.[61] The two branches were related to each other and eventually intermingled.

Inside the Chinese ethnic line, the Tongs comprised dozens of branches scattered throughout the Liaodong region. The most influential branch was the merchant house founded by Darhaci, known as Tong Dali in Chinese. He first settled in Kaiyuan, center of the Sanwan Guard, and then moved to Fushun, a meeting place of Chinese and Jurchens. In all likelihood, he was a sinicized Jurchen, despite the argument that he was of Chinese origin. As indicated, Darhaci was a Jurchen word. His Chinese name, Dali, meaning attainment of decorum, fits in the pattern of names often given to frontier tribal chiefs by the Ming. He, his son, and a grandson all married women nee Wang, a surname acquired by many Jurchens serving in the Ming government. More importantly, Chinese clans in Liaodong usually traced their pedigrees centuries back, but Tong Dali was the progenitor in the Tong genealogy. Like many other Jurchen leaders, he was recruited as an official by the Ming in the middle of the Hongwu reign to carry out diplomatic and military missions among the Jurchens. These duties were normally performed by Jurchen collaborators. After examining more than twenty Tong genealogical records, a Tong clansman recently confirmed that the clan was of Jurchen origin and composed of eleven groups with different names.[62] Doubtlessly they were transfrontiersmen. But after living among the Chinese for centuries, they had participated in Chinese ways of life and considered themselves Chinese.

One of Tong's most prominent descendants was Tong Deng (1526–1580s), a member of the Liaoyang branch founded in the early 1490s. Obtaining a military *jinshi* degree in 1553, Tong Deng served as the brigade general (*Zongbing guan*) in three regions, including Liaodong, and won many honors. Four of his sons were also warriors defending Liaodong from attacks by frontier tribes. Most of his descendants later joined the Nurhaci camp, served as Qing high officials, and even established nuptial relations with the imperial clan. According to a recent study, Nurhaci's first wife, Hahana Jacing (Tong Chunxiu in Chinese), was the daughter of Tong Deng. She gave birth to Cuyen (1580–1615) and Daišan, the first and second sons of Nurhaci. It is possible that she and her family reinforced what Nurhaci had learned from the Fushun frontier market about Chinese customs and language.[63]

But the line between the Tongs on the two sides of the frontier was never clear-cut since there were Tunggiyas who carried the name Tung (Tong in Chinese). Some Tong clansmen lived in the neighborhood of Jurchen villages. Tung Ki (Tong Qi) settled in Yarhū, the homeplace of sixteen Jurchen villages with different surnames. Tung Jy-siyan (Tong Zhixian) resided among seventy Jurchen settlements in the valley of the Long White Mountains. In the meantime, on the Chinese side, there were Tunggiya clansmen who under the name Tong inhabited the Dongning Guard with other Jurchens. Some Tunggiyas, also adopting the name Tong, served the Ming government as Jurchen-language specialists. As a consequence, some historians believe that the Tongs were descended from the Tunggiya clan, namely, of Jurchen origin.[64] All the above facts lead to the same conclusion: the Tongs were transfrontiersmen.

During the late Ming period the ethnic origin and political loyalty of the Tongs became a concern in official circles. The case of Tong Yangxing, a successful merchant, testified to the fact that the Tongs did not regard political loyalty as a serious matter, willing to work for either side of the frontier. From his Fushun settlement he supported

Nurhaci with money, materiel, and perhaps military intelligence. Imprisoned on a charge of treason in 1616, he was soon bailed out. When tipped off on the government's plan of persecution two years later, he jumped bail, joined Nurhaci, and won the latter's trust. Many clansmen, including his cousin, Tong Yangzhen (later Tong Yang-zheng; Tung Yangjeng in Manchu, d. 1621) followed suit. They fought for Nurhaci and contributed to his success.[65] The most controversial figure was Tong Bunian (1588–1625), a clansman of the Liaoyang branch. He earned his *jinshi* degree in 1616 and was a dutiful local administrator. Perhaps a victim of political struggle, he was imprisoned for three years and forced to commit suicide. During his confinement he submitted three memorials in defense against the charge of treason. While arguing for his father's innocence, Tong Guoqi (1609–1684) accepted Qing appointment as a regional administrator and felt proud because many clansmen served as high officials under the Manchus. Of such clansmen, Tong Yangzhen's branch was prominent during the Kangxi reign, for Tong Tulai (d. 1658), his son and a brave warrior, was the maternal grandfather of the emperor.[66]

The Tongs had been affiliated with Chinese Banners for decades because clansmen administered the Chinese subjects in the newly conquered areas. In 1688 a son of Tong Tulai petitioned the throne to transfer the Tong clansmen to the Manchu Banners, for they were of Jurchen descent. The Kangxi emperor switched the branch of Tong Tulai to the Manchu Bordered Yellow Banner. Since it was among the Three Superior Banners (*shang sanqi*) under direct command of the throne, the Manchu Bordered Yellow Banner carried more prestige. The other Tongs, too many to be reassigned, remained in the Chinese Banners.[67] This decision fitted in with the case of the Tong clan because as transfrontiersmen the Tongs belonged to both the Chinese and Manchu worlds and were assigned to the banners the same way.

The impact of the Tong connection on the early Qing deserves discussion. Of clansmen, Tong Yangxing stood out because he supervised the casting of cannons after the Ming model and organized the first artillery unit. Under his command this unit applied Chinese artillery warfare to defeat the Ming army. As stated, Kangxi's mother was the daughter of Tong Tulai. Although she died when Kangxi was only nine (ten *sui*), she seems to have influenced his attitude toward the Chinese and their culture. He took two consorts from her clan. One of them won his favor and was made empress. In his harem there were fifteen other consorts of Chinese descent, the largest number in Qing palace history. Of his twenty-four grown-up sons, seven were born to Chinese consorts. Kangxi was the first Qing ruler to found the palace school to educate imperial sons, from which emerged subsequent Qing emperors. Its curriculum included Chinese classics, philosophy, and history. When internalized with Chinese culture during childhood, Qing rulers sometimes even mistook Chinese tradition for Manchu heritage. Most importantly, Kangxi was also the first Qing emperor to visit Confucius's birthplace and prostrated himself in the sage's temple. He set the model for his grandson, the Qianlong emperor, who paid eight personal visits ro the Confucius temple in the sage's birthplace.[68] For all their political implications, these imperial visits served as an incentive to spread Confucianism among the Manchus.

Like the Tongs, the Shi (Ši in Manchu) clan had been active in Manchuria since the fifth century. Perhaps it was of Chinese origin, but in the frontier settlement it was enriched by non-Chinese elements. It is possible that for convenience some sinicized Jurchens adopted Shi as their surname.[69] With such complicated ethnic components, the Shi clansmen served under Chinese or non-Chinese frontier authorities.

Central figures of the Shi clan were Shi Tingzhu (Ši Ting-ju in Manchu, 1599–1661), an officer in the Ming garrison army in Guang-ning, and his two brothers. When Guang-ning was attacked by Nurhaci in 1622, the Shi brothers defected and later became high officers in the Chinese Banner forces. Of clan members, Shi Tingzhu and his descendants were prominent because of their successful careers. Shi Tingzhu was also associated with the application of Chinese artillery warfare. At first he served as an associate under Tong Yangxing. After the latter's death he took full charge of the division to fight for the Qing cause. In 1688, his third son, Hūwašan (Huashan in Chinese, d. 1695), petitioned the throne that the Shi clan descended from the Gūwalgiyas in Suwan, a place southwest of Jilin City. From the second half of the fifteenth century on, the petition states, the Ming made his ancestors officials of the guard-post system. His grandfather, Šihan (Shi Han in Chinese), moved the family to Liaodong and adopted the Chinese surname "Shi." To fullfil the dying commands of Šihan, the memorial goes on, the Shi clansmen joined Nurhaci. Hence Hūwašan petitioned the throne to transfer his clan to a Manchu Banner from the Chinese Plain White Banner, to which they had belonged. The court agreed to register the clansmen as Manchus, but were to remain in the Chinese forces.[70] The decision fit their transfrontiersmen's origin.

There is reason to believe Hūwašan's statement, although some scholars have raised questions. While chronicling the takeover of Guang-ning by Nurhaci, early Qing sources such as the veritable records mention one of Shi Tingzhu's full brothers as of Jurchen origin. Recent studies reach the same conclusion. Hūwašan's marriage may help support his claim because he was the son-in-law of Prince Dodo, fifteenth son of Nurhaci. From a legal perspective, one may believe the credibility of Hūwašan's memorial. The memorialist could not afford to risk his career or even his life by falsifying his ancestry, for false statements were severely punished.[71]

The Tong and Shi cases were not unique because a similar story was provided by Wang Guoguang (d. 1670). Descended from an obscure Wanggiya branch, the Wangs crossed the frontier, possibly in the early sixteenth century, settled in the Kaiyuan area, and served in the Ming army. In 1619, they switched allegiance to Nurhaci and were made members of the Chinese banner forces by Hong Taiji. Wang Guoguang was the first in the family to rise to eminence. Born a warrior, he began his military career at fourteen *sui* (age thirteen), winning many battles and holding high offices under three emperors from Hong Taiji to Kangxi. His son, also a brave soldier, played a role in the suppression of the Rebellion of the Three Feudatories and twice took part in the expeditions under Kangxi's personal command against the Dzungar Mongols. With imperial blessing the Wang sibs were reassigned to the Manchu Plain Red and Bordered White Banners in 1752.[72]

Korean transfrontiersmen had a role in transmitting Chinese ways of life to the Jurchens because of the close similarity between Korean and Chinese political institutions, religious and ethical concepts, and arts and letters. A large number of Korean transfrontiersmen originated in Korea's northern and northwestern regions, where Chinese influence was strong. Through frontier raids they were seized by the Jurchens as captives. After long captivity they willingly stayed with the Jurchens. They and their descendants became transfrontiersmen, some of whom were relocated in the area between Shenyang and Kaiyuan. Of the Korean transfrontiersmen, Chong Myong-su (fl. 1620s–1650s) was the most prominent. A slave in a local government, he was carried away as a captive by the invading Jurchens in 1627. Shortly afterward he won the trust of Hong Taiji, took the Manchu name Gūlmahūn, and served in the Literary Office. Because he served the Qing loyally and dealt with Korea arbitrarily, he was so hated by the Korean liaison office in Shenyang that two staff members plotted to kill him. But they failed and were executed by the Manchus.[73]

Korean fugitives, deserters, and other discontented individuals were also a source for transfrontiersmen. They crossed the Korean frontier and stayed in Liaodong, most likely the Dongning Guard, intermingling with Jurchen neighbors. One may believe that they made up the forty-three Korean clans in the Eight Banners. In 1589 a man named Chong, evidently of aristocratic origin, fled to the Jurchen region from Korea's capital because of a judicial case. All four of his sons served in the Jurchen army. He attuned himself to his host's customs so well that even other Koreans mistook him for a Jurchen when they met him in 1619. A witness testified that there were more than thirty Korean families residing in the "Korean Village" outside Nurhaci's headquarters. By early 1625 two young Korean nobles, Han In and his cousin Han Ui, joined the Jurchens because their families were involved in a coup and defeated. Nurhaci gave them offices, brides, servants, and land.[74]

Matrimonial relations seem to have been another source for Korean transfrontiersmen. Since its beginning the Yi dynasty had used marriage as a means of controlling Jurchen tribesmen along the northern frontier. Jurchen frontiersmen and immigrants were allowed to take Korean wives. Yi rulers also gave brides to Jurchen chieftains who served as their bodyguards or visited their courts. When staying in Korea, descendants of such unions were considered Korean subjects. After defeating Korea in 1637, Hong Taiji demanded their repatriation. Under pressure, Korea returned them but refused to let their Korean mothers go with them. Naturally these repatriates became transfrontiersmen.[75]

Assimilated Jurchens made up a special source for Korean transfrontiersmen As stated, Jurchens constituted a significant component of Korea's population along the northern frontier. In time they were assimilated and played a role in the founding of the Yi dynasty. Some served the Yi as high officials. For a variety of reasons many rejoined the Jurchens. Mafuta, a Tatara clansman, offers the most telling case. He and his kin crossed the Tumen River, settled inside Korea, and became its subjects. Under Mafuta they rejoined the Manchus around 1637. Since then they had cut off their social and cultural roots in Korea and followed the Manchu way. During the early Qing he became a ranking official and frequented Korea to carry out diplomatic missions. Mafuta and his men were certainly transfrontiersmen.[76]

There are numerous such cases in the *Genealogy of the Manchu Clans in the Eight Banners*. A great number of these Koreans joined the Jurchens and many adopted Manchu names and customs. All fought for the Manchu cause, even against their homeland. A member of a certain Chang family gave up his Korean name by adopting a new one, Dangini, and so did his offspring. Yatu, a third-generation member of the Chang family, served as commander (*dutong*, lieutenant general) of the Manchu Bordered Yellow Banner in 1706–1710. He lost imperial favor because he was involved in the succession struggle among the princes during the late Kangxi reign.[77]

The Han clan serves as another example. Under Han Un and his brother Han Ni, the clan joined Nurhaci and was organized into the banner forces. Although at first its members made up only half a company in the Manchu Plain Red Banner, by 1694 this small unit grew into a full company, whose command was inherited by the clansmen. Many members received high office and hereditary titles.[78]

Members of the Kim family were perhaps the most successful of Korean transfrontiersmen. Under its chief, Sindari (fl. 1620s–1640s), a Manchu name, the family collaborated with Hong Taiji in 1627, and Sindari reported to Hong Taiji all the plots his fellow Koreans developed against the Manchus. He and his descendants were bondservants attached to the Office of the Imperial Household, and most of them adopted Manchu names. They commanded two Korean companies. One of his grandsons, Canming (c. 1670s–1742), deserves special attention. In 1681, Canming was selected to attend a prince. Because he was a fine archer, he rose to a higher position. By the end of the Kangxi period he was made a second-rank imperial bodyguard and in 1735 a Chamberlain of the Imperial Bodyguard (*ling-shiwei nei-dachen*), a position usually held by Manchu nobles. He continued enjoying imperial trust in the Qianlong reign. His long service, altogether about sixty years, must have had some influence on the Qing court. This is attested to by the fact that when he was mortally ill the throne dispatched an imperial son to visit him and make arrangements for his funeral. Canming's cousin was Qianlong's favorite consort. Another cousin, Kim Kan (d. 1794), was entrusted by Qianlong to supervise the compiling and printing of the *Complete Library of Four Treasuries*, or *Siku quanshu*, the greatest literary project of the Qing.[79]

To end this chapter one may emphasize a few points. Because of geographical conditions and historical processes, Manchuria was a frontier, a meeting place of Chinese and non-Chinese cultures. Liaodong was China's administrative and cultural center for the region. There were Chinese, Korean, and Jurchen inhabitants, but the Chinese population dominated. The Chinese were under a centralized and bureaucratic administrative structure, Confucian-oriented, and protected by natural and artificial barriers. They lived mainly in villages, towns, and cities. Korean settlers concentrated in the southeast. Their way of life much resembled that of the Chinese. Under hereditary chieftains the Jurchens lived in small, dispersed communities. By various means they kept in contact with Chinese and Korean settlers and adopted their skills, technological know-how, and values.

One may regard all settlers in Liaodong as frontiersmen. Their activities shaped frontier life and contributed to sinicizing the Jurchens. The distinction between frontiersmen and transfrontiersmen is not always clear, but both contributed to great economic and technological changes among the Jurchens in the sixteenth and early seventeenth centuries. As slaves they brought Chinese farming methods to the base of Jurchen society. Farming was essential to the Jurchens and laid the foundation of Nurhaci's political power. From this background the Jurchens were able to plant cotton, tend silkworms, and produce silk goods. The Chinese blacksmiths Nurhaci acquired helped the Jurchens smelt iron and finally manufacture cannons, a technology hitherto monopolized by the Ming army.[80] In 1619, a Korean eyewitness testified that the blacksmiths were the most skillful craftsmen that Nurhaci possessed. As advisors, language specialists, or high officials, the frontiersmen and transfrontiersmen took Chinese values and ideals to the Jurchen ruling classes. Some even established matrimonial bonds with the imperial family and brought forth princes of mixed origins. The Kangxi emperor was one of them.

Notes

1. The prehistorical cultures that met in Manchuria include the culture of the Yellow River valley, the culture of the Mongolian desert and steppe, the culture of the Pacific Coast, and the taiga culture around Lake Baikal. See Chapter I, note 8, especially Chang's studies. For the quote, see Lattimore, *Studies in Frontier History*, 325.

2. For the definition of Franke and Twitchett, see *The Cambridge History of China*, volume 6, p. 9. For Lattimore, see his *Studies in Frontier History*, 469 and 489; and his *Inner Asian*, 238–42; *The Encyclopaedia of the Social Sciences* (New York: Macmillan Company, 1935, 15 volumes), 6: 500–506. For some other views, see Ladis K. D. Kristof, "The Nature of Frontiers and Boundaries," *Annals of the Association of American Geographers*, 49. 3 (1959): 269–70, especially 273; David J. Weber and Jane M. Rausch, eds., *Where Cultures Meet: Frontiers in Latin American History* (Wilmington, DE: Scholarly Resources Inc., 1994), xiv. According to Peter Perdue, the term can be defined either as "a broad zone of multiple cultural interactions or a linear border dividing two states." But he believes that in the case of China it has both connotations. See his *China Marches West*, 520.

3. For their differences, see Kristof, "The Nature of Frontiers and Boundaries," 269–82. For a fine analysis of the term "boundary," see Nicola Di Cosmo and Don J. Wyatt, eds., *Political Frontiers, Ethnic Boundaries, and Human Geographies in Chinese History* (London and New York: RoutledgeCurzon, 2003), 1–6.

4. For the relations between China and Manchuria before 1368, see Li, "Manchuria," 226–49.

5. For the system, see *Mingshi*, 8. 90: 2193. But two other sources provide different figures for the subunits. See Li, *Mingdai Dongbei*, 39; Lü Simian, *Zhongguo zhidu shi* (Shanghai: Shanghai jiaoyu chuban she, 1985), 794–95.

6. These two offices were introduced in 1436 and 1550. See *Mingshi*, 6. 73: 1777 and 1773. For a detailed discussion of the administrative institutions in the Liaodong area, see Yang, *Liaodong dusi*, 8–37. For the Commission's civilian functions, see Li Sanmou, "Mingdai Liaodong dusi weisuo di xing-zheng zhineng," *Liaoning shifan daxue xuebao (Sheke ban)*, 6 (1989): 73–77.

7. For the beginnings and development of the Nurkal Military Commission, see Yang, Yuan, and Fu, *Mingdai nuergan*, ch. 3; for the creation of many guards and their locations, see ibid., chs. 4–7.

8. For its population in Han times, see *Hanshu*, comp. Ban Gu (Taipei: SPPY ed., 1965, 8 volumes), 4. 28b: 8b. For the rise of the Chinese population in Liaodong, see Yang Yang, *Dongbei shikang* (Taipei: Taiwan Xuesheng shuju, 1993), 283–89. For the early fourth-century Chinese migrants, see James Lee, "Migration and Expansion in Chinese History." In William H. McNeill and Ruth S. Adams, eds., *Human Migration: Patterns and Policies* (Bloomington, IN: Indiana University Press, 1978), 29.

9. *Liaodong zhi*, first completed in 1443, reported that there were about 125,000 soldiers of all kinds, while their families and common people numbered 281,887. See ibid., 2.3: 1a–5a. Completed in 1565, its revised and enlarged edition is entitled *Quan Liao zhi*. It provides the figure of 381,532 (6. 2: 1a–6), which slightly differs from the summary it gives (6. 2: 1a), and also from the number given by Yang, *Liaodong dusi*, 111–14.

10. According to Liu Hanruo, by the mid-Ming period its population possibly reached three million. See his "Dongbei renkou shi chutan," *Xuexi yu tansuo*, 6 (1983): 35. This figure seems exaggerated. A high official reported that in 1622 as many as one million Chinese tried to flee to China proper from Manchuria. See *MSL*, vol. 18, Tianqi reign, 20: 19b, 2/3/renxu. This is also an inflated figure. But two million people at its height seems reasonable.

11. These figures are based on the registers of individual guards. See *Liaodong zhi*, 2. 3: 1a–5a, and *Quan Liao zhi*, 6. 2: 1a–6a. Although more than 100 years apart, these two sources occasionally provide the same figures. This suffices to indicate their faults.

12. For these exiles, see Yang Yang, Sun Yuchang, and Zhang Ke, "Mingdai liuren zai Dongbei," *Lishi yanjiu* 4 (1985): 54–66; Yang Yang, "Mingdai nanfang shaoshu minzu zheyu Liaodong qing-kuang," *Chong-yang minzu xueyuan xuebao* 3 (1987): 50–53.

13. For these 1635 exiles, see *MSL*, vol. 18, Xuande reign, 45: 6, 3/7/wuchen. In one case, out of 170 exiles, only 50 people survived the harsh journey. See ibid., vol. 21, Xuande reign, 107: 3a–b, 8/11/jihai.

14. For He Qin, see *DMB*, 1: 509–10; *Mingshi*, 24. 283: 7264–65.

15. There were numerous southward migrations. See *CKMT*, 467–97.

16. For the figure of about 7,500 people, see *CWS*, vol. 2, Reign of Sejong, 20: 538, 5/4/urhae. For the number of households, see *CWS*, vol. 6, Reign of Munjong, 9: 419, 1/8/kapsul. Kawachi Yoshihiro estimates that each Jurchen family had about seven members. See his *Mindai Joshin-shi*, 37. According to Li, *Mingdai Dongbei* (p. 163), each household had about six people. For the 1572 case, see *Wugong lu*, 4. 11: 997b. For the 1580 case, see *MTTS*, 119.

17. For the army under Wang Tai, see *Wugong lu*, 4.11: 996b. For the warriors under the two Yehe leaders, see ibid., 4.11: 1015a. For warriors under Bujantai, see *Nuer-haqi shilu*, 2: 6a.

18. For these Koreans, see *CWS*, vol. 7, Reign of Sejo, 34: 642, 10/8/imo. The memorialist mentioned that the first figure was taken from the *Liaodong zhi.*

19. For walls, forts, and beacon-mounds, see Zhi Xijun, "Mingdai Liaodong fangwei tixi ti jianshe," *Dongbei difang shi yanjiu* 1 (1991): 55–57. For the transportation network, see Yang, *Liaodong dusi*, 156–68. For the role played by the Chinese in the population, see *Liaodong zhi*, 1. 1: 21a.

20. For the importance of the Koreans and Jurchens in the entire population, see *Liaodong zhi*, 1. 1: 21a. For the Korean settlements, see *CWS*, vol. 7, Reign of Sejo, 34: 642, 10/8/imo. For the Jurchen settlements, see Zhu Chengru, "Mingdai Liaodong Nüzhen ren yu Hanren zaju zhuang-kuang di lishi kaocha,"*Liaoning shida xuebao: Shehui kexue ban* 1 (1984): 78–84. For the two centers: Anle and Zizai, see Qi, "Lun Mingchao neiqian Nüzhen anzhi zhengce—yi Anle Zizai zhou weili," 51–56.

21. There were many reports by Korean eyewitnesses about the size of Jurchen communities and travel difficulties. See *CWS*, vol. 4, Reign of Sejong, 77: 80, 19/6/kisa; vol. 7, Reign of Tanjong (*Nosan'gun ilgi*), 13: 23–28, 3/3/kisa. According to another eyewitness, there were only about sixty-seventy households under Li Manzhu, chieftain of the Jianzhou tribe, and their houses were thatched. See *CWS*, vol 11, Reign of Songjong, 217: 346, 19/6/pyongsin.

22. A Korean agent mentioned that he saw Jurchen farmers and oxen all over the countryside north of the Yalu River. See *CWS*, vol. 4, Reign of Sejong, 77: 80, 19/6/kisa. For the Hūlun Jurchens, see Feng, *Kaiyuan tushuo*, 2: 2b.

23. Information about these branches is based on *Jakūn gūsai manjusai mukūn hala be uheri ejehe bithe*, the Manchu version of the *Geneology of the Manchu Clans in the Eight Banners*, chs. 1–65. The first three clans might have more branches because each included clansmen without geographical origins. As a result these clansmen are not counted as branches. For the clans with rare surnames, see ibid., chs. 59–65.

24. These places, Jurchen groups, and clan names are from ibid., chs. 1–65. Besides the Manchu clans, the same source contains 525 Mongol, Chinese, and Korean clans. See ibid., chs. 66–80. Many inhabitants of the 351 clusters bore the same clan names. But there were only 232 clan names after eliminating duplicates.

25. For their traditions, see *MTTS*, 240–46. A Korean eyewitness reported that even Jurchen women and youngsters were used to horse riding and archery. See Yi, *Chaam Sŏnsaeng munjip*, 6. 5a–b. For the first code, see *Nuer-haqi shilu*, 1: 8a. Later more orders, decisions, and rules, possibly in oral form, were added to the earlier ones. Many of these were closely related to the conduct of soldiers. See *MBRT*, vol. 1, Taizu reign, 4: 51–53; Guang and Li, *Qing Taizu*, 2: 9–15.

26. Korean records provide numerous data on these slaves. For Chinese slaves, see *CWS*, vol. 4, Reign of Sejong, 78: 87, 19/7/kapo; 92: 331, 23/1/pyongo. For selling and purchase of Chinese slaves, see *CWS*, vol. 3, Reign of Sejong, 71: 669, 18/3/

imjin; vol. 4, 113: 697, 28/8/sinch'uk. For Korean slaves, see *CWS*, vol. 7, Reign of Sejo, 26: 493, 7/10/pyongja. A Korean account of 1491 suggests that the slaves lived with their masters. See *CWS*, vol. 12, reign of Sŏngjong, 255: 70–71, 22/7/chŏnghae. For marital bonds, see *CWS*, vol. 8, reign of Yejong, 8: 429, 1/11/kyesa.

27.   Korean and Mongol cultures were also related to the Liaodong frontier, but they will not be stressed here. What Owen Lattimore says of the Great Wall can be applied to the Liaodong defense works. See Lattimore, *Inner Asian*, 22–25, 238–42.

28.   William H. McNeill, *The Great Frontier: Freedom and Hierarchy in Modern Times* (Princeton: Princeton University Press, 1983), 10–11.

29.   Lattimore, *Studies in Frontier History*, 470.

30.   For the arrival of the first Ming army, see Li Luhua and Lü Wenlai, "Ming-jiang Ye Wang zai Dongbei," *KHCH*, 1 (1990): 234–37; also see the biography of "Ye Wang," *Mingshi*, 13. 134: 3899–901.

      For replacement regulations, see *Mingshi*, 8. 92: 2255–58; Yang, *Liaodong dusi*, 67. For a detailed survey of the military household in Liaodong, see Zhou Yuanlian and Xie Zhaohua, "Mingdai Liaodong junhu zhi chutan," *SHKH*, 2 (1980): 45–60.

31.   For geographical origins of the exiles, see Yang, *Dongbei shigang*, 52–59. For the Fan clan, see Li Hongbin, "Qingchu jiechu zhengzhi jia—Fan Wencheng," *KHCH*, 4 (1983): 201.

32.   For exiles sentenced to military service, see *Mingshi*, 8. 93: 2301–02. For a detailed treatment of Ming exiles, see Yang, *Dongbei shigang*, ch. 2, and cf. *MLTT*, 1: 1–45, 52–54. From 1533 onward, lawbreakers were exiled to Liaodong and places far north of it. See *MSL*, vol. 18, Jiajing reign, 157: 1a, 12/12/yihai. Many cases are included in *Zhongguo Mingchao dang'an zonghui*, vol. 86, pp. 1–2ff, 233ff.

33.   Saeki Tomi, "Shincho no koki to Sansei shōnin," *Shaka-bunka shigaku* 1 (March 1966): 11–41; also the same author's "Shindai ni okeru Sansei chōnin," *Shirin* 60. 1 (1977): 1–2ff.

34.   For Xiao Yongzao and his ancestry, see *TCCC*, 198: 12a–19b. But Xiao Cheng'en (possibly Xiao Yangyuan) was not included in the list of company leaders. See *TCCC*, 15: 6a.

35.   For the compulsory nature of migration, see Lee, "Migration and Expansion in Chinese History," 21–22. For the quote, see *Liaodong zhi*, 1. 1: 21a.

36.   For the Liu clan, see *Liushi jiapu*, 1a (postscript). For the Zu clan, see *Zushi jiapu*, comp. Zu Jianji, rev. ed. (N.p., 1707, handwritten, 8 volumes, unpaged), vol. 1, the preface. Zu Shirong and his descendants are largely covered in volume 3. For an English biography of Zu Dashou, see *ECCP*, 2: 769–70.

37.   *Wuqing tang chongxiu Caoshi zongpu*, generally known as *Cao Xueqin jiapu* (Peking: Yan-shan chuban she, 1990, unpaged). For unknown reasons, Cao

Xueqin, son of Cao Fu, does not show in the above genealogy. Also see *ECCP*, 2: 737–39; 740–42. For more information about the Cao clan, see Jonathan D. Spence, *Ts'ao Yin and the K'ang-hsi Emperor: Bondservant and Master* (New Haven and London: Yale University Press, 1966), ch. 1.

38. For frontier raids, see *CWS*, vol, 4, Reign of Sejong, 94: 364, 23/10/pyongin. For runaway slaves, see *CWS*, vol. 3, Reign of Sejong, 60: 463, 15/4/ulyu. For Chinese captives and their escapes, see *CWS*, vol. 4, Reign of Sejong, 92: 331, 23/1/pyŏngo; *CWS*, vol. 7, Reign of Sejo, 2: 78, 1/8/imcha. For the official mission, see *MSL*, vol. 27, Zheng-tong reign, 103: 8b–9a, 8/4/ gengxu. A Jurchen chieftain revealed that some farmers fled excessive corvée to the Jurchen region. See *CWS*, vol. 6, Reign of Tanjong (*Nosan'gun ilgi*), 12: 714, 2/ 12/kyesa. For deserters and mutinies, see *CWS*, vol. 4, Reign of Sejong, 94: 364, 23/10/pyŏngin; Kawachi, *Mindai Joshinshi*, 113. Five hundred soldiers in 1432 fled from a shipyard to the Hūlun Jurchens. See *MSL*, vol. 20, Xuande reign, 95: 10b, 7/9/jiashen. There were mutinies in Liaodong in 1509 and 1539, but the mutiny of 1600 was the most prominent. See Yang, *Liaodong dusi*, 222–30; *MSL*, vol. 111, Wanli reign, 350: 5a, 28/8/yiyou, and 351: 8a, 28/9/yichou.

   With the breakdown of the military farm system, displaced farmers crossed the ethnic line. See Cong Peiyuan, "Mingdai Liaodong juntun," *Zhongguo shi yanjiu* 3 (1985): 96–104. When Ming authorities decided to give up the new land outside Liaodong's southeast frontier in 1605, young able-bodied Chinese farmers defied the government and moved to Jurchen land. See Dong, *Shenmiao liuzhong zoushu*, ch. 11, Memorials of Song Yihan and Zhao Jie, 17b–23a and 23b–31a. For a private account, see Liu Ruoyu, *Zhuo-zhong zhi* (Congshu jicheng chubian, 1941, volumes 3966–67), 21: 181–82.

39. After capturing the Fushun area, Nurhaci enslaved about 300,000 Chinese residents. See Guang and Li, *Qing Taizu*, 1: 85. Hong Taiji enslaved even more captives. In 1639 he sent two armies to attack North China. Altogether, they took more than 460,000 captives. See *Shinkan ichiroku*, reign of Taizong, 7: 12b–13a, Chongde 4/3/bingyin.

   For the Korean's report, see Yi, *Chaam Sŏnsaeng munjip*, 6: 6a. Some defectors seem to have been the residents of the "Chinese Quarters" built by Nurhaci. See *MSL*, vol. 119, Wanli reign, 524: 4, 42/9/renxu. Chinese military defectors taught Jurchens the Chinese way of war. See *Chou-Liao shihua*, vol. 17, Memorial of Han Jun, 19: 23b–24b.

40. For the 1,580 Manchu households, see *CSL*, reign of Taizong, 14: 32a, Tiancong 7/7/xinmao.

41. For the Celge branch's marriage ties with Chinese bannermen, see *Xiang huangqi Niuhulu shi Hongyi gong jiapu*, vol. 4, 15b, 16b, 18b, 27a, 32a–33b. For mixed marriages of clanswomen from the Ilden branch, see ibid., vol. 6, 9a, 14a, 17b, 20a, 22a. For the Fuca clan, see *Nayin Fucha shi puzhuan*, comp. Fu Qishu et al. (N. P.: prefaced 1807, paging by the order of generations), 4th generation,

3b and 5th generation, 3b; 6th generation, 3a; 10th generation, 2a. For the Sakda clan, see *Zheng huangqi Neiwu fu Manzhou san jiala Ancun zuoling xia Huifa Sakeda shi jiapu* (N. P.: prefaced 1898), 31b–32a, 35b. 46ff. The Sakdas had served in the Office of the Imperial Household as bondservants since the beginning of the Qing.

42.   For Chang-ling and his four sons, see *Zheng huangqi Neiwu fu Manzhou san jiala Ancun zuoling xia Huifa Sakeda shi jiapu,* 20b–21b, 22b–29b For Zhongxiang, his son, and his grandson, see ibid., 22b–31a, 51b–53a. For Fuliang and his three sons, see *Nayin Fucha shi puzhuan,* 7th generation, 2b. For marriages of the three sons and the families of their sons, see respectively 8th generation, 2b, and 9th generation, 2a–3a. The three women whom the third son of Fuliang married seem to have carried non-Chinese surnames. See 8th generation, 2b. But the naming practices of the Sakdas may also result from the general trend of the time.

43.   For Fan Wencheng, see *Qingshi liezhuan* 2. 5: 257–61; Zhang, "Fa Wen-cheng," 141–46; *ECCP,* 1: 232. For the Confucian temple built in 1636, see *CSKC,* 4: 2743. For Fan's offering of sacrifices, see *MWLT,* 2: 1561.

44.   For Ning's background and public service, see *ECCP,* 1: 592–3; *TCCC,* 179: 2a–4a. For his contribution to sinicization of the Manchus, see Wang Dongfang, "Ning Wangwu di jinqu jingshen ji qi bianhua," *SHKH,* 2 (1984): 114–18. Besides Ning, there were a few other Chinese who urged Hong Taiji to adopt with modification the Ming ruling machinery (see Section 1, Chapter V of this study). According to official records, he translated the *History of the Three Kingdoms* (see *CSKC,* 10: 8097; *TCCC,* 179: 3b). But he actually translated the *Romance of the Three Kingdoms,* for these two works are often confused as one and the same. For this confusion, see Li Guangtao, "Qing Taizong yu Sanguo yanyi," *Bulletin of the Institute of History and Philology, Academia Sinica,* 12. 1–2 (1945): 256. Martin Gimm is of the same opinion. See Gimm, "Manchu Translations of Chinese Novels and Short Stories: An Attempt at an Inventory," *Asia Major* 1. 2 (1988): 103n90. Its translated version was completed in 1650. See *ECCP,* l: 593; *TCCC,* 179: 3b; *Qingshi biannian,* comps. Shi Song and Lin Tiejun (Peking: Zhongguo renmin daxue chuban she, 1985), 246.

       For frequent use of the *Romance of the Three Kingdoms* by the Manchus, see *Shangyu neige* (Palace ed., 1741, 32 volumes), 18: 5, Yongzheng 6/1/20; Li, "Qing Taizong yu Sanguo yanyi," 263. For the quoted sentence, see Gimm, "Manchu Translations of Chinese Novels and Short Stories: An Attempt at an Inventory," 103.

45.   For Gong's background, see Wada, "Shin no Taiso no komon Kyō Seiriku, *Tōyō gakuhō,* 35. 1 (1952): 40–49, and the same author's "Kyō Seiriku den hosei," *Tōyō gakuhō,* 40. 1 (1957): 110–11. For Gong as a teacher, see *CWS,* vol. 22. Reign of Sŏnjong, 70: 608, 28/12/kyemyo. By 1595, six sons of Nurhaci were at the school age and Hong Taiji was one of them.

For Abatai's selection of Chinese captive as teachers, see Zhaolian, *Xiaoting zalu* and *Xulu* (Taipei: Wenhai chuban she, 1968, CCST, No. 7, volume 63, 2 parts), part 1, 5: 12b–13a. For Yun-duan, see Xia Shi, "Yue-duan jiqi shige," *MANT*, 1 (1990): 55–69.

46. For the weakness of the army and the poverty of the frontier people, see *CWS*, vol. 16, Reign of Chungjong, 58: 544–45, 21/12/imsin; for Jurchen settlements inside the frontier, see *CWS*, vol. 4, Reign of Sejong, 82: 152, 21/7/kich'uk; for poor Koreans working for the Jurchens, see *CWS*, vol. 20, Reign of Myonjong, 29: 657, 18/8/kyech'uk. For the sable fur trade, see *CWS*, vol. 13, Yŏnsan'gun, 19: 308, 4/4/kyemi.

47. For Yi Song-gye's background and policy, see Robinson, "From Raiders to Traders," 97–100. For Korea's treatment of the Jurchen immigrants, see *CWS*, vol. 4, Reign of Sejong, 90: 313, 22/8/ muja. For frontier markets, see *CWS*, vol. 1, Reign of T'aejong, 11: 349, 6/2/kimyo. For the bodyguards, see *CWS*, vol. 1, Reign of T'aejong, 7: 292, 4/3/imsul; vol. 2, Reign of Sejong, 23: 577, 6/2/kiyu. For the bodyguard's duties and the number of entries, see Kawachi, *Mindai Joshinshi*, 172–73. For the Jurchen visitors, see *CWS*, vol 9, Reign of Songjong, 50: 175, 5/12/ulsa. For competition between the Ming and Korea, see Woodruff, "Foreign Policy and Frontier Affairs," 78–88; Yi Kung-ik, *Yollyosil kisul pyolchip* (N.p.: Handwritten, 1800s, unpaged), vol. 5 (see the entry of the fifth year, Reign of Sejo). For the two Ming decrees, see *MSL*, vol. 37, Tianshun reign, 300: 7, 3/2/yihai; 302: 7a, 3/4/ gengchen. Korea finally apologized to the Ming court. See *CWS*, vol. 7, Reign of Sejo, 17: 339, 5/7/pyongo.

48. For the origin and activities of transfrontiersmen, see Allen Isaacman and Barbara Isaacman, "The Prazeros as Transfrontiersmen: A Study in Social and Cultural Change," *International Journal of African Historical Studies*, 8.1 (1975): 1–39, especially 2n5, and 36–37. At the end of their article, the Isaacmans analyze the differences between frontiersmen and transfrontiersmen. See ibid., 36–37. For more discussion, see Franklin W. Knight, *The Caribbean: The Genesis of a Fragmented Nationalism* (New York: Oxford University Press, 2nd ed., 1990), 90; Philip D. Curtin, *The Rise and Fall of the Plantation Complex: Essays in Atlantic History* (Cambridge and New York: Cambridge University Press, 1990), 92–96. For the introduction of the term into the Asian field, see Wakeman, *The Great Enterprise*, I: 43–44 and 44n47.

49. This genealogy contains 645 Manchu, 235 Mongol, 247 Chinese, and 43 Korean clan names. Korean surnames appear in chapters 72–73, while the Chinese in chapters 74–80. These Korean and Chinese surnames also appear in *Jakū n gusan manjusai mukūn hala be uheri ejehe bithe*, chs. 72–73, 74–80. For the dates suggested by two scholars, see Wakeman, *The Great Enterprise*, I: 45; Li, *The Rise of the Early Manchu State*, 29–30.

50. The number of the places the 645 Manchu clans resided are drawn from *Jakūn gūsai manjusai mukūn hala be uheri ejehe bithe*, chs. 1–65. Among the eighty

Jurchen clans in Ula were the Irgen Gioro, Nara, and Tunggiya. For the two Chinese families, see *STTP*, 79: 4b and 5b. The Hešeri, Niohuru, Tatara, and Wanggiya clans were the most famous of the seventy-one Jurchen groups in the valley of the Long White Mountains. Among the eleven Chinese sibs were the Li, Zhao, Zhu, Dai, and Wang families. See *STTP*, 74: 7a; 75: 2b, and 7a–b; 76: 14b; 77: 5b, 16a, 17b, 19a, and 21a. The Gorolo, Šumuru, and Wanggiya groups were among the ten Jurchen clans in Zhanhe. For You and Zhao sibs, see *STTP*, 79: 6a and 7a. The twenty-four Jurchen groups in Ningguta included the Gūwalgiya, Magiya, and Sakda, to name only a few. For the three Chinese clans in Ningguta, see *STTP*, 77: 11b; 78: 3a; and 79: 2b.

51. For the Wang family, see *STTP*, 75: 2b; for the Yu branch, see ibid., 77: 11b.

52. For instance, Sangge of the Ren family from the Long White Mountains region served as a chief headman. See *STTP*, 77: 19a. Gabula, the son of Gahana, held the position of horse groom supervisor (ibid., 77: 11b). Ifona, a member of the Qin family from the valley of the Long White Mountains, was a bow-making inspector (ibid., 78:2b–3a).

53. Lio Sang-c'ai resided in Ligiya-holo, a small place in the Xinbin area of Liaoning, with the Joogiya and Ligiya clans. See *STTP*, 57: 3. The other Chinese family lived in Sintun, also a small place, in which a Gūwalgiya clan resided. See ibid.

54. For the case of twenty-one people, see *CWS*, vol. 13, Reign of Yŏnsan'gun, 17: 139, 2/8/kihae. For the second generation captive, see *CWS*, vol. 7, Reign of Sejo, 36: 698, 11/8/sinsa.

55. For his story, see *STTP*, 74: 7a. His posthumous title was *Qiduyu*, a hereditary designation of the seventh rank. See *TCCC*, 94: 18b. The case of Laohan resembles the story in *Xiaoting zalu* and *Xulu*, part 2, *Xulu*, 2: 16b. Laohan may be compared with the person names Luohan or Laohan, as recorded in *Nuer-haqi shilu*, 1: 6a. Laohan is possibly a Chinese term simply meaning an "old man."

56. For Dahai's biography, see *TCCC*, 236: 3a–6b; *Qingshi liezhuan*, 1. 4: 187–89. For Korean sources, see Cho Kyong-nam, *Nanjung chamnok; Sok chamnok* (Seoul: San-sŏ Nanjung chamnok Publication Office, 1964, 5 volumes), *Sok chamnok*, 1: 41; Yi Sŏng-nyŏng, *Ch'unp'a dang ilwollok* (Handwritten, 9 volumes, housed in Tōyō Bunko, Tokyo), 7. 8: 64b. For Yi Min-hwan's writing on Dahai's ethnic origin, see his *Chaam Sŏnsaeng munjip*, 5: 17b. Li Guang-tao argues that Dahai was of Chinese descent. See his "'Lao Man-wen shiliao' xu," *Bulletin of the Institute of History and Philosophy, Academia Sinica* 34 (1962): 327–29. Wakeman regards Dahai as the descendant of a transfrontier family. See his *The Great Enterprise*, I: 44.

57. For a short study of Dahai, see Chen Bolin, "Shilun Dahai," *Heilong-jiang wenwu congkan* 4 (1987): 56–58 and 44. His mastery of Chinese is among the reasons for Tatiana A. Pang to regard Dahai as a "Manchurised Chinese." See her "The Manchu Script Reform of 1632: New Data and New Questions." In

Juha Janhunen and Volker Rybatzki, eds., *Writing in the Altaic World* (Helsinki: The Finnish Oriental Society, 1999, Studia Orientalia 87), 202, 205.

58. For his appreciation of the Chinese style of dress, see *CSL*, reign of Taizong, 32: 9a, Chongde 1/11/guichou; 34: 26b–27a, Chongde 2/4/dingyou. For his translations, see *ECCP*, 1: 213–14; Durrant, "Sino-Manchu Translations at the Mukden Court," 654–56. For the importance of translation to acculturation, see Herbert Franke, *China under Mongol Rule* (Brookfield, VT: Variorum, 1994), 19 and 26.

59. For Meng Sen's study of Lio Aita, see his *Ming-Qing xubian*, 100–19; also a short study by Shang Hongkui (ibid., 119–22). For Liu's early relation with Nurhaci, see Mao Yuanyi, "Dushi jilüe," *Mingshi ziliao congkan*, 5 (1986): 44. For Liu's own statement, see *CWS*, vol. 34, Reign of Injo, 17: 221, 5/8/pyongo. According to a Korean source, he was on China's wanted list. Originally known as Yu Hae, he changed his name to Xingzuo in 1628. See Pan, Sun, and Li, *Qing ruguan qian shiliao*, 1: 463. For imperial credentials, see *MWLT*, 2: 920. For Hong Taiji's revelation, see *CSL*, reign of Taizong, 25: 13b, Tiancong 9/9/xinwei. Another source relates that Liu was born in Shensi Province, but lived in Kaiyuan, from where he joined Nurhaci. See *Beijing tushu guan guji zhenben congkan*, Beijing tushu guan guji chuban bianji zu (Peking: Shumu wenxian chuban she, 1987), vol.11, "Liaoshi shu," 690–91. For the other Liu brothers, see Qiao Zhizhong, ed., *Qingwen qianbian* (Peking: Beijing tushu guan chuban she, 2000, 6 volumes), 2: 102b–104a ff.

60. For Kūrcan's background, see *STTP*, 5: 13a; *TCCC*, 236: 9a–15b. Some sources, such as *CSKC* (10: 8004), maintain that his mother was a princess from the imperial clan, but the Qing imperial genealogy does not indicate this. See *Xingyuan jiqing*, 22–24. For his advice about the style of dress, see *CSL*, reign of Taizong, 32: 9a, Chongde 1/11/guichou; 34: 26b–27a, Chongde 2/4/dingyou. For Kūrcan's unswerving friendship with Lio Aita, see *CSKC*, 10: 8005.

61. The best genealogy of the Tong clan is Tong Guoqi, comp., *Xiang-ping Youfen xian-sheng lu* (Kanzhou, Kiangsi: Office of the Governor, 1656, 4 volumes, with various page numbers, housed in the Nanking Library, China), chs. 1 and 4. This book records the Tong clan from Tong Dali to the compiler, altogether ten generations. In his *Manzu zongpu yanjiu* (Shenyang: Liao-Shen Shushe, 1992), Li Lin provides a brief list of the Tong clansmen, but many names are inaccurate; Zhu Xizu divides the Tongs in three branches: Nurkal, Jianzhou, and the Sanwan Guard. See his "Hou Jin guohan xingshi kao." In *Qingzhu Cai Yuanpei xian-sheng liushiwu sui lunwen ji*, Part 1 (Peiping: Academia Sinica, 1933): 48–49. Okamoto Sae furnishes a genealogical chart of the Tong clan in his "Tou Koku-ki to Shinsho no Kōnan," *Tōyō bunka kenkyūji kiyō*, 101 (1988): 96–100. For the Mongol and Korean components, see Fu Yangyang, "Manzu Tongshi xingshi xing-cheng zai tan." In Fu, ed., *Manzu Tongjia shih yanjiu*, 52 and 56.

 For the twenty-nine locations, see *Jakūn gūsai manjusai mukūn hala be uheri ejehe bithe*, chs. 19-20. For the surname of the line from Menggetimur to Nurhaci, see Zhu, "Hou Jin guo-han," 38-42; Zheng Tianting, *Tanwei ji* (Peking: Zhonghua Book Company, 1980), 38-47. A recent study forcefully argues that Nurhaci's family name was Tung (Tong in Chinese). See Zhang, *Manzu fayuandi lishi yanjiu*, 346-47.

62.   For the Tong genealogy, see Tong, *Xiang-ping Youfen xian-sheng lu*, chs.1 and 4. For Tong Dali's career and duties, see ibid., ch. 4, "Preface to the Tong Genealogy," 2, "Tongshi jiapu," 1-2a. For the surnames of their wives, see "Tongshi jiapu," 1b-3. For the opinion about the Tongs as Chinese, see Wang, "Qingchao kaiguo gongchen Tong Yangxing," 34; Zheng, *Tanwei ji*, 53-59; Pamela Crossley, "The Tong in Two Worlds: Cultural Identities in Liaodong and Nurgan during the 13th-17th Centuries," *Qingshi wenti*, 4. 9 (1983): 22; Fu, *Manzu Tongjia shi yanjiu*, especially the papers on pp. 72, 97. Perhaps more works argue that the Tong clan was of Jurchen origin. See Fang, *Quanbian lüeji*, 10: 37a; Wang, *Qingshi xukao*, 62: Chen Yinke, *Liu Rushi biezhuan* (Shanghai: Shanghai guji chuban she, 1980, 3 volumes), 3: 980-81; Okamoto, "Tou Koku-ki," 96-100; many papers in Fu, *Manzu Tongjia shi yanjiu*, pp. 14-15, 31, 64, 236-37, are of the same opinion.

       For names given to frontier tribal leaders by the Ming court, see Zhang Hong-xiang, "Ming waizu cixing kao," *Furen xuezhi*, 3. 2 (1932): 1-40; 4. 2 (1934): 1-84. Tong Dali began to work for the Ming in 1383. For the recent article, see Tong Yonggong, "Guanyi Qingdai Tongshi jiazu di jige wenti." In Zhu Chengru, ed., *Qingshi lunji* (Peking: Zijin cheng chuban she, 2003), 447-48.

63.   For Tong Dali and Tong Deng, see Tong, *Xiang-ping Youfen xian-sheng lu*, ch. 1, "Youfen xian-sheng zhuan," 1-2; ch. 4, "Tongshi jiapu," 1, 5-6. The Liaoyang branch was founded by Tong Ying. See "Youfen xian-sheng zhuan," 1b. For Hahana Jacing's relationship with Nurhaci, see Zhang, *Manzu fayuandi lishi yanjiu*, 351 and 353; Fu et al., "Mingmen wanzu Tongjia shi, aiguo qinmin yu Zhonghua," 15-16. But in Qing official sources, such as *Xingyuan jiqing* (p. 15), she was recorded as the first consort of Nurhaci. For her being the mother of Cuyen and Daišan, see *ECCP*, 1: 598. For Nurhaci's knowledge of the Chinese language, see *Dongyi kaolüe*, 94: 11b; Yan, *Nuer-haci zhuan*, 19.

64.   Some scholars believe that the name "Tong" (Tung in Manchu) originated in Jiagu or Jiawen, a Jurchen surname during the Jin dynasty (1115-1234). See Meng, *Qingdai shi*, 9; Dong, *Qing Zhaozu*, 26. For the Tongs and the Tunggiyas, see *Jakūn gūsai manjusai mukūn hala be uheri ejehe bithe*, chs. 19-20. For Tung Ki and Tung Jy-siyang, see *STTP*, 19: 14b and 20: 20a. For these specialists with the name of Tong, see *Liaodong zhi*, 3. 6: 21b.

65.   For Tong Yangxing, see *ECCP*, 2: 797-98; *MWLT*, 2: 920. But the most detailed account about his collaboration with Nurhaci is included in Tong, *Xiang-ping Youfen xian-sheng lu*, ch. 1, "[Second] defense memorial," 11b-12a. For Tong

Yangzhen, see *ECCP*, 2: 797; *Qingshi liezhuan*, 1. 4: 177–78. Another clansman was Tong Henian (fl. 1610s), a Ming army officer in Shenyang. A contemporary source, *Wanli yehuo bian* (2. 19: 496), regards him as Jurchen. But he was mentioned as an officer in Liaoyang in Tong, *Xiang-ping Youfen xian-sheng lu*, ch. 4, "Tongshi jiapu," 19a.

66. For Tong Bunian's autobiography and troubles, see Tong, *Xiang-ping Youfen xian-sheng lu*, ch. 1, "Youfen xian-sheng zhuan," 1–16. In 1622 he submitted three memorials for his defense. See ch. 1, "Defense Memorials," 1–16. The article written by Tong Guoqi on his mother also reveals his own life. See ch. 1, "Xianbi Chen tai shuren xinglüe," 1–7. In his Preface to the Tong Genealogy (ch. 4, p. 4) he proudly mentioned positions taken by his clansmen in Qing officialdom. For Tong Tulai, see *Qingshi liezhuan*, 1. 4: 178–79; *ECCP*, 2: 796.

67. The petitioner was Tong Guogang (d. 1690), the eldest son of Tong Tulai. See *CSL*, Kangxi reign, 135: 2, 27/4/jiachen; *Qingshi liezhuan*, 3. 10: 728–29. For the validity of his claim, see Li, *Manzu zongpu yanjiu*, 166–67. Pamela Kyle Crossley seems to believe that the Sanwan branch of the Tongs were of Jurchen descent. See her *A Translucent Mirror*, 85–86. But in pages 112–13 of the same book she regards Tong Guogang's claim as false.

68. Under Tong Yangxing's supervision, forty cannons were cast. See *CSKC*, 10: 8069. For his commandership of the artillery unit, see ibid. For Kangxi's English biography, see *ECCP*, 1:327–31. For the two consorts from the Tong clan, see *Xingyuan jiqing*, 45–46. One of the seventeen women might be a Manchu. See *Xingyuan jiqing*, 45–48. For the seven imperial sons, see *Xingyuan jiqing*, 51–53. For the Palace School, see Zhao Zhiqiang, "Qinchao xing-shuai yu huangzi jiaoyu," *Manxue yanjiu*, 2 (1994): 83–89. For Kangxi's visit, see Sun, *Qianlong di*, 176; for Qianlong's visits, see ibid., 177–79.

69. For the early history of the Shi clansmen, see *Fengtian tongzhi*, comps. Wang Shunan, Wu Tingxie, and Jin Yufu (Shenyang: Shenyang Gujiu shudian, 1982, 5 volumes), 3. 102: 2332.

70. Shi Tingzhu's two brothers were Shi Guozhu (Ši Guwe-ju in Manchu, fl. 1620s–1630s) and Shi Tianzhu (Ši Tiyan-ju, fl. 1620s–1630s). For the three brothers' biographies, see *TCCC*, 176: 2a–11a, 176: 11, 176: 11b. For Shi Tingzhu's commandership of the artillery unit, see *CSKC*, 10: 8069. According to *CSL*, Kangxi reign (135: 2b, 27/4/jiachen), Hūwašan's petition was granted. Some other sources, such as *TCCC*, 196: 18b–19a, point out that he and his descendants were ordered to remain in the Chinese banner, but they were included in the Manchu registry.

71. Some scholars do not believe Hūwašan's statement and regard the Shi clansmen as ethnic Chinese. See Zheng, *Tanwei ji*, 58–59, and Jiang Qiao, "Qingchu di Hanjun jiang-ling Shi Ting-zhu," *Lishi dang'an*, 1 (1989): 81–83, and 94.

For these early Qing sources, see *Shinkan ichiroku*, reign of Taizu, 2: 17b, Tianming 7/1/ jiwei; *Nuer-haqi shilu*, 4: 1b; *CSL*, reign of Taizu, 8: 12b, Tianming 7/1/jiwei. For the studies of the same conclusion, see Chen Wan, "Shi Tingzhu shiji yu jiashi jikao," *Qingshi yanjiu tongxin*, 2 (1986): 33–37. For the marriage link, see *CSKC*, 10: 8430.

72.   The Wangs originated in the Wanggiya branch of Wang-to-lo-shu, a small place in the suburb of Kaiyuan. For the story, see *TCCC*, 179: 12b–15a. For Wang Guoguang's son, Wang Yong-yu (d. 1704), see *TCCC*, 197: 4b–6b.

73.   For the close similarity of the two cultures, see Reischauer and Fairbank, *East Asia*, 396–97. But there were also differences in spoken language, styles of clothing, national personalities. See ibid. For instance, a Korean named Kim was held by the Jurchens as a captive when he was a teenager. Later, he married a Jurchen woman and did not want to return to Korea. See *CWS*, vol. 3, Reign of Sejong, 71: 666, 18/2/kimi. For a similar case, see *CWS*, vol. 3, Reign of Sejong, 71: 667, 18/3/imsin. A private Korean source provides a case in 1624 about a captive who worked for the Jurchens bravely and loyally. See Hong Ik-han, *Hwap'o Sŏnsaeng yugo* (N.p.: with a postscript in 1709, 4 volumes), 2. 1: 41a. A Korean prince met such relocated people on a hunting trip with Hong Taiji. See *Shenyang zhuangqi*, 494, 500–501.

      For Gūlmahūn, see Tanaka Katsumi, "Tsūyaku Gūlmahūn." In Ishihama Sensei koki kinenkai, ed., *Ishihama Sensei koki kinen Tōyōgaku ronsō*, (Osaka: Ishihama Sensei koki kinenkai, 1953), 280–89. For the plot, see *Shenyang zhuangqi*, 142–43, 145–48, 165.

74.   For the forty-three Korean clans See *Jakūn gūsai manjusai mukūn hala be uheri ejehe bithe*, chs. 72–73. For the case of Chong and the Korean Village, see Yi, *Chaam Sŏnsaeng munjip*, 6: 6a. For Han In and Han Ui, see *MWLT*, 1: 620.

75.   For cases of Jurchen frontiersmen and immigrants, see *CWS*, vol. 7, Reign of Sejo, 21: 415, 6/8/imsul. For Korea's marriage policy, see ibid., vol. 2, Reign of Sejong, 19: 525, 5/2/ kimi; vol. 7, Reign of Sejo, 31: 590, 9/10/kapo; for Jurchen bodyguards and royal favors, see ibid., vol. 1, Reign of T'aejong, 7: 292, 4/3/imsul; vol. 4, Reign of Sejong, 106: 584, 26/9/pyongsul; vol. 7, Reign of Sejo, 19: 379, 6/3/kimyo. Descendants of such matrimonial relations created a diplomatic issue between Korea and the Jurchen kingdom. See *Shenyang zhuangqi*, 87–89, 312, 317.

76.   Many of them served in the military coalition to help Yi Song-gye ascend the throne. See John Duncan, "The Social Background to the Founding of the Chosŏn Dynasty: Change or Continuity," *Journal of Korean Studies* 6 (1988–89): 57–58. For Jurchen high officials in the Yi government, see ibid., 57. For the case of Mafuta, see *STTP*, 11: 20.

77.   For Dangini and his descendants, see *STTP*, 72: 9a. For Yatu's position in the Manchu Bordered Yellow Banner, see *TCCC*, 108: 14a–16b. For his factional activity, see *CSL*, Kangxi reign, 250: 6b–7b, 51/4/yichou.

78.   For the Han clan, see *STTP*, 72: 5. For Han Un, see *TCCC*, 158: 26a. Of the clansmen, Giyeyen (d. 1687), eldest son of Han Ni, reached the highest office.

He fought many battles and became a commander of imperial bodyguards. See *TCCC*, 158: 24b–25b.

79.   For Sindari and his clan, see *STTP*, 72: 1a–2a. For Canming's clan and the two companies, see *Eight Banners Archives*, "Miscellaneous Category," 3rd carton #81, under Šuwangboo, 4th division of the bondservants, Plain Yellow Banner; *TCCC*, 4: 38. For the last office Canming held, see *TCCC*, 114: 42a. For his various offices, see *Eight Banners Archives*, "Miscellaneous Category," 3rd carton #83. For the imperial favor and his death, see *CSL*, Qianlong reign, 170: 12b–13a, 7/7/bingyin. For Kim Kan and the imperial consort, see *STTP*, 72: 2a; *CSKC*, 11: 9225–26.

80.   By Nurhaci's order of 1616, the Jurchens began to plant cotton, tend silkworms, and produce silk goods. See Guang and Li, *Qing Taizu*, 2: 29. For iron smelting, see *Shinkan ichiroku*, reign of Taizu, 1: 11a, Wanli 27/3/jihai; *Nuer-haqi shilu*, 2: 1a. For their making of ironwares, see Hatada Takashi, "Mindai Joshinjin no tekki ni tsuite," *Tōhōgaku-hō*, Tokyo, 11. 1 (1940): 260–67. For Nurhaci's black-smiths, see Yi, *Chaam Sŏnsaeng munjip*, 6: 3b. Nurhaci even sent soldiers to locate and capture skilled Chinese blacksmiths. See *MBRT*, vol. 2, Taizu, 46: 675–76. For their industrial development, see Ch'en, *Ming-Qing zhengzhi*, 1: 283–325.

Chapter V

The Rise of Administrative
and Legal Institutions

CHINESE ADMINISTRATIVE AND LEGAL INSTITUTIONS helped greatly in
the sinicization of the Manchus because they functioned in relationship
with Chinese norms, mores, and values. With the fall of the Jin dynasty
in 1234, a gloomy chapter opened in the history of the Jurchens. There
were no effective indigenous administrative or legal institutions in
place that Nurhaci and Hong Taiji could use. Nor could they borrow
such institutions from their Mongol neighbors, who also suffered from
instability. China was the only provider of what the Jurchen frontier
state needed. As participants in the Ming guard-post system, the
Jurchens haunted the frontier markets and frequented the tributary
road to Peking. These contacts made it possible for them to acquire
knowledge of Chinese administrative and legal institutions and to
become accustomed to them. Both Nurhaci and Hong Taiji had Chinese
assistants, who naturally introduced Ming governing institutions to
their masters. With such institutions came Chinese norms, mores,
and ideals that made their assimilation of Chinese institutions possible.
Compared with his father, Hong Taiji was more China-oriented.
Because his Chinese subjects dramatically increased, he adopted more
Chinese political elements. Chinese administrative and legal institutions provided him not only with the governing machinery but the
legitimation he needed.

This chapter will cover Qing central administrative and legal institutions, focusing on their evolution from the Ming ruling machinery. It will not deal with provincial or local offices because they were
virtually an extension of the central government. Since the imperial
governing structure was composed of many offices and therefore in-

tricate, this study can cover only a few important agencies, such as the Literary Office, the Six Boards, and the censorial system. It was out of the Literary Office that the Grand Secretariat and the Hanlin Academy evolved. The Six Boards executed state affairs that were relevant to their respective responsibilities, while the censorial system was mandated to remonstrate, impeach, and check state papers. As for legal institutions, this chapter will analyze the development of the Qing judicial system and penal code in the light of their Ming model. The Manchu adoption of the Ming administrative and legal institutions may be considered a process of bureaucratization because the Ming state establishment was a bureaucracy.

1. Administrative Machinery

The frontier kingdom that Nurhaci founded and transformed in 1587–1616 was a creation of special circumstances. It appeared when traditional Jurchen society was undergoing change. There were only clans and tribes, and the line between the two was indistinct. In many cases a powerful clan was itself a tribe. To increase their strength, ambitious tribal chieftains made alliances and waged war against one another.[1] Because of warfare, internal growth, or economic needs, the traditional clan (*hala* in Manchu), originally a kinship unit, created subunits known as the *mukūn*. In time these *mukūn* developed into clans independent of their parental groups. During their expansion or division, the clan and the *mukūn* were frequently joined by outsiders and transformed into territorial units, in which traditional elements became less important. With the addition of outsiders, the territorial group was more powerful than the kinship unit. As recorded in the *Genealogy of the Manchu Clans in the Eight Banners*, many big and powerful clans, such as the Gūwalgiya, Fuca, and Hešeri, were territorial units. Clan cohesion disappeared with this old descent membership. Members of the same clan would become rivals for personal reasons. Suffice it to say that traditional Jurchen society was in a transition stage. At the same time, the Ming dynasty could no longer control the Jurchens because of poor leadership, among many other problems. Nurhaci and his frontier state arose out of this chaotic situation.[2]

Nurhaci's frontier state was a primitive political entity that took root in the Jurchen tribal and clan structure, along with Mongol and Chinese influences. Nurhaci was a minor tribal chieftain and head of his clan; this background affected the molding of his state. In view of its structure, the Eight Banners testified to such a relationship. In 1583–1626 he managed to control many Jurchen tribes and clans. From 1601 onward they were incorporated, one after another, according to their size and strength, into the Eight Banners, which was essentially the aggrandizement and perpetuation of the Jurchen clan's hunting formation. Chiefs and headmen were made officers, and their men served as warriors.[3] One may consider the Eight Banners as part of the administrative machinery because, in addition to military affairs, they took charge of civil matters concerning warriors and their families.

The Jurchen frontier state was organized in the same way. At its top stood Nurhaci and his clansmen, most of whom were made princes. Next were those tribal and clan chiefs who won his trust. From these people he appointed his chief administrators, the Five Councilors and the Ten *Jargūci*. Of the fifteen appointees, the five councilors were more important and laid the groundwork for the Council of Princes and High Officials (*yizheng wang dachen huiyi*). They evolved into a major policy-deliberating organization and a stronghold of the Manchu aristocracy, dominating the Qing court before 1722.[4] Whatever their offices, these men performed their jobs both as banner officers and as traditional tribal and clan chiefs. The state thus depended on functioning of the old elements. At least in its early stages, one may say, it amounted to a federation of clans.

In the Jurchen state there was no clear job differentiation. Military men were given responsibilities for civil affairs; nonmilitary people were sent into battle. All the five councilors, Anfiyanggu, Eidu, Fiongdon, Hohori, and Hurhan, and most of the Ten *Jargūci*, such as G'ag'ai (d. 1599)—a linguist who helped devise the Manchu old script—and Jaciba, were famous warriors. This lack of differentiation was also manifest in the fact that the same person concurrently worked in several offices, and agencies shared similar duties. Fiongdon was mainly a commander of the banner forces, but he served in offices of the Five Councilors and the Ten *Jargūci*. By 1623 Nurhaci had appointed eight *jargūci*, together with thirty-two judges in the Eight Banners. The forty appointees shared functions not only among themselves but with the earlier fifteen officials.[5]

The Jurchen kingdom under Nurhaci was influenced by Mongol culture. The title khan was conferred on him by some Mongol tribal chiefs in 1606, and he kept it. The Manchu old script, which he ordered devised in 1599, was an adaptation of the Mongol writing system.[6] He adopted Mongol terms for his offices and honorific designations. The *darugachi,* or *dalu huachi* in Chinese, an official appointed by Mongol rulers in China to cosign documents with the head of a government agency, was adapted by Nurhaci as his *jargū ci*, normally in charge of administrative and judicial affairs. The Manchu title *baksi* (scholar) had its origin in the Mongol language. He gave his warriors the designations *baturu* and *darhan* (*dargan*), also of Mongol origin, for their heroic performance in battles. More importantly, the banner system shared features with Mongol military institutions. The organization was similar, and in both cases there was no distinction between soldiers and civilians. Some scholars suggest that the Jurchens, a forest people, borrowed the tradition of raising and riding horses from the Mongols. With horses, the Manchus were able to organize a cavalry that helped them conquer the Ming dynasty.[7]

In contrast, the Jurchen state in its early stages did not adopt much from Ming political institutions. What Nurhaci borrowed from China included a few titles, such as the *zongbing guan*. Originally the designation for a regional commander in the Ming period, this title was adapted by Nurhaci as a nobility rank equivalent to viscount (*jingkini hafan* in Manchu).[8] Nurhaci borrowed Chinese imperial rituals, historical precedents, and the concept of heaven's support. Even before his formal proclamation of the Jurchen state he put on the dress of five-colored dragons, which Chinese rulers wore. Later he adopted the dragon to mark the flags of some military units. When his punitive army reached the Ula tribe in 1612, he appeared under a yellow umbrella, accompanied by a band of musicians. After 1616 his edicts and instructions frequently cited precedents from Chinese history. During the years 1612–1618 he and his advisors interpreted natural phenomena as heaven's approval of his imperial ambition. When he proclaimed the founding of his state he gave his reign period the designation *Tian-ming*, which means the Mandate of Heaven.[9]

The reasons why Nurachi did not adopt more from the Ming administrative structure can be explained. From 1583 onward, Nurhaci made efforts to unify the Jurchens, who were divided into groups all over Manchuria. Most Jurchen tribes were small, unstable, and less developed. The Ming governing machinery was highly centralized and bureaucratized. Naturally it was too sophisticated for a small and underdeveloped frontier state. It would be more feasible to unify the tribes on the basis of their traditional institutions. For centuries the Jurchens had been under the Ming guard-post system, but Nurhaci sought a unified Jurchen state independent of Chinese influence. It would be inappropriate to use Chinese ruling machinery when his kingdom was at a critical stage.[10]

Since his goal was to unify the Jurchens and found a state, Nurhaci devoted himself to building a powerful army, not an administrative structure. As stated, the Manchu Banners combined both military and administrative functions. It is possible that he did not see the necessity or urgency of adopting Chinese administrative machinery. Moreover, he was suspicious of his Chinese subjects, whom he thought unreliable. In 1622 he reprimanded Chinese officials for evasiveness, dereliction, and greed, and told them bluntly: "From now on you are not trusted." Oppressed and insecure, Chinese in southern Liaodong tried to run away, created sporadic incidents, and even rose in revolt in 1623 and 1625 against their conquerors. He massacred residents where uprisings occurred. He abandoned his policy of integration and discriminated against Chinese officials, especially the low-academic-degree scholars, who were believed to have incited the uprisings.[11]

But with more conquests there arose a state of competition between Nurhaci and his associates. He desired centralization and punished contenders, actual or alleged, among whom were his younger brother, Šurhaci, and the two chieftains of the Gorolo clan, Cangšu and Yangšu. A great warrior, Šurhaci was referred to as the *Darhan baturu* prince and had his own followers. Second only to Nurhaci, he found himself alienated. This finally caused his imprisonment and execution. As early as 1583 the two Gorolo chieftains joined Nurhaci, who swore to treat them as equals. Soon they became his subordinates, and Cangšu was punished on a dubious charge.[12]

During the latter part of Nurhaci's reign there were indications that he was planning to adopt Chinese political institutions. The first indication came with the rise of an informal secretariat filled with *baksi*, a term adopted by the Jurchens even before Nurhaci. In the Niohuru clan genealogy, Esulele, a granduncle of Eidu and two generations before Nurhaci, was referred to as a *baksi*. Nurhaci gave this title to more than a dozen people for their knowledge of the Mongol and Chinese languages. They served as secretaries, teachers, translators, interpreters, diplomats, and advisors. Although without this title, Gong Zheng-lu, who took care of communication in Chinese and taught Nurhaci's sons, was likely one of his earliest *baksi*. Among later *baksi* were Erde-ni, Dahai, Kūrcan, Hife, and Tusa (d. 1625). They formed a special group, within easy reach of their master and answerable to his call at any time. Their office, sometimes referred to as the *Shufang* (study), was the forerunner of the *Wen-guan* or Literary Office.[13]

A second indication pertained to Nurhaci's sponsorship of translating Chinese books into Manchu. Translators included *baksi* and people outside this group. Since his concern was governing, he selected Chinese books on government, law, and strategy. Under his order Dahai worked on the *Collected Statutes of the Ming Dynasty (Ming huidian)*, *Sushu,* and *Sanlüe.* Although authorship and dates of publication are controversial, the latter books concern leadership and political and military strategy. Whatever translated, reading translations was, as Herbert Franke argues, "a halfway stage on the way towards fuller sinicization." In 1621, Nurhaci asked a Manchu *jargūci* and several Chinese military men to submit a detailed report on Ming political and legal institutions that it could be used for his state. He demanded information about the Ming military establishment in Liaodong, the region's census figure, and registers of craftsmen, including carpenters and painters.[14]

Chinese influences greatly increased during the reign of Hong Taiji. After two attempts to designate an heir-apparent, Nurhaci finally decided that after his death the state should be ruled jointly by eight princes. They could select one of them as the khan. The new ruler should consult with the other princes and might be replaced if not satisfactory. For the first four years of his reign Hong Taiji sat together with Daisan, Amin, and Manggūltai to receive diplomats and decide state affairs. Not until 1632 was he able to clear his way to supremacy.[15] With the defeat of the Ming army at the battle of Jinzhou in 1642, a vast number of Chinese subjects came under his control. Unlike his father, whose thinking was conditioned by Jurchen traditions, Hong Taiji seems to have had a broader vision. He envisaged replacement of the Ming dynasty by the Manchu frontier kingdom. In all these cases he found solutions to his problems in Chinese administrative machinery.

Chinese administration reached from the local to the national level, with decisions made in reverse order. Administrators were recruited through civil service examinations. Without hereditary privileges or military backing, they were bureaucrats working for the ruler's interests and serving at his pleasure. Such machinery would help Hong Taiji consolidate his power and legitimize his rule over his Chinese subjects. After ascending the throne he moderated his father's harsh measures to pacify Chinese residents in the Liao valley. His policy benefited Chinese scholars, farmers, merchants, and even slaves. In 1629 he once gave official status to as many as fifty-six Chinese, among whom were merchants and dismissed, defecting, or captured Ming officers. Some of the new appointees were given hereditary offices. He organized Chinese Banner forces, many of whose soldiers were freedmen. All the above actions provided him with supporters indispensable for the adoption of Chinese political institutions.[16]

The rise of the Literary Office marked a new chapter in the history of Manchu accommodation to Chinese ruling machinery. This office had experienced a period of informal operation, roughly from the middle of Nurhaci's reign to 1632. An outgrowth of the aforesaid *Shufang*, it did not have a beginning date or rules of operation. Nor did it have a stipulated number of staff. It was institutionalized in 1632, instead of 1629 as commonly assumed. Under Hong Taiji the Literary Office had more members, divided into three grades: *baksi, bithesi,* and Chinese members. People with the title of *baksi* were senior members, many of whom, including Dahai and Kūrcan, had served Nurhaci and received this title from him. Perhaps because the title was abused, in 1633 Hong Taiji prohibited its use among men of letters unless conferred by the throne. It was replaced by the word *bithesi*, an occupation-oriented term meaning clerk or secretary.[17]

The *bithesi* were second-grade staff members, recruited chiefly from the Manchus. With the transformation of the Literary Office, the service of *bithesi* was required of branches of the bureaucratic structure and principal Manchu garrison headquarters. Although low in the hierarchy, the position might be a springboard for Manchus to reach high office. Zhaohui (1708–1764), a kinsman of an empress, and Omida (d. 1761), a member of an obscure clan, began their careers as *bithesi* in the Yongzheng reign and achieved distinction during the Qianlong period because of their performance. With resourcefulness, Zhaohui defeated the Moslem rebels in Sinkiang in a long war and became one of the greatest generals in Qing history. Omida served as governor-general in several regions and was promoted to assistant grand secretary.[18]

Chinese members joined the Literary Office, mainly after 1629, through examination, recommendation, or other means. They outnumbered others in the office, but belonged to the lowest grade. Such members as Gao Hong-zhong (fl. 1620s–1630s) and Wang Shun were originally Ming army officers. Most of the Chinese staffers were students or scholars holding the lowest academic degree, known as *xiucai* (men of high talents and ability). One may classify them in groups by when they began their relations with the Manchus. The earlier was selected from about three hundred people, slaves who had survived the massacre by Nurhaci in 1625. Among them were Ning Wanwo, Lei Xing (d. 1653), and Fan Wencheng. In 1629, Hong Taiji allowed them to take a civil service examination after the Chinese model, and two hundred students passed, some of whom were assigned to the Literary Office. The later group included individuals—Jiang Hede (d. 1670), Wang Wenkui (d. c. 1654)—captured by the Manchus early in the reign of Hong Taiji. Chinese staffers, including Ning Wanwo and Bao Chengxian (d. 1654), entered into service through recommendation.[19]

With more Chinese staff members, the characteristics of the Literary Office changed. Since they stressed hunting and fighting, the Jurchens did not acclaim literary or scholarly talent. The official status of linguists and scholars, such as Dahai, Erdeni (d. 1623) and Hife, was determined by military ranking. Chinese members, such as Ning

Wanwo and Fan Wencheng, also held military ranks. When more Chinese members were appointed, literary men dominated the office. Although not high officials, they enjoyed imperial trust and worked for the political cause of their master. Because of their cultural background they introduced more Chinese institutions and ideals to Hong Taiji's court.[20]

The Literary Office was the precursor of the Qing imperial administrative structure. In its early stages it focused on translating Chinese books into Manchu, keeping records, and compiling history. These responsibilities, especially the last two, remind one of the Hanlin Academy (*hanlin yuan*), a dynastic institution of traditional China. One may liken the office to the Ming Grand Secretariat because it took charge of preparing imperial decrees, drafting state communications, offering advice, and deliberating on state affairs. Like the Ming Transmission Office (*tong-zheng si*), the Literary Office also delivered memorials and foreign communications to the imperial desk. All in all, the Literary Office was similar to the above three Ming institutions. When Hong Taiji changed his frontier state to the Qing dynasty in 1636, it became the Inner Office of the State Historiographer (*nei guoshi yuan*), the Inner State Secretariat (*nei bishu yuan*), and the Inner Academy for Literary Advancement (*nei hongwen yuan*). These offices collectively were referred to as the Three Inner Courts, which underwent changes in the following reigns.[21]

During the Shunzhi reign the Three Inner Courts adopted more from Chinese political tradition and hired a large number of Chinese officials, many of whom had served the defunct Ming government. In a short period, from July 1644 to September of the following year, the prince regent, Dorgon, appointed 107 Chinese to help operate the Three Inner Courts. Among them were three former Ming grand secretaries, Feng Quan (1595–1672), Xie Sheng (d. 1645), and Li Jiantai (d. 1651). Naturally they ran these offices in a Chinese way. Of the three, Feng stayed in office for fifteen years, and this long service enabled him to exercise enormous influence on the Qing imperial administration. In 1644 he and Hong Cheng-chou memorialized the prince regent about the function of the Three Inner Courts, and their recommendations were accepted. By 1658 Shunzhi, the first Manchu ruler of China, changed the Three Inner Courts to the Grand Secretariat,

largely after the Ming model. With his domination over the tetrar-
chical regency following the death of the Shunzhi emperor, Oboi (d.
1669), a powerful regent during the minority of the Kangxi emperor,
reversed sinicization and reintroduced the Three Inner Courts. After
Oboi's fall in 1669, Kangxi reestablished the Grand Secretariat and the
Hanlin Academy. They remained in the Qing administrative structure
almost to the end of the dynasty.[22]

Members of the Literary Office formed a compact and informal
group serving as Hong Taiji's advisors and confidants. Because they
owed their positions to the throne, they were under his command and
competed for his attention. They received imperial orders and submitted memorials through the *baksi*. Many worked out military strategy,
and urged Hong Taiji to conquer the Ming dynasty, while others advised him to modify policies toward land and taxation. In 1632, Wang
Wenkui and Wang Shun suggested the introduction of an official dress
code and the classics colloquium. Ning Wanwo submitted many memorials, one of which advised Hong Taiji to adapt Ming statutes and
acquaint Manchu officials with the Chinese law. Ma Guozhu (d. 1664)
recommended the appointment of remonstrating or speaking officials.
At the throne's request Literary Office staffers studied issues or even
sat with princes to deliberate cases. When he wanted to end the co-
rulership in 1632, he ordered Dahai to sit in at a meeting to present his
view before the princes.[23]

The Literary Office was an important factor in sinicization. From
Chinese memorialists, especially members of the Literary Office,
Hong Taiji learned about Chinese political and social institutions and
their related values. They quoted from Chinese historical anecdotes
about wise and good rulers who knew how to select officials and care
for people. In 1628 and 1629, Hong Taiji twice requested a loan of Chinese classics from Korea. Among the classics Korea sent were the *Book
of Rites*, the *Spring and Autumn Annals*, and the *Comprehensive Mirror
for Aid in Government*. One may assume the requests were suggested
by Chinese advisors. In 1632 and 1635, Wang Wenkui and Ning Wanwo
reminded Hong Taiji of the importance of the Confucian classics.[24]
Moreover, it was mainly through their persistent petitions that Hong
Taiji began to adopt Ming political machinery.

The Six Boards were the administrative center of the traditional Chinese state. After conquering Liaodong, Nurhaci had to deal with many complicated problems, both military and nonmilitary. The *jargūci* and banner systems were no longer sufficient. In the second half of 1622 he put sixteen individuals in charge of judicial matters, presumably with an emphasis on civilian cases, and eight officials to handle other affairs, each attending to separate duties. Since their responsibilities matched the functions of five of the Six Boards—revenues, rites, war, punishment, and public works—one may regard these appointments as the prototype of the six offices and an adoption of Ming imperial administration. Hong Taiji seems to have created four offices: land and grain, weapons, animals, and punishments. Each seems to have had four *baksi*. In addition, the Office of Punishments had four interpreters, perhaps because it had to handle cases concerning Chinese and Mongol subjects.[25]

The installation of the Six Boards in 1631 marked another step in the development of Qing administration. It resulted in part from the advice of Ning Wanwo, Bao Cheng-xian, and Fan Wencheng, all members of the Literary Office. Hong Taiji needed the Six Boards to execute state affairs. He constructed new buildings to house them, made an inspection tour, and held ceremonies when they were completed in 1632. Each board was given a silver seal for identification and a placard showing its duties.[26]

Qing rulers from Hong Taiji to Shunzhi repeatedly adjusted the Six Boards for effective imperial control and efficient operation. In their early stage the Qing Six Boards were aristocratic as well as military, differing from their Ming predecessors. They were headed by princes who were lords of the Eight Banners. Next were officials later designated as presidents and vice-presidents. Below were mind-enlighteners (*qixin lang*), *bithesi*, secretaries (*janggin*), and runners. Whatever their rank or duty, these staff members, mostly Manchus, were also from the Eight Banners. In contrast, the officials of the Ming Six Boards were bureaucrats. Domineering and inexperienced, the princes handled the business of the board at home and gave priority to their own banners. As a result they transformed the Six Boards into another arena of power struggle at the expense of the throne. In 1644 their control over

the board was ended by Dorgon, the powerful regent, but it was restored in 1652, and came to a close in the following year.[27]

The office of the mind-enlighteners is worth exploring. Although it
was a minor and short-lived office, it was a unique Qing creation. Its
members were trusted by Hong Taiji, selected from among the Manchu and Chinese members of the Literary Office, and placed in the
Three Inner Courts and the Six Boards. The Manchu mind-enlighteners he placed in the Six Boards were to keep the princes under control, while their Chinese counterparts were charged with the duty of
maintaining justice and reporting unjust and lawbreaking cases. From
all accounts the mind-enlighteners, Manchu or Chinese, served as the
throne's personal agents and were awarded in 1652 the same rank as
vice-presidents of the Six Boards. Six years later, when Shunzhi felt his
control over the Six Boards was secure, he abolished the office of the
mind-enlighteners.[28]

The Six Boards underwent further major adjustments. In 1638, for
instance, their staff was downsized. A smaller staff would not only
make operation more efficient but also facilitate imperial control. Immediately after the Manchus took Peking Dorgon recalled the Chinese
who had served in the Six Boards under the Ming to guide the Manchu staff members in the operation of these offices because the latter did not have experience to deal with complicated problems in an
immense geographical area. During the Shunzhi reign the offices of
the presidents and vice-presidents were gradually standardized. Each
board ended up with two presidents, one Manchu and one Chinese,
and four vice-presidents on the same basis.[29] This ethnic balance, a
Qing innovation, extended to other offices, symbolizing joint rule of
China by Manchus and Chinese.

Under Hong Taiji the Qing dynasty adopted from the Ming the
Censorate (*ducha yuan*: lit. chief surveillance office), an institution
with broad responsibilities, civil and military.[30] The Qing Censorate
was likely founded between late 1635 and early 1636 at the advice of
Chinese staffers in the Literary Office. Although at first Hong Taiji
turned down their advice, he finally changed his mind at the persistent
advice of Chinese officials and by events after 1632; with the subjugation of the Chahar Mongols, he was able to control Inner Mongolia. A
large number of Ming officers and soldiers defected while many Chi-

nese scholars became collaborators. The great expansion of his state increased the volume of administrative affairs and needed the Censorate to oversee the operation of the Ming ruling machinery that he had decided to adopt.[31]

The early Qing Censorate underwent changes similar to those at the Six Boards. In 1638, staff was reduced. During the Shunzhi reign it was restructured, also following the practice of ethnic balance. Among its staff were two senior presidents (*zuo duyushi*), one Manchu and one Chinese. Below were two Manchu and two Chinese senior vice-presidents (*zuo fu duyushi*). The main body of staff consisted of fifty-six censors, organized into fifteen circuits to take care of provincial affairs and special assignments. On the whole, the Censorate operated in the same way as its Ming predecessor. Its staff could investigate and impeach officials for wrongdoing and scrutinize government actions. They could inform the ruler about events, urge action or inaction, and remonstrate with him on policies or personal conduct. However, the Censorate was weakened by the confidential memorial system, which began in the late Kangxi era, reached its height in the Yongzheng period, and carried out duties similar to those of the Censorate.[32]

At the suggestion of Chinese officials, Hong Taiji adopted another Ming censorial institution, the Six Offices of Scrutiny (*liuke jishi zhong*). Ma Guang-yuan (d. 1663), a Chinese banner officer, twice petitioned the throne in 1633 to establish this institution to improve the work of the Six Boards. Hong Taiji seems to have adopted these offices together with the Censorate. During Ming times they were independent of the Censorate but had a functional relationship. Staffed by a small group of supervising secretaries, the Six Offices paired with the Six Boards, each office focusing on its corresponding Board. Supervising secretaries had considerable authority, chiefly over the documents sent to and from the Six Boards. They could return such documents, even imperial decrees, for reconsideration. They appeared at imperial audiences, played a part in the deliberation of state affairs such as judicial cases, and took special assignments.[33]

The Qing Six Offices of Scrutiny were consolidated in the early Kangxi era. Each Office had two senior supervising secretaries and two supervising secretaries. Half of these appointees were Manchus and half Chinese. But the most important change occurred in 1723 when Yongzheng made efforts to suppress factionalism as a result of the succession struggle of the late Kangxi period. He incorporated the Six Offices of Scrutiny into the Censorate so as to keep them under central surveillance. Thus supervising secretaries lost their independence and had to perform the duties of censors. They were so busy that they could not do their best in either capacity. Their editorial and veto powers over imperial decrees were seriously compromised.[34]

In short, the Qing imperial administrative machinery that Hong Taiji installed was proposed mainly by Chinese aides. They introduced the Ming governing structure, with which they were familiar. It was through this adoption that the Qing established a legitimate link with China's dynastic tradition. But the Qing imperial administrative institutions were not merely copies, for they were characterized by Manchu features in organization, function, and personnel. The Translation Office, a unique component of the Qing Grand Secretariat, took charge of translating Chinese and Manchu documents. Functionally the Grand Secretariat was undercut first by the Southern Imperial Library (*nan shufang*), beginning in the early Kangxi era, and then by the Grand Council (*junji chu*), which was founded by Yongzheng and consolidated by the Qianlong emperor. Most offices in the Qing central government were filled with both Manchu and Chinese officials. From this practice came the principle of numerical equality between Manchu and Chinese appointees. Besides, the Qing had innovated its own institutions, such as the banner system, the Court of Dependent Peoples, and the Office of the Imperial Household.

2. Legal Institutions

The early Qing code, especially its penal regulations, was influenced by Ming statutes and became the foundation of Qing legal institutions. For centuries after the fall of the Jin dynasty the Jurchens did not have any written law. On the eve of the rise of Nurhaci, even their customary law was no longer effective because the traditional Jurchen social institutions had broken down. There were small groups under leaders entrenched in villages, forts, stockades. They organized alliances, changed sides, and waged ceaseless wars. It was from these chaotic circumstances that Nurhaci emerged. He tried to keep order and stability among his subjects by restoring customary law. This effort can be seen from his order of 1587, which forbade rebellion, robbery, and larceny. The most common forms of punishment were whipping, slapping the face, and piercing the nose or ears with arrows.[35] The more conquests Nurhaci made, the more he needed law.

The legal institutions that Nurhaci introduced during his lifetime were primitive, mainly of a tribal nature. Some of the aforesaid punitive methods were related to riding and archery, that is, to the Jurchen way of life. The tribesman sped up his horse with a whip, and the tribal chief used it to punish an offender. The arrow, chiefly a hunting tool, could be used to pierce the nose and ears of breakers of tribal rules. Although abolished in 1622, piercing as a punishment lingered until 1646. Many rules and commands Nurhaci issued in 1621–1623 were mainly administrative, prohibitory regulations or moral admonitions. In 1621 he asked people to live with their slaves on decent terms. He punished an officer for the breach of an agreement and ordered that Buddhist temples be protected. There was no clear distinction between administrators and judges, as in the case of the Five Councilors and Ten *Jargūci* appointed in 1615.[36] Nor was there much difference between military and civil cases, because he put all subjects under the Eight Banners. Officers at various levels of the banner system were leaders, administrators, and judges.

The conquest of Liaodong in 1621 was a milestone in early Qing legal development. With more Chinese and Mongol subjects, Nurhaci confronted more judicial cases. The need for a judicial system became urgent, and he freqently appointed judges. From April 1622 to March 1623 he made three such appointments, each including several people. In the first and third appointments were Chinese and Mongol judges. After one examines his decrees and the names of appointees, it appears that these appointments were temporary. In any case, frequent appointments testify to his endeavor to create a legal system. His ordinances and instructions suggest that he was aiming for a three-level judicial procedure based on collective decisions. One of his orders in 1622 indicates that judges carried out trials and reported the results to eight high officials, who presented their judgments to the eight princes for the final trial. At each level judges listened to cases and made decisions together.[37]

In addition to judicial personnel and procedures, Nurhaci needed a more advanced legal code. Shortly after his takeover of Liaodong he ordered some officials, mostly Chinese, to submit a detailed report on Ming statutes. At about the same time, he commissioned Dahai to translate the Ming penal code into Manchu. It is likely that Dahai finished the translation after the death of Nurhaci in 1626. But without question Nurhaci benefited from the Ming statutes known to him. In 1623, he issued rules for high officials on travel and regulated what caps and dress officials and attendants were allowed.[38] These rules were taken, with modifications, from the Ming statutes.

The above facts demonstrate that Nurhaci was a groundbreaker in the establishment of the early Qing legal system. First, his law was of a tribal, customary, and unwritten nature, but with creation of the Manchu script in 1599, it was written down. After 1621 he adopted more from the Ming statutes. Although he did not produce a comprehensive code for the early Qing, he accomplished a workable legal system with a focus on the penal code and trial procedure.[39]

Under Hong Taiji the early Qing legal system made great progress. In the beginning, he had to rule the state with other princes, as planned by Nurhaci. This created competition, and he had to struggle for supremacy. A few days after his enthronement he placed forty of his men in the Eight Banners, the power base of the princes. Eight of these appointees were made banner commanders, assisted by "sixteen high officers" (shiliu dachen), who functioned as deputy commanders with both military and judicial responsibilities. The other "sixteen high officers" concentrated on judicial matters. He also adopted many concepts from the Ming Code to enhance imperial power.[40]

The Manchu state under Hong Taiji was much more complex. Not only did it acquire more land but also more alien subjects. By diplomacy and force he won the cooperation of many Mongol tribes. He won over Chinese collaborators, many of whom were Ming army officers, such as Kong Youde (d. 1652) and Shang Kexi (d. 1676). Chinese and Mongol subjects outnumbered the Jurchens. With two military expeditions he made Korea a dependent state.[41] All these developments indicated that tribal Jurchen rules and values, the core of Nurhaci's law, were inadequate to meet the needs of a more complex Manchu state. Hong Taiji had to make new regulations and modify the old.

Hong Taiji's ambition to conquer the Ming dynasty played a role in the evolution of early Qing legal institutions. When he launched an attack on suburban Peking late in 1629 he announced that the Mandate of Heaven had been transferred from one house to another. Originally small frontier states, he further argued, the Liao, Jin, and Yuan dynasties ultimately turned into great empires. In light of these cases, he believed, his Jurchen state was qualified to be an empire. He proclaimed himself emperor of the Qing dynasty in 1636. He always had a high opinion of Ming institutions. In a full court audience in 1637 he pointed out that despite repeated military setbacks the Ming dynasty was able to avoid collapse because it had good administrative and legal foundations. It is not surprising, then, that he wanted to build a strong institutional foundation for his empire based on the Ming model.[42]

In several ways Hong Taiji upgraded early Qing legal institutions. He gradually replaced unwritten Jurchen customs and norms with written rules. It is likely that the new-script Manchu facilitated this transformation. From 1630 onward, he made regulations on Chinese runaways from their banner masters, hunting and marching, and marriage. Around 1636 he collected his regulations and commands in a book of statutes known as *Sheng-jing dingli* (Shenyang regulations). The collection consisted of penal and nonpenal articles incorporated into fifty-two provisions and was influenced by Confucian theory of law. For instance, it covered, among others, the "Ten Abominations" (*shio*), which included rebellion, treason and impious acts, all regarded as unpardonable offenses in the traditional Chinese penal code since the sixth century. It seems to have served as the basis on which officials dealt with 434 penal cases in 1638–1639, as contained in the *Archival Compilation of the Board of Punishments in Shenyang*. Perhaps the greatest improvement Hong Taiji made was the establishment of the Board of Punishments. Thereafter judicial matters were managed by professionals, who followed written rules and advocated standard practices.[43]

The *Shenyang Regulations* and the laws of the earlier conquest dynasties, such as the Liao, Jin and Yuan, shared common features, among which were multiethniciy, inequality, flexibility, and universality. As polyethnic states, they recognized the ethnic differences of their subjects and adopted the "personality principle," according to which, as Herbert Franke and Hok-lam Chan point out, different laws were applied to different ethnic groups. Even before 1644 the Qing dynasty was polyethnic and multilingual. The court issued important documents—for example, the calendar, a succession proclamation, and the *Veritable Records*—in three languages: Manchu, Chinese, and Mongol. It also emphasized the translation of state papers from one language to another. At different times, the Literary Office, the Three Inner Courts, and the Grand Secretariat translated Chinese and Manchu documents. It was via translation that the Manchus were able to borrow from the Ming Code of Law. The Court of Dependent Peoples, originally referred to as the Office of Mongol Affairs (*Menggu yamen*), rendered Mongol documents into Manchu and vice versa.[44]

Inequality and flexibility were important to the application of the "personality principle" because the conquest dynasties divided subjects into classes: conqueror and conquered. As conquerors the Manchus enjoyed, besides political and social advantages, judicial privileges. They were under the jurisdiction of the banners, separate from Chinese institutions. Local Chinese officials were not allowed to arrest, try, or punish them when they broke the Chinese law. Even if they were convicted by their own judges, their sentences were usually reduced. The Qing court also applied the *Shenyang Regulations* with flexibility, for the Manchus, Chinese, and Mongols had different ways of life. It was necessary to take into consideration their traditional norms and mores and broker a compromise between local usage and central commands within the framework of the statutes.[45]

The *Shenyang Regulations* also applied a universality or "territoriality" principle. It worked side by side with the personality principle, although they conflicted with each other. Hong Taiji made great efforts to universally apply his statutes to all his subjects. In 1636 he twice notified the Mongol leaders of the *Shengyang Regulations*. The Board of Punishments took charge of judicial cases involving Chinese or Manchus. When important cases occurred among Mongols, the Court of Dependent Peoples helped their leaders enforce the statutes. After 1644, it became the chief office to draft laws for the Mongols. Universal application of the law was essential to the claim of universal jurisdiction, a Chinese political tradition based on the Confucian theory of kingship. Hong Taiji needed it for legitimization of his rule on the eve of the Manchu conquest of China proper.⁴⁶

In the history of Qing legal institutions, the reign of Hong Taiji was a transitional phase because after 1644 Manchu components gradually gave way to Chinese elements. The banner system was a case in point. When organized into banners, the clan and tribal chiefs were made officers, with authority over their clansmen and tribesmen, who became the bannermen. All officers from the captain of the company to banner commanders played a part in the judicial process, and so did imperial princes.⁴⁷ Their role in the judicial process accentuated the Manchu components, which hindered the imperial effort to extend authority by application of law.

Clearing the tribal and clan elements from the judicial system was a part of the imperial plan to weaken the Manchu aristocracy. Naturally, this also meant adopting more Chinese institutions, which were centrally and bureaucratically oriented. From the reign of Hong Taiji on the early Qing monarchs struggled for political centralization. The Shunzhi and Kangxi emperors only made limited progress, for both experienced the domination of aristocratic regents during their minorities. Kangxi's work was disrupted by the heirdom crisis in 1708–1722, which involved almost all the Manchu nobles. As a determined, autocratic ruler, Yongzheng accomplished the most. He contained the aristocrats, bureaucratized the banner system, restricted the judicial privileges of the Manchus, and ordered provincial administrators to punish lawbreakers regardless of their ethnic background. As a rule, a Chinese subject would be sentenced to death if he killed a bannerman, on purpose or by accident. Yongzheng once rejected the death sentence of a Chinese on the ground that the bannerman he killed was guilty and the killing was not premeditated.⁴⁸ All this contributed to the reduction of Manchu components from Qing legal institutions.

A few more transitional Manchu components in the early Qing legal institutions are worth mentioning. Jurchen religious beliefs played a part in the legal process. Among early Qing documents were many religious affidavits made in a variety of circumstances. In 1619, Nurhaci asked banner officers to pledge loyalty and devotion. The same year, five Qalqa Mongol tribes decided to ally with Nurhaci by

exchanging written oaths. In one trial a defendant was allowed to take
an oath in front of a judge and the accuser to deny a charge that was
hard to prove. But this element was no longer applicable after 1644. As
a Jurchen social institution, ultimogeniture was an important factor
in judicial decisions. According to this principle, prior to adulthood
younger sons in the families of titled nobles stayed at home, enjoyed
their father's privileges, and finally inherited the family estates. On the
other hand, they would receive harsher punishment than their adult
brothers when the father was punished. This practice had disappeared
by the eighteenth century. Another Manchu component was *tuhere
weile*, a form of punishment by fine or whipping imposed on aristocratic offenders in accord with rank.[49] Started by Nurhaci and modified by Hong Taiji, this punishment lasted until the early Kangxi reign.

Frequent revisions of the Qing code after 1644 provided an opportunity for Chinese influence. The *Shenyang Regulations* was not logi-
cally organized, or exactly a code of law. As a product of a frontier
kingdom they became unfit for the situation arising after the conquest
of China in 1644. The Ming code of law that the Qing relied on during the Shunzhi period was no longer suitable for the new political and
social needs. At the request of officials the Qing government studied
the problem and in 1647 printed the *Da-Qing lü* (great Qing code),
the first formal Qing penal code, with a Manchu edition published
eight years later. It took much from the Ming code of law and also
followed the latter's format. The strong similiarity did not escape Tan
Qian (1594–1658), a noted historian who considered the *Great Qing
Code* merely a new name for the Ming code. His view has been shared
by other scholars, including Derk Bodde and Clarence Morris, authors
of *Law in Imperial China*.[50]

The Qing government continued to revise its code of law during
the next three reigns (1662–1795). These revisions revealed a problem
in the Qing legal institution. It gave precedence to substatutes (*li*) over
statutes (*lü*). In time substatutes increased as cases increased, becoming cumbersome. Traditional Chinese statutes were marked by brev-
ity liable to different interpretations. In consequence, the government
had to reinterpret statutes with commentaries and reclassify the substatutes so as to make them related. The result was the publication of
a code entitled *Xianxing zeli* (substatutes currently operative) in 1679.

During the Yongzheng reign an imperial commission devoted three years to examining statutes and substatutes. By the end of 1728 it developed a new code, *Da-Qing lü jijie fuli* (great Qing code with collected commentaries and appended substatutes), the most comprehensive of the early Qing dynasty, which included statutes and 815 substatutes.[51]

During his long reign the Qianlong emperor revised the Qing substatutes about nine times, and codified them. At first they were revised once every three years, but after 1746 every five years. Many substatutes were deleted or modified; numerous new ones were added. What made the Qianlong era distinct was that the Board of Punishments alone was charged with making the revisions, instead of a special imperial commission, which had characterized the earlier revisions.[52] Despite this change, one thing is certain: more revisions brought in more Chinese influence. This can been verified by the imperial edict of 1747, a six-point guideline on revision. Besides deletions and additions, the guideline called for consulting the Confucian classics on rites, earlier dynastic codes of law, and encyclopedic compilations. It also specified that the revision office was to select staff members from among appropriate scholar-officials and individuals with academic degrees. Obviously Confucian ideals were brought into the Qing code through consultation, for Chinese law had been Confucianized for centuries. Since the staff members were chiefly Confucian scholars, they were eager to introduce Confucian views of law into the Qing judicial system.[53]

Related to the above code were many other regulations. Almost every office in the central government had its own regulations. The most comprehensive was the *Da-Qing huidian* (collected institutes of the great Qing), which covered operational rules of all offices in the government. It was patterned after the collected Ming institutes, which had served Hong Taiji as the guidebook of his government, including the judicial process. The collected Qing institutes had five editions, the last of which, published in 1899, was the most detailed. Although its first edition appeared in the early Kangxi period, one may trace its beginning to the reign of Hong Taiji, who seems to have contributed to the regulations for the Board of Rites, a constituent part of the collected Qing institutes. To centralize his powers he made many rules, such as rites about the imperial inauguration and other matters about the emperor or his family, and regulations pertinent to relations between people of different ranks or social groups. Under his auspices and perhaps also with the support of Prince Sahaliyen (d. 1636), Icengge (fl. 1630s–1640s), a Manchu linguist and scholar, rendered the Ming regulations of the Board of Rites into Manchu. To be sure, the translation and the rules made by Hong Taiji laid the groundwork for the regulations of the Board of Rites.[54]

On the whole, Chinese administrative and legal institutions increased sinicization of the Manchus. Owing to administrative and political needs, the early Qing monarchs from Hong Taiji onward adopted Ming political institutions, which were the only ones available. But they modified the Ming institutions with Manchu components to meet the needs of a multiethnic empire. To operate Chinese institutions, they had to learn the elements that made their functioning possible. Beginning with Shunzhi, Qing emperors studied Chinese classics, history, and political tradition to facilitate their rule. They were hardly aware of the sinicization process and reinterpreted the components of Chinese culture in the context of their Manchu heritage. They supervised officials, many of whom were Manchus also influenced by Confucian ideals, to conduct state affairs in the Chinese way. A sinicized ruling class helped spread Chinese culture among the Manchu commoners.

Notes

1. According to the sources, his frontier state took shape as early as 1587. See *Nuer-haqi shilu*, 1: 8a; Teng, *Nuer-hachi*, 59–60.

2. For the *hala* and *mukūn* system, see Shirokogoroff, *Social Organization of the Manchus*, ch. 2 and pp. 153–55; Mitamura, *Shinchō zenshi no kenkyū*, ch. 3. Also see Pei Huang, "Monarchy and Aristocracy during the Early Ch'ing Dynasty (1644–1735)," in Graciela de la Lama, ed., *China* (Mexico City: El Colegio de Mexico, 1982), 344–46. For these clans, see *STTP*, chs.1–4, 9–10, and 25–27.

3. There are several studies on the *niru*. Two are mentioned here. Ch'en, "The Creation of the Manchu Niru," 11–46; Hatada Takashi, "Manshū hakki no seiritsu katei ni kansuru ichi kōsatsu—tokuni niru no seiritsu ni tsuite," *Tōa ronsō*, 2 (1940): 73–93. For the importance of the clan to the banner system, see Mo, *Manzushi luncong*, 63–68.

4. For their appointments, see *Nuer-haqi shilu*, 2: 9. For the rise and evolution of

the Council, see Zhao Zhijiang, "Qingdai qianqi di junguo yizheng yu Manzhou guizu," *Manxue yanjiu*, 1 (1992): 55–75. For the function, abolition, and
revival of the Council, see Beatrice S. Bartlett, *Monarchs and Ministers: The
Grand Council in Mid-Ch'ing China, 1723-1820* (Berkeley and Los Angeles:
University of California Press, 1991), 48–49, 311–12ns114 and 116.

5. For information about Anfiyangu, Eidu, Erdeni, and Fiongdon, see *ECCP*, 1: 13,
   221–22, 225–26, 247–48; also see *CSKC*, 10: 7935–37, 7924–28, 7998–99, 7929–31.
   For Jaciba, see *TCCC*, 201: 4a. For the forty appointments in 1623, see *MWLT*,
   1: 411; *MBRT*, vol. 2, Taizu, 45: 651. For the overlapping of their functions, see
   Sun Yan, "Qingchu yizheng wang dachen huiyi jiqi zuoyong," *SHKH*, 4 (1986):
   61.

6. For his being given this title, see *Nuer-haqi shilu*, 2: 2b; for the creation of the
   Manchu old script, see ibid., 2: 1a. For the close relationship between these two
   languages, see William Rozycki, *Mongol Elements in Manchu* (Bloomington,
   IN: Research Institute for Inner Asian Studies, Indiana University, 1994), 10ff.

7. For a detailed study of the *darugachi* office, see Elizabeth Endicott-West, *Mongolian Rule in China: Local Administration in the Yuan Dynasty* (Cambridge,
   MA and London: Council on East Asian Studies, Harvard University, and the
   Harvard-Yenching Institute, 1989), ch. 4. For the terms *Jargūci, baturu*, and
   baksi, see Zheng, *Tanwei ji*, 143–45, 151–59. For political, administrative, and
   legal terms, see Liu, *Manzu di buluo*, 149–50. For the similarity between the
   banner system and the Mongol army, see David M. Farquhar, "Mongolian versus Chinese Elements in the Early Manchu State," *Ch'ing-shih wen-t'i*, 2. 6
   (1971): 13–15. For the Jurchen borrowing of horse-raising and horse-riding, see
   the same article by Farquhar, 19; Liu, *Manzu di shehui yu shenghuo*, 380.

8. Eidu received this rank. See *Xiang-huang qi Manzhou Niuhulu shi Hongyi gong
   jiapu*, 1: 11b. Fiongdon was conferred with the same rank (*TCCC*, 141: 3b).
   Jaciba received the title of the *Youji*, equivalent to the *Adaha hafan* in Manchu,
   that is, two ranks below the *Zongbing guan* (*TCCC*, 201: 4a).

9. For his dress with dragons, see *CWS*, vol. 22, reign of Sonjo, 71: 641–42, 29/1/
   chŏngyu. In 1621 some of Nurhaci's army units carried banners with colored
   dragons. See *CWS*, vol. 33, reign of Kwanghaegun, 169: 9a, 13/9/musin. For his
   Ula expedition, see *MWLT*, 1: 12. For his citations from Chinese history, see
   MWLT, 1: 484 and 695–96. For interpretations of natural phenomena, see
   Roth, "The Manchu-Chinese Relationship," 7–8; Teng Shaozhen, "Cong 'Man-
   wen laodang' kan Nuer-hachi di tianming sixiang," *SHKH*, 1 (1986): 51–57. The
   designation "Tian-ming" has been a controversy among scholars. See Imanishi
   Shunjū "Temmei kengen kō," *Chōsen gakuhō*, 14 (1959): 599–621; Huang
   Zhang-jian, "Qing Taizu Tianming jianyuan kao," *Bulletin of the Institute of
   History and Philology, Academia Sinica*, 37. 2 (1967): 475–95. For his imperial
   emblems in 1612, see *MWLT*, 1: 12.

10. For the inapplicability of the Ming institutions, see Cai Meibiao, "Da-Qing guo jianhao qian di guohao, zuming, yu jinian," *Lishi yanjiu*, 3 (1987): 141.

11. For Nurhaci's harsh policy toward Chinese, see Roth, "The Manchu-Chinese Relationship," 20; Zhang Yuxing, "Lun Qingbing ruguan di wenhua beijing," *Qingshi yanjiu*, 4 (1995): 2–3. For the quoted remarks, see *MWLT*, 1: 287–88. For Chinese runaways, see *MWLT*, 1: 392, 423–24; and 516. For anti-Manchu incidents and massacres, see *MWLT*, 1: 386 and 503. In a highly confidential decree, he advised princes and high officials to discriminate against Chinese officials. See *MWLT*, 1: 492.

12. For the power and importance of Šurhaci, see *CWS*, vol. 22, reign of Sŏnjo, 71: 643–44, 29/1/chŏngyu; Yi, *Chaam Sŏnsaeng munip*, 6: 2a. For his execution, see Meng Sen, *Ming-Qing shi lunzhu jikan* (Taipei: Shijie shuju, 1961), 174–82. For the family background of the two Gorolos, see *Guololo shi qichuang fenxing: Ju Zhanhe shan* (Peking? Qing Guoshi guan? n.d., handwritten, 17 pp., unpaged), 1–2. For their cooperation with Nurhaci, see *Daicing gurun i manju yargiyan kooli*, 30–31; for Cangšu's punishment, see Guang and Li, *Qing Taizu*, 1: 4.

13. For the title of Esulele, see *STTP*, 5: 9a. For Gong Zhenglu, see Chapter I, note 57 above. Also see *CWS*, vol. 22, reign of Sŏnjo, 70: 608, 28/12/kyemyo. For Dahai and Kūrcan, see Chapter IV, section 3. Hife was a member of the Hešeri clan. For his and Dahai's service in the Literary Office, see *Qingshi liezhuan*, 1. 4: 187, 189. Tuša taught Nurhaci's sons Chinese and enjoyed easy access to his master. He was executed on the charge of adultery in 1625. See *MWLT*, 1: 327, 557–58, 633–34.

14. Dahai possibly translated a fourth book. See Durrant, "Sino-Manchu Translations," 654–55. For relations between reading translations and sinicization, see Franke, *China under Mongol Rule*, 19 and 26. These Chinese military men seem to have defected from the Ming army. For example, Li Yongfang was the commander of the Ming forces at Fushun before his defection. For the order by Nurhaci in 1621, see *MWLT*, 1: 189–90; *MBRT*, vol. 1, Taizu, 20: 305–306. For a fine work on administrative machinery, see Nakayama Hachirō, "Shinsho Nuruhachi ōkoko no tōchi kikō,"*Hitotsubashi ronsō*, 14. 2 (1944): 15–32.

15. For Nurhaci's attempts to designate an heir-apparent and plan for joint rule, see Zhou Yuan-lian, "Hou-Jin ba Heshi beile 'gongzhi guozheng' lun," *Qingshi luncong*, 2 (1980): 244–62. For his joint rule advice, see *MWLT*, 1: 345–48. For the termination of the joint rule, see Chen and Teng, "Lüelun Huang Taiji di lishi zuoyong," 117–18. For the succession of Hong Taiji, see Hidehiro Okada, "How Hong-taiji Came to the Throne," *Central Asiatic Journal*, 23. 3–4 (1979): 250–59.

16. For his action to pacify Chinese farmers, see *CSL*, reign of Taizong, 1: 9b–11a, Tianming 11/9/jiaxu, bingzi, and dingchou; He Puying and Xie Zhaohua, "Lun Huang Taiji di minzu yiti sixiang," *MANT*, 3 (1990): 23–24. For his policy toward scholars and his organization of the Chinese banner forces, see Sun and

Li, *Qing Taizong*, 309–20. For the fifty-six new appointees, see *MWLT*, 2: 920–29.

F.W. Mote rightly states that Qing political institutions were largely adopted from the Ming dynasty, with minor adjustments. See his *Imperial China, 900–1800* (Cambridge, MA and London: Harvard University Press, 1999), 918.

17. Qing official records only show the responsibilities of its members, not its inception date. See *CSL*, reign of Taizong, 5: 11b–12a, Tiancong 3/4/bingwu. For the date of its institutionalization, see Yuan, *Qingdai qianshi*, 2: 566–67. For prohibition from using the title of *baksi*, see *CSL*, reign of Taizong, 9: 12b, Tiancong 5/7/gengchen. For importance of the *baksi*, see Zhang and Guo, *Qing ruguan qian*, 119–26. Kanda Nobuo points out that it was created around 1616 and grew into a full-fledged office by about 1626. See his "Shinsho no bunkan ni tsuite," 49.

18. For the history and importance of the position of *bithesi*, see Chen, *Ming-Qing zhengzhi*, 2: 605–21. For Zhaohui, see *CSKC*, 11: 9132–36; *Wuya shi zupu*, by an anonymous compiler (N.p.: late Qing period, handwritten, 4 volumes, unpaged), vol. 2. For Omida, see *CSKC*, 11: 9240–42.

19. For a biography of Gao Hong-zhong, see *CSKC*, 10: 8100. For Wang Shun, see Pan, Sun, and Li, *Qing ruguan qian shiliao*, 2: 28–29. For an analysis of the Chinese members in the office, see Guo Cheng-kang, "Lun Wenguan Han ruchen jiqi dui Qingchu zhengzhi di ying-xiang," *Dongbei difang shi yanjiu*, 1 (1986): 68–75; Yuan, *Qingdai qianshi*, 2: 557–65. According to official sources, the office seems to have had ten members, who were the *baksi* and *bithesi*, not including Chinese scholars. See *CSL*, reign of Taizong, 5: 11b–12a, Tiancong 3/4/bingxu. But it is possible that the Chinese members joined the office at later dates. Among the ten people was Gūlmahūn, who was of Korean origin. See Chapter IV, note 73. For biographies of Ning, Lei, Jiang, and Wang, see *CSKC*, 10: 8094–98, 8224, 8198–99, and 8212–15. Wang Wenkui was originally known as Shen Wenkui. For recommendations, see *CSL*, reign of Taizong, 5: 16, Tiancong 3/6/yichou. Hong Taiji gave several examinations, two in 1634. See *CSL*, reign of Taizong, 18: 10b, 17b–18a, Tiancong 8/3/renzi and 8/4/xinsi. At first Ning Wanwo recommended himself and then suggested others, including Bao Cheng-xian, to the throne. See *CSKC*, 10: 8094; Pan, Sun. and Li, *Qing ruguan qian shiliao*, 2: 6–7.

20. For their low official status, see Guo, "Lun Wenguan Han ruchen," 70; Huang, *Autocracy at Work*, 138–39.

21. For its importance, see Wakeman, *Grand Enterprise*, I: 162–63. For its early responsibilities, see *CSL*, reign of Taizong, 5: 11b–12a, Tiancong 3/4/bingxu. For other duties, see Pan, Sun, and Li, *Qing ruguan qian shiliao*, 2: 21–22, 24, 40–42, and 61. For the functions of the Hanlin Academy, Grand Secretariat, and Transmission Office, see *Mingshi*, 6. 73: 1785–88; 6. 72: 1732–34; 6. 73: 1780–81. For the Three Inner Courts, see *CSL*, reign of Taizong, 28: 2a–3a, Tiancong

10/3/ xinhai. For their functions, see Zhang and Guo, *Qing ruguan qian*, 90–95; Kanda, "Shinsho no bunkan ni tsuite," 49–51.

22. For the 107 appointees, see *Qingdai dang'an shiliao congbian*, 13 (1990): 1–110. For Feng, Xie, and Li, see *CSL*, Shunzhi reign, 5: 7b, 1/5/xinchou; 7: 26a, 1/8/ renwu; 15: 7b, 2/3/gengzi. For the tenure of Feng and Xie, see *CSKC*, 7: 5269–71, 5273–76; 5279–81; 7: 5269.

 For an English biography of Shunzhi, see *ECCP*, 1: 255–59. For the change from the Three Inner Courts to the Grand Secretariat, see *CSL*, Shunzhi reign, 119: 6b–7a, 15/7/wuwu. For the change by Oboi, see *CSL*, Kangxi reign, 3: 9, Shunzhi 18/6/dingyou. For the restoration of the Grand Secretariat and the Hanlin Academy, see *CSL*, Kangxi reign, 33: 27a, 9/8/yiwei. For a succinct treatment of the Grand Secretariat, see Wang, *Qingshi xukao*, 321–22.

23. In a memorial dated 1633 Wang Wenkui revealed that a *baksi* passed the throne's words onto him. See Pan, Sun, and Li, *Qing ruguan qian shiliao*, 2: 54. For advice about military strategy, see, ibid., 2: 4–6, 14–17. For land and taxation, see ibid., 2: 42–43, 60, and 22. For suggestions by Wang Wenkui and Wang Shun, see ibid., 2: 18–20, 24, 29–30. Both Ning and Ma submitted memorials in 1633. See ibid., 2: 82 and 48–49. For such meetings, see *CSL*, reign of Taizong, 26: 5a–9b, Tiancong 9/12/xinsi. For a good article on the importance of the office, see Wei Jianxun and Yuan Lükun, "Shilun Huang Taiji di gaige jiqi zhinang duan," *Guang-ming ribao* (February 24, 1981): 4.

24. For the request for books, see Qiao, *Qingwen qianbian*, 2: 80b; *CWS*, vol. 34, reign of Injo, 19: 308, 6/12/kyongin; 19: 309, 6/12/sinmyo and imjin; 21: 352, 7/10/kapsul. For translations by Dahai, see *CSKC*, 10: 8001. For the memorials by Wang and Ning, see Pan, Sun, and Li, *Qing ruguan qian shiliao*, 2: 24 and 71–72. Durrant complained that the Confucian classics were not among the first texts to be translated, and that translations were not motivated by sinicization. See his "Sino-Manchu Translations," 653–57. For petitions for adopting Ming political machinery and Confucian ideals, see Yuan, *Qingdai qianshi*, 2: 577–79, 584–89, 608–11.

25. For the twenty-four appointments by Nurhaci, see *MWLT*, 1: 382–83; *MBRT*, vol. 2, Taizu, 42: 607–608. For the importance of these appointments, see Zhang and Kuo, *Qing ruguan qian*, 51–52. The *Veritable Records* mentions three offices: Land, Weapons, and Punishment. See *CSL*, reign of Taizong, 7: 3a, Tiancong 4/5/jichou. In *MWLT* (2: 1359) there were three offices: Grain, Punishment, and Animals. Very possibly the Office of Land and that of Grain were the same office.

26. For their installation, see *CSL*, reign of Taizong, 9: 11b–12b, Tiancong, 5/7/ gengchen; Yuan, *Qingdai qianshi*, 2: 607–11. For contributions of the three staff members, see Wang, "Ning Wanwo di jinqu jingshen jiqi bian-hua," 115. But Ning Wanwo perhaps contributed more. See *CSL*, reign of Taizong, 10: 32, Tiancong 5/12/renchen. For Hong Taiji's tour of the new offices and the celebration, see *MWLT*, 2: 1330–31.

27. For officials of the Six Boards, see Guang and Li, "Qing Taizu chao 'Lao Man-wen yuandang' yu 'Manwen laodang'," 154–65. For the control of the Six Boards by the princes and its demise, see *Lidai zhiguan biao*, comp. Ji Yun et al. (SPPY ed., 1965, volumes 313–316), 313. 5: 6a; for the characteristics of these boards, see Zhang and Guo, *Qing ruguan qian*, 68–72. For a brief discussion of these new offices and their contribution to sinicization, see Ch'en Chieh-hsien, "Cong Qingchu zhong-yang jianzhi kan Manzhou Hanhua." In *Jindai Zongguo chuqi lishi yantao hui lunwen ji,* ed. The Institute of Modern History, Academia Sinica (Taipei: Institute of Modern History, Academia Sinica, 1989, 2 volumes), 1: 189–98.

28. For the importance of the mind-enlighteners, see Zhang and Guo, *Qing ruguan qian*, 68–70; for their official rank, see ibid., 70. For their abolition, see *Lidai zhiguan biao*, 313. 5: 6a

29. For the 1638 reorganization, see *CSL*, reign of Taizong, 42: 21a–24a, Chongde 3/7/bingxu. For the recall of former Ming Six Boards officials, see ibid., Shunzhi reign, 5: 5a, 1/5/guisi. For the reappointing of former Ming grand secretaries, see ibid., Shunzhi reign, 5: 7b, 1/5/xinchou; 7: 26a, 1/8/renwu. For standardization of the number of presidents and vice-presidents, see *Lidai zhiguan biao*, 313. 5: 6a; 313. 6: 5ff. For its Chinese and Manchu staff, see Wang, *Qingshi xukao*, 323–34.

30. For the structure of the Ming Censorate, see Charles O. Hucker, *The Censorial System of Ming China* (Stanford: Stanford University Press, 1966), ch. 2; Guan Wenfa and Yan Guangwen, *Mingdai zhengzhi zhidu yanjiu* (Peking: Zhongguo shehui kexue chuban she, 1995), 128–35.

31. Generally, scholars believe that the Censorate was founded in the fifth month of the first year of the Chongde reign. But the text suggests that it had been created before that date. See *CSL*, reign of Taizong, 29: 6a–7a, Chongde 1/5/dingsi. For the memorial by Ma Guozhu in 1633, the response of Hong Taiji, subsequent memorials, and the mind-enlightener's function, see Pan, Sun, and Li, *Qing ruguan qian shiliao*, 2: 49, 90, 95–96, 111, and 39.

32. For the Qing Censorate, see *Lidai zhiguan biao*, 313. 18: 4a; Zhang Deze, *Qingdai guojia jigou kaolüe* (Peking: Zhongguo renmin daxue chuban she, 1981), 114–24. For the rise and effects of the confidential memorial system on the Qing Censorate and Six Offices of Scrutiny, see Huang, *Autocracy at Work*, 119–35.

33. For Ma's petitions, see Pan, Sun, and Li, *Qing ruguan qian shiliao*, 2: 40–41, 43–44. For the Six Offices of Scrutiny, see *Mingshi*, 6. 74: 1805–07.

34. For incorporation of the Six Offices into the Censorate and its effect, see Huang, *Autocracy at Work*, 113–19.

35. For his order of 1587, see *Nuer-haqi shilu*, 1: 8a. These forms of corporal punishment had appeared in various early Qing documents. For discussion of such punishments, see Li, "The Rise of the Early Manchu State," 149. For a comprehensive coverage of the forms of punishment, see Liu Shizhe, "Nuer-hachi shiqi xingfa leixiang jiqi tedian," *MTYC*, 6 (1987): 59–68.

36. For relations between these forms of punishment and the Jurchen way of life, see Wei Fuxiang and Du Shangxie, "Manzu falü zongshu," *MANT*, 3 (1994): 37. For his abolition of this punishment under Ming influence, see Yan, *Nuer-hachi zhuan*, 167. But it was not until after the request made by the Board of Punishments in 1646 that it was actually revoked. See *CSL*, Shunzhi reign, 25: 20a, 3/4/wuzi. For Nurhaci's orders in 1621, see *MWLT*, 1: 165, 172, and 267. For such rules issued in 1621–1623, see Liu Shizhe, "Nuer-hachi shidai fazhi shu-lun," *MTYC*, 6 (1986): 35.

37. For the appointments in 1621–1623, see *MWLT*, 1: 346–47, 382, and 411. There were Manchu, Chinese, and Mongol judges in the first and third appointments, but the number of Manchu appointees differed in these two appointments. Some appointees in the second and third appointments were the same people. These appointments do not seem to be permanent offices.

    For the three-level trial and collective decision, see *MWLT*, 1: 346–47. But when he appointed the Five Councilors and Ten *Jargūci* in 1615, Nurhaci pre-ferred a four-level procedure, with the eight princes and himself as the last two tiers. See *Nuer-haqi shilu*, 2: 9. Later he changed to the three-level procedure perhaps because he was too busy to be part of it.

38. For his order of Chinese officials to report on the Ming statutes, see *MWLT*, 1: 189–90. Dahai possibly finished the translation in 1630. See *ECCP*, 1: 213. For Nurhaci's rules on traveling officials and caps and dress, see *MWLT*, 1: 511–12.

39. For an article on the development of the penal code under Nurhaci, see Oshi-buchi, "Shin Taiso jidai keisei kō," 321–52.

40. This arrangement was made in a long conversation between Nurhaci and the eight princes. See *MBRT*, vol. 2, Taizu, 38: 554–58. Political centralization was a driving force for Hong Taiji's determination to improve the legal institution. See Zhang and Guo, *Qing ruguan qian*, 421. For these appointees, see *CSL*, reign of Taizong, 1: 11a–12a, Tianming 11/9/dingchou.

41. For his control of Inner Mongolia, see Sun and Li, *Qing Taizong*, 233–49. Many Chinese were forced to submit to the Manchus, while some willingly collabo-rated. For short biographies of Kong and Shang, see *ECCP*, 1: 435–36; 2: 635–36. For the two Korea expeditions, see Liu Chia-chü, *Qingchu zhengzhi fazhan shi lunji* (Taipei: Commercial Press, 1978): 33–173.

42. For his declaration, see *CSL*, reign of Taizong, 5: 38a–39, Tiancong 3/11/bing-shen; for his proclamation in 1636, see ibid., 28: 19, Chongde 1/4/yiyou. For his order to follow the Ming Code, see Pan, Sun, and Li, *Qing ruguan qian shiliao*, 2: 2. For his praise of the Ming foundation in 1637, see *CSL*, reign of Taizong, 37: 10b, Chongde 2/7/xinwei.

43. Since Nurhaci, the Manchu rulers had issued many regulations about Chinese runaways from the banner slavery. See Zhang and Guo, *Qing ruguan qian*, 513. For hunting and marching, see *MWLT*, 2: 1256–57. There were two decrees about marriage in a nine-month period (1635–36). See *Shinkan ichiroku*, reign

of Taizong, 5: 4a, Tiancong 9/3/gengshen; 5: 15b–16a, Tiancong 9/12/xinsi. For Hong Taiji's code, see *MWLT*, 2: 1447; Zhang and Guo, *Qing ruguan qian*, 436–39. The Chinese title for this archival compilation is *Sheng-jing xingbu yuan-dang* (Peking: Qunzhong chuban she, 1985). For the name *Sheng-jing dingli*, see *CSKC*, 5: 3967–68. For the Ten Abominations, see Zhang and Guo, *Qing ru-guan qian*, 510–12; T'ung-tsu Ch'ü, *Law and Society in Traditional China* (Paris and La Haye: Mouton, 1965), 42–43, 179n48.

44. When discussing the law of the Jin dynasty, Herbert Franke and Hok-lam Chan mention the ethnic differences and the personality principle. See Herbert Franke and Hok-lam Chan, *Studies on the Jurchens and the Chin Dynasties* (Aldershot, Hampshire, Great Britain: Ashgate, 1997), 215 and 387. For the calendar in three languages, see *CSL*, reign of Taizong, 39. 1b, Chongde 2/10/yiwei; for the enthronement proclamation, see *CSL*, reign of Taizong, 28: 21b–22a, Chongde 1/4/yiyou. For example, the *Veritable Records* of the reigns of Nurhaci, Hong Taiji, and Shunzhi were published in Chinese, Manchu, and Mongol languages (see their prefaces). For the translating function of the Literary Office, see the last two references in note 21 above. For the translation office in the Court of Dependent Peoples, see *Lidai zhiguan biao*, 17: 7b–8a.

45. For discussion of its characteristics, such as inequality and flexibility, see Oshibuchi, "Shin Taisō jidai keisei kō," 1–32; Zhang and Guo, *Qing ruguan qian*, 427–30, 443. For Manchu legal advantages, see *Shangyu baqi*, 6: 9b; 7: 2b, and Feng Erkang, *Yongzheng zhuan* (Peking: Renmin chuban she, 1985), 314–15.

46. For the application of Qing laws to the Mongols, see Nicola Di Cosmo, "Qing Colonial Administration in Inner Asia," *International History Review*, 20. 2 (June 1998): 287–309. For the role of the Court of Dependent Peoples in the drafting of laws for the Mongols, see Dorothea Heuschert, " Legal Pluralism in the Qing Empire: Manchu Legislations for the Mongols," *International History Review*, 20. 2 (June 1998): 314–15. In 1636, Hong Taiji sent missions to notify Mongol leaders of the new statutes. See *MWLT*, 2: 1447 and 1627. Mongol affairs were the chief duty of the Court of Dependent Peoples. He sometimes dispatched officials from both the Court and the Censorate to handle judicial matters among the Mongols. See *CSL*, reign of Taizong, 37: 17a, Chongde 2/7/guiwei, and 38: 11, Chongde 2/8/jiwei.

47. According to an entry dated Tianming 6/2/28 (*MWLT*, 1:161), the captain had the judicial authority. Before 1631 the captain had to report cases to the *Jargŭci* or such people as the Sixteen High Officers, appointed by Hong Taiji in the banners. Immediately after the establishment of the Board of Punishments Hong Taiji allowed the captain to handle trivial cases only, leaving important matters to the Board. See *CSL*, reign of Taizong, 9: 16b–17a, Tiancong 5/7/guisi.

48. For bureaucratization of the banner system, see Huang, *Autocracy at Work*, ch. 7. For Yongzheng's efforts to restrict the judicial privileges of the bannerman, see *Shangyu neige* 18: 8a and 19, Yongzheng 6/3/3 and 6/3/24. He forbade

princes from abusing their retainers. See *CSL*, Yongzheng reign, 9: 18b–19b, 1/7/guisi. For his ordering provincial administrators to punish lawbreakers regardless of ethnic origin, see *CSL*, Yongzheng reign, 8: 14a, 1/6/renshen. For his rejection of a death verdict, see *CSL*, Yongzheng reign, 56: 23, 5/4/dingwei.

49.   For the oaths taken by the banner officers in 1619, see *MWLT*, 1: 100–102. For the alliance, see ibid., 1: 121–26. For the defendant's oath, see *CSL*, reign of Taizong, 8: 14a–16b, Tiancong 5/2/ xinwei. For a detailed treatment of early Qing ultimogeniture, see Fang, "Qingchu Manzhou jiating, 1–16. Zheng Tianting regarded *tuhere weile* simply as a form of fine. See his *Tanwei ji,* 137–40. My explanation of this term is based on Zhang and Guo, *Qing ruguan qian,* 534–42.

50.   For the weaknesses of the *Shenyang Regulations,* see Zhang and Guo, *Qing ruguan qian,* 437–38. For Qing reliance on the Ming code, see *CSL*, Shunzhi reign, 5: 18b–19a, 1/6/jiaxu; 10: 11b, 1/10/yihai. Many officials made requests for a new code of law. See *CSL*, Shunzhi reign, 7: 3a–4b, 1/8/bingchen; 26: 21a, 3/6/guisi. Many sources insist that the Qing code was completed in 1646, but it actually occurred in 1647. See *CSL*, Shunzhi reign, 31: 8a, 4/3/yichou. For its Manchu version, see *CSL*, Shunzhi reign, 96: 7b, 12/12/yichou. For the view of Tan Qian, see his *Beiyou lu* (Peking: Zhonghua Book Company, 1960), "*Da-Qing lü,*" 378. Bodde and Morris provide a good evaluation of the Qing code; see their *Law in Imperial China: Exemplified by 190 Ch'ing Dynasty Cases, Translated from the Hsin-an hui-lan. With Historical, Social, and Juridical Commentaries* (Cambridge, MA: Harvard University Press, 1967), 59–62, 65–66.

51.   For the major problem of the Qing legal institution, see *CSKC*, 5: 3971–72. For revisions in the Kangxi era, see *CSL*, Kangxi reign, 84: 11b–12a, 18/9/bingwu. For revisions during the Yongzheng reign, see *CSL*, Yongzheng reign, 11: 22b–23a, 1/9/guisi; 76: 11b, 6/12/bingshen; Bodde and Morris, *Law in Imperial China,* 60, 65–66.

52.   For revisions during the Qianlong period, see *CSKC*, 5: 3971 and 4098.

53.   For the edict of 1747, see *CSL*, Qianlong reign, 282: 3b–6a, 12/1/pingshen. The *Book of Rites* was among the Confucian classics. The encyclopedic compilations were published during Ming and Qing times. For Confucianization of Chinese laws, see Ch'ü, *Law and Society in Traditional China,* ch. 6.

54.   For a long list of such regulations, see Wang, *Qingshi xukao,* 284–313. For a study of the *Da-Qing huidian,* see ibid., 314–20; also Kanda Nobuo, "Shinsho no kaiten ni tsuite." In *Wada hakushi koki kinen Tōyōshi ronsō* (Tokyo: Kodansha, 1960), 337–48. For the use of the Ming institutes, see Pan, Sun, and Li, *Qing ruguan qian shiliao,* 2: 2 and 82.

        For rites about the imperial inauguration, see *CSL*, reign of Taizong, 28: 15, Chongde 1/4/gengchen. For some other rites about the princely insignia, emperor's birthday, and titles for imperial consorts and daughters, see *MWLT*, 2: 1448–1449, 1462–1464ff. For propriety between officials of different ranks or people of different social status, see *CSL*, reign of Taizong, 30: 7, Chongde 1/6/ jimao. For Sahaliyen, see *CSKC*, 10: 7752–54; *ECCP*, 2: 631–32. Icengge was a member of the Sogiya clan. For his short biography, see *STTP*, 44: 10. The entry does not specify what kind of translation he did. But the context suggests that he translated the material from Chinese into Manchu.

Chapter VI

Transformation of Social Institutions

CHINESE INFLUENCE ON JURCHEN SOCIAL INSTITUTIONS perhaps played the most significant role in sinicization. Changes began before 1644 as a result of frontier contacts. The Liaodong region provided, among other things, a social basis for interaction between the Chinese and Jurchen frontiersmen. The wide cultural disparity did not hinder contacts, official or private. The Chinese were influenced by the culture of their counterparts; some even identified with Nurhaci's cause. But the Jurchens, both nobles and commoners, experienced far broader and deeper changes in their social institutions. If transformations of administrative and legal institutions had an effect on the upper structure of Jurchen culture, social changes also affected the very foundation of daily life. Working together, they deepened Chinese influence. My analysis will focus on changes in marriage, funerals, ultimogeniture, naming practices, and on the decline of Manchu martial values. All these are related to the family, which is a molder of a person's attitudes, manners, beliefs, and values.[1]

1. Changes in the Family and Customs

The Jurchen marital customs were influenced by neighboring tribes because Manchuria was a meeting place of peoples. Early marriage was common to the Jurchen people regardless of social status. In the harems of Nurhaci and Hong Taiji many women became imperial consorts at the ages of twelve to fourteen. These monarchs married off their daughters at similar ages, the youngest bride being a ten year old. In an edict of 1635, Hong Taiji forbade Jurchen girls from becoming brides before they were eleven (twelve *sui*). In all likelihood this decree was a result of Chinese cultural influence, since in China brides and bridegrooms were a little older. Shunzhi had only one grown princess, who became a bride at the age of thirteen.

The marriage age of imperial clanswomen generally increased from the Kangxi period onward. Kangxi had eight daughters, who married at ages seventeen to twenty-two. According to a report dated 1715, there were forty-three marriageable imperial clanswomen. They were between the ages of fifteen and thirty-two, averaging about nineteen and three-tenths. Yongzheng's daughter married at seventeen, while Qianlong married off his five daughters when they were between fourteen and sixteen. The marriage age of the female offspring of Dorgon, Hooge, and Yin-wu (also Yun-wu, 1693–1731), the fifteenth son of Kangxi, followed the same trend. Thirty-five of Dorgon's female offspring from the beginning to 1795 married at the average age of twenty and six-tenths. During the same period ninety-nine female descendants of Hooge, eldest son of Hong Taiji, married at the average age of nineteen and four-tenths. From the Yin-wu line came thirty-two princesses, born between the 1710s and 1795. Twelve of them married at the average age of eighteen and a half. The average marrying age for daughters of the Jiaqing and Daoguang emperors (r. 1796–1820; 1821–1850) was between seventeen and nineteen. In China proper, other Manchus seem to have followed the same pattern, but those in far-flung regions of Manchuria maintained the tradition of early marriage.[2]

Table 6. Average Marrying Age of Princesses, 1583–1795*

Emperor	Number of Married Daughters	Youngest Marrying Age	Average Marrying Age	Source: *Xingyuan jiqing*
Nurhaci	8	10	12.7–14.7*	pp. 22–23
Hong Taiji	14	11	12.7	pp. 30–33
Shunzhi	1	13	13	pp. 39–40
Kangxi	8	17	19	pp. 54–57
Yongzheng	1	17	17	p. 63
Qianlong	5	14	14.6	pp. 72–73

*Nurhaci's second daughter got married at the age of 29, but this seems incorrect. If counted, the average marriage age would be 14.7. If not, it would be 12.7.

Like ancestors in the Jin dynasty, the Jurchens before 1644 followed many matrimonial practices, including levirate, sororate, cross-cousin, incestuous, and cross-generational unions. All were popular among nomadic peoples in the steppes but were discouraged and even forbidden in China. My focus will be on the last two forms of matrimony because, one, they were related and, two, they were prohibited by Hong Taiji. Broadly, one may consider the incestuous marriage a form of matrimony between two closely related individuals of different or the same generations. After his father, Eidu, died, Turgei (1596–1645), a warrior, married his stepmother, a princess. Hooge, once nominated to succeed Hong Taiji, and Yoto (d. 1638), the eldest son of Daišan, took the consorts of their deceased uncle, Manggūltai, as their concubines. Hong Taiji decreed in 1631 that thereafter no one would be allowed to marry stepmothers, paternal uncles' wives, brothers' wives, or take widows within the same clan. Violators would be charged with adultery and punished accordingly because these practices amounted to beastly ways not tolerated in China or Korea, both of which he regarded as paragons of decorum. The decree did not have an immediate effect on the Manchus, for as late as 1648 the widow of Hooge was taken into the harem of Dorgon, his uncle and adversary. But incestuous marriage declined among the Manchus, nobles and commoners alike, after the Shunzhi period.[3]

Table 7. Average Marriage Age of Princesses
of Three Imperial Branches, 1630s–1810s*

Name of Branch	Number of Married Princesses	Youngest Marrying Age	Average Marriage Age	Source
Dorgon	35	14	20.6	See note 2 in this chapter
Hooge	99	12	19.4	Same
Yin-wu	12	14	18.5	Same

*The three genealogies, especially the first one, have errors in birth or marriage dates, but they show accurate trends.

There were marriages between related individuals of different generations. Bujantai, chieftain of the Ula tribe, married a niece to

Nurhaci, who, in return, gave a daughter and two nieces to the former. There were cases in which the uncle and his nephew became sons-in-law of the same family The matrimonial relations of Eidu, head of the Niohuru clan, were more complicated. He first married Nurhaci's cousin and then his daughter. Later Nurhaci gave away a daughter as the wife of Eidu's second son. Among the imperial consorts of Hong Taiji were a daughter of Eidu and two Mongol princesses: an aunt and a niece. There is no evidence that the early Qing rulers had issued any decree to stop this marriage practice. But one may reasonably assume that it gradually disappeared when other aspects of marriage underwent changes after 1644. Under Chinese influence the Manchus adopted more sophisticated engagement and wedding ceremonies.[4]

Since the fifteenth century, ultimogeniture, a custom unknown to the Chinese, had become a Jurchen social institution with political implications,. A nomadic practice, as the late Chaoying Fang argued, it was devised to protect younger sons in the family. Elder sons lived away and became independent when they reached adulthood. While at home, the younger ones and the father shared each other's belongings and privileges. With the death of the father, sons who did not have their own households inherited what he left. Naturally they shared their father's misfortunes. But this institution worked only with sons born by lawful wives of their father. Early Qing sources provide numerous cases. Ajige, Dorgon, and Dodo received more from Nurhaci because they were his younger sons by the lawful wife. In weddings, dress, and funerals, younger sons were allowed to follow the rules that regulated their fathers. When a powerful prince, Amin, was castigated by Hong Taiji in 1630, his younger sons received harsher punishment than their elder brothers. As late as 1680, ultimogeniture remained a factor in the punishment of officers found guilty in the war against the Rebellion of the Three Feudatories. But with changes in the family under Chinese influence, the institution of ultimogeniture, especially its political implications, faded away with time. Likely from the Yongzheng period, or at latest the Qianlong era, on it was no longer a consideration in the judicial process.[5]

Chinese culture infiltrated Manchu funeral customs. There were no elaborate mourning rules at the time of Nurhaci. He was buried one day after his death without rites appropriate for a dynastic founder.

This simplicity may have been a result of his wish against excessive mourning. More importantly, it was actually a manifestation of a long Jurchen tradition. The reign of Hong Taiji saw a change of Jurchen mourning customs, from simplicity to extravagance. It was hard to maintain the old, simple life style when the Jurchens seized more land and wealth from China. They became more exposed to Chinese culture, which emphasized funerals. It was possible that Prince Sahaliyen, as a China expert, added more Chinese components to regulations of the Board of Rites when he served as its president. Attended by Chinese scholars, Hong Taiji was interested in the grand imperial style that China's emperors enjoyed. He issued edicts to regulate mourning practices, which became refined and hierarchical. With sponsorship from the top, funerals of the Manchus, especially high officials, were so extravagant that as early as 1631 Prince Yoto proposed curtailing such excesses. After 1644 the Manchus adopted more Chinese funeral customs, including burial, mourning dress, the length of observances, and the soul-saving ritual.[6]

The Jurchens had long practiced cremation, a custom alien to the Chinese, who preferred to bury their dead. Nurhaci and Hong Taiji were cremated. The Shunzhi reign was a period of transition. In a decree of 1648, the emperor set rules for funerals of princes and made cremation optional. As a Buddhist, however, Shunzhi was cremated. During the Kangxi era, more Manchus adopted the burial practice. This practice began with the Manchus in the Peking area, where they could acquire graveyards. Bannermen, officers, and common warriors, in other regions of China proper continued with cremation, for their widows and children were required to return to Peking with their ashes. The Qianlong emperor fully supported the burial custom. In 1735 he decreed the prohibition of cremation on the ground that people of filial piety, unless they were too poor, should bury their deceased parents in graveyards in compliance to the ancient rule, The "ancient rule" he stressed here was in fact the Chinese burial tradition. Because he had internalized Confucian ideals and values at the palace school, he mistook Chinese tradition for Manchu heritage. Half a year later, in another decree, he allowed bannermen to bury the dead in their garrison areas, and so cremation disappeared, except in isolated communities in Manchuria.[7]

With the introduction of the practice of burial the Manchus adopted other related Chinese rites. Around the Qianlong period or even earlier, it was popular among Manchu officials to select grave sites using geomancy, a time-honored Chinese custom. There were clan and family cemeteries in which the dead were buried according to the branch and generation to which they belonged. Rich and prominent families set apart ritual land for sacrificial services. Many genealogical records provided details about cemetery locations, individual grave sites, and sacrificial ceremonies.[8]

The Manchu naming practices underwent a transformation after 1644. Manchus were used to naming sons after animals, plants, tools, and attributes such as bravery and honesty. In daily life, even in imperial decrees, Manchus referred to each other by their given names. This confused people because many had the same name. The problem was compounded when Manchu names were transliterated in the Chinese written language, a monosyllabic, nonalphabetic, and uninflective system in the form of characters, each unit with its own sound and meaning. Because of homonyms the same name may be represented by different Chinese characters and appear in a variety of names. Different Manchu names could be transliterated with the same characters. Therefore, Manchu names did not fit into the Chinese pattern of writing. When contact between Manchus and Chinese greatly increased after 1644, more problems arose. The best solution was to adopt the Chinese way of naming.[9] The change began during the Kangxi period.

The change of Manchu naming practices was intimately associated with the decline of their language. For all imperial efforts to resist it, the Manchu language continuously declined. Chinese scholars showed little interest in the language of their conquerors. A large number of government documents appeared in Chinese because Qing rulers since the Shunzhi emperor had learned the language of their subjects. Many Manchus, even the imperial bodyguards, preferred the Chinese tongue. This decline was a result of the sinicization of the Manchu way of life, including their naming practices.

The Manchus changed names in two stages. The first involved two developments, general and specific. The general pertained to transliteration, which involved choosing Chinese characters of appropriate sound and with good meanings. This can be seen from earliest documentary sources, such as the 1636 edition of the *Veritable Records* for the Nurhaci reign. It transliterated Fiongdon and Dorgon without paying attention to the meaning of the characters used. In later sources they were represented with more meaningful characters. In some cases a homophonic character was selected as if it were the person's surname. This development became a trend which the Qianlong emperor desperately tried to stop but failed.[10]

The Kangxi emperor was a pioneer of this trend. This was no accident—his mother was a daughter of Tong Tulai, a descendant of a transfrontiersman's family. During his boyhood, Kangxi devoted himself to the Chinese and specifically the Confucian classics. He was the first Manchu ruler to name his sons in the Chinese mode, each name consisting of two characters—Yin-lu and Yin-zhen—one of which was the generation indicator. In a decree of 1693, he enforced another Chinese practice among imperial clansmen. They were prohibited from naming sons and grandsons after their fathers and grandfathers. If already chosen, he decreed that these names be changed.[11] Naturally, this became the naming tradition of the imperial house.

Many other Manchu aristocratic families took up the practice. Hasan (1633?–1719), a member of the Fuca clan of Neyen, had eight sons whose names generally followed the widespread Chinese pattern. Tuhai (d. 1682), a great warrior from the Magiya clan, had seven grandsons by his eldest son. Active in the Yongzheng era, all seven were named in the Chinese fashion. In the early 1820s Magiya clan elders picked up sixteen characters as the common indicators in the names of their descendants. The Sakda family had served in the Office of the Imperial Household. From Chang-ling (1745–1817) on almost all Sakada male descendants took Chines given names. From the latter half of the Qianlong reign members of the Hešeri family in the Manchu Bordered Blue Banner were named in the same way.[12] In time, Manchu commoners came to follow the same naming practice.

Manchu clan names changed later than given names. Although some Jurchen leaders acquired Chinese surnames and given names during the early fifteenth century, these cases were uncommon because they were given such names by the Ming court for political reasons. The process seems to have begun by the late seventeenth century. The family of Oboi (fl. 1660s–1690s), a member of the Silin Gioro clan, deserves noting. Oboi studied the Confucian classics and once was put in charge of the Imperial Academy (*guozi jian*). Some of his sons, including Ortai (also Oertai, O-erh-tai, 1680–1745), a grand councilor trusted by the Yongzheng emperor, passed the Chinese civil service examinations. It was only natural that he would name his sons in the Chinese style. The first character was a family name common in China, with the second shared by siblings to mark horizontal relations. All his grandsons followed the Chinese way of naming. The situation became so alarming that in 1761 Qianlong attempted to reverse the trend. By the end of the dynasty, for both cultural and political reasons, all Manchu clan names had been replaced by Chinese family names. The Magiyas took the name Ma, the Fuca clansmen the names Fu and Li.[13]

By the seventeenth or early eighteenth century the Manchus had become interested in recording their pedigrees. Before then they passed stories of their ancestry onto younger generations orally. New developments finally whetted the Manchu desire for genealogical accounts. One related to the inheritance of privileges in the banner system. As early as the Kangxi era, some bannermen began to compile their genealogies, perhaps in response to this desire. With the growth of the system and its population, hereditary titles and ranks in the banners became more complicated and created disputes. In the first four years of his reign, the Yongzheng emperor gradually acted to address the problems and their relationship to genealogies. But not until 1733 did he sanction a proposal that people eligible to inherit such privileges should first deposit family records in the banner offices. All male members over nine years old (ten *sui*) were to sign records, and their accuracy had to be verified by the appropriate banner officers. The Qianlong emperor took another step by publishing the *Genealogy of the Manchu Clans in the Eight Banners* in 1745. An encyclopedic work based on archival sources as well as private records, it covered all the Manchu clans and those Mongol, Chinese, and Korean clans that joined the banner forces.[14]

The publication of the *Genealogy of the Manchu Clans in the Eight Banners* served several purposes. It was a permanent record kept in the imperial dossier. When combined with individual family records, it helped solve inheritance disputes. The Qianlong emperor had another goal in mind. As indicated in the preface, he hoped that through this work the Manchus would remember their origins, appreciate ancestors' achievements, and maintain their (ethnic) heritage. It also inspired the compilation of private Manchu genealogies, such as those of the Ligiya clan (of the Long White Mountains) ([*Golmin šanggiyan alin*] *Ligiya hala i mukūni dangse*), the Niohuru clan, and some others. But one should not overlook the Chinese impact on Manchu genealogies. Because genealogical records had long been esteemed in China as the depository of family history and values, almost all well-to-do Chinese families had genealogies, and frequently revised them. When encouraging Manchu subjects to keep their ethnic coherence, Qianlong implicitly cited this Chinese tradition to bolster his argument. Since then many Manchu family records had been compiled or revised. During the 1740s–1790s, for example, Niohuru clansmen had published four editions of their family records. Manchu genealogies had the same organizational features and contained the same kind of information as the Chinese genealogies. Today, hundreds of Manchu genealogical books, almost all in Chinese, still exist.[15]

2. Decline of Manchu Martial Values

In the shadow of Chinese culture the Manchus found it difficult to keep their traditional values intact. For generations the Jurchens had been hunters, gatherers, and fighters, even after agriculture dominated their economy. Horsemanship and archery (*qishe*), together with bravery, were long cherished as Manchu ethnic markers. The term *baturu* was a coveted title for warriors exhibiting exceptional bravery in fighting. In brief, these ideals were martial values cultivated by successive Qing rulers. They were the foundation of the banner institution, as well as one of the reasons for the Manchu conquest of China.

Signs of the decline of warrior values began in the seventeenth century. Manchu warriors deserted to the protection of the Ming army. An imperial decree of 1636 revealed that Manchu youths milled around marketplaces and tried to evade fighting and hunting. During the Rebellion of the Three Feudatories, which aimed to overthrow the Qing dynasty in 1673–1681, some Manchus joined rebels against their fellow warriors. The above cases, though not many, were of an allegorical nature, testifying to the weakening of Manchu martial values. Gone with these values were discipline and *esprit de corps*. It was largely Chinese soldiers that suppressed the Three Feudatories. When the Qing launched a war against the Dzungar Mongols in the Northwest in 1729–1734, the Manchu army on the northern front was almost annihilated. Only forces under Tsereng (d. 1750), a loyal Mongol general, were able to defeat the Dzungars and make a peace settlement possible.[16]

There was no way to revitalize the Manchu martial tradition. The Qianlong emperor could claim ten great military achievements, including the wars against the rebels in western Sichuan, the Miao ethnic minority group, the Dzungar Mongols, the Moslems, and the Burmese. In many cases the Manchus were not the core units of Qing forces, which were mostly composed of Chinese bannermen and soldiers from the Green Standard. Manchu commanders in chief were arrogant and inexperienced, making wars long and costly. The war against the Tibetan rebels in western Sichuan in 1747–1749 exemplified this. The emperor punished three commanders, executing one and forcing the two others to commit suicide. He punished more high commanders with death in other wars. According to a new study, nearly half of what he regarded as great military achievements were greatly exaggerated. When the Taiping Rebellion broke out in the next century, the Qing government could only rely on the Hunan and Anhwei armies organized and commanded by the Chinese.[17]

The explanation for the decline of Manchu martial values must be sought in three areas: socioeconomic, political, and cultural. Socioeconomic conditions during the frontier days had already exercised an important influence on the Jurchens. After 1644, the Manchus found themselves in an alien social milieu, namely China proper, in which they were overwhelmed numerically and culturally by the conquered. This can be seen from the fact that Qing rulers repeatedly warned the Manchus to stay away from "bad Chinese habits," a vague term. Examination of related imperial decrees shows that the term could mean insubordination, extravagance, slander, or something else, depending on the occasion. This was contrasted to the "good" Manchu heritage. Whatever the meaning of the term, the repeated imperial warnings highlighted the deepening of Chinese influence on the Manchus.[18]

The unfavorable socioeconomic conditions also found expression in Manchu quarters or cities (*Mancheng*). Beginning with the Shunzhi reign, the Qing government deployed Manchu Banner forces at strategic points all over China. In major garrisons soldiers, officers, and their families lived in special areas, later known as Manchu quarters and administered by their commanders. These quarters underwent two stages of evolution. Prior to the early 1700s they developed from temporary garrisons into enclosures, carved out of cities and separated from Chinese inhabitants by walls. They were "intramural" enclave-like settlements. Beginning in the Yongzheng period they were specially built, mainly outside cities and with walls and gates. Each quarter was a compound comprising three parts: training grounds and an armory, administrative offices, and residential sections. The construction of such compounds was an example of imperial policies of control and segregation. Each compound formed a world of its own, with many rules. Without permission, residents were not allowed to leave the compound. And if they did, they had to return to their quarters before the closing of the gate every night. Violators were severely punished. Clearly, the Manchu quarters facilitated Qing control of bannermen. Each compound was also segregated. Manchu bannermen were not permitted to have close associations, including marital relations, with neighboring Chinese residents, who were prohibited from entering the compound. Such restrictions were intended to keep Manchu heritage from being eroded by Chinese ways of life.[19]

For all its efforts, the Qing court failed to stop Chinese ideals and values from penetrating the Manchu compounds. In reality the Manchu quarters had adopted most of the structural characteristics of Chinese-administered cities, for example, city walls and religious institutions. Inside the quarters there were temples dedicated to such popular Chinese cults as the city god, the god of wealth, the god of fire, and a few others. Of these deities, the God of War, or the cult of Guan Yu, was the most influential. The compound also served as an indoctrination center modeled on imperial hortatory works, notably the *Amplified Instructions on the Sacred Edict,* which covered Confucian social, political, and economic themes. From the Yongzheng reign until the latter half of the nineteenth century, the work had been read and explained before Manchu warriors and officers in monthly sessions. Without doubt, after this long indoctrination, Confucian values got through to the Manchu bannermen.[20]

There are reasons to believe that it was nearly impossible to enforce the policy of segregation. Although damaged during the Ming-Qing transition, major garrison cities such as Kwang-chow, Chengdu, Tai-yuan, and Hangzhow were rebuilt between 1681 and 1735. Their bustling markets and colorful life tempted the warriors. There were no distinguishable physical differences between the Manchus and the Chinese, and this facilitated their contact with each other. With the passage of time, restrictions loosened. Chinese merchants were allowed to enter the Manchu quarters to engage in business; some peddlers were even permitted to open shops and lived in the compounds. A considerable number of Chinese slaves and servants worked for banner residents. Under population pressure, a problem that surfaced during the Yong-zheng period, the compounds had to let their residents spread into the surrounding Chinese sections. Young educated Manchus kept in touch with Chinese scholars because they wanted to take provincial examinations, instead of continuing military careers as they were expected to do by the throne.[21] All in all, the Manchu quarters were not as fully cut off from the Chinese world as one might believe.

Shortly after 1644 the Manchus confronted a serious financial problem. As hereditary warriors, they were a privileged class guaranteed military service, official positions, and fixed salaries. Such privileges hurt them because they were not allowed to engage in other occupations. With fixed stipends and limited service quotas, they were financially hard-pressed, and the problem was compounded by their spending habits. They indulged in luxury in the first half of each month, when they received their salaries. For the remaining days of the month they frequented pawnshops and dealt with loan sharks. The pawnshops in the Peking area, according to a noted Manchu author, were well structured and dominated by brokers from Shansi Province The Manchu bannermen sold land, even mortgaged their weapons, expected imperial relief, engaged in illicit behavior, and suffered loss of morale. Despite appropriations made by both Kangxi and Yongzheng to help, the financial situation of the Manchus continued to deteriorate.[22] Poverty distracted them from martial values.

Political conditions in China proper did not favor the Manchus. Prior to the conquest of China they were eager to fight because each campaign was an opportunity for looting and rewards.²³ After that they fought for the empire, which was characterized by hierarchy and regulations. They were not permitted to plunder and were subjected to more restrictions. Obviously, they were losers in the imperial order they helped to create. Qing emperors inculcated warrior virtues in the Manchus. They also frequently infused Manchus with Confucian political teachings, which justified the ruler's claim to the Mandate of Heaven and legitimized the centralization of power, a goal nurtured by the autocratic rulers. Confucianism also emphasized scholarly pursuits, sponsored civil careers, and despised the military, which of course contradicted the martial ideals encouraged by Qing rulers. Caught between these conflicting values, the Manchus, in particular low-ranking officers and common warriors, must have felt uprooted and alienated, with a strong sense of anomie. They tried to adjust to the new situation, but because their adjustments differed, the same problem appeared in different guises.

The overriding cause of the decline of Manchu values was cultural. Long before the rise of their state, the Jurchens had adjusted to Chinese culture. But the Chinese population was small on the frontier. After moving into China proper, the Manchus became an ethnic minority in an immense Chinese sociocultural configuration, which caught them off guard. Chinese urban life was more attractive and presented more opportunities, in contrast to the monotonous and melancholic life in the Manchu enclaves. It was difficult to break through the environment of their community because of imperial restrictions. Nor was it easy to suddenly reject their heritage. They must have been tormented. Despondency swept many of them into degenerative conduct—drinking, gambling, cockfighting. This resulted in scandal, financial problems, lapse of discipline, and decline of physical strength. Officers and men were not interested in work or strict drills. Many warriors did not even know how to use the bow. Time and again, Kangxi and Yongzheng expressed concern about these developments. So did the Qianlong emperor, who issued numerous edicts in the hope of reversing the course but was unsuccessful.²⁴

These developments forced a change of Manchu career patterns—from military to civil. The trend appeared shortly after they took control of China proper. The Shunzhi emperor revealed in 1657 that bannermen preferred a literary to a military career. Official and rich

Manchu families, he went on, asked servants to be surrogate soldiers for their sons. By the Kangxi period this had become common practice. The price of the *Zhaoming wenxuan*, a famous literary anthology compiled by Xiao Tong (501–531), skyrocketed because it was a favorite of young, educated Manchus. Anjuhū (fl. 1640s–1690s) was a case in point. A member of the Gūwalgiya clan from Suwan, he knew Manchu and Chinese and served in the Hanlin Academy. Because of his distinguished military service he was repeatedly promoted, and in 1678 achieved the rank of Tartar general, a position coveted by bannermen. But he told friends that he would rather serve in a civil position in Peking. Perhaps because he saw no possibility of attaining his goal, he requested retirement in 1683. This prompted the Kangxi emperor to dismiss him as a warning to others. In a long edict of 1724, Yongzheng argued that the Manchus, especially those in the northern part of Manchuria, should concentrate on martial values, not compete with Chinese for literary skills. The rise of Manchu power, according to him, resulted from action and military ability, not from literary knowledge. The Qianlong emperor was of the same opinion. When commending the writing ability of a young prince, he argued that literary skills were insignificant because the Manchu language, archery, and horsemanship were vital to the dynasty.[25]

Because the decline of Manchu martial values had become a trend that concerned Qing rulers from Kangxi to Qianlong, they took various measures to arrest it. With the situation deteriorating over time, each of the three monarchs focused on different aspects of the problem. Kangxi twice made large appropriations totaling about twelve million taels of silver to relieve the economic strain on the Manchus, especially the rank and file. Yongzheng followed a multifold approach. Among his measures were additional stipends, emergency allowances, low-interest loans, land reclamation in the metropolitan area, and organization of new banner units.[26]

Qianlong made further efforts to solve the problem. His policies were tailored to different Manchus according to their status. For the upper classes books on Manchu ethnic origins and heritage were published under his auspices. Among these were *Genealogy of the Manchu Clans in the Eight Banners*, *Book of Rites for Manchu Sacrifices and Offerings to Deities and Heaven*, and *Origins of the Manchus*. He also enforced Manchu tradition by punishing violators, even high officials. For the lower ranks of Manchus, he focused on their economic life. He continued and expanded what his father had started. Yongzheng, for instance, created a supernumerary banner force of about 8,000 men. Qianlong expanded the active service list to include more than 26,000 extra soldiers.[27] At the same time, he introduced two new measures. One was the founding of military settlements in Manchuria, which had almost become a deserted region, for nearly all the Manchus had been moved into China proper shortly after 1644. During the years 1644–1735 the Qing government allowed Chinese farmers to migrate to the region. At the suggestion of his officials, he opened the region to the Manchus only. In 1741–1754 he sent many unemployed Manchus and their families there to reclaim the land. The second measure was to downsize the Chinese Banner force by relieving many of its members of their hereditary warrior status At first he allowed some Chinese bannermen in the Peking area to become civilians. Then he permitted those in the provinces to leave the banners to find new jobs and filled the vacancies with Manchu bannermen. But none of these imperial efforts regenerated the Manchu martial spirit.[28]

The Qing rulers themselves were influenced by the same currents that engulfed their Manchu subjects. Nurhaci and Hong Taiji won support from their men because they were great warriors. Hong Taiji was also a good hunter and frequently made hunting trips. It is hard to judge if the Shunzhi emperor was a warrior because he died young. The records show that he only made one hunting trip. Kangxi twice led large forces to fight the Eleuth Mongols. He established the Imperial Hunting Preserves in Jehol. When he hunted there, he was joined by thousands of Manchu and Mongol warriors competing to display their horsemanship and archery. These were in fact military exercises. During his reign of sixty-one years Kangxi made a total of fifty-one such hunting trips. After his death, the Qing rulers made fewer such excursions and Manchu participants were less prepared.[29]

The Manchu emperors after Kangxi directed their attention to other problems or were more interested in Chinese culture than military exercises. Yongzheng, noted for his mastery of Chinese philosophy and religion and for writing long comments on memorials, did not travel to the hunting preserves. This may be due to the fact that he had to solve urgent political and social problems, notably the consolidation of his power. In his sixty-year reign, the Qianlong emperor made only twenty-eight hunting trips. In 1741 he chided high Manchu officials for evading hunting trips. Of course they were not interested in fighting for the dynasty either. In 1753 he punished a Chamberlain of the Imperial Bodyguard and two ranking bodyguards, all three from aristocratic families, because they acted cowardly in the Imperial Hunting Preserves. But Qianlong sponsored many Chinese cultural projects and wrote thousands of poems in Chinese. His successor, Jiaqing (r. 1796–1820), arranged fifteen military exercises in the hunting preserves. After his reign, these practices ceased in Jehol. In an attempt to revive this tradition, the Tongzhi emperor (r. 1862–1874) organized a small exercise in a park south of Peking. Manchu participants bought pheasants and rabbits and presented them to their superiors as if they had been harvested by their arrows. This case spoke eloquently to the fact that the Manchu bannermen, needed by the state, were no longer a coherent group of warriors. In addition, with increases in the population, they became a crushing financial burden for the court. In 1865 the Tongzhi emperor permitted them to leave the banners if they wanted to.[30] This was the end of the banner system for all intents and purposes.

Table 8. Hunting Trips by Qing Rulers, 1644–1820*

Name	Years in Office	Number of Trips	Other Related Activities
Shunzhi	18	1**	0
Kangxi	61	51	2 Mongol campaigns
Yongzheng	13	0	0
Qianlong	60	28	0
Jiaqing	25	15	0

*Sources: see note 29 in this chapter.
**Shunzhi did not hunt in the Imperial Hunting Preserves, which were established after his reign.

The story of the Jurchen pouch further documents the change of Manchu martial ideals to Chinese values. Made of leather and known in Manchu as *fadu*, the Jurchen pouch was originally a rustic and durable bag used by hunters to carry food. In early times, when they hunted in forests and mountains for days, the Jurchens carried quivers and food bags. Naturally the *fadu* suited the needs of warriors when in action. Jurchen warriors under Nurhaci, according to some sources, put rice flour in their *fadu*. The change seems to have begun as early as the reign of Hong Taiji, who frequently bestowed the *fadu*, together with other items, on Mongol nobles and a few others. The Shunzhi emperor continued the practice. By the late Kangxi period the *fadu* was replaced by the Chinese *hebao*, a small, elegant sachet, which possibly appeared during the Northern Song dynasty or earlier.[31]

The replacement of the *fadu* with the *hebao* resulted from political and cultural developments. After it took over China, the Qing government developed a better supply system for its soldiers. Following the defeat of the Rebellion of the Three Feudatories, China enjoyed peace and prosperity for decades. Since the *fadu* was no longer needed, it gave way to the *hebao*, which, made of Chinese satin, silk or fine leather, was highly adorned and came in many shapes. Included among the *hebao* Kangxi bestowed on officials were many kinds of beautifully made pouches, some of which appeared in twins, in yellow or other colors. Some were bordered or inlaid with other fancy materials.[32]

Functionally, the new pouch performed an aesthetic and sociopolitical purpose. Ofttimes it served as an imperial gift to officials or foreign envoys. By the end of 1720, Kangxi gave four pouches and a few other items to Carlo Ambrogio Mezzabarba, the Apostolic Legate of Pope Clement XI. Yongzheng gave pouches to officials as a display of imperial grace. Qianlong bestowed personal pouches on brave generals. On New Year's Day or other important festivals, the throne bestowed pouches on ranking courtiers, the size, number, and quality of which differed according to the status of the recipient. Nian Gengyao (d. 1726), a high official of the late Kangxi and early Yongzheng eras, owned ten pairs of *hebao* in various styles and seventy-four small ones. Officials used pouches to carry snacks, medicine, perfumes, or small amounts of silver. In time the pouch underwent more functional changes and was further refined. It symbolized friendship, happiness, good luck, and love between men and women. It now became popular among all social groups, in particular the Manchus, who carried it as an accessory.³³ The Manchus owned the new, graceful pouch but lost their *fadu*. Gone with the *fadu* were the virtues of the warrior.³⁴

In conclusion, as early as the frontier days Chinese culture had penetrated Jurchen society. Manchu traditions, as a famous author and thirteenth-generation descendant of Nurhaci pointed out, resulted from the combination of Jurchen and Chinese customs of the Liaodong region. Penetration by Chinese culture gained momentum after 1644, particularly in the eighteenth century, and reached almost every segment of Manchu society. Manchu customs, such as marriage, funerals, ultimogeniture, and naming of family members underwent changes. As a consequence of these changes, the Manchus lost their martial virtues and became a privileged, idle, and dissipated class. The transformation of Manchu society completed the changes the administrative and legal institutions left undone. Although the Manchus retained their status as a ruling class, there were no more cohesive ethnic ties among them. Instead they were deeply concerned with their economic life and became more and more an "embattled interest group," which further weakened their ethnic heritage. These developments brought them much closer to their conquered subjects. They and the Chinese stood on common ground. Today, the Manchus are one of the many ethnic minority groups in China.

Notes

1. For the importance of the family in this regard, see Jacqueline S. Mithun, "The Role of the Family in Acculturation and Assimilation in America: A Psychocultural Dimension," in William C. McCready, ed., *Culture, Ethnicity, and Identity: Current Issues in Research* (New York: Academic Press, 1983), 214.
2. For the Jurchen tradition of early marriage, see Huang Pei, "Qingchu di Manzhou guizu: Hunyin yu kaiguo," 605–606. For the decreee of 1635, see *CSL*, reign of Taizong, 23: 2a, Tiancong 9/3/gengshen. For the matrimonial age of Manchu princesses from Nurhaci to the Daoguang era, see *Xingyuan jiqing*, 22–24, 30–33, 39–41, 54–57, 63–64, 72–74, 79–81, 89–90. For the average marriage age of the forty-three imperial clanswomen during the Kangxi reign, see *Kangxi chao Manwen zhupi zouzhe quanyi*, 1096–97, #2772. For the female descendants of Dorgon, Hooge, and Yin-wu, see *Taizu Gao huangdi weixia heshi Ruizhong qinwang zhi zisun*, vol. 3, the first fifteen leaves; *Taizong Wen huangdi weixia diyi zi heshi Wusu qinwang zhi nüsun* (housed in the Tōyō Bunko, Tokyo, handwritten, unpaged), 1a–15b; *Huang shiwu zi duoluo Yuke junwang Yin-*

wu jiapu (housed in the Fu Sinian Library, Academia Sinica, Taipei, handwritten, unpaged, 2 volumes), vol. 2, the first five leaves. For the Chinese impact, see *MTTS*, 538; Teng Shaozhen, "Lun Mingdai Nüzhen di ji-zhong fengshu," *MTYC*, 6 (1986): 62–63. The Wanggiya family was a case in point. Linqing, a clansman and high official, married at age eighteen; his elder son, Chongshi, married at the same age. See Songshen, ed., *Changbai Wanyan shi jiude lu* (c. 1880s in 3 volumes), 1: 5b; 3A: 9b.

3. For cases of the incestuous marriage, see Huang Pei, "Qingchu di Manzhou guizu: Hunyin yu kaiguo," 602–604. For the decree of 1631, see *Shinkan ichiroku*, reign of Taizong, 2: 11a, Tiancong 5/7/gengchen. For the case of Dorgon, see *CSKC*, 10: 7808.

4. For these cases, see Huang Pei, "Qingchu di Manzhou guizu: Hunyin yu kaiguo," 603; Zheng, *Tanwei ji*, 80–81. For Chinese influence on the Manchu engagement and wedding ceremonies, see Yang, *Qingdai Manzu fengshu shi*, 26 and 28.

5. For its origin, function, and actual working, see Fang, "Qingchu Manzhou jiating," 1–9 and 15–16. For the case of Ajige, Dorgon, and Dodo, see *CSL*, reign of Taizong, 46: 24, Chongde 4/5/xinsi. Among Amin's younger sons were Gūlmahūn and Gunggan. They received more severe punishment. See *TCCC*, 137: 12b–13a. For the punishment of officers in 1680, see *CSL*, Kangxi reign, 93: 2b–3b, 19/11/xinyou.

   According to Fang, "Qingchu Manzhou jiating," 9, this political implication might have disppeared during the Qianlong reign. But the major judicial cases involving high Manchu officials during the Yongzheng period did not indicate the influence of ultimogeniture. This may suggest that it was discarded at that time.

6. For the simplicity of Nurhaci's funeral rites, see *Nuer-haqi shilu*, 4: 11b–12a. For Nurhaci's advice for simplicity, see *MWLT*, 1: 704–05. Sahaliyen had been in charge of the Board of Rites since its creation. See *CSKC*, 10: 7752–54. For the proposal of Yoto, see *CSL*, reign of Taizong, 8: 26a,Tiancong 5/3/yihai. For some edicts about the funeral affairs, see *CSL*, reign of Taizong, 11: 20, Tiancong 6/3/gengxu; 17: 28, Tiancong 8/2/renxu; Zhang and Guo, *Qing ruguan qian*, 461–65. For adoptions after 1644, see Zheng, *Tanwei ji*, 73–77; Yang, *Qingdai Manzu fengshu shi*, 51–62. For the Manchu adoption of Chinese funeral customs, see Aixin Gioro, *Lao Beijin yu Manzu*, 80–81, 88–89.

7. There were cremation and grave, tree, and water burials. But cremation became popular among the Jurchens who moved to southern Manchuria. See Qiu Xin, "Manzu chuan-tong fengshu," *MANT*, 2 (1987): 87. For the cremation of Nurhaci, Hong Taiji, and Shunzhi, see Tong Yue, "Qing ruguan qian Manzu sangzang xishu di shidai tezheng," *MANT* 3 (1993): 34. For the decree of 1648, see *CSL*, Shunzhi reign, 38: 2, 5/4/xinwei. For the beginning of the graveyard burial in the Kangxi era, see *MTTS*, 539. For Qianlong's decree, see *CSL*, Qian-

long reign, 5: 22b–23a, Yongzheng 13/10/yiyou. For his second decree, see *Baqi tongzhi*, introductory chapter 11: 8b–9b.

8.   For the case of geomancy, see *Xinxiu Fucha shi zhipu*, comps. Zhale-hali and Muke-dengbu (Wuchang: 1908, 3 volumes), 2: 27b–29 ff. For geomancy and the ritual land, see Soningan, *Manzhou sili ji* (Taipei: Tailian guofeng chuban she, 1969, reprint, vol. 11), 229, 249–50, 297–98. For clan cemeteries, and individual gravesites, see *Zheng-huang qi Neiwu fu Manzhou san jiala Ancun zuoling xia Huifa Sakeda shi jiapu*, 4b–12a.

9.   According to Liu Qinghua, there were 679 Manchu surnames, instead of 645, as recorded in the official genealogical compilation. See his *Manzu xingshi lu* (N. p.: Liaoning sheng Xinbin xian minzu shiwu weiyuan hui, 1982), 1–22. For a broad discussion of the Manchu naming and clan names, see ibid., 1–69. For the Manchu way of naming, see Wang, "Manzu renming di minshu tezheng he yuyan tezheng," 72–77. The name Nurhaci could be written in different Chinese characters. For a study of the change of Manchu naming practices, see Du Jiaji, "Manzu ruguan qianhou zhi quming ji xiang-guan zhu wenti fenxi," *Manxue yanjiu*, 2 (1994): 202–17.

10.   For the cases of Fiongdon and Dorgon, see *Nuer-haqi shilu*, 1: 8b; 4: 12a; Du, "Manzu ruguan qianhou zhi quming," 203–208. For the Qianlong emperor's attempt, see *Baqi tongzhi*, introducetory chapters 11: 44b–45a, and 12: 10b–11a, 58b–59a.

11.   For names of imperial sons from the Kangxi era onward, see *Xingyuan jiqing*, 49–54 ff. But when one of the princes became the emperor, his brothers had to change the common indicator in their given names. See Du, "Manzu ruguan qianhou zhi quming," 209–10. For Kangxi's decree of 1693, see *CSL*, Kangxi reign, 158: 10b–11a, 32/2/jiashen.

12.   For the eight sons of Hasan, see *Nayin Fucha shi puzhuan*, section on the 4th generation, p. 3b. The two oldest brothers kept in common the last two characters of their names, while the others kept the same first two characters. For the grandsons of Tuhai, see *Majia shi zupu*, comps. Ma Yanxi et al. (Peiping [?]: Jinghua yinshu ju, prefaced 1927, 5 volumes), vol. 4. 3: 15b. For the sixteen characters, see the same Magiya clan genealogy, vol. 1, "The Original Preface of Shengyin in 1822," 1.

      For the case of Chang-ling, see *Zheng-huang qi Neiwu fu Manzhou san jiala Ancun zuoling xia Huifa Sakeda shi jiapu*, 20–29 ff. For the Hešeri family, see *Hesheli shi jiapu*, comp. Chang-feng (Kwangchow: 1874, 2 volumes), 2: 4a–5a. Edward J. M. Rhoads also provides similar examples. See his *Manchus and Han: Ethnic Relations and Political Power in Late Qing and Early Republican China, 1861–1928* (Seattle and London: University of Washington Press, 2000), 55–56.

13.   For example, Aqaču is mentioned in Chapter 1, section 2. The Ming court gave him the name Li Cheng-shan, while his son Li Xian-zhong (d. ca.1420). Aqaču's grandson was known as Li Manzhu (d. 1476). See *DMB*, 1: 839–40. More Jur-

chen leaders received names from the Ming government. See Zhang, "Ming waizu cixing kao," 3. 2 (1932): 18–19, 23–24; 4. 2 (1934): 16–19. For the Oboi family, see *STTP*, 17: 2a–3a; *ECCP*, 1: 601–603. Qianlong complained in 1761 that the Niohuru clan changed to a Chinese surname "Lang." See *Baqi tongzhi*, introductory chapter 12: 10b. Through many ways the Manchus adopted Chinese family names. See *MTTS*, 527–29; Liu, *Manzu xingshi lu*, 14–69.

14. For a fine study of Manchu genealogy, see Elliott, *The Manchu Way*, 65–67, 326–29. Included among the bannermen who compiled their genealogies were the Bai and Wu families. The Bais were evidently of Manchu descent. See Li, *Manzu jiapu xuanbian*, 180–81. The Wus were likely of transfrontier origin, for with exception of only one clansman, all others were named after the Chinese style. All wives were of Chinese descent. See Li, *Manzu jiapu xuanbian*, 416–22. For Yongzheng's decrees and final decision, see *TCCC*, 37: 22b–26a. The official genealogical work is known in Chinese as the *Baqi Manzhou shizu tongpu*, including 645 Manchu, 235 Mongol, 247 Chinese, and 43 Korean clan names.

15. For a general discussion of Manchu genealogies, see Li, *Manzu jiapu xuanbian*, 7–9. For the imperial attempt to keep ethnic coherence, see the preface to the *Genealogy of the Manchu Clans in the Eight Banners*; Elliott, *The Manchu Way*, 65–67, 326–29. After its publication, many private Manchu genealogical records were compiled. Among these genealogies were the Niohuru clan records, the *Zheng-hong qi Manzhou Hada Guaerjia shi jiapu*, and [*Golmin šanggiyan alin*] *Ligiya hala i mukūni dangse* (Genealogical Record of the Ligiya Clan [of the Long White Mountains]), (1764, 4 volumes, housed in the Tōyō bunko). For the Chinese influence on Manchu genealogies, see *MTTS*, 522–23. For the four editions of the Niohuru family records, see the Introduction, note 33, of this work.

16. For Manchu deserters, see *CSL*, reign of Taizong, 8: 34b–35b, Tiancong 5/3/ jiawu. For Hong Taiji's revelation, see *MBRT*, vol. 6, Taizong, 23: 1211–12. For the Three Feudatory Rebellion, see Kai-fu Tsao, "K'ang-hsi and the San-fan War," *Monumenta Serica* 31 (1974–1975): 108–30. For the important contributions of the Chinese forces, see Shang Hongkui, "Lun Kangxi pingding San-fan," *Qingshi lunwen xuanji* 1 (1979): 381; for the Manchus joining the Chinese rebels, see *Kangxi qiju zhu* (Peking: Zhonghua Book Company, 1984, 3 volumes), 1: 653 and 667, dated 20/1/18; 20/2/15; 2: 823, and 1251, dated 21/ 2/13; 23/11/11.

Furdan (1683–1753) and Marsai (d. 1733) were both in charge of the war against the Dzungars, but they were incapable commanders. See *ECCP*, 1: 264–65. Tsereng, the loyal Mongol general, was made a prince for his defeat of the Dzungars. See *ECCP*, 2: 756–57. For the peace settlement, see Zhu, *Qingchao tongshi*, 8: 31–56.

17. For details of Qianlong's ten great military achievements, see Zhu, *Qingchao tongshi*, 9: 1–255, 275–438, 463–506. For their being exaggerations, see ibid., 8:

Introduction, 31–32. The three commanders included Qingfu, Zhang Guangsi, and Noqin. The very last of them was an arrogant and incapable field commander. For their being punished, see ibid., 9: 72. For other high commanders punished by him, see ibid., 8: Introduction, 22. For the principal organizers of the Hunan and Anhui armies and their importance, see *ECCP*, 2: 751–53; 1: 464–65.

18. For instance, the Yongzheng emperor frequently overstated the "good" Manchu heritage in contrast to the "bad" Chinese habits. See *Baqi tongzhi* introductory chapter 9, Decrees 3, 38a, 40a; introductory chapter 10, Decrees 4, 5a–6b. For a general coverage of the decline of their martial values, see Huang, *Autocracy at Work*, 164–67.

19. For the Manchu quarters, see Ma Xiedi, "Qingdai Mancheng kao," *MANT*, 1 (1990): 29–34. For the evolution and physical aspect of the Manchu quarters, see Ding Yizhuang, *Qingdai baqi zhufang zhidu yanjiu* (Tianjin: Tianjin guji chuban she, 1992), 162–68, especially 165; Elliott, *The Manchu Way*, 105–21. For the term "intramural" and the characteristics of the Manchu cities, see Rhoads, *Manchus and Han*, 38–9. For restrictions and segregation policy, including marital relations, see Ding, *Qingdai baqi zhufang*, 165–66, 215–17; Rhoads, *Manchu and Han*, 40–42; Ma, "Qingdai Mancheng kao," 33. But Chinese bannermen had a free hand to keep marital relations with Chinese without banner affiliations during the Yongzheng and Qianlong reigns. See Ding, *Qingdai baqi zhufang*, 215–17.

20. Elliott regards such quarters as "sites both of integration and of alienation" and also as "sites of re-formation of Manchu ethnicity" (see his *The Manchu Way*, 89–90). For the structural characteristics adopted by the Manchu quarters, see ibid., 115. For Chinese temples and cults, see ibid., 116. For the Chinese cults practiced by the Manchus and the indoctrination measure, see Chapter VIII.

21. For China's economic recovery, see Shang Hung-k'uei, "The Process of Economic Recovery, Stabilization, and Its Accomplishments in the Early Ch'ing, 1681–1735," *Chinese Studies in History* 15. 1–2 (1981–82): 19–61. For Chinese merchants in the compounds, see Ding, *Qingdai baqi zhufang*, 212; Rhoads, *Manchu and Han*, 38. For Chinese slaves and servants in the bannermen's households, see Elliott, *The Manchu Way*, 227–29. The Yongzheng emperor even forbade the bannermen from acquiring slaves and servants. See *CSL*, Yongzheng reign, 70: 6a–7b, 6/6/renchen. For banner residents spreading out of the quarters, see Elliott, *The Manchu Way*, 120. For the penchant of young Manchus for taking the provincial civil examinations, see *CSL*, Yongzheng reign, 121: 1b–2b, 10/7/yiyou.

22. For their financial problems, see Huang, *Autocracy at Work*, 176–77. For their mortgage and selling of land, see *CSL*, Yongzheng reign, 93: 14, 8/4/jiyou. Because of mortgage and negligence the banner forces were short of weapons. See

CSL, Yongzheng reign, 11: 16, 1/9/dinghai. For the structure and operations of pawnshops in the Peking area, see Aixin Gioro, *Lao Beijing yu Manzu*, 205–206, 226. What the author describes seems to have been heard from his father or grandfather and concerned the last few years of the dynasty. But it had been the lifestyle of the Manchus since the late seventeenth century. The Kangxi emperor twice appropriated about 12 million taels of silver to help the Manchu bannermen. See *CSL*, Yongzheng reign, 56: 13b–17a, 5/4/jihai. Some appropriations were invested in pawnshops. See Wei Qingyuan, *Ming-Qing shi bianxi* (Peking: Zhongguo shehui kexue chuban she, 1989), 166–228, 259–88. For high interest loans, see *Yuxing qiwu zouyi*, 1: 8b. Such illicit means included extortion and embezzlement. See *Shangyu baqi*, 1: 8; 2: 4.

23. For their eagerness to hunt and fight, see *MWLT*, 2: 1555; Yi, *Chaam Sŏnsaeng munjip*, 6: 5b.

24. For their drinking, gambling, cockfighting, see *Shangyu baqi*, 1: 3b; *CSL*, Kangxi reign, 44: 8a–9b, 12/12/xinchou; Yongzheng reign, 56: 16a, 5/4/jihai. Yongzheng lost his confidence in Manchu officials because many were corrupt. See *Gongzhong dang: Yongzheng chao zouzhe*. 21: 590, Memorial of Maiju. Kangxi and Yongzheng issued decrees about the Manchu dissipated life and its results. See *CSL*, Kangxi reign, 241: 4, 49/1/gengyin; Yongzheng reign, 56: 13b–17a, 5/4/jihai. For their neglect of military drill and skills, see *CSL*, Yongzheng reign, 6: 20, 1/4/dingmao; 12: 8b, 1/10/renzi. Some of Qianlong's edicts can be found in *Baqi tomgzhi* (introductory) ch. 11: 4b–6bff; ch.12: 7b–10b, 23a–26b.

25. For Shunzhi's edict, see *CSL*, Shunzhi reign, 106: 23b–25b, 14/1/jiazi. For the anthology, see Wang Shizhen, *Xiangzu biji* (N. p., n. d, 4 volumes), 5: 19a. For Anjuhū, see *STTP*, 1: 18; *TCCC*, 151: 3b–5b; *CSL*, Kangxi reign, 107: 6, 22/1/jiazi. For Yongzheng's edict, see *Shangyu baqi*, 2: 19a–20b; *CSL*, Yongzheng reign, 22: 21a–23b, 2/7/jiazi. For Qianlong's opinion, see *CSL*, Qianlong reign, 760: 11b–14a, 31/5/xinsi. The young prince was his 11th son.

26. For Kangxi's appropriations, see *CSL*, Yongzheng reign, 56: 13b–17a, 5/4/jihai. For Yongzheng's measures, see Huang, *Autocracy at Work*, 177–78.

27. For publication of these and other books in Manchu, see Sun, *Qianlong di*, 354–62. The Chinese titles for the three books are respectively, *Baqi Manzhou shizu tongpu, Qinding jishen jitian dianli* (1747), and *Qinding Manzhou yuanliu kao*, comps. Agui and Yu Minzhong (1783). Among those punished by the throne was a Manchu governor-general, who was forced to commit suicide because he violated the rule against cutting one's hair during the mourning period for the death of the empress. See Sun, *Qianlong di*, 223–25. For the creation of the extra banner force by Yongzheng, see Huang, *Autocracy at Work*, 177; Feng, *Yongzheng zhuan*, 302. For Qianlong's addition of 26,000 men, see Zhu, *Qingchao tongshi*, 8: 263–65.

28. For suggestions to create settlements in Manchuria, see *CSKC*, 11: 8999–9000, 9036, and 9141. For Qianlong's prohibition of Chinese migrants, see Sun, *Qian-*

long di, 225–28, 230. For his granting of permission for Chinese bannermen to be civilians, see Zhu, *Qingchao tongshi*, 8: 273–79. The Yongzheng emperor did permit young Chinese bannermen to be civilians, but the project did not continue. See Huang, *Autocracy at Work*, 178.

29. Shunzhi hunted once. See *CSL*, Shunzhi reign, 56: 14b–16 ff, 8/4/yimao; 57: 1b–3b, 7b–8a, 8/5/kuisi. For the military importance of hunting trips, see Wang, *Qingshi xinkao*, 59–62. In the same book (p. 61) Wang believes that Kangxi made forty-eight trips. But according to another study, he made fifty-one trips, one or two of which had been made before the creation of the preserves in Jehol. See Luo Yunzhi, "Kangxi di yu mulan weichang di guanxi." In *Jindai Zhongguo chuqi lishi yantao hui lunwen ji*, 1: 409–19.

30. For imperial hunting trips to Jehol from the Qianlong to the Jiaqing reigns, see Wang, *Qingshi xinkao*, 61. For Tongzhi's attempt, see ibid., 63. For his edict of 1741, see *CSL*, Qianlong reign, 151: 15b–17a, 6/9/gengyin. For punishment of the three officers, see *CSL*, Qianlong reign, 446: 13a–14a, 18/8/dingmao. For the purchase of these animals by the Manchus, see Zhenjun, *Tianzhi ouwen* (Taipei: Wenhai chuban she, CCST, No. 22, 1968, vol. 219), 1: 20a. For Tongzhi's permission of 1865, see *CSL*, Tongzhi reign, 144: 2b–3b, 4/6/jiawu.

31. For a general description of the *fadu*, see *Manzu da cidian*, 593–94; Teng Shaozhen and Bo Dagong, "Manzu di hebao," *Manzu wenhua*, 17 (1992): 55–56. A Korean captive reported that while in action, Nurhaci's soldiers carried rice flour. One may assume that these soldiers put their food in the *fadu*. See Yi, *Chaam Sŏnsaeng munjip*, 6: 5a. For pouches given by Hong Taiji, see *Qingchu Nei Guoshi yuan Manwen dang'an yibian* (Peking: Guangming ribao chuban she, 1989 in 3 volumes), 1: 20, 372; *Chongde sannian Manwen dang'an yibian*, trans. and comp. Ji Yonghai and Liu Jingxian (Shenyang: Liaoshen shushe, 1988), 129, 132, 213. For the case of the Shunzhi era, see *CSL*, Shunzhi reign, 81: 10a, 11/2/xinsi. The biography of Xie Xuan, a famous general of the Eastern Jin dynasty (317–420), helps explain the origin of *hebao*. As a young aristocrat, Xie liked to carry a purple sachet. See *Jinshu*, comps. Fang Xuanling et al. (Taipei: SPPY ed., 1965, 6 volumes), 4. 79: 7a. Also see Wei Song, *Yishi jishi* (Peking: Wenkui tang ed., 1891, 6 volumes), 5. 18: 5b–6a. For the origin of the term, see Meng Yuanlao, *Tongjing menghua lu* (Shanghai: Commercial Press, 1959), 75.

32. For pouches given by Kangxi, see *Gong-zhong dang: Kangxi chao zouzhe*, 6: 622, Memorial of Pan Yulong, 55/9/19; 7: 358, Memorial of Zuo Shiyong, 57/6/13; 7: 414, Memorials of Pan Yulong, 57/7/27. For Yongzheng's case, see *Gong-zhong dang: Yongzheng chao zouzhe*, 2: 671, Memorial of Li Weijun, 2/5/17. For the case of Qianlong, see Teng and Bo, "Manzu di hebao," 55–56. For its physical description, see Teng and Bo, "Manzu di hebao," 55–56.

33. For its functional change and new importance, see Teng and Bo, "Manzu di hebao," 55–56. For the gift to the Apostolic Legate, see *Kangxi yu Luoma shijie guanxi wenshu* (Taipei: Taiwan xuesheng shuju, 1973, reprint), 56. On New

Year's Day, the throne gave high courtiers pouches embroidered with the "Eight Treasures." See Fucha Dunchong, *Yanjing suishi ji* (Peking: Beijing chuban she, 1961, as the second part of the volume), 43. For the case of Nian Gengyao, see *Yongzheng chao Manwen zhupi zouzhe quanyi*, 1: 1226 (#2196).

34.   For the origin of Manchu customs, see Aixin Gioro, *Lao Beijing yu Manzu*, 42 and 298.

Chapter VII

Manchu Language and Literature

CHINESE INFLUENCE ON THE MANCHUS can be examined from the perspective of their language and literature. In the early years of the Qing the Manchu language took precedence over Chinese, although both were officially adopted. Specialists translated Manchu documents into Chinese and vice versa. The court encouraged young Chinese scholars to learn Manchu. Chinese officials were insulted by Manchu colleagues because they did not understand the latter's tongue. Shortly after 1644, Manchu became a minority language. For effective communication with the conquered, they had to use Chinese. Eventually they became accustomed to the Chinese tongue and forgot their native speech. For all their efforts, the Qing rulers could not prevent this from happening. True, the Manchus who forgot their mother tongue did not lose their ethnic identity, but a common language is important for maintaining close association between members of any group. In other words, without it, their sense of belonging to the same group would fade.[1]

Manchu literature better illustrates Chinese cultural influence. The rise of Manchu writers was chiefly the result of education. Because their own writing system was new and less sophisticated, Manchu writers used Chinese to express themselves. The Kangxi period was the beginning of the transition from written Manchu to written Chinese. Manchu traditional folklore existed in oral form only and was not helpful to Manchu writers. They had to turn to Chinese literature for inspiration. From the first half of the eighteenth century onward, many Manchu literarti emerged. Like language, literature links ways of thinking and expression. As a whole, therefore, Chinese language and literature penetrated the Manchu ethnic heritage and weakened it.

1. Language

Both the Jurchen and the Manchu languages belong to the Tungusic group, a branch of the Altaic linguistic family. In the early twelfth century the Jin dynasty developed two types of writing, large script and small script, both influenced by Khitan and Chinese characters. Large Jurchen script was devised in 1119 and was gradually supplanted by small script, which appeared in 1138. After the fall of the Jin dynasty the small script remained in use among the Jurchens in Manchuria and was possibly used for communication with China. The Ming government compiled Sino-Jurchen vocabularies as manuals for translators and interpreters. They were not always accurate, but might be regarded, as one specialist maintains, "as a late form of Jurchen or as a form of early Manchu." By the sixteenth century, small script had become obsolete. As a result the Jurchens either asked Ming interpreters for help, or used the Mongol system. Nurhaci relied on Chinese secretaries, notably Gong Zhenglu, to maintain communication with China and Korea.[2] In time, he needed a new writing system to symbolize the emergence of his state and serve as a bond between tribesmen.

Nurhaci ordered old-script Manchu to be devised in 1599, using Mongol phonetic symbols to mark the Jurchen language. According to tradition, Erdeni and G'ag'ai were its inventors, but it is possible that Kara, a member of the Nara clan from Ula, was also an inventor. With this new tool, the Jurchen frontier state began to compile its historical records, known today as the *Jiu Manzhou dang*, one of the best sources for early Qing history. But as one scholar argues, Nurhaci's motivation for creating the writing system was political; he failed to consider its linguistic aspects. Mongol symbols did not always accurately represent the Jurchen tongue. It could not distinguish certain sounds such as those of *g*, *h*, and *k*. This vagueness confused meanings of words, especially of personal and place names. In 1632, with imperial authorization, Dahai, perhaps with a few others, took charge of revision by adding circles, dots, and special consonants to the old-script system. Thus did new-script Manchu come into existence, and it lasted almost to the end of the dynasty. As discussed in Chapter II, the Manchu script, especially the revised version, made the translation of many Chinese classics and other books into Manchu possible. Such translations, notably of the *Romance of the Three Kingdoms*, greatly helped the dissemination of Chinese ideals and values among the Manchus. One can agree with Herbert Franke that "reading translations was but a half way stage on the way towards fuller sinicization."[3] The Manchu writing system evolved into a major component of Manchu ethnic identity.

The Manchu language traveled with banner forces from Manchuria to China, arriving in Peking first. It reached out to garrison centers of banner forces and offices of Manchu administrators in China proper. As the conqueror's language, Manchu outweighed Chinese in high levels of the bureaucracy, and on such occasions as imperial audiences, appointments, promotions, and performance evaluations. Early on, many documents were available only in Manchu, a language unknown to most Chinese officials. It was difficult for Manchu officials to perform their duties because they in turn did not understand Chinese. They needed interpreters and translators. The ability to speak or write Manchu helped Chinese officials carry on their work and advance their careers.

One may consider the examples of Li Wei (1625–84) and Wang Xi (1628–1703). After passing the metropolitan examination in 1647, they were made junior members of the Hanlin Academy and studied Manchu. Loyal and competent in both spoken and written Manchu, they won imperial confidence and rose rapidly in rank. In their early thirties they became grand secretaries, the highest position in the bureaucratic hierarchy. Wang's case is especially noteworthy because he, working alone, drafted the last will of the Shunzhi emperor. He was the first Chinese official without a banner background entrusted by the Kangxi emperor to read confidential Manchu reports during the war against the Three Feudatories. There are also the cases of Zhu Shi (1665–1736) and Zhang Tingyü (1672–1755). They learned Manchu when they were working in the Hanlin Academy. Their service spanned three reigns, from the Kangxi to the Qianlong. Zhang helped the Yongzheng emperor found the Grand Council and enjoyed unfailing imperial favor.[4]

During the early eighteenth century, both spoken and written Manchu declined, and by the end of the next century only a few Manchus knew their native tongue. This decline seems to have begun with spoken Manchu and appeared first in the south. The trend moved northward to Peking and ended in Manchuria, where it started from

Liaodong in the south and reached the Sungari-Amur region in the north. One may reasonably assume that the decline of spoken Manchu began with the Chinese bannermen. It was easier for them to give up Manchu and return to Chinese because they were born and grew up in a bilingual environment. When interviewed by the Yongzheng emperor, many Chinese bannermen could not relate their personal background in even rudimentary Manchu. In 1729, he ordered them to brush up their spoken Manchu within half a year, but more than a year later he found that the problem still existed.[5]

Clearly, the Manchus preferred Chinese to their native tongue. The Kangxi emperor's edict of 1671 attested to this situation. It abolished the office of interpreter throughout the country on the ground that Manchu officials and commanders fully understood spoken Chinese. The Yongzheng emperor complained that palace guards and soldiers spoke Chinese among themselves. By the next reign the situation had become worse. During the second half of his reign Qianlong was enraged by two Manchu officials. One served as a judicial commissioner in Kwangtung Province, the other as a prefect in Szechwan. They spoke no Manchu and behaved like Chinese before the throne. The two cases occurred twenty years apart, but they reflect the same chilling fact: the Manchus had no interest in their own language. Even imperial princes and the emperor's nephew forgot Manchu. In 1832, a Korean scholar, Kim Kyong-son, toured Peking and interviewed people there. He concluded that Chinese was the common language because young Manchus did not understand their mother tongue. Finally Manchuria, the homeland of the Manchus, was affected. In spite of official restrictions from the Qianlong period onward, Chinese farmers from Shantung and the metropolitan area continuously moved into Manchuria. The migrants changed the structure of the local population and made Chinese the dominant language. In the early nineteenth century, Xiqing, a Manchu writer and once a low-ranking official in Heilongjiang, testified that many Manchus spoke Chinese. Today, Manchu is almost extinct; only a tiny number of elderly Manchus in remote areas can speak the language. A *New York Times* reporter recently visited an isolated village of 1,054 residents in Heilongjiang. Three-fourths of villagers are ethnic Manchus. In a strict sense, only five or six of them, all over eighty years old, can speak fluent Manchu.[6]

Written Manchu suffered the same fate, which confronted the Chinese bannermen first. Li Linsheng (fl. 1680s–1710s) was a fifth-generation descendant of Li Cheng-liang, the clan's progenitor and a noted general of the Ming army in the Liaodong region. His clansmen later joined the Manchus and became members of the Chinese Plain Yellow Banner. While serving as commander in chief of Kansu, Li Linsheng in 1705 begged the throne to allow him to write confidential memorials in Chinese because of his incompetence in Manchu. A nephew of the Kangxi emperor's mother, Fahai (1671–1737), had the same problem. In a confidential memorial submitted in 1723 from his office in Chekiang, Fahai stated that he had to write in Chinese because he had not practiced his Manchu.[7]

The years from the 1680s to the 1780s witnessed the transition from written Manchu to written Chinese, a development related to the decline of Manchu. Like Chinese bannermen, many Manchus could not properly write in Manchu. Once, Kangxi even had to correct the written errors in a memorial submitted by Yin-ti (1688–1735), his fourteenth son and commander in chief of the Qing army dispatched to fight the Eleuth Mongols. In 1723 Pujoo, acting Tartar General of Sian, requested that Yongzheng permit him to submit confidential memorials in Chinese, for he could not write the regular style of Manchu. Fude (fl. 1720s–1730s), once a sub-chancellor of the Grand Secretariat, a position reserved for officials of scholarly accomplishment, was a similar case. Upon reading memorials submitted by Fude, who was serving in Kansu in the early 1720s, Yongzheng complimented him on his mastery of Chinese and asked if someone had assisted him. The language situation in Peking underwent the same change. In 1723–1724 officials there submitted reports in both Manchu and Chinese; toward the end of 1735 they used only Chinese. The Qianlong emperor took a compromising stand, allowing only bilingual reports. Since the Shenyang area was the homeland of the Manchus, its officials were required to write reports in Manchu. By the end of his reign, he permitted them to submit memorials in both languages if they found it difficult to use Manchu alone.[8]

There is no better evidence to illustrate the transition from written Manchu to written Chinese than the problem of translation. For the two centuries from Nurhaci to Qianlong, the Qing court kept rendering

Chinese works into Manchu. Indeed, translation played a major role in the transmission of Chinese culture to the Manchus. For administrative purposes, after 1644 the Qing translated Chinese documents into Manchu and vice versa. But with the decline of written Manchu, translation became a problem. In 1706 and again in 1711, Kangxi revealed that translations done by specialists in the Grand Secretariat were inaccurate. In a memorial of 1723, a Manchu official disclosed that many secretaries were incapable of writing in Manchu or translating Chinese documents into Manchu. Qianlong also complained about incapable translators. He twice censured examiners because they passed unqualified translators. Without qualified translators, many Chinese documents were probably left untouched. This may explain in part why the Grand Council's depository kept more copies of Chinese-language confidential memorials than those in Manchu.[9]

The imperial institutions in Peking experienced the same transition. In most cases the Court of Dependent Peoples used Manchu and Mongol, and occasionally Tibetan. By 1689, however, it had adopted Chinese as another official language. The Office of the Imperial Household, a guardian of Manchu values, followed the same trend. From 1644 to 1722 the branch office in Shenyang sent predominantly Manchu-language communications to its main office in Peking. But a few months, after ascending the throne, Yongzheng added twenty Chinese clerks to the main office and in 1725 allowed its divisions to use both Manchu and Chinese for communications. By the Qianlong period about half of the communications from the branch office were in Chinese. After the 1860s they were almost all in Chinese. During the Yongzheng era, imperial orders were often put in the form of court letters (*tingji*) and dispatched by the postal system directly to the provincial addressees. In the beginning such letters were largely in Manchu, but from the Qianlong reign onward they were mainly in Chinese.[10]

Qing emperors beginning with Yongzheng desperately tried to reverse the tide, but they did not succeed. After the Qianlong reign, even the imperial court did not sponsor major compilations in Manchu. Nor did Manchu aristocratic families have any interest in written Manchu. The Niohuru clan from the line of Eidu compiled four editions of the family genealogy during the 1747–1798 period. With the exception

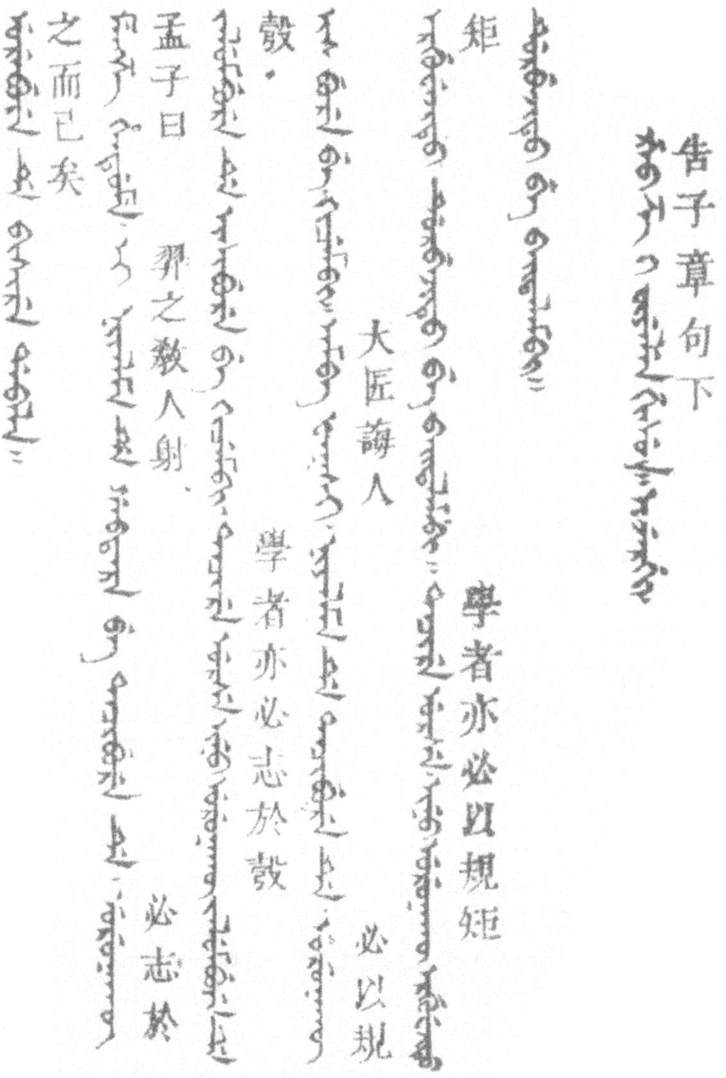

告子章句下

大匠誨人

矩

學者亦必以規矩

必以規

學者亦必志於彀

彀、

必志於

羿之教人射、

孟子曰

之而已矣

Figure 1. Manchu translation of the *Mencius*. Manchu is read from top to bottom and left to right.

of the first edition, which was bilingual, the others were in Chinese. As the late Joseph Fletcher, an expert in Mongol and Manchu, correctly observed, the Manchu language became "formalistic and lifeless" after the late eighteenth century. By the late Tongzhi period, commanders submitted military reports in Chinese. They were allowed to send memorials in Manchu only if they did not know Chinese. After officials finished oral reports while kneeling, Henry Pu-yi, the last Qing ruler, usually told them in Manchu that he "noted" what they said and asked them to "stand up." He confided to friends that "noted" and "stand up" were the only Manchu words he could speak.[11] Chinese had virtually supplanted Manchu by the second half of the nineteenth century.

Qing emperors emphasized the Manchu language because of its allegorical quality. Together with horsemanship and archery, it was regarded as a primary Manchu value, symbolizing the Qing order. Imperial promotion of Manchu blurred the picture and has created conflicting views among scholars toward the Manchu language. Gan Xi (fl. 1810s–60s) told a story involving a Manchu high official and a Chinese secretary in the early 1810s. The Chinese secretary was dismissed on the ground that he knew Manchu and had access to state secrets. The story seems to suggest that Manchu was still an effective language, serving as a code for keeping confidential matters from Chinese staff members. The Korean official Kim Kyong-son believed this to be the case. If true, these must have been isolated cases, not an imperial policy. Even in the seventeenth century, the Qing rulers generously rewarded Chinese officials who knew Manchu and permitted them to read state papers in that language.[12] Why, then, in the nineteenth century did the Qing government have to protect state secrets with a language that was no longer enforceable and most Manchus did not understand?

There are several reasons for the decline of the Manchu language. A chief reason concerns its structural weaknesses. Although it addressed the flaws of old-script Manchu, the new-script system was cumbersome, for it used circles, dots, and other symbols. In an attempt to arrest sinicization, the Qianlong emperor published many dictionaries, including both Manchu and Chinese (one of them contains five languages: Manchu, Chinese, Mongol, Tibetan, and Uigher), creating new words and phrases to replace Chinese loanwords. The term *jy-joo* is a Chinese loanword (*zhizhao*) for "license." In these dictionaries it became known as *temgetu bithe*. Difficult to grasp, such words and phrases drove more Manchus to use Chinese loanwords, which had been popular among them since the frontier days. Another structural problem is that the Manchu language was not adequate to expressing new or complex ideas. Naturally it could not compete with a language enriched for centuries by ideas and loanwords of various origins and spoken by a people far outnumbering the Manchus.[13]

The inconsistent language policies of the early Qing rulers contributed to the decline of Manchu. Throughout the Shunzhi reign and the Oboi regency, the Qing court vigorously maintained the dominant status of Manchu. Included in its measures were the integration of Manchu into the educational program for imperial clansmen and into civil service examinations for Manchu and Mongol bannermen. The Shunzhi emperor even went so far as to personally test the progress of Chinese scholars who learned Manchu. But after the fall of Oboi in 1669, as one study points out, Kangxi did not sponsor any works in Manchu about Manchu culture. He actually shifted focus to Chinese language and culture. The activities of the Imperial Printing Office and Bookbindery at Wuying Hall testified to this change of focus. The collected confidential Manchu memorials of the Kangxi reign consists of 4,297 memorials, of which more than 9 percent concerned the editing, printing, and binding of Chinese books on literature, history, geography, music, philology, and philosophy. Kangxi's enthusiasm for printing Chinese books and his naming imperial sons after the Chinese model, as stated in Chapter VI, evidenced his being deeply influenced by Chinese culture. Although Qianlong published some Manchu books and dictionaries, he was the patron of many more Chinese books. The most important of these was the monumental collection of books known as the *Complete Library of Four Treasuries*. No doubt the imperial sponsorship of Chinese language and culture helped shape the conduct of the Manchus and accelerate the decline of their native language.[14]

The influence of Chinese linguistic elements was another important reason for the decline of the Manchu language. Even in early times, Chinese shared certain linguistic elements with the Tungusic language family, from which the Manchu branch came. Among these elements are fire, fishing, hunting, and farming tools; such animals as goats, horses, bears, and dogs; and agricultural produce of various kinds. Given so many common elements, it is reasonable to infer that the relationship resulted from long contacts between speakers of the two languages. In the twelfth century, the Chinese language had contributed to the invention of the Jurchen scripts, both large and small. When Chinese and Jurchen frontiersmen came into frequent contact during Ming times, they adopted each other's languages and developed a *lingua franca*, referred to as the "Shenyang speech," which was used in the Liaodong region even among Chinese with mutually unintelligible dialects. With the Manchu conquest it reached Peking and interacted with the local dialect. The Kangxi emperor aptly used the Shenyang speech in his rescripts. By the Yongzheng era it had become a component of the Peking dialect, which was easily adopted by the Manchus.[15]

The aforesaid circumstances facilitated the rise of some Jurchens versed in the Chinese language. Wang Gao, an ambitious leader of the Right Jianzhou Guard, is said to have understood both spoken and written Chinese. Yangginu and Cinggiyanu, leaders of the Yehe tribe, once attempted to trick Ming soldiers using tribesmen who were able to speak Chinese. In 1613, one of their successors, Gintaisi, delivered to Ming authorities in Kaiyuan a Chinese report, possibly written by a clansman. A Qing official compilation lists thirteen bannerman-scholars: twelve Manchus, and one Chinese. All these Manchus, including Dahai, Erdeni, and Kūrcan, knew Chinese and helped spread Chinese culture among fellow Manchus.[16] Beyond question, Chinese linguistic elements had affected the Jurchen tongue.

The Chinese language influenced the pronunciation, vocabulary, and some other aspects of Manchu. Among the changes Dahai and others made for new-script Manchu were consonants designed to produce such Chinese sounds as "s," "z," and "tz." There are numerous Chinese loanwords in the Manchu vocabulary. These loanwords fall into three categories, each having subcategories. The first group includes titles, weights and measures, administrative terms, and proper names, such as "*fu*," pronounced the same in Chinese (*fu*), denoting prefecture, and *"huwangdi"* (*huangdi*), which means "emperor." In the second category are Chinese words with Manchu modifiers. The Manchu words for "horse" and "public notice" are *morin* (*ma*) and *bang bithe* (*bangwen*). The first parts of these two words originate in the Chinese vocabulary; the last parts are Manchu modifiers. The last category consists of Chinese ideas expressed in Manchu, such as *aliha amban* (*shang-shu*), president or minister of one of the Six Boards. After examining the content of the Manchu lexican, P. G. von Möllendorff believed that Chinese loanwords made up one-third of it. The work by von P. Schmidt, in which he identified hundreds of Chinese loanwords, is perhaps the most detailed study of Chinese components in the Manchu language. Richard J. Smith further points out: "Manchu, for instance, acquired far more from Chinese than Chinese gained from it."[17] The large quantity of Chinese loanwords must have left indelible marks on many aspects of the Manchu language.

There were grammatical and calligraphic relationships between the Manchu and Chinese languages. Recent studies demonstrate that both languages shared syntactic characteristics and other common elements. Like its Chinese counterpart, the Manchu verb remains unchanged, whatever the person or number of its subject. In both languages two or more nouns can stand together without connectors. The words "father and son" can be written as *ama jui* in Manchu and as *fuzi* in Chinese. The phrase "cows and goats" appear simply as *ihan honin* and *niu yang*, respectively. Among other similarities is the use of duplicate adjectives as adverbs. In its early stages Manchu had three calligraphic styles: regular, running, and cursive. During the Qianlong period, the seal script, an ancient Chinese style, was developed. Altogether, there were thirty-two styles of seal-script Manchu, all of which, it has been said, were patterned after their Chinese original.[18]

Overall, the Chinese language had a broad and deep influence on Manchu. But the greatest influence was sociopolitical. In references to the throne, for example, Chinese documents and books had to raise the characters one or two spaces above the column as a token of respect. Failure to follow this rule would be regarded as *lese majesty*. With the completion of the new-script system, a specialist argued, the Manchu language began to adopt Chinese formality.[19] Charged with

Chinese linguistic and sociopolitical elements, the Manchu language itself became an instrument of spreading Chinese ideas and values.

2. Literature

Manchu literature was a new field. The Manchu's ancestors, the Jurchens of the Jin dynasty, did have famous poets, most of whose works did not survive the ravages of violent dynastic transitions. The following pages will discuss Manchu literature after 1644, with a focus on poetry, the most popular literary form among Chinese and Manchu writers. For the purposes of this discussion, I will not catalog poets and masterpieces.

Early Manchu literature took the form of folklore, sagas and the founding myths of the Qing imperial house. Not until the invention of old-script Manchu were founding myths recorded, as seen in the *Jiu Manzhou dang*, which is written in a kind of prose. The reign of Hong Taiji saw the beginning of Manchu literature, with Omutu (1614–1662) as its representative.[20] During the next four reigns (1644–1795) it reached maturity.

The emergence of Manchu literature was a result of politics. After his succession to the throne, Hong Taiji confronted two problems: political centralization and the future of the frontier state. He needed to keep other powerful princes, especially the three senior princes, Daišan, Amin, and Manggūltai, under control. He had to decide whether the Jurchen state, which covered almost all of Manchuria, should remain a frontier kingdom or take a new direction. Under the influence of his Chinese advisors, mostly working in the Literary Office, he decided to conquer China. He was desperately in need of educated people to carry out administrative work and serve as advisors. Given these circumstances, he enlisted Chinese scholars through such means as emancipation and civil service examinations. Many worked on his personal staff; some in other offices of the Qing government.[21] In addition to political duties they helped spread Chinese ways of life. The larger their number, the more literary influence they exercised over their Manchu counterparts, for traditional China always emphasized poetry.

Education was an effective means of transmitting Chinese culture, and it made the rise of Manchu poets possible. Since the sixth century BC poetry had played a role in Chinese culture. Confucius (551–478 BC) is said to have edited the *Book of Songs,* one of the Five Classics.[22] Throughout the history of imperial China, education centered on the humanities, and poetry was a required subject. Every scholar was expected to know poems because, besides memorization, each was expected to learn how to compose poems.

Nurhaci and Hong Taiji sponsored education for political reasons. In 1595 an eyewitness reported that Nurhaci had his secretary, Gong Zhenglu, tutor his sons. At that time six of his sons were eligible for schooling. Classes might have included the Chinese language, culture, and history, because Gong was Chinese. Around 1621, Nurhaci founded a school in each banner, eight in all, for sons of its officers. Each school had a full-time teacher, a Manchu *baksi,* with a Chinese assistant. The following year Nurhaci rewarded these Chinese scholars, perhaps because of their good performance. Likely, subjects covered language and culture, Manchu, and Chinese. The eight schools lasted until the next reign.[23]

Hong Taiji increased the emphasis on education. To convince his officers of its importance, he issued a long edict comparing the performance of Manchu and Ming armies in two recent battles. Under their commander, Amin, he complained, the Manchu forces were more interested in looting than fighting, and thus were defeated. Surrounded and starving, Ming defenders in Jinzhou did not give up. Education made the difference, he concluded. It is not difficult to sense from the above argument his high opinion of Chinese education and interest in imitating it. In 1631 he ordered princes and high officers to send their sons between eight and fifteen *sui* to attend school so as to acquire knowledge and learn the principles of righteousness, loyalty to the ruler, and respect for superiors, all being moral ideals of a universal nature. But it is quite possible that he was inspired by the *Romance of the Three Kingdoms,* a popular Chinese historical novel glorifying the same ideals that the Ming defenders of Jinzhow displayed and known to him and Nurhaci. Both frequently cited episodes from this famous work to justify their actions or admonish subordinates. Hong Taiji held Guan Yu (162–220), a chief character of the novel and the embodiment of all such ideals, in high regard. (Fiction and Guan Yu will be further explored in Chapter VIII.) Confucian classics and Chinese were likely among the subjects taught because each school had two Chinese instructors, altogether sixteen.[24]

After 1644 the Qing court put greater stress on the education of Manchu sons. Schools appeared everywhere, centered in and around Peking. At the top was the Palace School for imperial sons. With the best scholars as teachers, this school kept rigid schedules and offered instruction in the Four Books and the Five Classics, the Manchu and Mongol languages, and military subjects. Negligent teachers were reprimanded, demoted, or even dismissed. Manchu emperors since Yongzheng had been educated there. As a result, most of the Qing rulers were versed in Chinese language, history, and penmanship. Figure 2 shows a piece of Yongzheng's handwriting taken from the *Zhu pi yu zhi*, a collection of select confidential reports from officials with his instructions in vermilion ink. There were schools for young male members from the branch imperial line and collateral relatives of the imperial house. The Imperial Academy admitted students from the Eight Banners. It later took charge of Government Schools for the Eight Banners (*Baqi guanxue*), which served more students. There were schools for imperial guard units such as the *Jianrui ying*. Since the Kangxi reign, sons of bondservants from the Office of the Imperial Household had been encouraged to study in their own schools. The Banner Charity Schools (*Baqi yixue*) were founded in the Yongzheng reign for students from poor families.[25]

Similar schools appeared in Manchuria, from the Shenyang area northward to the Amur valley. Garrison centers beyond Peking and Manchuria had their own banner schools. On the whole, schools for banner boys offered scholarships and taught language and military subjects. Some emphasized the Chinese language or translation. Records reveal that some schools were understaffed and poorly operated. But it was from these schools that hundreds of students became qualified to take civil service, translators, or other examinations. From 1651 to 1794, approximately 1,300 Manchu students passed examinations for the intermediate degree, *juren* (recommended or established man). Holders of this degree were entitled to take the metropolitan examina-

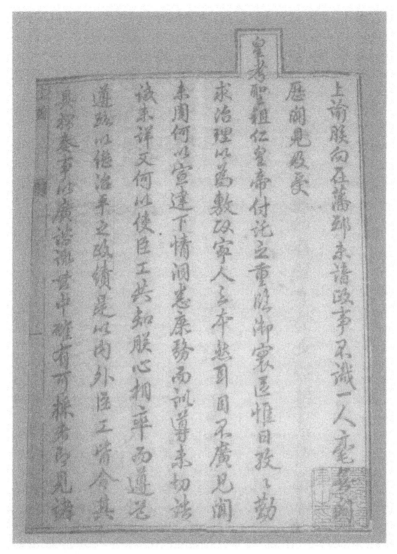

Figure 2. Yongzheng's handwriting.

Reproduced from the *Zhu pi yu zhi* by courtesy of Princeton University's East Asian Library.

tion. Between 1652 and 1795, about 380 received the *jinshi* degree, the
holders of which were immediately eligible to receive offices. All these
degree holders were scholars, writers, and poets, and many of them
composed poetic masterpieces.[26] Of course, many poets did not pass
the examinations.

In addition to schools there were private classes sponsored by individual Manchu nobles, officials, and even monarchs. Such classes
were comparable with the Chinese system known as *sishu*, essentially one-room schools with a few boys. Each school hired a scholar
to teach language, history, and classics. G'aose (1637–1670), the sixth
son of Hong Taiji and a noted poet, seems to have been taught by a
Chinese scholar. While leading an expedition into North China in
1642–1643, Abatai, the seventh son of Nurhaci, looted cities and took
prisoners, from whom he selected scholars as tutors for his sons. For
various reasons, the early Qing government exiled Chinese scholars
to Manchuria, many of whom ended up tutoring sons of local Manchu officials. Almost universally, Manchu officials in China proper
hired Chinese tutors for their sons. As stated earlier, Fude, a Manchu administrator in Kansu Province, had a Chinese scholar to tutor his son. With private classes so popular among Manchu officials,
the Yongzheng emperor became alarmed, advising these officials to
keep alert with such tutors, who, he warned, might be charlatans or
intriguers.[27]

It is difficult to provide details about the conducting of private
classes, but a sketch may be made. Pupils were at first asked to memorize the contents of textbooks by rote. After this stage, the teacher explained the contents. Eventually students learned how to write poems
and essays. Ortai (O-erh-t'ai), a high official active between the late
Kangsi and early Qianlong reigns, was a case in point. He attended
his first class immediately after Chinese New Year's Day in 1686, when
he was five years old (six *sui*). The *Four Books* and *Five Classics* were
among the first books he had to read and memorize. Two years later
the teacher began to tackle their contents. At age nine he learned to
write essays. Linqing (1791–1846), an official and writer, had a similar experience. He received education first from his Chinese mother,
a noted painter and poet. At age eleven he studied under a relative,
under whom he memorized textbooks by rote. He was taught to write
essays two years later.[28] The education of boys from childhood in Chi-

nese language, literature, and Confucian classics clearly weakened the ethnic heritage of the Manchus.

For all their differences, Manchu poets shared characteristics. With a few exceptions, they were aristocrats and officials. Qing emperors, particularly Qianlong, were prolific writers and poets. For cultural and political reasons they were interested in the culture of the conquered and schooled their sons in Chinese. They wrote in Chinese and followed the rules of Chinese poetry. Their poems were similar to those by Chinese writers, but frequently they explored new themes. Since they were members of the conquering class, early Manchu poets were warriors. Omutu participated in many campaigns; Singde was a noted archer and imperial bodyguard; Fukangan (d. 1796) was a noted general. Their works described not only conventional themes—such as happiness, sorrow, travel, natural beauty, and thinking of friends—but hunting, heroic deeds, frontier life.[29] These themes complemented the themes of most Chinese poets.

One may divide the rise of Manchu poets into three stages: beginning, imitating, and mature. The reign of Hong Taiji marked the beginning stage, and Omutu seems to have been the only Manchu poet then active. Born to the Janggiya clan, he was a member of the Manchu Plain Yellow Banner and well educated in Chinese language and literature. After passing the examination for the *juren* degree in 1641, he worked as a translator and compiler in the Inner State Secretariat. Among the Chinese books he translated into Manchu was the *Book of Songs*. He attained a high position in the government, but his literary achievement was even greater. In all likelihood he was the first Manchu to write poems in Chinese. His poems won high praise from famous Chinese poets.[30] One of his poems is translated as follows:

The Yellow River 黃河

I strain my eyes, seeing in the shadow of the sun
    the Yellow River stretch,   極目黃河日影開,
The high winds strike the bank;
    the surging waves press forward.   高風拍岸急浪催.
Who can command the often winding
    and always marching waters,   誰將百折長驅水,
To let [me] cross by horse
    to the southeast and compose verses? 渡馬東南作賦來.

The imitation stage, during the Shunzhi and Kangxi reigns (1644–1722), witnessed the rise of more Manchu poets, among whom were princes and even emperors. They kept in contact with Chinese scholars, poets, and artists through various means. Singde and Yun-duan (1671–1704), a grandson of Abatai, showed great hospitality to Chinese writers. The Kangxi emperor's sons, Yin-zhi (1677–1732), Yin-li (1697–1738), to name only two, also supported Chinese literary friends. Created in 1677, the Southern Imperial Study was the workplace of Chinese writers, scholars, poets, and artists under Kangxi's sponsorship. Kangxi himself was a fine poet.[31]

Manchu sponsors adopted other Chinese practices. For ages, educated Chinese had practiced the custom of taking courtesy, literary, pen, and other names. The same person might have four, five, or more names. The first four Manchu rulers after 1644 adopted this practice. Almost all Manchu nobles and high officials, among whom were poets, had courtesy and literary names. Because seal engraving were considered a form of art, Chinese scholars, writers, and artists had a penchant for personal seals made of jade or fine stone. Manchu officials and literati became fond of such seals. With more names a person might have more seals, with which he stamped the literary and artistic works he authored or collected. The Qianlong emperor had a great number of jade seals, the marks of which appeared on many paintings and calligraphic works in the imperial collection. During this stage, more Manchus became devotees of Chinese literature and arts and began to collect rare books and expensive art objects. Qing rulers and princes were the greatest collectors. When they were no longer blessed by fortune, owners placed collected items on the market. It took about twenty years, one source indicates, for the sixth inheritor of Yin-xiang (1686–1730), the thirteenth son of Kangxi, to empty his treasure house.[32]

The most prominent Manchu poet in this stage was G'aose, the sixth son of Hong Taiji. Unlike his brothers, he avoided the mundane. To pursue his interest in Chinese arts and literature, he once took up residence on Mount Yiwulü near Guang-ning in Liaodong. The mountain had been associated with intellectual activity during the Liao and Jin dynasties, when scholars and even princes maintained a library and built residences there for academic and literary pursuits. G'aose was the first prince versed in poetry, music, and painting. Seven of Kangxi's sons, such as Yin-zhi and Yin-xiang, were also active poets. But Abatai's descendants enjoyed the greatest literary fame among imperial clansmen during the Kangxi era. One of his grandsons, Yun-duan, was the most versatile. He was versed in poetry, painting, and drama. His two brothers, a sister, and a daughter were all talented writers and artists. Yun-duan died in his early thirties, but he has been remembered for his talents.[33] The compiler of *Xichao yasong ji,* an anthology of elegant poems by bannermen as well as imperial clansmen from the 1630s to the 1790s, selected fifty-three of his poems. The following is one of his poems:

Painting Chrysanthemums 畫菊

The rains stop just after the Qingming Festival,	清明才過雨初收,
Both laziness and sickness make me afraid to go out.	懶病相兼怕出遊.
Occasionally I paint three or four yellow chrysanthemum flowers,	偶畫黃菊三四朵,
Keeping the door closed and facing them alone, I feel it is late autumn.	閉門獨對似深秋.

No other Manchu literati of this period surpassed Singde, a member of the Plain Yellow Banner. He was the eldest son of Mingju (1635–1708), who once served as Grand Secretary and was a devotee of Chinese culture. Singde learned classics and literature from Chinese tutors and passed the examination for the *jinshi* degree in 1676. He participated in the compilation of important commentaries on the Chinese classics and also compiled anthologies of lyric verses (*ci*) by poets of various dynasties. He was a master of poetry, especially of *ci,* and a great prose writer. His poems and lyric verses have been studied by generations of scholars and aficionados. Many of his essays are included in the *Baqi wenjing*, a collection of essays by noted bannermen, including imperial princes. Singde's younger brother, Kuixu (1674?–1717), was also a famous poet.[34] The following is one of Singde's poems:

Recording the Words of the Warriors 記征人語

In the nightly solitude, tents spread over the sandy field,	列幕平沙夜寂寥,
Far off, the clouds of Hubei and the moon of Hobei	楚雲燕月兩迢迢.
Naturally warriors entertain no dreams of returning home,	征人自是無歸夢,
But resting their heads on their helmets, lie listening to the billowing tides.	卻枕兜鍪臥聽潮.

With the end of the Kangxi reign came the mature stage of Manchu poetry, an era destined to be different. The poets of that era formed a literary class comparable to their Chinese counterparts. The aristocratic poets of this stage were no longer as dominant as they had been. There were more banner schools, which prepared more poets. Since 1683, China had enjoyed decades of peace and prosperity, which contributed to an increase in the number of aristocrats. The government did not have enough positions for everyone, and they became unemployed. With the autocracy firmly established, they lost their political clout. These developments weakened the Manchu aristocrats and loosened their grip on the literary circles. In these circumstances a group of private Manchu poets appeared. Some had no interest in official careers; some were excluded from the government for political reasons; some had no opportunity for service. For the most part they were not in government service. Their poems described landscapes and pastoral life and were characterized by relaxation, nature, freshness, and harmony.[35]

Of the private Manchu poets, Canghai (1678?–1744) was the exemplar. Born to the Nara clan of the Hada tribe, he was a member of the Manchu Bordered White Banner. His father, Maki (d. 1696), had distinguished himself as a great warrior in the campaigns against

the Three Feudatories. Canghai declined official positions and hereditary privileges. He preferred a private life, surrounded by paintings
and books, and was familiar with the works of famous Chinese poets
before him. His poems focused on personal feelings, mountains, and
streams; were marked by sincerity, spontaneity, and naturalness; and
were praised by other poets.[36] Here is one of his poems:

The Single-Tree Temple 獨樹庵

Through the three peaks comes the distant sunlight,	三峰露遠光,
A single tree shades the temple.	獨樹遮蘭若.
From time to time I meet the monk of the mountain,	時與山僧期,
We saunter under the moonlight	婆娑明月下.

Sungšan was another famous private poet, a member of the Bordered White Banner and a nobleman from a family which had kept
marital bonds with the imperial clan. His wife was a descendant of
Šurhaci, Nurhaci's younger brother and competitor. Physically debili-
tated, he had no interest in any office, but devoted to writing poems
about serenity, natural surroundings, and eremite life. Despite his literary fame, Qing official records fail to keep sufficient information
about him. He seems to have been active during the late seventeenth
and early eighteenth centuries. He, his wife, and his younger brother
were all accomplished poets, whose verses are included in the *Xichao
yason ji*.[37] Below is one of Sungšan's poems:

Poem in Retirement 閑成

My hut faces the blue mountain, The green waters gird my vegetable garden.	茅屋青山向, 蔬園綠水圍.
In these leisure surroundings, urgent matters are diminished	境閑忙事少,
In the quiet, conventions are few.	人靜俗情稀.

After I wash the inkstone,
    fragrance arises from the water.   滌硯香生水,
When I stir the flowers,
    dewdrops moisten my cloak.   移花露上衣.
Naturally, there is an elegant,
    dispassionate atmosphere,   自成幽淡趣,
Where do I act against my
    original intention?   何處素心違?

Among the aristocratic poets in this era were the Yongzheng and Qianlong emperors and many imperial clansmen. One of Yongzheng's younger brothers, Yin-xi (1711–1758), was skilled in poetry and painting, and some of Yongzheng's sons, nephews, and grandsons were practicing poets. Qianlong himself wrote more than 43,000 Chinese poems.[38] Ortai may serve as an example of the aristocratic poets of this period because his clan had a scholarly tradition, produced high officials, and made complex marriages. A member of the Manchu Bordered Blue Banner, he was influenced by his father, Oboi, a noted scholar from the Silin Gioro clan who had served in the Hanlin Academy. Three clansmen held the *juren* degree; four, the *jinshi* degree. All were scholars, poets, and high officials. After passing the examination for the *juren* degree in 1699, Ortai began public service, but not until the Yongzheng and Qianlong reigns did his official career reach its peak. During his service in Kiangsu in 1723–1725, he made friends with Chinese writers and compiled an anthology that included their poems and his own. Ortai, his brother, two sons, and a nephew contributed 227 verses to the *Xichao yasong ji*.[39]

In short, Chinese language and literature were an effective means of sinicization. Out of necessity, the majority of Manchus adopted the language of the conquered and in time forgot their native speech. With this transition they unconsciously changed their attitudes and sentiments because, through the pervasive transmission of Chinese culture, Chinese ways of life were able to penetrate their ethnic tradition and weaken it. As an elite group, Manchu literati took great interest in both Chinese language and literature. They all studied under Chinese tutors in their boyhood. Since the age of ten, for example, Yun-duan had been taught by Chinese scholars brought in from Hunan Province. Kuixu was tutored by Cha Shenxing, a famous Chinese writer. Cang'an (fl. 1690s–1740s), a member of the Nara clan, was a noted poet who authored five literary works. He was a disciple of Han Tan, a high official and renowned essayist. A member of the Janggiya clan, Agui (1717–97) was a general, statesman, and poet. He learned from Shen Tong, a classicist. It is only natural that they followed their mentors and wrote in the Chinese way.[40]

Their close association with Chinese writers was perhaps the most prominent aspect of the rise of Manchu poets. The association further assisted them in adopting Chinese culture. Singde and Yun-duan were the best cases in point. They kept company with many Chinese writers and patronized them, regardless of their social and political status. Wu Zhaoqian (1631–1684), an accomplished poet, was falsely accused of an examination violation by the imperial court and exiled to northern Manchuria, where he stayed for more than two decades. After reading Wu's poems, Singde made great efforts to help the poet. In the end Wu was brought out of exile in 1681. Because of his generosity and friendliness to Chinese writers, he was even identified as the hero of the *Dream of the Red Chamber* by some scholars. Among Yun-duan's Chinese friends were wandering poets and writers, some of whom even refused to serve the Qing. No wonder he was degraded and finally deprived of his noble rank by the Kangxi emperor. Another example was Ochang (d. 1755), a high official and nephew of Ortai. He was ordered by Qianlong to commit suicide, for he had befriended a Chinese writer and together their poems were considered offensive to the dynasty.[41]

For an effective analysis, one has to examine the association between Manchu and Chinese writers from a different perspective because it went both ways. Manchu poets and writers eagerly befriended and sought advice and inspiration from brilliant Chinese poets. Wang Shizhen (1634–1711), a high official and prolific writer, posthumously recognized by Qianlong as the foremost poet of the Qing in 1765, was a very popular literary consultant. Many Manchu writers were either his students or friends. Zheng Xie (1693–1765) is another case. A well-known poet, painter, and calligrapher, he exchanged poems with Manchu poets, including Ortai and Prince Yin-xi, the twenty-first son of the Kangxi emperor. This close association demonstrates that poets ignored not only sociopolitical status but also ethnic boundaries. Chinese and Manchu poets belonged to the same cultural mainstream.[42]

Together with Chinese writers, Manchu poets enriched the literary history of the Qing period. This can be seen from the *Xichao yasong ji*, which contained the poems of 585 writers, of whom 353 were Manchus. Besides, many Manchu authors published individual collections of poems. True, their ability to write good Chinese poems or essays did not make them "Chinese," but it is also true that language and literature are related to patterns of thinking and values; they are not merely tools of communication. When coupled with changes in Manchu social institutions, Chinese language and literature further undermined the building blocks of the Manchu ethnic identity: language, horsemanship, and archery. Poetry and essays transformed Manchu warriors into literary men, who surely transmitted Chinese culture to other Manchus and accelerated the process of sinicization.[43]

Notes

1. For the language problems of Chinese officials, see *CSL*, reign of Taizong, 10: 35b, Tiancong 5/12/renchen. For the importance of a native language, see *International Encyclopedia of the Social and Behavioral Sciences*, 2: 846. George A. De Vos discusses close relations between language and a separate ethnic identity. See his "Ethnic Pluralism: Conflict and Accommodation." In Lola Romanucci-Ross and George A. De Vos, eds., *Ethnic Identity: Creation, Conflict, and Accommodation* (Walnut, CA: AltaMira Press, 3rd edition, 1995), 23.

2. For a detailed study of the Sino-Jurchen vocabulary, see Daniel Kane, *The Sino-Jurchen Vocabulary of the Bureau of Interpreters* (Bloomington, IN: Research Institute for Inner Asian Studies, Indiana University, 1989), chs. 3, 7, and 8. For the quote, see ibid., 99.

3. For the creation and weaknesses of old-script Manchu, see Guan and Wang, "Man yuwen di xing-shuai ji lishi yiyi," 208–11; *ECCP*, 1: 225–26. For the possible role of Kara, see Giovanni Stary, "Guanyu Manzu lishi he yuyen di ruogan wenti," *Manxue yanjiu* 2 (1994): 221–22. A new study questions the role of Dahai in the reform. See Pang, "The Manchu Script Reform of 1632," 201–206. For Nurhaci's motivation, see Perdue, *China Marches West*, 127. For the quote and a similar idea, see Franke, *China under Mongol Rule*, 19 and 26.

4. For biographies of Li and Wang, see, *ECCP*, 1: 493–94; 2: 819; *Qingshi liezhuan*, 2. 7: 477–79, 512–16. For Zhang, see *ECCP* 1: 54–56, and Bartlett, *Monarchs and Ministers*, 79–88. For Zhu, see *ECCP* 1: 188–90.

5. For a few detailed survey of the language problem, see Elliott, *The Manchu Way*, 290–304; Teng, "Ming-Qing liangdai Manyu Manwen," 21–28; Hanson Chase, "The Status of the Manchu Language in the Early Ch'ing" (Ph. D. Dis-

sertation, University of Washington, 1979), ch. 4; Chieh-hsien Ch'en, "The Decline of the Manchu Language in China during the Ch'ing Period (1644–1911)."
In Walther Heissig, ed., *Altaica Collecta; Berichte und Vortrage der XVII Permanent International Altaistic Conference, 3–8 Juni 1974 in Bonn and Honnef*
(Wiesbaden: Harrassowitz, 1976), 137–54. For Yongzheng's edict of 1729 and
his later findings, see *Shangyu baqi*, 7: 21b; 9: 1a.

6.   For abolition of the interpreter's office see *CSL*, Kangxi reign, 35: 5b–6a, 10/1/
dingchou; Lawrence D. Kessler, *K'ang-hsi and the Consolidation of Ch'ing Rule,
1661–1684* (Chicago and London: University of Chicago Press, 1976), 121. For
the palace guards and soldiers, see *Shangyu baqi*, 6: 2a; 10: 10. For the judicial
commissioner, see *CSL*, Qianlong reign, 844: 2a, 34/10/jichou. For the Manchu
prefect, see, *CSL*, Qianlong reign, 1347: 24, 55/1/xinhai. For imperial clansmen,
including the emperor's nephews, see *CSL*, Qianlong reign, 663: 19b–20a, 27/
[intercalary] 5/xinmao; 992: 12a–13a, 40/10/xinsi. For Kim's observation, see his
Yŏnwon jikchi in *Yŏnhaengnok sonjip* (Seoul: Sung Kyun Kwan University,
1960–62, 2 volumes), 1: 1176.

      For the language situation in Manchuria, see *CSL*, Qianlong reign, 735: 7a,
30/4/jisi; 1035: 4b–5a, 42/6/yimao; *MTTS*, 518. For Xiqing, see his *Heilong-jiang
waiji* (Taipei: Wenhai chuban she, Jindai Zhongguo shiliao congkan, Series 6,
1968, vol. 59), 6: 5a. A new study mentions that some old Manchu people in remote areas in Jilin and Heilongjiang kept their native tongue even in the last
three decades of the nineteenth century. See Rhoads, *Manchus and Han*, 53–54.
According to two recent reports, fewer than a hundred Manchu people can
speak the language. See *Shijie ribao*, "Shenzhou xiang-qing zhoukan" 49
(March 19, 2000): 1 and (August 14, 2000): A8. For the *New York Times* report,
see David Lague, "A Chinese Village Struggles to Save the Dying Language of a
Once Powerful Dynasty," *New York Times* (March 18, 2007). International
[section], 6.

7.   For Li Linsheng, see *Baqi tongzhi*, 194: 28b–30a. For his memorial, see *Gong-
zhong dang: Kangxi chao zouzhe*, 1: 43–44, 41/6/6. For the family history of
Fahai, see *Baqi tongzhi*, 141: 1a–4b. For his memorial, see *Gong-zhong dang:
Yongzheng chao zouzhe*, 1: 826, 1/10/7.

8.   For the memorial by Yin-ti, see *Kangxi chao Manwen zhupi zouzhe quanyi*,
1369 (#3344). For Pujoo, see *Yongzheng chao Manwen zhupi zouzhe quanyi*, 1:
355–56 (#658). For Fude, see *Baqi tongzhi*, 340: 19b; *CSL*, Yongzheng reign, 25:
13a, 2/10/xinmao; *Gansu tongzhi*, comps. Xu Rong et al. (Taipei: Wenhai chuban she, Zhongguo bian-jiang congshu, Series 2, 1966, 6 volumes), 3. 28: 23b.
For his memorials and the throne's compliments, see *Gong-zhong dang: Yongzheng chao zouzhe*, 1: 722–23, 1/9/16. In another memorial (2: 134, 1/12/6), he
told the emperor that because of a physical problem, he was helped by a Chinese scholar, but he essentially authored the memorials. For Qianlong's permission, see *Baqi tongzhi* (introductory) ch. 12, p. 64.

9. For Kangxi's dissatisfaction, see *TCCC*, 66: 15a and 18. For Qianlong's complaint, see *CSL*, Qianlong reign, 428: 15a, 17/12/bingshen. For officials who let unqualified students pass examinations, see *CSL*, Qianlong reign, 1362: 2, 55/9/jimao; 1451: 7, 59/4/yihai. For the official's report, see *Yongzheng chao Manwen zhupi zouzhe quanyi*, 1: 448 (#808). For the number of confidential memorial copies, see Bartlett, "Books of Revelations," 29–30.

10. For the languages used in the Court of Dependent Peoples, see Sun, *Qianlong di*, 209. For official reports in Chinese, see *CSL* [of the Qianlong era], 5: 40, Yongzheng 13/10/kuisi. For communications between the branch of the Office of the Imperial Household and its main office, see Tong Yonggong and Guan Jialu, "Sheng-jing Manwen xing-shuai tan," *Manyu yanjiu*, 1 (1985): 33. For Yongzheng's measures, see *Zongguan Neiwufu xianxing zeli* (Peiping: National Peiping Palace Museum, 1937, 7 volumes), 1. 1: 1a, 18b; 3. 1: 1b; 6. 1: 1b; 7. 1: 1b. For the court letters, see Huang, *Autocracy at Work*, 15; Sun, *Qianlong di*, 210.

11. For the four editions of genealogies by Eidu's descendants, see note 33 in the Introduction of this study. Of the four, the first or 1747 edition contains both languages. For Fletcher's view, see *The Cambridge History of China*, Volume 10: *Late Ch"ing, 1800–1911*, Part 1, eds., Denis Twitchett and John K. Fairbank (Cambridge and New York: Cambridge University Press, 1978), 44. For military reports in Chinese, see *CSL*, Tongzhi reign, 305: 4a, 10/2/xinwei. I heard Henry Pu-yi's story from Wang Zhonghan, Professor Emeritus of History, Central University of Nationalities, when I visited him in Newton, MA, in September 2000.

12. Gan Xi, *Baixia suoyan* (Nanking: reprint of the Gan family edition, 1926, 4 volumes), 1. 1: 23b. For the recent support of the theme, see Crossley and Rawski, "A Profile of the Manchu Language in Ch'ing History," 70–71. For Kim's opinion, see his *Yŏnwon jikchi*, 1: 1176.

13. For these dictionaries and many other examples of new words and phrases, see Tong and Guan, "Sheng-jing Manwen xing-shuai tan," 30–32. Kangxi ordered the compilation of a Manchu dictionary after the Chinese pattern. See *CSL* for his reign, 42: 2b–3a, 12/4/xinhai. For its completion, see *CSL*, Kangxi reign, 233: 9b–11b, 47/6/dingmao. For its structural weakness, see Chase, "The Status of the Manchu Language," 160–61.

14. For such inconsistent policies, see Chase, "The Status of the Manchu Language," ch. 4. For the compiling of the *Siku quanshu*, see R. Kent Guy, *The Emperor's Four Treasuries: Scholars and the State in the Late Ch'ien-lung Era* (Cambridge, MA: Council on East Asian Studies, Harvard University, 1987), ch. 4.

15. For such common elements, see Zhao, "Tonggusi," 1 (1986): 58–69; 2 (1986): 64–73; 1 (1987): 74–80. For the history and importance of the Shenyang speech, see Guan and Meng, "Manzu yu Shenyang yu, Beijing yu," 75–78.

16. For Wang Gao, Yangginu, and Cinggiyanu, see respectively *Wugong lu*, 4. 11:

1038b and 1017b. For the Chinese report by Gintaisi, see Dong, *Shenmiao liu-zhong zoushu*, ch. 9, Memorial of Zhang Tao, 47a. For these banner scholars, see *TCCC*, chs. 236–37.

17. Guang and Li, *Qing Taizu*, 1: 7 and 38. For examples from the three categories, see Ji, "Lun Manyu," 23–26; Tong and Guan, "Lun Manwen zhong di Hanyu jieci," 270–80. For the differences between Manchu and Jurchen, see Jin Qi-cong and Wula-xichun, "Nüzhen yu yu Manyu guanxi qiantan," *Minzu yuwen* 1 (1994): 11–16. For the Chinese sounds "s," "z," and "tz," see Li Deqi, "Man-zhou wenzi zhi laiyuan jiqi yanbian," *Guoli Beiping tushu guan guankan*, 5. 6 (1931): 9–10; Mao, "Manwen Hanhua kaolüe," 55–56, 62–68. Möllendorff's book, *Manchu Grammar, with Analysed Texts*, was published in Shanghai in 1892 by the American Presbyterian Mission Press. For his estimate see his book, p. 3. For Schmidt's study, see "Chinesische Elemente im Mandschu [Chinese Elements in Manchu]," *Asia Major* 7 (1932): 573–628; 8 (1933): 233–76, 353–436. For Richard J. Smith, see his *China's Cultural Heritage: The Qing Dynasty, 1644–1912* (San Francisco and Oxford: Westview Press, 1994, 2nd ed.), 101–102.

18. For common syntactic characteristics, see Liliya M. Gorelova, "Manchu-Chinese Syntactical Paralells," *Acta Orientalia Academiae Scientiarum Hungaricae*, 50 (1997): 99–106. For other common elements, see Mao, "Manwen Hanhua kaolüe," 71–74. For the new calligraphic styles, see Li, "Manzhou wenzi zhi laiyuan jiqi yanbian," 11–12; Mao, "Manwen Hanhua kaolüe," 55–56, 62–68. For a photocopy of the seal-style Manchu, see Elliott, *The Manchu Way*, 303, fig. 17b.

19. For this Chinese formality, see Li, "Manzhou wenzi zhi laiyuan ji qi yanbian," 8.

20. For a detailed study of Jurchen literature in the Jin dynasty, see Zhao Zhihui, Deng Wei, and Ma Qingfu, eds., *Manzu wenxue shi* (Shenyang: Shenyang chu-ban she, 1989, volume 1), ch. 5; for Jurchen poetry and poets, see ibid., 195–261, 287–330; for Manchu literary development, see ibid., 7–18. Omutu will be dis-cussed later. For a brief survey of Jurchen literature in the Jin dynasty, see Jin Qicong, "Jurchen Literature under the Chin." In Hoyt Cleveland Tillman and Stephen H. West, eds., *China under Jurchen Rule: Essays on Chin Intellectual and Cultural History* (Albany: State University of New York Press, 1995), 216–37.

21. For Hong Taiji's recruitment of Chinese scholars and their work in the Literary Office, see notes 17 and 19 in Chapter V. For importance of Chinese scholars to Hong Taiji, see Honey, "Stripping off Felt and Fur," 13 and 27.

22. The other four Classics are the *Book of History*, the *Book of Rites*, the *Book of Changes*, and the *Spring and Autumn Annals*. The first four Classics have dif-ferent translated titles.

23. For a survey of education under Nurhaci and Hong Taiji, see Zhao Zhan, *Manzu wenhua yu zongjiao yanjiu* (Shenyang: Liaoning minzu chuban she,

1993), 44–51. For Gong as a teacher, see *CWS*, vol. 22, reign of Sonjo, 70: 608, 28/12/kyemyo. The six sons were born in 1580–1589 and became eligible for school by 1595. For schools founded in 1621, see *MBRT*, vol. 1, Taizu, 24: 353–54. For the Chinese scholars rewarded by Nurhaci, see *MWLT*, 1: 286.

24.   For Hong Taiji's long edict of 1631, arguing the importance of education and ordering high officers to send sons to schools, see *CSL*, reign of Taizong, 10: 28a–29a, Tiancong 5/11 (intercalary)/gengzi. The sixteen Chinese he appointed were responsible for Chinese subjects. See *MWLT*, 2: 1338–39.

25.   For a survey of the education for the Manchus, see Adam Lui, "The Education of the Manchus, China's Ruling Race (1644–1911)," *Journal of Asian and African Studies* 6. 2 (1971): 126–33. The Palace School is also known as *Shang shufang*. See Fuge, *Tingyu congtan* (Hong Kong: Longmen shudian, 1969), 197–98; Zhao, "Qingchao xing-shuai yu huangzi jiaoyu," 83–89. The Four Books are the *Great Learning*, the *Doctrine of the Mean*, the *Analects*, and the *Mencius*. For Qianlong's education, see Harold L. Kahn, *Monarchy in the Emperor's Eyes: Image and Reality in the Qianlong Reign* (Cambridge, MA: Harvard University Press, 1971), ch. 7. In 1789, Qianlong reprimanded and penalized teachers for their failure to show up in the Palace School for a week. See *CSL*, Qianlong reign, 1324: 16b–18b, 54/3/yichou. The schools for sons from the branch imperial line and collateral relatives of the imperial house were known as the *Zongxue* and the *Jueluo-xue*. For these two types of school, the Government Schools for the Eight Banners, and those for the descendants of bondservants and poor bannermen, see Zhao, *Manzu wenhua*, 64–70, 70–76, 76–80, 82–83. See also *Baqi tongzhi*, 94: 3b–14a; chs. 95–96 and 97: 1a–7a, 7b–23b; ch. 98: 22a–27a.

26.   For the schools in Manchuria and garrison centers, see Zhao, *Manzu wenhua*, 84–98; *Baqi tongzhi*, 98: 27a–33b. For examinations, see *Baqi tongzhi*, chs. 99–101.

        During the Shunzhi era 50 Manchu and Mongol students received the *juren* degree and 100 the *jinshi* degree. It is impossible to tell their ethnic origins since the official rosters did not provide such information. But there were only very few holders of Mongol origin. According to a general pattern, I presume 10 Mongol students were holders of the intermediate degree, and 15 holders of the highest degree. From the Kangxi period onward, the rosters distinguished Manchu students from their Mongol counterparts. In 1663–1794, as many as 1,263 Manchu and 98 Mongol students received the *juren* degree. When added to the numbers of the Shunzhi reign, the figures should be 1,303 and 108. In 1670–1795, there were 296 Manchu and 25 Mongol holders of the *jinshi* degree. Combining the Shunzhi numbers, there should be 381 Manchu and 40 Mongol *jinshi* holders. For sources, see *Baqi tongzhi*, chs. 104–105; *Ming-Qing jinshi timing beilu suoyin*, 3: 2638–39, 2642–43.

27.   For some poems by G'aose, see Tiebao, *Xichao yasong ji* (Shenyang: Liaoning daxue chuban she, 1992), introductory chapter 1. For the expedition led by

Abatai in 1642–1643 and for some of his descendants, see *ECCP*, 1: 3–4; *Xiao-ting zalu*, part 1, 5: 12b–13a. For exiled Chinese scholars, see Xiqing, *Heilong-jiang waiji*, 7: 6a, 11b–12a. One of these exiled tutors was Wu Zhaoqian. See Fan Zhui-zheng, "Wu Zhaoqian nianpu," *Heilong-jiang wenwu congkan*, 2 (1984): 88. For Fude's case, see his memorial in *Gong-zhong dang: Yongzheng chao zouzhe*, 2: 134, 1/12/6. For Yongzheng's warning, see *Baqi tongzhi*, introductory chapter 9, p. 39b.

28. For the early education of Ortai, see Orong'an, "Xiangqin bo Owen-duan gong nianpu," *Qingshi ziliao*, 2 (1981): 57; for Linqing's schooling, see Songshen, *Changbai Wanyan shi jiude lu*, 1: 5a.

29. For principles of Manchu poetry, see Stary, "Fundamental Principles of Man-chu Poetry," 187–221. For characteristics of Manchu poets, see Zhao, Deng, and Ma, *Manzu wenxue shi*, 9–13; Xia Shi, "Shunzhi shiqi Manzu wenxue fazhan di beijing yu tiaojian," *MANT*, 4 (1994): 55–56. For Fukangan's biography, see *ECCP*, 1: 253–55. For some poems about deserts and frontiers, see *Xichao ya-song ji*, regular chapter 101: 1580 (poems by Fukangan); regular chapter 101: 1585 (poems by Kuilin).

30. For his biography, see *ECCP*, 1: 603–604; *STTP*, 40: 9b For some of his poems, see *Xichao yasong ji*, regular chapter 1: 328–31. The translated poem is taken from *Xichao yasong ji*, regular chapter 1: 330. The collection of his poems is known as *Beihai ji*. One of his admirers was Wang Shizhen, a famous poet.

31. In the last few years of his life, Shunzhi patronized Chan Buddhist monks, some of whom were writers. See *ECCP*, 1: 257. For Singde's clients, see Zhang Jiasheng, "Kangxi chao Manzu wenxue xing-sheng di yuanyin," *MANT*, 1 (1995): 55. For Yun-duan, see Xia Shi, "Yue-duan jiqi shige," 56–58. For Yin-zhi's Chinese friends, see Huang, *Autocracy at Work*, 74. Yin-li was the patron of Fang Bao. See Xia, "Shunzhi shiqi Manzu wenxue," 56. For the Southern Im-perial Study, see Huang, *Autocracy at Work*, 140–43. For Kangxi as a poet, see Bo Weiyi and Sun Peiren, eds., *Kangxi shixuan* (Shenyang: Chunfeng wenyi chuban she, 1984), 1–53 ff.

32. For examples of courtesy, literary, and other names, see the biographies of Akedun, Shunzhi, Kangxi, and Qianlong in *ECCP*, 1: 6, 255, 327, and 369. For Singde and Yongzheng, see *ECCP*, 2: 662 and 915. For Qianlong's seals, see Xu Qixian, "Qingdai baoxi lüetan," *Gugong bowu yuan yuankan*, 3 (1995): 64–65. For collections of rare books and artist objects, see *Tianzhi ouwen*, 4: 23.

33. For G'aose, see *ECCP*, 1: 3; *CSKC*, 10: 7814; Zhao, *Manzu wenhua*, 139–40. For Mount Yiwulü and its importance, see Chen Shu, "Liaodai jiaoyu shi lun-zheng." In Chen Shu, ed., *Liao-Jin shi lunji* (Shanghai: Shanghai guji chuban she, 1987), 149. For poems by G'aose and Kangxi's seven sons, see *Xichao yas-ong ji*, introductory chapters 1 and 2. Yun-duan's Manchu name was differently transliterated in Chinese. For removal of his princely status, see *CSL*, Kangxi reign, 188: 6, 37/4/jisi. Fifty-three poems of his are included in the *Xichao yas-*

ong ji, introductory chapter 14; for the translated poem, see the same chapter, p. 181. He is the focal point of several studies. See, for example, Xia, "Yue-duan jiqi shige," 55–69; Chen Guiying, "Yue-duan yu 'nan Hong bei Kong,'" *MANT*, 4 (1991): 55–60, 77; Song Ge, "Manzu shiren Yue-duan jiqi shige," *MANT*, 3 (1993): 55–60. For his daughter, see *Tianzhi ouwen*, 4: 40a.

34.　For Mingju's genealogy, see *Yehe Nala shi baqi zupu*, 17b–18a. For Mingju, see *ECCP*, 1: 577–78. For Singde, see *CSKC*, 14: 11165–66. Singde is the subject of many studies, a recent one being Zhao, "Nalan Xingde zhuzuo kao," 2 (1991): 53–62; 3 (1991): 56–69, 37; and 4 (1991): 47–54. For Kuixu, see *ECCP*, 1: 430–31. For Singde's poems, see *Xichao yasong ji*, regular chapter 4: 388–98; for the poem translated here, see the same chapter, p. 396. The poems by his brother, Kuixu, sixty-nine all told, see *Xichao yasong ji*, regular chapters 6–7.

35.　Zhang, "Qingdai qian, zhong qi," 140–42. For the rise of private Manchu poets, see ibid., 140–45.

36.　For Maki, see *STTP*, 23: 17a; *CSKC*, 11: 8479. For Canghai, see Sheng Yu and Yang Zhongxi, *Baqi wenjing* (Shenyang: Liao-Shen shushe, 1988, photocopy with punctuation), 412; *CSKC*, 14: 11178–79; Zhang, "Qingdai qian, zhong qi," 143–44. But the author erred in Canghai's banner affiliation. Some of Canghai's poems are included in the *Xichao yasong ji*, regular chapters 62–63. The translated poem is taken from *Xichao yasong ji*, regular chapter 63: 1128.

37.　Qing official records provide almost no information about Sungšan or his family. For a brief introduction to Sungšan, his brother Tungšan, his son Nengtai, and his wife Lanhiyan Nioiši, see *Xichao yasong ji*, respectively regular chapter 49: 956 and 961, complementary chapter 2:1684. See also Zhang, "Qingdai qian, zhong qi," 142–43. Since Nengtai was a member of the Bordered White Banner (see *Gansu tongzhi*, 3. 28: 23b), Sungšan must also belong to the same banner.

38.　For Yongzheng's poems, see Gong Wang, "Yongzheng huangdi di shiwen," *SHKH*, 1 (1990): 116–23. For Qianlong, see Wei Jianxun, "Lun Qianlong huangdi di shige," *MANT*, 4 (1990): 23–33, especially 24; Martin Gimm, *Kaiser Qianlong (1711–1799) als Poet: Anmerkungen zu seinem schrifstellerischen Werk* [Emperor Qianlong (1711–1799) as Poet: Comments on His Literary Work] (Stuttgart: Steiner, 1993), chs. 1–2. For Yin-xi, see *CSKC*, 10: 7842; Zhang Juling, "Zheng Xie yu Manzu renshi di hanmo yuan," *Zhong-yang minzu daxue xuebao*, 1 (1995): 43–44; *Xichao yasong ji*, introductory chapter 3 and ch. 4: 45–58.

　　　Among Yongzheng's sons, nephews, and grandsons were Hong-zhan (1733–1765), Hong-xiao (d. 1778), and Yong-rong (1744–1790). For their brief biographies, see *CSKC*, 10: 7841–42. Some of their poems are included in the *Xichao yasong ji*, introductory chapter 5: 68–80, chs. 9–10, and chapter 12: 153–59.

39.　For Ortai's clan, see *STTP*, 17: 2a–3a. For their degrees, see Orong'an, "Xiangqin bo Owen- duan gong nianpu," *Qingshi ziliao*, 2 (1981): 58–59, 65, 102, and 143.

For Ortai's biography, see *ECCP*, 1: 601–603; *CSKC*, 11: 8805–11. For the book Oertai (Ortai) edited, see his *Nanbang lixian ji* (N. p.: Shen shizai xian edition, 1725, 8 volumes). He received various honors. See John L. Mish, "Grand Secretary Ortai," *Bulletin of the New York Public Library*, 66. 8 (1962): 535–38. His younger brother, Orci (O-erh-ch'i, 1682–1735) once served as president of the Board of Revenue. See *Qingshi liezhuan*, 4. 14: 1026. Two of Ortai's sons, Orong'an (1714–1755) and Oshi (1718–1758), died in action against the Eleuths in Sinkiang. See *CSKC*, 11: 9127, 9163–64. Ortai married the daughter of Maiju, a Grand Secretary, while his sixth son's wife was the latter's granddaughter. His fifth son married the daughter of Prince Yin-lu. One of his nieces was the daughter-in-law of Prince Yin-xiang. See Orong'an, "Xiangqin bo Owenduan gong nianpu," 59, 74, 91, and 119. For the 227 poems by Ortai and his family members, see *Xichao yasong ji*, regular chapter 19, ch. 23: 627–28, ch. 40: 834–35, chs. 44–45, and ch. 56: 1047–53.

40. For unconscious changes of attitudes and sentiments, see *International Encyclopedia of the Social and Behavioral Sciences*, 2: 846. For Yun-duan's early education under Chinese tutors, see *ECCP*, 2: 934. For Cha Shenxing as Kuixu's tutor, see *ECCP*, 1: 21. For a short biography of Cang'an, see *CSKC*, 12: 9431–33. For his study under Han Tan (1637–1704), see *CSKC*, 12: 9433; *ECCP*, 1: 275. For publications by Cang'an, see Zhang, "Qingchu Manzu ciren ji chengjiu," 52. For Agui's being a student of Shen Tong (1688–1752). See *ECCP*, 1: 6–8; 2: 647–48.

41. For Singde's friendliness to Chinese scholars and writers, see *ECCP*, 2: 662; Zhang, "Qingchu Manzu ciren ji chengjiu," 48. For the story of Wu Zhaoqian and Singde's help, see *ECCP*, 2: 663; Fan, "Wu Zhaoqian nianpu," 84–91 For Yun-duan's friendship with Chinese writers, see Chen, "Yue-duan yu 'nan Hong bei Kong,'" 56–58; *ECCP*, 2: 934. For the case of Ochang, see *CSKC*, 12: 9427–28; *ECCP*, 1: 602.

42. For Wang Shizhen's biography, see *ECCP*, 2: 831–33; for his posthumous recognition by Qianlong, see ibid., 832.. For his influence on Manchu writers, see Zhang, "Kangxi chao Manzu wenxue xing-sheng di yuanyin," 54. For Zheng Xie's close association with Yin-xi, Ortai, and others, see Zhang, "Zheng Xie yu Manzu renshi di hanmo yuan," 43–47. For the general effect of Chinese literary men on Manchu writers, see Zhang, "Kangxi chao Manzu wenxue xing-sheng di yuanyin," 56.

43. These figures are from the *Xichao yasong ji*. Of the 353 Manchu poets, six were female. There were 206 Chinese bannermen poets, and 10 were Chinese bannerwomen writers. Only sixteen Mongol poets were included.

Chapter VIII

Architecture, Religion, and Confucianism

ARCHITECTURE SERVED AS ANOTHER VEHICLE for the sinicization of the Manchus because aesthetics is related to ethnic identity. Influenced by Bohai, Khitan, and Chinese cultures, the Jurchens made strides in architecture during the Jin dynasty. Their palaces, temples, and gardens in and around Peking attested to remarkable architectural achievements. But these achievements have been forgotten since the collapse of the Jin dynasty in 1234. Not until after the rise of Nurhaci were they able to resume architectural activities, centered in the Shenyang area. After conquering China the Manchus controlled more resources, acquired more Chinese influence, and brought their architecture to its zenith.

The Manchus practiced shamanism, an animistic religion popular among peoples in northern Asia. It did not have much theology or formal organization, promising no salvation. This made possible the penetration of Buddhism and such Chinese popular cults as the Jade Emperor, the city god, and the God of War. The Ming government constructed Buddhist temples in the Jurchen region in the early fifteenth century and recruited tribesmen as priests. Although of foreign origin, Buddhism had been adapted by China and carried Chinese values since the Tang dynasty. It was a factor in the sinicization of the Manchus.

Confucianism had been the chief source of Chinese norms, mores, and values since receiving state support in the second century BC. Under imperial sanction, Confucian temples appeared everywhere, and they held an annual memorial service performed as a religious ceremony. In traditional China, cultural identification overshadowed ethnic disparity. People who adopted the Confucian way of thinking and conduct would be considered Chinese even if of different ethnic origins. As one expert argues, this cultural orientation facilitated the frontier people's becoming new components of the Chinese.[1]

1. Architecture

One cannot appreciate the progress in architecture made by Nurhaci and his successors without examining the structure of traditional Jurchen houses. For centuries after the fall of their dynasty in 1234, the Jurchens had no administrative center, which was identified with the tribal chieftain's house. Jurchen houses were built on natural or man-made terraces, with mud walls and thatch- or birch-bark-covered roofs. A typical house faced toward the south and had a door only in one of its walls. With three sides of the house closed and only one side open, rooms looked like pockets. Windows were covered by Korean paper from outside. Against walls inside the house there were hollow clay blocks, known as the *kang*, under which the Jurchens burned fuels, with the chimneys outside. The *kang* became a radiant heating system to keep the house warm and served as beds or for other purposes as well. As described by eyewitness accounts, the Manchus lived in the same kind of houses.[2] This architecture had an impact on Nurhaci's early administrative and residential buildings.

Before 1644 the Manchus had constructed six administrative centers, which fall into three categories: traditional, transitional, and sinicized. The first four administrative centers were close to each other, all in the greater Xinbin area of Liaoning Province. Pragmatic and unpretentious, they exemplified traditional Jurchen architectural features. There was little difference between residences and government buildings. In 1596, a Korean envoy, Sin Ch'ung-il, visited Nurhaci in Fe Ala and saw structures with mud walls, thatch roofs, and heating clay blocks. Although referred to as the Rising Capital (Xingjing; Yenden) where Nurhaci proclaimed himself king of the Jurchen state in 1616, the administrative center in Hetu Ala was very much the same as the structure in Fe Ala. As for the third and fourth centers, there was almost no architectural improvement. At best, they were Nurhaci's command centers, not capitals in the general sense of the word. It was not until construction of the East Capital near Liaoyang in 1621–1622 that a new stage of architecture arose.[3]

Table 9. Nurhaci's Capitals, 1587–1644*

Name	Location	Dates
Fe Ala	Xinbin, Liaoning	1587–1603
Hetu Ala (Xingjing, Yenden in Manchu)	Same area	1603–1619
Jaifiyan	Northwest of Xinbin	1619–1620
Sarhū	West of Jaifiyan	1620–1621
East Capital (Dongjing)	Liaoyang	1621–1625
Prosperous Capital (Shen-jing)	Shenyang	1625–1644

*Sources: *Nuer-haqi shilu*, 1: 8a; 2: 2a; 3: 1a, 11b; 4: 2b; *MWLT*, 1: 72–73, 88, 164, 172, 290, 297, 353, 356, 626–27. And note 2 above.

Manchu adoption of Chinese architecture was the result of political necessity. With the conquest of three cities of strategic importance— Shenyang, Liaoyang, and Guang-ning—in 1621–1622, the Jurchen state greatly increased its political importance. It needed a more advanced administrative center. Nurhaci had led eight tributary missions to Peking, where he must have seen the splendid Ming palace complex and dreamed of building one for himself. After taking Liaoyang he stayed in office quarters of the Liaodong Military Commission. He must have admired the magnificence of Chinese office buildings and cherished plans to construct an administrative center. It is not surprising that after a short stay he ordered the construction of the East Capital in a suburb of Liaoyang. In the newly conquered region, moreover, he was able to acquire such building materials as glazed tiles and enlist Chinese craftsmen and architects.[4] The situation became more favorable when Hong Taiji succeeded to the throne. At the suggestion of Chinese advisors he adopted the Ming ruling machinery and took the imperial title. Naturally, he had to construct palaces and offices after the Ming model.

For an understanding of the Chinese influence on Manchu architecture, it would be appropriate to review the features of Ming palaces which the Manchus tried to imitate. In structure, Chinese palaces, including those of the Ming, were characterized by ridge roofs, flying rafters, checker-shaped ceilings, engraved columns, overhanging eaves, and bracket sets (*dougong*). The ridge roofs served aesthetic

Map 5. Jurchen-Manchu Capitals.

1. Fe Ala   2. Rising Capital (Hetu Ala)
3. Jaifiyan   4. Sarhū
5. East Capital (Liaoyang)   6. Prosperous Capital (Shenyang)
7. Peking

and practical purposes, while flying rafters conveyed a sense of spaciousness. Engraved columns manifested elegance and strength; overhanging eaves increased light in the building. The bracket set was a device sitting atop the column to determine the length and width of the structure. Outside, there were covered corridors to connect to the neighboring palace.

Building materials were cedar, stone, specially designed bricks, and glazed tiles. Rulers and architects in China had a passion for yellow and red. For centuries yellow had been the imperial color, with red suggesting power and blessing. The Jurchens traditionally preferred white. In Chinese palaces there are usually carvings of dragons on walls, columns, or ceilings to symbolize the throne and authority. These materials, designs, and craftsmanship produced splendid palaces—lofty, spacious, glittering.[5]

The East Capital marked a transitional stage politically and architecturally. Liaoyang, an important city during Liao and Jin times, was a military, political, and cultural center of the Ming dynasty in the Liaodong region. It was a transfrontier because there was a Jurchen community, Zizai-zhou. Nurhaci's capture of Liaoyang in 1621 was a fatal blow to the Ming court, assuring his control of Manchuria and making construction of a new capital possible. With strength and confidence, he transformed a primitive frontier state into an important kingdom. As the second capital, it was distinguished from earlier centers. With an octagonal structure at its center, the palace complex was larger and constructed with brick and stone, while earlier ones were stone and rammed earth. In contrast to older centers, the East Capital had walls equipped with battlements and watchtowers, surrounded by a moat. Palaces and administrative buildings were separate and had Chinese names. The East Capital was more like a Chinese capital.[6]

For political and security reasons, Nurhaci moved from his East Capital northward to Shenyang in 1625 beginning the last stage of Manchu architectural evolution. There he built the Prosperous Capital (Sheng-jing; Mukden), the third government seat he founded. Improved by Hong Taiji, it embodied many Chinese architectural elements. The palace complex, with two south-oriented wings, was the hub of the Prosperous Capital. The east wing included the octagonal Hall of Great Administration (*Dazheng dian*), the south yard was flanked by ten pavilions in two columns, with five pavilions in each column. It was in this hall that Hong Taiji declared the founding of the Qing dynasty in 1636. The pavilions served as offices for the Eight Banners. The centerpiece in the second wing was the Hall of Eminent Administration (*Chong-zheng dian*), in which Hong Taiji carried on most business because it was near his residential palace to the north.

Figure 3. Phoenix Hall (Feng-huang lou) at Shenyang Palace.

Source: Photo courtesy of Jin Jun, *Shenyang Daily*, Shenyang, China.

The Qianlong emperor constructed a third wing and renovated many buildings. In the process more Chinese architectural components were added to the palaces.[7]

The Shenyang palace complex adopted other Chinese elements, such as gates, couplets, tablets, and images of the door god. The gates stood as place markers or guideposts to the structure. With verses, maxims, or calligraphy, both the couplets and the tablets served an aesthetic purpose. The couplets were made of paper, silk, wood, or metal, while the tablets were largely made of wood, stone, or metal. Some of these couplets and tablets were written by the Qianlong emperor and his two immediate successors. The door god was supposed to protect the buildings. Palaces were designated with names to suggest moral qualities, literary tastes, or good omens. The *qingning gong* meant the palace of pure tranquility; the *guanju gong*, a term from the *Book of Songs*, suggested a happy marriage.[8] The Shenyang Palace was the most sinicized old Manchu capital, and it remains as a great architectural achievement in China today.

Chinese architectural features in Manchu palaces resulted mainly from Chinese craftsmanship and building materials. Hou Zhenju, a resident of the greater Liaoyang area, and his family provided both. Natives of Shansi, the Hou family moved to Liaodong during the Ming period. As a manufacturer of glazed wares, Hou Zhenju was ordered by Nurhaci to supply yellow glazed tiles and graphically designed blue bricks for the East Capital. He was also an architect of the project, and under his supervision the East Capital was completed. Then he carried out the construction of palaces in Shenyang. After 1626 he assisted Hong Taiji in completing the palace complex. His descendants provided both plans and materials for imperial construction until the end of the dynasty.[9]

With the construction of the Prosperous Capital the Manchus began to introduce court ceremonies and palace regulations. They were essential to the operation of the Qing court. Through symbols and deeds, court ceremonies made the throne unique and enhanced its authority. Palace regulations were devised to keep officials submissive. They perpetuated imperial supremacy. Perhaps content with a small frontier kingdom, Nurhaci did not pay much attention to imperial formalities. What he stressed was the security of palaces and the personal conduct of their residents. It was not until after Hong Taiji's rise to power that the Qing court developed ceremonies and regulations after the Ming model. In the beginning, high officials failed to sit or stand according to rank in court sessions. Related to such ceremonies and regulations were the court and official robes, also adapted from the Ming originals.[10] With determination and patience Hong Taiji succeeded in establishing an orderly court.

Prince Sahaliyen, who knew the Chinese language and culture and had been in charge of the Board of Rites since its beginning in 1631, must have contributed to the introduction of Qing court ceremonies and palace regulations. It was under his presidency that the board pre-

Figure 4. Hall of Great Administration (*Dazheng dian*) at Shenyang Palace.

Source: Photo courtesy of Jin Jun, *Shenyang Daily*, Shenyang, China.

pared imperial inauguration ceremonies for Hong Taiji in 1636. To be sure, these were adopted from the Ming court, since the Manchus did not have such elaborate procedures. One may believe that he introduced other Ming formalities—notably regular and special court sessions—to the Qing. Contributions of Chinese advisors should not be overlooked. In November of 1632 Wang Shun, a Chinese scholar working under Sahaliyen, memorialized the throne by proposing a dress code; it was instituted two months later. The court enforced a sophisticated system of imperial insignia. During the last two years of Hong Taiji's life the Board of Rites worked out rules for officials when the emperor was passing by and penalties for those who missed court sessions. A comparison shows that Qing ceremonies were almost the same as those of the Ming.[11] In view of so much Chinese architectural and operational features, one may say that the Qing court in Shenyang was not very different from the Ming court in Peking.

Other Manchu edifices, such as the imperial ancestral temple and the emperor's tomb, bore Chinese architectural elements. The imperial ancestral temple (*taimiao*) operated on the basis of Confucian political and social principles, symbolizing the ruling house as well as the state. Construction and destruction mirrored the transfer of the Mandate of Heaven. In response to the suggestion of a Chinese banner officer, Hong Taiji constructed the Manchu version of the imperial ancestral temple before proclaiming the Qing dynasty. In building materials, architectural style, and sacrificial ceremonies, it imitated the Ming imperial temple. When the court moved to Peking in 1644, the Manchus took the Ming imperial ancestral temple as theirs but retained the original in Shenyang.[12]

Qing imperial tombs provided another example of Chinese architectural influence. There were three clusters of Qing imperial mausoleums, each consisting of several individual tombs. The earliest cluster appeared in Liaodong and included the tombs of Nurhaci's ancestors near Xinbin. The tombs of Nurhaci and Hong Taiji were both in the Shenyang area. The second cluster, known as the Eastern Mausoleums, was to the east of Peking and contained the tombs of five emperors—including Shunzhi, Kangxi, and Qianlong—fourteen empresses, and many imperial concubines. Located west of Peking, the Western Mausoleums were the last cluster and included the tomb of the Yongzheng emperor. Designed and constructed by the Hou family, the mausoleums of Nurhaci and Hong Taiji resembled each other.[13]

The tombs of Nurhaci and Hong Taiji bore traces of the Chinese architectural layout and style. Their layout consisted of four divisions: gates, a long stone-paved road, a sacrificial hall, and a tumulus. To the south of each tomb complex stood the main gate, an imposing red structure, with a glazed and double-eaved roof. Behind the gate emerged the long stone road, or the Spirit Way, lined on both sides with stone animals such as horses, lions, and camels. Standing at the center of the tomb complex, the Hall of Eminent Favors (*longen dian*), a wooden structure on a sculptured terrace with a carved marble balustrade, functioned as the sacrifical building. The hall and its related structures made a rectangular compound surrounded by massive walls, with a tower at each corner. The four corner towers, each with an elegant gate, are said to be one of the chief differences between the

Manchu mausoleums and Ming imperial tombs. Enclosed in crescent walls and situated in the northernmost part of the complex was the tumulus. Beneath the mound is the lavish burial chamber.[14]

More magnificent Qing architecture appeared after 1644. The Manchus took over the Ming palace complex, making repairs and additions. Of the Qing rulers, Qianlong was the greatest sponsor of architectural undertakings. His masterpiece was the Yuanming Yuan, known to the West as the Summer Palace, an imperial landscape garden to the northwest of Peking. Originally a private estate of the Ming dynasty, it was redesigned by the Kangxi and Yongzheng emperors as a beautiful residence based on the Chinese cultural tradition. Under Qianlong's auspices it expanded to cover an area of about 780 acres marked by palaces, pavilions, gardens, streams, bridges, artificial hills, and forty scenic spots. With the help of the Jesuits, it acquired such European traits as baroque buildings and fountain springs. But the basic design was by Chinese architects from the Lei family and carried out by Chinese craftsmen in accordance with the best Chinese architectural tradition. Combining both northern and southern elements of Chinese architecture, the Summer Palace was an embodiment of architecture, gardens, and landscaping, synthesizing Ming-Qing aesthetic features and attesting, as a Qing historian puts it, to Qianlong's thinking on the Chinese scholar-official's way of life. It also symbolized the glory and strength of the Qing until its destruction by the invading Anglo-French forces in 1860.[15]

The above discussion clearly demonstrates that the Manchus had to operate their adopted administrative machinery in appropriate structures and according to regulations and ceremonies suitable to them. It was a Chinese dynastic practice, alien to the Manchus. The construction and renovation of magnificent palaces and gardens were mainly a result of Chinese design, craftsmanship, and building materials. Chinese aesthetic tastes infiltrated the Manchu ethnic heritage and weakened it.

2. Religion

Long before conquering China, the Manchus were aware of Chinese religious practices, which included Buddhism and popular cults. Like the Jurchens the Manchus practiced shamanism, a religion that began to evolve before the dawn of history and had been popular among such peoples as the Tungus and their subgroups in Northeast Asia. It later developed into versions based on clans or tribes. They were independent but shared characteristics: animistic, naturalistic, magical, and ritualistic. The shaman, or priest, was a sorcerer, doctor, and performer of such rituals as chanting, dancing, trances, and sacrificial offerings. He preserved and transmitted the clan's tradition and in times of crisis served as a political leader. Since the mid-Ming period, Jurchen clans had built shamanistic centers for holding services; the centers, known as the *tangzi*, with a divine post (*shengan*) beside it to symbolize their independence. Tribal or clan chiefs offered sacrifices before and after an important action or event. But after 1636 the term *tangzi* was monopolized by the imperial family.[16] Shamanism served as the bond between clansmen and was the fountainhead of Jurchen values.

Shamanism was weakened by the political process and infiltrated by other beliefs and practices even before 1644. With the founding of the frontier state by Nurhaci, it underwent a transformation. While unifying the Jurchen tribes, he found it necessary to regulate their independent shamanist activities, which ran counter to his political aims. Tribes lost their religious autonomy after their political independence disappeared. With the Ming empire as his model, Hong Taiji adopted Chinese political practices to control religious activities. He made rules for shamanistic sacrifices, standardized sacrificial odes, and forbade witching. Shamanism had ties to the Manchu aristocracy. In the effort to centralize, early Qing rulers tried to undercut the Eight Banners, the stronghold of aristocrats as well as the traditional clan system. With the bureaucratization of the Banner system by Yongzheng, shamanism lost ground. In 1747 the Qianlong emperor published the *Book of Rites for Manchu Sacrifices and Offerings to Deities and Heaven*, an effort to unify shamanist services. Its enforcement evidenced imperial control.[17]

Buddhism, a powerful belief and practice system, infiltrated shamanism and facilitated sinicization. Because it sought to adapt to local traditions, Buddhism appealed to whomever encountered it. In China, it became Chinese Buddhism, embodying elements of Confucianism and popular cults, and differing greatly from what it had been before in other cultures. It was also different from Lamaism, the Tibetan version of Buddhism marked with ritualistic, mystic, and magic features. From China it reached tribesmen in Manchuria, perhaps around the time of the Tang dynasty. In their rule of North China the Jurchens experienced more contact with Chinese Buddhism. Under the Mongols, however, Lamaism diminished the influence of Chinese Buddhism on the aristocratic Jurchens. Despite the disparities, Chinese Buddhism and Lamaism shared Buddhist principles. Early Qing rulers, using both to enhance their political cause, attempted to appease their Chinese subjects with Buddhism. Lamaism helped them succeed in bringing the Mongols, as well as the Tibetans, under control.[18]

During its early years the Ming dynasty revived Buddhism among the Jurchens as a means of political control. There were Jurchen monks, one of whom was Daoyuan (fl. 1390s–1410s). In 1407 he was invited by the Ming government to participate in a Buddhist convention in Peking. After returning to Liaodong he took charge of a temple and supervised more than forty monks. In 1413 the Yongle emperor built the Temple of Eternal Peace (*Yongning si*) in the lower Amur valley and dedicated it to the Goddess of Mercy (Guanyin), popular in China. By 1417 he had created the Jianzhou Buddhist Registry in the Liaodong Military Commission; the Registry was headed by a Jurchen monk to transmit Buddhism to his fellow tribesmen. Four months later he built another Buddhist temple in southeastern Jilin Province. Jurchen monks helped spread Chinese Buddhism and culture, for they frequently kept in touch with the Ming by sending tributary missions to Peking. A Ming source lists as many as ninety-seven Chinese Buddhist temples in the Liaodong region. There is no doubt that many Jurchens received Buddhist teachings at these temples.[19]

Buddhist influence on the Manchus was highly visible. Nurhaci wore Buddhist symbols, carried a rosary, and admonished his officials to practice Buddhist ethics. In 1615, he constructed in his capital, Hetu Ala, seven religious structures, including Buddhist and Lamaist temples, Taoist shrines, and buildings for other cults. He prohibited people from destroying or profaning temples. Hong Taiji, more politically oriented, focused on Lamaist monasteries. He protected old monasteries and constructed new ones, of which the Monastery of Ultimate Victory (*Shisheng si*) and Lasting Tranquil Temple (*Chang-ning si*) were the most famous. At the same time, he strictly regulated the lives and numbers of the lamas, as well as building permits for new temples. Of his successors, Qianlong carried out a similar policy. He built twelve Lamaist temples in the Peking area. With his blessing, Manchu lamas began to appear.[20]

After 1644, Chinese Buddhism spread among the Manchus. Despite his association with Father Adam Schall von Bell (1591–1666), a German Jesuit missionary, the Shunzhi emperor was deeply interested in Chan Buddhism, which stressed discipline, meditation, and sudden enlightenment. He befriended Chinese Chan monks and even contemplated joining the priesthood. His son, Kangxi, also sponsored Buddhism. In 1667, as a source records, there were 79,622 Buddhist temples throughout China proper. Of this figure, 12,482 were built by imperial order, the remainder using private funds. Of course, this huge number of temples delivered the Buddhist message far and wide. Yongzheng was the only Qing monarch who mastered Chan Buddhism and its paradoxes. He published works on the subject and organized a Chan study group of fifteen people, including himself, two of his brothers, two imperial sons—one of whom later became the Qianlong emperor—five princes, and five high officials. With imperial patronage, Chinese Buddhism had influence beyond ethnic and geographical boundaries. Chinese temples and shrines appeared in the interior and at the northernmost border of Heilongjiang Province. Chinese Buddhism was incorporated into shamanist literature and traditional Manchu religious services. Besides shamanist deities, the Qing imperial house even worshiped Sakyamuni Buddha and the Goddess of Mercy. Therefore, in a decree of 1747, Qianlong declared that the Manchus offered sacrifices to both Buddha and shamanist deities and demanded they offer sacrifices according to regulated procedures.[21]

Chinese popular cults played an important part in transmitting Chinese ways of life to the Manchus. Traditional China had local, regional, and national cults. Each cult developed versions tailored to the needs of various groups. Many were too complicated to be fully understood. The supreme ruler in the Taoist Heaven was the Jade Emperor. With a bureaucracy patterned after the temporal state administration, he extended his authority over all people, rich or poor. His imperial court enforced moral standards by rewards and punishments through the administrative system of the underworld. Apparently he was the last resort for the common man in case temporal authority failed. His shrine was among the seven religious structures built by Nurhaci in 1615. The cult of the city god (*cheng-huang*) possibly began in the sixth century and spread from the middle of the Yangtze valley to other parts of China. Basically a part of the bureaucratic hierarchy of the underworld and important to the well-being of people, this god had jurisdiction over individual cities and towns. The imperial court supported the cult for its political usefulness. Around 1808–1810, Xiqing, a Manchu official, mentioned various Chinese cults, one of which was about the city god, in Heilongjiang, especially in Tsitsihar, an administrative center in the southern part of that region. Xiqing and the local people—Manchus and Chinese—were among its worshipers.[22]

Of the Chinese cults Guan Yu was perhaps the most respected. Of obscure origin, he was a warrior active in the Three Kingdoms period (220–263). He served Liu Bei (162–223), founder of the kingdom of Han in Szechwan, one of the three states. Guan Yu was captured and executed by his master's rival, but beginning with the Tang dynasty he was elevated to as a figure of loyalty, bravery, and high moral standards. As the panegyric process continued, he became deified in Buddhist and Taoist beliefs. His sociopolitical potential did not escape the attention of rulers in China. From the Song and Ming governments he received royal and imperial posthumous titles. In the fourteenth century the historical fiction *Romance of the Three Kingdoms* made him a household word, worshiped by every group in China. He was protector of Buddhist temples, Taoist shrines, localities, the country. To traders and artisans he was the god of wealth. Members of secret societies respected him, for he symbolized what they needed from one another: devotion and selflessness. The virtues of loyalty and righteousness he was supposed to stand for fitted Confucian values. To most people he was the God of War. The cult of Guan Yu was integrated into China's society, state, and culture.[23]

This cult reached the Manchus through several channels before their conquest of China. By the Ming period its temples had appeared throughout China, including Liaodong. The cult became known to the Jurchens through frontier contacts. Possibly, Jurchen tributary missions learned about it in Peking, where the Ming government had dedicated a temple to Guan Yu. Of course, there must have been many temples sponsored by the private sector as well. It is said that Nurhaci understood Chinese and loved to read the *Romance of the Three Kingdoms*. One may assume that he heard stories about Guan Yu and his associates who were glorified in the book. Shortly before his death, he cited Zhuge Liang (181–234), Liu Bei's prime minister and chief strategist as an example to admonish officials. Among religious buildings in Hetu Ala, once the capital of Nurhaci, was a temple for Guan Yu. When the capital moved to Shenyang, there was another temple for the God of War, possibly built by Nurhaci.[24]

Hong Taiji knew about the book and the characters it eulogized. A Korean source asserted that of Nurhaci's sons he was the only one able to read. One can infer that he was able to read Chinese. That his Chinese advisors included in their memorials such protagonists as Liu Bei and Zhuge Liang confirms that the *Romance of the Three Kingdoms* was a favorite book. In edicts and communications, he liberally cited Guan Yu and others, persuading officials to accept his ideas. In 1633 he applied the story about Guan Yu to justify his warmly welcoming two Chinese defectors. It is believed that he was able to get rid of a capable Ming commander, Yuan Chong-huan, by a ruse taken from the book. *Romance of the Three Kingdoms* was one of the earliest Chinese books translated into Manchu. The translated version began to circulate in 1650 and attracted Manchu readers. It served the Manchus as a source of action and strategy deliberations. As late as the nineteenth century, it remained a sourcebook for Manchu commanders.[25]

Manchu interest in the *Romance of the Three Kingdoms* resulted in a commitment to the cult of Guan Yu. Commitment manifested itself in two ways. Prior to the Qing dynasty, Guan Yu had received ducal and imperial titles, and was known in China as Guangong or Guandi. Since the imperial title was the highest possible, Qing monarchs could only add adjectives or ennoble his ancestors. In 1725 Yongzheng conferred a ducal title on Guan Yu's father, grandfather, and great-grandfather. To demonstrate his enthusiasm, Qianlong issued decrees to add high-sounding words to Guan's posthumous title and correct what he regarded as inaccurate historical records. The Qing maintained, repaired, and built temples for Guan Yu as a state project, with Peking as the center of the cult. As a recent study shows, in Peking, temples to Guan Yu outnumbered those of all other cults. In Manchuria, such temples were first clustered in the Liaoning area. During the late eighteenth and early nineteenth centuries they spread to central and northern Manchuria. A gazetteer mentions forty-one temples around Jilin City. Another account mentions that there were such temples even in poor districts and isolated places in Heilongjiang. It can be argued that many of these temples had been there before the Qing. Nevertheless, Qing patronage reinforced the cult.[26] Manchus from the imperial family to common people became followers.

With the expansion of Manchu power, the Guan Yu cult spread throughout the Qing empire: China proper, and Mongol, Tibetan, and Moslem territories. Temples for Guan Yu and other Chinese gods appeared in many Manchu garrison compounds in China proper. The first half of the seventeenth century saw the rise of temples for Guan Yu in Jehol, a traditional Mongol region where the Qing imperial summer resort and hunting preserves were located. Probably, the cult was brought to Tibet by imperial forces after they defeated the Dzungar Mongol invaders in 1721–1722. There Manchu commanders renovated old temples and built new ones in the early 1790s. The cult appeared almost everywhere in Sinkiang, the home of Chinese Moslems of Turkic origin. Most temples were built during the second half of the eighteenth century as a result of the Qing campaign against the Moslem rebels. Some temples were close to the Manchu garrison camps and were honored by tablets with imperial handwriting.[27]

3. Confucianism

Jurchens and Mongols, foreign conquerors of China, furnish examples of the importance of Confucianism to sinicization. Gao Sirong, a descendant of an aristocratic Jurchen family that helped found the Jin dynasty, subscribed to Confucian ideals and married a Chinese wife. After the demise of the Jin he lived among the Chinese and was regarded as their model. Another case concerns a member of the Guaerjia (Gūwalgiya in Manchu) clan, also an aristocratic family. Born in the late Jin, he became an eremite during the early Yuan period. He acted in accord with Confucian values and was respected by Chinese in his community. During the Yuan era Confucianism remained a major intellectual and political current. As a young Mongol aristocrat, Bayan (1295?–1358) studied Neo-Confucianism under a Chinese scholar. He became a renowned Confucian scholar and attracted students. When compiling the Yuan history, Ming historians included him under "Confucian Scholars," a category usually reserved for Chinese savants.[28]

Together with other elements of Chinese culture, Confucian ideals spread among the Jurchens. This can be verified by the change of Nurhaci's political ideology. Because of his increasing contact with Chinese culture, he gradually switched from Mongol influence to Chinese institutions. Even in the early stage of his political career he adopted such Chinese imperial rituals as the dress with five-colored dragons, the yellow umbrella, and the concept of heaven's moral judgment. During the last years of his life, Nurhaci frequently admonished his sons and officials by using examples from Chinese history. In 1625 he cited Confucius' dictum that a person of filial piety and brotherliness would never be rebellious. He advised his sons to be kind to one another.[29] Under the influence of his Chinese advisors, mostly members of the Literary Office, Hong Taiji took further measures to sponsor Confucian ideals. For example, in the years 1632–1633 Wang Wenkui and Ning Wanwo, two members of the office, reminded their master of the importance of Confucian classics, especially the *Four Books*, to country-governing and world-pacification. Hence, they urged him to study the Confucian tenets through translations and special seminars. Apparently Hong Taiji put their suggestions into practice. He introduced the civil service examination, which was based on Confucian precepts. In addition to filial piety and fraternity, he lectured officials about the cultivation of personal virtues, the foundation of the orderly family in Confucian values. In turn the orderly family was indispensable for state administration. After making himself emperor of the Qing in 1636, he continued the dynastic practice of the Chinese state, revering Confucius. He built a Confucian temple in Shenyang and sent an official to offer sacrifices to the sage. Thereafter the Qing adopted Confucianism as a state philosophy.[30]

Hong Taiji's effort helped him not only achieve centralization but spread Confucian ideals among his Manchu subjects. Manchu poets and scholars laid the groundwork for their accomplishment through the Confucian classics. Omutu was a scholar as well as translator educated in Confucian subjects. Mahū (d. 1676), a member of the Jebe clan, began his academic career at the banner school founded by Hong Taiji and earned a *jinshi* degree in 1652. He was in charge of the Imperial Board of Astronomy. But the most famous Confucian scholar from the same school system was a member of the Wanggiya clan, Asitan (c. 1630s–1684), who became a *jinshi* in 1652. For a long time he served as a translator and language teacher. His translations included the *Great Learning (Daxue)* and the *Canon of Filial Piety (Xiaojing)*, all based on Confucian precepts. His descendants kept this family academic tradition until the second half of the nineteenth century.[31]

Qing monarchs from Shunzhi to Yongzheng took measures to popularize Confucius' teachings to enhance their political cause. Included in the measures were citings from Confucian classics and projects of compiling, revising, and reprinting related works. The Shunzhi emperor filled the *Important Reading for Aid in Government* and the *Imperial Admonitions on the Conduct of Officials and Subjects* with Confucius' sayings and ideals. Both works were attributed to him. Kangxi patronized the Neo-Confucian School of Principle, a rigid interpretation of Confucianism. Under his auspices, as mentioned in Chapter VII, officials at the Imperial Printing Office and Bookbindery kept working hard. Among the books they printed were the *Essence of the Doctrines of the Neo-Confucian School of Principle* and the *Book of Changes*. Many works were translated into Manchu in the years 1661–1795.[32] These translated versions furnished Manchus with easy access to Confucian precepts.

Of the Qing rulers, perhaps Yongzheng made the greatest contribution to the spread of Confucian teachings among the Manchus. As a prince he was interested in philosophy and religious studies and became aware of the political usefulness of Confucianism. After accession to the throne he cited passages from the *Five Classics* and eagerly inculcated Confucian ideals, such as loyalty and submission, in his Chinese and Manchu subjects. Because his succession created controversies, he struggled to consolidate his power, with Manchu aristocrats in particular as the primary target. He bureaucratized the Banner institution, the chief source of their power. Many of his edicts and the memorials from the Banners were printed in both Chinese and Manchu. It was by his order that the *Baqi tongzhi chuji* (General history of the Eight Banners, first series) and the *Genealogy of the Manchu Clans in the Eight Banners* were compiled, although they were not printed until the early Qianlong era. All carried not only imperial injunctions but Confucian teachings.[33]

The most effective instrument that passed Confucian ideals onto the Manchus was the *Amplified Instructions on the Sacred Edict,* or *Shengyu guangxun,* a hortatory work resulting from the combined efforts of three emperors. To stabilize Qing rule, Shunzhi ordered his Chinese and Manchu subjects to observe the *Six-Maxim Edict* (*Liuyu*), which he promulgated in 1652. It incorporated Confucian social, political, and economic themes in the simplest terms. In 1670, Kangxi reworked his father's edict and produced the *Sacred Edict* of sixteen maxims based on Confucian ideals, as interpreted by the Neo-Confucian School of Principle. Maxims 1–3, 9–11, and 15–16 covered society; numbers 4–5 were economic. Items 8 and 12–14 concerned relations between people, while Maxims 6–7 were relevant to the literati. Kangxi intended to apply the *Sacred Edict* to the entire country, but at first only civil officials were required to study it. From 1686 onward military officials and hereditary headmen of ethnic minority peoples were asked to study it. To aid comprehension the text had vernacular and illustrated editions. By an imperial order of 1700 local officials began to read and explain the maxims before gatherings of the general public on the first and fifteenth of every month, while teachers did the same before students. Yongzheng added his mark to the work by writing a long commentary on each maxim and incorporating them in a text under the title *Amplified Instructions on the Sacred Edict.*[34]

Yongzheng redoubled his efforts to enforce the sixteen maxims. Shortly after his succession, printed copies of his amplified work were distributed among officials and schools. It was required reading for students, Chinese or Manchu. In district and prefectural examinations, students had to correctly write, by rote, one of the maxims and its commentary. In each locality he increased the number of people who prepared semimonthly lecture meetings. In 1729 the imperial court ordered a permanent lecture facility in large and densely populated towns and villages. The Manchus had their own lecture meetings; their text was available in both Chinese and Manchu versions.

Beginning in 1725, Manchu officers and common warriors at the company level held a session on the first day of each month. Extra lectures were given on the day of the periodic archery exercise. If illiterate and aged eighteen *sui* or older, collateral imperial clansmen (*jueluo*) attended semimonthly lectures at the administrative office of each Banner. At first, Manchus who were not in military or government service received lectures from their clan head at the end of each year. From 1725 onward they had to attend monthly sessions. All in all, this was a nationwide indoctrination lasting to the nineteenth century. It was through this process that Confucian values reached the Manchu masses. By the end of the dynasty, according to a field survey, some Manchus even considered Confucianism their own heritage.[35]

Another important action taken by early Qing rulers was to show respect for Confucius. They added eulogies to the sage's posthumous title and developed sumptuous sacrificial ceremonies. Kangxi visited Confucius' birthplace and offered sacrifices. He knelt and saluted in front of officials and the sage's descendants. The veneration of Confucius reached a new stage during the Qianlong reign. The throne visited the sage's birthplace more frequently than any monarch in Chinese history. In the years 1748–1790 he paid eight visits. Each time he knelt, offered a sacrifice, and held a brief seminar with representatives of the Confucius' descendants. His frequent visits may suggest his genuine respect for the sage, not merely a political show. Whatever his motivations, these visits appealed to Chinese and Manchu intellectuals and deepened their faith in Confucianism.[36]

The Qianlong reign was also known for its great literary projects. The emperor himself liked to read, collect, and annotate rare Chinese books. He indeed deserved to be regarded as a bibliophile. The most famous literary project he sponsored was the *Complete Library of Four Treasuries*, an encyclopedic collection of about 3,450 important books on almost all categories of learning that had existed before the Qianlong era. The project brought together thousands of scholars, proofreaders, and copyists, and it took about ten years (1772–1782) to complete the first manuscript copy. Later six more copies were made. In undertaking this monumental compilation, according to some scholars, Qianlong was motivated by the desire to suppress works with anti-Manchu remarks or ideas. As a consequence, numerous books were destroyed or partially expunged. Nevertheless, one should also point out, the project preserved many rare books and encouraged historical scholarship. Above all, the entire collection was relevant to Confucian norms.[37]

Qianlong's commitment to Confucian ideals can be further examined. While his father, Yongzheng, emphasized filial piety, Qianlong made efforts to promote loyalty. Both filial piety and loyalty were pillars of the five Confucian human relationships underlying the Chinese state and society. In 1775 he ordered the collection of data on officials who lost their lives for the cause of the Ming during the dynastic transition. Finally he honored 3,600 people with posthumous titles and included their biographies in a special compilation. Of these Ming officials, he singled out Xiong Tingbi, Yuan Chong-huan, and Shi Kefa (d. 1645) for highest commemoration since they bravely fought against the Manchus. For the purpose of contrast he sponsored the compilation of the *Biographies of Officials who Served Two Dynasties* (*Erchen zhuan*) in 1777. This work covered 124 officials, including Hong Cheng-chou and Zu Dashou, all of whom had switched their allegiance from the Ming to the Qing and contributed to the Manchu takeover of China. They, however, were condemned by Qianlong as men of disloyalty. In spite of its political implication, Qianlong's emphasis on loyalty did help spread Confucian values among his subjects.[38]

Under the influence of Confucianism the status of Manchu widows underwent a significant change after 1644. After the rise of Neo-Confucianism, widows, however young, were discouraged from remarrying. Known as *jiefu* (chaste widows), those who conformed won public praise or official commendation. For centuries Jurchen widows could freely remarry.[39] But during the reign of Hong Taiji a few chaste Manchu widows, mainly of aristocratic origin, appeared. With the passage of time, there were more such widows, many of whom were from the rank and file. From the Shunzhi reign onward they were included in the *Veritable Records* (*CSL*) and the *General History of the Eight Banners, First Series,* and its enlarged version. The throne commemorated each with an arch erected at or near her residence. Tables 10 and 11 show how many widows were commemorated from 1644 to 1795 and 1627 to 1795, respectively. The figures are not always complete because the sources did not follow consistent rules of compilation. The

Veritable Records supplied the sum total, failing to distinguish their ethnic origin, while the other two gave names of individual widows. Unlike other sources, the Qianlong *Veritable Records* included 7,195 chaste Manchu widows from the Office of the Imperial Household, Manchuria, as well as from some other areas. As a result, they are, in aggregate, a large number. In view of poor statistical knowledge, one may assume that many qualified Manchu widows were left out. For all their shortcomings, the figures show the deepening of Chinese cultural influence on the Manchus.

Table 10. Statistics of Chaste Manchu Widows, 1644–1795
Based on the *Veritable Records**

Reign title	Reign period	Number of chaste Manchu Windows	Average	Source
Shunzhi	1644–1661	27 (for 1661 only)	?	CSL
Kangxi	1662–1722	2,279	38	CSL
Yongzheng	1723–1735	1,466	113	CSL
Qianlong	1736–1795	13,353	222	CSL

*The *Veritable Records* provides the year-end statistics, such as population, on chaste widows. For such statistics, see the last chapter (*juan*) of each year. For instance, the annual statistical figure of chaste widows from the Eight Banners for the first year of the Kangxi reign appears in chapter 7, page 26a. The figures here are the grand totals, including only the ethnic Manchu widows. For the Shunzhi reign, there is only the figure for 1661. The average is the nearest round number.

To conclude, one may stress a few points. Aesthetics and religion were among the major components of the Manchu ethnic identity. Their transformations echoed sinicization more convincingly than anything else. After conquering the Liaodong Valley, Nurhaci began to build his capital. In style and design it was virtually a replica of the Ming model. Of his construction projects, the Shenyang palace complex was the most magnificent. With renovations and additions by his successors, from Hong Taiji to Qianlong, it remains a significant architectural achievement. Naturally, the Qianlong emperor's enthusiasm for writing couplets and tablets to decorate the palace was yet more

Table 11. Statistics of Chaste Manchu Widows, 1627–1795
Based on *TCCC* (1985) and *Baqi tongzhi**

Reign title	Reign period	Number of chaste Manchu widows	Average	Source *TCCC* (1985)
Reign of Hong Taiji	1627–1643	8	?	8. 239: 5366; 241: 5409, 5415, 5420–21
Shunzhi	1644–1661	119	7	8. 239: 5367–72; 240: 5382–98
Kangxi	1662–1722	817	13	8. 240–46 (chs.)
Yongzheng	1723–1735	358	27	8: 246–49 (chs.)
Qianlong	1736–1795	4,833	80	*Baqi tongzhi*, 42. 247–50; 43. 251–54; 44. 255–57 (chs.)

*A large number of widows were Chinese women who married Manchus. Since my focus falls on widows of Manchu origin, I count out widows of other ethnic backgrounds. But in some cases it is difficult to trace the widow's ethnic origin merely by her name. Cf. Mark C. Elliott, "Manchu Widows and Ethnicity in Qing China," *Comparative Studies in Society and History* 41. 1 (1999): 35 (Table 1.1). Elliott's figures include all the widows of the Manchu, Mongol, and Chinese Eight Banners.

evidence of his being deeply influenced by Chinese culture. The earliest Manchu ancestral temples and mausoleums, following the Chinese style, were in the Shenyang area. Under Hong Taiji, the Manchus adopted Chinese court ceremonies and regulations, for they were necessary for the palace to function. The Yuanming Yuan tells a different story. It was an immense imperial garden, characterized by the Chinese aesthetic tradition. Captivated by its sublime beauty, five emperors from Yongzheng to Xianfeng (1723–1861) made it their principal residence and frequently handled state business there.[40]

The Manchus practiced shamanism, the major source of their ethics. With the infiltration by Buddhism, popular cults, and Confucianism, its role diminished. Buddhism began to spread quickly among the Jurchens during the Ming period and was adopted by the Manchus of all social groups. For political reasons, however, Qing rulers patronized Tibetan Buddhism. Of Chinese popular cults, Guan Yu was

the most influential among the Manchus. His temples appeared everywhere, especially around the garrison camps.

The Manchu adaptation to Confucianism was essential to the continuity of the Qing dynasty. After Kangxi, Qing rulers were thoroughly
educated in the Chinese classics and history, and became bearers of
the Confucian tradition. They realized its importance to their rule.
There is no stronger evidence than Yongzheng's testimonials to this
relationship. In an edict of 1727 he discussed the value of Confucianism to the state and society and frankly admitted that the ruler himself
benefited the most from it. Beginning with the Kangxi era, Qing monarchs strove to indoctrinate their subjects, Chinese and Manchus alike,
with Confucian precepts, as represented in the Sacred Edict and its
amplified version and in other imperial works. Confucianism helped
them to enlist the loyalty of the Chinese elite, civil and military, who
were willing to serve any ruler who respected Confucian tenets. Manchu ethnic cohesion or the banner forces alone did not prolong Qing
rule. In reality, Confucianism and its subscribers, the Chinese elite,
steered the dynasty through many turbulent times. Chinese almost
everywhere revolted against the Qing in its early years, but this anti-
Manchu sentiment died down during the Kangxi reign, mainly because of that monarch's conciliatory measures, among which was the
veneration of Confucianism. The Chinese elite also played the chief
role in the defeat of the Three Feudatories, the conquest of Taiwan,
and the victory over the mid nineteenth-century rebels, including the
Taipings.

Confucianism functioned as a binding force among the Manchus
and facilitated imperial control over them. After 1644, out of necessity, the Manchus had to learn the language and culture of the conquered, who far outnumbered the conquerors. With the onslaught of
Chinese culture, the Manchu ethnic heritage was greatly weakened.
In time the Manchus forgot their native speech and forsook their military virtues, including archery and horsemanship. Under intense imperial indoctrination, which was carried out under the terms of Confucian tenets, they were further driven to Chinese cultural influence;
under these circumstances it would have been virtually impossible
to restore their ethnic tradition. Like their Chinese counterparts, the
Manchus venerated Confucius and followed his teachings. They were

thus brought into the Chinese mainstream. Under imperial patronage and manipulation, Confucianism became the linchpin of the Qing state and society.

Notes

1. See Yao, *Dongbei shi luncong*, 1: 1–26.
2. For architectural features of traditional Jurchen houses, see Xu, *Sanchao bei-meng*, 1. 3: 3a; Du Ruo, "Manzu di jushi yu jianzhu," *MANT* 2 (1992): 82–83. For eyewitness reports, see *CWS*, vol. 12, reign of Sŏngjong, 259: 116, 22/11/muja; vol. 22, reign of Sŏnjo, 71: 641 and 643, 29/1/ chongyu; Yi, *Chaam Sŏnsaeng munjip*, 6: 3a. For Manchu houses in Heilongjiang, see Xiqing, *Heilong-jiang waiji*, 6: 9b–10b. For the *kang*, see *Illustrated Dictionary of Historic Architecture*, ed. Cyril M. Harris (New York: Dover Publications, 1977), 314.
3. For a survey of the six centers, see Tie, "Lun Qing ruguan qian ducheng," 638–50; Jiang and Tong, *Sheng-jing huang-gong*, Introduction (unpaged [1–22]). For discussion about the location and importance of these six centers and Peking, see Yan Chong-nian, *Yanbu ji* (Peking: Yanshan chuban she, 1989), 365–93. For pictures of the last five capitals, see Giovanni Stary, *On the Tracks of Manchu Culture, 1644–1994: 350 Years after the Conquest of Peking* (Wiesbaden: Harrossowitz, 1995), 4–7 for Hetu Ala, 12 for Jaifiyan, 13–14 for Sarhū, 15 for the East Capital, 18–25 for the Prosperous Capital.
4. For Nurhaci's tributary missions, see Yan, *Nuer-hachi zhuan*, 149–52; also Yan, "Nuer-hachi rujing," 2–5. For his stay in the office compound of the Liaodong Military Commission, see Jiang and Tong, *Sheng-jing huang-gong*, "Introduction" [18–19]. Among the technicians recruited by Nurhaci for palace construction was the Hou family, which was made a hereditary house to produce glazed tiles. See Jiang and Tong, *Sheng-jing huang-gong*, 99–105.
5. For technical terms and structural analysis of Chinese architecture, see Liang Ssu-ch'eng, *A Pictorial History of Chinese Architecture: A Study of the Development of Its Structural System and the Evolution of Its Types*, ed. Wilma Fairbank (Cambridge, MA: MIT Press, 1984), 8–17.

   For the traditional Jurchen color, see Jiang Xiang-shun, "Cong Manzu di wenhua xishu kan Shenyang gugong di menshen he bianlian," *MANT*, 4 (1990): 42.
6. For this contrast, see Tie, "Lun Qing ruguan qian ducheng," 644–58; Zhi Yun-ting, "Cong Qing qianji huang-gong jianzhu yishu fengge kan Manzu wenhua di fazhan qushi," *Qingshi yanjiu*, 3 (1997): 62–63.
7. For the beginnings of the Shenyang palace complex, see Jiang and Tong, *Sheng-jing huang-gong*, 24–80; Tie Yuqin and Shen Changji, *Shenyang gugong* (Shenyang: Liaoning renmin chuban she, 1985), ch. 3; Murata, "Hōten kyūden

kenchikushi kō," 1–52. The English names for the two major administrative halls are taken from Swart and Till, "Nurhachi and Abahai," 148.

The Hall of Great Administration is an octagonal structure, with a pyramidal roof and Mongol style of ornament. The other hall had a flushed gable roof and was lacking any Mongol type of decoration. For the common features and characteristics of the palaces, see Jiang and Tong, *Sheng-jing huang-gong*, 38–80. For an interesting report on the Shenyang palace, with pictures, see Swart and Till, "Nurhachi and Abahai," 149–51, 154 (pictures on pp. 148 and 151). For additions and renovations by Qianlong, see Jiang and Tong, *Sheng-jing huang-gong*, 301–25; Stary, *On the Tracks of Manchu Culture*, 18–25.

8.   One of such gates was the Great Qing Gate. See Jiang and Tong, *Sheng-jing huang-gong*, 48–49. For the naming of palaces and gates, see *CSL*, reign of Taizong, 28: 41a, Tiancong 10/4/ dinghai; Murata, "Hōten kyūden kenchikushi kō," 20–31. For the couplets and tablets, see Jiang, "Cong Manzu di wenhua xishu kan Shenyang gugong di menshen he bianlian," 42–45.

9.   For the Hou family, see Jiang and Tong, *Sheng-jing huang-gong*, 99–105.

10.   No records indicate such ceremonies during the reign of Nurhaci. But there was a security problem—once a Mongol intruder was found in the palace. See *MWLT*, 1: 235. For his measures to strengthen palace security and deal with wrongdoers, see ibid., 1: 490–91; 631–32. For instance, on the Chinese New Year's days of 1627 and 1632 the court followed special ceremonies. See ibid., 2: 805, 1187–88. But toward the end of 1632 Hong Taiji complained about the disorder of court sessions. See ibid., 2: 1349. For the Qing court and official robes, see Schuyler Cammann, "Origins of the Court and Official Robes of the Qing Dynasty," *Artibus Asiae*, 12 (1949): 189–201.

11.   For Sahaliyen, see *CSKC*, 10: 7752–54; *ECCP*, 2: 631–32. For his introduction of imperial inauguration ceremonies, see *CSL*, reign of Taizong, 28: 15, Tiancong 10/4/gengchen. For Wang's suggestion and its adoption, see Pan, Sun, and Li, *Qing ruguan qian shiliao*, 2: 30; *CSL*, reign of Taizong, 12: 37a–39a, Tiancong 6/12/yichou. For other rules, see *CSL*, reign of Taizong, 28: 40, Tiancong 10/4/ dinghai; 62: 11, Chongde 7/9/wuchen; 65: 21, Chongde 8/7/renyin. For a comparison of Ming and Qing ceremonies, see *Mingshi*, 5. 53: 1345–65; 54: 1367–87; *CSKC*, 4: 2800–13. For the early Qing insignia system, see Li Li, "Lun Qingchu yizhang zhi zhi di yanbian," *Liaoning daxue xuebao*, 5 (1992): 42–46.

12.   For the suggestion by the Chinese banner officer, see *CSL*, reign of Taizong, 21: 24a–28b, Tiancong 8/12/jiachen; Pan, Sun, and Li, *Qing ruguan qian shiliao*, 2: 101. For a study of the Qing temple in Shenyang, see Tong Yue, "Qing Sheng-jing taimiao kaoshu," *Gugong bowu yuan yuankan*, 3 (1987): 24–29. Sources indicate that the Manchus had removed the tablet of the Ming founder to another temple by the end of July 1644. About two months later, references to the Qing imperial temple began to appear in official records. This may suggest that the Manchus changed the Ming imperial temple to theirs. See *CSKC*, 1: 74 and

75. For a detailed study of the Qing imperial temple, see Jiang Shunyuan, "Qingdai di zongmiao zhidu," *Gugong bowu yuan yuankan*, 3 (1987): 15–23 and 57.

13. In Qing history they are referred to respectively as *Fuling* and *Zhaoling*. For their design and construction by the Hou family, see Jiang and Tong, *Shengjing Huang-gong*, 101–2. For their resemblance, see Swart and Till, "Nurhachi and Abahai," 154–55.

14. For a detailed description of the two tombs, see Swart and Till, "Nurhachi and Abahai," 154–55. See also *Qingchu sanling*, ed. Shenyang shi wenwu guanli bangong shi (Peking: Wenwu chuban she, 1982), 3–33.

15. For a good study of the design and history of the Yuanming Yuan, see Youngtsu Wong, *A Paradise Lost: The Imperial Garden Yuanming Yuan* (Honolulu: University of Hawai'i Press, 2001), chs. 1–2; For a Chinese study, see Zhu, *Qingchao tongshi*, 9: 517–23. For the comments from a recent study, see Smith, *China's Cultural Heritage: The Qing Dynasty, 1644–1912*, 199.

16. For a critical discussion of the definition and nature of shamanism, see Margaret Nowak and Stephen Durrant, *The Tale of the Nišan Shamaness: A Manchu Folk Epic* (Seattle and London: University of Washington Press, 1977), 3–38; Rawski, *The Last Emperors*, 231–34. For the evolution of shamanism and the role of the shaman, see Fu and Meng, *Manzu saman jiao yanjiu*, ch. 1. For imperial monopoly of the *tangzi*, see Mo, *Manzu shi luncong*, 194.

17. For the effect of political unification on shamanism, see Fu and Meng, *Manzu saman jiao yanjiu*, 53–54 and 56; Zhao, *Manzu wenhua*, 325–26. For the rules set by Hong Taiji, see *MWLT*, 2: 1514; for his standardization of sacrificial odes, see *MWLT*, 2: 1521. For his prohibition of witching practices, see *CSL*, reign of Taizong, 63: 24b–26b, Chongde 7/10/jiazi. For his punishment of those who practiced or sponsored witchcraft, see *Chongde sannian*, 167–68. For Hong Taiji's efforts to weaken shamanism, see Zhao, *Manzu wenhua*, 326, 330–31.

    For bureaucratization of the banner system, see Huang, *Autocracy at Work*, ch. 7. The *Book of Rites for Manchu Sacrifices and Offerings to Deities and Heaven* is known in Chinese as *[Qinding] Manzhou jishen jitian dianli*. For its completion, see *CSL*, Qianlong reign, 294: 13a–14a, 12/7/dingyou. For a detailed analysis of this book, see Liu, *Qingtai gongting saman jisi*, 41–214. For shamanistic rituals and code and palace rites, see Di Cosmo, "Manchu Shamanic Ceremonies at the Qing Court," 359–98.

18. For the coming of Lamaism to China and Qing sponsorship of it, see Rawski, *The Last Emperors*, 244–63. For the influence of Lamaism among the Jurchen upper class, see *MTTS*, 249.

19. For the Buddhist Registry, see *MSL*, vol. 13, Yongle reign, 184: 1b, 15/1/jihai. The new temple was built in today's Antu, Jilin. See Yang, *Liaodong dusi*, 47–48; *CWS*, vol. 2, reign of T'aejong, 33: 157, 17/4/sinmi; 33: 163, 17/5/ulmyo; 34: 180, 17/7/kimyo. For tributary missions by Jurchen monks, see *MSL*, vol. 18, Xuande

reign, 47: 9a, 3/10/yiyou; vol. 20, 89: 5a, 7/4/bingwu; 90: 1b, 7/5/kuihai. For these Chinese Buddhist temples, see *Quan Liao zhi*, 4: 55b–57a. For Daoyuan, see Yang, *Liaodong dusi*, 280.

20.　For Nurhaci's wearing of Buddhist symbols, see *CWS*, vol. 22, reign of Sŏnjo, 71: 642, 29/1/ chongyu. A Korean witness reported that both Nurhaci and his commanders carried rosaries. See Yi, *Chaam Sŏnsaeng manjip*, 6: 4b. For his admonition in Buddhist terms, see *MWLT*, 1: 38–39. For construction of seven religious structures, see *Daicing gurun i Manju yargiyan kooli, 169–70*. For his prohibition of destroying or profaning temples, see *MWLT*, 1: 267.

　　　For Hong Taiji's protection of old Lamaist temples, see *CSL*, reign of Taizong, 11: 29b, Tiancong 6/4/yiwei; 12: 5b, 6/6/xinwei; 20: 15b–16a, 8/(intercalary) 8/kuimao. For his construction of new temples, see *Chongde sannian*, 165 and 180–83; Wang Peihuan, "Huang-taiji yu Chang-ning si," *Beifang wenwu* 2 (1986): 82–85. For his regulations, see *CSL*, reign of Taizong, 10: 29b–31a, Tiancong 5/11/gengxu; 64: 11, Chongde 8/2/gengyin; Zhang and Guo, *Qing ruguan qian*, 467–68. For a fine study of Qianlong's sponsorship of Lamaism, see Xiangyun Wang, "The Qing Court's Tibet Connection: Lcang skya Rol pa'i rdo rje and the Qianlong Emperor," *Harvard Journal of Asiatic Studies* 60. 1 (2000): 125–63. See also Wang, "'Manzhou' yu 'Wenshu' di yuanyuan," 101–104.

21.　For Shunzhi's interest in Chan Buddhism, see *ECCP*, 1: 255–57. For the statistical figure, see Qu Xuanying, *Zhongguo shehui shiliao congchao* (Shanghai: Commercial Press, 1938, 3 volumes), 1: 233. For Yongzheng's commitment to Chan Buddhism, see Huang, *Autocracy at Work*, 43–45. Two of his works best represent his Chan ideas. In the *Jianmo bianyi lu* (Palace ed., 1733, 4 volumes), he refuted liberal interpretations of Chan Buddhism. Another book, *Yu-xuan yulu,* is a selection of sayings, mostly of Chan monks, including Yunzheng's own words. See also Yang Qiqiao, *Yongzheng di jiqi mizhe zhidu yanjiu* (Hong Kong: Sanlian shudian, 1981), 20–26.

　　　Most of these temples and shrines in Heilongjiang were built between the late Qianlong and early Jiaqing era (1796–1820). See Xiqing, *Heilong-jiang waiji*, 2: 13b–17b. For the worshiping of Sakyamuni Buddha and the Goddess of Mercy, see the document in Liu, *Qingdai gongting saman jisi*, 230. A Manchu folk epic records that Nišan, a shaman, once listened to a bodhisattva about the karmic consequence. See Nowak and Durrant, *The Tale of Nišan Shamaness*, 81. For Chinese Buddhism in Manchu religious services, see Soningan, *Manzhou sili ji*, 27, 32–33 ff. For Qianlong's point, see *CSL*, Qianlong reign, 294: 13a–14a, 12/7/dingyou.

22.　For the Jade Emperor's temple, see *MWLT*, 1: 29. For origins of the cult of city god, see Huang Pei and Tao Jinsheng, eds., *Deng Siyu xian-sheng xueshu lunwen xuanji* (Taipei: Shihuo chuban she, 1980), 55–95. For the City God Temple in Hetu Ala, see Tie, "Lun Qing ruguan qian ducheng," 649. For various Chinese cults in Heilongjiang, see Xiqing, *Heilong-jiang waiji*, 2: 13b–14b.

23. For Guan's biography, see *Sanguo zhi*, comp. Chen Shou (Taipei: SPPY ed., 1965, 4 volumes), 3:.1a–3b. For the evolution of his cult and its importance, see Robert Ruhlmann, "Traditional Heroes in Chinese Popular Fiction" in Arthur F. Wright, ed., *The Confucian Persuasion* (Stanford: Stanford University Press, 1960), 173–75; Prasenjit Duara, "Superscribing Symbols: The Myth of Guandi, Chinese God of War," *Journal of Asian Studies* 47. 4 (1988): 778–95, especially 780–90; Guo Songyi, "Lun Ming-Qing shiqi di GuanYu chongbai," *Zhongguo shi yanjiu*, 3 (1990): 127–39.

24. For Ming patronage of the cult, see Duara, "Superscribing Symbols," 783. The Ming government built temples for Guan Yu at battle sites because he was the God of War. See ibid. Most of the seventy-four Guan temples listed in the *Qinding Sheng-jing tongzhi* (ch. 26) were built before the Qing dynasty. According to *Mingshi* (5. 50: 1305), the Guan temple was one of the nine officially supported temples in Peking. For Nurhaci's ability to read Chinese and the *Romance of the Three Kingdoms*, see Huang, *Bowu dianhui*, 6. 20: 15a. For his citing of Zhuge Liang, see *CSL*, reign of Taizu, 10: 15b, Tianming 11/6/yiwei. For the temples in Hetu Ala and Shenyang, see Tie, "Lun Qing ruguan qian ducheng," 649, and *CSKC*, 4: 2749.

25. For the Korean source, see Yi, *Chaam Sŏnsaeng munjip*, 6: 4b. For some memorials by his Chinese advisors, see Pan, Sun, and Li, *Qing ruguan qian shiliao*, 2: 24 (Wang Wenkui's memorial) and 35–36 (the memorial by Hu Gongming). For Hong Taiji's citing from the book to support his decision, see *Qingchu Nei guoshi yuan*, 1: 19. For the book as a source of tricks used by Hong Taiji to get rid of Yuan Chong-huan and by Manchu commanders to outmaneuver enemies, see Li, "Qing Taizong yu Sanguo yanyi," 251–72.

  For the translation of the book into Manchu, see Gimm, "Manchu Translations of Chinese Novels and Short Stories: An Attempt at an Inventory," 78–79; Durrant, "Sino-Manchu Translations," 656. For Shunzhi's endorsement, see *Qingshi biannian*, 246. For its use by officials to justify their action, see *Shangyu neigo*, 18: 5, Yongzheng 6/1/20.

26. His royal title was conferred in 1129; his imperial title in 1590. See Guo, "Lun Ming-Qing shiqi di Guan Yu chongbai," 127–28. For ennoblement of Guan's ancestors, see *CSL*, Yongzheng reign, 31: 2b–3a, 3/4/gengwu. For Qianlong's addition and correction, see *CSKC*, 4: 2749–50. For the temples around Kirin City, see *Jilin tongzhi*, 26: 3a–7b. For the temples in Heilongjiang, see Xiqing, *Heilongjiang waiji*, 2: 15b and 17a. Guan Yu was among the deities worshiped by the imperial family and other Manchus. See Liu, *Qingdai gongting saman jisi*, 230; Soningan, *Manzhou sili ji*, 3a, 5b–6a, 12ff For Guan Yu's temples in Peking, see Susan Naquin, *Peking: Temples and City Life, 1400–1900* (Berkeley and Los Angeles: University of California Press, 2000), 327–28, 500, and Table 2.2.

27. For Guan Yu's temples in many Manchu garrison compounds, see Elliott, *The Manchu Way,* 116 and 239. For the Jehol case, see *Qinding Rehe zhi*, comp. He-

shen et al. (Taipei: Wenhai chuban she, 1966, Zhongguo bian-jiang congshu, Series 2, 6 volumes), 5. 81: 2a, 3b, 4a, 5a, 6a. For its spread to Tibet, see *Wei Zang tongzhi*, comp. Helin (Taipei: Wenhai chuban she, 1965, Zhongguo bian-jiang congshu, Series 1, 2 volumes), 1. 6: 10a, 12a, 23a. For the cult in Sinkiang, see Qi Qingshun, "Qingdai Xinjiang di Guan Yu chongbai," *Qingshi yanjiu*, 3 (1998): 101–106.

28. For the two Jurchen cases, see Hu, *Zishan daquan ji*, 56. 18: 15; 18: 19a–20b ("Guaerjia yinshi muzhi ming"). For Confucianism as a current under Yuan rule, see David Gedalecia, "Wu Ch'eng and the Perpetuation of the Classical Heritage in the Yuan." In John D. Langlois, Jr., ed., *China under Mongol Rule* (Princeton: Princeton University Press, 1981), 186–211. For the controversy about the abolition of the civil service examination, see Dardess, *Conquerors and Confucians*, chs. 3–4. For Bayan as a Confucian scholar, see *Yuanshi*, 10. 190: 10b–11a.

29. For his adoption of Chinese imperial rituals, see the first section in Chapter V. For his stress on filial piety and brotherliness, see *MWLT*, 1: 630.

30. For the advice of Wang Wenkui, Ning Wanwo, and another member of the Literary Office, see Pan, Sun, and Li, *Qing ruguan qian shiliao*, 2: 24–25, 71–72, 114–15; Yuan, *Qingdai qianshi*, 2: 584–89. For Hong Taiji's patronage of the civil service examination, see *CSL*, reign of Taizong, 18: 10b, 17b–18a, Tiancong 8/3/ renzi and 8/4/xinsi. For his citation of Confucian precepts from the *Great Learning*, one of the *Four Books*, see *CSL*, reign of Taizong, 34: 23b–27b, Chongde 2/4/ dingyou. For the Confucian temple he built, see *CSKC*, 4: 2743. He sent Fan Wencheng to offer sacrifices to Confucius. See *MWLT*, 2: 1561.

31. For Mahū, see *TCCC*, 186: 24b–25b. For Asitan, see *ECCP*, 1: 13–14; *TCCC*, 237: 6b–13a. For the family academic tradition Asitan established, see Songshen, *Changbai Wanyan shi jiude lu*, 1: "Xingshu," 3a–5a; also see the biography of Lioboo, *CSKC*, 11: 8839.

32. For Qing imperial policy toward Confucius and his teachings, see Lü, "Qingdai di chongru yu Hanhua," 533–42; *CSKC*, 4: 2743–48. For Kangxi's gesture, see *CSKC*, 4: 2747–48. For Kangxi's patronizing Confucianism and winning acclaim from his subjects, see Chin-shing Huang, *Philosophy, Philology, and Politics in Eighteenth-Century China: Li Fu and the Lu-Wang School under the Ch'ing* (New York: Cambridge University Press, 1995), ch. 7. Yong-zheng took various measures to honor Confucius. Among them was conferment of royal posthumous titles on the latter's ancestors. See Feng, *Yongzheng zhuan*, 422–31. For imperial sponsored compilations, see *CSKC*, 5: 4000, 4005, 4008ff.

Shunzhi's work is known as *Renchen jingxin lu*. See *ECCP*, 1: 258. The *Essence of the Doctrines of the Neo-Confucian School of Principle* is known as the *Xingli jingyi*, printed in 1715. For the translated Confucian books, see *CSKC*, 5: 4027, 4028, and 4031. For translation of the three classics, see Qinggui, Dong Gao *et al.*, *Guochao gongshi xubian* (Peking: Beijing guji chuban she, 1994),

842–43. Many of those translated books are available in the Library of Congress; see Matsumura Jun, "Beikoku gikai toshukan shozō manshūgo bunken mokuroku," *Tōyō gakuhō.* 1–2 (1976): 37–40.

33. For Yongzheng's interest in philosophy and religious studies, see Huang, *Autocracy at Work*, 33–34, 36–39, and 42–48. For his succession controversies and consolidation of power, see ibid., chs. 3, 4 and 7. His edicts and the memorials from the Banners, all filled with Confucian norms, were included in three books: *Shangyu baqi, Dergi hesei wesimbuhe gūsai baita be dahūūme gisurefi wesimbuhengge (Shangyu qiwu yifu)*, and *Hesei yabubuha hacilama wesimbuhe gūsai baita (Yuxing qiwu zouyi)*. All the three books were printed during the Yongzheng period. See Pei Huang, "Five Major Sources for the Yongzheng Period, 1723–1735," *Journal of Asian Studies* 27. 4 (1968): 954–55. For the compilation on the Eight Banners, see *TCCC* and *TCCC* (1985) in the bibliography. For the genealogical compilation, see *STTP* in the bibliography.

34. The Six-Maxim Edict was issued in 1652. See *CSL*, Shunzhi reign, 63: 3a, 9/2/gengxu. For the *Sacred Edict*, see *CSL*, Kangxi reign, 34: 10a–11a, 9/10/guisi. For a comparison between these two edicts, see Kung-chuan Hsiao, *Rural China: Imperial Control in the Nineteenth Century* (Seattle and London: University of Washington Press, 1960), 186–88.

For Kangxi's intention to enforce the *Sacred Edict*, see *CSL*, Kangxi reign, 34: 21, 9/11/jimao. The imperial action of 1686 was a response to the suggestion of a provincial commander. See *CSL*, Kangxi reign, 126: 4a–5a, 25/(intercalary) 4/jiazi. For the imperial order of 1700, see Ōmura Kōdō, "Shinchō kyōiku shisōshi ni okeru 'Seiyu kokun' no chii ni tsuite." In Hayashi Tomoharu, ed., *Kinsei Chūgoku kyōikushi kenkyū: sono bunkyō seisaku to shomin kyōiku* (Tokyo: Kokudosha, 1958), 256–57. For Yongzheng's contribution to the *Sacred Edict*, see Huang, *Autocracy at Work*, 190–95.

35. For Yongzheng's redoubled effort, see Victor H. Mair, "Language and Ideology in the Written Popularization of the Sacred Edict." In David Johnson, Andrew J. Nathan, and Evelyn S. Rawski, eds., *Popular Culture in Late Imperial China* (Berkeley and Los Angeles: University of California Press, 1985), 325–59; Huang, *Autocracy at Work*, 192–95; Hsiao, *Rural China*, 185–86. For the lecture system and its continuation, see Ōmura, "Shinchō kyōiku shisoshi," 257–66.

For the Manchu version of the amplified *Sacred Edict*, see Matsumura, "Beikoku gikai toshukan," 40. For lectures at the company level, see *Yuxing qiwu zouyi*, 3: 5. For lectures to the collateral imperial clansmen, see *Shangyu qiwu yifu*, 7: 18a–20a. For the ordinary Manchus, see *Yuxing qiwu zouyi*, 3: 9b–10b. For the field survey, see Shirokogoroff, *Social Organization of the Manchus*, 148.

36. For Qianlong's visits, see Sun, *Qianlong di*, 178–79.

37. For a detailed treatment about the beginning, completion, effect on historical scholarship, and related literary inquisition of the project, see Guy, *The Em-*

peror's Four Treasuries, chs. 4–6; Zhu, *Qingchao tongshi,* 9: 555–93. For a succinct coverage of the project, see *ECCP,* 1: 122 and 371.

38. For Yongzheng's stress on filial piety, see Huang, *Autocracy at Work,* 195–96.
     For Qianlong's love of books, see Qinggui, *Guochao gongshi xubian,* 720–74.
     For Qianlong's praise of loyal Ming officials, see *CSL,* Qianlong reign, 996: 17a–
     20a; 1000: 22a–23a, 40/11/guiwei; 41/ 1/jimao. For the posthumous honors
     given to them, see *CSL,* Qianlong reign, 1002:15b–19b, 41/2/gengxu. Shi commanded the Ming army in Yangzhou against the Manchu invaders. He was executed, for he refused to collaborate. Qianlong eulogized him as a model of
     loyalty. See *CSL,* Qianlong reign, 996: 17b; 1035: 2, 40/11/guiwei; 42/6/jiayin. He
     showed concern for the descendants of Xiong and Yuan. See *CSL,* Qianlong
     reign, 1175: 12a; 1181: 4b–5a, 48/2/wuzi and 48/5/wushen. Wing-ming Chan regards Qianlong's honoring of Ming martyrs as a concession to the Han Chinese. See his "The Qianlong Emperor's New Strategy in 1775 to Commend
     Late-Ming Loyalists," *Asia Major,* Third Series, 13. 1 (2000): 109–36.

     For compilation of the *Erchen chuan,* see *CSL,* Qianlong reign, 1022: 2b–4b,
     41/12/gengzi. One edition of the *Erchen zhuan* was published by Liuyi shuju,
     Shanghai, in four volumes. For Hong, see Wang, *The Life and Career of Hung
     Ch'eng-ch'ou (1593–1665),* chs. 8–9.

39. Mark C. Elliott emphasizes an ethnic and political interpretation of the chaste
     Manchu widows, although he recognizes Confucian influence on them. See his
     "Manchu Widows and Ethnicity in Qing China," *Comparative Studies in Society and History* 41. 1 (1999): 33–71.

40. For the driving force behind Qianlong's enthusiasm for writing many things
     such as inscriptions, see Smith, *China's Cultural Heritage: The Qing Dynasty,
     1644–1912,* 215 and 220. For the function of the Yuanming Yuan, see Wong, *A
     Paradise Lost,* 3, 16, 118–20.

Conclusion

THE MANCHUS HAD A LONG ANCESTRAL LINE originating in Northeast China, also known as Manchuria. Geographical barriers in that region created diverse ecologies and, consequently, special economic enclaves. The barriers also resulted in scattered political centers comprising tribes or tribal alliances. Because of intertribal rivalry, such centers made political unification difficult. Disunity invited intervention from China and nomadic invaders from the steppes of Mongolia and Central Asia. In brief, Manchuria constituted the northeastern flank of China, an East Asian frontier, and as such played a frontier role.

As a huge region strategically situated, Manchuria was close to Siberia, Mongolia, the Pacific coast, Korea, and China proper. Each neighboring region represented a culture, such as forest hunting, steppe-pastoral, fishing, and agriculture. Manchuria became their meeting place, and the interaction had a great impact on its inhabitants. With the exception of Liaodong, which most of the time was under China's control, China's cultural influence in Manchuria fluctuated with its political strength.

It is from this background that the Manchu ancestors arose three thousand years ago. The early ancestors were heterogeneous, including components from all the inhabitants of ancient Manchuria. More recently they comprised the Jurchens, who founded the Jin dynasty in the early twelfth century. In time Mongol, Chinese, and Korean components were added to the Jurchens. The Manchus therefore were not a homogeneous people. It is nearly impossible to discover the origin and meaning of the term "Manchu," although there are numerous interpretations. One thing is certain: Hong Taiji adopted the term as a new ethnic label to meet his political needs when he founded the Qing dynasty in 1636.

The early seventeenth century marked a new era in the history of Manchuria. Nurhaci emerged out of the internal chaos that had confronted the Jurchens for almost three centuries. The Mongols were divided; the Ming dynasty was in turmoil. There was a power vacuum on the Liaodong frontier. Nurhaci developed agriculture, attracted more supporters, and created his war machine, the Eight Banners. With war and diplomacy he was able to establish outside the weakening Ming orbit a frontier kingdom, the first Jurchen state since the conquest of the Jin dynasty by the Mongols. His subjects were bound not only by his leadership but by a language which was devised in 1599. Firmly grounded, the kingdom was destined to become important.

The subsequent reign of Hong Taiji was crucial to the Jurchen state because he gave it direction. With strength and resourcefulness, he pacified the Mongols, humiliated the Koreans, and defeated the Chinese, laying the foundation of the Qing dynasty. He appreciated the service of Chinese advisors, whom he recruited from enslaved or captured scholars and through recommendations or civil service examinations. Because of their advice, he envisioned the conquest of the Ming dynasty. He repeatedly invaded China proper, consolidated his power, and created a bureaucracy after the Ming model. Compared with Nurhaci, who was the unifier and groundbreaker, Hong Taiji was the centralizer, empire builder, and farsighted statesman. Under the regency of Dorgon, the Manchus moved into China and became founders of the last conquest dynasty in Chinese history.

Sinicization of the Manchus had been an ongoing and complex process arising from frontier activities between Chinese and Jurchens in the Liaodong valley. The Jurchens were active on China's frontier as early as the Yongle period of the Ming. Their activities were many, carried on through private and official channels and characterized by chronic conflict. Of these activities, agriculture was perhaps the most important for sinicization. Because of geography, the Jurchens depended on a mixed economy of hunting, fishing, and gathering, as well as farming. The plain encouraged inhabitants to develop agriculture. By the fifteenth century the Jianzhou and Hūlun Jurchens, in particular those close to Chinese and Korean settlements, were engaged in agriculture. Farming changed the Jurchen lifestyle. They became accustomed to a sedentary life, grew grain as their staple, and became more receptive to Chinese culture. To improve their farming they sought iron implements and plow animals and took captives and harbored fugitives, deserters, and hard-pressed individuals from the Chinese and Korean sides of the frontier.

Trade was another important frontier activity. The Ming opened frontier markets as a means to control the Jurchens, who were eager to improve their lives. With patents from the Ming government, they brought horses, pearls, furs, and ginseng to market or took them on tributary missions to Peking. There was also unofficial or private trading in the official markets, as well as at frontier walls and in other places as permitted by the Ming government. Jurchen traders purchased textiles, salt, oxen, and farming implements from their Chinese counterparts. Such frontier trade stimulated trade among the Jurchen tribes. Trade upgraded the Jurchen economy, narrowed the disparity between societies, and offered opportunities for increased contact. Chinese and Jurchen traders exchanged not only commodities but the ideas and values that produced them. Chinese loanwords found their way into the Manchu language.

As a frontier, Manchuria attracted adventurers, invaders, and migrants, who settled among the natives. There was also constant internal migration from northern to southern Manchuria. This population movement transformed frontier lives. During the last years of the Yuan dynasty, three Jurchen tribes—the Odoli, Hurha, and Taowen—began southward migrations and eventually settled in the Liaodong region, where their neighbors were Chinese and Koreans. There were changes on the other side of the frontier, too. After the overthrow of the Yuan dynasty in China, Korea threw off its Mongol fetters and sought to expand to the north. To protect its northeastern flank, the Ming dynasty dispatched soldiers and convicts, and encouraged migrants to Liaodong to man garrisons and become farmers. Moreover, traders came to the region from other parts of China. It was from this environment that frontiersmen and transfrontiersmen appeared.

Chinese frontiersmen helped in the sinicization of the Jurchens. As farmers, craftsmen, and traders they brought the Jurchens farming skills, implements, and commodities for daily needs. As the sources suggest, Chinese captives, fugitives, and deserters lived in the Jurchen settlements. In war, Nurhaci and Hong Taiji took hundreds of thousands of Chinese captives from Liaodong and other places. The Chinese thus were able to keep in broad contact with Jurchen society and to transmit Chinese culture. They and their descendants were organized into the Eight Banners as officers or common warriors. Some even became advisors and teachers of Manchu leaders.

Chinese transfrontiersmen also played a role in spreading Chinese culture among the Manchus. These were frontiersmen who crossed ethnic boundries to settle amid the Jurchens. In new settlements they became a minority group prone to the influence of local culture. But, as Charles Keyes argues, it took time, perhaps more than a generation, for them to incorporate new elements into their cultural heritage. Hence they were able to introduce Chinese traditions such as language and farming skills to the dominant group.[1] They and their descendants made up the earliest units of the Eight Banners and were treated as Manchus by the Qing court. On the other hand, Jurchen immigrants on the Chinese side of the frontier also served as transmitters of Chinese culture. According to Ming official records, the number of such immigrants was considerable, although no precise statistical figure is available. They appeared in many places, especially the Dongning Guard near Liaoyang. There they mingled with Chinese and Korean residents and became sinicized. From these immigrants the Ming government recruited interpreters. When the Ming was defeated in Liaodong, they joined Nurhaci and some served as high officials. Their long stay in China enabled them to spread Chinese values among the Manchus. The Tong and Shi families were cases in point. A clanswoman of the Tong family was the mother of the Kangxi emperor.

Chinese administrative and legal institutions helped transform the Jurchen frontier state into a centralized and bureaucratized empire. The state founded by Nurhaci was a superstructure based on Jurchen family, clan, and tribal relations, all working as decentralizing agents. An ambitious ruler, Hong Taiji spent the first six years of his reign breaking up the joint rulership designed by his father. By adopting such Ming administrative institutions as the Six Boards, the Censorate, and the Six Offices of Scrutiny, he steered the state toward a centralized polity. The central administrative structure he introduced lasted almost to the end of the dynasty. Qing rule was consolidated after the defeat of the anti-Manchu forces in the early 1680s. This enabled the Kangxi emperor to undercut clan and tribal elements from the state structure. An autocratic ruler, the Yongzheng emperor eliminated them, and the Qing became a unitary polity. Qianlong did not change the state administrative machinery, but he operated it with energy and flexibility. Under him the Qing reached the climax of its power.

Adoption of Ming administrative machinery necessitated the employment of Chinese legal institutions, for the two were interdependent. The legal institution that Nurhaci first tried to restore was traditional Jurchen tribal law. There was no distinction between administrators and judges, or between military matters and civil cases. When his state became more complex after the takeover of the Liaodong region, he needed a better legal system. With ideas and practices from Ming statutes, he introduced a workable penal code. His successor, Hong Taiji, borrowed more from Ming statutes because he knew their advantages through their translation by Dahai. The result was the collection of Qing statutes known as the *Shenyang Regulations*, marked by multi-ethnicity, inequality, flexibility, and universality. After 1644, the Qing court revised its code many times, and with each revision there were more Chinese components. In addition to the code, the Qing compiled comprehensive regulations based on Ming institutions to govern operations of all offices in the central government.

As early as the frontier days, Chinese culture infiltrated Jurchen social institutions, and the process increased when the Manchus moved into China. In China proper, the Manchus found such Chinese influences as marital customs, funeral rites, family relations, and naming patterns penetrating their lives. More importantly, the Manchus forgot their martial virtues: horsemanship and archery. To change the situation, Qing rulers repeatedly issued decrees, appealing to group honor and individual pride. They failed to influence their Manchu subjects because the Manchu cultural identity in their day had incorporated Chinese cultural elements. The Manchus continued to choose civil careers, evade military obligations, and pursue personal interests. Qing emperors, especially those after Jiaqing, showed little interest in military exercises. The decline of the Manchus as warriors can be seen in the turning of the *fadu* from military interests to social and aesthetic concerns. Indeed, changes in Manchu customs served as chilling testimony of sinicization.

There were clear indications not only of Chinese influence on the Manchu language, but also on literature, architecture, and religion. A century after its creation in 1599, the Manchu language lost its vitality as a means of communication, official or private. One may identify many reasons for its decline, but sinicization is the most telling. There had been links between the Chinese and Jurchen languages. Manchu included many Chinese loanwords and grammatical elements. After the Kangxi era, many Manchus, including imperial clansmen and officials from Manchuria, could not speak or understand their mother tongue. They preferred Chinese to their native speech. This became an irreversible trend, spreading from private to official circles.

By the Yongzheng era, many officials, who were supposed to submit Manchu memorials, wrote them in Chinese. Among the memorialists were princes, grand secretaries, Tartar generals, governors-general, commanders in chief, and members of the Office of the Imperial Household. A compilation of confidential memorials of the Yongzheng period contains memorials by a Chinese Tartar general and a Manchu lieutenant general, eighty-three memorials by Prince Yinxiang and forty-three by Nian Gengyao, who was once commander in chief of imperial forces against the rebels in Kokonor. All these memorials were written in Chinese. During the Qianlong reign many Manchu princes, Tartar generals, and grand secretaries also wrote Chinese memorials. An imperial decree of 1871 indicated that commanders should send memorials to the throne in Chinese unless they did not know it.[2] For political considerations, Manchu remained a required language, but the requirement was only nominal. Of course, for Manchus who forgot their mother tongue this did not necessarily mean loss of ethnic identity. It should be noted, however, that they lost an important connection with their culture and became more susceptible to Chinese cultural influence.

Chinese literature greatly inspired Manchu literati and their works. They learned rules and writing skills from classical Chinese literature, wrote on the same subjects in the same language, and expressed themselves in the Chinese way. Poetry was the dominant form of Manchu literature. Throughout the Qing dynasty there were many Manchu poets, among whom were emperors, princes, high officials, banner officers, and private individuals. It is difficult to distinguish literary works by Manchu writers from those by Chinese.

Manchu architecture was characterized by the Chinese aesthetic elements. Construction of the East Capital or Dongjing in 1621–1622 marked a transition from Jurchen patterns to Chinese traditions. With the conquest of the Liaodong valley, Nurhaci decided to build a new capital with Chinese architectural features, such as magnificence, spaciousness, symmetry, and harmony, to symbolize the glory of his frontier state. The rise of Shenyang as the Prosperous Capital in 1625 signified a new stage of Manchu architectural evolution. With renovations by Hong Taiji and his successors, the Shenyang palace became the most sinicized old Manchu capital. Both capitals were results of Chinese craftsmanship, epitomized by the Hou family. Manchu imperial tombs and ancestral temples were also built along Ming imperial models. The palace complex in Peking was mainly adopted from the Ming dynasty. But the greatest Qing architectural achievement after 1644 was the Summer Palace, completed by Qianlong. It represented the best Chinese architectural and aesthetic tradition and was executed by Chinese architects and designers. In addition to its other functions, it served as the principal imperial residence from 1723 to 1860.[3]

Chinese religion and philosophy, too, left their imprint on Manchu life. The Manchus practiced shamanism, an animistic, ritualistic belief. Without a theology or the promise of salvation, shamanism was nearly defenseless against the advance of such alien beliefs as Chinese Buddhism and popular cults. Patronized by the early Ming, Buddhism soon played a part in the lives of the Manchus. The Goddess of Mercy, a popular deity in China, became well known. Of the popular Chinese deities, Guan Yu was the most worshiped by Manchus, from the emperor to the common people. Related to the cult was the *Romance of the Three Kingdoms*, one of the favorite pieces of historical fiction in China. For the Manchus it became a household word and a multipurpose sourcebook. For political control over Tibet and Mongolia the Qing court cultivated Lamaism, the Tibetan version of Buddhism.

Hong Taiji was the first Manchu ruler to identify the dynastic interests of the Qing with Confucianism, which had become China's state philosophy since the second century BC, monopolizing moral teachings and legitimatizing political centralization. He followed the Chinese dynastic practice of offering sacrifices to the sage. His successors continued the practice. Despite his leanings toward Buddhism, the Shunzhi emperor continued the sponsoring of Confucianism, as evidenced in his *Six-Maxim Edict*. With the Kangxi emperor's blessing, the Neo-Confucian School of Principle dominated the intellectual scene. The imperial court compiled, revised, and reprinted works on Confucianism. Kangxi issued the *Sacred Edict*, interpreting social, economic, and political matters in Confucian terms and intended for nationwide application.

No Qing ruler was more devoted to the inculcation of Confucian values in his Manchu subjects than Yongzheng. In many decrees he exaggerated traditional Manchu values and urged the Manchus to preserve them. He wrote *Amplified Instructions on the Sacred Edict*, which incorporated his comments on his father's hortatory work. Available in Chinese and Manchu, it was required reading for students and was the text that scholars and officials had to explain before semimonthly gatherings of townspeople or villagers. There were special lecture sessions for the Manchus.[4] This kind of indoctrination continued almost until the end of the dynasty. Indeed, through this long and intensive process, Confucian norms, mores, and values were widely and deeply instilled in the broad masses of the Manchus.

In like manner, the Qianlong emperor took every possible measure to rekindle his Manchu subjects' consciousness of their heritage and glorious past. He sponsored special compilations on Manchu origins and traditions. Officials who forgot their mother tongue, avoided hunting, or were defeated in the battlefield were demoted or punished with death. At the same time, he did everything he could to improve the lives of the common Manchu warriors.

But none of the Qing emperors, from Hong Taiji to Qianlong, succeeded in reviving the Manchu ethnic heritage. The main reason for their failure lay in the fact that they politicized the issue too much. As an ethnic group, the Manchus were not merely a political association. They were chiefly a cultural and social group responding to new conditions. When they extended their political and ethnic boundary from Manchuria to China proper, they confronted a new cultural and social environment, in which the conquered had long traditions and a huge population. As a conquering minority, the Manchus were in constant contact with the Chinese and had to accommodate themselves to the latter's ways of life. The late Kangxi reign saw the rise of a new group of Manchus, who belonged to the second or third generation of the conquest elite. Born and raised in China proper, they were remoter from their ancestors and closer to the Chinese. As they adopted more from Chinese culture, they lost more of their own cultural heritage. This process could not be stopped by Manchu quarters or imperial edicts.

One may draw a few points from the above discussion. Chinese influence and the Manchu ethnic identity are not mutually exclusive because, as experts agree, ethnicity is a subjective perception changeable with time and conditions. Therefore, sinicization of the Manchus is a relative term. It would be futile to pin down precisely how sinicized the Manchus were. They continuously adapted themselves to the Chinese ways of life, even after the fall of the Qing At the same time, a sinicized Manchu could retain some of his own cultural traits. As late as the 1910s the Manchus in Xinbin, Liaoning, retained a shaman to oversee sacrifices, while in Peking, even in the 1950s, they kept traditional formality in dealing with senior family members. But these remnants are not enough to prove the separation of the Manchus from the larger population of China.[5]

There is ample evidence that Manchu traditions lingered in the Qing state structure. The Eight Banner system originated in the Jurchen clan system and hunting practices. It combined military, political, and social functions and was alien to Chinese experience. The Office of the Imperial Household was another example. It was an outgrowth of the Eight Banners, staffed with bondservants, and it differed from the Chinese institution of eunuchs. The Qing central government was also marked by the Court of Dependent Peoples, which was in charge of Mongol, Tibetan, and Moslem affairs and, founded before 1644, originally known as the Office of Mongol Affairs. All these institutions preserved Manchu characteristics and lasted to the end of the Qing.

Another point is worth mentioning. It is nearly impossible to determine which group, elite or commoners, was more affected by Chinese culture, for Chinese influence marks all Manchus, without distinction. But it is certain that the upper-class Manchus became sinicized through education, government service, interest in the Chinese classics and art, and association with Chinese literati. Through their broad contacts, ordinary Manchus learned the Chinese language and other cultural elements. The difference between the Chinese and the Manchus diminished with time. During the second half of the nineteenth century, matrimonial relations between them became common. To relieve the financial strain, in 1865 the Qing court allowed Manchus to leave the banners to look for new opportunities. It is difficult to determine how many Manchus left the banners, but one may assume that the legal and social cleavage between the two groups was further diminished after the 1865 edict.[6]

Sinicization was not a one-way street because the Manchus left indelible marks on the Chinese. Frontier contacts created a hybrid language, referred to in a recent study as the Shenyang dialect. It was widely spoken among people on both sides of the Liaodong frontier. After 1644 its elements, together with many Manchu words, penetrated the Peking dialect, which evolved into National Spoken Chinese (*guoyu*), known in the West as Mandarin. Many place names in Manchuria are of Manchu origin. The Manchu script system inspired scholars to refine Chinese philology. Manchu novels, folk literature, and other literary works such as the *Dream of the Red Chamber* and the *zidi shu*, which combined ballads with folktales, brought Manchu ideas and values to a Chinese audience.[7]

There were marked Manchu influences on Chinese society. Indeed, these Manchu influences should be studied in detail, for they cover many aspects. But the present study only concerns itself with the Manchu adoption of Chinese culture. It is hoped that Manchu influence on China will be treated as a separate subject in the near future. I can cite a few examples here. As hunters and warriors, the Manchus had worn long, wide gowns. In the nineteenth century, women's gowns were tightened to fit the figure and were bordered with lace. From such gowns evolved the *qipao* (lit. banner gown), popular among Chinese women today. The riding jacket or *magua* was another style of Manchu dress. With many styles, it was worn at first by soldiers, and it became popular in China from the Kangxi era on, and it was adopted by Chinese men, even after 1912. The most egregious was the queue, the Manchu hairstyle imposed on Chinese men, some of whom wore it until the 1920s. Manchus loved sweet snacks, one of which was *sacima* (in Chinese, *saqima*). The dynasty is gone, but the beloved *sacima* remains.[8]

In closing this study it is worth exploring how the Manchus reacted to Chinese culture. One may first examine the reaction of the Qing monarchs. As shown in many edicts, their reaction followed a substance-and-application formula. As Manchu rulers, they regarded the Manchu heritage as substance, which they tried to maintain. As emperors, they used Confucian precepts to win the support of their Chinese subjects and keep the imperial order. At the beginning, Nurhaci focused on Mongol institutions, such as the writing system and official titles. Not until the last few years of his reign did he turn to Chinese cultural ideals. To transform his frontier state to an empire, Hong Taiji adopted many Chinese political and social institutions. But he considered the Manchu language and martial virtues to be the essence of Manchu tradition. He prohibited subjects from using Chinese for titles and place names, forbade Manchu women to follow the hairstyle and foot-binding practices of the "other people" [Chinese women], and rejected advice to replace Manchu dress with Chinese styles.[9]

Qing monarchs from Shunzhi to Qianlong all studied the Chinese language, history, and classics and sponsored projects to compile and print books on Chinese culture. At the same time, they did their best to uphold Manchu tradition. Shunzhi enforced the fugitive law, which pertained to the Manchu institution of slavery. Kangxi made special appropriations to help Manchu bannermen out of financial trouble so as to maintain their martial virtues.[10] The Yongzheng and Qianlong emperors became more concerned about progressing sinicization than had their predecessors. In many edicts, the two emperors demanded, with anger, nostalgia, and expectation, that the Manchus preserve their virtues, improve their military skills, refrain from Chinese customs, and commit themselves to the state. As one can see, these demands were made largely in terms of such Confucian precepts as loyalty, filial piety, and dutifulness.[11]

In the early years of the dynasty, Manchu aristocrats reacted to Chinese influence unfavorably. The battlefield conduct of Prince Amin serves as an example. In 1630 he was ordered to hold four cities east of Peking. When pressed by the Ming army, he fled his command center and slaughtered its residents, including Ming defectors. One of the reasons for this cruelty, according to official sources, was his displeasure with Hong Taiji's effort to win the support of Chinese. One may detect a similar reaction from another case, in which a prince and two officials were angry because defecting Ming officers received high positions and enjoyed a good life.[12]

The behavior of the four regents in the early Kangxi reign further attests to the unfavorable aristocratic reaction to sinicization. While he lay dying in 1661, Shunzhi appointed four regents to execute state affairs during the minority of his successor, Kangxi. In all likelihood, with the cooperation of Shunzhi's mother, Empress Xiao-zhuang (1613–1688), the regents altered the imperial will into a document of self-denunciation. In the new will Shunzhi blamed himself for fourteen blunders. The first was his adoption of Chinese customs, while the fifth concerned his giving precedence to Chinese bureaucrats over Manchu officials. Under the influence of Ming institutions Shunzhi changed the Office of the Imperial Household to the Thirteen Eunuch Offices (*shisan yamen*) in 1654 and, five years later, changed the Three Inner Courts to the Grand Secretariat. In the name of restoring ancestral institutions, the regents reinstituted the two earlier organizations. Not until 1670 did Kangxi reintroduce the Office of the Imperial Household and the Grand Secretariat.[13]

Further adverse Manchu aristocratic responses occurred during the late Kangxi and early Qianlong periods. In 1713 a Manchu president of the Board of War memorialized to the throne that the key to a gate in Peking should be taken away from the Chinese officer there and entrusted to the Manchu commander. As a rule, in another example, the last imperial will was announced to the court in the Manchu, Chinese, and Mongol languages, but Kangxi's last will was read in Manchu only. To pacify the Chinese officials the Yongzheng emperor issued a long edict to explain away the incident. In 1728, a Manchu lieutenant general petitioned that the Manchus should be made eligible to hold the ranks between lieutenant colonel and lieutenant in the Chinese military units in Peking. The petition was turned down by Yongzheng on the ground that Chinese soldiers helped defeat the Three Feudatories and thus deserved to keep their positions. During the early Qianlong reign a similar petition was made about the grades between colonel to second captain in the Chinese Green Standard units stationed along the Great Wall. The throne granted the petition and assigned ninety-three of the 133 positions to Manchus.[14] One may believe that similar cases occurred frequently, but they failed to diminish Chinese influence among the Manchus.

Manchu scholars and literary men seem to have favored Chinese culture even before 1644. The famous linguists Dahai and Kūrcan learned Chinese and appreciated the Chinese style of dress, which they advised Hong Taiji to adopt for the Manchus. A scholar and poet, Singde was active in literary circles, keeping in touch with many Chinese. He and his father, Mingju, helped a Chinese writer in exile in Manchuria. Yun-duan and Yin-xi, imperial clansmen, were fond of Chinese poems and paintings. Both kept company with Chinese men of letters and collected Chinese art objects. The matrimonial bond between Tinglu (1772–1820) and Yun Zhu provides another pertinent case. Tinglu was a Manchu scholar-official from the Wanggiya clan, which produced a number of celebrated scholars and translators, such as Asitan and Hesu (1652–1718). Yun Zhu was a poetess and painter descended from a Chinese family noted for its scholastic and artistic tradition. For academic and professional reasons the families were friendly, their relations furthered by marriage.[15]

Ordinary Manchus, mostly anonymous individuals without access to power or wealth, had mixed feelings about Chinese customs and ideals. Initially, they must have felt excitement when exposed to an exotic way of life, tantamount to comfort and opportunity. Through daily contact with the conquered, they picked up the latter's language and customs. As hereditary soldiers, they were given legal and financial privileges and were not allowed to engage in any other way of life. But the situation changed. With increasing numbers, limited income, and prodigal habits, they confronted financial problems. As autocratic rule was consolidated, the government introduced more regulations. They were under more control and must have had a feeling of loss, a sense of emptiness.

There was an escapist trend among Manchu commoners, as shown in Qing sources. The lifestyle of the Manchu bannermen—such as a decline of martial virtues, rise of individual inclination, and desire for nonmilitary careers—which Qing rulers from Kangxi to Qianlong sought to correct, was in part a manifestation of their need for escape. Drinking seems to have been one means of escape. Before 1644, drinking was not a major problem. Nevertheless, late in the Kangxi reign it was a cause for concern. An imperial edict stated that excessive drinking changed facial features. Visiting ancestral tombs, Yongzheng stopped in Shenyang, which had about a thousand drinking establishments. The city was not only the old Qing capital but also the brewery capital of Manchuria.[16]

Considering the discussion above, one may say that the Qing dynasty was not that different from any Chinese dynasty before it. There are seeming differences because throughout the Qing the Manchus were a privileged class. Imperial clansmen and banner officials were positioned over Chinese bureaucrats, and Manchu commanders controlled strategic points. But this dominance did not change the course of sinicization. For all their privileges and influence, Manchu officials and commanders adopted the Chinese language, followed the Chinese way of naming, venerated Confucian teachings, and valued civil jobs. They were sinicized individuals, no longer Manchu warriors. Like Chinese bureaucrats, they carried out decisions made by emperors who perhaps were even more sinicized. Under continuous indoctrination, the Manchus, both officials and commoners, became thoroughly imbued with orthodox Confucianism. In northernmost Manchuria, as Shirokogoroff reported, the Manchu residents regarded Confucianism as their heritage.[17]

In discussing the Tungus, Lattimore has pointed out that "both in Manchuria and in Siberia," they had "always been distinguished by their cultural adaptability."[18] One may describe the Manchus in the same way. Sinicization was a result of cultural contact that neither prohibition nor protection could stop. Adoption of the Chinese ways of life by the Manchus meant a reorientation. They did not have to be hereditary warriors or confine themselves to Manchu quarters. They were able to join the people surrounding them. China also benefited from the Manchu heritage, which enriched Chinese culture.

Notes

1. See his "The Dialectics of Ethnic Change," in Charles F. Keyes, ed., *Ethnic Change* (Seattle: University of Washington Press, 1982), 15. But what the author

mentions here is a general view, not directly related to the Jurchens or Manchus.

2. During the Kangxi period Chinese Tartar generals occasionally submitted memorials in Chinese. See *Gong-zhong dang: Kangxi chao zouzhe*, 7: 354–57, Memorials of Guan Yuan-zhong, 57/6/7. For the memorials by Yin-xiang and Nian Gengyao, the Tartar general and the Manchu lieutenant general, respectively, see *Gong-zhong dang: Yongzheng chao zouzhe*, 26: 250–87, 425–50, 674, 927. For Chinese confidential memorials during the Qianlong reign, see *Gong-zhong dang: Qianlong chao zouzhe*, 1: 45–47, 70–72, and 229. For the decree of 1871, see *CSL*, Tongzhi reign, 305: 4a, 10/2/xinwei.

3. For Yuanming Yuan's various functions, see Wong, *A Paradise Lost*, 3, 16.

4. For Yongzheng's efforts, see Huang, *Autocracy at Work*, 173, 175–76. For his exaggeration, see *CSL*, Yongzheng reign, 22: 21b–23b, 2/7/jiazi; 44: 2b, 4/5/renchen; *Baqi tongzhi*, introductory chapter 9: 38. Qianlong also overstated traditional Manchu values. See *Baqi tongzhi*, introductory chapter 11: 4b, 42a. Elliott uses the term "Manchu way" to cover traditional Manchu values. See his *The Manchu Way*, ch. 7.

5. For specialists' opinions about ethnicity, see Eller, *From Culture to Ethnicity to Conflict*, 9. McCready, *Culture, Ethnicity, and Identity*, xxi. As late as the 1910s the Manchu community in Xinbin, Liaoning, remained under the clan chief (*mukūnda*), and the shaman took charge of sacrificial services. See *Manzu shehui lishi diaocha*, 46. Long after the overthrow of the Qing dynasty the Manchus in Peking maintained traditional formality to deal with senior members in the family. See Ibid, 120. Edward Rhoads maintains that even by "the end of the nineteenth century Manchus and Han were still separate peoples . . . who retained some distinctive cultural traits . . . " See his *Manchus and Han*, 63. But one may point out that distinctive cultural traits also exist among Han Chinese themselves.

6. For the decree of 1865, see *CSL*, Tongzhi reign, 144: 2b–3b, 4/6/jiawu. In his *Manchus and Han* (pp. 35–36, 68), Rhoads argues that this decree had never been carried out because a similar decree was issued in 1898. But the last decree was too brief (*CSL*, 425: 22, Guangxu 24/7/gengchen). It needs to be further studied.

7. For the hybrid speech, see Guan and Meng, "Manzu yu Shenyang yu, Beijing yu," 73–81. A recent study provides thirty-three examples of Sino-Manchu words in the Peking speech. See Zhao Jie, "Beijing hua zhong di Man-Han yonghe ci tanwei," *Zhongguo yuwen* 4 (1993): 281–87. But Zhao's findings have been challenged. See Zhou Yimin and Zhu Jiansong, "Guanyu Beijing hua zhong di Manyu ci, 1–2," *Zhongguo yuwen* 3 (1994): 201–205. *For* more studies, see Jerry Norman, "Four Notes on Chinese-Altaic Linguistic Contacts," *Tsing Hua Journal of Chinese Studies* 14. 1–2 (1982): 245–46; Stephen A. Wadley, "Altaic Influences on [the] Beijing Dialect: The Manchu Case," *Journal of the*

American Oriental Society 116. 1 (1996): 102–104. Aixin Gioro Ying-sheng provided many examples for penetration of Manchu words into the Peking dialect. See his *Lao Beijing yu Manzu*, 20–29. For some Manchu terms such as *jalan*, *janggin*, and *niru*, see Rhoads, *Manchus and Han*, 62.

For its philological feedback, see Luo Xindian, "Zhongguo yinyun xue di wailai yingxiang," *Dongfang zazhi* 32. 14 (July 1935): 38–40. For the *Dream of the Red Chamber* and the *zidi shu*, see Guan and Meng, "Manzu yu Shenyang yu, Beijing yu," 78–81; *MTTS*, 504–12; Chen Jinzhao, "Zidi shu zhi zuojia jiqi zuopin," *Zhongguo shumu jikan* 12. 1 and 2 (1978): 21–56.

8. For the banner gown and the riding jacket, see Zhou Xibao, *Zhongguo gudai fushi shi* (Peking: Xinhua shudian, 1984), 464–65, 484–85, 533, 535; Zheng, *Qingshi tanwei*, 366–68.

9. For Hong Taiji's effort to preserve the Manchu language, dress, and military virtues, see *CSL*, reign of Taizong, 18: 13a–14a, Tiancong 8/4/xinyou; 32: 8b–9b, Chongde 1/11/guichou; 34: 26b– 27a, Chongde 2/4/dingyou. For the hairstyle and foot-binding rule, see *CSL*, reign of Taizong, 42: 10b, Chongde 3/7/ dingchou; Chase, "The Status of the Manchu Language," 13.

10. Since the Kangxi reign, imperial sons received education in the palace school. For Shunzhi's adoption of Chinese culture, see Jin, "Lun Shunzhi," *Wen-shi-zhe*, 46–48; *ECCP* 1: 256. For the fugitive law, see *CSL*, Shunzhi reign, 119: 6b– 7a, 15/7/wuwu.

    For Kangxi's education and boyhood, see Jonathan D. Spence, "The Seven Ages of K'ang-hsi (1645–1722)," *Journal of Asian Studies* 26. 2 (1967): 205–206; Bai, *Kangxi huangdi quan-zhuan*, ch. 1. For Kangxi's appropriations, see Huang, *Autocracy at Work*, 166–67.

11. For demands made by Yongzheng and Qianlong, see *Baqi tongzhi*, 9: 13b, 38; 11: 4b, 42a.

12. For the first case, see *CSL*, reign of Taizong, 7: 4a–5a, 18a–19b, Tiancong 4/5/ renchen and 4/6/yimao. For the second case, see ibid., 64: 7b–8a, Chongde 8/1/ xinyou.

13. For the text of Shunzhi's last will, see *CSL*, Shunzhi reign, 144: 2a–6a, 18/1/ dingsi. The four regents were Oboi, a member of the Gūwalgiya clan, Soni, Suksaha, and Ebilun. For their biographies, see *CSKC*, 10: 8353–59, 8361–65. For the change of Shunzhi's last will and the restoration of the two old offices, see Oxnam, *Ruling from Horseback*, 52, 54–59, 67–69, 76–78; Kessler, *K'ang-hsi and the Consolidation of Ch'ing Rule*, 25–30. For Shunzhi's replacing the Office of the Imperial Household with the Thirteen Eunuch Offices and the Three Inner Courts by the Grand Secretariat, see *CSL*, Shunzhi reign, 76: 16a–18a, 10/6/gui-hai; 119: 6b–7a, 15/7/wuwu.

    By 1670 Kangxi had reintroduced the Office of the Imperial Household and the Grand Secretariat, which since then stayed. See *CSL*, Kangxi reign, 1: 21a– 22b, (Shunzhi) 18/2/yiwei; Kangxi reign, 33: 27a, 9/8/yiwei.

14. For the memorial of the Manchu president of the Board of War, see *Kangxi chao Manwen zhupi zouzhe quanyi*, 83(#2084). For the case about Kangxi's last will, see *Shang-yu neige*, 1: 7b. For the petition of 1728, see *Baqi tongzhi*, introductory chapter 10: 17b-19a. For the petition of the early Qianlong reign, see *CSL*, Qianlong reign, 8:12b-13b, Yongzheng 13/12/xinwei; 18: 10b, Qianlong 1/4/gengwu.

15. Wu Zhaoqian was the Chinese writer. With the help of Singde and Mingju, he was able to return home from exile. See Fan, "Wu Zhaoqian nianpu," 89-91. For Tinglu,Yun Zhu, and their marriage, see Songshen, *Changbai Wanyen shi jiude lu*, 1: "*Xingshu*," 2b-5b; 2: "*Beiming*," 2: 3b-7b. For Asitan and Hesu, see *ECCP*, 1: 13-14, 281.

16. For the drinking problem, see *Shangyu baqi* 1: 3; *CSL*, Yongzheng reign, 31: 13b-14b, 3/4/gengchen. For the study of the brewing business in Shenyang, see Kawakubo Teirō, "Shindai Manshū ni okeru shōka no zokusei ni tsuite" in *Wada Hakushi koki kinen Tōyōshi ronsō* (Tokyo: Kōdansha, 1960), 303-13.

17. Shirokogoroff, *Social Organization of the Manchus*, 148.

18. For this quote, see Lattimore, *Manchuria*, 18-19.

Glossary

This glossary covers all names and terms in the text and notes. With a few exceptions authors, books, and articles are included in the Bibliography. For clarity I divide long romanized names and terms by one or two hyphens if each is more than eight letters (see the Preface). But names of Qing imperial clansmen follow the pattern, as set in Arthur W. Hummel's *Eminent Chinese of the Ch'ing Period (1644–1912)*. After Yongzheng's enthronement, all his brothers changed the first character of their given names from "Yin" to "Yun." For consistency, I keep using the character Yin. For instance, I use Yin-zhi, instead of Yun-zhi.

Abatai	阿巴泰	Anfiyanggu	安費揚古
Adaha hafa	阿達哈哈番	Anjuhū	安珠護, 安珠瑚
Adai	阿台	Anlezhou	安樂州
Aguda	阿骨打	Antu	安圖
Agui	阿桂	Aqača	阿哈出
Aha	阿哈	Asitan	阿什坦
Aibida	愛必達		
Aisin	愛新	Bai	白
Aisin Gioro	愛新覺羅	Baigiya	白佳
Aiyang	靉陽	Baishan	白山
Ajige	阿濟格	*baksi*	巴克式
Akedun	阿克敦	*bangwen*	榜文
Alikun	阿里袞	Bao Cheng-xian	鮑承先
Amin	阿敏	Baqi	八旗
Aminrtu	阿敏爾圖	*Baqi dang*	八旗檔

313

Baqi guanxue	八旗官學	Celge	車爾格
Baqi Manzhou	八旗滿洲氏族通	*chang*	常
shizu tongpu	譜	Chang (Korean	張
Baqi tongzhi	八旗通志	surname)	
Baqi tongzhi chuji	八旗通志初集	Chang-ling	長齡
Baqi yixue	八旗義學	Chang-ning si	長寧寺
baturu	巴圖魯	Changbai shan	長白山
Bayan	伯顏	Cha Shenxing	查慎行
Bayara	巴雅拉	chen	陳
Bayote	把岳忒	Chen Wangting	陳王庭
Bede	柏德	Chen Yuan	陳垣
Beihai ji	北海集	cheng-huang	城隍
beile	貝勒	Cheng Kaihu	程開祜
beiming	碑銘	Chengdu	成都
Beizhen	北鎮	Chŏng	鄭
Bi Gong	畢恭	Chŏng Myŏng-su	鄭命壽
Bingbu	兵部	Chong-zheng	崇禎
bithesi	筆帖式	Chong-zheng dian	崇政殿
Boersun	把兒遜	Chongde	崇德
Bohai	渤海	Chŏngjong	定宗
Boku-jiang	孛苦江	Chongshi	崇實
Borji	博爾濟	Chosŏn	朝鮮
Boyisuo	波乙所	*Chou-Liao shihua*	籌遼碩畫
Bujai	布察，布寨	ci	詞
Bujantai	布占泰	Cinggiyanu	逞加奴，清佳砮
Bukūri Yongson	布庫里雍順	Cungsan	充善
Burni	布爾尼	Cuyen	褚英，褚宴
Caku	察庫，查庫	*Da-Qing huidian*	大清會典
Cang'an	常安	*Da-Qing lü*	大清律
Canghai	長海	*Da-Qing lü jijie fuli*	大清律集
Cangšu (also	常 書		解附例
Cangšiu)		Da-shun	大順
Canling	參領	Dahai	達海，大海
Canming	常明	Dahurs	達斡爾
Cao	曹	Dai	戴
Cao Fu	曹頫	Daišan	代善
Cao Jun	曹俊	Dalu huachi	達魯花赤
Cao Xueqin	曹雪芹	Dangini	檀濟尼
Cao Zhan	曹霑	Daoguang	道光
ce	冊	Daoyuan	道圓
Cecen	車臣	Dargan, Darhan	達爾漢

Darhaci	達爾哈齊	Fan Yue	范岳
Darugachi	達魯花赤	Fanca	凡察，范察
Datong	大同	Fanca	范嗏
datong (Grand Unity)	大同	Fang Bao	方苞
		Fang Kongzhao	方孔炤
Dazheng dian	大政殿	*Fanli*	凡例
Delu	德祿	Fe Ala	費阿拉
Deyun	德雲	Fekulen	佛古倫，佛庫倫
Dodo	多鐸	Feng-huang lou	鳳凰樓
Dong-zheng yuan-shuai fu	東征元帥府	Feng Quan	馮銓
		Fiongdon	費英東，非英凍
Donggo	董鄂	Former and Later Han periods	前、後 [東] 漢
Donghai	東海		
Donghu	東胡	Former Han dynasty	前 [西] 漢
Dongjing	東京		
Dongkang	東康	Fu	福 [王]
Dongning	東寧	Fu	富，傅
Dongyi	東夷	fu	府
Dorgon	多爾袞，多里哄	Fu duyushi	副都御史
dougong	斗拱	Fuca	富察
Du yushi	都御使	Fude	傅德
Du zhihui shi	都指揮史	Fukangan	富康安
Ducha yuan	都察院	Fuliang	傅良
Dunhua	敦化	Fulin	福臨
Duoyen	朵顏	Fuling	福陵
Dusi	都司	Funing	富寧
Dutang	都堂	Furdan	傅爾丹
Dutong	都統	Fushun	撫順
Dutong yamen	都統衙門	*Fusi nikan*	撫順尼堪
		Fuyu	福餘
Ebilun	遏必隆	fuzi	父子
Eidu	額亦都		
Eleuth	厄魯特	Gabula	噶布拉
Erchen zhuan	貳臣傳	G'ag'ai	噶蓋
Erdeni	額爾德尼	Gahana	噶哈納
Esen	也先	Gan Xi	甘熙
Esulele	額素勒勒	Gao Hong-zhong	高鴻中
		Gao Sirong	高嗣榮
Fadu	See *hebao*	G'aose	高塞
Fahai	法海	Gilyaks	費雅喀，基里亞克
Fan	范		
Fan Wencheng	范文程	Gintaisi	金台石

Giocangga	覺昌安，叫場，教場	Hailar	海拉爾
		Hairtu	海爾圖
Giolca	覺爾察	Haixi	海西
Girin Ula	吉林烏喇	Hala	哈拉
Giyeyen	傑殷	Han	韓
Gong Zhenglu	龔正陸	Han In	韓潤
Gong-zhong dang: Kangxi chao zouzhe	宮中檔：康熙朝奏摺	Han Jun	韓浚
		Han Ni	韓尼
		Han Tan	韓菼
Gong-zhong dang: Yongzheng chao zouzhe	宮中檔：雍正朝奏摺	Han Ŭi	韓義
		Han Un	韓雲
		Hangchow	杭州
Gorolo	郭絡羅	Hanhua	漢化
Guaerjia	瓜爾佳	Hanlin yuan	翰林院
Guaerjia yinshi muzhi ming	瓜爾佳隱士墓誌銘	Hasan	哈山
		He	貉
Guan Donggui	管東貴	He Erjian	何爾健
Guan Yu	關羽	He Qin	賀欽
Guan Yuan-zhong	管源忠	He Zhu	何珠
Guandi	關帝	*hebao*	荷包
Guan'yin	觀音	Hedong	河東
Guang Lu	廣祿	Heishui	黑水
Guang-ning	廣寧	Heje	赫哲
Guang-shun	廣順	Hešeri	赫舍里
Guangong	關公	Hesu	和素
Guangxu	光緒	Hetu Ala	赫圖阿拉
Guanju gong	關雎宮	Hexi	河西
Gui	桂 [王]	Hife	希福
Gūlmahūn	顧爾瑪洪	Hoeryong	會寧
Gunggan	恭安	Hohori	何和禮
Guo Cheng-kang	郭成康	Hoifa	輝發
Guozi jian	國子監	Hong Bok-wǒn	洪福源
Guoyu	國語	Hong Cheng-chou	洪承疇
Gure	古勒	Hong-guang	弘光
gusa	固山	Hong Taiji	皇太極
Guwalca	卦爾察	Hongwu	洪武
Gūwalgiya	瓜爾佳	Hong-xiao	弘曉
Guwei	骨嵬	Hong-zhan	弘瞻
		Honglou meng	紅樓夢
Hada	哈達	Hongwu	洪武
Hahana Jacing	哈哈納扎青	Hooge	豪格
haidong qing	海東青	Hou	侯

Hou Jin	後金	Jianrui ying	健銳營
Hou Zhenju	侯振舉	Jianzhou	建州
Hu Gongming	胡貢明	Jiaqing	嘉慶
Huahua	華化	Jiawen	夾溫
Huang Daozhou	黃道周	Jiefu	節婦
huangdi	皇帝	Jilimi	吉里迷
Huashan	See Hūwasan	Jilin	吉林
Hūgiya	瑚佳	Jimi	羈縻
Huitong guan	會同館	Jin	金
Hulan	呼蘭	Jin dynasty	金朝
Hulawen	忽剌溫	Jin Sheng-huan	金聲桓
Huligai	胡里改	Jingkini hafa	精奇尼哈番
Hūlun	扈倫	Jinliang	金梁
Hurha	火兒阿	Jinshi	進士
Hurha [Hurka]	呼爾哈	Jinzhou	錦州
Hūrhan	扈爾漢	Jirgalang	濟爾哈朗
Hūwangiya	黃佳	Jishen	稷慎
Hūwašan	華善	Jiu	舊
Hyojong	孝宗	*Jiu Manzhou dang*	舊滿洲檔
		Jokis	卓啟斯
Ice	伊徹	Joogiya	兆佳，肇佳
Icengge	伊成額	*juan*	卷
Ifona	伊佛訥	Jucangge	朱長格
Ilari	伊拉里	Jueluo	覺羅
Ilden	宜爾登	Jueluo xue	覺羅學
Injo	仁祖	Jugiya	朱佳，珠佳
Irgen Gioro	伊爾根覺羅	Junji chu	軍機處
Isu	伊蘇	Jürčed	女真
		juren	舉人
Jaciba	扎齊巴	Jūsen	諸申
Jaifiyan	界藩 [凡]		
Jaisai	宰賽	Kaiguo shiliao	開國史料
Jalan	扎攔，甲喇	Kaiyuan	開原
janggin	章京	Khalkha	喀爾喀
Janggiya	章佳，張佳	*kang*	炕
Jargūci	扎爾固齊	Kangxi	康熙
Jebe	哲柏	Kara	喀喇
Ji	紀	Kerde	克爾德
Ji Yingju	吉應舉	Kim	金
Jiagu	夾谷	Kim Kan	金簡
Jiang Hede	蔣赫德	Kim Kyong-mum	金慶門
Jiang Xiang	姜瓖	Kim Kyong-son	金景善

Koguryŏ	高句驪	Liao	遼
Kong Youde	孔有德	Liao dynasty	遼朝
Kŏnju mun'gyonnok	建州聞見錄	Liaodong	遼東
Koryŏ dynasty	高麗	Liaodong dusi	遼東都司
Kuaihuo	快活 [州]	*Liaodong zhi*	遼東志
Kuandian	寬甸	*Liaohai congshu*	遼海叢書
Kuilin	奎林	*Liaoshu shu*	遼事述
Kuixu	揆敘	Liaoyang	遼陽
Kūrcan	庫爾纏	Lifan yuan	理藩院
Kurka	庫爾喀	Ligiya	李佳
Kuyala	庫雅喇	Ligiya-holo	李佳和羅
Kuyi	苦夷	Ling-shiwei nei-	領侍衛內大臣
Kwang-chow	廣州	dachen	
Kwanghaegun	光海君	Lindan Khutuktu	林丹汗
Kyonghung	慶興	Khan	
		Linqing	麟慶
Laili-hong	來力紅	Lio Aita	劉愛塔
Lailuhūn	賴盧渾	Lio Jy-heng	劉志恆
Lanhiyan Nioisi	蘭軒女史	Lio Sang-c'ai	劉尚彩
lang	郎	Lioboo	留保
Laohan	老漢	Liogiya	劉佳
Lei	雷	Liu	劉
Lei Xing	雷興	Liu Bei	劉備
Leping	樂平	Liu Jie	劉節
li	例	Liu Xingzuo	劉興祚
Li	李	Liubu	六部
Li Cheng-liang	李成梁	Liuke jishi zhong	六科給事中
Li Cheng-shan	李誠善	Liuyu	六諭
Li Fu	李輔	Longen dian	隆恩殿
Li Guohan	李國翰	Longshan	龍山
Li Ji	李濟	Loohan	勞翰
Li Jiantai	李建泰	Loosa	勞薩
Li Jiugao	李九羔	*lü*	律
Li Jixue	李繼學	Lü Zhi	呂熾
Li Linsheng	李林盛	Luo	羅
Li Manzhu	李滿住	Luo Zhenyu	羅振玉
Li Qingshan	李青山	Luohan	洛翰
Li Wei	李爵		
Li Weijun	李維鈞	Ma	馬
Li Xian-zhong	李顯忠	ma	馬
Li Xuezhi	李學智	Ma Guozhu	馬國柱
Li Yongfang	李永芳	Ma Guang-yuan	馬光遠
Li Zicheng	李自成	Maca	馬察

Mafuta	馬福他，瑪福他	mukūn	穆昆
Magiya	馬佳，瑪佳	mukūnda	穆昆達
Magua	馬褂	Munjong	文宗
Mahū	馬祜，瑪琥	Myŏngjong	明宗
Maiju	邁柱		
Maki	馬奇，瑪奇	Naiman	奈曼
Mamun Rōtō	滿文老檔	Nan shufang	南書房
Mana	瑪納	Nanchang	南昌
Mancheng	滿城	Nara	納喇
Manggūltai	莽古爾泰	Nei bishu yu*an*	內秘書院
Manjusri	曼殊師利	Nei guoshi yuan	內國史院
Manwen laodang	滿文老檔	Nei hongwen yuan	內弘文院
Manzhou	滿洲	Nei sanyuan	內三院
Manzi cheng	蠻子城	Neige	內閣
Manzu tongshi	滿族通史	Neiwu fu	內務府
Mao Ruizheng	茅瑞徵	Nengtai	能泰
Mao Wen	毛汶	Neyen	訥殷
Mao Wenlong	毛文龍	Ni	倪
Maolian	毛憐	Nian Gengyao	年羹堯
Marsai	馬爾賽	Niju	尼珠
Meng Sen	孟森	Nikan Wailan	尼堪外蘭
Meng'an	猛安	Ning Wanwo	寧完我
Menggebulu	孟骨孛羅， 孟格布祿	Ningan	寧安
		Ningguta	寧古塔
Menggetimur	猛哥帖木兒	Ningyuan	寧遠
Menggu yamen	蒙古衙門	Niohuru	鈕祜祿
Mengtem	孟特穆	niru	牛彔
Mergen Daicing	墨爾根戴青	Niru ejen	牛彔額真
mergen hiya	墨爾根轄	*niuyang*	牛羊
Ming dynasty	明朝	Noqin	訥親
Ming huidian	明會典	Northern Song dynasty	北宋朝代
Ming shilu	明實錄		
Mingju	明珠	Northern Wei dynasty	北魏朝代
Mingqing dang'an	明清檔案		
Mingqing shiliao	明清史料	*Nosan'gun ilgi*	魯山君日記
Mingshi	明史	Nuergan dusi	奴兒干都司
Mitamura Taisuke	三田村泰助	Nunjiang	嫩江
Mo	貊	Nurhaci	努爾哈赤，努爾 哈齊，努爾哈 奇，奴兒哈赤
Mohe	貊貉		
Monggolji	蒙古爾濟		
mou	畝	Nurkal dusi. See Nuergan dusi	
mouke	謀克		
Mudan	牡丹	Nüxilie	女奚列

Nüzhen	女真	*Qingshi ziliao*	清史資料
Nüzhen shi	女真史	qipao	旗袍
Nüzhi	女直	qishe	騎射
		Qixing lang	啟心郎
Oba	奧巴	Qorčin	科爾沁
Oboi	鄂拜 (Silin Gioro)	*Quan Liao zhi*	全遼志
Oboi (d. 1669)	鰲拜		
(Gūwalgiya)		Ren	任
Ochang	鄂昌	*Renchen jingxin lu*	人臣儆心錄
Odoli	吾都里，幹朵里		
O-erh-tʼai	鄂爾泰	Sahalcas	薩哈爾察
(Ortai, Oertai)		Sahalien	薩哈連
Ojo	鄂卓	Sahaliyen	薩哈璘
Oltute	鄂爾圖忒	Sakda	薩克達
Omida	鄂彌達	Sanfan (Three	三藩
Omutu	鄂貌 [穆] 圖	Feudatories)	
Orci (O-erh-chʼi)	鄂爾奇	Sangge	桑額 [Li family]
Oronchons	鄂倫春	Sangge	桑格 [Ren family]
Orongʼan	鄂容安	*Sanguo zhi yanyi*	三國志演義
Ortai		*Sanlüe*	三 略
See O-erh-tʼai		Sanwan	三萬
Oshi	鄂實	Saqima	薩其瑪
		Sarhū	薩爾滸
Pan Yulong	潘育龍	Sartu	薩爾圖
Pujoo	普照	Sejo	世祖
Pʼyongyang	平壤	Sejong	世宗
		Shang and	商周時期
Qaračin	喀喇沁	Zhou periods	
Qianlong	乾 隆	Shang dynasty	商朝
Qidahen	七 大恨	Shang Hongkui	商鴻逵
Qiduyu	騎都尉	Shang Kexi	尚可喜
Qienjia zhuang	千家莊	Shang sanqi	三旗
Qin (family name)	秦	Shang-shu	尚書
Qin dynasty	秦朝	Shang shufang	上 [尚] 書房
Qinding Manzhou	欽定滿洲祭神	Shang-yang bao	尚 陽堡
jishen jitian	祭天典禮	*Shangyu baqi*	上諭八旗
dianli		Shen Defu	沈德符
qing	頃	Shen Tong	沈 彤
Qing dynasty	清朝	Shen Wenkui	沈文奎
Qingfu	慶復	Shengan	神杆
Qinghe	清河	*Shenguan lu*	瀋館錄
Qingning gong	清寧宮	Shenyang	瀋陽

Shenyang zhuangqi	瀋陽狀啟	Sŏnjo	宣祖
Shenyang riji	瀋陽日記	Sŏngjong	成宗
Sheng-jing	盛京	Šoongkoro baturu	碩翁科洛 巴圖魯
Sheng-jing dingli	盛京定例	songzi	松子
Shengyin	昇寅	Soni	索尼
Shengyu	聖諭	Sonoda Kazuki	園田一龜
Shengyu guangxun	聖諭廣訓	Šose	碩色
Shi (Ši)	石	Suhete	速黑忒
Shi Guozhu	石國柱	sui	歲
(Ši Guwe-ju)		Suibin	綏賓
Shi Kefa	史可法	Suksaha	蘇克薩哈
Shi Tianzhu	石天柱	Suksuhu	蘇克素滸
(Ši Tiyan-ju)		Šumuru	舒穆祿
Shi Tingzhu	石廷柱	Sun Yat-sen	孫逸仙
(Ši Ting-ju)		Sŭngjŏngwŏn	承政院
Shi-e	十惡	Sungšan	嵩山
Shiliu dachen	十六大臣	Sungta	松塔
Shilu	實錄	Sunid	蘇尼特
shisan yamen	十三衙門	Šurhaci	舒爾哈齊
Shisheng si	實勝寺	Šuru	舒祿，舒魯
Shu nüzhen	熟女真	Sushen	蕭慎
Shufang	書房	*Sushu*	素書
Shui-dada	水達達	Suwan	蘇完
Shuihu zhuan	水滸傳	Šuwangboo	雙保
Shunzhi	順治	Suzi	蘇子
Sian	西安		
Sibe	錫伯	Taehae	大海 [達海]
Šihan (Shi Han)	石翰	T'aejo	太祖
Siku quanshu	四庫全書	T'aejong	太宗
Silin Gioro	西林覺羅	Taichang si	太常寺
Sin Ch'ung-il	申忠一	taimiao	太廟
Sindari	新達里，辛達里	Taining	泰寧
Singde	性德	Taiyuan	太原
Singgen Dargan	星根達爾漢	Taksi	塔克世，塔失，
Sintun	新屯		他失
Sishu	私塾	Talumu	塔魯木
Siyi guan	四夷館	Tan Qian	談遷
Socoro	索綽羅	Tang dynasty	唐朝
Sogiya	索佳	tangzi	堂子
Solon	索倫	Taoer	洮兒 [河]
Song-Liao	松遼	Taowen	桃溫
Song Yihan	宋一韓	Tashan	塔山

Tatara	他塔喇	Tümed	土默特
Tenghis	騰吉思	Tung Jy-siyan	佟智賢
Tianming	天命	(Tong zhixian)	
Tiancong	天聰	Tung Ki (Tong Qi)	佟啟
Tiancong chao	天聰朝臣工奏議	Tunggiya	佟佳
chengong zouyi		Tungsan	童山，童倉
Tianshun	天順	Tuo-wo-lian	脫斡憐
Tiebao	鐵保	Turgei	圖爾格
Tieli	鐵利，鐵驪	Tuša	圖沙
tingji	廷寄	Tusi zhidu	土司制度
Tinglu	廷璐		
Tong	佟	Ugiya	吳佳，武佳
Tong Bunian	佟卜年	Ujala	兀扎拉
Tong Chunxiu	佟春秀	Ula	烏喇
Tong Dalaha	佟答剌哈	Urate	吳拉忒
Tong Dali	佟達禮	Ulhan	烏爾漢
Tong Deng	佟登	Usu	烏蘇
Tong Fanca	童凡察	Wan	萬
Tong Guoqi	佟國器	Wanhu fu	萬戶府
Tong Guogang	佟國綱	Wanli period	萬曆時期
Tong Henian	佟鶴年	Wang Gao	王杲
Tong Tulai	佟圖賴	Wang Guoguang	王國光
Tong Yangzhen	佟養正	Wang Shizhen	王士禛
(Tong Yang-		Wang Shun	王舜
zheng, Tung		Wang Tai	王台
Yang-jeng)		Wang-to-lo-shu	王多羅樹
Tong Yangxing	佟養性	Wang T'ung-ling	王桐齡
(Tung		Wang Wenkui	王文奎
Yang-sing)		Wang Wutang	王兀堂
Tong Yangze	佟養澤	Wang Xi	王熙
Tong Ying	佟瑛	Wang Yongyu	王永譽
Tong-zheng si	通政司	Wang Zhonghan	王鍾翰
Tongren	同仁	Wanggiya	完顏
Tungšan	峒山	Wanyan	蜿蜒
Tongshi	通事	Wanyan clan	完顏
Tongshi jiapu	佟氏 家譜	(Wanggiya)	
Tongzhi	同治	Warka	瓦爾喀
Toogiya	陶佳	Warring States	戰國時期
Tsereng	策棱	period	
Tsitsihar	齊齊哈爾	Weisuo	衛所
Tuhai	圖海	*Wen-guan*	文館
tuhere weile	土黑勒威勒	Wo-to-lian	斡朵憐

Wu	吳	Xu Yue	徐月
Wu Chaoqian	吳兆騫	Xuande	宣德
Wu dachen	五大臣	Xuantong	宣統
Wu-liang-ha	兀良哈	Xue Guoyong	薛國用
Wu Sangui	吳三桂	Xue Sancai	薛三才
Wuji	勿吉，渥集,窩集，沃且	Xunfu	巡撫
Wure	烏惹，兀惹，烏舍	Ya	雅
		Yalai	雅懶
Wuying Hall	武英殿	Yan	燕
Wuzhe	兀者	Yang Hao	楊鎬
		Yang Jingshi	楊景時
Xianbei	鮮卑	Yangginu	仰加奴，楊吉砮
Xianbi Chen Tai shuren xinglüe	先妣陳太淑人行略	Yangshao	仰韶
		Yangšu (Yangšiu)	楊書
Xianfeng	咸豐	Yangzhou	揚州
Xianxing zeli	現行則例	Yao Congwu	姚從吾
Xiao Cheng'en	蕭承恩	Yarhū	雅爾湖
Xiao Tong	蕭統	Yatu	雅圖
[Xiao] Yangyuan	[蕭]養元	Yehe	葉赫
Xiao Yongzao	蕭永藻	Yejong	睿宗
Xiao-zhuang	孝莊	Yenden (Hetu Ala)	興京
Xiaojing	孝經	Yengge	英額
Xiaowen	孝文 [帝]	Yeren	野人
Xichao yasong ji	熙朝雅頌集	Yi dynasty	李朝
Xiduan	西團 [山]	Yi Min-hwan	李民寏
Xie Sheng	謝陞	Yi Song-gye	李成桂
Xie Xuan	謝玄	Yi Song-nyong	李星齡
xin	新	Yi Wang	李氵山王
Xin'an	新安	Yilan	依蘭
Xinbin	新賓	Yilou	挹婁
Xing-cheng	興城	Yin	胤
Xingjing	興京	Yin-li	胤禮
Xingkai hu	興凱湖	Yin-lu	胤祿
Xingli jingyi	性理精義	Yin-ti	胤禵
"Xingshu"	行述	Yin-wu	胤䄉
Xiong Tingbi	熊廷弼	Yin-xi	胤禧
Xiongnu	匈奴	Yin-xiang	胤祥
Xiqing	西清	Yin-zhen	胤禛
Xishen	息慎	Yin-zhi	胤祉
Xixing	稀姓	Yiwulü	醫無閭 [山]
xiucai	秀才	Yixian	義縣

Yizheng wang dachen huiyi	議政王大臣會議	Zhao Jie	趙楫
		Zhaohui	兆惠
Yizhou	義州	Zhaoling	昭陵
Yizhou	易州	*Zhaoming wenxuan*	昭明文選
Yong-rong	永瑢		
Yongdian	永甸	Zhaozu yuan-huangdi	肇祖原皇帝
Yongji	永吉		
Yongle	永樂	Zhenbei	鎮北
Yongli	永曆	Zheng-dong yuan-shuai fu	征東元帥府
Yongning si	永寧寺		
Yongping	永平	Zheng Xie	鄭燮
Yongzheng	雍正	Zhihui shi	指揮使
Yŏnsan'gun	燕山君	*zhizhao*	執照
Yŏnwon jikchi	燕轅直指	Zhongguo hua	中國化
Yoto	岳託	Zhong-xiang	中祥
You	尤	Zhou dynasty	周朝
Youfen xian-sheng zhuan	幽憤先生傳	Zhu	朱
		Zhu pi yu zhi	硃批諭旨
Youji	游擊	Zhu Shi	朱軾
Yu	俞	Zhu Youlang	朱由榔
Yu Hae (Liu Hai in Chinese)	劉海	Zhu Yuan-zhang	朱元璋
		zhuanti	篆體
Yuan Conghuan	袁崇煥	Zhuge Liang	諸葛亮
Yuan dynasty	元朝	*zidi shu*	子弟書
Yudie	玉牒	Zizai-zhou	自在州
Yue-duan	岳端	Zongbing guan	總兵官
Yun	允	Zongdu	總督
Yun-duan	蘊端	Zongxue	宗學
Yun Zhu	惲珠	Zu	祖
Yupi dazi	魚皮韃子	Zu Dashou	祖大壽
Yuxuchu	於虛出	Zu Shirong	祖世榮
		Zungar (Dzungar)	準噶爾
Zhang Guangsi	張廣泗	Zuo duyushi	左都御史
Zhang Tao	張濤	Zuo fu duyushi	左副都御史
Zhang Tingyu	張廷玉	Zuo Shiyong	左世永
Zhang Xian-zhong	張獻忠	*zuoling*	佐領
Zhanhe	沾河		
Zhao	趙		

Bibliography

I. Bibliographical Note

This Bibliography includes only the materials cited in the notes or the text. I do not adopt the traditional criteria of "primary" and "secondary" sources, for they are relative terms. Rather, I divide the sources into two categories: basic and monographic. In either case, all sources are interfiled, without regard to their language. The basic category comprises three subdivisions.

- In the first subdivision are archival sources, such as Manchu archives, confidential memorials, and their translations, if any.
- The second subdivision consists of veritable records (*shilu*), dynastic histories—including Tan Qian's *Guoque*—official publications, local histories, and personal accounts of the Ming and Qing periods.
- The last group contains official and private genealogies, most of which pertain to Manchu and Chinese bannermen's families or clans.

In the monographical category are books, articles, and others, such as conference papers and news reports. They cover various subjects relative to the Jurchens, Manchus, and the Qing dynasty, representing the results of international scholarship. For the sake of convenience they are listed alphabetically, without divisions.

In the Bibliography, Chinese, Korean, and Japanese sources are not translated into English, for they are provided with appropriate characters, which scholars and advanced students in the field of Asian studies will understand. German sources are rendered into English, however. Manchu materials are also translated into English unless they are accompanied with Chinese titles or Chinese editions.

A great number of the sources are arranged by authors or compilers. Most archival materials, local histories, government publications, books known usually by their titles, and those whose authors or compilers cannot be identified, are listed by title. Sources referred to in the abbreviated form in the notes appear in the Bibliography as cited, followed by the titles in full. Since some Chinese authors romanize their names using different practices, the Bibliography follows their original forms instead of the *pin-yin* system. Because the Manchus are always mentioned only by given names, I cite their works the same way, such as Orong'an instead of Silin Gioro Orgong'an, unless their clan names appear on the title page.

If a source consists of two or more volumes, the number of volumes is indicated at the end of the entry. The word "volume" stands for 冊 in Chinese.

II. Basic Sources

1. Archival Materials

Baqi dan 八旗檔 consists of many files and subfiles on genealogical, hereditary, service, and others, housed in Number One Historical Archives in Beijing.

Chongde sannian Manwen dang'an yibian 崇德三年滿文檔案譯編. Trans. and comp. Ji Yonghai 季永海 and Liu Jingxian 劉景憲. Shenyang: Liao-Shen shushe, 1988.

CMCT. See *Jiu Manzhou dang.*

Di Cosmo, Nicola, and Dalizhabu Bao. *Manchu-Mongol Relations on the Eve of the Qing Conquest: A Documentary History.* Leiden and Boston: Brill, 2003.

Dong Qichang 董其昌, comp. *Shenmiao [Wanli Reign] liuzhong zoushu huiyao* 神廟 留中奏疏彙要. N.p., Ming period, handwritten, in microfilm, Library of Congress.

Gong-zhong dang: Qianlong chao zouzhe 宮中檔: 乾隆朝奏摺. Taipei: National Palace Museum, 1982–1986, 75 vols. Vol. 1.

Gong-zhong dang: Kangxi chao zouzhe 宮中檔: 康熙朝奏摺. Taipei: National Palace Museum, 1976, 7 vols. in Chinese.

Gong-zhong dang: Yongzheng chao zouzhe 宮中檔: 雍正朝奏摺. Taipei: National Palace Museum, 1977–1980, 27 vols. in Chinese.

Guang Lu 廣祿 and Li Xuezhi 李學智, trans. *Qing Taizu chao lao Manwen yuandang* 清太祖朝老滿文原檔. Taipei: Institute of History and Philology, Academia Sinica, 1970–1971, 2 vols.

Jinliang 金梁. *Manzhou laodang bilu* 滿洲老檔秘錄. Peiping: 1929, 2 vols.

Jiu Manzhou dang 舊滿洲檔. Taipei: National Palace Museum, 1969, 10 vols.

Jiu Manzhou dang yizhu 舊滿洲檔譯註. Taipei: Guoli gugong bowu yuan, 1977–1980, 2 vols., for the years 1627–1630.

Kangxi chao Manwen zhupi zouzhe quanyi 康熙朝滿文硃批奏摺全譯. Trans. and ed.

Zhongguo diyi lishi dang'an guan 中國第一歷史檔案館. Beijing: Zhongguo shehui kexue chuban she, 1996.

Kangxi qiju zhu 康熙起居注. Ed. Zhongguo diyi lishi dang'an guan 中國第一歷史檔
案館. Beijing: Zhonghua Book Company, 1984, 3 vols.

Kangxi yu Luoma shijie guanxi wenshu 康熙與羅馬使節關係文書. Taipei: Taiwan
Xuesheng shuju, 1973. Reprint.

Mambun rōtō 滿文老 檔. Tokyo: The Tōyō bunko, 1955–1963, 7 vols.

Manwen laodang 滿文老 檔. Trans. and annot. *Zhongguo diyi lishi dang'an guan* 中國
第一歷史檔 案館 and *Zhongguo shehui kexue yuan lishi yanjiu suo* 中國社會科學
院歷史研究所. Beijing: Zhonghua Book Company, 1990, 2 vols.

Manzu lishi dang'an ziliao xuanji 滿族歷史檔案資料選輯. Comp. Zhongguo kexue
yuan minzu yanjiu suo Liaoning shaoshu minzu shehui lishi diaocha zu 中國科學
院民族研究所遼寧 少數民族社會歷史調查組. N.p., 1963.

MBRT. See *Mambun rōtō*.

Ming-Qing shiliao 明清史料. Comp. and published by the Institute of History and
Philology, Academia Sinica. Peiping: 1930–1936; Shanghai: 1936-48; Taipei: 1949–
1972, 10 series.

Ming-Qing dang'an 明清檔案 . Ed. Zhang Weiren 張偉仁. Taipei: Institute of History
and Philology, Academia Sinica, 1986–1992, 261 vols. Vol. 1.

Mingdai Liaodong dang'an huibian 明代遼東檔案匯編. Eds. Liaoning sheng dang'an
guan 遼寧省檔案館 and Liaoning sheng shehui kexue yuan lishi yanjiu suo 遼寧
省社會科學院 歷 史研究所. Shenyang: Liao-Shen shushe, 1985, 2 vols.

MLTT. See *Mingdai Liaodong dang'an huibian*.

MWLT. See *Manwen laodang*.

Pan Zhe 潘喆, Sun Fangming 孫方明, and Li Hongbin 李鴻 彬, comps. *Qing ruguan
qian shiliao xuanji* 清入關前史料選輯. Beijing: Chinese People's University Press,
1989.

Qiao Zhizhong 喬治中, ed. *Qingwen qianbian* 清文前編. Beijing: Beijing tushu guan
chuban she, 2000, 6 vols.

Qingchu Nei Guoshi yuan Manwen dang'an yibian 清初內國史院滿文檔案譯編.
Comp. Zhongguo diyi lishi dang'an guan 中國第一歷史檔案館. Beijing: Guang-
ming ribao chuban she, 1989, 3 vols.

Qingdai dang'an shiliao congbian 清代檔案史料叢編, 13 and 14. 1990.

Sheng-jing xingbu yuandang 盛京刑部原檔. Trans. and comp. Zhongguo renmin
daxue Qingshi yanjiu suo 中國人民大學清史研究所 and Zhongguo diyi lishi
dang'an guan 中國第一歷史檔案館. Beijing: Qunzhong chuban she, 1985.

Shiliao congkan chubian 史料叢刊初編, ed. Luo Zhenyu 羅振玉. N.p., Dongfang xuehui, 1924, vols. 2–3.

Yongzheng chao Manwen zhupi zouzhe quanyi 雍正朝滿文硃批奏摺全譯. Trans.
and ed. Zhongguo diyi lishi dang'an guan 中國第一歷史檔案館. Hefei, Anhui:
Huang-shan shushe, 1998, 2 vols.

Zhongguo Mingchao dang'an zonghui 中國明朝檔案總匯. Eds. Zhongguo diyi lishi

dang'an guan 中國第一歷史檔案館 and Liaoning sheng dang'an guan 遼寧省檔
案館. Guilin, Guangxi: Guangxi shifan daxue chuban she, 2001, 101 vols.

2. Documentary Materials, Official Compilations, and Local Histories

Agui 阿桂 et al. *Huang-Qing, kaiguo fanglüe* 皇清開國方略. Taipei: Wenhai chuban
she, 1966. CCST, no. 14, 2 vols.

Agui and Yu Minzhong 于敏中, comps. *Qinding Manzhou yuanliu kao* 欽定滿洲源流
考. Taipei: Wenhai chuban she, 1966. CCST, no. 14, vol. 131.

Baqi tongzhi 八旗通志. Comps. Tiebao 鐵保 et al. Taipei: Taiwan xuesheng shuju,
1968 reprint, 60 vols.

Baqi tongzhi chuji 八旗通志初集. Comps. Ortai 鄂爾泰 et al. Taipei: Taiwan Xuesheng shuju, 1968, reprint, 40 vols.

Baqi tongzhi chuji 八旗通志初集. Comps. Ortai 鄂爾泰 et al. Chang-chun: Dongbei
shifan daxue chuban she, 1985, 8 vols. With punctuation by Li Xun 李洵 and Zhao
Degui 趙德貴.

Bi Gong 畢恭 et al. *Liaodong zhi* 遼東志. Dailien: Liaohai shushe, 1934, Liaohai congshu. Series 2, vols. 1–14.

Cheng Kaihu 程開祜, comp. *Chou-Liao shihua* 籌遼碩畫. Peiping: National Peiping
Library Rare Books, Series 1, 1936, preface dated 1620, 44 vols.

Cho Kyŏng-nam 趙慶男. *Nanjung chamnok* 亂中雜錄 *sok chamnok* 續 雜錄. Seoul:
San-sŏ Nanjung chamnok Publication Office, 1964, 5 vols.

Chŏng In-ji 鄭麟趾. *Koryŏsa* 高麗史. Seoul: Yŏnsei taehakkyo, 1955, 3 vols.

Chosŏn wangjo sillok 朝鮮王朝實錄. Comp. Kuksa P'yonch'an wiwonhoe 國史編纂
委員會. Seoul: T'aeback-san edition, 1955–1958, 48 vols.

Chou-Liao shihua. See Cheng Kaihu.

CSKC. See *Qing shigao jiaozhu*.

CSL. See *Da-Qing lichao shilu*.

CWS. See *Chosŏn wangjo sillok*.

Daicing gurun i Manju yargiyan kooli [for Taizu's reign] 大清滿洲實錄. Taipei: Hualian chuban she, 1964 reprint.

Da-Ming huidian 大明會典. Comps. Li Tongyang 李東陽 et al. Revised by Shen Shixing 申時行 et al. Taipei: Dongnan shubao she, 1964, 5 vols.

Da-Qing lichao shilu 大清歷朝實錄 (Taipei: Hualian chuban she, 1964, reprint,
94 vols.

Dergi hesei wesimbuhe gūsai baita be dahūme gisurefi wesimbuhengge (10 vols.). See
Shangyu qiwu yifu.

Erchen zhuan 貳臣傳. Comp. Qing Guoshi guan 清國史館. Shanghai: Liuyi shuju,
4 vols.

Feng Yuan 馮瑗. *Kaiyuan tushuo* 開原圖說. Ed HLTS, 1941, vols. 26–27.

Fengtian tongzhi 奉天通志. Comps. Wang Shunan 王樹枏, Wu Tingxie 吳廷燮, and
Jin Yufu 金毓黻. Shenyang: Shenyang gujiu shudian, 1982, 5 vols.

Gansu tongzhi 甘肅通志. Comps. Xu Rong 許容 et al. Taipei: Wenhai chuban she, Zhongguo bian-jiang congshu, series 2, 1966, reprint, 6 vols. Vol. 3.

Hanshu 漢書. Comp. Ban Gu 班固. Taipei: SPPY ed., 1965, 8 vols.

Hauer, Eric, trans. *Huang-Qing kaiguo fanglüe* 皇清開國方略. Berlin and Leipzig: Walter de Gruyter, 1926.

He Erjian 何爾健. *An-Liao yudang sugao* 按遼御璫疏稿. Eds. He Ziquan 何兹全 and Guo Liangyu 郭良玉 [Zheng-zhou]: Zhong-zhou shuhua she, 1982.

Hesei yabubuha hacilama wesimbuhe gūsai baita (6 vols.). See *Yuxing qiwu zouyi.*

Jakūn gūsai tung ji sucungga weilehe bithe. See *Baqi tongzhi chuji.*

Jiang Liangqi 蔣良騏. *Donghua lu* 東華錄. Beijing: Zhonghua Book Company, 1980.

Jilin tongzhi 吉林通志. Comps. Chang-shun 長順 et al. Taipei: Wenhai chuban she, 1965, Zhongguo bian-jiang congshu, series 1, 10 vols.

Jinshi 金史. Comp. Tuotuo 脫脫. Taipei: SPPY ed., 1965, 4 vols.

Jinshu 晉書. Comps. Fang Xuanling 房玄齡 et al. Taipei: SPPY ed., 1965, 6 vols.

Kim Kyong-son 金景善. "Yonwon jikchii" 燕轅直指. In *Yŏnhaengnok sonjip* 燕行錄選集. Seoul: Sung Kyun Kwan University, 1960–1962, 2 vols.

Li Fu 李輔. *Quan Liao zhi* 全遼志. Dailian: Liaohai shushe, 1934, Liaohai congshu, series 2, vols. 5–10.

Liaodong zhi. See Bi Gong.

Liaoshi 遼史. Comp. Tuotuo 脫脫. Taipei: SPPY ed., 1965, 2 vols.

Lidai zhiguan biao 歷代職官表. Comps. Ji Yun 紀昀 et al. Taipei: SPPY ed., 1965, vols. 313–16.

Manzhou yuanliu kao. See Agui and Yu Minzhong.

Manzu shehui lishi diaocha 滿族社會歷史調查. In "Minzu wenti wuzhong congshu 民族問題五種叢書." Comp. Liaoning sheng bianji weiyuan hui 遼寧省編輯委員會. Shenyang: Liaoning renmin chuban she, 1985.

Mao Chengdou 毛承斗. *Tong-jiang shujie tangbao jiechao* 東江疏揭塘報節抄 [combined with two other titles]. N.p., Zhejiang guji chuban she, 1966.

Mao Yuanyi 茅元儀. "Dushi jilüe 督師紀略," *Mingshi ziliao congkan* 明史資料叢刊 5 (1986).

Min Jin-wŏn 閔鎮遠. "Yŏnhaengnok" 燕行錄. In *Yŏnhaengnok sonjip* 燕行錄選集. Seoul: Sung Kyun Kwan University, 1960–1962, 2 vols.

Ming shilu 明實錄. Taipei: Institute of History and Philology, Academia Sinica, 1962–1968, 133 vols.

Mingshi 明史. Comps. Zhang Tingyu 張廷玉 et al. Beijing: Zhonghua Book Company, 1974, 28 vols.

MSL. See *Ming shilu.*

Nuer-haqi shilu. See *Qing Taizu Wu Huangdi Nuer-haqi shilu.*

(*Qinding*) *Manzhou jishen jitian dianli* (欽定) 滿洲祭神祭天典禮. Beijing: Palace edition, 1747, 2 vols.

Qinding Rehe zhi 欽定熱河志. Comps. Heshen 和珅 et al. Taipei: Wenhai chuban she, 1966, Zhongguo bian-jiang congshu, series 2, 6 vols.

Qinding Sheng-jing tongzhi 欽定盛京通志. Comps. Lü Yaozeng 呂耀曾 and Song Yun 宋筠. Taipei: Wenhai chuban she, 1965, Zhongguo bian-jiang congshu, series 1, 3 vols.

Qing shigao jiaozhu 清史稿校注. Comp. Qing shigao jiaozhu bianzuan xiaozu 清史稿校注編纂小組. Taipei: Academia Historica, 1986–1991, 16 vols.

Qing shilu 清實錄. Beijing: Zhonghua Book Company, 1986, 60 vols.

Qing Shizong 清世宗. *Enduringge tacihiyan be neileme badaramabuha bithe* (Yong-zheng period). See the same author's *Shengyu guangxun.*

———. *Jianmo bianyi lu* 揀魔辨異錄. Palace edition, 1733, 4 vols.

———. *Shengyu guangxun* 聖諭廣訓. 1724 and other editions.

———. *Yuxuan yulu* 御選語錄. Palace edition, 1733, 14 vols.

Qing Taizu Wu huangdi Nuer-haqi shilu 清太祖武皇帝弩爾哈奇實錄. Peiping: Pal-ace Museum, 1932.

Qinggui 慶桂, Dong Gao 董誥 *et al. Guochao gongshi xubian* 國朝宮史續編. Beijing: Beijing guji chuban she, 1994.

Qingshi liezhuan 清史列傳. Beijing: Zhonghua Book Company, 1987, 20 vols.

Qinzheng pingding shuomo fanglüe 親征平定朔漠方略. Comps. Wenda 溫達 (Unda in Manchu) et al. Beijing: Zangxue chuban she, 1994, reprint of 1708 edition, 2 vols.

Qüan Liao zhi. See Li Fu.

Sanguo zhi 三國志. Comp. Chen Shou 陳壽. Taipei: SPPY ed., 1965, 4 vols.

Shangyu baqi 上諭八旗. Palace edition, c. 1735, 8 vols.

Shangyu neige 上諭內閣. Palace edition, 1741, 32 vols.

Shangyu qiwu yifu 上諭旗務議覆. Yongzheng period, 8 vols.

Shenguan lu 瀋館錄. Taipei: Tailian guofeng chuban she, 1970, Qingshi ziliao 清史資料, series 3, Kaiguo shiliao 開國史料 3. vol. 7. Known as *Simgwannok* in Korean.

Shenyang riji i 瀋陽日記. Taipei: Tailian guofeng chuban she, 1970. Qingshi ziliao 清史資料, series 3, Kaiguo shiliao 開國史料 3. vol. 8. Known as *Simyang ilgi* in Korean.

Shenyang zhuangqi 瀋陽狀啟. Taipei: Tailian guofeng chuban she, 1970. Qingshi ziliao 清史資料, series 3, Kaiguo shiliao 開國史料 3. vol. 7. Known as *Simyang changgye* in Korean.

Shinkan ichiroku 清鑑易知錄. Eds. Murayama Shio 村山芝塢 and Nagane Hyosai 永根冰齋. 1860 ed., 8 vols.

Shunzhi shilu 順治實錄. N.p., handwritten, housed in the Fu Sinian Library, Acade-mia Sinica; n.d., 119 leaves.

Simgwannok. See *Shenguan lu.*

Simyang changgye. See *Shenyang zhuangqi.*

Simyang ilgi. See *Shenyang riji.*

Taidzu hūwangdi ming gurun i cooha be sarhū alin de ambarame efulehe baita be tacibume araha bithe [A record of the defeat of the Ming army by Emperor Taizu at the Battle of Sarhū]. 1776 edition.

Taidzung hūwangdi ming gurun i cooha be sung šan de ambarame efuleme afaha baita be ejeme araha bithe [An account of the defeat of the Ming army by Emperor Taizong at the Battle of Songsan]. Qianlong period.

Tan Qian 談遷. *Guoque* 國榷. Beijing: Guji chuban she, 1958, 6 vols.

TCCC. See *Baqi tongzhi chuji*. Comps. Ortai et al. Taipei: 1968.

TCCC (1985). See *Baqi tongzhi chuji*. Comps. Ortai et al. Chang-chun: 1985.

Wanli bielu 萬曆別錄. Taipei: handwritten, unpaged, housed in the Fu Sinian Library, Academia Sinica, 9 vols.

Wei Zang tongzhi 衛藏通志. Comp. Helin 和寧. Taipei: Wenhai chuban she, 1965. Zhongguo bian-jiang congshu, series 1, 2 vols.

Xiong Tingbi 熊廷弼. *An-Liao shugao* 按遼疏稿. Handwritten, 12 vols. in microfilm, Library of Congress.

Xiqing 西清. *Heilong-jiang waiji* 黑龍江外記. Taipei: Wenhai chuban she, 1968. CCST, no. 6, vol. 59.

Yi Jun 李濬. *Songgye Simyang illok* 松溪 瀋陽日錄. N.p., handwritten, unpaged.

Yi Kung-ik 李肯翊. *Yollyosil kisul pyolchip* 燃藜室記述別集. N.p., handwritten, 1800s.

Yi Min-hwan 李民寏 *Chaam Sŏnsaeng munjip* 紫巖先生文集. N.p., with a postscript dated 1886, 3 vols.

Yi Sŏng-nyŏng 李星齡. *Ch'unp'a dang ilwŏllok* 春坡堂日月錄. Handwritten, 9 vols., housed in Tōyō Bunko, Tokyo.

Yijo sillok 李朝實錄. Tokyo: Gakushūin, Tōyō Bunka Kenkyūjo, 1953–1967, 56 vols.

Yŏnhaengnok sonjip 燕行錄選集. Seoul: Sung Kyun Kuan University, 1960–1962, 2 vols.

Yuanshi 元史. Comp. Song Lian 宋濂. Taipei: SPPY ed., 1965, 10 vols.

Yuxing qiwu zouyi 諭行旗務奏議. Comps. Yun-lu [Yin-lu] 允祿 et al. Palace edition, 4 vols.

Zongguan Neiwufu xianxing zeli 總管內務府現行則例. Peiping: National Peiping Palace Museum, 1937, 7 vols.

3. Genealogical Records

Aixin Gioro zongpu 愛新覺羅宗譜. Comp. Aixin Gioro xiupu chu 愛新覺羅修譜處. Shenyang: 1938, in 8 vols. Vol. 1: *Xingyuan jiqing* 星源集慶.

Baqi Manzhou Niuhulu shi tongpu 八旗滿洲鈕祜祿氏通譜. Comp. Noqin 訥親. Preface dated 1747, handwritten, 12 vols.

Baqi Manzhou shizu tongpu 八旗滿洲氏族通譜. Comps. Ortai 鄂爾泰 and Lü Zhi 呂熾. Palace ed., 1745, 24 vols. Its new printing was made available by Liao-Shen shushe, Shenyang, 1989.

[*Golmin šanggiyan alin*] *Ligiya hala i mukūni dangse* (Genealogical record of the Ligiya Clan [of the Long White Mountains]), 1764, housed in Tōyō bunko, Tokyo, 4 vols.

Guololo shi jiazhuan bing lao baqi tongpu 郭絡羅氏家傳並老八旗通譜. N.p., 1877, handwritten, unpaged (33 sheets).

Guololo shi qichuang fenxing: Ju Zhanhe shan 郭絡羅氏起創奮興: 居沾河山. Beijing? Qing guoshi guan 清國史館, n.d., handwritten, unpaged (17 sheets).

Guololo shi shizong tongpu 郭絡羅氏世宗同譜. N.p., n.d., handwritten, unpaged (26 sheets).

Hesheli shi jiapu 赫舍里氏家譜. Comp. Chang-feng 長豐. Kwangchow: 1874, 2 vols.

Huang shiwu zi duoluo Yuke junwang Yin-wu jiapu 皇十五子多羅愉恪郡王胤禑家譜. Housed in the Fu Sinian Library, Academia Sinica, Taipei, handwritten, unpaged, 2 vols. Vol. 2.

Jakūn gūsai manjusai mukūn hala be uheri ejehe bithe. Palace ed., 1745, 26 volumes. This is the Manchu version of the *Baqi Manzhou shizu tongpu,* as listed above.

Kaiguo zuoyun gongchen Hongyi gong jiapu 開國佐運功臣弘毅公家譜. Comp. Fu-lang 福朗. Handwritten, 1786, 16 vols.

Li Lin 李林, ed. *Manzu jiapu xuanbian* 滿族家譜選編. Shenyang: Liaoning minzu chuban she, 1988.

———. *Manzu zongpu yanjiu* 滿族宗譜研究. Shenyang: Liao-Shen shushe, 1992.

———. Hou Jinbang 侯錦邦 et al. *Benqi xian Manzu jiapu yanjiu* 本溪縣滿族家譜研究 Shenyang: Liaoning minzu chuban she, 1988.

Liushi jiapu 劉氏家譜. Comp. Liu Anguo 劉安國. N.p., 1684, various page numbers.

Majia shi zupu 馬佳氏族譜. Comp. Ma Yanxi 馬延喜 et al. Peiping [?]: Jinghua yinshu ju, preface dated 1927, 5 vols.

Nayin Fucha shi puzhuan 訥殷富察氏譜傳. Comps. Fu Qishu 富啟書 et al. N.p.: preface dated 1807.

Nayin Fucha shi zengxiu zhipu 訥殷富察氏增修支譜. Comp. Dexing 德馨. 1889–1890, handwritten.

Orong'an 鄂容安. "Xiangqin bo Owenduan gong nianpu 襄勤伯鄂文端公年譜." *Qingshi ziliao* 清史資料 2 (1981).

STTP. See *Baqi Manzhou shizu tongpu.*

Songshen 嵩申, ed. *Changbai Wanyan shi jiude lu* 長白完顏氏舊德錄. c. 1880s, in 3 vols. Vol. 2: "*Beiming* 碑銘."

Taizong Wen huangdi weixia diyi zi heshi Wusu qinwang zhi nüsun 太宗文皇帝位下第一子和碩武肅親王之女孫. Housed in the Tōyō bunko, Tokyo, handwritten, unpaged.

Taizu Gao huangdi weixia heshi Ruizhong qinwang zhi zisun 太祖高皇帝位下和碩睿忠親王之子孫. Handwritten, housed in the Tōyō bunko, Tokyo, unpaged, 3 vols. Vol. 3.

Tang Bangzhi 唐邦治. *Qing huangshi sipu* 清皇室四譜. Taipei: CCST, Series 8, 1966, vol. 71.

Tong Guoqi 佟國器. Xiang-ping Youfen xian-sheng lu 襄平幽憤先生錄. Kanzhou: Kiangsi: Office of the Governor, 1656, 4 vols. Various page numbers. Housed in the Nanking Library.

Wuqing tang chongxiu Caoshi zongpu 五慶堂重修曹氏宗譜. Generally known as *Cao Xueqin jiapu* 曹雪芹家譜. Beijing: Yanshan chuban she, 1990, unpaged.

Wuya shi zupu 烏雅氏族譜. Anonymous compiler. N.p., late Qing period, handwritten, 4 vols., unpaged.

Xiang huangqi Niuhulu shi Hongyi gong jiapu 鑲黃旗滿洲鈕祜祿氏弘毅公家譜. Comp. Aligun 阿里袞. 1765, 10 vols.

Xiang huangqi Manzhou Niuhulu shi Hongyi gong jiapu 鑲黃旗滿洲鈕祜祿氏弘毅公家譜. Handwritten, 1798, 15 vols.

Xingyuan jiqing. See *Aixin Gioro zongpu.*

Xinxiu Fucha shi zhipu 新修富察氏支譜. Comps. Zhale-hali 扎勒哈哩 and Muke-dengbu 穆克登布. Wuchang: 1908, 3 vols.

Yehe Nalan shi baqi zupu 葉赫那蘭氏八旗族譜. Comp. Etenge 額騰額. N.p., handwritten, unpaged, 1823.

Zhangshi jiapu 張氏家譜. Comps. Zhang Chaolin 張朝璘 and Zhang Chaozhen 張朝珍. Preface dated 1679.

Zheng hongqi Manzhou Hada Guaerjia shi jiapu 正紅旗滿洲哈達瓜爾佳氏家譜. Comp. 恩齡. Preface dated 1849, in 8 vols.

Zheng huangqi Neiwu fu Manzhou san jiala Ancun zuoling xia Huifa Sakeda shi jiapu 正黃旗內務府滿洲三甲喇安存佐領下輝發薩克達氏家譜. N.p.: preface dated 1898.

Zushi jiapu 祖氏家譜. Comp. Zu Jianji 祖建極. N.p.: 1707, rev. ed., handwritten, 8 vols., unpaged.

III. Monographic Works

Abe Takeo 安部健夫. "Hakki Manshū niru no kenkyū" 八旗滿洲牛条の研究. *Tōa jimbun gakuhō* 東亞人文學報 1.4 (February 1942); 2.2 (July 1942).

———. "Hakki Manshū niru no kenkyū—tokuni Temmei shoki no niru ni okeru jōbu jin teki kōzō—kōshi no hen" 八旗滿洲ニルの研究—とくに天命初期のニルにおはる上部人的構造—甲士の篇. *Tōhō gakuhō* 東方學報. Kyoto, 20 (1951).

———. *Shindai shi no kenkyū* 清代史の研究. Tokyo: Sōbunsha, 1971.

Aixin Gioro Ying-sheng 愛新覺羅瀛生. *Lao Beijing yu Manzu* 老北京與滿族. Beijing: Xueyuan chuban she, 2005.

Anami Korehiro 阿南惟敬. "Shin no Taisō no Kokuryūkō seitō ni tsuite" 清の太宗の黑龍江征討について. *Bōei Daigakkō kiyō* 防衛大學紀要 6 (1962).

———. "Tensō ku-nen no Mōko hakki seiritsu ni tsuite" 天聰九年の蒙古八旗成立について. *Rikishi kyōiku* 歷史教育 13.4 (1965).

Athenaeum, a literary weekly published in London (November 26, 1898): 747 (3rd column); (September 28, 1899): 414 (2nd column).

Bai Shouyi 白壽彝, ed. *Qingshi guoji xueshu taolun hui lunwen ji* 清史國際學術討論會論文集. Shenyang: Liaoning renmin chuban she, 1990.

Bai Xinliang 白新良, ed. *Kangxi huangdi quan-zhuan* 康熙皇帝全傳. Beijing: Xueyuan chuban she, 1994.

Barfield, Thomas J. *The Perilous Frontier: Nomadic Empires and China*. Cambridge, MA: Basil Blackwell, 1989.

Bartlett, Beatrice S. "Books of Revelations: The Importance of the Manchu Language Archival Record Books for Research on Ch'ing History," *Late Imperial China* 6.2 (1985).

———. *Monarchs and Ministers: The Grand Council in Mid-Ch'ing China, 1723–1820*. Berkeley: University of California Press, 1991.

Bawden, C. R. "The Mongol Rebellion of 1756–1757," *Journal of History* 2.3 (1968).

Beijing tushu guan guji zhenben congkan 北京圖書館古籍珍本叢刊. Ed. Beijing tushu guan guji chuban bianji zu 出版編輯組. Beijing: Shumu wenxin chuban she, 1987. Vol. 11: "Liaoshi shu 遼事述."

Bi Zisu 畢自肅. *Liaodong shugao* 遼東疏稿. CCST xubian, Series 64, 1979, vol. 631.

Bo Weiyi 卜維義 and Sun Peiren 孫丕任, eds. *Kangxi shixuan* 康熙詩選. Shenyang: Chunfeng wenyi chuban she, 1984.

Bodde, Derk, and Clarence Morris, *Law in Imperial China: Exemplified by 190 Ch'ing Dynasty Cases, Translated from the Hsin-an hui-lan. With Historical, Social, and Juridical Commentaries*. Cambridge, MA: Harvard University Press, 1967.

Bol, Peter K. " Seeking Common Ground: Han Literati under Jurchen Rule," *Harvard Journal of Asiatic Studies* 47.2 (1987).

Cai Meibiao 蔡美彪. "Da-Qing guo jianhao qian di guohao, zuming, yu jinian" 大清國建號前的國號, 族名, 與記年. *Lishi yanjiu* 歷史研究 3 (1987).

The Cambridge History of China, Volume 6: Alien Regimes and Border States, 907–1368. Eds. Herbert Franke and Denis Twitchett. Cambridge and New York: Cambridge University Press, 1994.

The Cambridge History of China, Volume 10: *Late Ch'ing, 1800–1911*, Part 1. Eds. Denis Twitchett and John K. Fairbank. Cambridge and New York: Cambridge University Press, 1978.

The Cambridge History of Early Inner Asia. Ed. Denis Sinor. Cambridge and New York: Cambridge University Press, 1990.

Cammann, Schuyler, "Origins of the Court and Official Robes of the Ch'ing Dynasty," *Artibus Asiae* 12 (1949).

CCST. Jindai Zhongguo shiliao congkan, 近代中國史料叢刊, comp. Shen Yunlong 沈雲龍. Taipei, Wenhai chuban she, in various series and dates.

Chan, Albert. *The Glory and Fall of the Ming Dynasty*. Norman, OK: University of Oklahoma Press, 1982.

Chan, Hok-lam. *Legitimation in Imperial China*. Seattle: University of Washington Press, 1984.

Chan, Wing-ming. "The Qianlong Emperor's New Strategy in 1775 to Commend Late Ming Loyalists," *Asia Major*, third series, 13.1 (2000).

Chang, Kwang-chih. "A Classification of Shang and Chou Myths (Abridgement)," *Bulletin of the Institute of Ethnology, Academia Sinica* 14 (1962).

———. "Neolithic Cultures of the Sungari Valley, Manchuria," *Southwestern Journal of Anthropology* 17.1 (1961).

Chang Kwang-chih 張光直. "Dongbei di shiqian wenhua" 東北的史前文化. In Institute of History and Philology, Academia Sinica, and Chinese Ancient History Editorial Committee, *Zhongguo shanggu shi daiding gao* 中國上古史待定稿, vol. 1: *Shiqian bufen* 史前部分. Taipei: Academia Sinica, 1972.

Chase, Hanson. "The Status of the Manchu Language in the Early Ch'ing," Ph.D. dissertation, University of Washington, 1979.

Chen Bolin 陳伯霖. "Shilun Dahai" 試論達海. *Heilong-jiang wenwu congkan* 黑龍江文物叢刊 4 (1987).

Ch'en, Chieh-hsien. "The Decline of the Manchu Language in China during the Ch'ing Period (1644–1911)." In Walther Hessig, ed., *Altaica Collecta; Berichte und Vorträge der XVII Permanent International Altaistic Conference,* 38 June 1974 in Bonn and Honnef. Wiesbaden: Harrassowitz, 1976.

Ch'en Chieh-hsien 陳捷先. *Manzhou congkao* 滿洲 叢考. Taipei: College of the Arts, National Taiwan University, 1963.

———. "Cong Qingchu zhong-yang jianzhi kan Manzhou Hanhua" 從清初中央建置看滿洲漢化. In *Jindai Zhongguo chuqi lishi yantao hui lunwen ji* 近代中國初期歷史研討會論文集. Ed. The Institute of Modern History, Academia Sinica. Taipei: Institute of Modern History, Academia Sinica, 1980, 2 vols.

Chen Guiying 陳桂英. "Yue-duan yu 'nan Hong bei Kong'" 岳端與 "南洪北孔." *MANT* 4 (1991).

Chen Jiahua 陳佳華. "Baqi zhidu yanjiu shulüe" 八旗制度研究述略. *SHKH* 5 (1984); 6 (1984).

Chen Jinzhao 陳錦釗. "Zidi shu zhi zuojia jiqi zuopin" 子弟書之作家及其作品. *Zhongguo shumu jikan* 中國書目季刊 12.1–2 (1978).

Chen Kejin 陳克進 and Teng Shaozhen 滕紹箴. "Lüelun Huang-taiji di lishi zuoyong" 略論皇太極 的歷史作用, *SHKH* 2 (1982).

Chen Qi 陳 祺. "Mingdai Liaodong mashi jiqi lishi ying-xiang" 明代遼東馬市及其歷史影響. *Dongbei shida xuebao* 東北師大學報 (*Zhexue shehui kexue ban* 哲學社會科學版) 1 (1987).

Chen Shu 陳述. "Liaodai jiaoyu shi lunzheng." 遼代教育史論証. In Chen Shu, ed. *Liao-Jin shi lunji* 遼金史論集. Shanghai: Shanghai guji chuban she, 1987.

Chen Wan 陳浣. "Shi Tingzhu shiji yu jiashi jikao" 石廷柱事跡與家世輯考. *Qingshi yanjiu tongxin* 清史研究 通 訊 2 (1986).

Ch'en Wen-shih 陳文石. "The Creation of the Manchu Niru," *Chinese Studies in History* 14.4 (1981).

———. *Ming-Qing zhengzhi shehui shilun* 明清政治社會史論. Taipei: Taiwan xuesheng shuju, 1991, 2 vols.

Chen Yinke 陳寅恪. *Liu Rushi biezhuan* 柳如是別傳. Shanghai: Shanghai guji chuban she, 1980, 3 vols.

Chen Yuan 陳垣. *Liyun shuwu congke* 勵耘書屋叢刻. Beijing: Beijing shifan daxue chuban she, 1982, 3 vols.

Chia, Ning. "The Lifanyuan and the Inner Asian Rituals in the Early Qing (1644–1795)," *Late Imperial China* 14.1 (1993): 60–92.

Chiu Ling Yeong 趙令揚 (Zhao Lingyang). "Ji Mingdai Huitong guan" 記明代會同館. *Dalu zazhi* 大陸雜誌 4.5 (September 15, 1970).

Ch'ü, T'ung-tsu. *Law and Society in Traditional China*. Paris and La Haye: Mouton, 1965.

CKMT. See Wang Zhonghan, ed. *Zhongguo minzu shi*. CLST. *Jilin shida xuebao: Shehui kexue ban* 吉林師大學報: 社會科學版.

Cong. "Chishu zhizheng." See Cong Peiyuan. "Mingtai Nüzhen di chishu zhizheng."

Cong Peiyuan 叢佩遠. *Hūlun sibu xing-cheng gaishu* 扈倫四部形成概述. *MTYC* 2 (1984).

———. "Hūlun sibu shixi kaosuo" 扈倫四部世系考索. *KHCH* 2 (1984).

———. "Mingdai Liaodong juntun" 明代遼東軍屯. *Zhongguo shi yanjiu* 中國史研究 3 (1985).

———. "Mingdai Nüzhen di chishu zhizheng" 明代女真的敕書之爭, *Wenshi* 文史 26 (1986).

Corradini, Piero. "Civil Administration at the Beginning of the Manchu Dynasty," *Oriens Extremus* 9.2 (1962).

Cressey, George Barcock, *China's Geographical Foundations: A Survey of the Land and Its People*. New York and London: McGraw-Hill, 1934.

Crossley, Pamela Kyle. *The Manchus*. Cambridge, MA: Blackwell, 1997.

———. *Orphan Warriors: Three Manchu Generations and the End of the Qing World*. Princeton: Princeton University Press, 1990.

———. "Thinking about Ethnicity in Early Modern China," *Late Imperial China* 11.1 (1990).

———. "The Tong in Two Worlds: Cultural Identities in Liaodong and Nurgan during the 13th–17th Centuries," *Ch'ing-shih wen-t'i* 4.9 (1983).

———. *A Translucent Mirror: History and Identity in Qing Imperial Ideology*. Berkeley, Los Angeles, and London: University of California Press, 1999.

Crossley, Pamela Kyle, and Evelyn S. Rawski. "A Profile of the Manchu Language in Ch'ing History," *Harvard Journal of Asiatic Studies* 53.1 (1993).

Curtin, Philip D. *The Rise and Fall of the Plantation Complex: Essays in Atlantic History*. Cambridge and New York: Cambridge University Press, 1990.

Dardess, John W. *Conquerors and Confucians*. New York and London: Columbia University Press, 1973.

de Crespigny, R. R. C. *China: The Land and Its People*. New York: St. Martin's, 1971.

De Vos, George A. "Ethnic Pluralism: Conflict and Accommodation." In Lola Romanucci-Ross and George A. De Vos, eds., *Ethnic Identity: Creation, Conflict, and Accommodation*. Walnut Creek, CA: AltaMira Press, 3rd ed., 1995.

Di Cosmo, Nicola. "Manchu Shamanic Ceremonies at the Qing Court." In Joseph P. McDermott, ed., *State and Court Ritual in China*. Cambridge and New York: Cambridge University Press, 1999.

———. "Qing Colonial Administration in Inner Asia," *International History Review* 20.2 (1998).

Di Cosmo, Nicola, and Don J. Wyatt, eds. *Political Frontiers, Ethnic Boundaries, and Human Geographies in Chinese History*. London and New York: RoutledgeCurzon, 2003.

Diao-shang yugong 苕上愚 公 (also Mao Ruizheng 茅瑞徵). *Dongyi kaolüe* 東夷考略. HLTS, 1941. Vols 94–95.

Dictionary of Ming Biography, 1368–1644. Eds L. Carrington Goodrich and Chaoying Fang. New York and London: Columbia University Press, 1976, 2 vols.

Ding Yizhuang 定宜莊. *Qingdai baqi zhufang zhidu yanjiu* 清代八旗駐 防制度研究. Tianjin: Tianjin guji chuban she, 1992.

DMB. See *Dictionary of Ming Biography, 1368–1644*.

Dong Wanlun 董萬崙. *Qing Zhaozu zhuan* 清肇祖傳. Shenyang: Liaoning renmin chuban she, 1991.

Dongyi kaolüe. See Diao-shang yugong.

Du Jiaji 杜家驥. "Qingdai huangzu yu Meng-Han guizu lianyin di zhidu he zuoyong" 清代皇族與蒙漢貴族聯姻的制度和作用. *Nankai xuebao: Zhexue shehui kexue ban* 南開學報：哲學社會科學版 4 (1990).

———. "Manzu ruguan qianhou zhi quming ji xiang-guan zhu wenti fenxi" 滿族入關 前後之取名及相關諸問題分析. *Manxue yanjiu* 滿族研究 2 (1994).

Du Ruo 杜若. "Manzu di jushi yu jianzhu" 滿族的居室與建築. *MANT* 2 (1992).

Duncan, John. "The Social Background to the Founding of the Chosŏn Dynasty: Change or Continuity?" *Journal of Korean Studies* 6 (1988–1989).

Duara, Praserjit. "Superscribing Symbols: The Myth of Guandi, Chinese God of War," *Journal of Asian Studies* 47.4 (1988).

Durrant, Stephen. "Sino-Manchu Translations at the Mukden Court," *Journal of the American Oriental Society* 99.4 (1979).

———. "Repetition in the Manchu Origin Myth as a Feature of Oral Narrative," *Central Asiatic Journal* 22.1–2 (1978).

ECCP. *Eminent Chinese of the Ch'ing Period (1644–1912)*. Ed. Arthur W. Hummel. Washington, DC: Government Printing Office, 1943–1944, 2 vols.

Ejima Hisao 江島壽雄. "Anraku Jizai nishū ni tsuite" 安樂自在二州に就て. *Shien* 史淵 48 (1951).

———. "Mimmatsu Ryōtō no goshijō" 明末遼東 の互市場. *Shien* 史淵 90 (1963).

———. "Min Seitōki ni okeru Jochoku chōkō no seigen" 明正統期に於ける女直朝貢の制限. *Tōyō shigaku* 東洋史學 6 (1952).

———. "Mindai Jochoku chōkō bōeki no gaikan" 明代女直朝貢貿易の概觀. *Shien* 史淵 77 (1958).

———. "Minsho Jochoku chōkō ni kansuru nisan no mondai" 明初女直朝貢に關する 二 三 の 問 題. *Shien* 史淵 58 (1953).

Eller, Jack David. *From Culture to Ethnicity to Conflict: An Anthropological Perspective on International Ethnic Conflict.* Ann Arbor: University of Michigan Press, 1999.

Elliott, Mark C. "The Limits of Tartary: Manchuria in Imperial and National Geographies," *Journal of Asian Studies* 59.3 (2000).

———. "The Manchu-Language Archives of the Qing Dynasty and the Origins of the Palace Memorial System," *Late Imperial China* 22.1 (2002).

———. *The Manchu Way: The Eight Banners and Ethnic Identity in Late Imperial China.* Stanford: Stanford University Press, 2001.

———. "Manchu Widows and Ethnicity in Qing China," *Comparative Studies in Society and History* 41.1 (1999).

Encyclopedia Americana. Danbury, CT: Grolier, 2003, International ed., 30 vols.

The Encyclopedia of the Social Sciences. New York: Macmillan Company, 1935, 15 vols. Vol. 6.

Fairbank, John King, and Ssu-yu Teng. *Ch'ing Administration: Three Studies.* Cambridge: Harvard University Press, 1960.

Fan Jingwen 范景文. *Zhaodai wugong bian* 昭代武功編. Bingbu ban 兵部版 (1638– 1642).

Fan Zhui-zheng 范垂正, "Wu Zhaoqian nianpu" 吳兆騫年譜. *Heilong-jiang wenwu congkan* 黑龍江文物叢刊 2 (1984).

Fang Chaoying 房兆楹. "Qingchu Manzhou jiating lidi fenjiazi he wei fenjiazi" 清 初滿洲家庭裡的分家子和未分家子. *Guoli Beijing daxue wushi zhounian jinian lunwen ji* 國立北京大學五十週年紀念論文集. Peiping: Beijing University Press, 1948. College of Arts, no. 3.

Fang Kongzhao 方孔炤. *Quanbian lüeji* 全邊略記. Peiping: National Peiping Library, 1930, 6 vols.

Fang Yan 方衍, ed. *Heilong jiang shaoshu minzu jianshi* 黑龍江少數民族簡史. Beijing: Central College of Nationalities Press, 1993.

Farquhar, David M. "Mongolian versus Chinese Elements in the Early Manchu State," *Ch'ing-shih wen-t'i* 2.6 (1971).

Feng Erkang 馮爾康. *Yongzheng zhuan* 雍正傳. Beijing: Renmin chuban she, 1985.

Feng Jichang 馮季昌. "Mingdai Liaodong dusi jiqi weisuo jianzhi kaobian" 明代遼東 都司及其衛所建置考辨. *Lishi dili* 歷史地理 14 (1998).

Fletcher, Joseph. "Ch'ing Inner Asia c. 1800." In Denis Twitchett and John K. Fairbank, eds., *The Cambridge History of China, Volume 10: Late Ch'ing, 1800–1911, Part 1.* New York: Cambridge University Press, 1978.

Franke, Herbert. *China under Mongol Rule.* Brookfield, VT: Variorum, 1994.

———. "The Forest Peoples of Manchuria: Kitans and Jurchens." In Denis Sinor, ed., *The Cambridge History of Early Inner Asia.* New York: Cambridge University Press, 1990.

Franke, Herbert and Hok-lam Chan, *Studies on the Jurchens and the Chin Dynasty* (Aldershot, Hampshire, Great Britain: Ashgate Publishing Limited, 1997).

Franke, Wolfgang, comp. *An Introduction to the Sources of Ming History*. Kuala Lumpur: University of Malaya Press, 1968.

Fu Bo 傅波, ed. *Manzu Tongjia shi yanjiu* 滿族佟佳氏研究. Shenyang: Liaodong minzu chuban she, 2003.

Fu Bo 傅波, Bian Zuoqing 邊佐卿, and Wang Pinglu 王平魯. "Mingmen wangzu Tongjia shi, aiguo Qinmin yu Zhonghua" 名門望族佟佳氏, 愛國親民譽中華. In Fu, *Manzu Tongjia shi yanjiu* 滿族佟佳氏研究. Shenyang: Liaoning minzu chuban she, 2003.

Fu Kedong 傅克東 and Chen Jiahua 陳佳華. "Qingdai qianqi di zuoling" 清代前期的佐領. *KHCH* 5 (1982).

Fu Langyun 傅朗云 and Yang Yang 楊暘. *Dongbei minzu shilüe* 東北民族史略. Chang-chun: Jilin renmin chuban she, 1983.

Fu Sinian 傅斯年. *Fu Meng-zhen xian-sheng ji* 傅孟真先生集. Taipei: National Taiwan University, 1952, 6 vols.

Fu Yangyang 傅洋洋. "Manzu Tongshi xingshi xing-cheng zai tan" 滿族佟氏姓氏形成再探. In Fu Bo, *Manzu Tongjia shi yanjiu*. Shenyang: Liaoning minzu chuban she, 2003.

Fu Yueguang 富育光 and Meng Huiying 孟彗英. *Manzu saman jiao yanjiu* 滿 族薩滿教研究. Beijing: Beijing daxue chuban she, 1991.

Fucha Dunchong 富察敦崇. *Yanjing suishi ji* 燕京歲時記. Beijing: Beijing chuban she, 1961, as the second part of the volume.

Fuchs, Walter. "Fan Wencheng 范文程, 1597–1666, und sein Diplom (誥命)," *Shigaku kenkyū* 史學研究 10.3 (1939).

Fuge 福格. *Tingyu congtan* 聽雨叢談. Hong Kong: Longmen shudian, 1969.

Gan Xi 甘熙. *Baixia suoyan* 白下瑣言. Nanking: 1926, reprint of the Gan Family, 4 vols.

Gan Zhigeng 干志耿 and Sun Xiuren 孫秀仁. *Heilong jiang gudai minzu shigang* 黑龍江古代民族史綱. Harbin: Heilong jiang renmin chuban she, 1986.

Gedalacia, David, "Wu Ch'eng and the Perpetuation of the Classical Heritage in the Yuan." In John D. Langlois, Jr., ed., *China under Mongol Rule*. Princeton: Princeton University Press, 1981.

Gernet, Jacques. *A History of Chinese Civilization*. Trans. J. R. Foster. Cambridge and New York: Cambridge University Press, 1982.

Gimm, Martin. *Kaiser Qianlong (1711–1799) als Poet: Anmerkungen zu seinem schriftstellerischen Werk* [Emperor Qianlong (1711–1799) as poet: Comments on his literary work]. Stuttgart: Steiner, 1993.

———. "Manchu Translations of Chinese Novels and Short Stories: An Attempt at an Inventory," *Asia Major* 1.2 (1988).

Gong Wang 公望. "Yongzheng huangdi di shiwen" 雍正皇帝的詩文. *SHKH* 1 (1990).

Gorelova, Liliya M. "Manchu-Chinese Syntactical Parallels," *Acta Orientalia Academiae Scientiarum Hungaricae* 50 (1997).

Grousset, René. *The Empire of the Steppes: A History of Central Asia*. Trans. Naomi Walford. New Brunswick, NJ: Rutgers University Press, 1970.

Grupper, Samuel Martin. "The Manchu Imperial Cult of the Early Ch'ing Dynasty: Text and Studies on the Tantric Sanctuary of Mahakala at Mukden." Ph.D. dissertation, Indiana University, 1980.

Guan Donggui 管東貴. "Guanyu Manzu Hanhua wenti di yijian ditaolun" 關於滿族漢化問題的意見的討論. *Dalu zazhi* 大陸雜誌 40.3 (1970).

———. "Manzu ruguan qian di wenhua fazhan dui tamen houlai Hanhua di yingxiang" 滿族入關前的文化發展對他們後來漢化的影響. *Bulletin of the Institute of History and Philology, Academia Sinica* 40.1 (1968).

———. "Manzu di ruguan yu Hanhua" 滿族的入關與漢化. *Bulletin of the Institute of History and Philology, Academia Sinica* 43.3 (1971).

Guan Jialu 關嘉祿. "Qingchao kaiguo xunchen Fei-ying-dong jianlun" 清朝開國勳臣費英東 簡論. *Gugong bowu yuan yuankan* 故宮博物院院刊 1 (1985).

Guan Jixin 關紀新 and Meng Xianren 孟憲仁. "Manzu yu Shenyang yu, Beijing yu" 滿族與瀋陽語, 北京語. *MANT* 1 (1987).

Guan Kexiao 關克笑 and Wang Peihuan 王佩環. "Manyu-wen di xing-shuai ji lishi yiyi." 滿語文的興衰及歷史意義. In *Qingzhu Wang Zhonghan xian-sheng bashi shouchen xueshu lunwen ji* 慶祝王鍾翰先生八十壽辰學術論文集. Ed. Qingzhu Wang Zhonghan xian-sheng bashi shouchen xueshu lunwen ji weiyuan hui 委員會. Shenyang: Liaoning daxue chuban she, 1993.

Guan Wenfa 關文發, and Yan Guangwen 嚴廣文. *Mingdai zhengzhi zhidu yanjiu* 明代政治制度研究. Beijing: Zhongguo shehui kexue chuban she, 1995.

Guang Lu 廣祿 and Li Xuezhi 李學智. "Qing Taizu 'Lao Manwen yuandang' yu 'Manwen laodang' zhi bijiao yanjiu" 清太祖 '老滿文原檔' 與 '滿文老檔' 之比較研究. *Zhongguo Dongya xueshu yanjiu jihua weiyuan hui nianbao* 中國東亞學術研究計劃委員會年報 4 (1965).

Guo Cheng-kang 郭成康. "Lun Wenguan Han ruchen jiqi dui Qingchu zhengzhi di ying-xiang 論文館漢孺臣及其對清初政治的影響. *Dongbei difang shi yanjiu* 東北地方史研究 1 (1986).

———. "Yetan Manzu Hanhua" 也談滿族漢化. *Qingshi yanjiu* 清史研究 2 (2000).

Guo Songyi 郭松義. "Lun Ming-Qing shiqi di Guan Yu congbai" 論明清時期的關羽崇拜. *Zhongguo shi yanjiu* 中國史研究 3 (1990).

Guy, R. Kent. *The Emperor's Four Treasuries: Scholars and the State in the Late Ch'ien-lung Era* (Cambridge, MA: Council on East Asian Studies, Harvard University, 1987).

Haneda Torū 羽田亨. *Manwa jiten* 滿和辭典. Taipei: Xuehai chuban she, 1974, reprint.

Hatada Takashi 旗田巍. "Manshū hakki no seiritsu katei ni kansuru ichi kōsatsu—tokuni niru no seiritsu ni tsuite "滿洲八旗の 成立過程 に關する一考察一特 に 牛条の 成立について. *Tōa ronsō* 東亞論叢, 2 (1940).

———. "Mindai Joshinjin no tekki ni tsuite" 明代女真人の鐵器について. *Tōhō Gakuhō*, Tokyo 東方學報, 東京 11.1 (1940).

Hauer, Eric. "Prinz Dorgon," *Ostasiatische Zeitschrift* 13 (1926).

He Puying 何溥瀅 and Xie Zhaohua 謝肇華. "Lun Huang taiji di minzu yiti sixiang." 論皇太極的民族一體思想. *MANT* 3 (1990).

Heilong jiang sheng bowu guan 黑龍江省博物館. "Dongkang yuanshi shehui yizhi fajue baogao." 東康原始社會遺址發掘報告. *Kaogu* 考古 3 (1975).

Heuschert, Dorothea, "Legal Pluralism in the Qing Empire: Manchu Legislation for the Mongols," *International History Review*, 20.2 (1998).

HLCM. See Gan Zhigeng and Sun Xiuren.

HLTS. See Xuanlan tang congshu 玄覽堂叢書. Comp. Zheng Zhenduo 鄭振鐸. N.p., The Zheng Family photo-lithographic edition, 1941, 120 vols.

Ho, Ping-ti. "In Defense of Sinicization: A Rebuttal of Evelyn Rawski's 'Reenvisioning the Qing,'" *Journal of Asian Studies* 57.1 (1998).

———. "The Significance of the Ch'ing Period in Chinese History," *Journal of Asian Studies* 26.2 (1967).

Honey, David B. "Stripping off Felt and Fur: An Essay on Nomadic Sinification." *Papers on Inner Asia*. Bloomington, IN: Research Institute for Asian Studies, Indiana University 21, 1992.

Hong Ik-han 洪翼漢. *Huap'o sōnsaeng yugo* 花浦先生遺稿. N.p., postscript dated 1709, 4 vols.

Hosie, Alexander. *Manchuria: Its People, Resources, and Recent History*. Boston and Tokyo: Millet Company, 1910.

Hou Shou-chang 侯壽昌. "Qianlun Tong Yangxing" 淺論佟養性. *Lishi dang'an* 歷史檔案 2 (1986).

Hsi, Angela N. S. "Wu San-kuei in 1644: A Reappraisal," *Journal of Asian Studies* 34.2 (1975).

Hsiao, Ch'i-ch'ing. *The Military Establishment of the Yüan Dynasty*. Cambridge: Council on East Asian Studies, Harvard University, 1978.

Hsiao, Kung-chuan. *Rural China: Imperial Control in the Nineteenth Century*. Seattle and London: University of Washington Press, 1960.

Hu Zhiyu 胡祇遹. *Zishan daquan ji* 紫山大全集. Beijing: Zhongguo shudian, 1990, Sanyi tang congshu 三怡堂叢書. Ed. Zhang Fengtai 張鳳台. Vols. 51–60.

Hua Li 華立. "Qingdai di Man-Meng lianyin" 清代的滿蒙婚姻. *MTYC* 2 (1983).

Huang, Chin-shing. *Philosophy, Philology, and Politics in Eighteenth-Century China: Li Fu and the Lu-Wang School under the Ch'ing*. New York: Cambridge University Press, 1995.

Huang Daozhou 黃道周. *Bowu dianhui* 博物典彙. Preface dated 1635, 6 vols. Vol. 6.

Huang-Ming siyi kao. See Zheng Xiao.

Huang, Pei. *Autocracy at Work: A Study of the Yung-cheng Period, 1723-1735*. Bloomington, IN: Indiana University Press, 1974.

———. "Five Major Sources for the Yung-cheng Period, 1723–1735," *Journal of Asian Studies* 27.4 (1968).

———. "Monarchy and Aristocracy during the Early Ch'ing Dynasty (1644–1735)." In Graciela de la Lama, ed., *China*. Mexico City: El Colegio de Mexico, 1982.

———. "New Light on the Origins of the Manchus," *Harvard Journal of Asiatic Studies* 50.1 (1990).

Huang Pei 黃培. "Qingchu di Manzhou guizu: Hunyin yu kaiguo" 清初的滿洲貴族: 婚姻與開國 (1583–1661). In Tao Xisheng xian-sheng jiuzhi rongqing zhushou lunwen ji bianji weiyuan hui 陶希聖先生九秩榮慶祝壽論文集編輯委員會, ed., *Tao Xisheng xian-sheng jiuzhi rongqing zhushou lunwen ji* 祝壽論文集. Taipei: Shihuo chuban she, 1988, 2 vols. Vol. 2.

Huang Pei 黃培 and Tao Jing-shen 陶晉生, eds. *Deng Siyu xian-sheng xueshu lunwen xuanji* 鄧嗣禹先生學術論文選集. Taipei: Shihuo chuban she, 1980.

Huang, Ray. "The Liao-tung Campaign of 1619," *Oriens Extremus* 28.1 (1981).

Huang Xihui 黃錫惠. "Manyu diming fanyi di yuyuan, yinbian wenti" 滿語地名翻譯的語源、音變問題. *Manyu yanjiu* 滿語研究 2 (1991).

Huang Zhang-jian 黃彰健. "Qing Taizu Tianming jianyuan kao" 清太祖天命建元考, *Bulletin of the Institute of History and Philology, Academia Sinica* 37.2 (1967).

Hucker, Charles O. *The Censorial System of Ming China*. Stanford: Stanford University Press. 1966.

Hwang, Kyung Moon. "From the Dirt to Heaven: Northern Koreans in the Chosŏn and Early Modern Eras," *Harvard Journal of Asiatic Studies* 62.1 (2002).

Illustrated Dictionary of Historic Architecture. Ed. Cyril M. Harris. New York: Dover Publications, 1977.

Imanish Shunju 今西春秋. "Jušen kokuiki kō" Jušen 國域考. *Tōhōgaku kiyō* 東洋學紀要 2 (1967).

———. "Temmei kengen kō" 天命建元考. *Chōsen gakuhō* 朝鮮學報 14 (1959).

Inaba Iwakichi 稻葉岩吉, ed. *Kōkyō nidōkashi kyūrōjō* 興京二道河子舊老城. Changchun: Kenkoku daigaku kenkyūin, 1939.

International Encyclopedia of the Social and Behavioral Sciences. Amsterdam and New York: Elsevier, 2001, 26 vols.

Isaacman, Allen, and Barbara Isaacman. "The Prazeros as Transfrontiersmen: A Study in Social and Cultural Change," *International Journal of African Historical Studies* 8.1 (1975).

Ishibashi, Hideo. "On Irgen, Jušen and Aha in the Early Ch'ing," *Acta Asiatica* 53 (1988).

Ji Yonghai 季永海. "Lun Manyu zhongdi Hanyu jieci" 論滿語中的漢語借詞. *Manyu yanjiu* 滿語研究 1 (1985).

Jia Jingyan 賈敬顏. "Hanren kao" 漢人考. In Fei Xiaotong 費孝通 et al., eds. *Zhonghua minzu duoyuan yiti geju* 中華民族多元一體格局. Beijing: Zhong-yang minzu xueyuan chuban she, 1989.

———. "Lishi shang shaoshu minzu zhong di Hanren chengfen" 歷史上少數民族中的漢人成分. In Fei Xiaotong 費孝通 et al., eds., *Zhonghua minzu duoyuan yiti geju* 中華民族多元一體格. Beijing: Zhong-yang minzu xueyuan chuban she, 1989.

Jia Lanpo 賈蘭坡 and Yan Yin 顏訚. "Xituan shan rengu di yanjiu baogao" 西團山人骨的研究報告. *Kaogu xuebao* 考古學報 2 (1963).

Jiang Ning 江寧. "Lun Ning-Jin dajie" 論寧錦大捷. *Qingshi yanjiu tongxin* 清史研究通訊.1 (1989).

Jiang Qiao 江橋. "Qingchu di Hanjun jiang-ling Shi Tingzhu" 清初的漢軍將領石廷柱. *Lishi dang'an* 歷史檔案 1 (1989).

Jiang Shoupeng 姜守鵬. "Mingdai Liaodong jingji" 明代遼東經濟. *KHCH* 3 (1990).

Jiang Shunyuan 姜舜源. "Qingdai di zongmiao zhidu" 清初的宗廟制度. *Gugong bowu yuan yuankan* 故宮博物院院刊 3 (1987).

Jiang Xiang-shun 姜相順. "Cong Manzu di wenhua xishu kan Shenyang gugong di menshen he bianlian" 從滿族的文化習俗看瀋陽故宮的門神和匾聯 *MANT*, 4 (1990).

Jiang Xiang-shun 姜相順 and Tong Yue 佟悅. *Sheng-jing huang-gong* 盛京皇宮. Beijing: Zijin cheng chuban she, 1987.

Jiang Xiusong 蔣秀松. "Mingdai Nüzhen di chigong zhi" 明代女真的敕貢制. *MTYC* 4 (1984).

———. "Qingchu di Huerha bu" 清初的呼爾哈部 *KHCH* 1 (1981).

———. "Shilun Jianzhou Nüzhen di jiju he zuhe" 試論建州女真的集聚和組合. In *Qingshi guoji xueshu.*

Jin Chengji 金成基. "Fan Wencheng jianlun" 范文程簡論. *Lishi yanjiu* 歷史研究 5 (1982).

———. "Lun Shunzhi" 論順治. *Wen-shi-zhe* 文史哲 5 (1984).

Jin, Qicong. "Jurchen Literature under the Chin." In Hoyt Cleveland Tillman and Stephen H. West, eds., *China under Jurchen Rule: Essays on Chin Intellectual and Cultural History.* Albany: State University of New York Press, 1995.

Jin Qicong 金啟琮. "Shilun Qingdai di Man-Meng-Han guanxi" 試論清代的滿蒙漢關係. In *Qingshi guoji xueshu.*

Jin Qicong 金啟琮 and Wula Xichun 烏拉熙春, "Nüzhen yu yu Manyu guanxi qiantan" 女真語與滿語關係淺談. *Minzu yuwen* 民族語文 1 (1994).

Jin Yufu 金毓黻. "Manwen laodang kao" 滿文老檔考. *Shenyang bowu yuan choubei weiyan hui huikan* 瀋陽博物院籌備委員會彙刊 1 (1947).

Jindai Zhongguo chuqi lishi yantao hui lunwen ji 近代中國初期歷史研討會論文集, ed., The Institute of Modern History, Academia Sinica. Taipei: Institute of Modern History, Academia Sinica, 1989, 2 vols.

Kahn, Harold L. *Monarchy in the Emperor's Eyes: Image and Reality in the Ch'ien-lung Reign.* Cambridge: Harvard University Press, 1971.

Kanda, Nobuo, "The National Name 'Manju,'" *Proceedings of the Fourth East Asian Altaistic Conference.* Taipei: December 26–31, 1971.

Kanda Nobuo 神田信夫, "Shinsho no bunkan ni tsuite" 清初の文館. *Tōyōshi kenkyū* 東洋史研究 19.3 (1960).

———. "Shinsho no kaiten ni tsuite" 清初 の會典について. In *Wada hakushi koki kinen Tōyōshi ronsō* 和田博士古稀紀念東洋史論叢. Tokyo: Kodansha, 1960.

Kane, Daniel. *The Sino-Jurchen Vocabulary of the Bureau of Interpreters.* Bloomington, IN: Research Institute for Inner Asian Studies, Indiana University, 1989.

Kang Yuming 康右銘. "Man-Meng guizu lianmeng yu Qing diguo" 滿蒙貴族聯盟與清帝國. *Nankai xuebao* 南開學報 2 (1986).

Kawachi Yoshihiro 河内良弘. "Kenshū Jochoku no idō mondai" 建州女真の移動問題. *Tōyōshi kenkyū* 東洋史研究 19.2 (1960).

———. *Mindai Joshinshi no kenkyū* 明代女真史の研究. Kyoto: Dōhōsha, 1992.

————. "Mindai Ryōyō no Tōneii ni tsuite" 明代遼陽の東寧衛 について. *Tōyōshi kenkyū* 東洋史研究 44.4 (1986).

————. "Mingdai dongbei Ya di diaopi mouyi" 明代東北亞的貂皮貿易. In *Qingzhu Wang Zhonghan xian-sheng bashi shouchen xueshu lunwen ji* 慶祝王鍾翰先生八十壽辰學術論文集. Ed Qingzhu Wang Zhonghan xian-sheng bashi shouchen xueshu lunwen ji weiyuan hui 委員會. Shenyang: Liaoning daxue chuban she, 1993.

————. "Ri-chō shoki no Joshinjin jiei" 李朝初期の女真人侍衛. *Chōsen gakuhō* 朝鮮學報 14 (1959).

Kawakubo Teirō 川久保悌郎. "Shindai Manshū ni okeru shōka no zokusei ni tsuite." 清代滿洲における燒鍋の簇生 について. In *Wada Hakushi koki kinen Tōyōshi ronsō* 和田博士古稀紀念東洋史論叢. Tokyo: Kodansha, 1960.

Kessler, Lawrence D. *K'ang-hsi and the Consolidation of Ch'ing Rule, 1661–1684.* Chicago and London: University of Chicago Press, 1976.

Keyes, Charles F. "The Dialectics of Ethnic Change." In Charles F. Keyes, ed., *Ethnic Change.* Seattle: University of Washington Press, 1982.

KHCH. *Shehui kexue zhanxian* 社會科學戰線.

King, J. R. P. "The Korean Elements in the Manchu Script Reform of 1632," *Central Asiatic Journal* 3–4 (1987).

Knight, Franklin W. *The Caribbean: The Genesis of a Fragmented Nationalism.* New York: Oxford University Press, 2nd ed., 1990.

Kolarz, Walter W. *The Peoples of the Soviet Far East.* Hamden, CT: Archon Books, 1969.

Kristof, Ladis K. D. "The Nature of Frontiers and Boundaries," *Annals of the Association of American Geographers* 49.3 (1959).

Kuhn, Philip A. *Soulstealers: The Chinese Sorcery Scare of 1768.* Cambridge, MA, and London: Harvard University Press, 1990.

Lague, David. "A Chinese Village Struggles to Save the Dying Language of a Once Powerful Dynasty," *New York Times*, Sunday, March 18, 2007, p. 6. "International."

Larichev, V. Ye. "Ancient Cultures of Northern China." In Henry N. Michael, ed., *The Archaeology and Morphology of Northern Asia: Selected Works.* Toronto: University of Toronto Press, 1964.

————. "Neolithic Remains in the Upper Amur Basin at Ang-ang-hsi in Tungpei." In Henry N. Michael, ed., *The Archaeology and Geomorphology of Northern Asia: Selected Works.* Toronto: University of Toronto Press, 1964.

Lattimore, Owen. *Inner Asian Frontiers of China.* New York: American Geographical Society, 1951, 2nd ed.

————. *Manchuria: Cradle of Conflict.* New York: MacMillan Company, rev. ed., 1935.

————. *Studies in Frontier History: Collected Papers, 1928–1958.* London and New York: Oxford University Press, 1962.

Lee, James. "Migration and Expansion in Chinese History." In William H. McNeill and Ruth S. Adams, eds., *Human Migration: Patterns and Policies.* Bloomington, IN: Indiana University Press, 1978.

Lee, James Z., and Cameron D. Campbell. *Fate and Fortune in Rural China: Social Or-*

ganization and Population Behavior in Liaoning 1774–1873. New York: Cambridge University Press, 1997.

Lee, Robert H. G., *The Manchurian Frontier in Ch'ing History*. Cambridge, MA: Harvard University Press, 1970.

Leonard, Jane Kate. *Wei Yuan and China's Redicovery of the Maritime World*. Cambridge: Council on East Asian Studies, Harvard University, 1984.

Li Chi. "Manchuria in History," *Chinese Social and Political Science Review* 16.2 (1932).

Li Deqi 李德啟. "Manzhou wenzi zhi laiyuan jiqi yanbian" 滿洲文字之來源及其演變. *Guoli Beiping dushu guan guankan* 國立北平圖書館館刊 5.6 (1931).

Li Ge 李格. "Duoergun yu Qingchao tongzhi di jianli" 多爾袞與清朝統治的建立. *Qingshi luncong* 清史論叢 3 (1982).

Li, Gertraude Roth. "The Rise of the Early Manchu State: A Portrait Drawn from Manchu Sources to 1636." Ph.D. dissertation, Harvard University, 1975.

Li Guangtao 李光 濤. "Qing Taizong yu Sanguo yanyi" 清太宗與三國演義. *Bulletin of the Institute of History and Philology, Academia Sinica* 12.1–2 (1945).

———. " 'Lao Manwen shiliao' xu" '老滿文史料' 序. *Bulletin of the Institute of History and Philology, Academia Sinica* 34 (1962).

———. *Mingji liukou shimo* 明季流寇始末. Taipei: Institute of History and Philology, Academia Sinica, 1965.

Li Hongbin 李鴻彬. "Duoergun yu Shanhai-guan dazhan" 多爾袞與山海關大戰. *Qingshi yanjiu* 清史研究 5 (1986).

———. "Qingchu jiechu zhengzhi jia—Fan Wencheng" 清初杰出政治家一范文程. *KHCH* 4 (1983).

———. "Shilun 'Dingmao zhiyu'" 試論 '丁卯之役'. *KHCH* 4 (1987).

Li Hongbin 李鴻彬 and Guo Cheng-kang 郭成康. "Qing ruguan qian baqi zhuqi beile di yanbian" 清入關前八旗主旗貝勒的演變. *KHCH* 5 (1982).

Li Jiancai 李健才. *Mingdai Dongbei* 明代東北. Shenyang: Liaoning renmin chuban she, 1986.

Li Li 李理. "Lun Qingchu yizhang zhi zhi di yanbian" 論清初儀仗之制的演變. *Liaoning daxue xuebao* 遼寧大學學報 5 (1992).

Li Luhua 李陸華, and Lü Wenlai 呂文來. "Ming-jiang Ye Wang zai Dongbei" 明將葉旺在 東北. *KHCH* 1 (1990).

Li Qi 李頎, and Jin Jihao 金基浩. "Yehe bu shi chutan" 葉赫部史初探. *MTYC* 3 (1983).

Li Sanmou 李三謀. "Mingdai Liaodong dusi, weisuo di xing-zheng zhineng" 明代遼東都司, 衛所的行政職能. *Liaoning shifan daxue xuebao* 遼寧師範大學學報 (*Sheke ban* 社科版) 6 (1989).

Li Shilong 李士龍. "Wu Sangui xiang Qing shi lishi shishi" 吳三桂降清是歷史事實. *Beifang luncong* 北方論叢 2 (1987).

Li Wenzhi 李文治. *Wan-Ming minbian* 晚明民變 (Hong Kong: Yuandong tushu gongsi, 1966).

Li Xinda 李新達, "Guanyu Manzhou qizhi he Hanjun qizhi di shijian shijian wenti" 關於滿洲旗制和漢軍旗制的始建時間問題. *Qingshi luncong* 清史論叢 4 (1982).

Li Xuezhi 李學智. "Shi Manwen zhi 'zhushen' yu 'aha'" 釋滿文之'諸申'與'阿哈'. *Bian-zheng yanjiu suo nianbao* 邊政研究所年報 12 (1981).

Li Xun 李洵, and Xue Hong 薛虹, eds. *Qingdai quanshi* 清代全史 (vol. 1). Shenyang: Liaoning renmin chuban she, 1991.

Li Yanguang 李燕光, and Guan Jie 關捷. *Manzu tongshi* 滿族通史. Shenyang: Liaoning minzu chuban she, 1991.

Li Yuping 李宇平. "Qing ruguan qian di Hanhua—Taizu Taizong shiqi" 清入關前的漢化—太祖太宗時期. *Shixue huikan* (Shida) 史學彙刊 (師大) 23 (1979).

Li Yunxia 李云霞. "Shilun Mingdai Guang-ning di mashi" 試論明代廣寧的馬市. *MANT* 4 (1984).

Li Zongtung 李宗侗. "Qingdai zhong-yang zheng-quan xingtai di yanbian" 清代中央政權形態 的演變, *Bulletin of the Institute of History and Philology, Academia Sinica* 7.1 (1967).

Liang, Ssu-ch'eng. In Wilma Fairbank, ed., *A Pictorial History of Chinese Architecture: A Study of the Development of the Structural System and the Evolution of Its Types.* Cambridge: MIT Press, 1984.

Light, Ivan. "Ethnic Succession." In Charles F. Keyes, ed., *Ethnic Change.* Seattle and London: University of Washington, 1981.

Lin, T. C. "Manchuria Trade and Tribute in the Ming Dynasty," *Nankai Social and Economic Quarterly* 9.3 (1936).

Lin Dingqing 林廷清. "Lun Mingdai Liaodong mashi cong guanshi dao minshi di zhuan-bian" 論明代遼東馬市從官市到民市的轉變. *MTYC* 4 (1983).

Ling Chunsheng 凌純聲. *Songhua jiang xiayou di Heizhe zu* 松花江下游的赫哲族. Nanking: Academia Sinica, 1934, 2 vols.

Linke, Bernd-Michael. *Zur Entwicklung des mandjurischen Khanats zum Beamten-staat: Sinisierung und Burokratisierung des Mandjuren wahrend der Eroberungszeit* [The evolution of the Manchu Khanate into a bureaucratic state: Sinicization and bureaucratization of the Manchus during the period of conquest]. Wiesbaden: Franz Steiner, 1982.

Lissner, Ivar. *Man, God, and Magic.* New York: Putnam's Sons, 1961.

Liu, Chia-chü. "The Creation of the Chinese Banners in the Early Ch'ing," *Chinese Studies in History* 14.4 (1981).

Liu Chia-chü 劉家駒. *Qingchao chuqi di Zhong-Han guanxi* 清朝初期的中韓關係. Taipei: Wen-shih-zhe chuban she, 1986.

———. *Qingchu zhengzhi fazhan shi lunji* 清初政治發展史論集. Taipei: Commercial Press, 1978.

Liu Dan 劉丹. "Lun Nuer-hachi yu Mingchao di guanxi" 論努爾哈赤與明朝的關係. *Liaoning daxue xuebao: Zhexue shehui kexue ban* 遼寧大學學報: 哲學社會科學版 5 (1978).

Liu Hanruo 劉含若. "Dongbei renkou shi chutan 東北人口史初探. *Xuexi yu tansuo* 學習與探索 6 (1983).

Liu Housheng 劉厚生. *Qingdai gongting saman jisi [yanjiu]* 清代宮廷薩滿祭祀 [研究]. Chang-chun[?]: Jilin wenshi chuban she, 1992.

Liu Jianxin 劉建新. "Lun Ming-Qing zhiji di Song-Jin zhizhan" 論明清之際的松錦之戰. *Qingshi yanjiu ji* 清史研究集 4 (1986).

Liu Lu 劉潞. "Qing Taizu Taizong shi Man-Meng hunyin kao" 清太祖太宗時滿蒙婚姻考. *Gugong bowu yuan yuankan* 故宮博物院院刊 3 (1995).

Liu Qinghua 劉慶華. *Manzu xingshi lu* 滿族姓氏錄. N.p., Liaoning sheng Xinbin xian minzu shiwu weiyuan hui, 1982.

Liu Ruoyu 劉若愚. *Zhuo-zhong zhi* 酌中志. Congshu jicheng chubian 叢書集成初編, 1941. Vols. 3966–67.

Liu Shizhe 劉世哲. "Mingdai Nüzhen jizhong wuchan shuchu shuyi" 明代女真幾種物產輸出述議. *MTYC* 6 (1984).

———. "Mingdai Nüzhen wuchan shuru jizhong" 明代女真物產輸入幾種. *Heilong jiang wenwu congkan* 黑龍江文物叢刊 4 (1984).

———. "Nuer-hachi shidai fazhi shulun" 努爾哈赤時代法制述論. *MTYC* 6 (1986).

———. "Nuer-hachi shiqi xingfa leixiang jiqi tedian" 努爾哈赤時期刑罰類項及其特點. *MTYC* 6 (1987).

Liu Xiaomeng 劉小萌. "Guanyu Qingdai 'Xin Manzhou' di jige wenti" 關於清代'新滿洲'的幾個問題. *MANT* 3 (1987).

———. *Manzu di buluo yu guojia* 滿族的部落與國家. Chang-chun: Jilin wenshi chuban she, 1995.

———. *Manzu di shehui yu shenghuo* 滿族的社會與生活. Beijing: Beijing tushu chuban she, 1998.

Liu Zhiyang 劉志揚. "Qing zhengfu jianli hou Han wenhua dui Manzu wenhua di ying-xiang" 清政府建立後漢文化對滿族文化的影響. *Heilong jiang minzu congkan* 黑龍江民族叢刊 4 (1992).

Lü Shipeng 呂士朋. "Qingdai di chongru yu Hanhua" 清代的崇儒與漢化. In *Zhongyang yanjiu yuan Guoji Hanxue huiyi lunwen ji* 中央研究院國際漢學會議論文集. Taipei: Academia Sinica, 1981, 7 vols. in 10. Vol. 3A.

Lü Simian 呂思勉. *Zhongguo zhidu shi* 中國制度史. Shanghai: Shanghai jiaoyu chuban she, 1985.

Lui, Adam. "The Education of the Manchus, China's Ruling Race (1644–1911). *Journal of Asian and African Studies* 6.2 (1971).

———. *Two Rulers in One Reign: Dorgon and Shun-chih 1644–1660*. Canberra: Faculty of Asian Studies, Australian National University, 1989.

Luo Xianyu 羅賢佑. "Jin-Yuan shiqi Nüzhen ren di neiqian ji yanbian" 金元時期女真人的內遷及演變. *MTYC* 2 (1984).

Luo Xintian 羅莘田. "Zhongguo yinyun xue di wailai ying-xiang" 中國音韻學的外來影響, *Dongfang zazhi* 東方雜誌 32.14 (July 1935).

Luo Yunzhi 羅運治. "Kangxidi yu mulan weichang di guanxi" 康熙帝與木蘭圍場的關係. In *Jin-dai Zhongguo chuqi lishi yantao hui lunwen ji* 近代中國初期歷史研討

會論文集, ed., The Institute of Modern History, Academia Sinica. Taipei: Institute of Modern History, Academia Sinica, 1989, 2 vols. Vol. 1.

Ma Xiedi 馬協弟. "Qingdai Mancheng kao" 清代滿城考. *MANT* 1 (1990).

Ma Yueshan 馬越山. "Manzhou zuming yanjiu zongshu" 滿洲族名研究綜述. *MANT* 3 (1988).

Mair, Victor H. "Language and Ideology in the Written Popularization of the Sacred Edict." In David Johnson, Andrew J. Nathan, and Evelyn S. Rawski, eds., *Popular Culture in Late Imperial China*. Berkeley and Los Angeles: University of California Press, 1985.

Man-Han dacidian 滿漢大辭典. Eds. An Shuang-cheng 安雙成 et al. Shenyang: Liaoning minzu chuban she, 1993.

Manzhou yuanliu kao. See Agui and Yu Minzhong.

Manzu da cidian 滿族大辭典. Eds. Sun Wenliang 孫文良, Liu Wanquan 劉萬泉, and Li Zhiting 李治亭. Shenyang: Liaoning University Press, 1990.

MANT. Manzu yanjiu 滿族研究.

Mao Ruizheng 茅瑞徵. See Diao-shang yugong.

Mao Wen 毛汶. "Manwen Hanhua kaolüe" 滿文漢化考略. *Guoxue lunheng* 國學論衡 9 (1937).

Matsumura Jun 松村潤. "Beikoku gikai toshukan shozō manshūgo bunken mokuroku" 米國議會圖書館所藏滿洲語文獻目錄. *Tōyō gakuhō* 東洋學報 5.1-2 (1976).

———. "The Founding Legend of the Qing Dynasty Reconsidered," *Memoirs of the Research Department of the Toyo Bunko* 55 (1997).

McCready, William C., ed. *Culture, Ethnicity, and Identity: Current Issues in Research*. New York: Academic Press, 1983.

McNeill, William H. *The Great Frontier: Freedom and Hierarchy in Modern Times*. Princeton: Princeton University Press, 1983.

Meng, *Ming-Qing xubian*. See Meng Sen, *Ming-Qing shi lunzhu jikan xubian*.

Meng Sen 孟森. *Ming-Qing shi lunzhu jikan* 明清史論著集刊. Taipei: Shijie shuju, 1961.

———. *Ming-Qing shi lunzhu jikan* xubian 明清史論著集刊續編. Beijing: Zhonghua shuju, 1986.

———. *Qingdai shi* 清代史. Taipei: Zheng-zhong shuju, 1960.

Meng Xiangang 孟憲剛. "Baqi qizhu kaoshi" 八旗旗主考實. *MANT* 2 (1986).

Meng Yuanlao 孟元老. *Dongjing menghua lu* 東京夢華錄. Shanghai: Commercial Press, 1959.

Michael, Franz. *The Origin of Manchu Rule in China: Frontier and Bureaucracy as Interacting Forces in the Chinese Empire*. Baltimore: Johns Hopkins University Press, 1942.

Michael, Henry N., ed. *The Archaeology and Geomorphology of Northern Asia: Selected Works*. Toronto: University of Toronto Press, 1964. Arctic Institute of North America Anthropology of the North: Translations from Russian Sources No. 5.

Ming-Qing Jinshi timing beilu suoyin 明清進士題名碑錄索引. Comps. Zhu Baojiong 朱保炯 and Xie Peilin 謝沛霖. Shanghai: Shanghai guji chuban she, 1980, 3 vols.

Mish, John L. "Grand Secretary Ortai," *Bulletin of the New York Public Library* 66.8 (1962).

Mitamura Taisuke 三田村泰助. "Manju koku seiritsu katei no ichi kōsatsu" 滿珠國成立過程 の一考察. *Tōyōshi kenkyū* 東洋史研究 2.2 (1936).

———. *Shinchō zenshi no kenkyū* 清朝前史の研究. Kyoto: Tōyōshi kenkyūkai, 1965.

———. "Shoki Manshū hakki no seiritsu katei ni tsuite—Mindai kenshū Jochoku no gunsei." 初期滿洲八旗 の成立過程 について一明代建州女真 の軍制. In Shimizu hakushi tsuitō kinen Mindai shi ronsō hensan iinkai 編纂委員會, ed., *Shimizu hakushi tsuitō kinen Mindaishi ronsō* 清水博士追悼記念明代史論叢. Tokyo: Daian, 1962.

Mithun, Jacqueline S. "The Role of the Family in Acculturation and Assimilation in America: A Psychocultural Dimension." In William C. McCready, ed., *Culture, Ethnicity, and Identity: Current Issues in Researc*, 214. New York: Academic Press, 1983.

Mo Dongyin 莫東寅. *Manzu shi luncong* 滿族史論叢. Beijing: Sanlian shudian, 1979, reprint.

Möllendorff, P. G. von. *Manchu Grammar, with Analysed Texts*. Shanghai: American Presbyterian Mission Press, 1892.

Morioka Yasu 森岡康. "Chōsen horyo no Shinkoku no kaku ni tsuite" 朝鮮捕虜 の清國 の價格 について, *Tōyō gakuhō* 東洋學報 66.1–4 (1985).

Mote, F.W. *Imperial China, 900–1800*. Cambridge, MA, and London: Harvard University Press, 1999.

MTTS. See Li Yanguang and Guan Jie.

MTYC. *Mingzu yanjiu* 民族研究.

Murata Jirō 村田治郎. "Hōten kyūden kenchikushi kō" 奉天宮殿建築史考. *Manshū gakuhō* 滿洲學報 2 (1933).

Nakayama Hachirō 中山八郎. "Hakki engen shishaku" 八旗淵源考釋. *Jimbun kenkyū* 人文研究 10 (1959).

———. "Shinsho Nuruhaci ōkodo no tōchi kikō" 清初 ヌルハチ王國 の統治機構 *Hitotsubashi ronsō*.一橋論叢 14.2 (1944).

Naquin, Susan. *Peking: Temples and City Life, 1400-1900*. Berkeley; Los Angeles: University of California Press, 2000.

NCS. See Sun Jinji et al.

Niu Zhonghan 牛仲寒 and Wang Jiandang 王建黨. "Yue Fei Jin Wozhu houren shouci jushou bajiu gonghua duanjie yu hexie" 岳飛金兀朮後人首次聚首把酒共話團結與和諧. *Sina News* [Internet] (27 February 2007), "Global News."

Norman, Jerry. *A Concise Manchu-English Lexicon*. Seattle and London: University of Washington Press, 1978.

———. "Four Notes on Chinese-Altaic Linguistic Contacts." *Tsing Hua Journal of Chinese Studies* 14.1–2 (1982).

Nowak, Margaret, and Stephen Durrant. *The Tale of the Nišan Shamaness: A Manchu Folk Epic*. Seattle and London: University of Washington Press, 1977.

Oertai (Ortai) 鄂爾泰. *Nanbang lixian ji* 南邦黎獻集. N.p., Shen-shizai xian ed., 1725, 8 vols.

Ogawa Hiroto 小川裕人. "Sanjūbu Joshin ni tsuite" 三十部女真 について. *Tōyō gakuhō* 東洋學報 24.4 (1937).

Okada, Hidehiro. "How Hong Taiji Came to the Throne," *Central Asiatic Journal* 23.3–4 (1979).

Okamoto Sae 岡本さえ. "Tou Koku-ki to Shinsho no Kōnan" 佟國器と清初の江南. *Tōyō bunka kenkyūjo kiyō* 東洋文化研究所紀要 106 (1988).

Ōmura Kōdō 大村興造. "Shinchō kyōiku shisōshi ni okeru 'Seiyu kokun' no chii ni tsuite" 清朝教育思想史 に於ける '聖諭廣訓' の地位について. In Hayashi Tomoharu 林友春, ed., *Kinsei Chūgoku kyōikushi kenkyū: sono bunkyō seisaku to shomin kyōiku* 近世中國教育史研究 その文教政策と庶民教育. Tokyo: Kokudosha, 1958.

Oshibuchi Hajime 鴛淵一. "Shin Taiso jidai keisei kō" 清太祖時代刑政考. In *Haneda hakushi shōju kinen Tōyōshi ronsō* 羽田博士頌壽記念東洋史論叢. Kyoto: Kyoto University Tōyōshi Kenkyūkai, 1950.

———. "Shin Taisō jidai keisei kō" 清太宗時代刑政考. *Jimbun kenkyū* 人文研究 2 (1951).

The Oxford English Dictionary. Oxford: Clarendon Press, 2nd edition, 1989, 20 vols. Vol. 15.

Oxnam, Robert B., *Ruling from Horseback: Manchu Politics in the Oboi Regency, 1661–1669*. Chicago and London: University of Chicago Press, 1970.

Pang, Tatiana A. "The Manchu Script Reform of 1632: New Data and New Questions." In Juha Janhunen and Volker Rybatzki, eds., *Writing in the Altaic World*. Helsinki: The Finnish Oriental Society, 1999, Studia Orientalia 87.

Parsons, James Bunyan. *The Peasant Rebellion of the Late Ming Dynasty*. Tucson: University of Arizona Press, 1970.

Peng Sunyi 彭孫貽. *Shan-zhong wenjian lu* 山中聞見錄. Yujian-zhai congshu 玉簡齋叢書, 1910? Vols. 4–5, with various editions.

Perdue, Peter C. *China Marches West: The Qing Conquest of Central Eurasia*. Cambridge, MA, and London: The Belknap Press of Harvard University Press, 2005.

Qi Qingshun 齊清順. "Qingdai Xinjiang di Guan Yu chongbai" 清代新疆的關羽崇拜. *Qingshi yanjiu* 清史研究 3 (1998).

Qi Wenying 奇文瑛. "Lun Mingchao neiqian Nüzhen anzhi zhengce—yi Anle, Zizai zhou weili" 論明朝內遷女真安置政策--以安樂自在州為例. *Zhong-yang minzu daxue xuebao*中央民族大學學報 (Zhexue shehui kexue ban 哲學社會科學版) 29.2 (2002).

Qian Shifu 錢實甫. *Qingdai zhiguan nianbiao* 清代職官年表. Beijing: Zhonghua Book Company, 1980, 4 vols. Vol. 1.

Qingchu sanling 清初三陵. Ed. Shenyang shi wenwu guanli bangong shi 瀋陽市文物管理辦公室. Beijing: Wenwu chuban she, 1982.

Qingshi biannian 清史編年. Comps. Shi Song 史松 and Lin Tiejun 林鐵鈞. Beijing: Zhongguo renmin daxue chuban she, 1985.

Qingshi guoji xueshu. See Bai Shouyi.

Qiu Xin 秋心. "Manzu chuan-tong fengshu" 滿族傳統風俗. *MANT* 2 (1987).

Qu Jiusi 瞿九思. *Wanli Wugong lu* 萬曆武功錄. Taipei: Yiwen yinshu guan, 1980, reprint, 5 vols.

Qu Xuanying 瞿宣穎. *Zhongguo shehui shiliao congchao* 中國社會史料叢鈔. Shanghai: Commercial Press, 1938, 3 vols.

The Random House Dictionary of the English Language Unabridged. New York: Random House, 2nd ed., 1987.

Rawski, Evelyn S. *The Last Emperors: A Social History of Qing Imperial Institutions.* Berkeley and Los Angeles: University of California Press, 1998.

———. "Presidential Address: Reenvisioning the Qing: The Significance of the Qing Period in Chinese History," *Journal of Asian Studies* 55.4 (1996).

Reischauer, Edwin O., and John K. Fairbank. *East Asia: The Great Tradition.* Boston: Houghton Mifflin, 1960.

Ren Chang-zheng 任長正. "Qing Taizu, Qing Taizong shidai Ming-Qing hezhan kao" 清太祖,清太宗時代明清和戰考. *Dalu zazhi* 大陸雜誌 14.4 (1957); 14.5–8 (1957).

Rhoads, Edward J. M. *Manchus and Han: Ethnic Relations and Political Power in Late Qing and Early Republican China, 1861–1928.* Seattle and London: University of Washington, 2000.

Robinson, Kenneth R. "From Raiders to Traders: Border Security and Border Control in Early Chosōn, 1392–1450," *Korean Studies* 13 (1992).

Rossabi, Morris, *The Jurchens in the Yuan and Ming.* Ithaca, NY: Cornell East Asia Series vol. no. 27, 1982.

Roth, Gertraude. "The Manchu-Chinese Relationship, 1618–1636." In Jonathan D. Spence and John E. Wills, Jr., eds., *From Ming to Ch'ing: Conquest, Region, and Continuity in Seventeenth-Century China.* New Haven and London: Yale University Press, 1979.

Rozycki, William. *Mongol Elements in Manchu.* Bloomington, IN: Research Institute for Inner Asian Studies, Indiana University, 1994.

Ruhlman, Robert. "Traditional Heroes in Chinese Popular Fiction." In Arthur F. Wright, ed., *The Confucian Persuasion.* Stanford: Stanford University Press, 1960.

Saeki Tomi 佐伯富. "Shinchō no koki to Sansei shōnin" 清朝の興起と山西商人. *Shakai-bunkai shigaku* 社會文化史學 1 (March 1966).

———. "Shindai ni okeru Sansei chōnin" 清代における山西商人. *Shirin* 史林 60.1 (1977).

Schmidt, von P. "Chinesische Elemente im Mandschu [Chinese elements in Manchu]," *Asia Major* 7 (1932); 8 (1933).

Serruys, Henry. *Sino-Jürčed Relations during the Yung-lo Period (1403–1424)*. Wiesbaden: Otto Harrassowitz, 1955.

Shang Hongkui 商鴻逵. "Lun Kangxi pingding Sanfan" 論康熙平定三藩. *Qingshi lunwen xuanji* 清史論文選集 1 (1979).

Shang, Hung-k'uei. "The Process of Economic Recovery, Stabilization, and Its Accomplishments in the Early Ch'ing, 1681–1735." In Pei Huang, ed., *The Early Ch'ing Dynasty: State and Society, 1601–1722 (II)*. Special issue of *Chinese Studies in History* 15.1–2 (1981–1982).

Shen Defu 沈德符. *Wanli yehuo pian* 萬曆野獲篇. Beijing: Zhonghua Book Company, 1959, 3 vols.

Sheng Yu 盛昱, and Yang Zhongxi 楊鍾羲, comps. *Baqi wenjing* 八旗文經. Shenyang: Liao-Shen shushe, 1988, photocopy with punctuation.

Shijie ribao 世界日報. "Shenzhou xiang-qing zhoukan" 神州鄉情周刊 49 (March 19, 2000).

Shirokogoroff, S. M. *Social Organization of the Manchus: A Study of the Manchu Clan Organization*. Shanghai: 1924.

SHKH. *Shehui kexue jikan* 社會科學季刊.

Sin Ch'ung-il 申忠一. "Kŏnju kijŏng togi" 建州紀程圖記. *Chin-tan Hakpo* 震檀學報 10 (1939), annotated and commented upon by Yi In-yŏng 李仁榮.

Sinor, Denis. "Some Remarks on Manchu Poetry." In Denis Sinor, ed., *Studies in South East and Central Asia, Presented as a Memorial Volume to the Late Professor Raghu Vira by Members of the Permanent International Altaistic Conference*. New Delhi: International Academy of Indian Culture, 1968.

Siyi kao. See Ye Xianggao.

Smith, Richard J. *China's Cultural Heritage: The Qing Dynasty, 1644–1912*. Boulder, San Francisco, and Oxford: Westview Press, 1994.

Song Dejin 宋德金. "Jindai Nüzhen zushu shulun" 金代女真族俗述論. *Lishi yanjiu* 歷史研究 3 (1982).

Song Ge 宋戈. "Manzu shiren Yue-duan jiqi shige" 滿族詩人岳端及其詩歌. *MANT* 3 (1993).

Soningan 索寧安. *Manzhou sili ji* 滿洲四禮集. Taipei: Tailian Guofeng chuban she, Zhongguo bian-jiang shidi congshu chubian, 1969. Reprint, vol. 11.

Sonoda Kazuki 園田一龜. *Mindai Kenshū Jochoku shi kenkyū* 明代建州女直史研究. Tokyo: Kokuritsu shoin, 1948.

Spence, Jonathan D. *Ts'ao Yin and the K'ang-hsi Emperor: Bondservant and Master*. New Haven and London: Yale University Press, 1966.

SPPY. Sibu beiyao 四部備要. A series of books published in Taipei by the Zhonghua Book Company in 1965

Stary, Giovanni. "Fundamental Principles of Manchu Poetry." In Lin En-shean 林恩顯, ed., *Proceedings of the International Conference on China Border Area Studies*. Taipei: National Chengchi University, 1985.

———. "Guanyu Manzu lishi he yuyan di ruogan wenti" 關於滿族歷史和語言的若干問題. *Manxue yanjiu* 滿學研究 2 (1994).

———. "Manzhou jiuming xinshi" 滿洲舊名新釋. *Zhong-yang minzu xueyuan xue-bao* 中央民族學院學報 6 (1988).

———. *Manchu Studies: An International Bibliography*. Wiesbaden: Otto Harrassowitz, 1990, 3 vols.

——— et al. *On the Tracks of ManchuCulture, 1644–1994: 350 Years after the Conquest of Peking*. Wiesbaden: Harrassowitz, 1995.

Struve, Lynn A. *The Ming-Ch'ing Conflict, 1619–1683: A Historiography and Source Guide*. Ann Arbor, MI: Association for Asian Studies, Monograph and Occasional Paper Series, Number 56, 1998.

———. *The Southern Ming, 1644–1662*. New Haven and London: Yale University Press, 1984.

Sun Jinji 孫進己 et al. *Nüzhen shi* 女真史. Chang-chun: Jilin wenshi chuban she, 1987.

———. "*Nüzhen yuanliu kao*" 女真源流考. *Shixue jikan* 史學集刊 4 (1984).

Sun Wenliang 孫文良. "Lun Manzu di jueqi" 論滿族的崛起. *MTYC* 1 (1986).

——— et al. *Qianlong di* 乾隆帝. Chang-chun: Jilin remin chuban she, 1993.

Sun Wenliang 孫文良 and Li Zhiting 李治亭. "Qing kaiguo xunchen Heheli" 清開國勛臣何和禮. *KHCH* 2 (1984).

———. *Qing Taizong quan-zhuan* 清太宗全傳. Chang-chun: Jilin renmin chuban she, 1983.

Sun Yan 孫琰. "Qingchu yizheng wang dachen huiyi jiqi zuoyong" 清初議政王大臣會議及其 作用. *SHKH* 4 (1986).

Sun Zhanwen 孫占文. *Heilong jiang sheng shi tansuo* 黑龍江省史探索. Harbin: Heilong jiang renmin chuban she, 1983.

Swart, Paula, and Barry Till. "Nurhachi and Abahai: Their Palace and Mausolea, the Manchu Adoption and Adaptation of Chinese Architecture," *Arts of Asia* 18.3 (May–June 1988).

Symons, Van Jay. *Ch'ing Ginseng Management: Ch'ing Monopolies in Microcosm*. Tempe, AZ: Center for Asian Studies, Arizona State University, 1981.

Taga Akigorō 多賀秋五郎. *Sofu no kenkyū* 宗譜の研究. Tokyo: The Tokyo Bunko, 1960.

Tan Qian 談遷. *Beiyou lu* 北游錄. Beijing: Zhonghua Book Company, 1960, "*Da-Qing lü*" 大清律.

Tanaka Hiromi 田中宏己. "Shin Taiso jidai no hakki seido" 清太祖時代の八旗制度, *Bōei Daigakko kiyō* 防衛大學校紀要 53 (1976).

Tanaka Katsumi 田中克己. "Mimmatsu no yajin Jochoku ni tsuite" 明末の野人女直について. *Tōyō gakuhō* 東洋學報 42.2 (1959).

———. "Tsūyaka gulmahūn" 通譯グルマフン. In Ishihama Sensei koki kinenkai 石濱先生古稀紀念會, ed., *Ishihama Sensei koki kinen Tōyōgaku ronsō* 東洋學論叢. Osaka: Ishihama Sensei koki kinenkai, 1953.

Tao, Jing-shen. *The Jurchen in Twelfth-Century China: A Study of Sinicization.* Seattle: University of Washington Press, 1976.

Taylor, Romeyn. "Yuan Origins of the Wei-so System." In Charles O. Hucker, ed., *Chinese Government in Ming Times: Seven Studies.* New York: Columbia University Press, 1969.

Teng Shaozhen 滕紹箴. "Lun Mingdai Nüzhen di jizhong fengshu" 論明代女真的幾種風俗, *MTYC* 6 (1986).

———. "'Manzhou' ming-cheng kaoshu" '滿洲'名稱考述. *MTYC* 4 (1996).

———. "Ming-Qing liangdai Manyu Manwen shiyong qingkuan kao" 明清兩代滿語滿文使用情況考. *Minzu yuwen* 民族語文 2 (1986).

———. *Nuer-hachi ping-zhuan* 努爾哈赤評傳. Shenyang: Liaoning renmin chuban she, 1985.

———. "Shilun Mingdai Nüzhen yu Menggu di guanxi" 試論明代女真與蒙古的關係. *MTYC* 4 (1983).

———. "Cong 'Manwen laodang' kan Nuer-hachi di tianming sixiang" 從 '滿文老檔' 看努爾哈赤的天命思想. *SHKH* 1 (1986).

Teng Shaozhen 滕紹箴 and Bo Dagong 博大公. "Manzu di hebao" 滿族的荷包. *Manzu wenhua* 滿族文化 17 (1992).

Terauchi Itarō 寺内威太郎. "Kyōngwon kaishi no Konshun" 慶源開市の 琿春. *Tōhōgaku* 東方學 70 (July 1985).

Tiebao 鐵保. *Xichao yasong ji* 熙朝雅頌集. Shenyang: Liaoning daxue chuban she, 1992, reprint of the 1804 edition.

Tie Yuqin 鐵玉欽. "Lun Qing ruguan qian ducheng chengguo yu gongdian di yanbian" 論清入關前都城城郭與宮殿的演變. In Ming-Qing shi guoji xueshu taolun hui mishu chu lunwen zu 明清史國際學術討論會秘書處論文組, ed., *Ming-Qing shi guoji xueshu taolun hui lunwen ji* 論文集. Tianjin: Tianjin renmin chuban she, 1982.

Tie Yuqin 鐵玉欽 and Shen Changji 沈長吉. *Shenyang gugong* 瀋陽故宮. Shenyang: Liaoning renmin chuban she, 1985.

Tianzhi ouwen. See Zhenjün.

TMSL. See Fu Langyun and Yang Yang.

Tong Yonggong 佟永功. "Guanyu Qingdai Tongshi jiazu di jige wenti" 關於清代佟氏家族的幾個問題. In Zhu Chengru 朱誠如, ed., *Qingshi lunji: Qinghe Wang Zhonghan jiaoshou jiushi huadan* 清史論集: 慶賀王鍾翰教授九十華誕. Beijing: Zijin cheng chuban she, 2003.

Tong Yonggong 佟永功 and Guan Jialu 關嘉祿. "Lun Manwen zhong di Hanyu jieci" 論滿文中的漢語借詞. *Manxue yanjiu* 滿學研究 1 (1992).

———. "Sheng-jing Manwen xing-shuai tan" 盛京滿文興衰談. *Manyu yanjiu* 滿語研究 1 (1985).

Tong Yue 佟悅. "Qing ruguan qian Manzu sangzang xishu di shidai tezheng" 清入關前滿族喪葬習俗的時代特徵. *MANT* 3 (1993).

———. "Qing Sheng-jing taimiao kaoshu" 清盛京太廟考述. *Gugong bowu yuan yuankan* 故宮博物院院刊 3 (1987).

Tong Zheng 佟錚. "Cong Nuer-hachi di jingji yaoqiu kan Ming yu Hou-Jin jian di guanxi" 從努爾哈赤的經濟要求看明與後金間的關係. *SHKH* 6 (1987).

Tregear, T. R. *A Geography of China.* Chicago: Aldine Publishing Co., 1965.

Tsao, Kai-fu. "K'ang-hsi and the San-fan War," *Monumenta Serica* 31 (1974).

Wada Sei 和田清. "Kyō Seiriku den hosei" 龔正陸傳補正. *Tōyō gakuhō* 東洋學報 40.1 (1957).

———. "The Natives of the Lower Reaches of the Amur River as Represented in Chinese Records," *Memoirs of the Research Department of the Tōyō Bunko* 10 (1938).

———. "Shin no Taiso no komon Kyō Seiriku" 清の太祖 の顧問龔正陸. *Tōyō gakuhō* 東洋學報 35.1 (1952).

———. *Tōashi kenkyū: Manshū hen* 東亞史研究: 滿洲篇. Tokyo: Tōyō Bunko, 1955.

Wadley, Stephen A. "Altaic Influences on Beijing Dialect: The Manchu Case," *Journal of the American Oriental Society* 116.1 (1996).

Wakeman, Frederic, Jr., *The Fall of Imperial China.* New York: The Free Press, 1975.

———. *The Great Enterprise: The Manchu Reconstruction of Imperial Order in Seventeenth-Century China.* Berkeley and Los Angeles: University of California Press, 1985, 2 vols.

Wang. "Tong Yangxing." See Wang Gesheng.

Wang Bin 王彬. "Heizhe zu yu Donghai Nüzhen" 赫哲族與東海女真. *Zhong-yang minzu xueyuan xuebao* 中央民族學院學報 2 (1988).

Wang, Chen-main. *The Life and Career of Hung Ch'eng-ch'ou (1593–1665): Public Service in a Time of Dynastic Change.* Ann Arbor, MI: Association for Asian Studies, Monograph and Occasional Paper Series, no. 59, 1999.

Wang Chengli 王承禮. "Mohe di fazhan he Bohai wangguo di jianli" 靺鞨的發展和渤海王國的建立. *CLST* 3 (1979).

Wang Dongfang 王冬芳. "Lianyin zhengce zai Nüzhen tongyi zhong di zuoyong" 聯姻政策在女真統一中的作用. *SHKH* 5 (1987).

———. "Ming Liaodong Nüzhen Han—Wang Tai" 明遼東女真汗—王台. *Dongbei difang shi yanjiu* 東北地方史研究 4 (1986).

———. "Ning Wanwo di jinqu jingshen jiqi bianhua" 寧完我的進取精神及其變化. *SHKH* 2 (1984).

Wang Gesheng 王革生. "Qingchao kaiguo gongchen Tong Yangxing" 清朝開國功臣佟養性. *Beifang luncong* 北方論叢 6 (1985).

Wang Huo 王火. "Manzu renming di minshu tezheng he yuyan tezheng" 滿族人名的民俗特徵和語言特徵. *MANT* 4 (1993).

Wang Junzhong 王俊中. "'Manzhou' yu 'Wenshu' di yuanyuan ji Xizang zheng-jiao sixiang zhong di lingxiu yu fupusa" '滿洲' 與 '文殊' 的淵源及西藏政教思想中的領袖與佛菩薩. *Bulletin of the Institute of Modern History, Academia Sinica* 28 (1997).

Wang Mouhe 汪茂和. "Zaoqi Manzu shehui di aha shenfen wenti" 早期滿族社會的阿哈身份問題. *Nankai xuebao* 南開學報 5 (1982).

Wang Peihuan 王佩環. "Huang Taiji yu Chang-ning si" 皇太極與常寧寺. *Beifang wenwu* 北方文物 2 (1986).

Wang Shizhen 王士禎. *Xiangzu biji* 香祖筆記. N.p., Saoye shanfang, 1911, 4 vols.

Wang Tongling 王桐齡. "Shina ni okeru Gairai Minzoku no kanka ni tsuite" 支那に於ける外來民族 の 漢化に就いて. *Shigaku zasshi* 史學雜誌 47. 11 (1936); *Harvard Journal of Asiatic Studies* 2 (1937).

Wang, Xiangyun. "The Qing Court's Tibet Connection: Lcang skya Rol pa'i rdo rje and the Qianlong Emperor," *Harvard Journal of Asiatic Studies* 60.1 (2000): 125–63.

Wang Xiaoming 王曉銘 and Wang Yongxi 王詠曦. "O-lun-chun yu O-wen-ke zu tongyuan kao" 鄂倫春與鄂溫克族同源考. *Heilong jiang minzu congkan* 黑龍江民族叢刊 1 (1987).

Wang Zhong-han [Wang Zhonghan]. "The Question of the Place Where the Manchu Ancestors Originated," *Central Asiatic Journal* 33.3–4 (1991).

Wang Zhonghan 王鍾翰. *Qingshi xinkao* 清史新考. Shenyang: Liaoning daxue chuban she, 1990.

———. *Qingshi xukao* 清史續考. Taipei: Huashi chuban she, 1993.

———, ed. *Zhongguo minzu shi* 中國民族史. Beijing: Zhongguo shehui kexue chuban she, 1994.

Wanli yehuo pian. See Shen Defu.

Weber, David J., and Jane M. Rausch, eds. *Where Cultures Meet: Frontiers in Latin American History*. Wilmington, DE: Scholarly Resources Inc., 1994.

Webster's Third New International Dictionary of the English Language Unabridged. Springfield, MA: Merriam Company, 1971.

Wei Fuxiang 魏福祥 and Du Shangxie 杜尚俠. "Manzu falü zongshu" 滿族法律綜述. *MANT* 3 (1944).

Wei Jianxun 魏鑒勛. "Huang Taiji shiqi Hou Jin zheng-quan di xingzhi" 皇太極時期後金政權的性質. *SHKH* 5 (1980).

———. "Lun Qianlong huangdi di shige" 論乾隆皇帝的詩歌. *MANT* 4 (1990).

Wei Jianxun 魏鑒勛 and Yuan Lükun 袁閭琨. "Shilun Huang Taiji di gaige jiqi zhinang duan" 試論皇太極的改革及其智囊團. *Guang-ming ribao* 光明日報 (February 24, 1981).

Wei Qingyuan 韋慶遠. *Ming-Qing shi bianxi* 明清史辨析. Beijing: Zhongguo shehui kexue chuban she, 1989.

Wei Song 魏崧. *Yishi jishi* 壹是紀始. Beijing: Wenkui tang, 1891, 6 vols.

West, Elizabeth Endicott. *Mongolian Rule in China: Local Administration in the Yuan Dynasty*. Cambridge and London: Council on East Asian Studies, Harvard University, and the Harvard-Yenching Institute, 1989.

Wittfogel, Karl A., and Chia-sheng Feng. *History of Chinese Society: Liao, 907–1125*. Philadelphia: American Philosophical Society, 1949.

Wong, Young-tsu. *A Paradise Lost: The Imperial Garden Yuanming Yuan*. Honolulu: University of Hawai'i Press, 2001.

Woodruff, Phillip H. "Foreign Policy and Frontier Affairs along the Northeastern Frontier of the Ming Dynasty, 1350–1618: Tripartite Relations of the Ming Chinese, Korean Koryo and Jurchen-Manchu Tribesmen." Ph.D. dissertation, The University of Chicago, 1995.

Wright, Mary Clabaugh. *The Last Stand of Chinese Conservatism: The T'ung-chih Restoration, 1862–1874*. Stanford: Stanford University Press, 1957.

Wu, David Y. H. "Culture Change and Ethnic Identity among Minorities in China." In Chien Chiao and Nicholas Tapp, eds., *Ethnicity and Ethnic Groups in China*. Hong Kong: New Asia College, The Chinese University of Hong Kong, 1989.

Wugong lu. See Qu Jiusi.

Wula Xichun 烏拉熙春. "Cong yuyan lunzheng Nüzhen, Manzhou zhi zucheng" 從語言論證女真, 滿洲 之族稱. *Manzu wenhua* 滿族文化 14 (December 1, 1990).

Xia Shi 夏石. "Shunzhi shiqi Manzu wenxue fazhan di beijing yu tiaojian" 順治時期滿族文學發展的背景與條件. *MANT* 4 (1994).

———. "Yue-duan jiqi shige" 岳端及其詩歌. *MANT* 1 (1990).

Xiao Yishan 蕭一山. *Qingdai tongshi* 清代通史. Taipei: Taiwan Commercial Press, 1962–1963, 5 vols.

Xiaoting zalu. See Zhaolian.

Xichao yasong ji. See Tiebao.

Xie Guozhen 謝國楨. *Nan-Ming shilüe* 南明史略. Shanghai: Shanghai renmin chuban she, 1988 edition.

Xie Jingfang 謝景芳. "Baqi Hanjun di jianli jiqi lishi zuoyong" 八旗漢軍的建立及其歷史作用. *SHKH* 3 (1987).

Xu Jianzhu 徐健竹. "Lun Jianzhou zuowei di jianli yu bianqian" 論建州左衛的建立與變遷. *SHKH* 1 (1983).

Xu Mengxin 徐夢莘. *Sanchao beimeng huibian* 三朝北盟會編. Taipei: Wenhai chuban she, 1962, 4 vols.

Xu Qixian 徐啟憲. "Qingdai baoxi lüetan" 清代寶璽略談. *Gugong bowu yuan yuankan* 故宮博院院刊 3 (1995).

Xu Zhongshu 徐中舒. "Mingchu Jianzhou Nüzhen judi qianxi kao" 明初建州女真居地遷徙考. *Bulletin of the Institute of History and Philology, Academia Sinica* 6.2 (1936).

Xue Hong 薛虹. "Nuer-hachi di xingshi he jiashi" 努爾哈赤的姓氏和家世. *Qingshi yanjiu tongxin* 清史研究通訊 4 (1989).

———. and Liu Housheng 劉厚生. "'Jiu Manzhou dang' suo ji Da-Qing jianhao qian di guohao" '舊滿洲檔' 所記大清建號前的國號. *SHKH* 2 (1990).

Yan Chong-nian 閻崇年. "Nuer-hachi rujing jingong kao" 努爾哈赤入京進貢考. *Qingshi yanjiu tongxin* 清史研究通訊 2 (1983).

———. *Nuer-hachi zhuan* 努爾哈赤傳. Beijing: Beijing chuban she, 1983.

————. *Yanbu ji* 燕步集. Beijing: Yanshan chuban she, 1989.

Yan Congjian 嚴從簡. *Shuyu zhouzi lu* 殊域周咨錄. Taipei: Taiwan Huawen shuju, 1969, reprint, Zhonghua wenshi congshu Series 3, vols. 36–37.

Yang Baolong 楊保隆. "Qiantan Yuandai di Nüzhen ren" 淺談元代的女真人. *MTYC* 3 (1984).

————. *Sushen Yilou hekao* 肅順挹婁合考. Beijing: Zhongguo shehui kexue chuban she, 1989.

Yang, Lien-sheng. "Historical Notes on the Chinese World Order." In John King Fairbank, ed., *The Chinese World Order: Traditional China's Foreign Relations*. Cambridge: Harvard University Press, 1968.

Yang Mousheng 楊茂盛. "Guanyu Shuidada di fenbu yu zushu wenti" 關於水達達的分布與族屬問題. *Dongbei difang yanjiu* 東北地方研究 2 (1989).

Yang Qiqiao 楊啟樵. *Yongzheng di jiqi mizhe zhidu yanjiu* 雍正帝及其密摺制度. Hong Kong: Sanlian shudian, 1981.

Yang Xuechen 楊學琛 and Zhou Yuanlian 周遠廉. *Qingdai baqi wanggong guizu xing-shuai shi* 清代八旗王公貴族興衰史. Shenyang: Liaoning renmin chuban she, 1986.

Yang Yang 楊暘. *Mingdai Dongbei shigang* 明代東北史綱. Taipei: Taiwan xuesheng shuju, 1993.

————. *Mingdai Liaodong dusi* 明代遼東都司. Zheng-zhou: Zhong-zhou guji chuban she, 1988.

————. "Mingdai nanfang shaoshu minzu zheyu Liaodong qing-kuang" 明代南方少數民族謫寓遼東情況. *Zhong-yang minzu xueyuan xuebao* 中央民族學院學報 3 (1987).

————, Sun Yuchang 孫與常, and Zhang Ke 張克. "Mingdai liuren zai Dongbei 明代流人在東北 *Lishi yanjiu* 歷史研究 4 (1985).

————. Yuan Lükun 袁閭琨 and Fu Langyun 傅朗云. *Mingdai Nuergan dusi jiqi weisuo yanjiu* 明代奴爾干都司及其衛所研究. Zheng-zhou: Zhong-zhou shuhua she, 1982.

Yang Yingjie 楊英杰. *Qingdai Manzu fengshu shi* 清代滿族風俗史. Shenyang: Liaoning renmin chuban she, 1991.

Yang Yulian 楊余練. "Mingdai houqi di Liaodong mashi yu Nüzhen zu di xingqi" 明代後期的 遼東馬市與女真族的興起. *MTYC* 5 (1980).

Yao Congwu 姚從吾. *Dongbei shi luncong* 東北史論叢. Taipei: Zheng-zhong shuju, 1959, 2 vols.

————. "Guoshi kuoda mianyan di yige kanfa" 國史擴大綿延的一個看法. In the same author's *Dongbei shi luncong*, vol. 1.

————. "Jin Shizong duiyu Zhong-yuan Hanhua yu Nüzhen jiushu di taidu" 金世宗對於中原漢化與女真舊俗的態度. In Yao Congwu, *Dongbei shi luncong*, vol. 2.

————. "Jinchao shang-jing shiqi di Nüzhen Wenhua yu qian Yan hou di zhuan-bian 金朝上京時期的女真文化與遷燕後的轉變. In Yao Congwu, *Dongbei shi luncong*, vol. 2.

————. "Nüzhen Hanhua di fenxi" 女真漢化的分析. *Dalu zazhi* 6.3 (1953).

———. "Qidan Hanhua di fenxi" 契丹漢化的分析. In *Dalu zazhi shixue congshu* 大陸雜誌史學 叢書, series 1 (Taipei: Dalu zazhi she, 1960, 8 volumes). Vol. 5: *Song-Liao-Jin shi yanjiu lunji* 宋遼金史研究論集.

———. *Yao Congwu xian-sheng quanji* 姚從吾先生全集. Taipei: Zheng-zhong shuju, 1982, 10 vols. Vol. 7.

Ye Xianggao 葉向高. *Siyi kao* 四夷考. Peiping: Wendian ko, 1934, Guoxue wenku 國學文庫, no. 13.

Ying Yunping 瀛云萍. "Manzu jiujing fayuan yu hedi" 滿族究竟發源於何地. *MTYC* 2 (1986).

Yongzheng Emperor (as author). See Qing Shizong.

Yu, Ying-shih. "The Hsiung-nu." In Denis Sinor, ed., *The Cambridge History of Early Inner Asia* (Cambridge and New York: Cambridge University Press, 1990).

———. *Trade and Expansion in Han China: A Study in the Structure of Sino-Barbarian Economic Relations.* Berkeley and Los Angeles: University of California Press, 1967.

Yuan Lükun 袁閭琨 et al. *Qingdai qian shi* 清代前史. Shenyang: Shenyang chuban she, 2004, 2 vols.

Yuan Senpo 袁森坡. "Lun Huang Taiji tongyi Chahaer di douzheng" 論皇太極統一察哈爾的鬥爭. *Qingshi yanjiu* 清史研究 6 (1988).

Yuan Tsing 袁清. "Qingjun ruguan qian Nüzhen zu di jingji qianli" 清軍入關前女真族的經濟潛力. *Qingshi yanjiu* 清史研究 1 (1996).

Zhang Cunwu 張存武. "Qing-Han guanxi 清韓關係: 1631–1636." *Hanguo xuebao* 韓國學報 1 (1981).

———. "Qing-Han guanxi 清韓關係 (1636–1644)." *Gugong wenxian* 故宮文獻 4.2 (1973).

———. *Qing-Han zongfan maoyi* 清韓宗藩貿易 (*1637–1894*). Taipei: Institute of Modern History, Academia Sinica, 1978.

Zhang Deyu 張德玉. *Manzu fayuandi lishi yanjiu* 滿族發源地歷史研究. Shenyang: Liaoning minzu chuban she, 2001.

———. "Saerhu zhiyu Hou Jin canzhan bingli zaitan" 薩爾滸之役後金參戰兵力再探. *MANT* 3 (1989).

Zhang Deze 張德澤. *Qingdai guojia jigou kaolüe* 清代國家機構考略. Beijing: Zhongguo renmin daxue chuban she, 1981.

Zhang Hong-xiang 張鴻翔. "Ming waizu cixing kao" 明外族賜姓考. *Furen xuezhi* 輔仁學誌 3. 2 (1932); 4.2 (1934).

Zhang Jiasheng 張佳生. "Kangxi chao Manzu wenxue xing-sheng di yuan yin" 康熙朝滿族文 學興盛的原因 *MANT* 1 (1995).

———. "Qingchu Manzu ciren ji chengjiu" 清初滿族詞人及成就. *MANT* 1 (1991).

———. "Qingdai qian, zhong qi Manzu buyi shiren shulüe" 清代前，中期滿族布衣詩人述略. *SHKH* 1 (1990).

Zhang Jinfan 張晉藩 and Guo Cheng-kang 郭成康. *Qing ruguan qian guojia falü zhidu shi* 清入關前國家法律制度史. Shenyang: Liaoning renmin chuban she, 1988.

Zhang Juling 張菊玲. "Zheng Xie yu Manzu renshi di hanmo yuan" 鄭燮與滿族人士的翰墨緣. *Zhong-yang minzu daxue xuebao* 中央民族大學學報 1 (1995).

Zhang Taixiang 張太湘. "Cong zuixin kaogu xue chengqiu kan lishi shang di Sushen Yilouren" 從最新考古學成就看歷史上的肅慎挹婁人. *Dongbei shida xuebao: Zhexue shehui kexueban* 東北師大學報: 哲學社會科學版 5 (1982).

Zhang Yuxing 張玉興. "Fan Wencheng gui Qing kaobian" 范文程歸清考辨. *Qing-shi luncong* 清史論叢 6 (1985).

———. "Lun Qingbing ruguan di wenhua Beijing" 論清兵入關的文化背景. *Qingshi yanjiu* 清史研究 4 (1995).

Zhao Dong-sheng 趙東升. "Guanyu Yehe bu shouling di zushu wenti" 關於葉赫部首領的族屬問題. *MANT* 4 (1995).

Zhao Duo 趙 鐸. Qing kaiguo jingji fazhan shi 清開國經濟發展史. Shenyang: Liao-ning renmin chuban she, 1992.

Zhao Jie 趙杰. "Beijing hua zhong ti Man-Han yongheci tanwei" 北京話中滿漢融合詞探微. *Zhongguo yuwen* 中國語文 4 (1993).

Zhao Lianwen 趙連穩. "Kuang-shui jian Gao Huai luan-Liao shiping" 礦稅監高淮亂遼事評. *Dongbei difang shi yanjiu* 東北地方史研究 3 (1991).

Zhao Xiuting 趙秀亭, "Nalan Xingde zhuzuo kao" 納蘭性德著作考. *MANT* 2 (1991); 3 (1991); 4 (1991).

Zhao Zhan 趙展. *Manzu wenhua yu zongjiao yanjiu* 滿族文化與宗教研究. Shenyang: Liaoning Minzu chuban she, 1993.

Zhao Zhencai 趙振才. "Tonggusi-Manyu yu wenhua" 通古斯- 滿語與文化. *Manyu yanjiu* 滿語研究 1 (1986); 2 (1986); 1 (1987).

Zhao Zhenji 趙振紀. "Qingshi guoyu jie" 清史國語解. *Xueyi zazhi* 學藝雜誌 15.4 (1936).

Zhao Zhihui 趙志輝, Deng Wei 鄧偉, and Ma Qingfu 馬清福, eds. *Manzu Wenxue shi* 滿族文學史. Shenyang: Shenyang chuban she, 1989. Vol. 1.

Zhao Zhijiang 趙志強. "Qingchao xing-shuai yu huangzi jiaoyu 清朝興衰與皇子教育. *Manxue yanjiu* 滿學研究 2 (1994).

———. "Qingdai qianqi di junguo yizheng yu Manzhou guizu" 清代前期的軍國議政與滿洲貴族. *Manxue yanjiu* 滿學研究 1 (1992).

Zhaolian 昭槤. *Xiaoting zalu* 嘯亭雜錄 and *Xulu* 續錄. Taipei: Wenhai chuban she, 1968, *CCST* no. 7, vol. 63, 2 parts.

Zheng Xiao 鄭 曉. *Huang-Ming siyi kao* 皇明四夷考. Peiping: Wendian ge, 1933. *Guoxue wenku* 國學文庫, no. 1.

Zheng Tianting 鄭天挺. *Qingshi tanwei* 清史探微. Beijing: Beijing University Press, 1990.

———. *Tanwei ji* 探微集. Beijing: Zhonghua Book Company, 1980.

Zhenjun 震鈞. *Tianzhi ouwen* 天咫偶聞. Taipei: Wenhai chuban she, 1968, *CCST* no. 22, vol. 219.

Zhi Xijun 智喜君. "Mingdai Liaodong fangwei tixi di jianshe" 明代遼東防衛體系的建設. *Dongbei difang shi yanjiu* 東北地方史研究 1 (1991).

Zhi Yunting 支運亭. "Cong Qing qianqi huang gong jianzhu yishu fengge kan Manzu wenhua di fazhan qushi 從清前期皇宮建築藝術風格看滿族文化的發展趨勢. *Qingshi yanjiu* 清史研究 3 (1997).

Zhongguo tongshi jianbian 中國通史簡編. Ed. Zhongguo lishi yanjiu hui 中國歷史研究會 under Fan Wenlan 范文瀾. Shanghai: Huadong renmin chuban she, 1952.

Zhou Xibao 周錫保. *Zhongguo gudai fushi shi* 中國古代服飾史. Beijing: Xinhua shu-dian, 1984.

Zhou Yimin 周一民 and Zhu Jiansong 朱建頌. "Guanyu Beijing hua zhong di Manyu ci" 關於北京話中的滿語詞. *Zhongguo yuwen* 中國語文 3 (1994).

Zhou Yuanlian 周遠廉. "Cong 'zhushen' shenfen di bianhua kan ruguan qian Manzu di shehui xingzhi" 從 '諸申'身份的 變化看入關前滿族的社會性質. *SHKH* 1 (1979).

———. "Hou Jin ba Heshi beile 'Gongzhi guozheng' lun" 後金八和碩貝勒 '共治國政' 論. *Qingshi luncong* 清史論叢 2 (1980).

———. *Qingchao kaiguo shi yanjiu* 清朝開國史研究. Shenyang: Liaoning renmin chuban she, 1981.

———. *Qingchao xingqi shi* 清朝興起史. Chang-chun: Jilin wenshi chuban she, 1986.

Zhou Yuanlian 周遠廉 and Xie Zhaohua 謝肇華. "Mingdai Liaodong junhu zhi chu-tan" 明代遼東軍戶制初探. *SHKH* 2 (1980).

Zhou Yuanlian 周遠廉 and Zhao Shiyu 趙世瑜. *Huangfu shezheng wang Duoergun quan zhuan* 皇父攝政王多爾袞全傳. Chang-chun: Jilin wenshi chuban she, 1986.

Zhu Chengru 朱誠如. *Guankui ji: Ming-Qing shi sanlun* 管窺集: 明清史散論. Bei-jing: Zijin cheng chuban she, 2002.

———. "Mingdai Liaodong Nüzhen ren yu Hanren zaju zhuang kuang di lishi kao-cha" 明代遼東女真人與漢人雜居狀況的歷史考察. *Liaoning shida xuebao: She-hui kexue ban* 遼寧師大學報 : 社會科學版 1 (1984).

———, ed. *Qingchao tongshi* 清朝通史. Beijing: Zijin cheng chuban she, 2002–2003, 14 vols.

Zhu Xizu 朱希祖. "Hou Jin guohan xingshi kao" 後金國汗姓氏考. In *Qingzhu Cai Yuanpei xian-sheng liushiwu sui lunwen ji* 慶祝蔡元培先生六十五歲論文集, part 1. Peiping: Academia Sinica, 1933.

Zhuang Jifa 莊吉發. *Qingshi lunji* 清史論集. Taipei: Wen-shi-zhe chuban she, 1997, 2 vols.

Zuo Shuo 左書諤. "Zailun Wu Sangui 'xiang Qing' wenti" 再論吳三桂 '降清'問題. *Beifang luncong* 北方論叢 3 (1987).

Index

Page numbers in *italics* indicate illustrations and tables

CORNELL EAST ASIA SERIES

103 Sherman Cochran, ed., *Inventing Nanjing Road: Commercial Culture in Shanghai, 1900-1945*
104 Harold M. Tanner, *Strike Hard! Anti-Crime Campaigns and Chinese Criminal Justice, 1979-1985*
105 Brother Anthony of Taizé & Young-Moo Kim, trs., *Farmers' Dance: Poems by Shin Kyŏng-nim*
106 Susan Orpett Long, ed., *Lives in Motion: Composing Circles of Self and Community in Japan*
107 Peter J. Katzenstein, Natasha Hamilton-Hart, Kozo Kato, & Ming Yue, *Asian Regionalism*
108 Kenneth Alan Grossberg, *Japan's Renaissance: The Politics of the Muromachi Bakufu*
109 John W. Hall & Toyoda Takeshi, eds., *Japan in the Muromachi Age*
110 Kim Su-Young, Shin Kyong-Nim & Lee Si-Young: *Variations: Three Korean Poets;* trs. Brother Anthony of Taizé & Young Moo Kim
111 Samuel Leiter, *Frozen Moments: Writings on Kabuki, 1966-2001*
112 Pilwun Shih Wang & Sarah Wang, *Early One Spring: A Learning Guide to Accompany the Film Video February*
113 Thomas Conlan, *In Little Need of Divine Intervention: Scrolls of the Mongol Invasions of Japan*
114 Jane Kate Leonard & Robert Antony, eds., *Dragons, Tigers, and Dogs: Qing Crisis Management and the Boundaries of State Power in Late Imperial China*
115 Shu-ning Sciban & Fred Edwards, eds., *Dragonflies: Fiction by Chinese Women in the Twentieth Century*
116 David G. Goodman, ed., *The Return of the Gods: Japanese Drama and Culture in the 1960s*
117 Yang Hi Choe-Wall, *Vision of a Phoenix: The Poems of Hŏ Nansŏrhŏn*
118 Mae J. Smethurst & Christina Laffin, eds., *The Noh Ominameshi: A Flower Viewed from Many Directions*
119 Joseph A. Murphy, *Metaphorical Circuit: Negotiations Between Literature and Science in Twentieth-Century Japan*
120 Richard F. Calichman, *Takeuchi Yoshimi: Displacing the West*
121 Fan Pen Li Chen, *Visions for the Masses: Chinese Shadow Plays from Shaanxi and Shanxi*
122 S. Yumiko Hulvey, *Sacred Rites in Moonlight: Ben no Naishi Nikki*
123 Tetsuo Najita & J. Victor Koschmann, *Conflict in Modern Japanese History: The Neglected Tradition*
124 Naoki Sakai, Brett de Bary & Iyotani Toshio, eds., *Deconstructing Nationality*
125 Judith N. Rabinovitch & Timothy R. Bradstock, *Dance of the Butterflies: Chinese Poetry from the Japanese Court Tradition*
126 Yang Gui-ja, *Contradictions,* trs. Stephen Epstein and Kim Mi-Young
127 Ann Sung-hi Lee, *Yi Kwang-su and Modern Korean Literature:* Mujŏng
128 Pang Kie-chung & Michael D. Shin, eds., *Landlords, Peasants, & Intellectuals in Modern Korea*
129 Joan R. Piggott, ed., *Capital and Countryside in Japan, 300-1180: Japanese Historians Interpreted in English*
130 Kyoko Selden & Jolisa Gracewood, eds., *Annotated Japanese Literary Gems: Stories by Tawada Yōko, Nakagami Kenji, and Hayashi Kyōko* (Vol. 1)
131 Michael G. Murdock, *Disarming the Allies of Imperialism: The State, Agitation, and Manipulation during China's Nationalist Revolution, 1922 1929*
132 Noel J. Pinnington, *Traces in the Way: Michi and the Writings of Komparu Zenchiku*
133 Charlotte von Verschuer, *Across the Perilous Sea: Japanese Trade with China and Korea from the Seventh to the Sixteenth Centuries,* Kristen Lee Hunter, tr.
134 John Timothy Wixted, *A Handbook to Classical Japanese*
135 Kyoko Selden & Jolisa Gracewood, with Lili Selden, eds., *Annotated Japanese Literary Gems: Stories by Natsume Sōseki, Tomioka Taeko, and Inoue Yasushi* (Vol. 2)
136 Yi Tae-Jin, *The Dynamics of Confucianism and Modernization in Korean History*
137 Jennifer Rudolph, *Negotiated Power in Late Imperial China: The Zongli Yamen and the Politics of Reform*
138 Thomas D. Loooser, *Visioning Eternity: Aesthetics, Politics, and History in the Early Modern Noh Theater*
139 Gustav Heldt, *The Pursuit of Harmony: Poetry and Power in Late Heian Japan*
140 Joan R. Piggott & Yoshida Sanae, *Teishinkōki: The Year 939 in the Journal of Regent Fujiwara no Tadahira*
141 Robert Bagley, *Max Loehr and the Study of Chinese Bronzes: Style and Classification in the History of Art*
142 Edwin A. Cranston, *The Secret Island and the Enticing Flame: Worlds of Memory, Discovery, and Loss in Japanese Poetry*
143 Hugh de Ferranti, *The Last Biwa Singer: A Blind Musician in History, Imagination and Performance*
144 Roger Des Forges, Gao Minglu, Liu Chiao-mei, Haun Saussy, with Thomas Burkman, eds., *Chinese Walls in Time and Space: A Multidisciplinary Perspective*
145 George Sidney & Hye-jin Juhn Sidney, trs., *I Heard Life Calling Me: Poems of Yi Sŏng-bok*
146 Sherman Cochran & Paul G. Pickowicz, eds., *China on the Margins*
147 Wang Lingzhen & Mary Ann O'Donnell, trs., *Years of Sadness: Autobiographical Writings of Wang Anyi*
148 John Holstein, trans. *A Moment's Grace: Stories from Korea in Transition*
149 Sunyoung Park with Jefferson J.A. Gatrall, *On the Eve of the Uprising and Other Stories from Colonial Korea*
150 Brother Anthony of Taizé & Lee Hyung-Jin, *Walking on a Washing Line: Poems of Kim Seung-Hee*
151 Matthew Fraleigh, *New Chronicles of Yanagibashi and Diary of A Journey to the West: Narushima Ryūhoku Reports from Home and Abroad*
152 Pei Huang, *Reorienting the Manchus: A Study of Sinicization, 1583 1795*
153 Karen Gernant & Chen Zeping, trs., *White Poppies and Other Stories by Zhang Kangkang*
154 Marina Svensson & Mattias Burrell, eds., *Making Law Work: Chinese Laws in Context*

DVD Monica Bethe & Karen Brazell: "Yamanba: The Old Woman of the Mountains" to accompany CEAS volume no. 16 *Noh As Performance*

CORNELL
East Asia Series

Order online at www.einaudi.cornell.edu/eastasia/publications